Business & Sustainability

Second Edition

Scott T. Young
Western Washington University

K. Kathy Dhanda
Sacred Heart University

Steve Hollenhorst
Western Washington University

WAVELAND PRESS, INC.
Long Grove, Illinois

For information about this book, contact:
   Waveland Press, Inc.
   4180 IL Route 83, Suite 101
   Long Grove, IL 60047-9580
   (847) 634-0081
   info@waveland.com
   www.waveland.com

Copyright © 2024 by Scott T. Young, K. Kathy Dhanda, and Steve Hollenhorst

10-digit ISBN 1-4786-5024-9
13-digit ISBN 978-1-4786-5024-9

All rights reserved. No part of this book may be reproduced, stored in a retrieval system, or transmitted in any form or by any means without permission in writing from the publisher.

Printed in the United States of America

7   6   5   4   3   2   1

Contents

Preface *xv*

PART I   1

SUSTAINABILITY: ESSENTIALS FOR BUSINESS

Introduction 2
- What Is Sustainability? *3*
- Sustainability-Related Definitions *4*
- History of Industrial Capitalism and the Environmental Movement *5*
    - The First Wave: Conservation *6*
    - The Second Wave: Pollution and Sprawl *7*
    - The Third Wave: Bargaining and Dealmaking *9*
- Environmental Leaders *10*
    - The Transcendentalists *10*
    - John Muir *11*
    - John James Audubon *11*
    - The Wilderness Society Leaders *11*
    - Rachel Carson *12*
    - Gaylord Nelson *12*
    - George Washington Carver *12*
    - Robert Bullard *12*
    - Alice Hamilton *13*
    - Wangari Maathai *13*

Chico Mendes *13*
Vandana Shiva *13*
David Suzuki *13*
Greta Thunberg *13*

Ten Myths About Sustainability *13*

The Case for Being Sustainable *15*
Profitability *15*
Linking Profitability to Development *16*
Competitiveness *17*
Consumer Loyalty *17*
Global Warming Concerns *17*
International Pressures *17*
Public Exposure *18*
Greening the Supply Chain *18*
Minimizing Waste *18*
A Note of Caution, However *18*

Why Sustainable Strategy? *19*

Five Stages on the Path to Sustainability *21*

Triple Bottom Line *21*
The Importance of Triple Bottom Line *23*

Chapter Outline *23*
Part I: Sustainability: Essentials for Business *24*
Part II: Earth and Environmental Systems *24*
Part III: Stakeholder Interest and Choices *26*
Part IV: Strategies for a Sustainable Future *27*

Conclusion *28*

Keywords *28*   *Discussion Questions* *29*
Recommended Websites *29*   *Endnotes* *29*

PART *II* *33*

EARTH AND ENVIRONMENTAL SYSTEMS

Chapter 1: Overview of Earth and Environmental Systems *34*

Chapter Overview *34*

Earth Systems   *35*
    The Geosphere   *35*

Ecosystems   *42*
    Basic Ecological Concepts   *42*

The Carbon Cycle   *45*

Conclusion   *48*

Keywords   48   Discussion Questions   49   Endnotes   49

Chapter 2: Climate Change   50

Chapter Overview   *50*

Human Impact on the Earth's Carbon Cycle   *51*

The Science of Climate Science   *54*
    What Causes Climate Change   *54*
    Greenhouse Gases   *55*
    Global Warming Potential   *60*

GHG Emission Sources and Mitigation Strategies   *61*
    Electricity Production   *62*
    Agriculture Sector   *63*
    Industry   *64*
    Transportation   *66*
    Commercial and Residential Buildings   *67*

Consequences of Climate Change   *69*
    Temperature and Precipitation   *69*
    Sea Level Rise   *70*
    Ocean Acidification   *71*
    Ecosystems   *72*
    Indirect Consequences of Climate Change   *72*

Climate Solutions   *72*
    Mitigation Strategies   *73*
    Adaptation Strategies   *73*

International Cooperation   *74*

Conclusion   *76*

Keywords   77   Discussion Questions   77
Recommended Websites   78   Endnotes   78

Chapter 3: Energy — 80

Chapter Overview 81
The Basics of Energy Science 81
    Categories and Forms of Energy 81
    Laws of Energy 81
Sources of Energy 83
    Non-Renewable Energy 83
    Renewable Energy 94
Energy Storage 119
    Gravity Batteries 120
    Flow Batteries 121
    Compressed Air Energy Storage 121
    Thermal Energy Storage 121
    Solid-State Batteries 121
    Hydrogen 122
    Flywheels 122
Implications for Businesses 122
    Cost Parity 122
    Energy Price Fluctuations Exposure 122
    Increased Demand in Other Sectors 123
    Investment Opportunities 123
Conclusion 123

Keywords 123   Discussion Questions 125
Recommended Websites 125   Endnotes 126

Chapter 4: Ecosystem Services: — 128
Water, Forests, Wildlife, and Biodiversity

Chapter Overview 129
Types of Ecosystem Services 130
    Biospheric Services 130
    Ecological Services 131
    Social Services 131
    Amenity Services 131
    Resource Services 132
Ecosystem Management 132

Forest Ecosystems and
Forest Ecosystem Management *133*

    Why are Temperate Forests Increasing While
Tropical Forests Continue to Decline? *134*

    Bringing an End to Our Long History of Deforestation *135*

    Forest Product Supply and Demand Trends *136*

    Forest Ownership and the Delivery of Ecosystem Services *137*

    Sustainable Forestry *138*

    Sustainable Forest Certification *140*

    Urban Forests *141*

Biodiversity *142*

    Endangered and Threatened Species *144*

Business Implications *145*

Conclusion *146*

Keywords 147   *Discussion Questions 147*
Recommended Websites 148   *Endnotes 148*

Chapter 5: Sustainable Agriculture and Food 150

Chapter Overview *150*

A Brief History of
Agriculture and Food Systems *151*

    Intensive Agriculture and The Green Revolution *152*

    Socioeconomic Impacts of Conventional Agriculture *152*

    Environmental Impact of Conventional Agriculture *153*

Trends Shaping the Future of Sustainable Agriculture *156*

    Biotechnology *156*

    Drones *157*

    Blockchain Technology *157*

    Artificial Intelligence *157*

What the World Eats *157*

    Malnutrition *158*

Conventional versus Sustainable Agriculture *159*

    Organic Farming and Food *161*

    Buy Local: The Local Food Movement *162*

How and What Should We Eat? *163*

Sustainability at Food Companies 164
Monsanto and "Roundup Ready" Crops 165
McDonald's and the Climate Impacts of Beef 166
Cargill and Deforestation 167
Kraft Heinz and Shareholder Pressure 168
Walmart, Scope 3 Emissions, and Transport 169
Danone and ESG Disclosure 170

Conclusion 172

Keywords 172   Discussion Questions 173
Recommended Websites 173   Endnotes 174

PART III   177

STAKEHOLDER INTEREST AND CHOICES

Chapter 6: Sustainable Strategies and Frameworks   178

Chapter Overview 178
Why Sustainable Strategy? 179
Sustainable Value Creation 179
Global Drivers of Sustainability 180
Ladder of Sustainability 182
Players Within the Organization 182

Natural Capitalism 183

Natural Step 184
Four System Conditions for Sustainability 185
The Funnel 185
Strategies for Action 186

Industrial Ecology 187
Systems Analysis 188
Material and Energy Flows and Transformations 188
Multidisciplinary Approach 188
Analogies to Natural Systems 188
Linear (Open) Versus Cyclical (Closed) Loop Systems 189
Examples of Industrial Ecology 190
Life Cycle Assessment 193

Cradle-to-Cradle and Biomimicry   *194*

    Cradle-to-Cradle   *195*

    Biomimicry   *195*

Environmental Stewardship and Sustainability   *197*

    The Environmental Protection Agency's Approach to Environmental Stewardship   *198*

Tools for Sustainability   *200*

    Environmental Management System   *200*

    Total Quality Environmental Management   *201*

    Sustainable Value Stream Mapping   *202*

    Sustainable Operating System   *202*

    Sustainability Balanced Scorecard   *203*

    Circular Economy   *203*

    Example: Renault, Europe's First Circular Economy Factory for Vehicles   *204*

Conclusion   *205*

Keywords   205   Discussion Questions   205
Recommended Websites   206

Chapter 7: Role of the Consumer   207

Chapter Overview   *207*

Limits to Consumption   *208*

    Global Drivers   *208*

    Link to Earth's Ecosystems   *209*

    Ecological Impact   *209*

Consumption Choices   *210*

    Food and Drink   *210*

    Housing   *213*

    Clothing   *215*

    Transportation   *216*

Role of Consumers   *217*

    Barriers to Change   *217*

    Ecological Footprint and Carbon Footprint   *218*

Project Drawdown   *219*

Future of Consumption   *220*

Conclusion   221

Keywords   221   Discussion Questions   221
Mini Case: Carbon Footprint   222   Mini Case Questions   222
Recommended Websites   223

Appendix   223
    Top Ten Sustainable Steps   223
    Household Cleaners   224
    Personal Care   225

Chapter 8: Role of the Corporation   227

Chapter Overview   227

The Chrysalis Economy   228
    Corporate Locusts   228
    Corporate Caterpillars   229
    Corporate Butterflies   229
    Corporate Honeybees   229

Sustainability Is More Than Green   230

Corporate Social Responsibility   230
    Definition   231
    History of Corporate Social Responsibility   231
    Phases of Corporate Social Responsibility   232
    Making the Case for Corporate Social Responsibility   234
    Relevance of Corporate Social Responsibility   235
    Key Corporate Social Responsibility Areas   237
    Corporate Social Responsibility Policies   237
    Benefits of Corporate Social Responsibility   238
    Challenges of Corporate Social Responsibility   239

The World's Most Sustainable Companies   240

Green, Sustainable Supply Chains   241
    Align the Green Supply Chain with Business Goals   241
    Use the Green Supply Chain to Improve Processes   241
    Green Suppliers and Material Refurbishment   241
    Ten Steps to Creating a Sustainable Supply Chain   242
    Facility Design, Equipment, and Systems   243
    Logistics and Transportation   244
    Green Procurement   245

A Business Case for Sustainability   247
    Patagonia   248

Conclusion 248

Keywords 249   Discussion Questions 249
Recommended Case Studies 250   Recommended Websites 250

Chapter 9: Role of Governments and Nongovernmental Organizations 251

Chapter Overview 252

Role of Governments 252
- Changing Role of Governments 253
- Policy Instruments 254
- Role of the Environmental Protection Agency 255
- List of Environmental Protection Agency Programs for Sustainability 255
- Local Governments for Sustainability 256

Nongovernmental Organizations 256
- Definition 256
- History of the Nongovernmental Organizations Movement 257
- Top 10 Most Influential NGOs in the World 257
- Growth in Power 259

Role of Nongovernmental Organizations 260
- Social Development 260
- Sustainable Community Development 261
- Sustainable Development 262
- Sustainable Consumption 262
- Business Partnerships 264
- Other Examples 264
- Caveats 266

Environmental Nongovernmental Organizations 268
- Role of Environmental Nongovernmental Organizations 268
- The Split: From Two Groups to Five 269

Blessed Unrest 270

Conclusion 271

Keywords 271   Discussion Questions 271
Recommended Websites 272

Appendix 273
- *Programme Area 274*

Part IV — 279

Strategies for a Sustainable Future

Chapter 10: Transparent Reporting, Measurement, and Standards — 280

Chapter Overview *280*

Reporting *281*
- Why Companies Report on Sustainability Performance *282*
- Benefits of Sustainability Reporting *282*
- Why Companies Do Not Report on Issues *282*

Frameworks *284*
- Global Reporting Initiative (GRI) *284*
- GRI Standards *284*
- Who Reports and Why? *285*
- Benefits of the Global Reporting Initiative *285*
- Limitations of the Global Reporting Initiative *286*

UN Global Compact *286*
- Carbon Disclosure Project *287*
- World Business Council for Sustainable Development *288*
- GHG Protocol *288*

Standards *288*
- International Organization for Standardization Standards *288*
- ISO 14001 *289*
- ISO 26000: Social Responsibility *290*
- AA1000 *291*

Ratings and Indices *292*
- Dow Jones Sustainability World Index (DJSI World) *292*
- FTSE4Good Index Series *292*
- MSCI KLD Database (Formerly KLD) *293*

Other Registries *293*
- Ceres *294*
- Corporate Register *295*
- Corporate Knights Global 100 *295*
- Caveats of Reporting *296*

Conclusion   *296*

Keywords   297   Discussion Questions   297
Recommended Websites   298

Appendix   298
- Global Compact Speech, Kofi Annan, Secretary General, UN, January 31, 1999   *298*

Chapter 11: Carbon Markets: Offsets and Standards   302

Chapter Overview   *302*

International Climate Agreements   *303*
- Net Zero versus Carbon Neutrality   *304*
- Carbon Markets   *305*
- Carbon Offset Programs   *308*

Conclusion   *309*

Keywords   310   Discussion Questions   310
Recommended Website   311   Endnotes   311

Appendix   312
- Carbon Calculators   *312*

Chapter 12: Designing Sustainable Cities and Communities   313

Chapter Overview   *313*

A City Sustainability Portfolio   *314*
- Los Angeles   *315*
- Salt Lake City   *316*
- Seattle   *317*
- Phoenix   *317*
- Chicago   *319*
- Boston   *319*
- New York City   *320*
- Atlanta   *321*
- Washington, D.C.   *323*
- San Francisco   *324*
- Portland   *325*
- New Orleans   *326*
- Top Sustainable Cities   *328*
- London   *329*
- Paris   *329*

      Hong Kong *330*
      Montreal *331*
      Vancouver *332*
      Mexico City *333*
      Mumbai *335*
      Curitiba *336*
      Melbourne *337*
      Best Cities to Survive the Zombie Apocalypse *338*

Business Implications *338*

LEED Certification *339*

Conclusion *339*

Keywords 340   Discussion Questions 340
Recommended Websites 340   Endnotes 341

Chapter 13: Green Marketing   342

Chapter Overview *342*

Green Marketing *343*
      Paths to Developing Sustainable Products *345*
      The Rules of Green Marketing *345*
      Greenwashing *346*
      The Seven Sins of Greenwashing *346*
      Green Marketing Segments *347*

The Ogilvy Earth Handbook *348*
      Planning Your Approach *348*
      Developing Communications *348*
      Launching and Beyond *348*

Corporate Examples *349*

Fifty Years of Green Marketing *349*

Ecotourism *350*

The Federal Trade Commission Environmental Standards *350*
      The General Principles *350*

Business Implications *352*

Conclusion *353*

Keywords 353   Discussion Questions 353
Recommended Websites 354

References *355*

Index *385*

Preface

The first edition of *Business and Sustainability* was published in 2012 by Sage Publications under the title *Sustainability: Essentials for Business*. Kathy Dhanda and Scott Young, colleagues at that time at DePaul University, collaborated on this book, realizing there was no textbook for business students covering the basics of sustainability. The first edition was adopted by both business and environmental studies programs. Almost ten years passed when Waveland Press approached us about a second edition.

Much has changed since the first edition was published. Sustainability issues have taken a front stage in the media and the discussions around global climate change. Most of the world's largest economic entities are corporations, not countries. This immense power calls for greater responsibility, and society can hold global businesses accountable for their actions and results. For this reason, companies need to develop and execute sustainability strategies that consider every dimension of the business environment: social, economic, cultural, and natural.

True sustainability is much more than a public relations campaign or an occasional agreement for short-term gain. If sustainability is realized fully and implemented well, it can drive a bottom-line strategy to save costs, a top-line strategy to reach a new consumer base, and a talent strategy to find, retain and develop creative, dedicated employees.

Consider climate change, which requires a multi-pronged global response. Governments and regulatory agencies must align public policy and investments that favor clean, renewable energy and wean themselves away from heavily polluting or endangered resource- and energy-consuming industries. Businesses ought to invest in natural capital, preserve natural resources, and align their reporting to reflect their social and environmental intentions and outcomes. Similarly, individuals should reflect upon personal consumption options and their impact on climate and the Earth. For example, many Americans are vacationing closer to home while Europeans wander more by rail than by air.

In this second edition, we added a third author, Steve Hollenhorst. Steve is the Associate Vice President of Facilities, Professor, and former Dean at the College of the Environment at Western Washington University. Steve did a substantial rewrite of the environmental science chapters, making this a major revision of the first edition. We feel this edition is appropriate for Business and Environmental Studies students and retitled the book to conform with Western's academic program of the same name.

On the campus where Scott and Steve work, the Business College and Environmental College buildings are separated by a lovely red-brick pedestrian walkway. For decades, this narrow distance might as well have been a deep chasm. The inhabitants of each building saw each other as irrelevant at best and, at worst, the enemy. They rarely interacted intellectually and academically, held starkly different worldviews, and saw little value in each other's curriculum and scholarship.

Over time, this rift has narrowed, and the differences dissolved. This is mainly attributed to new generations of students who don't see or accept the divide. An environmental major today is just as likely to aspire for a career at Costco, decarbonizing its supply chain, as they are for an environmental organization. Conversely, many business majors want to make the environment and sustainability a foundational element of their careers.

Similarly, the business world increasingly expects sustainability to be part of new employees' knowledge and skill set, while environmental organizations expect graduates to have fundamental business skills. The faculty have been pulled along, and over time, the curricula have come closer together, blending and merging business and environmental content in ever-evolving and exciting ways.

The closing of the chasm will undoubtedly continue to narrow. But more work is needed. This textbook is designed to be one scaffold in the bridge that narrows the divide.

Our team of three educators, who are passionate advocates for the environment, feel that all students need to be exposed to sustainability since the solutions to address the challenges need to be diverse and cross-disciplinary, creative, and synergistic.

We are grateful to Don Rosso at Waveland for providing the opportunity to update this book. We hope students will benefit from the content of this book.

Scott T. Young
Western Washington University

K. Kathy Dhanda
Sacred Heart University

Steve Hollenhorst
Western Washington University

Part I

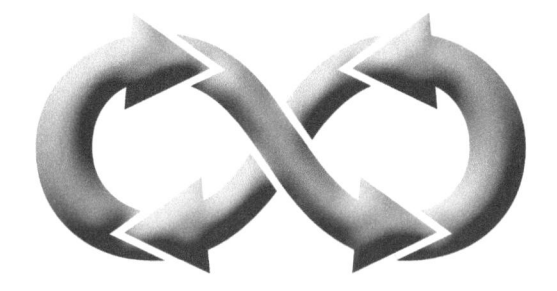

Sustainability: Essentials for Business

Introduction

Greta Thunberg, a courageous teenage student, stood outside the Swedish Parliament in the Spring of 2016, boycotting school to protest the slow reaction of Sweden to climate change. In drawing attention to the issue, she came to embody the concern of young people worldwide for the planet's future. Their alarm was magnified by a series of climate disasters, culminating with July of 2021 recording the hottest month in recorded history.

Global forces such as the climate crisis, deforestation, toxic contamination, loss of biodiversity, and extreme weather disasters, along with their inherent inequities, have propelled the sustainability movement's growth in importance. With its origins in environmental management, the business sector is key to solving these challenges. Sustainability has emerged as a new business discipline—one that must find its way into the curriculum of business schools.

The position of the organization and the individual consumer in relation to the natural world has caused a new awareness of our collective need for sustainability to be front and center in business enterprise. This book represents an introduction to the field. It will introduce the critical business interactions with sustainability while providing essential background on environmental science.

We write this book during a global pandemic. Many of us worked remotely for more than a year and watched as political divisiveness across the globe permeated our consciousness and concern about the Earth's future. Industry, policy, and individuals are at the heart of the critical issue of global climate change and how the world of business can adapt to save the planet. This book is intended as an introductory text on the business world's environmental and sustainability issues.

What Is Sustainability?

Sustainability has become a buzzword applied to everything from business practices to natural ecosystems. Yet it remains an elusive and evolving concept. Like other ideas such as democracy and globalization, sustainability is one of the most "ubiquitous, contested and indispensable concepts of our time."[1] As our understanding of the ecological, social, and economic dimensions of environmental issues grows, so does our conception of sustainability. But where did the word come from? What does it mean for something to be sustainable?

The concept of sustainability has been around for as long as humans have taken actions to restrict the use of their resources to maximize their chance of survival. Food, water, fiber, and minerals must come from somewhere, and early cultures had to think about what would happen if the resources they depended upon disappeared.[2]

The concept of sustainability in the literature can be traced to the German term *Nachhaltigkeit* coined by Hans Carl von Carlowitz (1645–1714) to describe the practice of restricting timber harvests to what the forest could regenerate. The translated term appeared in English beginning in the mid-19th century.[3]

Once ecology became a discipline, the concept of sustainability became more inclusive, referring now not just to forests but to all biological systems. Ecological sustainability, then, is the ability of an ecosystem to maintain its essential functions and to retain biodiversity over time.[4] For human beings, sustainability is about the "potential for long-term maintenance of well-being, which in turn depends on the maintenance of the natural world and natural resources."[5]

In a very general sense, the term *sustainability* means to endure. Today there are more than 500 definitions of sustainability, and most of these pertain to the specific discipline or field—for example, sustainable community or sustainable design. Despite the varied definitions of sustainability, the concepts include these basic precepts:

- Living on Earth has environmental limits.
- The economy, environment, and society are interconnected and interdependent.[6]
- Humans have the responsibility of preventing environmental impacts.

The most common definition of sustainability is one from the area of sustainable development provided by the World Commission on Environment and Development (WCED), also known as the Brundtland Report, that states, "Sustainable development is the development that meets the needs of the present without compromising the ability of future generations to meet their own needs."[7]

SUSTAINABILITY-RELATED DEFINITIONS

Ecological sustainability: "The capacity of ecosystems to maintain their essential processes and function over time and to retain their biological diversity without impoverishment."[8]

Environmental sustainability: "Sustainability means using, developing and protecting resources at a rate and in a manner that enables people to meet their current needs and also provides that future generations can meet their own needs."[9]

Just sustainability: "The need to ensure a better quality of life for all, now and into the future, in a just and equitable manner while living within the limits of supporting ecosystems."[10]

Sustainable agriculture: "[Sustainable agriculture is] an agriculture that can evolve indefinitely toward greater human utility, greater efficiency of resource use, and a balance with the environment that is favorable both to humans and to most other species."[11]

Sustainable city: "Sustainable urban development is improving the quality of life in a city, including ecological, cultural, political, institutional, social and economic components without leaving a burden on the future generations—a burden which is the result of reduced natural capital and excessive local debt. Our aim is that the flow principle, that is based on an equilibrium of material and energy and financial input/output, plays a crucial role in all future decisions upon the development of urban areas."[12]

Sustainable community development: "Sustainable community development is the ability to make development choices which respect the relationship between the three 'E's'—economy, ecology, and equity: Economy—Economic activity should serve the common good, be self-renewing, and build local assets and self-reliance. Ecology—Humans are part of nature, nature has limits, and communities are responsible for protecting and building natural assets. Equity—The opportunity for full participation in all activities, benefits, and decision-making of a society."[13]

Sustainable design: "Sustainable design is the set of perceptual and analytic abilities, ecological wisdom, and practical wherewithal essential to making things that fit in a world of microbes, plants, animals, and entropy. In other words, (sustainable design) is the careful meshing of human purposes with the larger patterns and flows of the natural world, and careful study of those patterns and flows to inform human purposes."[14]

Sustainable development: "Sustainable development is development that meets the needs of the present without compromising the ability of future generations to meet their own needs."[15]

Sustainable economy: "An ideal and sustainable economy is one which provides for the greatest amount of general well-being with the least amount of resource use and environmental harm. In economic terms, to be truly sustainable, the overall demand for natural resources (also known as ecological footprint) must be less than the nature's renewable supply of resources (also known as biocapacity)."[16]

Sustainable education: "Sustainable education involves active participation to create economic and social development programs and goals that will help balance and generate long-standing improvements of a nation's basic quality of life standards and needs. This can help generate empowerment to the nation's citizens."[17]

Sustainability ethics: "A thing is right when it tends to preserve the integrity, stability, and beauty of the biotic community. It is wrong when it tends otherwise."[18]

Sustainable food: "Food that is healthy for consumers and animals, does not harm the environment, is humane for workers, respects animals, provides a fair wage for the farmer, and supports and enhances rural communities."[19]

Sustainability in commerce: "Leave the world better than you found it, take no more than you need, try not to harm life or the environment, make amends if you do."[20]

Sustainable processes: "A transition to sustainability involves moving from linear to cyclical processes and technologies. The only processes we can rely on indefinitely are cyclical; all linear processes must eventually come to an end."[21]

Sustainable society: "A sustainable society is one which satisfies its needs without diminishing the prospects of future generations."[22]

Sustainable university: "A higher education institution, as a whole or as a part, that addresses, involves and promotes, on a regional or a global level, the minimization of environmental, economics, societal, and health negative effects in the use of their resources to fulfill its main functions of teaching, research, outreach & partnership, and stewardship among others as a way to helping society make the transition to sustainable lifestyles."[23]

Sustainable value: "As a value, it refers to giving equal weight in your decisions to the future as well as the present. You might think of it as extending the Golden Rule through time, so that you do unto future generations as you would have them do unto you."[24]

HISTORY OF INDUSTRIAL CAPITALISM AND THE ENVIRONMENTAL MOVEMENT

The relationship between the economy and the environment has a long and complicated history. Today, it is generally acknowledged that industrialization and the rise of modern capitalism have played a central and controversial role in the planet's condition. In a mere 150 years, the world has gone from a primarily agrarian society to the highly mechanized, industrialized, and urbanized world we know today. While the human benefits from this transformation are undeniable, it also resulted in overwhelming environmental challenges: resource depletion, energy use, greenhouse gas emissions, pollution, loss of biodiversity, waste generation, etc.

Alfred Chandler was the first business historian to explain how the organization of the modern industrial enterprise had coevolved with the use of fossil energy, locking business and the world economy into an unsustainable growth trajectory.[25] Often described as the "Great Acceleration,"[26] this trajectory has pushed the planet into a new geological epoch—the Anthropocene—caused by the accumulated human impact on Earth's life support systems.[27]

The modern environmental movement is often described as a societal response to the negative environmental impacts of our fossil-fuel-based economy. The roots of environmentalism are interwoven with those of industrial capitalism. Since the earliest days of industrialization, some have observed—and often criticized—the dramatic transformation of not only land and water but also socioeconomic systems, the nature of work, and the structure of family, communities, and government.

THE FIRST WAVE: CONSERVATION

These concerns focused on the great change industrialization brought to natural and agrarian landscapes. This concern became the "first wave" of environmentalism—the conservation movement.

The early conservation movement was somewhat elitist and narrowly focused on the interests of its adherents, who tended to be male, white, affluent, and Protestant. Their primary concern was to protect wildlife and habitat for hunting and fishing and preserve open space for aesthetics and recreation. Around the world, complex systems evolved to protect these interests, involving government regulatory and land management agencies, non-profit organizations, and a combination of public and private philanthropic financing mechanisms.

The roots of the conservation movement are intertwined with European colonialism and imperialism, both of which were fueled by industrialization. From the earliest days of the movement, writers took note of the dramatic change occurring to the European landscape and the regions of colonization, particularly North and South America, South Asia, and Australia. John Evelyn's work *Sylva*,[28] published in 1662, marks the first publication on the depletion of natural resources, particularly forests, and advocated they be conserved by controlling the harvest rate so that it did not exceed regrowth. This was critical since trees were an essential resource for the Royal Navy, which was undergoing massive expansion in support of the British imperial agenda. Attention was mainly focused on the forests of the British Isles and the colonies in India and North America.

In the United States, transcendentalist Henry David Thoreau was writing about the loss of the wilderness and the negative impact of industrialism on nature and the human spirit. In 1864, George Perkins Marsh's book *Man and Nature; or Physical Geography as Modified by Human Action*,[29] sounded the alarm on how human activity was causing permanent damage to the Earth.

These concerns eventually crystallized into what we know today as the conservation movement. The basic idea underlying the movement is that the nation's natural resources—forests, lands, and waters—should be conserved to benefit the public interest, not just those of the industrialists. Beyond this overarching principle, the movement was divided by conflicting values and perceptions of the relationship between nature and humanity.

On one side were the preservationists, represented by John Muir. Preservationists generally wanted to set aside land to protect its intrinsic and instrumental value to humans. Muir believed that everything in the universe was "hitched" to everything else and that extractive activities like logging and mining disrupted the great cosmic plan. To support the cause of preservation, Muir founded the Sierra Club, the first of the major voluntary non-profit organizations to advocate for the protection of the environment. Many similar preservation-oriented organizations followed: the National Audubon Society, the National Parks and Conservation Association, the Izaak Walton League of America, The Wilderness Society, the National Wildlife Federation, Ducks Unlimited, and Defenders of Wildlife. The legacy of the preservationists can be seen in the suite of federal legislation that created the National Park System, the National Wilderness Preservation System, the National Wildlife Refuge System, the National Wild and Scenic River System, and the National Trail System. It can also be seen in parallel protection systems created at the state and local level and in the private land protection systems of The Nature Conservancy and local land trusts.

On the other side were the conservationists, led by Gifford Pinchot. Conservationists generally advocated for the "wise use" of nature, including the sustainable extraction of natural resources for human benefit. They agreed with the preservationists that large swaths of land should be kept in public ownership. But they differed in that they thought these lands should be scientifically managed to serve direct material needs, including future generations. While they appreciated intrinsic values of nature, those values had to be balanced with direct use values. Conservationists were instrumental in placing vast areas of the public domain under permanent federal protection for multiple-use purposes, including the National Forest System, the Bureau of Land Management, and the dam projects managed by the Bureau of Reclamation and the Army Corps of Engineers. Similar multiple-use lands were also protected at the state and local levels.

The public debate over these competing views is encapsulated in the legacy of a third character, President Theodore Roosevelt. Roosevelt believed that the two approaches were different sides of the same conservation coin. He sought to reconcile the tensions through public policy that recognized both sentiments. The vast public land system in the United States, including areas for both preservation and multiple-use, are the legacy of that public policy compromise.

THE SECOND WAVE: POLLUTION AND SPRAWL

Over time, expanding industrialization created increasingly difficult and hazardous environmental challenges that traditional conservation tools could not address. Raw sewage and industrial waste were dumped into our rivers and streams, leading to cholera outbreaks. The use of coal caused deadly smog to envelop London in 1880, killing 3,000 people, and again in 1952, killing 4,000 people. Similarly, a deadly fog killed 1,063 in Glasgow, Scotland, in 1909. The death toll goes way beyond the immediate counts due to the daily breathing of toxic materials. A grandmother of one of the authors of this book, a nonsmoker, died of lung cancer in 1946, most likely caused by her living and breathing the air in Glasgow, Scotland.

History is full of catastrophic events that cause immediate changes in process once the damage has already been done. In 1977, rainfall in a community in New York resulted in corroding underground containers full of chemical waste. The resultant pollution leaked into homes and schools, leading to cancer, congenital disabilities, and miscarriages. The Love Canal scandal exposed the damage caused by toxic waste and the care taken in its disposal. In 1984, a Union Carbide plant in India released chemical gases that killed thousands of people. In 1989, the Exxon Valdez tanker spilled oil off the coast of Alaska, decimating the area's marine ecosystem. Twenty-four years later, an even costlier spill by British Petroleum (BP) wreaked havoc with the Gulf Coast. In 1986, the Chernobyl nuclear reactor in the Soviet Union exploded. Combined with an incident in the United States at Three Mile Island, Pennsylvania, nuclear energy as a fuel source became threatened, if not discarded.

Other impacts also rose to crisis levels, including biodiversity loss, soil loss, urban sprawl, and disappearing farmland. Public concern about the environment's decline became a flood that could not be contained. It burst over the dam on April 22, 1970—the first Earth Day, marking the emergence of new environmentalism onto the world stage as an unmistakable mass social movement. The anger and fear of the public had finally crystallized into a potent political and economic force.

The underlying cause of these environmental challenges is often described as the "misalignment" between private and public interests. The obvious solution was to look to the police powers of the state, in the form of legislation and regulation, to protect the public interest. In short, government intervention could be used to balance these conflicting incentives. This road to environmental regulation took many forms, including limits on water and air pollution emissions, restrictions on the disposal of chemical waste, habitat destruction, and protection of vulnerable species.[30]

In the United States, Congress established the Environmental Protection Agency (EPA) in 1970, which consolidated numerous federal pollution control responsibilities divided among several federal agencies. The EPA's responsibilities grew over time as Congress enacted various environmental statutes and major amendments to these statutes. Usually administered in partnership with the states, these major laws include:

The **Clean Air Act** (1963) authorizes the EPA to set standards for air quality, hazardous air pollutant emissions, and new pollution sources. Through ensuing amendments, it also allows the agency to administer a cap-and-trade program to reduce acid rain, and phase out substances that deplete the Earth's stratospheric ozone layer.

The **Clean Water Act** (1977), along with earlier legislation and later amendments, authorizes the EPA to regulate and enforce limits to waste discharges into U.S. waters.

The **Ocean Dumping Ban Act** (1988) regulates the intentional disposal of materials into ocean waters.

The **Safe Drinking Water Act** (1974) authorizes the EPA to establish drinking water standards, regulate underground injection disposal practices, and administer a groundwater control program.

The **Solid Waste Disposal Act** (1965) and **Resource Conservation and Recovery Act** (1976) regulate solid and hazardous waste disposal and corrective actions to prevent improper waste management practices.

The **Comprehensive Environmental Response, Compensation, and Liability Act** (1980) focuses on the cleanup of contamination resulting from the past release of hazardous substances (excludes petroleum).

The **Oil Pollution Act** (1990) regulates the cleanup of petroleum leaked from underground storage tanks that are not covered under CERCLA.

The **Toxic Substances Control Act** (1976) and the **Federal Insecticide, Fungicide, and Rodenticide Act** (1988) regulate commercial chemicals to reduce risks to human health and the environment.

The **Pollution Prevention Act** (1990) regulates pollution by reducing the generation of pollutants at the point of origin.

The **Emergency Planning and Community Right-to-Know Act** (1986) requires industrial reporting of toxic releases and encourages chemical emergency response planning.

THE THIRD WAVE: BARGAINING AND DEALMAKING

Against this backdrop, the relationship between business and the environment has evolved over time. From the earliest days of the environmental movement, the business community has often dismissed environmental concerns and opposed regulatory reforms. Companies have often resisted public policies that incentivize or force them to internalize the cost of adverse environmental and human health externalities resulting from their operations. Caught off guard by the new environmentalism that emerged in the 1960s and 1970s, corporate America began to mount an effective resistance. The business community employed sophisticated skills, like those it had developed to fight trade unions and antitrust laws, to thwart environmental regulation and make counter-accusations of environmentalists.

In response, the environmental community, led by national and international organizations and a number of environmental organizations, adapted their skills and tactics. Often referred to as the "third wave" of environmentalism, these strategies employed more sophisticated economic and political analysis, effective media, and public outreach strategies. They also began expanding their political base to include poor and minority populations, underscoring the disproportionate ecological ills heaped on these groups. Some environmental groups began to seek out negotiated settlements to environmental problems instead of lawsuits. They also started looking at market forces—as opposed to command-and-control regulation—as a tool for protecting environmental assets.

Not surprisingly, the business community has promoted and supported this third wave model, with many businesses engaging in visible and effective voluntary activities. It also seemed to fit well with the sustainability concept, as it promised to bridge the divide between the public environmental interest and economic growth. Corporate leaders have expressed environmental concern and awareness, particularly around climate change. We've also seen the advent of entrepreneurs creating new markets, consumers and investors changing their preferences, and big business shifting from being seen solely as profit-seeking polluters to being regarded as agents capable of meeting the world's needs, including creating sustainable development voluntarily.

As promising as this sounds, voluntary business action has not kept pace with the rate of environmental damage,[31] bringing into question whether this new approach can work effectively enough to deal with global crises like climate change.

Environmental Leaders

While the world has become awash with pollution and natural resources are depleted, there have been key defenders of nature and the environment whose words and deeds have influenced legislation and thinking.

The Transcendentalists

There are many points in history that one could point to as the beginning of the sustainability movement. The transcendentalists of the 19th century, including Ralph Waldo Emerson, Henry David Thoreau, Bronson Alcott, and Margaret Fuller, emphasized the interaction of humans and nature in their writings and saw the world in a holistic sense.

Emerson's essays made him an influential figure in his lifetime, which was not the case of his young protégé, Henry David Thoreau, whose famous work *Walden*[32] would not receive acclaim until many years after his death. Thoreau's venture to spend two years in a cabin, primarily living off the land, was a total immersion in nature and solitude and was an important work in influencing such future leaders as Mahatma Gandhi. His friend Bronson Alcott, the father of Louisa May Alcott, started one of the first communes, called Fruitlands, an idealistic effort to live off the land as vegetarians.

Thoreau wrote in *Walden*:

> I went to the woods because I wished to live deliberately, to front only the essential facts of life, and see if I could not learn what it had to teach, and not, when I came to die, discover that I had not lived. I did not wish to live what was not life, living is so dear; nor did I wish to practice resignation, unless it was quite necessary. I wanted to live deep and suck out all the marrow of life, to live so sturdily and Spartan like as to put to rout all that

was not life, to cut a broad swath and shave close, to drive life into a corner, and reduce it to its lowest terms, and if it proved to be mean, why then to get the whole and genuine meanness of it, and publish its meanness to the world; or if it were sublime, to know it by experience, and be able to give a true account of it in my next excursion.

John Muir

The Scottish immigrant John Muir was an important figure in taking a stance to protect wilderness. Muir helped found the Sierra Club and was instrumental in the designation of Yosemite as a national park. Muir, like Thoreau, was a long-distance hiker, once chronicling his walk from Indiana to the Gulf in "A Thousand Mile Walk to the Gulf."[33] The Muir Woods and Muir Beach in California were named for him in appreciation of his efforts to protect forests.

Today, the Sierra Club still maintains a strong presence in lobbying efforts to protect the wilderness, plus sponsoring eco-friendly tours.

John James Audubon

When it comes to notable historical figures of the environmental movement, we must also acknowledge and contend with the complex circumstances of their legacies. John James Audubon is a case in point. Audubon was a 19th-century French immigrant naturalist/painter known as a champion of birds. He cataloged his paintings into the opus *Birds of America*, a collection of over 400 illustrations of North American birds. Today we see his legacy preserved in the name of the National Audubon Society, formed in 1905 with the goal "To conserve and restore natural ecosystems, focusing on birds, other wildlife, and their habitats for the benefit of humanity and the Earth's biological diversity."

While Audubon's contributions to ornithology, art, and culture are enormous, he's also a disturbing character who did inexcusable things, even by 19th-century standards. He was a fabulist who committed academic fraud and plagiarism to advance his work and reputation. But far worse, he was an unapologetic slaveholder who wrote critically about emancipation. He stole human remains and sent them to a colleague to assert that white people were superior to non-white people.[34]

Today, many National Audubon Society chapters have denounced these actions, and some have removed his name from their organizations. We debated omitting his name from this chapter but included it to make the point that many historical figures have controversial and complex legacies with which we must contend.

The Wilderness Society Leaders

Four individuals formed the Wilderness Society in 1935: (1) Robert Sterling Yard, who helped create the National Park Service; (2) Benton MacKay, the father of the Appalachian Trail; (3) Robert Marshall, chief of recreation for the Forest Service; and (4) Aldo Leopold, an ecologist at the University of Wisconsin. Together they helped steer the Wilderness Act through Congress in 1964. As defined in the Act, "WILDERNESS, in contrast with those areas where man and his own works dominates the landscape, is hereby recognized as an area where the Earth and its community of life are untrammeled by man, where man himself is a visitor who does not remain."[35]

Rachel Carson

Rachel Carson, a naturalist and scientific writer, wrote *Silent Spring*, which pointed out the harm caused to plants and wildlife by pesticides.

The initial reaction to her book was that it was unfounded nonsense, but further research validated her arguments, and the government acted to halt the use of DDT.

Carson's (1962) book was the beginning of awareness that consumers should be more careful about what they put into their bodies. For many years, the populace had been operating under the assumption that their health was safe if they ate the recommended diet approved by the USDA. Although Carson cannot be considered the first environmentalist, she probably had the most impact.

Gaylord Nelson

Gaylord Nelson (1970), a U.S. senator from Wisconsin, had witnessed how the timber industry had entered his region's white pine forest and "wiped it out in an eyewink of history and left behind fifty years of heartbreak and economic ruin." He came to be known as the "conservation governor" for his efforts to preserve the natural resources of his state. Inspired by the teach-ins across colleges to protest the Vietnam War, he came up with the idea for Earth Day. The first Earth Day was held in 1970 and attracted 20 million participants. Since then, Earth Day has been observed worldwide.[36]

George Washington Carver

George Washington Carver (1865–1943) was noted for his many agricultural innovations. The first African American to receive a Bachelor of Science degree, he started the Agricultural School at the Tuskegee Institute in Alabama. Among his many inventions was crop rotation to improve cotton yields and over 300 uses for peanuts. He was dedicated to improving the quality of life for poor farmers by helping them grow crops such as sweet potatoes and peanuts as a source of their own food. He is credited with being one of the first agriculture scientists to promote farming practices that today would be considered ecologically grounded and sustainable.[37]

Robert Bullard

Robert Bullard, Ph.D., deserves his title of "the Father of Environmental Justice." He is an award-winning author of eighteen books that address sustainable development, environmental racism, urban land use, community resilience, smart growth, and regional equity. He is cofounder of the HBCU Climate Change Consortium and is currently a Distinguished Professor at Texas Southern University.[38]

ALICE HAMILTON

Dr. Alice Hamilton was a pioneer in the field of occupational health. She was the first woman appointed professor to the Harvard School of Medicine, where she researched the effects of industrial metals and chemicals in the workplace on health.[39]

WANGARI MAATHAI

Dr. Wangari Maathai was a Nobel Peace Prize Laureate known for founding the Green Belt Movement—a collaborative involving community-based tree planting, poverty reduction, and environmental conservation. She was based in Nairobi, where she chaired the Department of Veterinary Anatomy at the University of Nairobi.[40]

CHICO MENDES

Chico Mendes was a defender of the Amazon Rainforest who led a movement in Brazil to establish forest reserves that would benefit indigenous communities. He was murdered for his efforts to protect the forest.[41]

VANDANA SHIVA

Dr. Vandana Shiva is a leading proponent of sustainable agriculture practices in India. She argued that large corporations provided seed strains that required large amounts of fertilizer and pesticides and were genetically engineered, forcing farmers to purchase new seeds every year.[42]

DAVID SUZUKI

Dr. David Suzuki is a retired Canadian academic and broadcaster known for vocal environmental advocacy. Retired from the University of British Columbia, he has authored fifty books on environmental topics and produced the CBC television show, "The Nature of Things." A vociferous critic of human-caused climate change, he has received twenty-nine honorary doctorates recognizing his contributions to environmental causes.[43]

GRETA THUNBERG

Greta Thunberg is the teenage climate activist who gained international attention for her three-week strike outside the Swedish Parliament to protest a lack of effort to prevent climate change. Her strike went viral and led to her current role as spokesperson for youth seeking a better tomorrow.[44]

TEN MYTHS ABOUT SUSTAINABILITY

1. *Nobody knows what sustainability really means.* There is international consensus on the meaning and need for sustainability. The UN (Brundtland

Report) definition states that sustainable development is "development that meets the needs of the present without compromising the ability of the future generations to meet their own needs."[45] People everywhere realize there is a future price to pay if we do not act now.

2. *Sustainability is all about the environment.* The focus of the original UN commission was to help developing nations catch up. Poverty often contributes to environmental degradation—ending poverty goes hand-in-hand with strategies that improve health and education, reduce inequality, and spur economic growth—all while tackling climate change and working to preserve natural ecosystems.[46] Today there are actually seventeen interrelated sustainability goals, ranging from environmental to economic and social equity.

3. *Sustainable is a synonym for green.* The term *green* usually suggests a preference for the natural over the artificial. However, to meet the needs of our population, there is a heavy reliance on technology.

4. *It's all about recycling.* Recycling, by itself, is a small part of the larger issue, as energy and transportation are the most significant aspects of sustainability.

5. *Sustainability is too expensive.* Although sustainability efforts may require an initial capital outlay, it has a significant long-term impact. W. Edwards Deming fought the same battle with quality. Detractors argued that quality was expensive. Deming argued that not having quality is more costly.

6. *Sustainability means lowering our standard of living.* Improving people's standard of living is recognized as a key element of sustainability. It may mean a shift of employment, as withering industries lose jobs to innovative sustainable industries.

7. *Consumer choices and grassroots activism, not government intervention, offer the fastest, most efficient routes to sustainability.* Government policy and regulation often favor environmentally damaging business activity. For instance, petroleum-dependent transportation and energy systems are primary drivers of climate change. Yet powerful lobbies exist to advance and perpetuate legislation and policy that keeps these companies active.

8. *New technology is always the answer.* There are cases where a creative business model might offer a better solution.

9. *Sustainability is ultimately a population problem.* Not entirely, though the best way to curb population is by educating women and raising the standard of living. However, a larger focus needs to be placed on less waste of precious resources.

10. *Once you understand the concept, living sustainably is a breeze to figure out.* A practice cannot be termed sustainable without a complete life-cycle analysis of all the costs involved.[47]

Within business schools, academic majors are organized around the traditional major functional disciplines: management, marketing, finance, accounting, economics, and operations management. Where does sustainability fit within business schools—and further, within the organizational structure of the firm?

In terms of the organization, we see the eventual place for sustainability as a distinct function, equal to operations, accounting, and the other dimensions of business. Since sustainability is strategic in nature, its home may be found either in the business strategy domain or since it is very involved with process and maintenance within operations management.

In the business school curriculum, it should have a similar evolution. As it grows in importance, it brings more students and more courses. Some would argue that sustainability is a topic within business ethics, but that implies that operating sustainably is an ethical choice. It is not a choice. Business ethics is a topic that crosses all functional boundaries. We do not get into business ethics in sustainability until we have a case in which ethics is breached.

THE CASE FOR BEING SUSTAINABLE

What forces companies to think about sustainability? The most obvious cause is the link to profitability: The other reasons are image enhancement, response to shareholders, and business strategy, among others.

PROFITABILITY

Businesses that focus on sustainability can be more innovative and increase profits. A report from BT and Cisco states that sustainability can create commercial success and lead businesses to develop new products and services. The ten steps that companies can take to become sustainability-driven are as follows:[48]

1. Make innovating for sustainability part of an overall corporate vision.
2. Formulate a strategy with sustainability at its heart.
3. Embed sustainability in every aspect of your business.
4. Emphasize actions, not words.
5. Set up effective board-level governance to make sustainability matter.
6. Set firm rules.
7. Bring stakeholders on board by engaging them.
8. Use people power through recruitment, staffing, training, and rewards.
9. Join networks focused on sustainability.
10. Think beyond reporting—align all business systems with the company's sustainability vision.

Stakeholders want to know more about what companies are doing to improve the world and lessen their impact on the planet. Though profit is still important, it is not the sole criterion for ranking companies.

Linking Profitability to Development

Companies can contribute to global sustainable development through their core businesses to be profitable and help development. A recent report from the World Business Council for Sustainable Development (WBCSD) provides perspectives on critical challenges and opportunities for developing nations. The report advances eight fundamental foundations of sustainability that we need to realize.[49]

Global warming is stabilized at no more than 1.5°C and clear air is available for everyone. Global anthropogenic greenhouse gas emissions have reached net-zero; improved air quality supports better health and environmental outcomes; aerosol emissions to the atmosphere have been minimized; the ozone layer in the stratosphere has stabilized and is repairing.

The biosphere is protected and restored. The biosphere's ecosystems are sufficiently resilient to sustain and regulate the environment; regulatory services (such as pollination) are thriving; afforestation and habitat creation are embraced; conservation plans for species threatened by climate change are implemented; the spread of invasive species is limited; habitats and ecosystems are enhanced and connected.

Healthy land and soils are stewarded in an equitable and sustainable way. Expansion of land used for agricultural and food production is halted, conserving forests, grasslands, wetlands, and peatlands; the importance of land and forest restoration is universally recognized; innovative technologies ensure the wide practice of land management and stewardship.

The oceans and cryosphere are protected and restored. Ocean temperature increase and acidification, sea-level rise and marine heatwaves are kept within manageable bounds; ocean ecosystems regenerate and thrive; losses from ice sheets and glaciers, reductions in snow cover and arctic sea ice, and increases in permafrost temperatures are limited to those that cannot be avoided at 1.5°C of global warming, and black carbon emissions are eliminated.

The freshwater cycle is safeguarded, and clean water is available for all. Sustainable management of water systems allows for groundwater to be restored; local water storage capacity is optimized for equitable and efficient use; freshwater systems, including wetlands, are conserved and restored, storing carbon and encouraging nature to thrive.

Land, oceans, waterways, and coastlines are free from waste and pollution. Plastic pollution has been eliminated; emissions of other toxic, persistent, and bio-accumulative substances have ceased; biogeochemical cycles of nitrogen and phosphorous have been returned to a sustainable balance, protecting waterways from eutrophication.

Natural resources are consumed sustainably. The true value of resources is recognized; service-oriented and circular material flows have enabled people to use natural resources sustainably; the ecological footprint of production and consumption has been reduced by more than half; waste is minimized; efficient and sustainable food systems deliver nutritious food and clean water for all; everyone has access to clean, affordable energy.

Nature is valued. People value nature in its own right, recognizing the intrinsic and existential value of the natural world; governments, companies, and financial institutions consider the value of nature in making all decisions; everyone enjoys access to nature, which continues to inspire ingenuity and creativity.

COMPETITIVENESS

Another reason for companies to think about sustainability is their need to be competitive. A recent study by *As you Sow* found that "Clean200" companies continue to outperform the MSCI ACWI Global Index.[50] The Clean200 is comprised of 200 publicly traded companies leading the way with solutions for the transition to clean energy. A study by Morningstar in 2016 rated the sustainability portfolios of mutual funds. After their ratings, money flowed out of funds with the lowest rating ($12 to $15 billion) and into funds with the highest rating ($24 to $32 billion). Researchers at the University of Chicago's Booth School of Business speculated that this movement was motivated by two things: performance expectations and altruistic or environmental concerns.[51]

CONSUMER LOYALTY

Consumers are also providing a big push for companies to become sustainable. Specifically, consumers worried about sustainability seek more environmentally friendly products and tell companies to lessen their impact on the planet. Incorporating sustainable supply chain practices can increase profit, help the industry work with government agencies to create regulations, and build consumer loyalty.[52]

GLOBAL WARMING CONCERNS

There is more interest in sustainability/green construction because of concerns about global warming and oil prices. It is estimated that as of 2018, 5.2% of commercial buildings are LEED (Leadership in Energy and Environmental Design) certified, and 11.5% are Energy Star labeled. People in Japan are expected to have grass on their roofs, computerized light systems, and an HVAC system. Prologis plans to create minimum design standards for new developments to meet the requirements for environmental certification. Simon has reduced $18 million a year in operating costs by green retrofitting and other projects. It reduced 110,000 metric tons of carbon dioxide emissions per year. The U.S. Environmental Protection Agency (EPA) encourages green environment measures by providing a free software tool called Portfolio Manager. The benefits of green buildings are lowering consumption and costs, attracting more tenants, tax credit, and insurance discounts.[53]

INTERNATIONAL PRESSURES

The European Commission's new biofuels target for the European Union increases pressure on tropical forests and peatlands. The UN Food and Agriculture Organization plans to develop bioenergy guidelines, and École Polytechnique Fédérale de Lausanne plans to draft global standards on sustainable biofuels.

There is concern that growing more palm oil in Asia for bioenergy and food use will increase emissions of GHGs.

PUBLIC EXPOSURE

The Massachusetts Institute of Technology (MIT) awards an annual Lemelson–MIT Prize and the Lemelson–MIT Award for Sustainability. The Lemelson–MIT Prize is given to inventors who make a product or process that can offer significant value to society. The sustainability award is given to inventions that expand economic opportunity and community well-being in developing and developed countries.[54]

GREENING THE SUPPLY CHAIN

An increasing number of multinational corporations have committed to working with their suppliers to adopt social and environmental standards. This usually begins with the companies' first-tier suppliers, who in turn push for compliance from *their* suppliers—who ideally ask the same from *their* suppliers, and so on. The basic idea is to create a cascade of sustainable practices that flows smoothly throughout the supply chain, or, as we prefer to call it, the supply network.[55] Unfortunately, these commitments tend to break down with the second- and third-tier suppliers, posing a huge challenge to even the most sustainability-conscious corporations.

MINIMIZING WASTE

Sonoco plans to help manufacturing companies save money by eliminating and reusing waste streams. The Sonoco Sustainability Solutions (S3) Zero Waste goal is to reduce waste entering landfills. Sonoco develops custom programs for their customers to reduce the amount of waste generated. S3 will find new ways to use the waste to generate a new revenue stream.[56]

A NOTE OF CAUTION, HOWEVER

Despite all the progress made by corporations and organizations, one needs to be careful. Many companies are being criticized for *greenwashing*, a practice of appearing green without incorporating actual, measurable goals toward sustainability.

Real sustainability is complicated and more positive in that it aims to have humans and other life flourish on the planet forever. Sustainability is gained when everything is working well with everything else. A primary reason why the environment can't be fixed easily is consumption. Even though companies have created programs to reduce waste, they are continuing to feed the beast. Companies need to offer products and services that help consumers restore and maintain their ability to care, flourish, and be aware. Sustainability will help stop the addiction by providing carefully designed products and services that lead people toward responsible choices.[57]

Why Sustainable Strategy?

The increase in fuel price, concern over global warming, and increased consumer demand for environmentally friendly products are just some of the factors that have made sustainability a strategic focal point in industry after industry. Whether for-profit or not-for-profit, all organizations compete for customers, and increasing awareness has altered the competitive landscape. All one needs to do is compare the websites in any industry—automobile manufacturing, hospitality, publishing, pharmaceuticals, food products, even ice cream—and it is quite easy to see a growing emphasis on sustainability. Given the strategic importance of this area, we have devoted an entire chapter (Chapter 6) to reviewing the various frameworks that try to define and classify sustainability.

As with any trend, some skeptics are doubtful and resistant. Then, the early adopters embrace the trend and incorporate it within their organizations. Sustainability is no different; it has its share of believers and skeptics. As this trend unfolds, we shall see organizations that will be skeptical and do as much of the minimum as possible. Other organizations will not want to be perceived as laggards and will attempt to be more engaged. But there will also be the organizations that will genuinely walk the talk and will embrace the concept and incorporate it throughout the ranks.

In his book *The Necessary Revolution*, Peter Senge discusses how organizations and individuals can work together to create a sustainable world.[58] Indeed, plenty of organizations are huddled together in paralysis and inaction. Rather than being proactive, these organizations think that doing nothing is the safe way to go. However, other organizations believe that they need to incorporate sustainability into their long-term goals to survive in the future. How does sustainability become a priority for organization leaders? The initial step is to change the view and refocus the vision. The traditional, accepted industrial-age view is one wherein the largest and most important circle is the economy that contains smaller subareas of society and the environment. The only way to change this view is to shift priorities and integrate sustainability into the organization. This can be done by reconsidering the traditional view. In the new way of looking at the world, the largest circle is the environment, which contains a circle of human activity. The circle representing the economy, the industrial systems, is the smallest circle within the others (see Figure 0.1).

> *The economy is the wholly-owned subsidiary of nature, not the other way around.*
>
> —U.S. Senator Gaylord Nelson,
> quoted by Ray Anderson (Senge, 2008)

All the stakeholders of an organization—from customers to suppliers, employees to shareholders—care about the environment and social issues. With information being instantly disseminated on the web, blogs, and Internet, the organizations have no place to hide. Indeed, organizations that ignore sustainability issues run the risk of losing market share, losing talented employees,

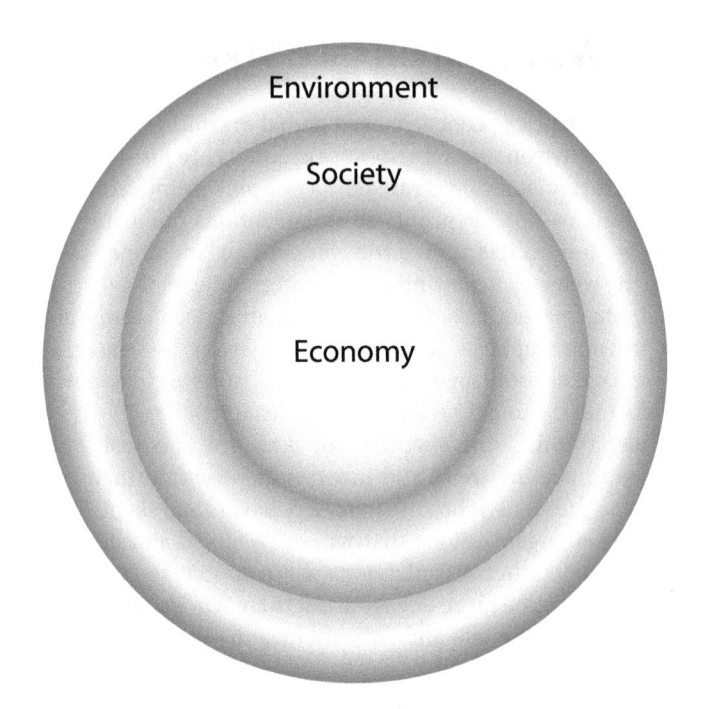

Figure 0.1 | The Real, Real World.
Source: Adapted from Senge (2008).

and incurring damage to their reputations. For those organizations that want to be on the front lines, there needs to be enough evidence for opportunities to embrace sustainability. The following is a small list advanced by Senge:

- Gaining competitive advantage from goodwill
- Preference for green brands by consumers
- Recruiting and retaining good employees
- Saving money from efficiency and waste reduction
- Making money from creative forms of waste regeneration
- Sustainability as a point of differentiation
- Shaping future of industry
- Becoming preferred supplier
- Providing a competitive edge to customers
- Changing image and brand.

FIVE STAGES ON THE PATH TO SUSTAINABILITY

For any organization, Senge argues there are five stages to go from noncompliance to full integration of sustainability into a company's strategy and purpose.

Stage 1 is noncompliance, in which an organization is essentially getting fined for not complying with local emission regulations.

Stage 2 is compliance, in which, perhaps in a reaction to external pressure from nongovernmental organizations (NGOs) and regulators, the organizations begin to comply. Still, the actions are primarily aimed at compliance to avoid incurring fines or taxes. At this point, the organization is meeting minimum legal requirements regarding air emissions, water effluents, or toxic waste emissions.

Stage 3 is beyond compliance. Organizations discover that the savings and payoffs of going further than compliance can far outweigh the initial investments. This reinforces the win-win scenario, or the snowball effect, wherein reinvestment of initial savings leads to positive gains, including improved brand value and reputation.

Stage 4 is when sustainability is fully integrated into strategy. This happens when organizations decide to proactively integrate sustainability factors into every aspect of their business strategy. In addition, sustainability is also factored into the core of the investment and decision-making process across the organization. Numerous companies from Alcoa, General Electric (GE), Walmart, and DuPont have moved to Stage 4.

Stage 5 is when organizations step into sustainability without passing through other stages, usually due to a mission to make a change or contribute to society. Examples are Patagonia, Seventh Generation, The Body Shop, and several others. Ray Anderson, the CEO of Interface, the carpet tile company, set out to make his company a restorative enterprise, "a sustainable operation that takes nothing out of the earth that cannot be recycled or quickly regenerated, and that does no harm to the biosphere" (Dean, 2007). More organizations move to Stage 5 as their mission begins incorporating sustainability. A movement from Stage 4 to 5 can also result from a natural progression as the leaders can learn from the experiences of launching new initiatives that get positive feedback from employees.

TRIPLE BOTTOM LINE

Triple bottom line (TBL) states that the success of a company needs to be measured along three lines— (1) economic, (2) social, and (3) environmental. It also goes by the term *3P*, which stands for people, planet, and profits; it states that companies need to measure their impacts not only on the bottom line (profits) but also on the community (people) and the environment (planet). The phrase was first used in 1989 by John Elkington, co-founder of a consultancy focused on sustainability.

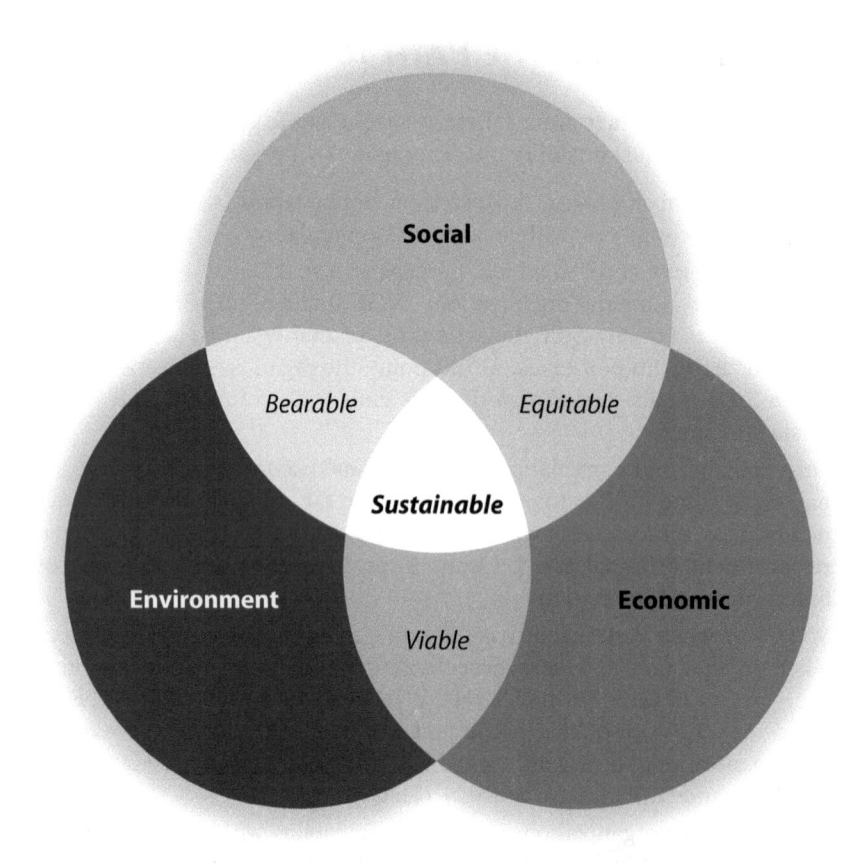

Figure 0.2 | Triple Bottom Line.
Source: Dreo (2006).

The TBL is a form of reporting that states the business's responsibility extends to all its stakeholders, not merely to its shareholders. In other words, it considers the impact of the company in terms of social and environmental values along with financial returns. Whereas traditional models were about making money and garnering profits, TBL accounting recognizes that without satisfied employees and a clean environment, business is doomed to be unsustainable in the long run.[59]

People: This is also known as human capital, and it relates to fair and beneficial business practices toward labor and the community and region in which a corporation conducts its business. In simplest terms, it means treating your employees right. In addition, companies should pay fair wages and reinvest some of their gains into the surrounding community through sponsorships, donations, or projects that go toward the common good.[60]

Planet: This is natural capital, and it refers to the company's environmental practices. A business will strive to minimize its environmental impact in all areas—from sourcing raw materials to production processes, shipping and administration. It's a *cradle to grave* approach and, in some cases, *cradle to cradle* (C2C)—that is, taking some responsibility for goods after they've been sold, such as offering a recycling or take-back program. In addition, a TBL business will also not be involved in the production of toxic items.[61]

Profit: "This is more about making an honest profit than raking a profit at any cost—it must be made in harmony with the other two principles of People and Planet." The profit aspect is the real economic value created by the company, one that deducts the cost of all inputs.[62]

THE IMPORTANCE OF TRIPLE BOTTOM LINE

Of the 100 largest economies globally, fifty-one are businesses, and the other forty-nine are countries. In terms of financial power, "General Motors is now bigger than Denmark; DaimlerChrysler is bigger than Poland; Royal Dutch/Shell is bigger than Venezuela; IBM is bigger than Singapore; and Sony is bigger than Pakistan."[63]

Instead of being an award, accreditation, or certification, the Triple Bottom Line is an ongoing process that helps a company in running a greener business. It demonstrates to the community that they are working not just towards riches but the greater common good. Green business is good business in practice.

CHAPTER OUTLINE

The purpose of this book is to provide a comprehensive treatment of the relationship between business and sustainability. Our goal is that this book serves as a key source for instructors and students wanting to learn about sustainability within a business context. The opening chapters address the major issues confronting our environment and climate. It is essential to get a grounded perspective on these critical issues before addressing the strategic issues of the firm. Businesses must clearly understand the consequences of ecosystem degradation, unsustainable natural resource exploitation, and human-caused climate change.

Therefore, we begin this journey here in Part I, Chapter 1 with this overview of sustainability. In Part II, we present a basic introduction to environmental and Earth science concepts, including the science behind climate change, energy, ecosystem services (Air, Water, Forests, Wildlife, and Biodiversity), and agriculture and food. Throughout this material we integrate relevant socioeconomic issues and concerns (see Figure 0.2). This discussion provides a starting point so that the later chapters on environmental challenges can be framed appropriately.

The book's next section is Part III: Stakeholder Interest and Choices. The first chapter in this section provides a comprehensive discussion of strategies and frameworks used to understand and implement sustainability. The rest of this section presents various stakeholder perspectives such as the role of consumers (what people buy), the role of corporations (what companies sell), and the role of governments and NGOs (how people organize and govern). This section also presents the concept of ecological footprint and illustrates how to compute an individual carbon footprint. The book's last section is Part IV: Strategies for a Sustainable

Future. This section of the book presents chapters on reporting and measurement, carbon markets, the design of sustainable cities, and green marketing.

Part I: Sustainability: Essentials for Business

In this introduction we explore the basic concept of sustainability in relation to the economy and business. We also look historically at the development of industrial capitalism and its relationship to the environment and natural resources, particularly the role of "ecosystem services" in our modern economy.

Part II: Earth and Environmental Systems

The first bottom line is the one that concerns the planet. The planet is our natural capital, and together we need to preserve the planet and its resources. This section includes a basic introduction to environmental and climate science, and how our Earth and environmental systems are related to society and our economy. The following chapters are included in this section.

Chapter 1 – Overview of Earth and Environmental Systems

In this chapter, we will do the following:

- Explain the concepts of Earth systems and subsystems or spheres.
- Understand the components of the geosphere and how human activity impacts them.
- Understand the components of the biosphere and how human activity impacts them.
- Explain basic ecological concepts.
- Explain the hydrologic cycle and its mechanisms.
- Explain the carbon cycle and how human activity impacts it.

Chapter 2 – Climate Change

In this chapter, we will do the following:

- Describe how human activity disrupts the Earth's carbon cycle.
- Describe the causes and consequences of climate change. List the major greenhouse gases and identify their sources and impacts.
- Identify strategies for reducing greenhouse gas emissions to limit global warming.
- Describe global efforts to combat climate change.

Chapter 3 – Energy

In this chapter, we will do the following:
- Define "energy."
- Describe the various forms of potential and kinetic energy.
- Describe the laws of energy.

- List specific examples of non-renewable energy sources.
- Explain what makes an energy source non-renewable.
- Describe the main types of fossil fuels and how they formed.
- Explain the environmental impacts associated with exploration, extraction, and use of the different types of fossil fuels.
- Discuss the need for clean energy.
- Present the four types of conventional energy.
- Explain the different types of renewable energy.
- Compare and contrast solar and wind energy.
- Evaluate the promise of plant-based energy from ethanol to wood waste.
- Discuss other forms of energy, such as tidal to geothermal.
- Explain why energy storage is critical to the renewable energy transition
- Evaluate the most viable alternative energy and fuel sources for businesses today.

Chapter 4 – Ecosystem Services: Water, Forests, Wildlife, and Biodiversity

In this chapter, we will do the following:

- Define ecosystem services.
- Discuss the relationship between various ecosystem services and climate.
- Discuss the various methods of forest stewardship.
- List the certification programs for sustainable forestry.
- Understand the importance of urban forests.
- Explain the importance of preserving wilderness.
- Discuss the Endangered Species Act of 1973 (ESA).
- Research the issues concerning economics and biodiversity.

Chapter 5 – Sustainable Agriculture and Food

In this chapter, we will do the following:

- Describe the role of innovation in the development of our modern agriculture and food systems.
- Discuss sustainable agriculture.
- Discuss the foods we eat.
- Describe the difference between conventional and sustainable agriculture.
- Recognize the differences between natural and organic foods.
- Examine companies involved in the food industry
- Discuss malnutrition.

PART III: STAKEHOLDER INTEREST AND CHOICES

In this section, the book's focus moves away from renewable resources to issues faced by stakeholders. How does the degradation of our natural resources impact the various stakeholders? Are some communities or nations at a higher risk than other, more affluent communities or nations? What can consumers, organizations, and governments do to prepare for a sustainable future? The second bottom line concerns the people that inhabit the planet. The people as a collective are our human capital. Like natural capital, this human capital also needs to be treated fairly and beneficially to the entire community. This section will present some of the strategies and frameworks used to understand sustainability. In addition, this section will discuss the role of consumers, the corporation's role, and the role of NGOs and governments.

Chapter 6: Sustainable Strategies and Frameworks

In this chapter, we will do the following:

- Explain the concept of sustainable value creation.
- Understand the precepts of natural capitalism.
- Examine activities via the natural step.
- Discover examples of industrial ecology and biomimicry.
- Compare and contrast the principles of the cradle to cradle (C2C) approach with biomimicry.
- Explain environmental management system (EMS) and environmental stewardship.
- Compare and contrast various tools and processes used for sustainable strategies.

Chapter 7: Role of the Consumer

In this chapter, we will do the following:

- Discuss consumption and its link to ecosystem services.
- Evaluate the link between consumption and the environment.
- Detail the sustainable choices in food, drink, housing, clothing, and transportation.
- Explain the role of consumers.
- Discuss the ecological footprint and compute the carbon footprint.
- Examine the future of consumption.

Chapter 8: Role of the Corporation

In this chapter, we will do the following:

- Present the chrysalis economy.
- Discuss why sustainability is more than green.
- Define corporate social responsibility (CSR) and link it to sustainability.

- Understand the phases of CSR and how to make a case for CSR.
- Discuss the benefits and challenges of CSR.
- Explain green supply chains and sustainable value chains.
- Examine the role of logistics, transportation, and green procurement.
- Map out a business case for sustainability.

Chapter 9: Role of Governments and Nongovernmental Organizations

In this chapter, we will do the following:

- Understand the role of governments in promoting sustainability.
- Present the role of the U.S. Environmental Protection Agency (EPA).
- Explain Agenda 21 and the role of local governments.
- Discuss the history, growth, and funding of nongovernmental organizations (NGOs).
- Expand on the role of NGOs in social development, community development, and sustainable development.
- Explore NGOs and business partnerships.
- Discuss the role of NGOs and sustainable consumption.
- Present the five types of environmental NGOs.

PART IV: STRATEGIES FOR A SUSTAINABLE FUTURE

The third bottom line concerns the profits derived from the corporations' operations. The basic idea is that corporations ought to be focused on making an honest profit rather than raking in a profit at any cost—it must be made in harmony with the other two principles of people and planet. The profit aspect is the fundamental economic value created by the company—one that deducts the cost of all inputs. This section focuses on the role of transparency and reporting and discusses carbon markets and green marketing.

Chapter 10: Transparent Reporting, Measurement, and Standards

In this chapter, we will do the following:

- Understand the need for reporting and transparency.
- Present voluntary reporting on sustainability.
- Discuss frameworks such as GRI, CDP, and UN Global Compact.
- Compare and contrast various standards such as ISO 14001 and AA1000.
- Present other ratings and indices such as DJSI and FTSE.

Chapter 11: Carbon Markets: Offsets and Standards

By the end of this chapter, you should be able to do the following:

- Present the concept of carbon neutrality.
- Explain the Kyoto Protocol.
- Discuss the details of carbon markets.
- Compare and contrast the various types of offsets.
- Present the market standards.
- Discuss proceedings of Conference of the Parties (COP1 7) Durban.

Chapter 12: Designing Sustainable Cities and Communities

In this chapter, we will do the following:

- Discuss the sustainability plan highlights of major cities across the world.
- Understand the components of a sustainable city plan.
- Discuss the city's contribution to corporate sustainability.

Chapter 13: Green Marketing

In this chapter, we will do the following:

- Know the basic rules of green marketing.
- Understand greenwashing: trying to pass a company off as green when it is questionable.
- Explain the five green Ps.
- Discuss the consumer groups that marketers target.

CONCLUSION

This book will explore ideas and concepts for a future that is more sustainable. The range of ideas is multipronged—investing in alternative energy sources, going back to the old methods of purchasing seasonal food from local farms, designing our communities to encourage people to work and live in common areas, encouraging walking and public transportation, and aiming development globally with a vision for reducing poverty and population hot spots.

Keywords

- » Brundtland Report
- » Carbon Beta and Equity Performance
- » Clean Water Act of 1972 (CWA)
- » Exxon Valdez
- » Human capital
- » Natural capital
- » Sustainability
- » Triple bottom line (TBL)

Discussion Questions

1. What is sustainability?
2. Why is sustainability important?
3. What are the sustainability practices of companies you are familiar with?
4. Is sustainability the same as green?
5. Do a cost-benefit analysis of a hybrid automobile compared to the same non-hybrid model.
6. If all automobiles were hybrids in the United States, what would be the cumulative effect?
7. Is there any evidence of a sustainability program at your college or university?

Recommended Websites

- The Natural Step – www.naturalstep.org/
- Sustainable Measures – www.sustainablemeasures.com/
- United Nations Documents: Report of the World Commission on Environment and Development – www.un-documents.net/wced-ocf.htm
- UNESCO – www.unesco.org/new/en/unesco/

Endnotes

[1] Tavanti, M. (2010, September 30). Defining sustainability. *Sustainable DePaul, DePaul University*. https://sustainabledepaul.blogspot.com/p/defining-sustainability.html.

[2] United Nations Environment Programme. (2017). Indigenous people and nature: A tradition of conservation. *United Nations Environment Programme*. Retrieved from https://www.unep.org/news-and-stories/story/indigenous-people-and-nature-tradition-conservation.

[3] Von Carlowitz, H. C. (1713). *Sylvicultura Oeconomica, Oder Haußwirthliche Nachricht Und Naturmäßige Anweisung Zur Wilden Baum Zucht*. Leipzig: J. Fr. Braun.

[4] Callicott, J. B., & Mumford, K. (1997). Ecological sustainability as a conservation concept. *Conservation Biology, 11*(1), 32–40. https://doi.org/10.1046/j.1523-1739.1997.95468.x.

[5] Bromley, D. W. (2008). Sustainability. In S. N. Durlauf & L. E. Blume (Eds.), *The new Palgrave dictionary of economics* (2nd ed.). New York: Palgrave Macmillan.

[6] Tavanti, M. (2010, September 30). Defining sustainability. *Sustainable DePaul, DePaul University*. https://sustainabledepaul.blogspot.com/p/defining-sustainability.html.

[7] World Commission on Environment and Development. (1987). *Our common future: Report of the World Commission on Environment and Development*. Oxford, UK: Oxford University Press.

[8] Callicott, J. B., & Mumford, K. (1997). Ecological sustainability as a conservation concept. *Conservation Biology, 11*(1), 32–40. https://doi.org/10.1046/j.1523-1739.1997.95468.x.

[9] Morelli, J. (2011). Environmental sustainability: A definition for environmental professionals. *Journal of Environmental Sustainability, 1*(1), 1–10. https://doi.org/10.14448/jes.01.0002.

[10] Agyeman, J., Bullard, R. D., & Evans, B. (Eds.). (2003). *Just sustainabilities: Development in an unequal world*. Cambridge, MA: MIT Press.

[11] Harwood, R. R. (1990). A history of sustainable agriculture. In C. A. Edwards, R. Lal, J. P. Madden, R. H. Miller, & G. House (Eds.), Sustainable agricultural systems (pp. 3–19). Ankeny, IA: Soil and Water Conservation Society.

[12] Anastasiadis, P., & Metaxas, G. (2010). *Sustainable city and risk management.* Paper presented at the first WIETE Annual Conference on Engineering and Technology Education, Pattaya, Thailand. Retrieved from www.wiete.com.au/conferencesnst_wiete/11-07-Metaxas.pdf

[13] Mountain Association for Community Economic Development. (n.d.). Retrieved from https://mtassociation.org/.

[14] Orr, D. W. (1992). Ecological literacy: Education and the transition to a postmodern world. SUNY series in constructive postmodern thought. Albany, NY: State University of New York Press.

[15] World Commission on Environment and Development. (1987). *Our common future: Report of the World Commission on Environment and Development*. Oxford, UK: Oxford University Press.

[16] Econation. (2021, November 28). Sustainable economy: What is a sustainable economy. *Econation.* https://econation.one/sustainable-economy/

[17] UNESCO. (2002). Education for sustainable development. https://www.unesco.org/en/education/sustainable-development

[18] Leopold, A. S. (1949). The land ethic. In *A Sand County Almanac and Sketches Here and There*. New York: Oxford University Press.

[19] MeetGreen. (2021). Glossary. *MeetGreen.com*. https://meetgreen.com/event-resources/glossary/

[20] Hawken, P. (1994). *The ecology of commerce: How business can save the planet*. London, UK: Weidenfeld & Nicolson.

[21] Karl-Henrik, R. (2022). *The Natural Step story: Seeding a quiet revolution*. Gabriola Island, BC: New Society Publishers.

[22] Brown, L. R. (1981). *Building a sustainable society*. New York: Norton.

[23] Velazquez, L., et al. (2006). Sustainable university: What can be the matter? *Journal of Cleaner Production, 14*(9–11), 810–819.

[24] Gilman, R., & Gilman, D. (1991). *Ecovillages and sustainable communities: A report for Gaia Trust*. Gaia Trust.

[25] Chandler, A. D. (1980). Industrial revolutions and institutional arrangements. *Bulletin of the American Academy of Arts and Sciences, 33*(8), 33. https://doi.org/10.2307/3823248.

[26] McNeil, J., & Engelke, P. (2014). The great acceleration: An environmental history of the anthropocene since 1945. Cambridge, MA: Harvard University Press.

[27] Crutzen, P. J., & Stoermer, E. F. (2000). The Anthropocene. *Global Change Newsletter, 41*, 17–18.

[28] Evelyn, J. (1670). Sylva, or A discourse of forest-trees, and the propagation of timber in His Majesties dominions: As it was deliver'd in the Royal Society the XVth of October, [MD]CLXII, upon occasion of certain quæries propounded to that illustrious assembly, by the honourable the principal officers, and Commissioners of the Navy.

Published by expresse order of the Royal Society. London: Printed for Jo. Martyn and Ja. Allestry. http://name.umdl.umich.edu/A38811.0001.001

[29] Marsh, G. P. (1864). *Man and nature: Or, physical geography as modified by human action*. New York: Scribner.

[30] Andrews, R. N. L. (2006). *Managing the environment, managing ourselves: A history of American environmental policy*. New Haven, CT: Yale University Press.

[31] Lyon, Thomas P., Delmas, M. A., Maxwell, J. W., Bansal, P., Chiroleu-Assouline, M., Crifo, P., Durand, R., Gond, J.-P., King, A., Lenox, M., Toffel, M. W., Vogel, D., & Wijen, F. (2018). CSR needs CPR: Corporate sustainability and politics. *California Management Review, 60*(4), 5–24.

[32] Thoreau, H. D. (1854). *Walden; Or, life in the woods*. Boston, MA: Ticknor and Fields.

[33] Muir, J. (1916). *A thousand-mile walk to the Gulf*. Boston and New York: Houghton Mifflin Company.

[34] National Audubon Society. (n.d.). John James Audubon: A complicated history. National Audubon Society. Retrieved 29 Apr. 2021, from https://www.audubon.org/content/john-james-audubon

[35] Wilderness History. (n.d.). History. Wilderness.net. Retrieved from https://wilderness.net/learn-about-wilderness/history/default.php

[36] Wilderness History. (n.d.). History. Wilderness.net. Retrieved from https://wilderness.net/learn-about-wilderness/history/default.php

[37] History.com Editors. (2009, Oct. 27). George Washington Carver. History.com, A&E Television Networks. Retrieved from https://www.history.com/topics/black-history/george-washington-carver.

[38] Dr. Robert Bullard. (n.d.). Dr. Robert Bullard: Father of Environmental Justice. *DrRobertBullard.com*. https://drrobertbullard.com/.

[39] Changing the Face of Medicine. (2015, 3 June). Alice Hamilton. *U.S. National Library of Medicine, National Institutes of Health*. https://cfmedicine.nlm.nih.gov/physicians/biography_137.html.

[40] The Green Belt Movement. (n.d.). Wangari Maathai: Biography. *The Green Belt Movement*. https://www.greenbeltmovement.org/wangari-maathai/biography.

[41] Ramalho, Tania. (2013). Chico Mendes: Brazilian labour leader and conservationist. *Encyclopædia Britannica*. Chicago, IL: Encyclopædia Britannica, Inc. Retrieved from https://www.britannica.com/biography/Chico-Mendes.

[42] Specter, M. (2014, August 18). Seeds of doubt. *The New Yorker*.

[43] David Suzuki Archives. David Suzuki Foundation. https://davidsuzuki.org/expert/david-suzuki/.

[44] Tikkanen, Amy. (2020). Greta Thunberg: Swedish activist. *Encyclopædia Britannica*. Chicago, IL: Encyclopædia Britannica, Inc. Retrieved from https://www.britannica.com/biography/Greta-Thunberg.

[45] World Commission on Environment and Development. (1987). *Our common future: Report of the World Commission on Environment and Development*. Oxford, UK: Oxford University Press.

[46] United Nations Department of Economic and Social Affairs. (n.d.). The 17 Goals: Sustainable Development. *United Nations*. https://sdgs.un.org/goals.

[47] Lemonick, M. D. (2009). Top 10 myths about sustainability. *Scientific American, 19*(1), 40–45. https://doi.org/10.1038/scientificamericanearth0309-40.

48. Strandberg, C. (2013, October 23). 10 steps to developing an industry sustainability program. *Greenbiz*. Retrieved from https://www.greenbiz.com/article/10-steps-developing-industry-sustainability-program
49. World Business Council for Sustainable Development. (2021). Vision 2050: Time to transform. *World Business Council for Sustainable Development (WBCSD)*. https://www.wbcsd.org/Overview/About-us/Vision-2050-Time-to-Transform.
50. As You Sow. (2022, February 16). *Clean200 continues to outperform MSCI ACWI Global Index, leaves index of dirty energy companies in the dust*. https://www.asyousow.org/press-releases/2022/2/15/clean200-outperform-msci-acwi-global-index
51. Lambert, E. (2021, February 23). *When green investments pay off*. Chicago Booth Review. Retrieved from https://www.chicagobooth.edu/review/when-green-investments-pay?sc_lang=en.
52. Consumer trends. (2012). Greenbiz. Retrieved September 10, 2022, from https://www.greenbiz.com/topics/consumer-trends?page=22
53. Marino, V. (2007, April 29). A starring role for "green" construction. *The New York Times*. Retrieved September 10, 2022, from https://www.nytimes.com/2007/04/29/realestate/commercial/29sqft.html
54. Lemelson. (n.d.). A national leader in advancing invention education. *Lemelson-MIT*. Retrieved September 10, 2022, from https://lemelson.mit.edu/
55. A more sustainable supply chain. (2020, November 16). *Harvard Business Review*. Retrieved September 10, 2022, from https://hbr.org/2020/03/a-more-sustainable-supply-chain
56. Sonoco. (n.d.). *Zero waste consulting*. Retrieved September 10, 2022, from https://www.sonoco.com/capabilities/recycling/zero-waste-consulting
57. Ehrenfeld, J. (2008). *Sustainability by design: A subversive strategy for transforming our consumer culture*. New Haven, CT: Yale University Press.
58. Senge, P. M., Smith, B., Kruschwitz, N., Laur, J., & Schley, S. (2008). *The necessary revolution: How individuals and organizations are working together to create a sustainable world*. New York: Penguin Random House.
59. A more eco friendly existence. (2018, October 27). *Green Living Tips*. Retrieved September 10, 2022, from https://www.greenlivingtips.com/
60. A more eco friendly existence. (2018, October 27). *Green Living Tips*. Retrieved September 10, 2022, from https://www.greenlivingtips.com/
61. A more eco friendly existence. (2018, October 27). *Green Living Tips*. Retrieved September 10, 2022, from https://www.greenlivingtips.com/
62. A more eco friendly existence. (2018, October 27). *Green Living Tips*. Retrieved September 10, 2022, from https://www.greenlivingtips.com/
63. Anderson, S., & Cavanagh, J. (2000, December 4). *Top 200: The rise of corporate global power*. Institute for Policy Studies. Retrieved from http://www.corpwatch.org/article.php?id=377

PART II

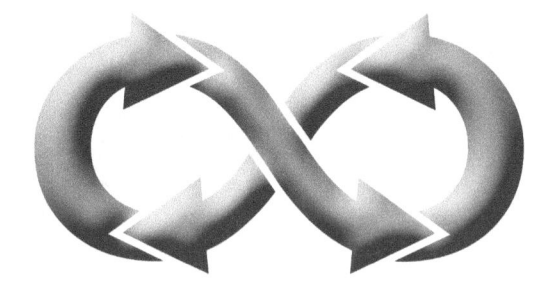

Earth and Environmental Systems

CHAPTER 1

Overview of Earth and Environmental Systems

LEARNING OBJECTIVES

By the end of this chapter, you should be able to do the following:

» Explain the concepts of Earth systems and subsystems or spheres.
» Understand the components of the geosphere and how human activity impacts them.
» Understand the components of the biosphere and how human activity impacts them.
» Explain basic ecological concepts.
» Explain the hydrologic cycle and its mechanisms.
» Explain the carbon cycle and how human activity impacts it.

CHAPTER OVERVIEW

Understanding the relationship between sustainability and business requires a basic understanding of Earth and environmental systems. Business and the global economy impact these systems, and vice versa. This chapter aims to provide a foundational introduction to the Earth's environmental systems and the ecosystem services that flow from these systems. The concepts and terms in this section will be used throughout the book to draw the connection between the business world and the environment.

EARTH SYSTEMS

What we understand as "the environment" is comprised of two main systems, the geosphere and biosphere, and four subsystems, or spheres. All things near the surface of the Earth fit into these systems.

THE GEOSPHERE

The *geosphere* includes all the *abiotic* or non-living things. The geosphere comprises three subsystems or spheres: the *lithosphere, atmosphere,* and *hydrosphere.*

Lithosphere

The *lithosphere* refers to all the Earth's rocks. The term comes from the Greek word *lithos*, meaning stone. It includes the Earth's two outermost hard layers, the crust and the mantle. The lithosphere ends where the solid mantle becomes viscous and fluid because of heat and pressure. The lithosphere varies from 40 km to 280 km in thickness.

The lithosphere is made up of tectonic plates. Geologists generally agree that there are about eight major plates and fifteen minor plates. Plate tectonics is the large-scale movement of these plates, forming mountains, ocean trenches, and volcanoes.

Human Impacts on the Lithosphere. Human activity can have significant direct and indirect impacts on the lithosphere. Farming, urbanization, building roads, mining, and oil and gas development are examples of activities that change the structure of the crust and upper mantle. Indirectly, deforestation and grazing can result in erosion and soil loss.

Hydrosphere

The *hydrosphere* is comprised of all the water on Earth, in all three of its states: liquid, solid, and gas. In liquid form, water is found in oceans, lakes, ponds, rivers, streams, and wetlands, along with underground aquifers. As a gas, it is found in the form of water vapor in the atmosphere. In solid form, it is found as ice and snow. In this frozen solid state, it is often referred to as the *cryosphere*.

Scientists estimate there are about 332 million cubic miles of water on the planet. About 97 percent is in the oceans, with the remaining 3 percent appearing as water vapor, ice caps, glaciers, and in rivers and lakes. The globe illustration below (Figure 1.1) shows the amount of water relative to the size of the Earth. The largest sphere represents all the water. The middle sphere represents all the liquid water. The smallest sphere represents the surface freshwater—the water in lakes and rivers—that most people on the planet depend on every day for survival.

Water is constantly circulating through what is known as the *hydrological cycle.* This cycle involves the movement of water from the surface of the Earth to the atmosphere and back again (Figure 1.2). The primary mechanisms of this movement are *evaporation, transpiration, condensation, precipitation,* and *runoff.* The cycle requires energy, primarily from the sun.

FIGURE 1.1 | The World's Water.
Source: https://www.usgs.gov/media/images/all-Earths-water-a-single-sphere

Human Impacts on the Hydrosphere. Human impact on the hydrosphere has had a profound worldwide impact. Human-induced climate change results in the melting of glaciers, ice caps, and arctic sea ice. This, in turn, results in changes in the thermohaline circulation of the oceans. Often referred to as the "conveyer belt," deep-ocean currents are controlled by temperature (*thermo*) and salinity (*haline*). Disruption from global warming can result in worldwide climatic and weather changes.

This melting, along with the expansion of water from rising temperatures, also results in sea-level rise that affects coastal communities and ecosystems worldwide. Data already shows a 15–20 cm (6–8 inch) increase in sea level from pre-industrial levels. Even if we reduce greenhouse gas (GHG) emissions dramatically, sea levels are likely to rise at least 0.3 meters (12 inches) above the year 2000 levels by 2100, even on a low-emissions pathway by the end of the century. In a worst-case scenario, sea-level rise could be as high as 2.5 meters (8.2 feet) by 2100.[1]

Rising temperatures are also causing the permafrost of the tundra to melt. Not only does this directly affect people who live in these regions as buildings, roads, and infrastructure sink and become unstable, but scientists estimate it will also release massive amounts of carbon dioxide (CO_2) and methane (CO_4) previously trapped in the frozen ground into the atmosphere, further accelerating climate change.

Other human impacts on the hydrosphere include water pollution from the discharge of toxic chemicals, radioactive substances, and other industrial wastes and the seepage of fertilizers, herbicides, and pesticides from agriculture into water systems. The damming of rivers, wetland drainage, reduction in streamflow from

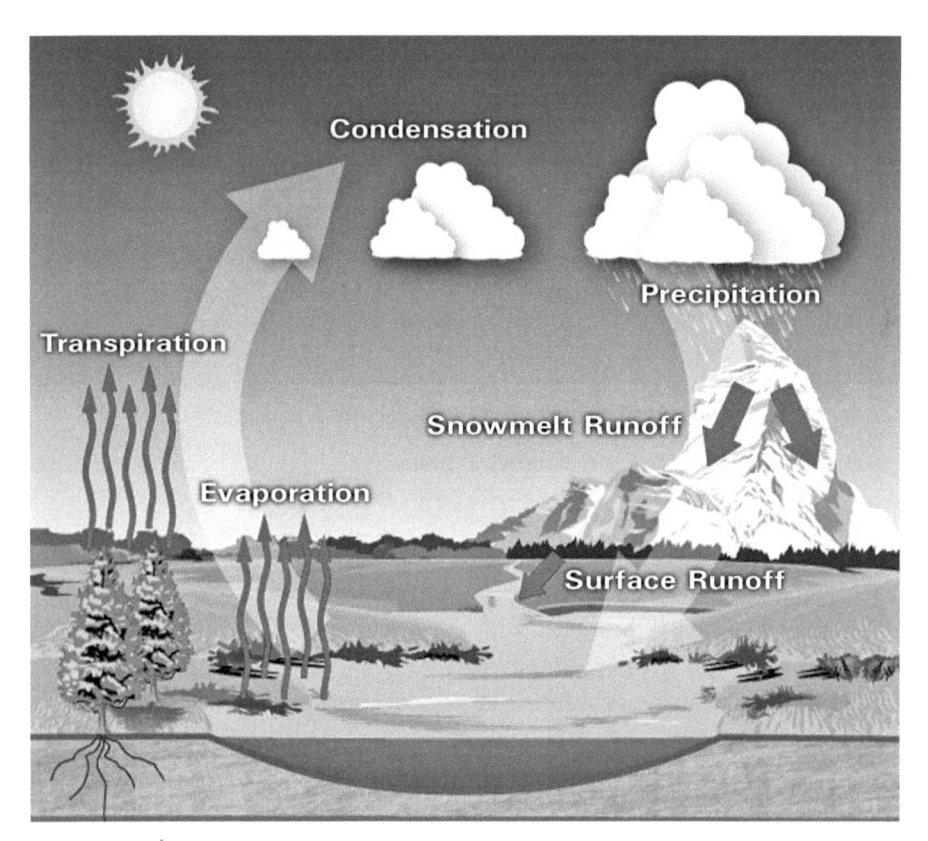

FIGURE 1.2 | The Earth's Hydrological Cycle.
Source: https://www.weather.gov/jetstream/hydro

diversions, and irrigation have degraded existing freshwater systems. Acid rain, in the form of sulfur dioxide and nitrogen oxides from the burning of fossil fuels, has acidified freshwater systems around the globe, resulting in dramatic decreases in fish populations. Eutrophication or excess nutrients from agriculture, sewage, and industry have damaged animal life in these systems from lack of oxygen.

Atmosphere

The *atmosphere* is the gaseous layer surrounding the planet and is held in place by gravity. Commonly referred to as air, the atmosphere is composed primarily of nitrogen (79 percent) and oxygen (21 percent), with the remaining atmosphere composed of argon, CO_2, CO_4, ozone, and other trace gasses. Most of these gasses are located near the bottom layer, the *troposphere*. The troposphere includes the air we breathe and most of the clouds. Beyond that, the atmosphere gets thinner and thinner.

The next layer is the *stratosphere*, where most of the Earth's ozone is located. Beyond that is the *mesosphere*, the highest layer to still contain gasses. There are enough gases to create friction, which causes meteors to break up. Above that is the *thermosphere*. With no gas molecules to transfer heat, temperatures can be 4,500 degrees Fahrenheit in the thermosphere. This is the layer where most satellites and the International Space Station are found. The uppermost layer is the *exosphere*, with extremely low concentrations of hydrogen and helium. The *ionosphere* overlaps the mesosphere, thermosphere, and exosphere. This layer of electrons and ionized atoms and molecules grows and shrinks based on solar conditions. The ionosphere is a critical link in the chain of Sun-Earth interactions and makes radio communications possible.

Human Impact on the Atmosphere. One of the most profound environmental impacts of our industrial economy is on the Earth's atmosphere. The earliest forms of atmospheric impact were in the form of air pollution and remain a problem today. *Air pollution* is the term used to describe harmful gas or particulate substances in the air. Most air pollution occurs through industrial activity and internal combustion engines in vehicles. Primary atmospheric pollutants include:

- **Carbon oxides** include carbon monoxide (CO) and carbon dioxide (CO_2). Both are colorless, odorless gases. Both are greenhouse gases. CO is toxic to both plants and animals.
- **Nitrogen oxides** take the form of gas emissions from vehicles, power plants, and factories. Nitrogen oxide (NO) and nitrogen dioxide (NO_2) are greenhouse gases. Nitrogen oxides contribute to acid rain.
- **Sulfur oxides** include sulfur dioxide (SO_2) and sulfur trioxide (SO_3). These form when sulfur from burning coal reaches the air. Sulfur oxides also contribute to acid rain.
- **Particulates** are solid particles such as ash, dust, and fecal matter. They are commonly formed from the combustion of fossil fuels and can produce smog. Particulates can contribute to asthma, heart disease, and some types of cancers.

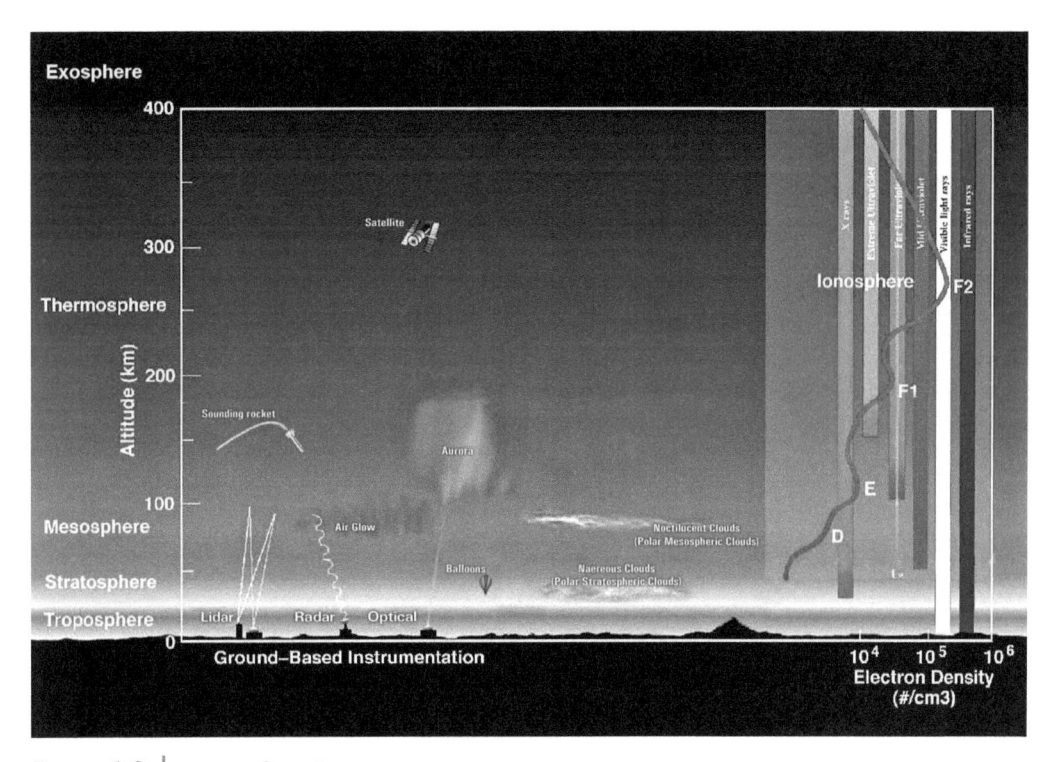

CHAPTER 1 ∞ OVERVIEW OF EARTH AND ENVIRONMENTAL SYSTEMS | 39

FIGURE 1.3 | Atmosphere Layers.
Source: https://www.nasa.gov/mission_pages/sunearth/science/atmosphere-layers2.html

- *Lead* was once widely used in automobile fuels, paint, and pipes. This heavy metal can cause brain damage and blood poisoning.
- *Volatile organic compounds (VOCs)* include CO_4, chlorofluorocarbons (human-made compounds that are being phased out because of their effect on the ozone layer), and dioxin (a byproduct of chemical production harmful to humans and other organisms).
- *Ozone* is created by exhaust and in the presence of sunlight. It is a significant problem in large, dry, hot cities. Ozone is also a greenhouse gas.

The Biosphere

The *biosphere* is composed of all the *biotic* or living things, including all animals, plants, and one-celled organisms. Most of the aquatic life in the oceans and freshwater bodies can be found from the surface to about 200 meters deep. Most terrestrial life can be found from 30 meters above the surface to 3 meters below. However, some animals live far beyond that range, with some fish living 8 kilometers below the surface and some birds flying 8 kilometers above. Some microorganisms can live far beyond these ranges.

The biosphere is comprised of between 20 million and 100 million different species, organized in 100 *phyla* and five *kingdoms* of lifeforms, and can be found throughout the lithosphere, hydrosphere, and atmosphere. The biosphere comprises *biomes*, a large community of plants and animals adapted to a specific climate and geosphere. The five major biome types are *aquatic, grassland, forest, desert*, and *tundra*.[2]

Aquatic Biomes

Aquatic biomes are divided into freshwater and marine (saltwater). *Freshwater biomes* are bodies of water located on land, including lakes, ponds, rivers, streams, and wetlands. They make up only 1 percent of the Earth's surface but provide habitats for many species. Covering close to three-quarters of the Earth's surface, *marine biomes* include the oceans, seas, coral reefs, and estuaries.

Human impacts on freshwater biomes have been particularly pronounced in fish populations, which have declined by 20 percent over the past twenty years. This happens when freshwater habitats are destroyed by filling them in, pollution, or withdrawing or diverting water. Dams and water diversions block fish migration routes and cause damage to plant and animal systems. Expanding human population and water consumption needs bring ever-increasing pressures on this finite resource.

Grassland Biomes

Grassland biomes occur in dry, warm climates and are dominated by grasses. They cover approximately 31–43 percent of the Earth's land area. The two main types are *temperate grasslands* and *tropical grasslands*, or *savannas*. Temperate grasslands occur further away from the equator, typically have few or no trees or shrubs, and are extremely dry. Savannas are closer to the equator and may have a few scattered trees. *Prairies* and *steppes* include two types of temperate grasslands; prairies have taller grasses, while steppes have shorter grasses.

Human population growth and the resulting need for more land have negatively affected grassland ecosystems worldwide. Urban development and agriculture are the biggest drivers of grassland conversion. The grazing of grasslands by domestic cattle can also negatively impact wildlife habitats and lead to the depletion of nutrients from the soil. Global warming also threatens grassland ecosystems, leading to successional changes. Drier conditions increase the frequency of fire, further accelerating this change.

Forest Biomes

Forest biomes are dominated by trees and cover about one-third of the Earth's land area. Much of the world's terrestrial biodiversity occurs in forest biomes. The three major forest biomes are primarily divided by latitude and climate. Tropical forests are warm, humid, and found close to the equator. Boreal forests are found at even higher latitudes and have the coldest and driest climate. Temperate forests are found at mid-latitudes and experience all four seasons.

Before the industrial revolution, 52 percent of the world's habitable land was forested. By 2018, one-third of the world's forests were lost, driven by *deforestation*, primarily for conversion to agriculture. For instance, in the United States, 46 percent of the area was forested. Today it's just 34 percent.

Each year, an additional ten million hectares of forests are lost, an area about the size of Guatemala. About half of that is offset by *afforestation*—establishment of forests where there was no previous tree cover, and *reforestation*—bringing trees back to previously forested areas.

Most of the world's deforestation (95 percent) occurs in the developing countries of the tropics. However, this is driven by economic forces in the world's wealthiest nations. Demand for wood and paper products from these forests is one such force. But the primary demand is for beef, cooking oils, cocoa, coffee, and other agricultural products produced on deforested land.

Desert Biomes

Desert biomes receive less than 50 centimeters (20 inches) of precipitation per year. Covering about 20 percent of Earth's surface, most deserts are found in subtropical areas. The biodiversity is relatively low because of the arid and hot conditions. Plants and wildlife living in a desert have adaptations for surviving in a dry environment.

The arid condition of deserts means that their fragile soils and habitat take an extremely long time to recover from human impact. Climate change reduces the snowpack and glaciers that provide much of the water that desert communities depend on.

The amount of desert land on the planet is expanding through *desertification*. This occurs when arid lands, typically grasslands or agricultural lands, lose their productivity due to drought, overfarming, overgrazing, and fire. Typically, once desertification occurs, these lands are unable to recover. An estimated 6 and 12 million square kilometers of land have been impacted by desertification. Approximately 1 billion people are under threat from further desertification.[3]

Tundra Biomes

Tundra biomes have the lowest average temperatures of any of the five major biomes. They also have low precipitation, poor quality soil nutrients, and short summers. The main types of tundra are *arctic* and *alpine*. The tundra is found north of boreal forests, and the alpine tundra is in the mountains above the tree line. The biodiversity of the tundra generally comprises simple communities of shrubs, grasses, mosses, and lichens. This is partly due to a frozen layer under the soil surface called *permafrost*. Tundra biomes also include some of the world's most recognized wildlife species: polar bears, gray wolves, caribou, musk ox, snow geese, and arctic fox.

Climate change is already radically changing tundra ecosystems and is expected to increase as the Earth warms further. The tundra is also susceptible to air pollution. Black carbon from diesel engines darkens the snow and decreases its ability to reflect sunlight, leading to warmer microclimatic conditions. Chemicals from refrigerants deplete ozone over the poles, increasing UV radiation. Toxic mercury from coal-fired power plants and industry accumulates in tundra ecosystems, threatening wildlife and humans. On top of that, the fossil fuel and mining industries are continually developing these resources, resulting in a host of damages from road and infrastructure development, toxic spills, and habitat loss.

Ecosystems

Ecology is the study of how living things interact with each other and their environment. It involves the interactions of organisms, the flow of energy and recycling of matter through living things, and the biodiversity and distribution of organisms. *Ecosystems* are geographic areas where living and non-living things interact to form a bubble of life. Understanding these basic ecological and ecosystem phenomena and concepts is critical to the practice of sustainability.

Basic Ecological Concepts

All living things have the same basic needs: energy and matter. To obtain these needs, organisms must interact with their environment, which comprises two primary components or factors:

- *Biotic factors* are the living aspects of the environment, plants, animals, and other organisms.
- *Abiotic factors* are the nonliving aspects of the environment. They include factors such as sunlight, rocks, temperature, and water.

Every factor in an ecosystem depends directly or indirectly on every other factor. For instance, a change in the amount or quality of the water in an ecosystem can directly affect what plants will grow there. Animals that depend on those plants for food and shelter are then indirectly affected and will have to either adapt to the new water conditions, move to another ecosystem where water conditions are more favorable, or die.

Ecological Hierarchy

One way to think of the biosphere is as a nested hierarchy. Below the level of the individual organism, the hierarchy levels include genes, cells, tissue, and organs. Ecological hierarchies typically focus on the levels at and above the individual organism. These levels are generally defined as:

- *Population.* A population consists of all the individual organisms of the same species living and interacting in the same area.
- *Community.* A community refers to all the populations of different species living and interacting in the same area.
- *Ecosystem.* An ecosystem includes all the biotic and abiotic things in a given area and their interactions. Ecosystems can be vast, like a forest or wetland, or very small, like a pond.
- *Biome.* A biome is a group of similar ecosystems with the same general type of physical environment anywhere in the world. As described earlier in this chapter, the major biome types are *aquatic, grassland,* forest, *desert,* and *tundra.*

- *Biosphere.* The biosphere is the largest ecological category, and it consists of many different biomes. The biosphere comprises all the life on the planet, including the land, water, and air where living things are found.

Ecosystems

The *ecosystem* is one of the essential concepts in ecology. Ecosystems vary in size from small areas like a pond or rock outcrop to large areas like a forest or prairie. Ecosystems are not closed but need constant energy inputs, usually from sunlight. Ecosystems also receive matter inputs like water, carbon, and nitrogen, but they are also constantly recycling matter within the system. Ecosystems are usually continually changing over time. They are often disturbed by natural events such as droughts and human actions such as deforestation.

Niche

A *niche* is a role a species plays in its ecosystem, including how it interacts with the biotic and abiotic factors of that system. Niches have three main components: environmental conditions, resources for survival, and interaction with other niches. Species with narrow niches are called *specialists*, while those with broad niches are *generalists*.

An example of a specialist species is the red-cockaded woodpecker, which makes its nest holes only in large old longleaf pine trees. Examples of generalists are cockroaches, mice, rats, whitetail deer, raccoons, coyotes, and humans. Species with narrow niches are susceptible to human-induced changes, such as pollution, habitat conversion, or invasive species that compete for the same niche. Many generalists thrive in niches created by human disturbance.

Habitat

Habitat is the natural environment in which a species lives and to which it is adapted. As with niches, species may have general or specific habitat requirements. Microhabitats are small areas with somewhat different environmental factors than the larger areas in which they occur, such as sun exposure, temperature, and moisture. South-facing hillsides may be primarily grassland because of the hot, dry conditions. However, it may also have a microhabitat of trees or shrubs where spring brings water to the surface.

Food Chains

A *food chain* is a simplified model that describes how energy flows through an ecosystem. Organisms at the bottom of the food chain are producers like grasses in *terrestrial systems* and phytoplankton in *aquatic systems*. Producers are consumed by herbivores, which become the prey of carnivores, which themselves are the prey of other carnivores. The top organism in each food chain is called an apex predator, not preyed upon by any other species.

Decomposers like fungi and bacteria are components of the food chain in every ecosystem. Decomposers break down organic matter (whether from producers or consumers), using some of the energy it contains and releasing excess nutrients back into the environment.

Food Webs

A *food web* is a simplified model that describes the multiple pathways by which energy flows through an ecosystem. It generally includes many intersecting food chains. Although food webs (like food chains) are usually simplifications of reality, they do demonstrate that most organisms eat—and are eaten by—more than one species.

Trophic Levels

Trophic levels are the different feeding positions in a food chain or food web. The primary trophic levels can be seen in the diagram below. Most food chains and food webs have between two and five trophic levels. The first trophic level is typically *producers*. Most *consumers* feed at more than one trophic level. For instance, humans are *primary consumers* when eating plants, such as grains. They are *secondary consumers* when eating meat from herbivores, such as cattle. They are *tertiary consumers* when they eat secondary consumers, such as salmon, which eat smaller fish.

Trophic Levels and Energy. Energy is passed up a food chain or food web from lower to higher trophic levels. However, about 90 percent of energy at each trophic level is used by organisms at that level for survival and reproduction. In the process, they generate heat (thermal energy) that is lost to the environment. This is why "eating lower on the food chain" results in less human impact on the environment.

Trophic Levels and Biomass. *Biomass* is the total mass of organic matter in a given area or volume. The decrease in numbers and biomass of organisms from lower to higher trophic levels can be seen in the ecological pyramid above (Figure 1.4). Although individual organisms tend to be larger in size at higher trophic levels, their smaller numbers result in less biomass at higher levels.

While humans make up only about .01 percent of the total global biomass, we have dramatically impacted the amount and distribution of biomass on the planet. Since the dawn of the Agricultural Revolution 3,000 years ago, human civilization has reduced the amount of marine and terrestrial wildlife by six times and the amount of plant matter by half.[4] Humans account for 36 percent of the mammal biomass on the planet. Domesticated livestock, mostly cows and pigs, account for 60 percent. Wild mammals account for only 4 percent. For birds, the biomass of poultry is three times that of wild birds.

Keystone Species

In many ecosystems, certain species are known as *keystone species*. These species play a crucial function, often as *apex predators*, like wolves, orca whales, and humans. Human impacts that influence the population of a keystone species affect many other species in the community, either directly or indirectly. For example, when wolves were removed from the Yellowstone ecosystem, populations of *herbivores* such as elk and deer exploded, resulting in the overgrazing of many plant species. With no food or building supply, the population of herbivores like beaver declined. The depleted vegetation also resulted in soil erosion. When wolves were reintroduced, the population of large herbivores and the plant communities that had declined from overgrazing also started to recover, as has the beaver population.

Trophic levels are split by a who-eats-who system.

(Heterotrophs)
Tertiary Consumers
10 Kcal/m²/year

The vast majority of energy is lost as heat to the environment. Said heat is produced by cellular respiration, a necessary function for life.

Secondary Consumers
100 Kcal/m²/year
(Heterotrophs)

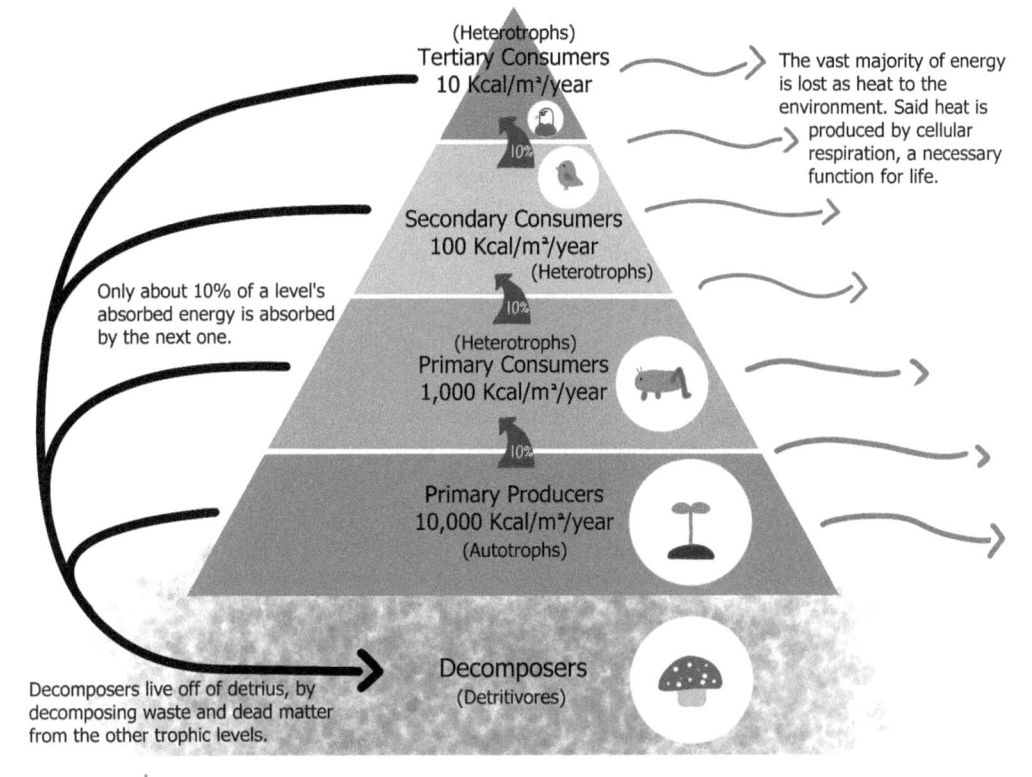

Only about 10% of a level's absorbed energy is absorbed by the next one.

(Heterotrophs)
Primary Consumers
1,000 Kcal/m²/year

Primary Producers
10,000 Kcal/m²/year
(Autotrophs)

Decomposers
(Detritivores)

Decomposers live off of detrius, by decomposing waste and dead matter from the other trophic levels.

FIGURE 1.4 | Trophic Levels & Energy Transfer.
Source: https://upload.wikimedia.org/wikipedia/commons/1/16/Diagram_of_Trophic_Layers_%26_Energy_Transfer_in_an_Ecosystem.svg

THE CARBON CYCLE

Carbon is the fourth most abundant element in the Universe. It's the chemical backbone of all life on the planet, including every photosynthesizing plant, every animal, and every microbe. It's found in every ocean, lake, river, and stream. It's in the soil and every sedimentary rock. It's in the air we breathe and the bubbles rising to the surface of a swamp. Carbon regulates the Earth's temperature, makes up the food we eat, and provides the energy that fuels the world's economy.

Most of the Earth's carbon, about 99.985%, is stored in the lithosphere in the form of sedimentary rocks (see Table 1.1 below). These rocks are composed of plants and animals that lived millions of years ago. Two basic processes form them. The first is when sediment containing organic matter hardens into shale over geologic time. Under high temperatures and pressure, the accumulations can be transformed into hydrocarbons like coal, oil, and natural gas. The second is when the sediment comprises shells and the skeletons of marine organisms, resulting in limestone.

The remaining carbon is found in the hydrosphere (.0076%), soils (.0031%), frozen tundra (.0018%), the atmosphere (.0015%), and the biosphere (.0012%).

The *carbon cycle* is how carbon is exchanged between these spheres. Carbon is also continually cycling throughout the biosphere. It is stored in carbon pools or reservoirs and moves between these reservoirs through various processes, including respiration, photosynthesis, combustion, decomposition, and sedimentation. *Carbon sinks* are those pools where more carbon is added than leaves. *Carbon sources* are those pools where more carbon leaves than is added. Expressed mathematically:

Carbon Sink = Carbon Inputs > Carbon Outputs

Carbon Source = Carbon Outputs > Carbon Inputs

The movement of carbon between pools is called a *flux*. If all sources are equal to all sinks, the carbon cycle is in *dynamic equilibrium* (or in balance) and there is no change in the size of the pools over time. Before the industrial revolution, the Earth's carbon cycle was relatively in balance for at least the last several hundreds of thousands of years.

Scientists describe two main types of carbon cycling (Figure 1.5). The fast (or biogenic) carbon cycle operates in the biosphere moving carbon from the atmosphere to the biosphere and back to the atmosphere. It includes annual cycles of photosynthesis and decadal cycles involving plant growth and decomposition. Human impacts to the fast carbon cycle are primarily deforestation and land-use change and have a relatively immediate impact on atmospheric carbon levels.

The slow (or geologic) carbon cycle occurs across millions of years, moving carbon through the ocean, rocks, soil, and the atmosphere. Plants and animals in the ocean die and settle on the ocean floor, where sedimentary rock is formed

TABLE 1.1 | Major stores of carbon by percent of the total.

Store of Carbon	% of total carbon	Forms of carbon
Lithosphere	99.985	Sedimentary rocks like limestone Organic carbon Hydrocarbons such as fossil fuels Marine sediments
Hydrosphere	0.0076	Carbonate ions Bicarbonate ions Dissolved CO_2
Pedosphere (soils)	0.0031	Soil organisms Plant remains
Cryosphere	0.0018	Frozen mosses Methyl clathrates
Atmosphere	0.0015	Gaseous carbon
Biosphere	0.0012	Living plants and animals

Source: https://www.coolgeography.co.uk/advanced/Stores_of_Carbon.php

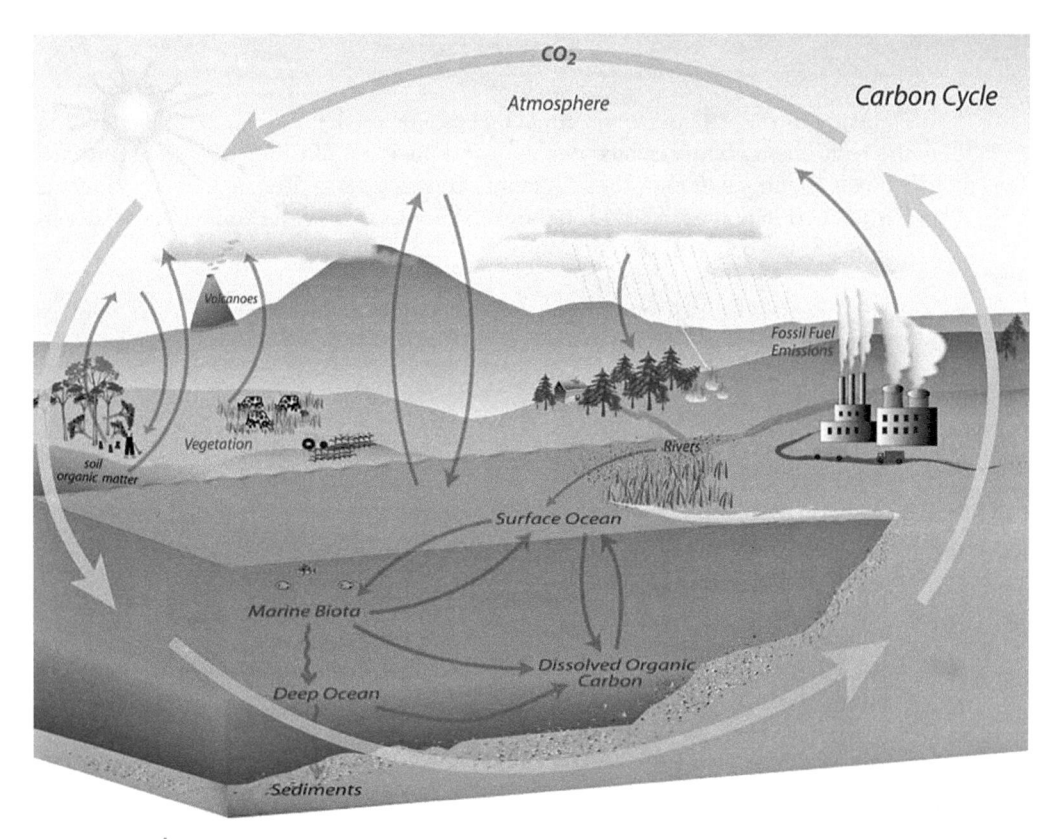

FIGURE 1.5 | The Fast (Biogenic) and Slow (Geologic) Carbon Cycles.
Source: https://www.noaa.gov/education/resource-collections/climate/carbon-cycle

over time. While volcanoes and other geologic processes return carbon directly to the atmosphere in the form of CO_2, this is a tiny proportion (less than 1 percent) of total emissions.

Since the beginning of the industrial revolution, humans have drastically disturbed the carbon cycle by extracting fossil carbon (coal, oil, gas, limestone) from the lithosphere and emitting it into the atmosphere. By 2020, the amount of CO_2 in the atmosphere had increased nearly 52 percent over pre-industrial levels, greater than at any time in the last 3.6 million years,[5] resulting in human-caused climate change. Most of those emissions have occurred in the past half-century, and rates continue to rise rapidly. Carbon sinks in the land and the ocean take up about one-quarter of anthropogenic carbon emissions each year, far less than needed to offset rising atmospheric CO_2 levels.

The largest consequences are still set to unfold in the coming decades and centuries. Restoring balance to this natural system is an international priority, as described in the Paris Climate Agreement and Sustainable Development Goal 13.

Conclusion

Knowing how Earth and environmental systems work is crucial to understanding the relationship between sustainability and business. Business decisions and our global economics impact these systems, and vice versa. The concepts and terms in this section will be used throughout the book to draw the connection between the business world and the environment.

Keywords

- Abiotic
- Air Pollution
- Apex Predator
- Aquatic Biomes
- Aquatic System
- Atmosphere
- Biomass
- Biome
- Biosphere
- Biotic
- Carbon Cycle
- Carbon Dioxide (CO_2)
- Carbon Oxides
- Carbon Sinks
- Carbon Sources
- Community
- Condensation
- Consumers
- Cryosphere
- Decomposers
- Desert Biomes
- Dynamic Equilibrium
- Ecological Hierarchy
- Ecology
- Ecosystems
- Evaporation
- Exosphere
- Fast (or Biogenic) Carbon Cycle
- Flux
- Food Chain
- Food Web
- Forest Biomes
- Generalists
- Geosphere
- Grassland Biomes
- Habitat
- Herbivore
- Hydrological Cycle
- Hydrosphere
- Ionosphere
- Keystone Species
- Lead
- Lithosphere
- Mesosphere
- Niche
- Nitrogen Oxides
- Ozone
- Population
- Precipitation
- Primary Consumers
- Producers
- Runoff
- Secondary Consumers
- Slow (or Geologic) Carbon Cycle
- Specialist
- Stratosphere
- Sulfur Oxides
- Terrestrial Systems
- Thermosphere
- Transpiration
- Trophic Levels
- Troposphere
- Tundra Biomes
- Volatile Organic Compounds (VOCs)

Discussion Questions

1. What are the two main Earth systems and four subsystems or spheres?
2. Describe the impact of human activity on each of the four subsystems or spheres.
3. Explain the hydrologic cycle and its mechanisms.
4. What differentiates the geosphere from the biosphere?
5. What is a biome, and what are the different forms of biomes?
6. Explain the concept of *ecological hierarchy*.
7. Contrast the concept of a *niche* from a *habitat*.
8. Contrast the concept of a *food chain* from a *food web*.
9. In ecological terms, explain why "eating lower on the food chain" results in less human impact on the environment.
10. Explain the concept of a keystone species and how its presence or absence can impact an ecosystem. Use an example not given in this chapter.
11. Describe the Earth's carbon cycle. How has human activity impacted it?

Endnotes

[1] Sweet, W. V., Kopp, R. E., Weaver, C. P., Obeysekera, J., Horton, R. M., Thieler, E. R., & Zervas, C. (2017). *Global and regional sea level rise scenarios for the United States: NOAA Technical Report NOS CO-OPS 083*. NOAA/NOS Center for Operational Oceanographic Products and Services.

[2] Klappenbach, L. (2021). The Biomes of the World. *ThoughtCo*. thoughtco.com/the-biomes-of-the-world-130173.

[3] Johnson, P. M., & Mayrand, K. (Eds.). (2006). *Governing global desertification: Linking environmental degradation, poverty, and participation*. Oxfordshire, UK: Routledge.

[4] Bar-On, Y. M., Phillips, R., & Milo, R. (2018). The biomass distribution on Earth. *Proceedings of the National Academy of Sciences of the United States of America, 115*(25), 6506–6511. ISSN 0027-8424. PMCID PMC6016768.

[5] NOAA Global Monitoring Laboratory. (n.d.). The NOAA annual greenhouse gas index (AGGI): An introduction. *NOAA Global Monitoring Laboratory/Earth System Research Laboratories*. Retrieved 30 October 2020 from https://gml.noaa.gov/aggi/.

CHAPTER 2

Climate Change

LEARNING OBJECTIVES

By the end of this chapter, you should be able to do the following:

- » Describe how human activity disrupts the Earth's carbon cycle.
- » Describe the causes and consequences of climate change. List the major greenhouse gases and identify their sources and impacts.
- » Identify strategies for reducing greenhouse gas emissions to limit global warming.
- » Describe global efforts to combat climate change.

CHAPTER OVERVIEW

Since the beginning of the industrial revolution, humans have drastically disrupted the carbon cycle by extracting fossil carbon (coal, oil, gas, limestone) from the lithosphere and emitting it into the atmosphere in the form of *greenhouse gases* (GHGs). The result is human-caused global warming and climate change. This chapter aims to provide an overview of climate change science and the role human activity plays in it. The topics covered include the carbon cycle, causes of climate change, consequences of this change, mitigation and adaptation strategies, and international efforts to solve the climate crisis.

Human Impact on the Earth's Carbon Cycle

Before the industrial revolution, all economies could be described as "organic" in that they were dependent on *insolation* (exposure to the sun's rays) and the resulting process of photosynthesis in plants. The entire world economy was based on the *fast (or biogenic) carbon cycle* (described in Chapter 1), whereby carbon moves back and forth between the biosphere and the atmosphere. It includes annual cycles of photosynthesis and decadal cycles involving plant growth and decomposition. Virtually all forms of energy were mechanical in the form of work done by human labor and animals. Biomass produced from photosynthesis provided the energy source for food and forage for both, along with thermal energy for heating and cooking. Hydropower and wind in the form of watermills and windmills were present but contributed a marginal amount for specific purposes like milling grain.

Therefore, growth was severely constrained by the amount of energy available from the biogenic carbon cycle. People living in these economies would have been acutely aware of these environmental limits. Early economic theorists like Thomas Malthus and Adam Smith saw land productivity as a significant limit to growth. As Smith remarked:[1]

> In a country which had acquired that full complement of riches which the nature of its soil and climate, and its situation concerning other countries, allowed it to acquire; which could, therefore, advance no further, and which was not going backwards, both the wages of labour and the profits of stock would probably be very low.

This all began to change in the early 19th century with the industrial revolution. Two factors are generally recognized as co-evolving to create this societal transformation. The first was the emergence of modern capitalism, which allowed for vastly increased productivity. But that alone was not sufficient to produce the industrial revolution, given the limits posed by biogenic energy sources. A new form of capital was needed for that to occur: fossil energy, particularly coal extracted from the lithosphere.

Ironically, fossil energy is also produced by plant photosynthesis. The difference is that it was created over 300–400 million years as part of the slow or *geologic carbon cycle* and stored in the lithosphere. Utilizing this new form of capital was critical since it meant that energy could be expanded on a scale not available from the biogenic carbon cycle.

The graph below (Figure 2.1) describes the dramatic increase in coal consumption in England as the Industrial Revolution grew. The chart also compares energy use patterns with Italy, which remained largely an agrarian society dependent on biogenic energy sources during this period.

During this first significant human disruption of the Earth's carbon cycle, coal was used to generate thermal energy to produce mechanical energy, primarily by steam engines but increasingly over time for industrial power plants. One steam horsepower fueled by coal was equivalent to 21 human laborers, and by 1840 in

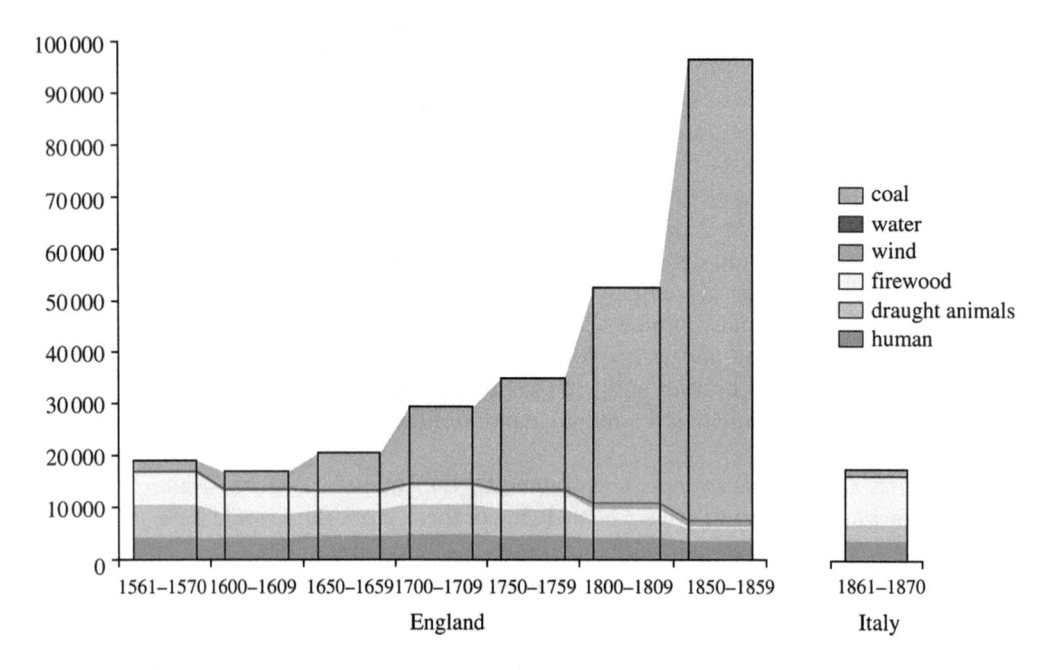

FIGURE 2.1 | Energy Consumption in England and Wales, 1561–1870.
Source: Wrigley, E. A. (2010). *Energy and the English Industrial Revolution*, Cambridge University Press.

France, steam engines performed the work of 1.2 million workers. By the 1880s, that figure rose to 98 million workers.[2]

This second major disruption saw the introduction of internal combustion engines to power transportation (particularly for rail and ships, and later for automobiles and aviation) and industry. The following graph illustrates this shift to fossil energy sources, spurring the development of a global trade network. By the 1950s, nuclear energy became part of the world energy portfolio, along with electrical production from large hydropower developments. However, overall energy consumption was dominated primarily by fossil energy sources.

While this economic transformation from the biogenic carbon cycle to the geological carbon cycle has had a profound impact on all the Earth's systems, arguably the biggest problem is its impact on the climate from *global warming*. Global warming is defined as the increase in combined surface air and sea surface temperatures averaged over the globe over a 30-year period. It is expressed relative to the years 1850–1900 as a measure of pre-industrial temperatures.[3] In contrast to global warming, *climate change* is a long-term shift in temperatures and weather patterns. These shifts may be natural, such as through variations in the solar cycle. But since the 1800s, global warming from human activity has been the primary cause of climate change.

The United Nations *Intergovernmental Panel on Climate Change* (IPCC) has concluded that global warming must be limited to 1.5°C to avoid "tipping points" where the Earth's support systems pass a threshold, triggering climate *feedback loops* and irreversible cascading impacts.[4] Climate feedback loops are processes that either amplify or diminish *forcing* from GHG emissions. Examples of negative feedback loops include:

- *Water vapor.* As the Earth warms, more water evaporates into the atmosphere. Warming air can also hold more water vapor. The additional water vapor has more heat, which leads to a cycle of more warming and more evaporation.
- *Ice sheets.* Ice cover regulates global temperatures by the albedo effect, the reflecting of solar radiation away from Earth. Less sea ice leads to a cycle of further warming and even less sea ice.
- *Permafrost.* Global warming melts the Earth's permafrost, releasing the methane and carbon within, creating a feedback loop for even greater warming.

And we're already well on our way to reaching the 1.5°C tipping point. The IPCC has concluded that human-induced global warming reached approximately 1°C in 2017 and is increasing at a rate of .2°C per decade.[5] Higher warming levels have already occurred in many regions.

In the following section, we will explore how human-induced disruptions to the Earth's carbon cycle result in climate change.

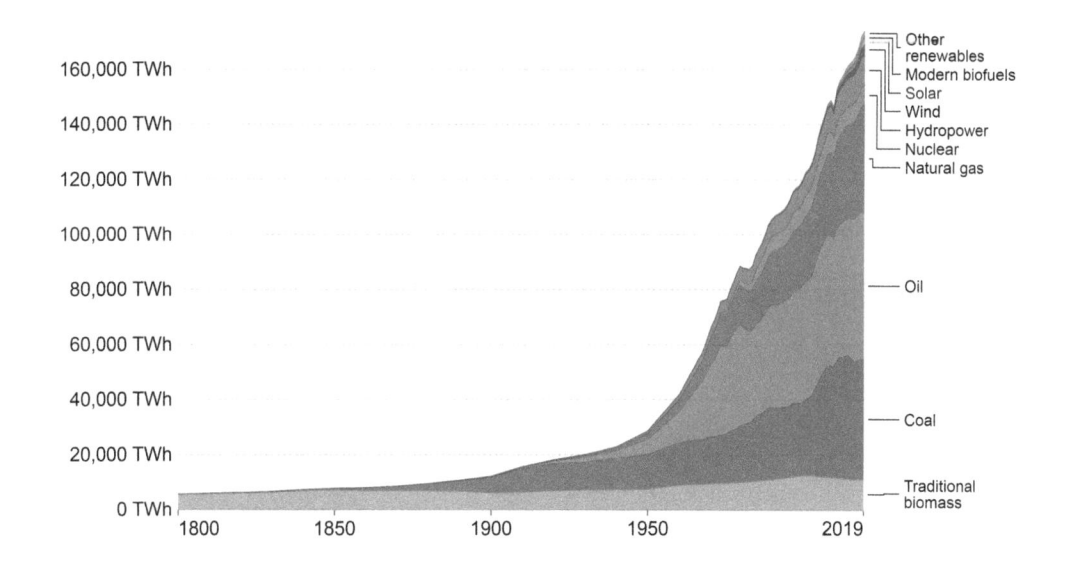

FIGURE 2.2 | Global Primary Energy Consumption.
Source: https://ourworldindata.org/energy-production-consumption

The Science of Climate Science

What Causes Climate Change

The relative stability of the Earth's temperature is called *thermal equilibrium*. This happens when the solar energy received from the sun is offset by the energy radiated back into space. The *greenhouse effect* slows the heat transfer from Earth to space, like a blanket of insulation that keeps the surface warmer. Without it, the Earth would be far too cold to support life.

The figure below (Figure 2.3) describes how the greenhouse effect works. Some solar radiation is reflected by the Earth and atmosphere back into space without contributing to warming. Some solar radiation passes through the Earth's atmosphere, is absorbed by the Earth's surface, and re-emitted as *infrared radiation* (heat) that escapes into space. However, some of this heat is intercepted by greenhouse gases and trapped in the atmosphere. The left side of Figure 2.3 shows how pre-industrial levels of greenhouse gases trap some of the sun's heat, making the Earth habitable.

The increase of greenhouse gases from fossil fuel emissions is causing slightly more heat to be absorbed by the Earth than is radiated into space. This slight imbalance is changing the planet in dangerous ways. On the right of Figure 2.3, the burning of fossil fuels traps additional solar radiation, increasing the planet's average temperature.

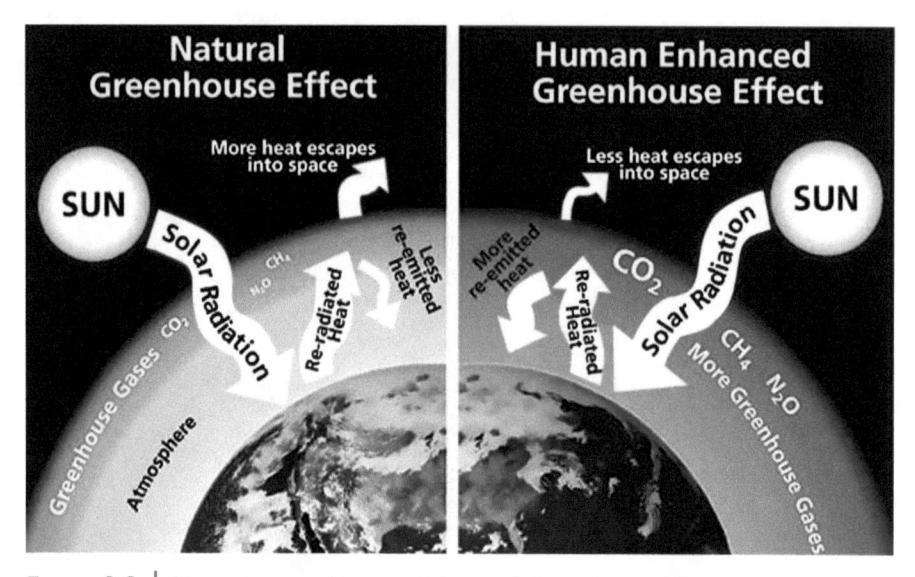

FIGURE 2.3 | Natural versus Human-Enhanced Greenhouse Effect.
Source: https://www.nps.gov/grba/learn/nature/what-is-climate-change.htm

GREENHOUSE GASES

There are four leading greenhouse gases emitted by human activity, *carbon dioxide* (CO_2), *methane* (CH_4), *Nitrous oxide* (N_2O), and *synthetic fluorinated gases*, including *hydrofluorocarbons* (HFCs), *perfluorocarbons* (PFCs), and *sulfur hexafluoride* (SF_6). These gases vary in their source and contribution to the greenhouse effect. (Note: All emission estimates are from the Inventory of U.S. Greenhouse Gas Emissions and Sinks: 1990–2019.)[6] Water vapor is also a greenhouse gas but is not directly affected by human activity.

Carbon Dioxide

The chart below shows that CO_2 emissions were very low before the Industrial Revolution. From 1990 to 2020, emissions rose from 6 to 34 billion metric tons per year. At the same time, we can see that atmospheric CO_2 concentrations were below 300 ppm before the Industrial Revolution. As of 2020, atmospheric CO_2 concentration set a record high of 412.5 ppm.

Today CO_2 emissions are the primary driver of climate change, accounting for about 76 percent of GHG emissions from human activity. Since most CO_2 emissions come from fossil fuel combustion, emission levels vary according to various socioeconomic factors, such as economic growth, population, energy prices, technological innovation, consumer behavior, and seasonal temperatures.

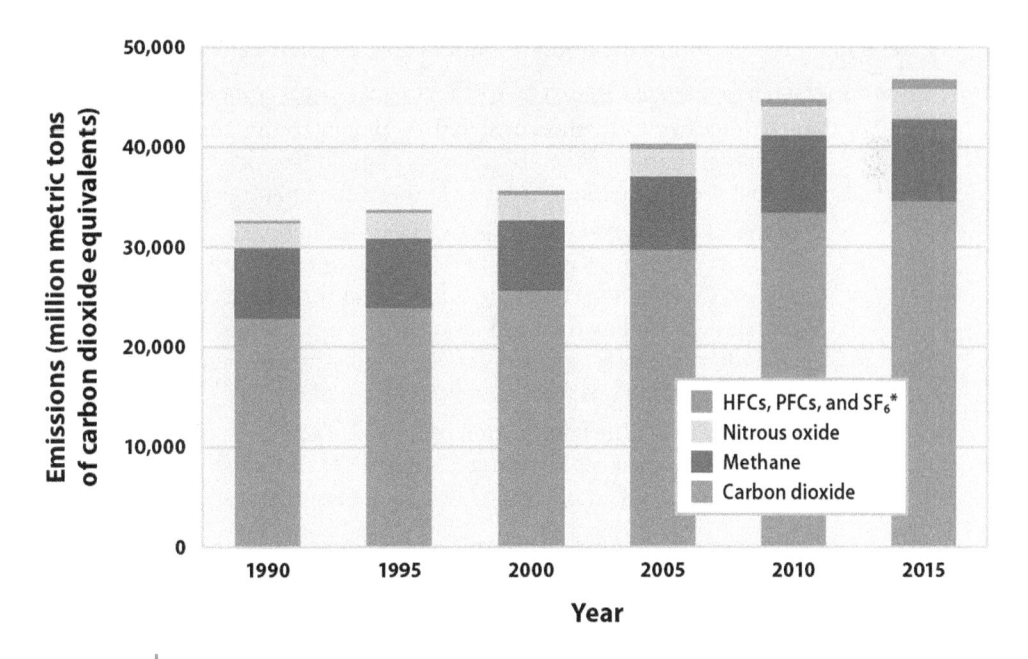

FIGURE 2.4 | Global GGH Emissions by Gas, 1990–2015.
Source: https://www.epa.gov/climate-indicators/climate-change-indicators-global-greenhouse-gas-emissions

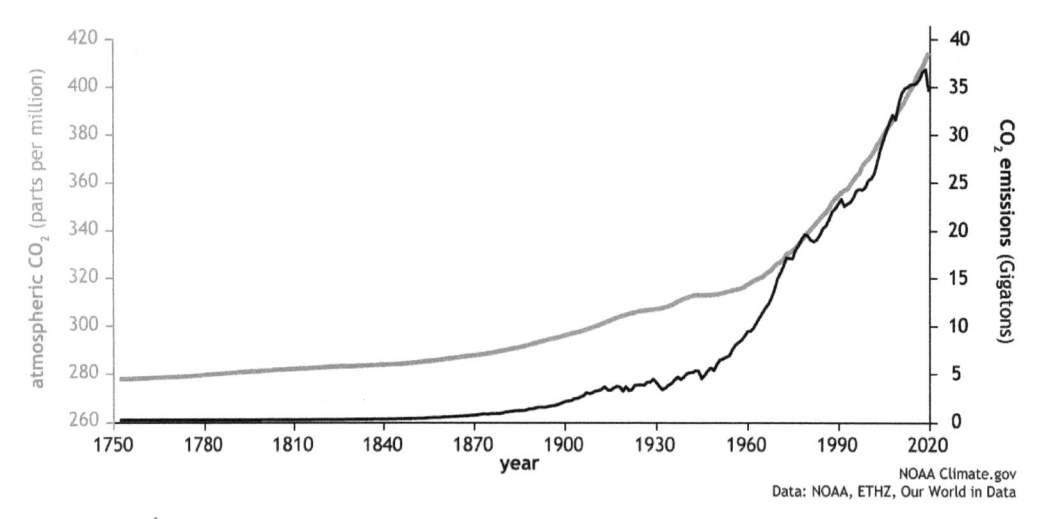

FIGURE 2.5 | CO₂ Emissions and Atmospheric Concentration (1750–2020).
Source: https://www.climate.gov/news-features/understanding-climate/climate-change-atmospheric-carbon-dioxide

There are both natural and human sources of CO_2 emissions. The primary natural sources are decomposition, ocean release, and respiration. About 87 percent of the human-produced CO_2 comes from burning fossil fuels like coal, oil, and natural gas. Of this, the primary sources are (see chart below):

- ***Electricity and heating.*** Electrical and heat production make up the largest source of CO_2 emissions, with 37 percent of the total. The types of fossil fuels used to generate electricity emit different amounts of CO_2, with coal producing more CO_2 per kilowatt than natural gas or oil.
- ***Industry.*** Fossil fuel combustion from various industrial processes accounted for about 25 percent of CO_2 emissions. Several processes also produce CO_2 emissions through chemical reactions that do not involve combustion, including the production of cement, metals, and chemicals. Many industrial processes also use electricity, thereby indirectly contributing to CO_2 emissions from electricity generation.
- ***Transportation.*** The combustion of fossil fuels to drive our transportation systems accounts for about 23 percent of CO_2 emissions. This includes trucks and automobiles, air travel, marine transport, and rail.

The remaining CO_2 emissions come from other activities, primarily deforestation and land-use changes. This is because forests absorb tremendous amounts of CO_2 from the atmosphere through photosynthesis, where it is stored in biomass and the soil. Deforestation and land-use change reduce the capacity of natural sinks like forests and soils to remove and store CO_2 from the atmosphere.

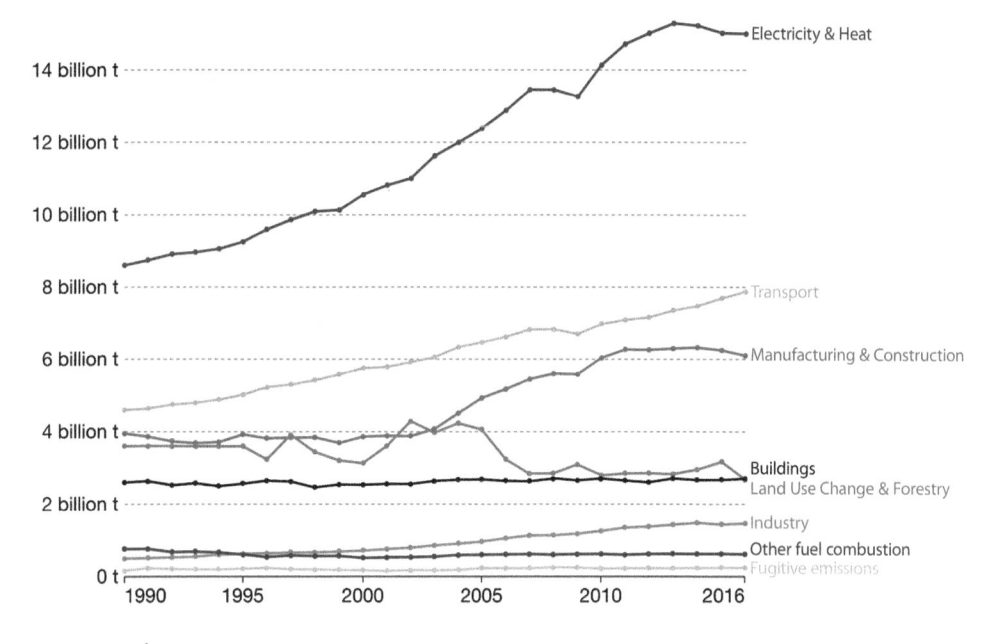

FIGURE 2.6 | Global CO$_2$ Emissions by Economic Sector.
Source: https://ourworldindata.org/emissions-by-sector

Methane

CH$_4$ accounts for 16 percent of global GHG emissions. Methane exists in the atmosphere for a much shorter time than CO$_2$ but is far more efficient at trapping radiation. While most CO$_2$ is produced by combustion and respiration, most CH$_4$ is emitted from the following human activities:

- *Agriculture.* The agriculture sector is the largest source of global CH$_4$ emissions. Domestic livestock produces CH$_4$ as part of normal digestive processes. It is also produced from animal manure in lagoons and holding tanks. While not shown and less significant, emissions of CH$_4$ also occur due to land use and land management activities in the Land Use, Land-Use Change, and Forestry sector (e.g., forest and grassland fires, decomposition of organic matter in coastal wetlands, etc.).

- *Energy and Industry.* A primary component of natural gas, methane emissions occur through venting and unintentional leaks. Such *Fugitive emissions* occur at all levels of the supply chain, including wells, pipelines, storage tanks, and appliances.

- *Waste.* Waste comprises the third-largest source of CH$_4$ emissions. Methane is generated in landfills as waste from homes and businesses decomposes. It is also a product of domestic and industrial wastewater treatment, composting, and anaerobic digestion.

- *Land-use change.* Methane is also emitted from various natural sources, such as wetlands, where it is emitted from anaerobic bacteria that decompose organic matter. As the Earth warms, this process is accelerated by the thawing of the permafrost.

Nitrous Oxide

N_2O accounts for about 6 percent of all global GHG emissions from human activities, with over three-quarters of those emissions coming from agriculture. It is also part of the Earth's nitrogen cycle and naturally present in the atmosphere. N_2O emissions occur naturally through many sources associated with the nitrogen cycle, particularly from bacteria breaking down nitrogen in soils and the oceans. N_2O is removed from the atmosphere when absorbed by certain bacteria or destroyed by ultraviolet radiation or chemical reactions. N_2O stays in the atmosphere for over 100 years before being removed by a sink or destroyed through chemical reactions. The impact of 1 pound of N_2O on warming the atmosphere is almost 300 times CO_2.

The primary human sources of N_2O include:

- *Agriculture.* The agriculture sector is by far the largest source of N_2O emissions. N_2O emissions result from various soil management activities, such as applying synthetic and organic fertilizers and other cropping practices, managing manure, and burning agricultural residues.

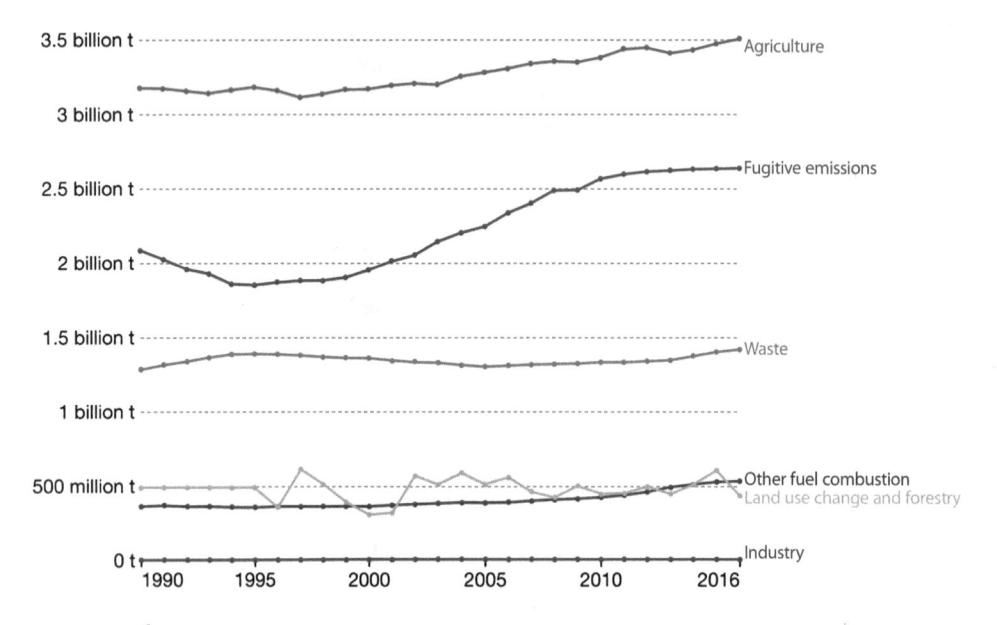

FIGURE 2.7 | Global CH_4 Emissions by Economic Sector.
Source: https://ourworldindata.org/emissions-by-sector

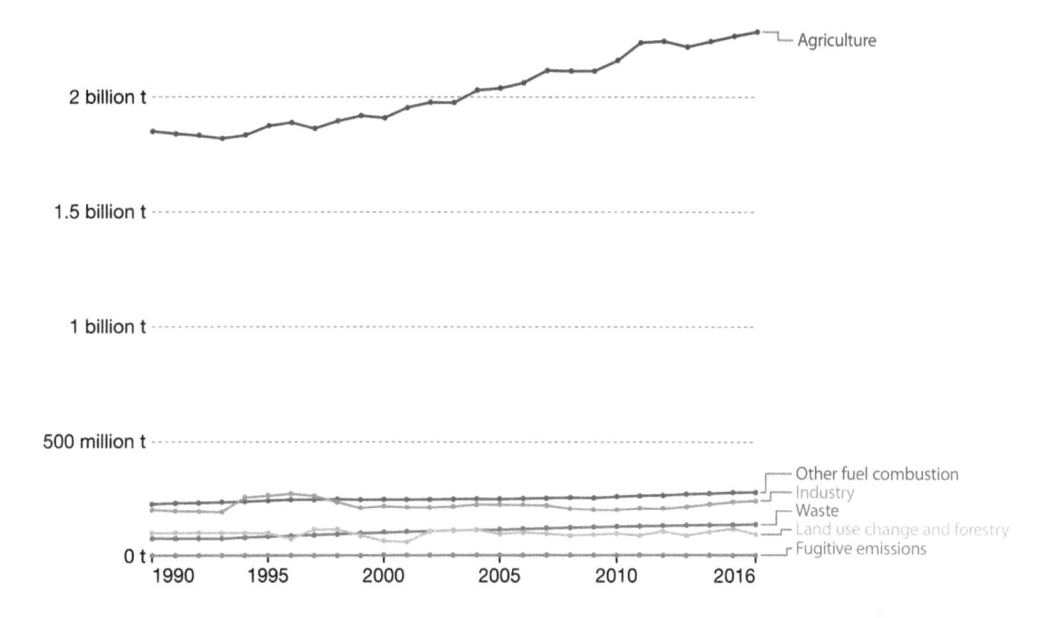

FIGURE 2.8 | Global N$_2$O Emissions by Economic Sector.
Source: https://ourworldindata.org/emissions-by-sector

- ***Fossil Fuel Combustion.*** Nitrous oxide is emitted when fuels are burned. The amount of N$_2$O emitted from burning fuels depends on the type of fuel and combustion technology, maintenance, and operating practices.
- ***Industry.*** N$_2$O is generated as a byproduct during the production of chemicals such as nitric acid, which is used to make synthetic commercial fertilizer, and in the production of adipic acid, which is used to make fibers like nylon and other synthetic products.
- ***Waste.*** N$_2$O is also generated from domestic wastewater treatment during nitrification and denitrification of the nitrogen present, usually in the form of urea, ammonia, and proteins.

Fluorinated Gases

Fluorinated gases include a suite of synthetic (do not exist in nature), potent greenhouse gases emitted from various industrial processes. There are four main categories of fluorinated gases: hydrofluorocarbons (HFCs), perfluorocarbons (PFCs), sulfur hexafluoride (SF$_6$), and nitrogen trifluoride (NF$_3$). Ironically, they are produced as substitutes for ozone-depleting refrigerant chemicals (e.g., chlorofluorocarbons, hydrochlorofluorocarbons, and halons) and through various industrial processes such as manufacturing aluminum and semiconductors. SF$_6$ is used as an insulating gas in electrical transmission equipment and circuit breakers.

The primary human sources of fluorinated gases include:

- **Substitution for Ozone-Depleting Substances.** HFCs are used as refrigerants, aerosol propellants, foam blowing agents, solvents, and fire retardants. Refrigerants used in air conditioning refrigerator systems are the primary source of these emissions. These chemicals were developed to replace chlorofluorocarbons (CFCs) and hydrochlorofluorocarbons (HCFCs) because they do not deplete the stratospheric ozone layer. Given their extreme impact as a greenhouse gas, they are being phased out by the next generations of hydrofluoroolefins (HFOs) with shorter atmospheric lifetimes.
- **Industry.** PFCs are a byproduct of aluminum production and are used to manufacture semiconductors. SF_6 is used in magnesium processing, semiconductor manufacturing, and tracer gas for leak detection.
- **Transmission and Distribution of Electricity.** SF_6 is an insulating gas in electrical transmission equipment and circuit breakers. SF_6 is the most potent greenhouse gas, 22,800 times that of an equal amount of CO_2.

Global Warming Potential

Different GHGs have different effects on the Earth's warming. The two critical factors by which GHGs differ are their *radiative efficiency* (the amount of energy they can absorb) and their lifetime (how long they stay in the atmosphere). *Global Warming Potential* (GWP) is a standard unit for measuring the global warming impacts of different greenhouse gases. CO_2 serves as the baseline, with 1 ton of CO_2 having a GWP of 1, regardless of the time period used since it remains in the climate system for thousands of years. GWP measures how much energy that 1 ton of gas will absorb over a given period, usually 100 years, relative to 1 ton

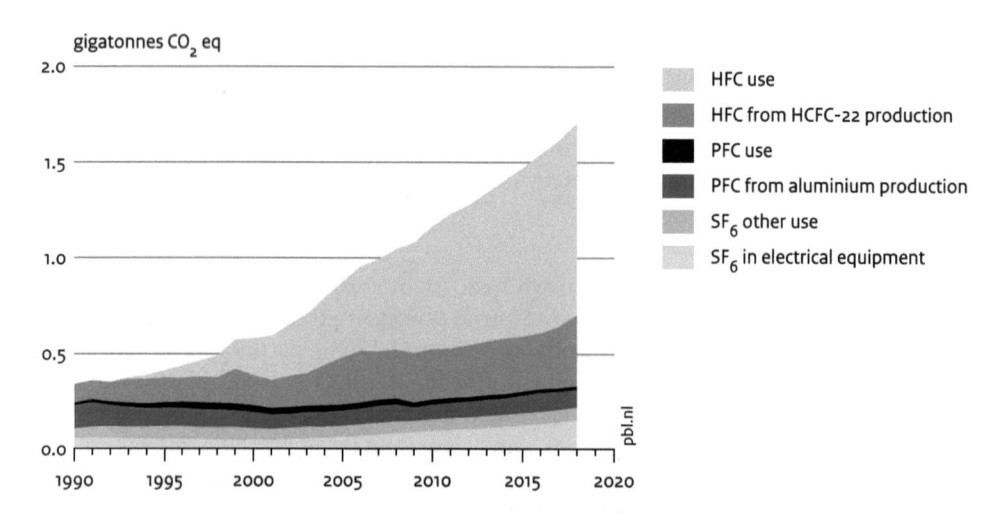

Figure 2.9 | Global Fluorinated Gas Emissions by Gas Type.
Source: https://edgar.jrc.ec.europa.eu/

TABLE 2.1 | Greenhouse gas emissions and properties.

Green House Gas	Chemical Formula	Emissions	Emissions Trend (since 1990)	Lifetime in Atmosphere (in years)	Global Warming Potential (GWP) (100-year period)
Carbon dioxide	CO_2	6,558 million metric tons	+3%	Thousands of years	1
Methane	CH_4	13 million metric tons	−15%	12 years	28
Nitrous Oxide	N_2O	7.9 million metric tons	+0%	114 years	265
Fluorinated Gases[1]	HFCs PFCs SF_6 NF_3	185 million metric tons	86%	HFCs: 270 years PFCs: 2,600–50,000 years NF_3s: 740 years SF_6s: 3,200 years	HFCs: up to 14,800 PFCs: up to 12,000 NF_3: 17,200 SF_6: 22,800

[1] Over 80 substances controlled by the Montreal Protocol. SAR

of CO_2 emissions. GWPs enable us to add up emissions and different gases into GHG inventories, allowing for comparing emissions and reduction strategies across economic sectors and gases.

The table below shows 2019 GHG emissions, trends in emissions since 2000, and the GWP properties of each GHG. While CH_4, N_2O, and fluorinated gas emissions are much lower than CO_2, their GWP is much higher. In the case of some fluorinated gases, the GWP is between 12,000 and 22,800 times that of CO_2. Even more troubling, the emission trend of these fluorinated gases has increased dramatically since 2000.

GHG Emission Sources and Mitigation Strategies

The primary sources of global GHG emissions are electricity and heat production (25 percent); agriculture, forestry, and land use (24 percent); industry (21 percent); transportation (14 percent); other energy, i.e., fuel extraction, refining, processing, and transportation (10 percent); and commercial and residential buildings (6 percent). *Mitigation strategies* are actions to reduce GHG emissions (see the section on mitigation later in the chapter for a full description of climate change mitigation and adaptation).

FIGURE 2.10 | Global Greenhouse Gas Emissions by Economic Sector. *Source:* https://www.epa.gov/ghgemissions/global-greenhouse-gas-emissions-data

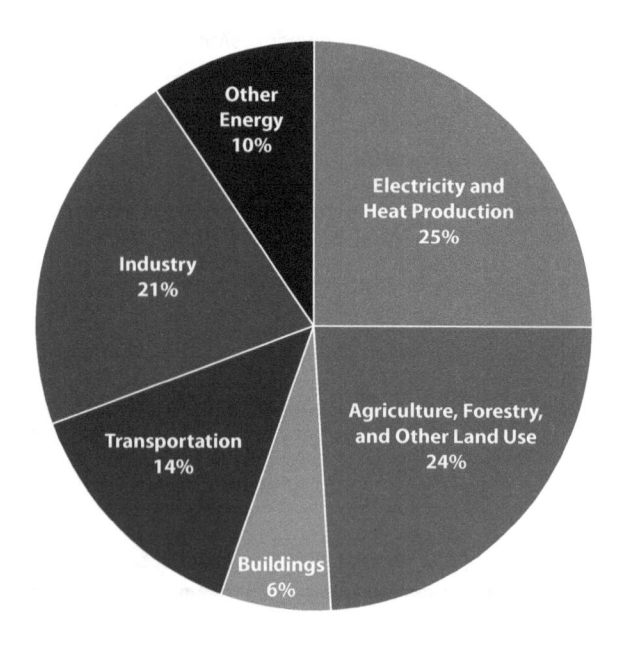

ELECTRICITY PRODUCTION

Emissions and Trends

Electricity production accounts for about 25 percent of global GHG emissions, with CO_2 comprising the vast majority, although CH_4 and N_2O are also emitted. These emissions result from the combustion of fossil fuels (coal, natural gas, oil) to produce electricity. A small fraction (about 1 percent) are fluorinated chemicals used as insulation in electricity transmission equipment.

Producing electricity from coal is much more emission-intensive than other fossil fuels. While coal accounted for about 34 percent of global electricity generated, it comprises over two-thirds of GHG emissions. Natural gas accounted for 23 percent of electricity generated, and petroleum less than 5 percent. The remaining 37 percent comes from low emission sources, including hydropower (17 percent), nuclear (10 percent), and renewables (11 percent). Renewables are composed of hydropower, wind, solar, and biomass.

CO_2 emissions declined by 3.3 percent in 2020, the most significant decrease on record. While the pandemic reduced demand, expansion of renewables was the biggest contributor to lower emissions, followed by a decline in coal. The share of renewables in global electricity generation rose from 27 percent in 2019 to 29 percent in 2020, the biggest annual increase on record. The rise of renewables has been having a growing impact on the electricity sector's emissions. Other reasons for the decrease are increased efficiency of both power generation and end-use appliances and lighting.

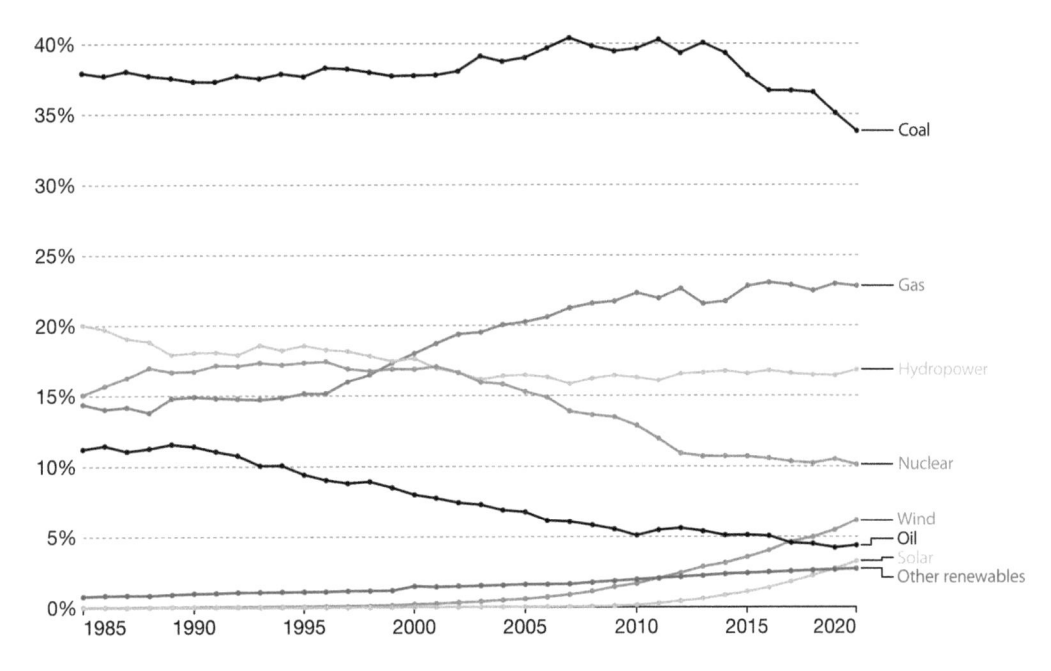

FIGURE 2.11 | Share of World Electricity Production by Fuel Type.
Source: https://ourworldindata.org/electricity-mix

Mitigation Strategies

The IPCC has identified five main strategies for reducing emissions from the electricity sector. The following table (Table 2.2) describes these strategies and provides examples for implementation.

AGRICULTURE SECTOR

Emissions and Trends

Agriculture, forestry, and land-use practices account for about 24 percent of global emissions. Techniques such as applying fertilizers, growing nitrogen-fixing crops, drainage of wet areas, and irrigation can result in N_2O. Such practices contribute over half of the emissions from the agriculture sector. Beyond that, livestock, particularly ruminants, produce CH_4 as part of the *enteric fermentation* digestive process, accounting for another quarter of agriculture emissions. Manure is also a significant source, emitting both CH_4 and N_2O. The remaining emissions come from applying lime and urea on fields, burning crop residue, and rice cultivation. Deforestation also continues to be a significant contributor.

This estimate does not include the CO_2 that ecosystems remove from the atmosphere by sequestering carbon in biomass, dead organic matter, and soils, which offset approximately 20 percent of emissions from this sector.[7]

TABLE 2.2 | Emission Reduction Strategies in the Electricity Sector.

Type	How Emissions Are Reduced	Examples
Fuel Switching and Increased Efficiency of Fossil-fired Power Plants	Substituting less carbon-intensive fuels; shifting to lower-emitting power plants; advanced power generation technologies	• Convert from coal-fired to natural gas boilers • Shift generators to lower-emitting units or power plants • Convert from single-cycle to combined-cycle gas turbines
Renewable Energy	Using renewable energy sources rather than fossil fuel to generate electricity	• Increase generating capacity from renewables (wind, solar, hydro, and geothermal sources, biofuels)
Increased End-Use Energy Efficiency	Increasing energy efficiency and conservation in homes, businesses, and industry	• ENERGY STAR® program (efficient appliances, lighting, water heaters, heat pumps) • Smart metering
Nuclear Energy	Generating electricity from nuclear energy rather than fossil fuels	• Extend the life of existing nuclear plant • Building new nuclear generating capacity
Carbon Capture and Sequestration (CCS)	Capturing CO_2 at the power plant source and injecting it into suitable subsurface geologic formations	• Capture CO_2 from the stacks of a coal-fired power plant • Injection into abandoned oil fields

Source: Modified from https://www.epa.gov/ghgemissions/sources-greenhouse-gas-emissions

Mitigation Strategies

The IPCC has identified three main strategies for reducing emissions from the agriculture sector. The following table describes these strategies and provides examples for implementation.

Other strategies for reducing on-farm emissions include:

- Zero-emission farm machinery and equipment (i.e., using methane produced on-site)
- Low- and no-tillage practices
- Optimize animal feed mix
- Controlled release and stabilized fertilizers

INDUSTRY

Emissions and Trends

The industrial sector produces the goods and raw materials we consume every day. It comprises manufacturing, mining, construction, fisheries, and forestry. Agriculture is also usually included, but because emissions from agriculture are so large, we have separated them above.

GHG emissions from the industry sector fall into two categories:

- *Direct emissions* that are produced at the facility. Most direct emissions result from burning fossil fuel for power or heat, chemical reactions, and leaks during the industrial process. A smaller amount comes from leaks during the industrial process, producing materials such as plastics and chemical reactions during the production of chemicals, iron and steel, and cement.
- *Indirect emissions* occur off-site, notably fossil fuel burning at power plants to make electricity, which is then used to power industrial processes.

Direct industrial emissions are the third largest (21 percent) sources of global emissions. If indirect emissions are included, industry is the largest contributor of greenhouse gases of any sector. Direct and indirect emissions from industry have continued to increase, despite implementing more efficient processes, fuel switching, combined heat and power, increased use of renewable energy, and more efficient use of materials, including material recycling.

TABLE 2.3 | Emission Reduction Strategies in the Agriculture Sector.

Type	How Emissions Are Reduced	Examples
Plant-Rich Diet	Plant-rich food systems produce fewer emissions and require fewer resources.	• Protein from beans instead of beef • Meat substitutes • End price subsidies for animal agriculture • Shift social norms away from meat consumption
Land and Crop Management	Adjusting the methods for managing land and growing crops.	• Fertilize crops with the appropriate amount of nitrogen since over-application leads to higher nitrous oxide emissions • Drain water from wetland rice soils during the growing season to reduce methane emissions
Livestock Management	Adjusting feeding practices and other management methods to reduce the amount of methane from enteric fermentation.	• Improve pasture quality to reduce the amount of methane emitted • Increase productivity/efficiency through improved breeding practices
Manure Management	Controlling the way in which manure decomposes to reduce nitrous oxide and methane emissions. Capturing methane from manure decomposition to produce renewable energy.	• Store and handle manure as a solid rather than liquid (lagoons) to reduce methane emissions • Store manure in anaerobic lagoons to maximize methane production, then capture and use as substitute for fossil fuels.

Source: Modified from https://www.epa.gov/ghgemissions/sources-greenhouse-gas-emissions

Mitigation Strategies

The IPCC has identified four main strategies for reducing emissions from the industrial sector. The following table describes these strategies and provides examples for implementation.

TRANSPORTATION

Emissions and Trends

The transportation sector is the fourth largest contributor to global GHG emissions, accounting for about 14 percent of total emissions. Transportation emissions come from burning fossil fuels to power cars, trucks, ships, trains, and airplanes. Over 90 percent of this fuel comes from petroleum, which is refined into various transportation fuels, including gasoline, diesel, jet fuel, and residual fuel oil (or bunker fuel, used in ships). Propane and natural gas are also fossil fuels used in the transportation sector. Light-duty and heavy-duty vehicles account for 72 percent of transportation emissions, with the remaining coming from aviation (11 percent), maritime transport (11 percent), rail (2 percent), and pipelines (2 percent).

Emissions from transportation have increased about 45 percent since 1990, primarily because of increased demand for travel. The *vehicle miles traveled* (VMT) increased by 48 percent, resulting from multiple factors, including population growth, economic growth, urban sprawl, and relatively low fuel prices. Modest annual increases in fuel economy have offset this since 2005.

GHG emissions from transportation are primarily in the form of CO_2 (97.4 percent) produced by burning fossil fuels in internal combustion engines. Smaller amounts of N_2O (0.6 percent) and CH_4 (0.1 percent) are also emitted during fuel

TABLE 2.4 | Emission Reduction Strategies in the Industrial Sector.

Type	How Emissions Are Reduced	Examples
Energy Efficiency	Upgrade to more energy-efficient technologies in manufacturing processes	• ENERGY STAR® program • Local utility incentive programs
Fuel Switching	Switching to less carbon-intensive fuels	• Convert from coal to natural gas to run machinery • Electricity from renewable sources
Recycling	Switch from use of raw materials to recycled materials in the manufacturing process	• Recycled feedstock materials: metals, paper, plastic, glass, tires, electronic waste, construction and demolition waste, batteries, paints, organic waste
Training and Awareness	Education and training programs aimed at reducing a company's emissions	• Instituting handling policies and procedures for fluorinated gases • Implement strategies for waste reduction

Source: Modified from https://www.epa.gov/ghgemissions/sources-greenhouse-gas-emissions

TABLE 2.5 | Emission Reduction Strategies in the Transportation Sector.

Type	How Emissions Are Reduced	Examples
Mode Shift	Using lower-carbon transport systems	• Public transport • Non-motorized infrastructure (walking, cycling) • Telepresence technology
Fuel Switching	Switching to fuels that emit less CO_2, including electricity from renewable sources, biofuels, and hydrogen	• Electric or hybrid automobiles • Low-carbon biofuels • Compressed natural gas to replace gasoline and diesel
Improved Fuel Efficiency	Using advanced technologies, design, and materials to develop more fuel-efficient vehicles	• Electric and hybrid vehicles • Reduce vehicle weight • Reduce aerodynamic resistance • Fuel efficiency standards
Improved Operating Practices	Adopting practices that minimize fuel use	• Reduce aircraft taxi time • Efficient transport routing • Reduce engine-idling • Weather routing of ships to increase fuel efficiency
Reducing Travel Demand	Reducing vehicle miles traveled through urban planning and land use management	• Improve low-carbon transportation infrastructure (public transportation, sidewalks, and bike lanes, telework technology) • Mixed use zoning to reduce travel distances from residences to schools, stores, and businesses

Source: Modified from https://www.epa.gov/ghgemissions/sources-greenhouse-gas-emissions

combustion. HFC emissions (2 percent) result from vehicle air conditioners and refrigerated transport.

Mitigation Strategies

The IPCC has identified four main strategies for reducing emissions from the transportation sector. The following table describes these strategies and provides examples for implementation.

COMMERCIAL AND RESIDENTIAL BUILDINGS

Emissions and Trends

This part of the economy includes businesses that don't manufacture or transport, such as health services, retail sales, entertainment, education, and financial services. It also includes all the activity around people living their lives in their homes). This sector includes all homes and commercial businesses (excluding agricultural and industrial activities). GHG emissions from this part of the economy fall into two categories:

- *Direct emissions* result from burning fossil fuels for heating and cooking, which emit CO_2, CH_4, and N_2O. These emissions account for 80 percent of direct emissions from this sector. Direct emissions also are created by waste and sewage management. Organic waste sent to landfills emits CH_4. Wastewater treatment plants emit CH_4 and N_2. Fluorinated gases used in refrigeration and air conditioning equipment also can leak into the atmosphere.

- *Indirect emissions* are produced offsite when fossil fuel is used to make electricity, used in residential and commercial activities such as lighting, appliances, heating, and cooling.

TABLE 2.6 | Emission Reduction Strategies in the Commercial and Residential Sector.

Type	How Emissions Are Reduced	Examples
Homes and Commercial Buildings	Reducing energy use through energy efficiency	• Better insulation • Energy-efficient heating, cooling, ventilation, and refrigeration systems • Efficient lighting • Passive heating and lighting to take advantage of sunlight • Energy-efficient appliances and electronics (learn more about ENERGY STAR®)
Wastewater Treatment	Making water and wastewater systems more energy-efficient	• Use efficient pumping systems • Efficient aeration and anaerobic digestion equipment • Capture energy from water moving downhill • Host solar and wind farms for renewable electricity generation
Waste Management	Reducing solid waste sent to landfills. Capturing and using methane produced in current landfills.	• Improved recycling, waste reduction, composting programs • Fleet efficiency (fuel switching, efficient routing) • Landfill methane capture programs • Host solar and wind farms for renewable electricity generation
Air Conditioning and Refrigeration	Reducing leakage from air conditioning and refrigeration equipment. Using refrigerants with lower global warming potentials.	• Implement programs to avoid leaks • Recover and destroy refrigerants at end of life • Alternatives to HFC refrigerants • Increased appliance efficiency, thereby lowering use of refrigerants

Source: Modified from https://www.epa.gov/ghgemissions/sources-greenhouse-gas-emissions

Direct GHG emissions from businesses and homes compose 6 percent of total U.S. emissions. When indirect emissions are included, the total is closer to 20 percent. Total emissions from this sector have increased by about 3 percent since 1990. This is due to many factors, including a growing population, economic growth, construction of buildings for businesses and homes, aging, and inefficient building stock. The demand for cooling of buildings in an increasingly warmer climate will likely push emissions higher. However, overall, continued efficiency improvements are expected to offset future population and economic growth and may even result in modest reductions in emissions.

Mitigation Strategies

The IPCC has identified four main strategies for reducing emissions from the commercial and residential sectors. The following table describes these strategies and provides examples for implementation.

CONSEQUENCES OF CLIMATE CHANGE

Global climate change from human activity has already had observable impacts on the environment. While these impacts are far-ranging, they can be grouped into four broad categories: 1) temperature and precipitation; 2) ecosystems; 3) sea-level rise, and; 4) ocean acidification.

TEMPERATURE AND PRECIPITATION

The Earth's average atmospheric temperature has already increased by about 1°C. As the graph below demonstrates, virtually all this increase results from human drivers. Warming from human sources will persist for hundreds if not thousands of years and is estimated to be increasing at a rate of .2°C per decade. At this rate, the world will reach 1.5°C of warming sometime between 2030 and 2052 and 3–4°C of warming by 2100.

The big question is, how hot will the planet get in the future? The Sixth Assessment Report of the IPCC uses several scenarios or *Shared Socioeconomic Pathways* (SSPs) to develop projections (see chart below). The best-case climate scenario, called SSP1, involves a global shift toward sustainable management of global resources and reduced inequity. SSP2 is a business-as-usual path with slow and uneven progress toward sustainable development goals and persisting income inequality and environmental degradation. SSP3 envisions heightened global conflict with countries focusing on their short-term domestic best interests, resulting in persistent and worsening inequality and environmental degradation. SSP5 is a dire scenario in which countries reverse their current commitments to the Paris Agreement and burn all the fossil fuels possible.

The model includes two SSP1 scenarios for achieving the Paris targets limiting global warming to 1.5 and 2°C. The SSP2 scenario predicts temperatures approaching 3°C in the year 2100. The SSP3 scenario predicts about 4°C global warming by the end of the century. The SSP5 scenario results in close to 5°C by 2100.

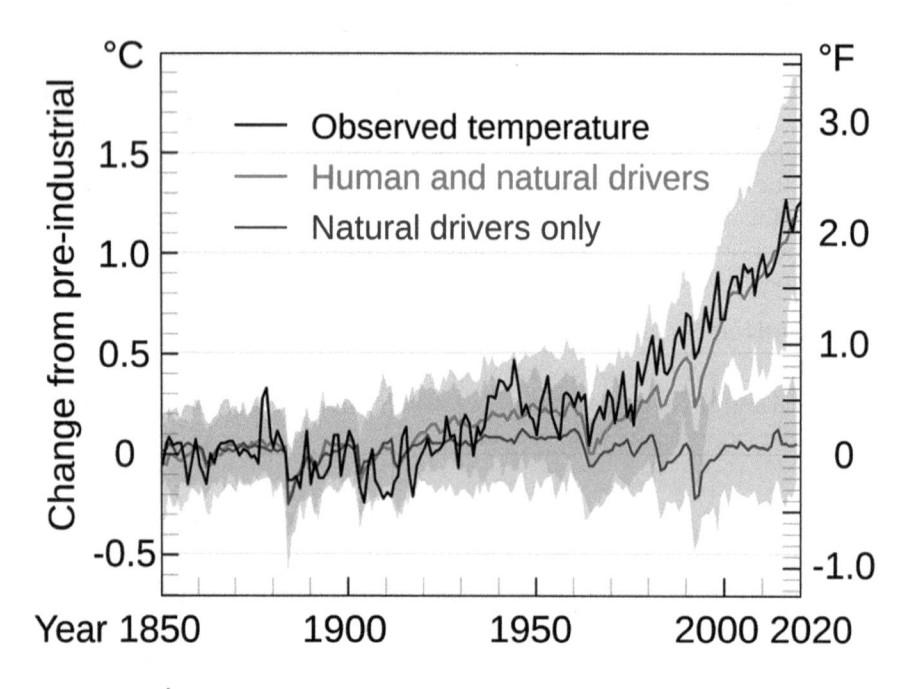

FIGURE 2.12 | Global Surface Temperature.
Source: https://data.giss.nasa.gov/gistemp/graphs_v4/#

Global warming can also affect the intensity of the Earth's water cycle. As we learned earlier, water vapor is a major component of the Earth's atmosphere. Warmer air holds more water than cooler air. As the air cools, its ability to hold water vapor decreases, resulting in precipitation. Furthermore, as the temperature rises, the evaporation on the Earth's surface also increases, increasing evaporation and surface drying.

Increased atmospheric moisture and precipitation will not fall evenly across the planet, with drier areas generally becoming drier and wet regions becoming wetter. Precipitation events are also expected to become more intense. With more precipitation falling in the form of rain rather than snow, less *snowpack* will accumulate in the mountains, reducing the flow of freshwater to the valleys below as it melts in the spring and summer.

SEA LEVEL RISE

Global warming causes sea levels to rise in two ways. First, the melting of glaciers and ice sheets adds water to the ocean. Second, the volume of the ocean expands as the water gets warmer. Sea level has risen about 9 inches since 1880, with about one-third of that occurring in the last 20–30 years. By the end of the century, sea levels are expected to rise between 1.7 and 3.2 feet above 2000 levels, even if GHG emissions are limited to 1.5°C pathways. Beyond 2100, sea levels will continue to rise for centuries and remain elevated for thousands of years.

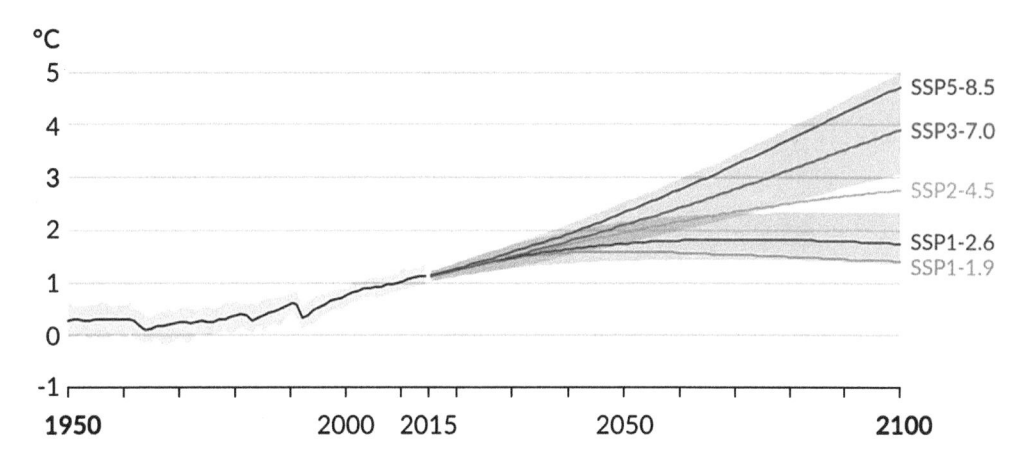

°C
```
5                                                           SSP5-8.5
4                                                           SSP3-7.0
3                                                           SSP2-4.5
2
1                                                           SSP1-2.6
0                                                           SSP1-1.9
-1
  1950        2000  2015        2050              2100
```

FIGURE 2.13 | Global Surface Temperature Projections.
Source: Figure SPM.8, Panel (a) of IPCC, 2021: Summary for Policymakers. In: *Climate Change 2021: The Physical Science Basis.* Contribution of Working Group I to the Sixth Assessment Report of the Intergovernmental Panel on Climate Change. Cambridge University Press, Cambridge, United Kingdom and New York, NY, USA, pp. 3–32, doi:10.1017/9781009157896.001.

The impacts of rising sea-levels fall into several broad categories: 1) submergence and flooding of coastal land, 2) more frequent and intense coastal flooding, saltwater intrusion into soils, surface waters, and groundwater, 3) loss and change of coastal ecosystems, 4) increased erosion, and 5) impeded drainage. Virtually all the Earth's coastal zones and low-lying islands face risk from these impacts.

OCEAN ACIDIFICATION

Ocean acidification refers to the increased acidity of the ocean over an extended period, caused primarily by the uptake of carbon dioxide (CO_2) from the atmosphere. The ocean absorbs about 30 percent of the CO_2 released into the atmosphere. When CO_2 is absorbed by seawater, the concentration of hydrogen ions increases, while carbonate ions become relatively less abundant. Carbonate ions are the building block for calcifying organisms such as oysters, clams, sea urchins, corals, and calcareous plankton. Decreases in carbonate ions make it difficult for these organisms to build and maintain shells and other calcium carbonate structures. Many species of plankton also need a specific pH to grow. If the ocean is too acidic, these species can no longer build their calcareous skeletons and have trouble developing. Ocean acidification also affects some fish's ability to detect predators. The entire ocean food web is impacted when these organisms are at risk.

Ocean acidification affects the entire world's oceans, including coastal estuaries and waterways. Coral reef ecosystems are particularly affected by ocean acidification. Many economies are dependent on fish and shellfish, and people worldwide rely on food from the ocean as their primary source of protein.

Ecosystems

Global warming impacts the Earth's ecosystems in a variety of ways. It may shift the habitat range to higher latitudes or higher elevations. In North America, both land and aquatic animals and plants have moved to higher elevations at the rate of 36 feet per decade and to higher latitudes at 10.5 miles per decade. Since this rate of movement is not possible for some species, the result can be local extinctions of both plants and animals. Similarly, as sea levels rise, saltwater intrusion into a freshwater system may change the entire ecosystem to a saltwater habitat.

Other impacts of a warming planet on ecosystems include disruptions to food webs, reduction of buffering capacity, the spread of pathogens, parasites, diseases, and species extinction.

Indirect Consequences of Climate Change

The direct consequences of climate change described above lead to a cascading set of indirect effects that directly affect our socioeconomic systems and us as humans. While the list is long, notable consequences include:

- hunger and water crises, especially in developing countries
- health risks from rising air temperatures and heatwaves
- cost of relocating from coastal areas
- mass migration
- higher insurance costs
- higher food prices
- reduced work productivity due to heat
- lower agricultural productivity
- economic impacts of extreme weather, drought, and wildfire events
- spread of disease, pests, and pathogens
- loss of biodiversity
- reduced productivity of marine resources from ocean acidification
- cost of adaptation (e.g., agriculture, forestry, energy, infrastructure, tourism, etc.)
- national security

Climate Solutions

Climate change *mitigation* consists of actions to limit global warming and resulting climate change. It involves avoiding and reducing GHG emissions and increasing carbon sequestration of GHGs already in the atmosphere. In contrast, climate change *adaption* consists of actions that enable us to adjust to life in a changing climate. It involves altering our behavior, public policies, and business practices to reduce our vulnerability to the harmful effects of climate change.

MITIGATION STRATEGIES

Climate change mitigation strategies focus on three general approaches to reducing atmospheric carbon concentrations:

- ***Conventional Mitigation Strategies.*** The first approach is to stop burning fossil fuels, using a mix of supply-side and demand-side technologies to decarbonize all aspects of the world economy. This generally involves scaling up renewables and nuclear energy production, fuel switching, efficiency gains, point-source carbon capture and storage, and energy storage. Specific strategies were discussed earlier in the chapter for each economic sector.

- ***Negative Emission Mitigation Strategies.*** The second approach involves strategies to capture and sequester GHGs from the atmosphere, sometimes referred to as *negative emission technologies* or *carbon removal methods*. This approach includes a collection of *natural climate solutions* that use photosynthesis to capture and store carbon, such as afforestation, reforestation, soil carbon sequestration, and wetland restoration. It also includes complex technologies for *direct air capture and storage* (DAC+S), in which large fans push ambient air through a chemical filter to capture and fix CO_2.

- ***Geoengineering Mitigation Strategies.*** Geoengineering approaches involve modifying the Earth's radiation balance by reflecting solar radiation back to space. Examples include stratospheric aerosol injection, cirrus cloud thinning, marine sky brightening, space-based mirrors, surface-based brightening. These technologies are all theoretical and come with a great deal of risk and uncertainty about their effectiveness and unintended negative consequences. As such, they are not part of any current international mitigation frameworks.

Various political/economic mitigation measures are used to implement the above mitigation strategies. To date, these efforts include regulations requiring low-carbon energy and increased energy efficiency in products, consumer incentives, carbon pricing such as carbon taxes and cap and trade programs, tax incentives, and eliminating fossil fuel subsidies.

ADAPTATION STRATEGIES

Climate change is already occurring, making it essential to adapt to our changing environment. Adaptation refers to ecological, social, or economic adjustments in response to climatic change and its impacts. It involves changing processes, practices, and structures to moderate potential damages. Countries, communities, and businesses need to develop and implement adaptation actions to respond to the impacts of climate change that are already happening and prepare for future consequences.

The best climate change adaptation strategies simultaneously achieve other societal goals, such as sustainable development, disaster risk reduction, and improvements in quality of life. As such, adaptation strategies can provide multiple benefits when incorporated into existing decision-making processes. Adaptation actions can be implemented proactively to prepare for projected changes or reactively after climate changes occur. Proactive preparation can reduce the vulnerability to shifting temperature and precipitation patterns on water supplies, air quality, and habitat. Reactive strategies may be necessary when unanticipated consequences occur.

Adaptation can take many shapes and forms, depending on the unique context of a community, business, or country. Adaptations can include reducing wildfire fuel loads, setting up early warning systems for flooding, switching to drought-resistant crops, business operations, and government policies. Many nations and communities are already building climate-resilient societies and economies. Still, considerably greater action and ambition will be needed to manage the risks cost-effectively, both now and in the future.

INTERNATIONAL COOPERATION

Since climate change is a global problem, international negotiations and agreements have been critical to mitigation efforts. Since the groundbreaking *Rio Earth Summit* in 1992, the United Nations has recognized climate change as a serious issue, leading to a series of negotiations and agreements. The Rio Summit resulted in the *United Nations Framework Convention on Climate Change* (UNFCCC). The ultimate objective of the UNFCCC is to stabilize atmospheric concentrations of GHGs below 2°C relative to the pre-industrial level. While the UNFCCC does not legally bind signatories to reduce greenhouse gas emissions and gives no targets or timetables, it required frequent meetings between the ratifying countries, known as the Conference of the Parties, or COP, which led to additional agreements and firmer commitments. As of 2022, UNFCCC has been ratified by 197 countries.

The first legally binding climate treaty happened in 1997 at COP3 in Japan. The *Kyoto Protocol* requires developed countries to reduce emissions by 5 percent below 1990 levels and establishes a system to monitor countries' progress. Acknowledging systemic inequities in emissions, it did not compel developing countries, including high carbon emitters China and India, to act. It did create a carbon market for countries to trade emissions units in a system known as "cap and trade."

The successor to the Kyoto Protocol was supposed to be finalized at COP15 in Copenhagen, but the parties only reached a nonbinding agreement, the *Copenhagen Accord*. The accord does acknowledge that global temperatures should not increase by 2°C (3.6°F) above preindustrial levels, though representatives from developing countries sought a target of 1.5°C. Some countries later vowed to follow the accord and make non-binding pledges.

What followed were a series of COP meetings that also did not result in agreements, including Cancún (2010), Durban (2011), Doha (2012), and Warsaw (2013). Finally, in 2015, the landmark *Paris Agreement* was reached. Unlike past accords, it requires nearly all developed and developing countries to set emissions reduction goals, essentially confirming commitments made at the Rio Earth Summit and Kyoto.

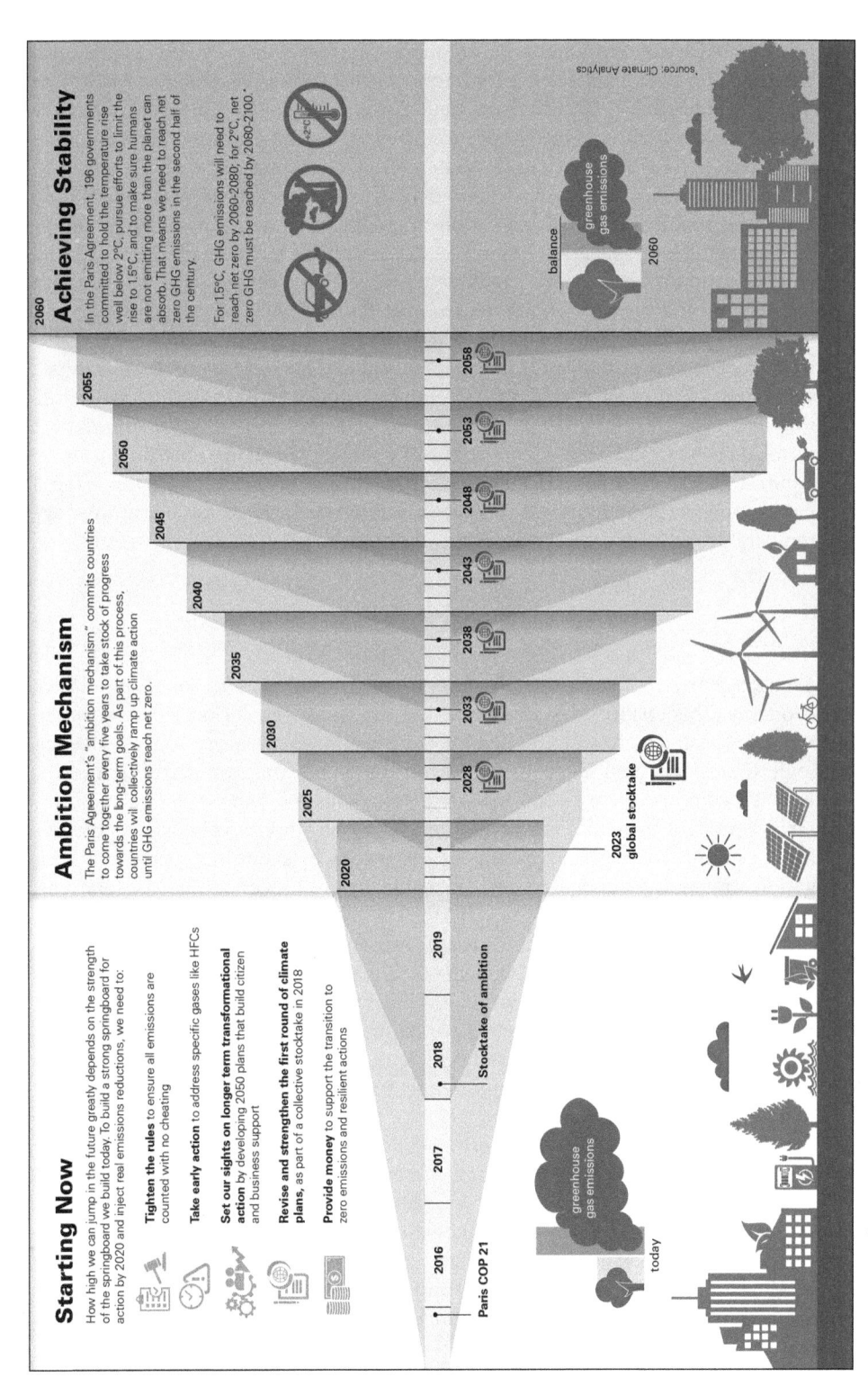

FIGURE 2.14 | Timeline for Paris Agreement Ambition Mechanism.
Source: https://www.e3g.org/publications/the-paris-agreement-ambition-mechanism/

Current Paris Agreement commitments are insufficient to keep global temperature increases below 2°C. Therefore, raising ambition over time is key to the agreement. It establishes a ratcheting mechanism wherein countries come together every five years to take stock of progress and ramp up emission reduction obligations accordingly to reach net-zero GHG emissions by 2050. A key to the mechanism is comprehensive *monitoring, reporting, and verifications* (MRV) and implementing international carbon markets, finance systems, and technology transfer. However, countries were still allowed to choose their targets and no enforcement mechanisms were included. Under the agreement, countries submit targets known as *nationally determined contributions* (NDCs).

COP26 in 2021 resulted in the *Glasgow Climate Pact*, which calls for countries to reduce coal use and fossil fuel subsidies—both firsts for a UN climate agreement—and urges governments to submit more ambitious emissions-reduction targets by the end of 2022. In addition, delegates finally established rules for a global carbon market. Smaller groups of countries made notable side deals on deforestation, methane emissions, coal, and more. But analysts note that even if nations follow through on their pledges for 2030 and beyond, the world's average temperature will still rise 2.1°C (3.8°F).

Conclusion

Climate change is fundamentally an outcome of our modern fossil fuel-driven economy. This chapter describes how the industrial revolution led to a fundamental transformation of the economy from biogenic energy sources to geologic sources or fossil fuels. This shift resulted in a significant disruption to the Earth's carbon cycle. We then explored the science of climate change and how GHG emissions from fossil fuels result in global warming and climate change. We looked in-depth at the sources of GHG emissions by economic sector and mitigation strategies for reducing emissions. Finally, we looked at climate solutions, including international efforts to solve the climate crisis.

Achieving net-zero emissions is a massive global undertaking and only possible with the widespread involvement of businesses. To reach net-zero goals, it is estimated that 2 percent of global GDP will need to be dedicated to the effort. The required infrastructure investments are estimated to be $7 trillion per year up to 2030. However, the impact of inaction is much worse. Economists estimate that if current trajectories continue and temperatures rise 3.2°C by 2050, global GDP will decrease by 18 percent.

Decarbonization is the most critical and challenging aspect of sustainability that the business community faces. It comes with enormous obligations but also opportunities. Many organizations have already begun the journey. In the short term, the first step is to develop a holistic understanding of the company's climate impacts, risks, and opportunities. This requires a science-based approach to quantify the company's emissions and sources and infuse awareness of these impacts across every part of the organization. From that base understanding, a comprehensive mitigation plan can be developed that injects decarbonization into every critical decision and every point in the value chain. Eventually, firms will need to adapt governance mechanisms to build decarbonization into roles, responsibilities, remuneration, and accountability.

In the long term, climate action represents new business opportunities. The zero-emission transition creates demand for new goods and services worth trillions of dollars across all sectors. Opportunity exists not only for companies to develop products and services that mitigate climate change but also to help other companies decarbonize their operations, products, and services.

Keywords

- » Albedo Effect
- » Climate Change Adaptation
- » Climate Change Mitigation
- » Carbon Dioxide (CO_2)
- » Climate Feedback Loops
- » Climate Forcing
- » Conference of the Parties (COP)
- » Copenhagen Accord
- » Direct Air Capture and Storage (DAC+S)
- » Direct Emissions
- » Enteric Fermentation
- » Fast (or Biogenic) Carbon Cycle
- » Fluorinated Gases
- » Fuel Switching
- » Geologic Carbon Cycle
- » Glasgow Climate Pact
- » Global Warming
- » Global Warming Potential (GWP)
- » Greenhouse Effect
- » Greenhouse Gases (GHGs)
- » Hydrofluorocarbons (HFCs)
- » Indirect Emissions
- » Infrared Radiation (Heat)
- » Insolation
- » Intergovernmental Panel on Climate Change (IPCC)
- » Kyoto Protocol
- » Methane (CH_4)
- » Monitoring, Reporting, And Verifications (MRVs)
- » Nationally Determined Contributions (NDCs)
- » Natural Climate Solutions
- » Nitrous Oxide (N_2O)
- » Ocean Acidification
- » Paris Agreements
- » Perfluorocarbons (PFCs)
- » Rio Earth Summit
- » Sea Level Rise
- » Shared Socioeconomic Pathways (SSPs)
- » Slow (or Geologic) Carbon Cycle
- » Snowpack
- » Sulfur Hexafluoride (SF_6)
- » Thermal Equilibrium
- » United Nations Framework Convention on Climate Change (UNFCCC)
- » Vehicle Miles Traveled (VMT)

Discussion Questions

1. How has human activity disrupted the Earth's carbon cycle?
2. Why is 1.5°C of global warming such a critical threshold?
3. Describe the greenhouse effect.
4. What are the leading greenhouse gases (GHGs) and their primary sources of emission?

5. Explain Global Warming Potential (GWP)? How do the leading greenhouse gases compare regarding their GWP?
6. What are the primary GHG emissions from the transportation sector, and what strategies could be employed to reduce these emissions?
7. What are the primary GHG emissions from the electricity production sector, and what strategies could reduce these emissions?
8. What are the primary GHG emissions from the industry sector, and what strategies could be employed to reduce these emissions?
9. What are the primary GHG emissions from the commercial and residential sectors, and what strategies could reduce these emissions?
10. What are the primary GHG emissions from the agriculture sector, and what strategies could be employed to reduce these emissions?
11. Why is electrification such a critically important strategy for reducing emissions?
12. What are the consequences, both direct and indirect, of climate change?
13. Describe international efforts to combat climate change.

Recommended Websites

- Intergovernmental Panel on Climate Change – https://www.ipcc.ch/
- United Nations Climate Action – https://www.un.org/en/climatechange/
- National Center for Atmospheric Research (National Science Foundation) – https://ncar.ucar.edu/
- The European Environment Agency (EEA) – https://www.eea.europa.eu/
- National Centers for Environmental Information (NOAA) – https://www.ncei.noaa.gov/
- Skeptical Science – https://skepticalscience.com/
- Center for Climate & Energy Solutions (C2ES) – https://www.c2es.org/
- Global Change (U.S. Global Change Research Program) – https://www.globalchange.gov/
- EPA Climate Change Page – https://www.epa.gov/climate-change

Endnotes

[1] Smith, A. (2002). *The wealth of nations*. Oxford, England: Bibliomania.com Ltd.
[2] Levasseur, É. (1889). *La population française: Histoire de la population avant 1789 et démographie de la France comparée à celle des autres nations au XIX siècle, précédée d'une introduction sur la statistique*. Vol. 1. Paris, France: Arthur Rousseau.
[3] NASA. (n.d.). Global warming versus climate change. *NASA*. https://climate.nasa.gov/resources/global-warming-vs-climate-change/

[4] Intergovernmental Panel on Climate Change. (n.d.). *IPCC.* https://www.ipcc.ch/.
[5] Intergovernmental Panel on Climate Change. (2018). Special report: Global warming of 1.5°C. *IPCC.* https://www.ipcc.ch/sr15/.
[6] EPA. (2022, April 14). Inventory of U.S. greenhouse gas emissions and sinks: 1990–2019. *United States Environmental Protection Agency.* https://www.epa.gov/ghgemissions/inventory-us-greenhouse-gas-emissions-and-sinks
[7] Tubiello, F. N., Salvatore, M., Cóndor Golec, R. D., Ferrara, A., Rossi, S., Biancalani, R., Federici, S., Jacobs, H., & Flammini, A., (2014). Agriculture, forestry and other land use by sources and removals by sinks. *United Nations Food and Agricultural Organization.* Retrieved from https://www.fao.org/3/i3671e/i3671e.pdf

CHAPTER 3

Energy

LEARNING OBJECTIVES

By the end of this chapter, you will be able to do the following:

- Define "energy."
- Describe the various forms of potential and kinetic energy.
- Describe the laws of energy
- List specific examples of non-renewable energy sources.
- Explain what makes an energy source non-renewable.
- Describe the main types of fossil fuels and how they formed.
- Explain the environmental impacts associated with exploration, extraction, and use of the different types of fossil fuels.
- Discuss the need for clean energy.
- Present the four types of conventional energy.
- Explain the different types of renewable energy.
- Compare and contrast solar and wind energy.
- Evaluate the promise of plant-based energy from ethanol to wood waste.
- Discuss other forms of energy, such as tidal to geothermal.
- Explain why energy storage is critical to the renewable energy transition
- Evaluate the most viable alternative energy and fuel sources for businesses today.

Chapter Overview

Energy poses one of the biggest sustainability challenges. Energy is fundamental to our civilization and the prosperity of nations. Its production, distribution, and utilization are deeply embedded in the fabric of our economies and businesses. Yet there is growing public awareness of the unsustainable impacts of non-renewable energy, from GHG emissions, air and water pollution, and land degradation, to geopolitical instability.

Fortunately, Renewable sources of energy have grown at an unprecedented rate in the last decade. In combination with energy efficiency, renewables now form the leading edge of a far-reaching energy transition. This transition is not just a shift from one set of fuels to another. It involves a much more profound transformation of the world's energy systems that will have far-reaching social, economic, and geopolitical implications beyond the energy sector. The term *energy transition* captures the global phenomenon.

This chapter begins with a discussion of basic energy science. We then discuss conventional non-renewable energy sources and their challenges. We then examine renewable energy resources and how the transition to these sources fundamentally changes our global energy systems.

The Basics of Energy Science

Energy is the ability of a system to do work. Modern civilization is possible because we have learned how to change energy from one form to another and then use it to do work. We use energy to move, heat, and cool our buildings, manufacture products, grow and cook our food, and light our homes and offices. In the process, energy is transferred from one system to another, and at least some energy is also transformed from one type to another.

Categories and Forms of Energy

There are two categories that all energy falls into: *kinetic* and *potential*. Kinetic energy refers to types of energy associated with motion, such as objects, substances, waves, electrons, atoms, and molecules. Potential energy is stored energy in an object or system due to its position in space relative to another object or system, such as water stored behind a dam or a person on a bicycle at the top of a hill.

Within each of these categories are several forms of energy, described in Table 3.1.

Laws of Energy

There are two fundamental physical laws of energy that are important to understand:

1. *Conservation of Energy*. To scientists, conservation of energy does not mean saving energy. Instead, the law of conservation of energy says that energy

is neither created nor destroyed. When people use energy, it doesn't disappear; it changes from one form of energy into another form of energy. When we walk, chemical energy in our bodies is converted to mechanical energy. Energy changes form, but the total amount of energy in the universe stays the same.

2. *Energy Efficiency.* Energy efficiency is the amount of useful energy obtained from a system. A perfectly energy-efficient machine would convert all the energy put into the machine to useful work. Not all energy can be converted into work. Converting one form of energy into another always involves converting it into usable (or useful) and unusable (or unuseful) forms of energy. Most energy transformations are not efficient. For example, the human body is less than 5 percent efficient at converting food into work. The rest of the energy is converted to heat.

TABLE 3.1 | Categories and Forms of Energy.

Potential energy	Kinetic energy
Chemical energy is energy stored in the bonds of atoms and molecules. Batteries, biomass, petroleum, natural gas, and coal are examples of chemical energy. Chemical energy is converted to thermal energy as coal is burned in a powerplant or gasoline in a car's engine.	**Radiant Energy** is electromagnetic energy that travels in transverse waves. Radiant energy includes visible light, x-rays, gamma rays, and radio waves. Sunshine is radiant energy, which provides the fuel and warmth that make life on Earth possible.
Mechanical energy is energy stored in objects by tension. Compressed springs and pressurized air and liquids are examples of mechanical energy.	**Thermal energy**, or heat, is the energy that comes from the movement of atoms and molecules in a substance. Heat increases when these particles move faster. Geothermal energy is the thermal energy in the Earth.
Nuclear energy is energy stored in the nucleus of atoms. Large amounts of energy are released when the nuclei are combined or split apart.	**Motion energy** is energy stored in the movement of objects. The faster they move; the more energy is stored. It takes energy to get an object moving, and energy is released when an object slows down. Wind is an example of motion energy.
Gravitational energy is energy stored in an object's height. Hydropower is an example of gravitational energy, where gravity forces water down through a hydroelectric turbine to produce electricity.	**Sound** is energy that can be heard by living things. Sound is produced when a force causes an object or substance to vibrate. The energy is transferred through a substance, like air or water in a wave.
	Electrical energy is delivered by tiny, charged particles called electrons, typically moving through a wire. Lightning is an example of electrical energy in nature.

Source: Adapted from https://www.eia.gov/energyexplained/what-is-energy/forms-of-energy.php

Sources of Energy

There are two main categories of energy: *non-renewable* and *renewable*. In the following sections, we will describe the various sources of non-renewable and renewable energy, their challenges and pitfalls, and their prospects as society transitions away from non-renewables and toward renewables.

Non-Renewable Energy

Non-renewable energy is energy derived from finite resources extracted from the Earth that are not replaced quickly enough to keep up with the speed of consumption. These energy sources will not be replenished in our lifetime or even many human lifetimes. Most non-renewable energy sources are fossil fuels that formed 100–500 million years ago from the buried remains of ancient sea plants and animals. These dead plants and animals slowly decomposed in *anaerobic* (low to no oxygen) conditions and concentrated their chemical energy. The organic compounds in their tissue were chemically changed under high pressures and temperatures.

There are three main types of fossil fuels—*coal, oil,* and *natural gas*. Coal was created from dead trees, ferns, and other plants that lived 300 to 400 million years ago. In some areas, coal was formed from swamps covered by seawater containing a high concentration of sulfur. As the seas dried up, the sulfur was left behind in the coal. However, some coal deposits were formed from freshwater swamps, which had very little sulfur.

In contrast, oil and natural gas were created from marine organisms—plankton—that accumulated on the bottoms of oceans and rivers and were buried under sediments. Over time, these organisms were transformed into oil and natural gas by the combined forces of heat, pressure, and bacteria. Some of this oil and natural gas worked upward through the Earth's crust until running into rock formations called "caprocks" that prevented seepage to the surface. Most oil and natural gas extracted today are from these concentrations under caprocks.

Nuclear energy is also generally classified as nonrenewable since it is derived from uranium, a finite resource. Scientists think uranium was created billions of years ago when stars formed.

Coal

Coal is a combustible black or dark-brown sedimentary rock comprised primarily of carbonized plant matter. Coal is classified into four main types, or ranks, based on the amounts of carbon present and thus the amount of heat energy it can produce. In order from least- to most energy-intensive, these types are:

Peat, a precursor of coal.

Lignite contains 25–35 percent carbon and has the lowest energy content of all coal ranks. Lignite is mainly used to generate electricity. Lignite is also most harmful to human health, given the high number of pollutants emitted per unit of energy produced.

Subbituminous coal properties range between lignite and bituminous coal and are used primarily as fuel for steam-electric power generation.

Bituminous coal contains 45–86 percent carbon and is used primarily for steam-electric power generation and coke production.

Anthracite contains 86–97 percent carbon and generally has the highest heating value of all ranks of coal.

Coal Production Trends Global coal production increased dramatically in the early 2000s, led by enormous electrification projects in China. Global production peaked in about 2013 at about 167 metric million tons but has declined since then. Declines have been most dramatic in North America and Europe, where coal-fired power plants have been closed or converted to natural gas.[1]

Coal Mining, Processing, and Transport The first step in the coal supply chain is mining. There are two primary methods of coal mining: *strip mining* and *underground mining*. Strip mining, or surface mining, removes the soil and layers of rock known as overburden to expose coal seams. It is typically used when the coal is near the surface. *Mountaintop removal* is a form of surface mining where the tops of mountains are removed to access coal seams. The overburden is typically placed in nearby valleys, called *valley fill*.

Underground mining, or deep mining, is used when the coal is deeper below the surface. Underground coal mining involves tunneling into the Earth to the coalbed, which is then mined with underground mining equipment such as cut-

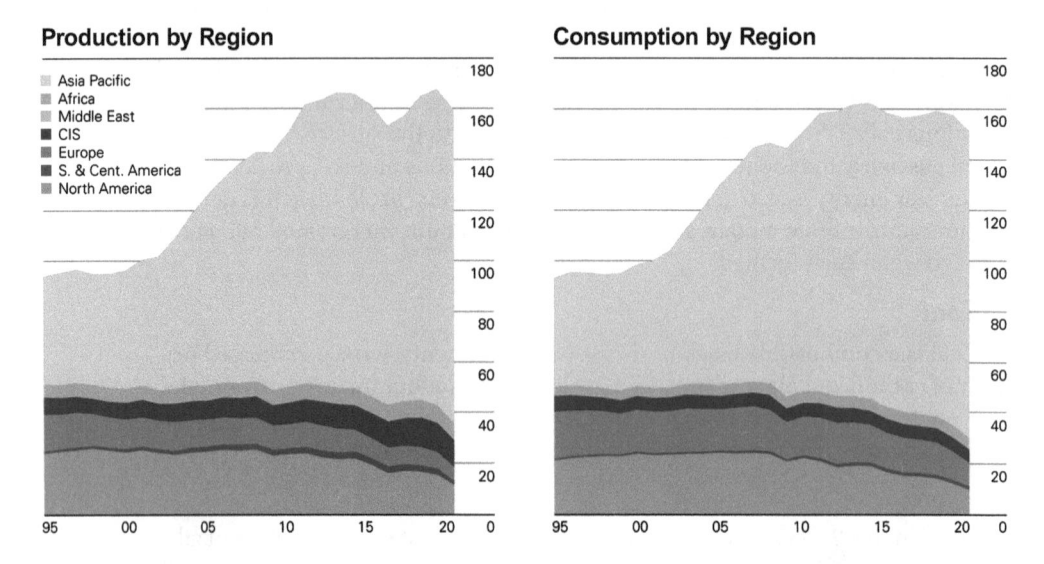

FIGURE 3.1 | Coal Production by World Region (Million metric tons of oil equivalent).
Source: https://www.bp.com/en/global/corporate/energy-economics/statistical-review-of-world-energy.html

ting machines and continuous, longwall, and shortwall mining machines and transported to the surface. Some underground mines are thousands of feet deep and extend for miles.

Once mined, coal usually goes to a processing plant located near the mine, where it is cleaned to remove impurities, thereby increasing its heating value. The processed coal is then transported to consumers. In North America, about 70 percent of coal is transported by train. Coal can also be transported by conveyor, tram, barge, ship, or truck. Coal-fired electric power plants are sometimes built near coal mines to lower transportation costs.

Electric power generation is the primary use for coal worldwide. *Thermal* coal is burnt to create steam that drives turbines and generators that produce electricity. Metallurgic (coking) coal is a main ingredient in making steel and other metals like aluminum and copper. Coal is also used to produce cement, chemicals, paper, textiles, and carbon fiber.

Environmental and Health Impacts of Coal Mining and Burning As discussed in earlier chapters, GHG emissions are among the most severe impacts of coal mining, primarily CO_2. Coal is the number one producer of CO_2 emissions, at 14 billion metric tons annually. However, numerous other environmental and health impacts occur from mining, preparation, combustion, waste storage, and transport.

- *Acid mine drainage (AMD)* refers to the outflow of sulfuric acid water from coal mines that drain into nearby rivers and streams.
- *Air pollution* from mining and burning coal includes sulfur dioxide, nitrogen oxides, particulate matter, and heavy metals, leading to smog, acid rain, toxins in the environment, and numerous respiratory and cardiovascular effects. Coal combustion is the largest source of mercury released into the environment.
- *Coal dust* created during mining and transport can cause deadly respiratory problems, also referred to as *black lung disease.*
- *Coal combustion waste* is disposed of in landfills or "surface impoundments," where toxic metals are leached out into the local environment
- *Coal sludge,* also known as slurry, is the liquid coal waste generated by washing coal and disposed of at impoundments near coal mines, where toxins leak out into the surrounding environment.
- *Deforestation* caused by mountaintop removal mining.
- *Floods* caused by mountaintop removal mining and failures of coal mine impoundments.
- *Groundwater hydrology* loss or degradation occurs when mining changes the groundwater hydrology.
- *Mountaintop removal* drastically alters the landscapes, destroys habitat, and damages water supplies.
- *Subsidence* is caused by underground mining, particularly longwall mining.

- *Thermal pollution* occurs when water used as a coolant at powerplants is returned to the natural environment at a higher temperature, damaging those ecosystems.
- *Water consumption* from coal plants is the second-largest consumer of domestic water after agriculture.

Reducing the Impacts of Coal   The most significant action we can take to reduce the impact of coal is to stop using it. Phasing out coal from the electricity sector is the most crucial step to align with 1.5°C. To reach this, global coal use in electricity generation must fall by 80 percent below 2010 levels by 2030, and all coal-fired power stations must be shut by 2040 at the latest. The 2021 Glasgow Climate Pact (COP26) calls for countries to reduce coal use, a first for international agreements. The strategies for this transition include fuel switching, renewable energy, energy efficiency and conservation, and nuclear energy. There are also efforts to capture CO_2 at the powerplant source and sequester it in underground formations. Given the high cost of carbon capture technology relative to other energy sources like renewables, it is unlikely this strategy will gain much traction.

By removing coal from the world energy portfolio, most other damaging impacts are also eliminated. There will be legacy impacts for decades to come, but at least we will not be adding to this damage.

Oil

Crude oil exists in liquid or gaseous form in underground pools or reservoirs, in tiny spaces within sedimentary rocks, and near the Earth's surface in tar (or oil) sands. In reservoirs, it usually is found in association with natural gas, which, being lighter, forms a gas cap over the oil. *Petroleum* products are fuels made from crude oil and hydrocarbons contained in natural gas. Petroleum means "rock oil" or "oil from the Earth."

Oil Production Trends   Global oil production peaked in 2018 at about 95 million barrels per day but has begun to decline since then. Demand declined precipitously during the COVID-19 pandemic but is expected to grow again as mobility increases.[2]

Oil Extraction, Processing, and Transport   Oil is mainly obtained by onshore or offshore drilling. Offshore drilling rigs can operate in water as deep as two miles. Wells are drilled on stationary or floating platforms, which are also used to lower drilling equipment to the ocean floor. These platforms hold all required drilling equipment and housing and storage areas for the work crews. Offshore production is much more expensive than land-based production.

Regulations require both onshore and offshore producers to take precautions to prevent pollution, spills, and significant changes to terrestrial and ocean environments. Offshore rigs are designed to withstand hurricanes. When oil wells are no longer productive enough to be economical, they are sealed and abandoned according to applicable regulations.

Hydraulic fracturing, or "fracking," is a drilling process that involves injecting water, sand, and chemicals under high pressure into a bedrock formation. This process creates new fractures in the rock and increases the size and connectiv-

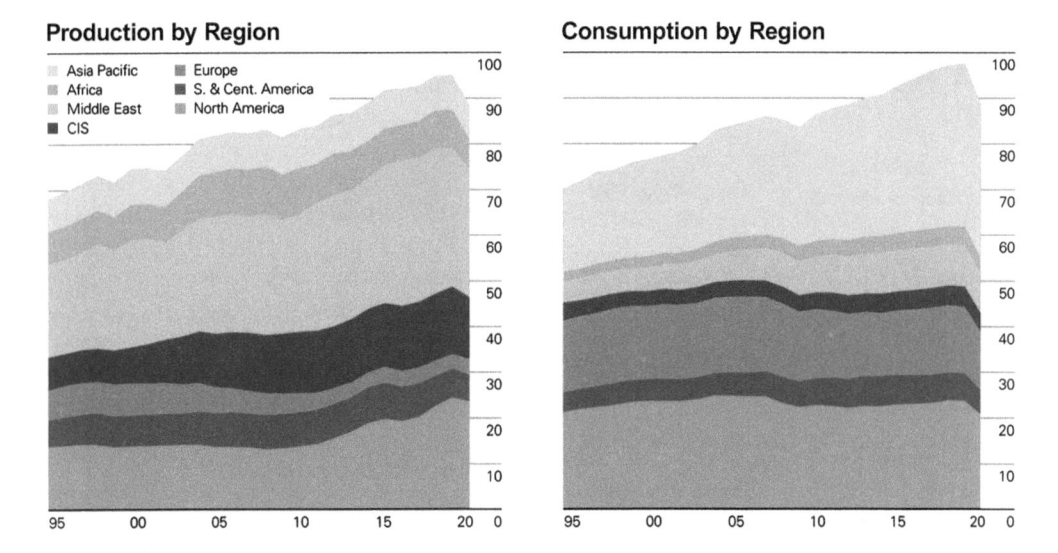

FIGURE 3.2 | Coal Production by World Region (millions of barrels per day).
Source: https://www.bp.com/en/global/corporate/energy-economics/statistical-review-of-world-energy.html

ity of existing fractures. It is commonly used in low-permeability rocks like tight sandstone, shale, and some coal beds to increase oil flow to a well from petroleum-bearing rock formations.

The oil then needs to be sent to refineries for processing. Oil can be transported long distances by tanker ship over water or by pipeline over land. Both have the potential for leaks and spills.

Unprocessed crude oil is not generally usable until separated into different usable products at a *refinery*. All refineries perform three basic steps:

Separation. The first step is to separate the crude oil into different components, called fractions. This process is called fractional distillation, which involves heating the crude to vaporize it and condensing the vapor. The lightest components have the lowest boiling temperature and rise to the top, while the heaviest, which also have the highest boiling temperature, remain at the bottom.

Conversion. Conversion is the chemical process by which some of the fractions are transformed into other products, such as turning diesel fuel into gasoline. Conversion can involve cracking larger hydrocarbon chains into smaller ones, combining smaller chains into larger ones (unification), or rearranging the molecules to create other products (alteration).

Treatment. Each fraction is then treated to remove sulfur, nitrogen, and water impurities. Refineries also combine the various fractions into mixtures to make desired products, such as gasoline with different octane ratings.

Petroleum products made from a barrel of crude oil, 2020
gallons

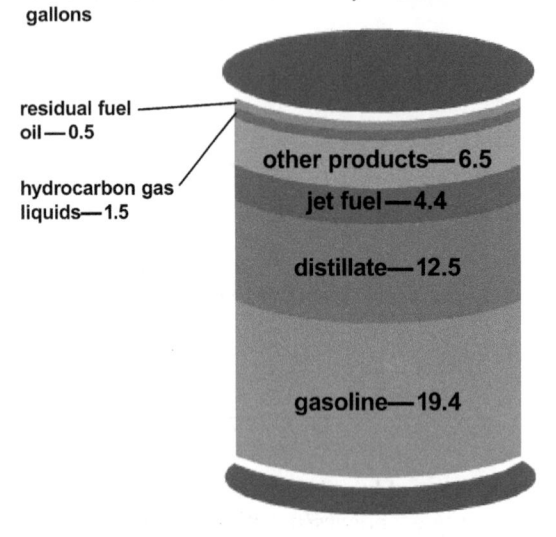

- residual fuel oil—0.5
- hydrocarbon gas liquids—1.5
- other products—6.5
- jet fuel—4.4
- distillate—12.5
- gasoline—19.4

FIGURE 3.3 | Petroleum Products Made From a Barrel of Crude Oil, 2020.
Source: https://www.energy.gov/

Petroleum products made from crude oil Petroleum products made from crude oil include gasoline, distillates such as diesel fuel and heating oil, jet fuel, petrochemical feedstocks, waxes, lubricating oils, and asphalt. A U.S. 42-gallon barrel of crude oil yields about 45 gallons of petroleum products because of refinery processing gain. This increase in volume is like what happens to popcorn when it is popped. A corn kernel is smaller and denser than a popped kernel. The number of individual products produced varies as refineries adjust production to meet market demand and maximize profitability. Typically, about 19 gallons of gasoline and 10 gallons of diesel fuel are produced. Other products such as jet fuel and heating oil make up the remaining one-third.

Environmental and Health Impacts of Oil The oil and petroleum industry constitutes the second-largest global producer of CO_2 emissions, emitting about 11.5 billion metric tons annually. However, there are numerous other environmental and health impacts that occur from mining, preparation, combustion, waste storage, and transport:

- *Air pollution.* Air pollutants are emitted in every step of the oil-producing process. In the extraction and combustion phases, emissions include methane and carbon dioxide, but other pollutants like nitrous oxides, sulfur dioxide (acid rain) aerosols, carbon monoxide, and methanol also occur. When oil or petroleum is combusted, the combustion is usually incomplete, and the chemical reaction leaves these by-products.

- *Microplastics.* Petroleum is the primary ingredient used to create the massive amounts of plastic the world consumes each year. This consumption is primarily driven by single-use plastics, which are not recycled. Over time these products fragment into smaller and smaller pieces. Microplastics are observable in air, water, and soil samples gathered from nearly every location on Earth and in marine organisms. They usually end up in tissues such as the digestive glands, circulatory system, gills, and guts.

- *Oil spills.* The term is usually applied to spills released into the ocean or coastal waters, but spills may also occur on land. Spills may be released by oil tankers, pipelines, railcars, offshore platforms, drilling rigs and wells, and spills of refined petroleum products such as gasoline and diesel. The oil penetrates the structure of the plumage of birds and the fur of mammals, reducing insulating ability, and making them more vulnerable to temperature fluctuations and affecting their buoyancy. It may take weeks, months, or even years for ecosystems to recover from spills.

- ***Produced water and drilling waste discharges.*** Produced water (PW) discharge from extraction results in Poly-aromatic Hydrocarbon (PAH) emissions in the ocean. PW discharge from offshore oil and gas production is the largest source of PAH emissions into the marine environment. PAHs released in PW are responsible for biological changes in mussels and fish. PAHs also pose a serious threat to human health, such as lung, skin, bladder, and gastrointestinal cancer.
- ***Toxic compounds.*** Benzene is the petroleum-related product with the highest level of toxicity. Benzene is present in crude oil and gasoline and is known to cause leukemia, Hodgkin's lymphoma, and other blood and immune system diseases within 5–15 years of exposure.
- ***Other highly toxic compounds include toluene, methylbenzene, and xylenes.***
- ***Waste oil.*** Examples of waste oil are used oils such as hydraulic oil, transmission oil, brake fluids, motor oil, crankcase oil, gearbox oil, and synthetic oil. When waste oil from vehicles drips out of engines over streets and roads, the oil travels into the water table along with toxins like benzene. This poisons both soil and drinking water. Runoff from storms carries waste oil into rivers and oceans, poisoning them.

Reducing the Impacts of Oil   As with coal, the most significant action we can take to reduce the impact of oil is to stop using it. Most of the world's remaining oil reserves need to stay in the ground if we are to reach 1.5°C. Since virtually all oil is used in the transportation sector, the primary strategy is to transition from petroleum to electricity or other low-carbon fuels. Electric vehicles are currently the most effective technology for making this possible. Beyond electrifying transportation, we must also make progress on the energy efficiency of vehicles, reduce black carbon emissions from diesel engines, and find ways to decarbonize the aviation and international marine transport industries. By removing oil from the world energy portfolio, most other damaging impacts can also be eliminated.

Natural Gas

Natural gas contains many different compounds, the most significant being methane. *Conventional natural gas* is found in large cracks and spaces between rock layers. *Unconventional natural gas* occurs in the tiny pores (spaces) within some formations of shale, sandstone, and other types of sedimentary rock. This natural gas is also referred to as *shale gas* or *tight gas. Associated natural gas* occurs with deposits of crude oil. A type of natural gas found in coal deposits is called *coalbed methane*. Natural gas deposits are located both on land and offshore. We use natural gas as a fuel and to make materials and chemicals.

Natural Gas Extraction, Processing, and Transport Natural gas is extracted using vertically and horizontally drilled wells. In conventional natural gas deposits, the natural gas generally flows easily up through wells to the surface. In shale gas formations, hydraulic fracturing or fracking is used to force water, chemicals, and sand down a well under high pressure and releases the natural gas from the rock to flow up to the surface. At the top of the well, natural gas is put into gathering pipelines and sent to natural gas processing plants.

Water vapor and nonhydrocarbon compounds are removed at the processing plant, and *natural gas liquids* (NGLs) are separated and sold separately. Chemicals called odorants are added so that leaks can be detected. The refined product is then sent through pipelines to underground storage fields, distribution companies, and consumers. In places where pipelines are not available to transport the natural gas produced from oil wells, the gas is either reinjected into the oil-bearing formation or vented or burned (flared).

Uses of Natural Gas About 50 percent of the natural gas demand is for electrical power generation. This demand is primarily driven by the conversion of coal-fired power plants to natural gas. While burning natural gas does emit greenhouse gases, it contributes far less CO_2 and air pollutants than coal. Therefore, it is often referred to as a *bridge fuel* to a carbon-neutral energy future. As China transitions from coal-fired power plants and industrial plants, natural gas demand is expected to increase dramatically.[3]

Other uses of natural gas include industry, where it is used as a fuel for process heating and to make chemicals, fertilizer, and hydrogen. It is used for heating buildings and water, cooking, drying clothes, and residential and commercial refrigeration systems. In transportation, it is used to operate compressors to move gas through pipelines and as a vehicle fuel in compressed and liquid form. Nearly all vehicles that use natural gas are government or private vehicle fleets.

Environmental and Health Impacts of Natural Gas Natural gas emits 50 to 60 percent less carbon dioxide (CO_2) when combusted efficiently than emissions from a typical new coal plant. In vehicles, tailpipe emissions from natural gas are 15 to 20 percent less than gasoline. But that is not the whole story.

The drilling and extraction of natural gas from wells and its transportation in pipelines result in the leakage, or fugitive emissions, of methane, the primary component of natural gas. Methane is 34 times stronger than CO_2 at trapping heat over 100 years and 86 times stronger over 20 years. When their total lifecycle is considered, these fugitive methane emissions account for up to 9 percent of total GHG emissions. As with other GHGs, reducing methane emissions is essential to reach the 1.5°C goals.

Beyond the climate impact, there are numerous other environmental and health impacts associated with natural gas:

- *Air pollution.* The combustion of natural gas produces nitrogen oxides and sulfur, mercury, polycyclic aromatic hydrocarbons, carbon monoxide, carbon dioxide, volatile organic compounds, and particulate matter. This includes gas well sites, power plants and industry, and residential use of gas appliances and furnaces. The resulting health risks include cancer, decreased lung function, worsening asthma, chronic obstructive pulmonary disease, heart disease symptoms, nervous system damage, and delayed neurodevelopment in children.

- *Land use and wildlife.* The land disturbance required for gas drilling can alter land use and harm local ecosystems. Hydraulic fracturing can cause erosion and sedimentation, aquatic contamination from chemical spills or runoff, and habitat fragmentation.

- *Water use and pollution.* Gas development may pose health risks by contaminating drinking water with hazardous chemicals used in drilling, hydraulically fracturing the well, processing and refining the oil or gas, or disposing of wastewater. Gas development also poses contamination risks to surface waters through spills and leaks of chemical additives, diesel fuel, or other fluids from equipment on-site. Spills and leaks also occur at wastewater storage, treatment, and disposal. Hydraulic fracturing also requires enormous volumes of water, with a single well requiring from 3 to 12 million gallons. Similar amounts of water are needed each time a well is refractured to maintain pressure and gas production.

Reducing the Impacts of Natural Gas The role of natural gas in the world's transition to carbon-neutral energy is complicated. On the one hand, natural gas enables us to reduce the use of coal and some petroleum products, which have much higher global warming potential. Yet, in the end, natural gas is also a fossil fuel that generates substantial GHG emissions. To reach our 1.5°C goals, most of the world's remaining natural gas reserves will need to stay in the ground.

Since projections estimate that a vast amount of natural gas will be used in the future for electricity generation, the big challenge is to transition to renewables, along with battery storage capacity, and possibly nuclear energy. Natural gas for heating and cooking needs to be replaced by clean electric appliances, heat pumps, and furnaces in commercial and residential settings. Potential also exists for *green gas*—low-carbon substitutes for conventional natural gas, including biomethane produced from waste products and agricultural residues and *green hydrogen* made via water electrolysis using renewable electricity.

In the short term, the natural gas industry needs to tackle the leakage and flaring problems from fugitive methane emissions. We also need to commit to deep efficiencies in all aspects of energy production and use to reduce the demand for natural gas. Removing natural gas from the world energy portfolio will also mitigate or eliminate other damaging environmental and health impacts.

Nuclear Energy

For over half a century, the debate around nuclear energy has inspired impassioned discourse on all sides. Given the urgent imperative to rapidly decarbonize our energy systems, it is more important than ever to have an even-handed, impartial reckoning with nuclear power.

High-profile accidents like Chernobyl, Fukushima, and Three Mile Island have helped to make both the public and policymakers wary of nuclear energy, even though fatalities from fossil fuel-derived energy dwarf the number of combined fatalities from nuclear energy. Deaths associated with nuclear power are estimated from the low tens of thousands to the low hundreds of thousands. In contrast, deaths by fossil fuels are in the tens or hundreds of millions, just based on air pollution deaths alone. Even considering the significantly higher proportion of energy generated by fossil fuels, fossil fuels are still considerably more dangerous. That said, the consequences of catastrophic accidents are what often grab the attention of the public and policymakers. From this catastrophe perspective, the argument can be made that nuclear energy should not be part of our clean energy future.

Conversely, proponents of nuclear power often downplay the risks while proclaiming the climate benefits. Advocates suggest that nuclear energy can provide a steady energy supply with a relatively small land footprint. New technological innovations make nuclear even safer and more efficient than earlier-generation facilities. Indeed, there is a serious argument that nuclear energy should—even must—be a significant component of our efforts at decarbonization.

In short, we urgently need a clear-eyed, balanced understanding of the overall costs and benefits of pursuing nuclear energy. As more coal and gas plants are decommissioned, nuclear may become an attractive alternative for some policymakers, so it is essential to weigh the risks and benefits now. The debate speaks to consequential questions about the kind of decarbonized society we want to create. A full accounting of the risks and benefits of nuclear can enlighten our understanding and offer some ways forward.

The question may be moot because of the immense cost and time required to stand up nuclear power compared to renewables. Nuclear power plant construction takes an average of ten years, and the energy it will produce costs between $112 and $189 per megawatt-hour (MWh), in contrast to $29 to $56 per MWh for wind and $36 to $44 per MWh for solar. Since nuclear power plants may cost more to build and operate than they earn, the private sector investors are reluctant to invest in a nuclear transition. The alternative would be massive government investment, which is unrealistic in many countries. It just might be too late to scale up nuclear power, even if future innovations could overcome the problems of slowness, cost, and safety.

How does a nuclear power plant work? Nuclear power comes from nuclear fission. In nuclear fission, atoms are split to form smaller atoms, releasing immense energy. Fission takes place inside the reactor of a nuclear power plant. At the center of the reactor is the core, which contains uranium for nuclear fuel. The uranium is processed into small ceramic pellets and stacked into sealed metal tubes called fuel rods. More than 200 rods are bundled together to form a fuel assembly. A reactor core is generally made up of several hundred assemblies, depending on power level.

Nuclear power plants use heat from nuclear fission to heat water and produce steam to spin large turbines that generate electricity. The steam is cooled back into water in a separate structure called a cooling tower or using water from ponds, rivers, or the ocean. The cooled water is then reused to produce steam.

Mining, enrichment, and disposal of uranium Uranium is a slightly radioactive metal found in rocks all over the world. There are several areas around the world where the concentration of uranium in the ground is sufficiently high that extraction of it for use as nuclear fuel is economically feasible. Both surface (generally open pit) and underground mining techniques recover uranium ore. Open-pit mining is usually used where deposits are close to the surface, and underground mining is typically used for deposits at deeper depths. Milling generally carried out close to the mine extracts the uranium from the ore, producing uranium oxide concentrate, sometimes referred to as "yellowcake." The tailings are usually returned to a mined-out pit for safe storage.

In the enrichment process, the uranium oxide is converted to a gas and fed into centrifuges to separate the uranium-235, then converted to uranium dioxide powder. This powder is then pressed and heated into small fuel pellets inserted into thin tubes known as fuel rods. Fuel rods are then grouped to form fuel assemblies. Up to 200 fuel rods can be used to make each fuel assembly, depending on the type of reactor. Once loaded, the fuel normally stays in the reactor core for several years.

The used fuel rods, or spent fuel, are generally stored at the reactor or nearby storage. The rods are either enclosed in steel-lined concrete pools of water or steel and concrete containers, known as dry storage casks. Used nuclear fuel can be recycled to make new fuel and byproducts since more than 90 percent of its potential energy remains, even after five years of operation in a reactor.

Environmental and Health Impacts of Nuclear Power GHG emissions from nuclear power plants are much smaller than those from fossil fuels, and the routine health risks are much lower. Yet the risk of a catastrophic accident if containment fails could wipe out the benefits. The most long-lived radioactive wastes, including spent nuclear fuel, must be contained and isolated from the environment for extremely long periods. Spent nuclear fuel could also be reused, yielding even more energy, and reducing the amount of waste to be contained. Overall, the environmental and health risks associated with nuclear power are as follows:

- *GHG emissions.* While nuclear power creates significantly lower emissions than fossil fuels, emissions are still associated with building and running the plants. Uranium mining, processing, transport, and radioactive waste management result in GHG emissions.
- *Uranium Mining.* Uranium mining produces radioactive tailings that pose serious environmental and health risks like windblown dust dispersal and leaching of contaminants, including heavy metals and arsenic released into the water.
- *Low-Level Radiation.* Nuclear power plants constantly emit low levels of radiation into the environment. There is a differing opinion among scientists over the effects caused by constant low levels of radiation. Various scientific studies have shown an increased cancer rate among people near nuclear power plants. Long-term exposure to low-level radiation has been shown to damage DNA. The damage caused to wildlife, plants, and the ozone layer is not fully understood.

- *Radioactive Waste.* Radioactive waste is a huge concern. Waste from nuclear power plants can remain active for hundreds of thousands of years. Much of the radioactive waste from nuclear power plants is stored at the power plant. Due to space constraints, the radioactive waste will eventually need to be relocated. While plans have been proposed to bury the radioactive waste in casks in Nevada's Yucca Mountains, there is significant opposition to the strategy.
- *Cooling Water System.* Cooling systems are used to keep nuclear power plants from overheating. There are two main environmental problems associated with nuclear power plant cooling systems. First, the cooling system pulls water from an ocean or river source. Fish are inadvertently captured in the cooling system intake and killed. Second, after the water is used to cool the power plant, it is returned to the ocean or river. The returned water is approximately 25 degrees warmer than it is at the intake. The warmer water kills some species of fish and plant life.
- *Nuclear Accidents.* If a nuclear power plant accident occurs, the environment and surrounding people could be exposed to high radiation levels. The 2011 accident at the nuclear power plant in Fukushima, Japan, is one of the worst nuclear disasters in history. A tsunami following a major earthquake destroyed the reactors. Terrorism threats are another concern that needs to be addressed. Effective plans to protect nuclear power plants from terrorism are often not in place.

Reducing the Impacts of Nuclear Energy If nuclear energy is to have a future beyond the life of current facilities, technological innovation will be vital in reducing risk. This includes advanced reactor designs and safer fuels, which can be paired with renewable generating sources, are much less expensive, and can process nuclear waste into an energy source. Solutions will also need to be found for the long-term storage of nuclear waste. There is now only one deep waste repository in the United States: the Waste Isolation Pilot Plant in New Mexico. Finding and constructing additional repository sites is possible but requires overcoming immense political hurdles, as no community wants such a facility located nearby.

RENEWABLE ENERGY

Renewable energy is energy collected from sources replenished by natural processes on a human timescale. All renewable energy is derived directly or indirectly from the sun or heat within the Earth. Renewable sources include sunlight, wind, rain, tides, waves, and geothermal heat. Renewable energy stands in contrast to fossil fuels, which are used far more quickly than they are replenished.

Renewable energy accounts for about 11.2 percent of global energy consumption, including almost 30 percent of electricity generation. In many nations, renewable sources are already contributing well over 20 percent of their energy supply.[4] Some generate over half their electricity from renewables, and a few generate all their electricity using renewables. But even with this strong growth, renewables will only be able to meet around half the projected increase in global

World consumption
Exajoules

- Renewables
- Hydroelectricity
- Nuclear energy
- Coal
- Natural gas
- Oil

Shares of global primary energy
Percentage

- Oil
- Coal
- Natural gas
- Hydroelectricity
- Nuclear energy
- Renewables

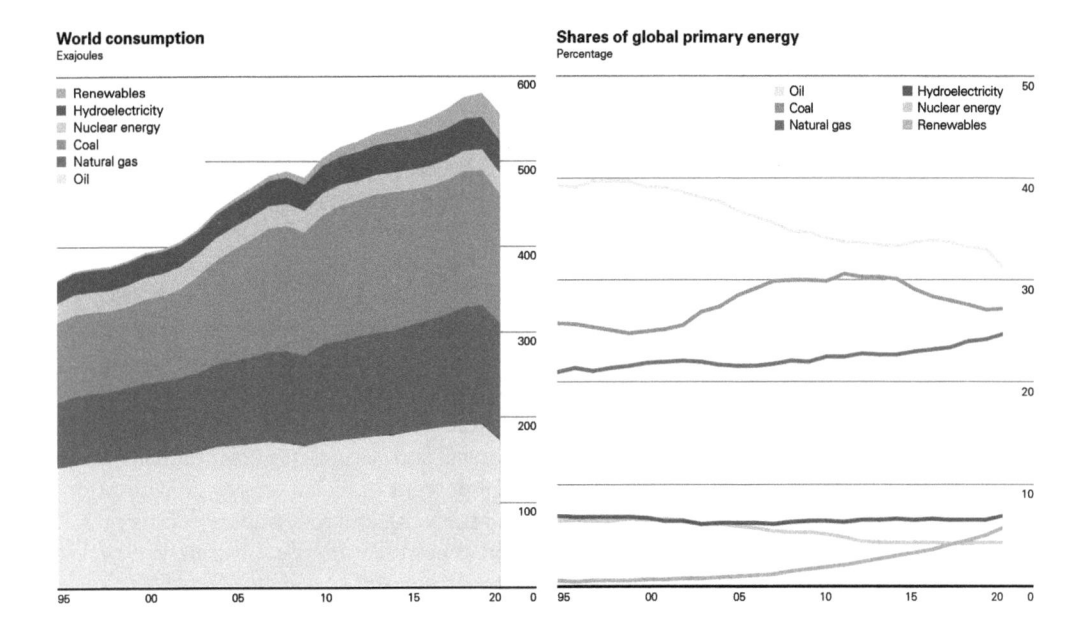

FIGURE 3.4 | World Renewable Energy Consumption.
Source: https://www.bp.com/en/global/corporate/energy-economics/statistical-review-of-world-energy.html

electricity demand. Fossil fuel sources are expected to cover the other half of this growth, which will drive carbon emissions even higher.

Renewable energy markets are projected to grow strongly in the 2020s and beyond. The primary reasons for this growth include the following drivers:

1. ***Growing Concern over Climate Change.*** Policymakers, business leaders, and citizens worldwide are increasingly aware of the need to combat climate change more aggressively. Rapid deployment of renewable energy is seen as key to limiting global warming to 1.5°C. This has translated into strong public support for public policies and regulations that drive the expansion of renewable energy.

2. ***Increasing Corporate Commitments.*** Businesses are helping lead the charge with renewable energy growth and publicly committing to more aggressive renewable energy and sustainability targets. Over 60 percent of Fortune 500 companies have made climate commitments related to GHG emissions, energy efficiency, and renewable energy sourcing. This represents a significant increase from just 6 percent in 2016. The largest companies continue to lead the way, with 76 percent of the Fortune 100 making substantial climate commitments.

3. ***Declining Costs.*** The costs for renewable energy—particularly solar and wind generation—have fallen dramatically. The cost of utility-scale solar (generally one megawatt or higher) has dropped 78 percent since 2010. Utility-scale wind costs have dropped about 71 percent over the past decade. Costs have fallen to the point that—on an unsubsidized, *levelized cost of energy* (LCOE)

basis—wind and solar are now cheaper than all non-renewable forms of power generation, including natural gas and coal-fired generation.

4. **Energy Security.** Fossil energy resources are concentrated in a limited number of countries, some of which may pose security risks to other countries. In contrast, renewable energy resources are available virtually everywhere on the planet. Renewable energy can bolster regional or national energy security by reducing reliance on fossil fuel imports while contributing to domestic economic development.

Renewable Energy Consumption Trends The figures below show the trends in low-carbon energy sources relative to fossil fuels. While renewables are the fastest-growing energy sector, research shows they still make up only a sliver of world energy demand. Oil continues to hold the largest share of the energy mix (31.2 percent), followed by coal (27.2 percent) and natural gas (24.7 percent). Low carbon energy sources compose about 18 percent of world energy consumption, including hydro (6.9 percent), nuclear (4.3 percent), and renewables (5.7 percent).[5]

Below is a breakdown of sources of renewable energy. Overall, renewable energy is the fastest-growing global source of energy.

The International Renewable Energy Agency (IRENA) has estimated that different types of renewable energy will provide 86 percent of the global primary energy by 2050).[6] The largest renewable energy source in the world is hydropower. However, among the various types of renewable energies, wind and solar

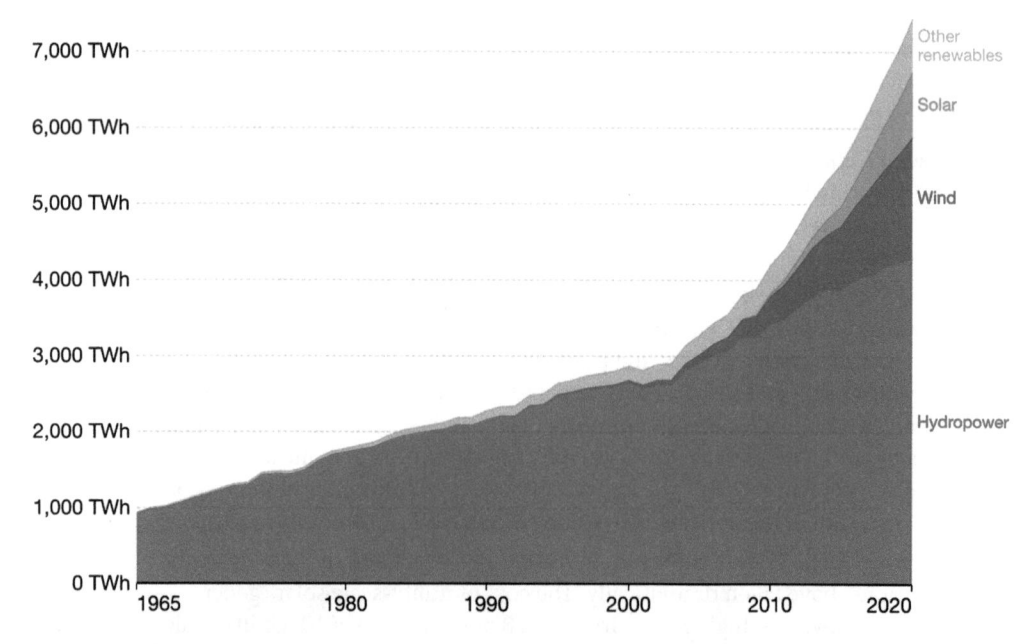

FIGURE 3.5 | World Renewable Energy Generation.
Source: BP: Statistical Review of World Energy

energy technologies have grown at the fastest rate in the past two decades and are expected to continue. Renewable electricity technologies are projected to continue to be deployed at record levels. Still, government policies and financial support are needed to incentivize even greater deployments to give the world a chance to achieve its net-zero climate goals.

Wind Energy

Wind is the movement of air caused by the uneven heating of the Earth by the sun. In this way, *wind energy* is an indirect form of solar energy. Because the Earth's surface is made up of different types of land and water, it absorbs the sun's heat at different rates, resulting in differences in atmospheric pressure. Wind is the great equalizer of these pressure differences. *Aeolian processes* relate to the wind's ability to erode landforms and transport and deposit eroded material at great distances around the Earth. Wind energy is a form of *kinetic energy*.

The total amount of economically extractable power from the wind is much more than current world energy consumption from all sources combined. Wind energy is a sustainable solution for many disparate reasons. Because it is widely distributed around the Earth, wind energy has the potential to reduce dependence on fossil fuels in virtually every country. The conversion of wind power to wind energy is relatively inexpensive and produced at a fraction of the cost of other power sources. Wind energy systems are highly efficient and can share space with other land uses such as farming and ranching. They can provide an additional revenue stream for landowners and economic development activity for rural communities. Wind energy produces minimal waste over the course of its life cycle.

Windmills can be built anywhere there is wind, and wind turbines can be planted on interior farmlands, coastal boundaries, and the ocean by deep-sea wind currents. Small wind turbines are designed for simplicity, ruggedness, and low maintenance and are primarily used for household and small farm or business applications. Most modern windmills are operated by computers at central command locations and need occasional repairs or upgrades. Wind turbines work according to airspeed and do not consume additional power to generate electricity.

Wind turbines have significant economies of scale. While small farm or residential scale turbines cost less overall, they are more expensive per kilowatt of energy-producing capacity. The initial cost for installing a small turbine is between $50,000 and $80,000 per kilowatt capacity. In contrast, the initial cost of a large turbine is between $1.3 and $2.2 million per megawatt of capacity. Often there are tax exemptions and other incentives that can dramatically reduce the cost of a wind project. Utilities offer wind-generated electricity at a 2 to 3 cents per kilowatt-hour premium. A household that uses wind power for 25 percent of its energy needs would spend an additional $4 or $5 per month.[7]

Wind Energy Capacity Trends Wind is the second-largest renewable source of electric power generation worldwide, behind hydropower. In 2021, wind supplied over 6 percent of worldwide electrical generation and over 2 percent of total energy consumption.[8] China had the largest installed capacity of wind generation, with around 290 MW in 2021. The United States is second with 122.5 GW of installed capacity.

Wind energy installation costs have fallen rapidly over the past decade and are now less expensive than the cheapest coal or natural gas projects. As a result, wind capacity has increased rapidly, particularly in China. This growth in wind capacity is not on pace to help meet the net-zero goals of the Paris Agreement (see figure below). To attain 8,000 TWh capacity by 2030, generation must increase 18 percent per year from 2021 to 2030. Currently, capacity is growing at about 11 percent annually. Much stronger efforts are needed to achieve this level of sustained capacity growth. The most critical areas for improvement are cost reductions and technology improvements for offshore wind and facilitating permitting for onshore wind. Fossil fuel subsidies hinder the expansion of wind power.[9]

Wind Energy Technology The most common way to collect and convert wind energy into usable form is through *wind turbines*. Like an aircraft wing, wind flows over the turbine *blades*, creating lift and causing the blades to turn. The blades are connected to a *nacelle*, or housing, containing a *rotor*, *driveshaft*, and *gearbox* that turns an *electric generator* that produces electricity. The nacelle is affixed at the top of a *tower*, which is then attached to the ground or the ocean floor, or floating structures cabled to the ocean floor. Since winds generally are stronger higher

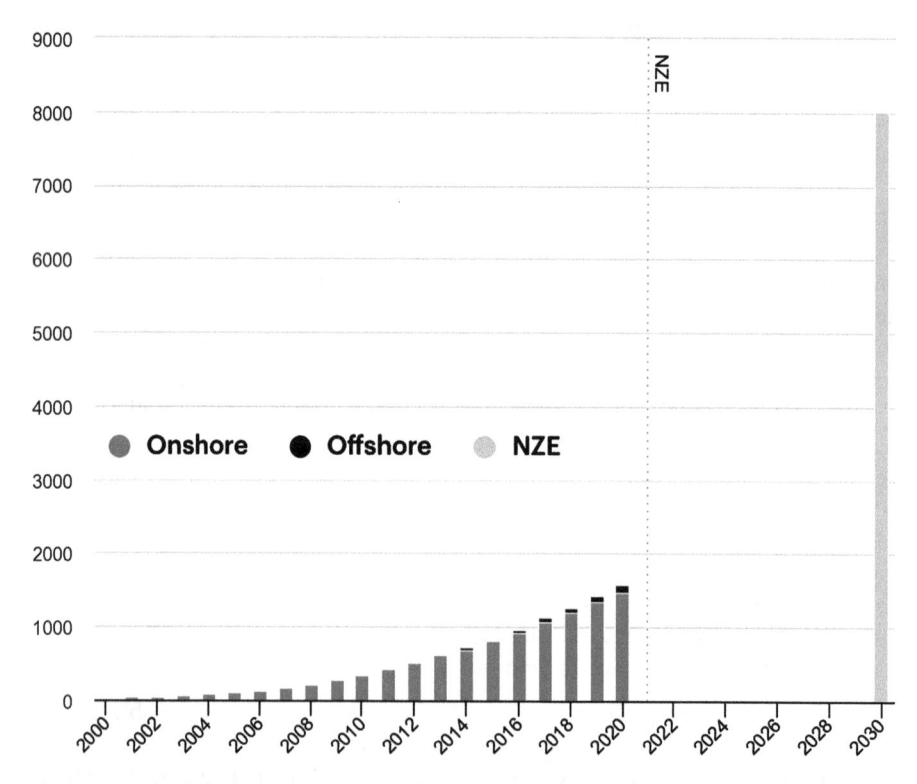

FIGURE 3.6 | Wind Power Generation in the Net-zero Scenario, 2000–2030.
Source: https://www.iea.org/data-and-statistics/charts/wind-power-generation-in-the-net-zero-scenario-2000-2030

up in the atmosphere, towers and blades are getting longer. Onshore towers now average over 90 meters (295 feet). Offshore towers average over 150 meters (500 feet), or about the height of the Washington Monument. Taller towers allow for larger blades, which produce more lift and, therefore, more electricity.

A group of wind turbines is referred to as a *wind farm*, also called a *wind park* or *wind power station*. The size of wind farms varies from a small number to several hundred wind turbines covering an extensive onshore or offshore area. The wind turbines in a wind farm are wired together to a *transformer*, which then is connected to the *electrical grid*. Onshore wind farms tend to be sited on the tops of smooth round hills, ridges, and mountain passes, where the topography accelerates the wind.

There are two basic types of wind turbine installations. *Onshore wind farms* are large installations of wind turbines located on land. *Offshore wind farms* are in bodies of water. Wind speed and consistency differ considerably between onshore and offshore wind farms. Offshore wind speeds are typically higher and more consistent. Therefore, offshore wind farms have the potential to generate more electricity at a steadier rate than their onshore counterparts. The downside is that offshore wind farms are far more expensive to build and maintain. Offshore technologies are improving and getting cheaper. Offshore installations will likely become more appealing at some point soon because of the higher and more consistent generation capacity. Onshore wind farms need to be carefully sited to ensure sufficient wind speeds and consistency.

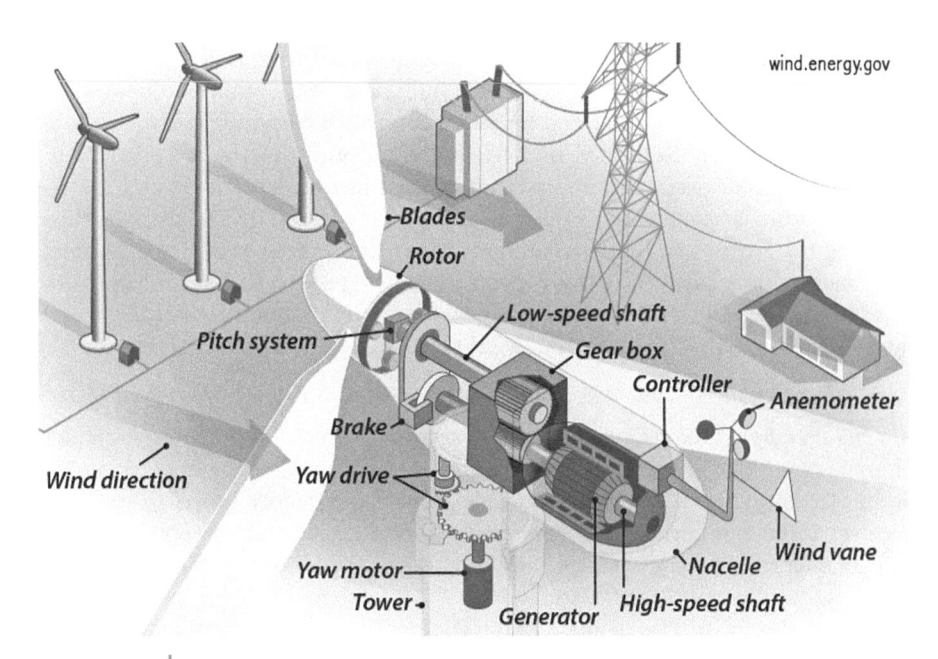

FIGURE 3.7 | Wind Turbine Components.
Source: https://www.energy.gov/eere/inside-wind-turbine

Environmental Impacts of Wind Energy   How green is wind power? It's not a simple question. While wind turbines do not produce direct GHG emissions, there are indirect emissions. Manufacturing and installation of wind turbines require hundreds of tons of material, including steel for the towers, concrete for the foundations, and carbon fiber and epoxy resins for the blades. Copper, neodymium, and dysprosium are used to manufacture the magnets in the generators. Mining the raw materials is energy intensive. Making the steel and copper requires the combustion of metallurgical coal in blast furnaces. And the manufacture of concrete emits lots of carbon dioxide. Emissions are also created in the transport, installation, and eventually the decommissioning of the wind turbines.

Except for decommissioning, the emissions from wind installations are one-time and front-loaded. In contrast, the emissions from fossil-fueled electric power plants occur continuously as fuels are combusted. Amortizing the carbon cost over the decades-long lifespan of a wind farm, wind power has a carbon footprint of 99 percent less than coal-fired power plants, 98 percent less than natural gas, and a surprising 75 percent less than solar. More specifically, wind turbines average 11 grams of CO_2 emission per kilowatt-hour, compared to 44 g/kwh for solar, 450 g/kwh for natural gas, and an enormous 1,000 g/kwh for coal.[10] As wind farms become larger and more efficient, GHG emission are expected to fall further.

Other human and environmental impacts of wind farms also need to be considered. Criticisms of wind farms include visual and noise impacts, land-use conflicts, impacts on resident and migratory birds, disruption of local surface air and temperature patterns, and electromagnetic interference. These impacts are typically mitigated through careful siting and design. For instance, care can be taken to locate onshore installations away from population centers and migratory flyways. Offshore installations are located far from humans, usually resulting in less conflict.

Onshore wind farms need to be carefully sited to minimize impacts on humans and the environment and be easily connected to power grids. Onshore windfarms are often co-located on agriculture and forest lands, contributing to rural economic development and providing extra income to farmers and ranchers. The turbines occupy only 1 percent of the land covered by a wind farm, thus enabling the farmers and ranchers to grow grain and graze cattle. These farmers and ranchers typically receive royalties for each wind turbine without any up-front investment. Wind farms also hold promise for rural communities because wind farms yield local jobs, royalties from wind turbines, and additional tax revenue.

Solar Power

Solar energy is the radiant light and heat from the sun. It is the most abundant energy resource on Earth. The large magnitude of available solar energy, known as insolation, makes it a highly appealing renewable energy source. The Earth receives 173,000 terawatts of energy from the sun every hour, enough to supply human energy needs for one year.[11] Solar energy installations have been cheaper than fossil fuels since 2021.[12]

Solar energy produces no direct GHG emissions, operates silently, and requires very little maintenance since they have few movable parts. Solar power systems have operating lifespans of 20 to 30 years and low operation costs. It is also a scalable technology in that the systems can be small or large, depending upon the needs of the community. The technology is flexible in that more solar energy capacity can be added as needed.

Globally, over 1.2 billion people are not connected to electrical grids, still relying on energy sources from the 1800s that are expensive, inefficient, and hazardous. These consumers spend over $30 billion (USD) annually on candles, disposable batteries, firewood, diesel fuel, and kerosene to meet lighting and power needs. Nonetheless, developing countries are increasingly well-positioned to benefit from solar energy technologies. They generally have abundant domestic distributed renewable energy sources, notably sunshine. They lack legacy fossil-fueled energy systems. Solar energy systems are far less expensive than centralized fossil-fueled systems and grids. They are experiencing rapid increases in energy demand. Finally, they are often characterized by relatively large and dispersed rural populations with limited access to centralized electrical systems and grids. For these reasons, developing countries have a significant opportunity to leapfrog directly to solar energy technologies that are modular, decentralized, low cost, reliable, environmentally friendly, and well suited to serving dispersed rural populations.

Solar Energy Capacity Trends Solar power is the third largest renewable electricity technology behind hydropower and onshore wind. Solar power currently generates 4 percent of the world's electricity, compared to 1 percent in 2015 when the Paris Agreement net-zero goals were adopted. Along with onshore wind, utility-scale solar is now the cheapest type of electricity to build, surpassing coal in 2021.

In 2020, electricity generation from solar was estimated to have increased by a record 156 TWh, a 23 percent increase from 2019. Reaching the Paris Agreement net-zero goals of 6,970 TWh by 2030 will require yearly average generation growth of 24 percent from 2020 to 2030. Although this rate is lower than the current expansion rate, it will be increasingly difficult to maintain this momentum as the photovoltaics market grows.[13]

Mainstream Solar Energy Technologies Technologies that harness solar energy are classified as either *passive* or *active*. Passive solar uses windows, walls, and floors to collect, store, reflect, and distribute solar energy. Passive systems collect heat in the winter and reject solar heat in the summer. Passive solar systems do not use mechanical and electrical devices. Building design, orientation, and materials are used to control inside temperatures. Large south-facing windows, shade trees, and Trombe walls (made of absorptive materials that store heat during the day and slowly release it at night) are examples of passive solar techniques. They can provide up to 60 percent of a home's winter heating.

Active solar systems use various electrical and mechanical devices to produce *solar power*. Solar power is defined as the conversion of solar energy into electricity. Solar power systems generate electricity either directly using *photovoltaics* (PVs) or indirectly using *concentrated solar power* (CSP). Active solar systems typically include a mix of PVs, collectors, voltage controllers, blowers, and pumps that work together to collect and process solar energy.

In PV systems, *photovoltaic cells* convert light into an electric current using the photovoltaic effect. This process generates an electric current in a photovoltaic cell when exposed to sunlight. Exposing the PV cell to sunlight produces an electric current by stimulating electrons (negative charges) in a cell layer designed to give up electrons easily. The electric field in the solar cell pulls these electrons to another layer connected to an external load.

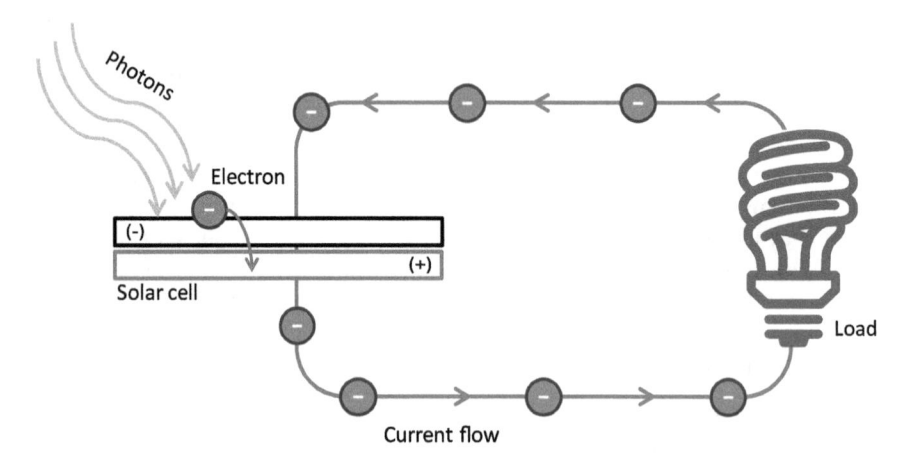

FIGURE 3.8 | Generation of Electricity from a Photovoltaic Cell.
Source: National Renewable Energy Institute. Facility-Scale Solar Photovoltaic Guidebook

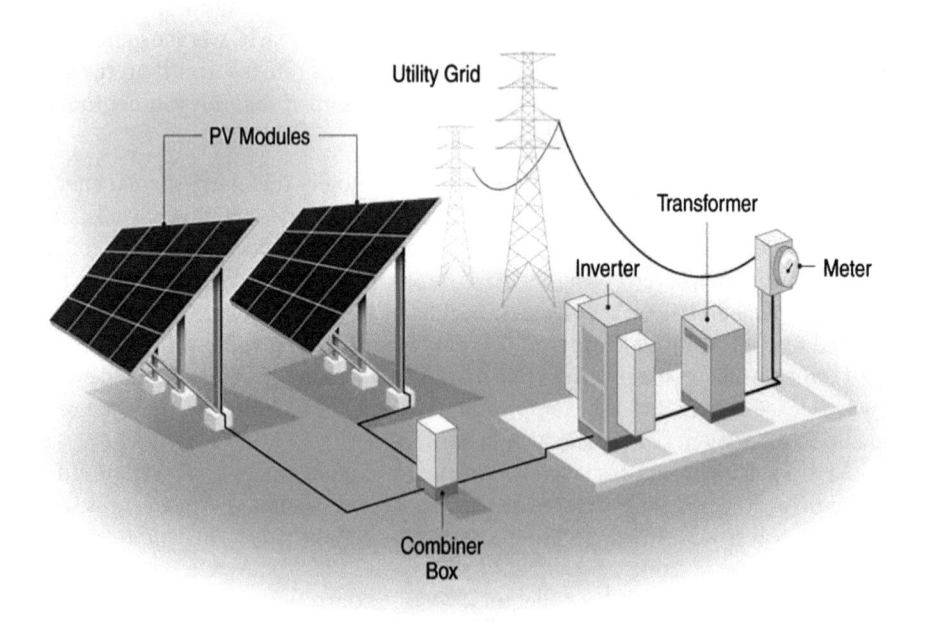

FIGURE 3.9 | Utility-Scale Photovoltaic System Components.
Source: National Renewable Energy Institute. Facility-Scale Solar Photovoltaic Guidebook

A *solar panel* is a collection of photovoltaic cells arranged in a grid-like pattern. A *photovoltaic system* consists of solar arrays comprised of several solar panels, an inverter to convert the output from direct to alternating current, and mounting, cabling, and other electrical devices. It may also use a solar tracking system to improve overall performance.

PV systems range from small rooftop-mounted systems to large utility-scale power stations of hundreds of megawatts. Most PV systems are grid-connected, with off-grid or standalone systems serving a small niche market. In 2021, prices for residential, commercial rooftop, and utility-scale PV systems continued to fall by 3 percent, 11 percent, and 12 percent, respectively.[14]

Concentrated Solar Power (CSP) systems use lenses or mirrors and solar tracking systems to focus a large area of sunlight onto a receiver. This concentrated light is converted to heat, which is used to drive a steam turbine connected to an electrical power generator. There are four main types of CSP technologies. The two main approaches are *Solar Power Towers* and *Parabolic Troughs*. Others include *Dish Stirling* and *Concentrating Linear Fresnel Reflectors*.

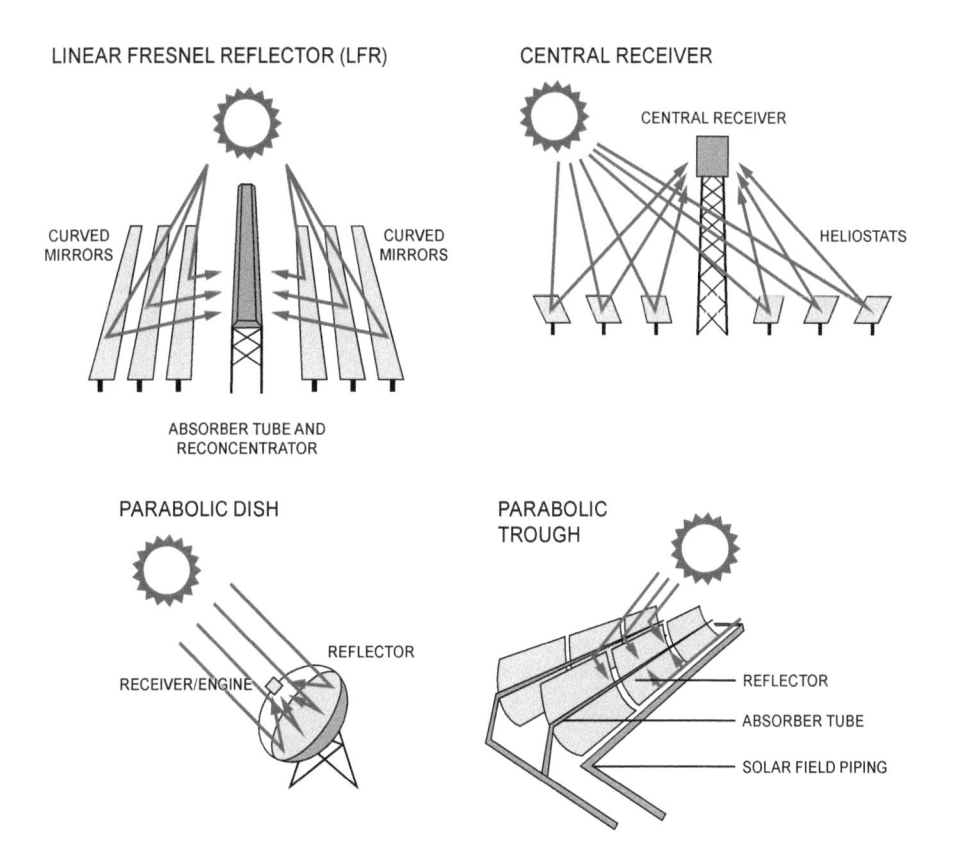

FIGURE 3.10 | Concentrated Solar Power Systems.
Source: National Renewable Energy Laboratory

Although utility-scale CSP plants have been operating long before commercial scale solar PV systems, they have largely been overtaken by PVs due to their declining costs. Global CSP capacity grew only 1.6 percent in 2020 to 6.2 GW. CSP is not on track to help meet net-zero emissions goals, which would require almost 31 percent between 2020 and 2030. Policies emphasizing the value of CSP plant storage to reduce costs will be key to attracting additional investment.

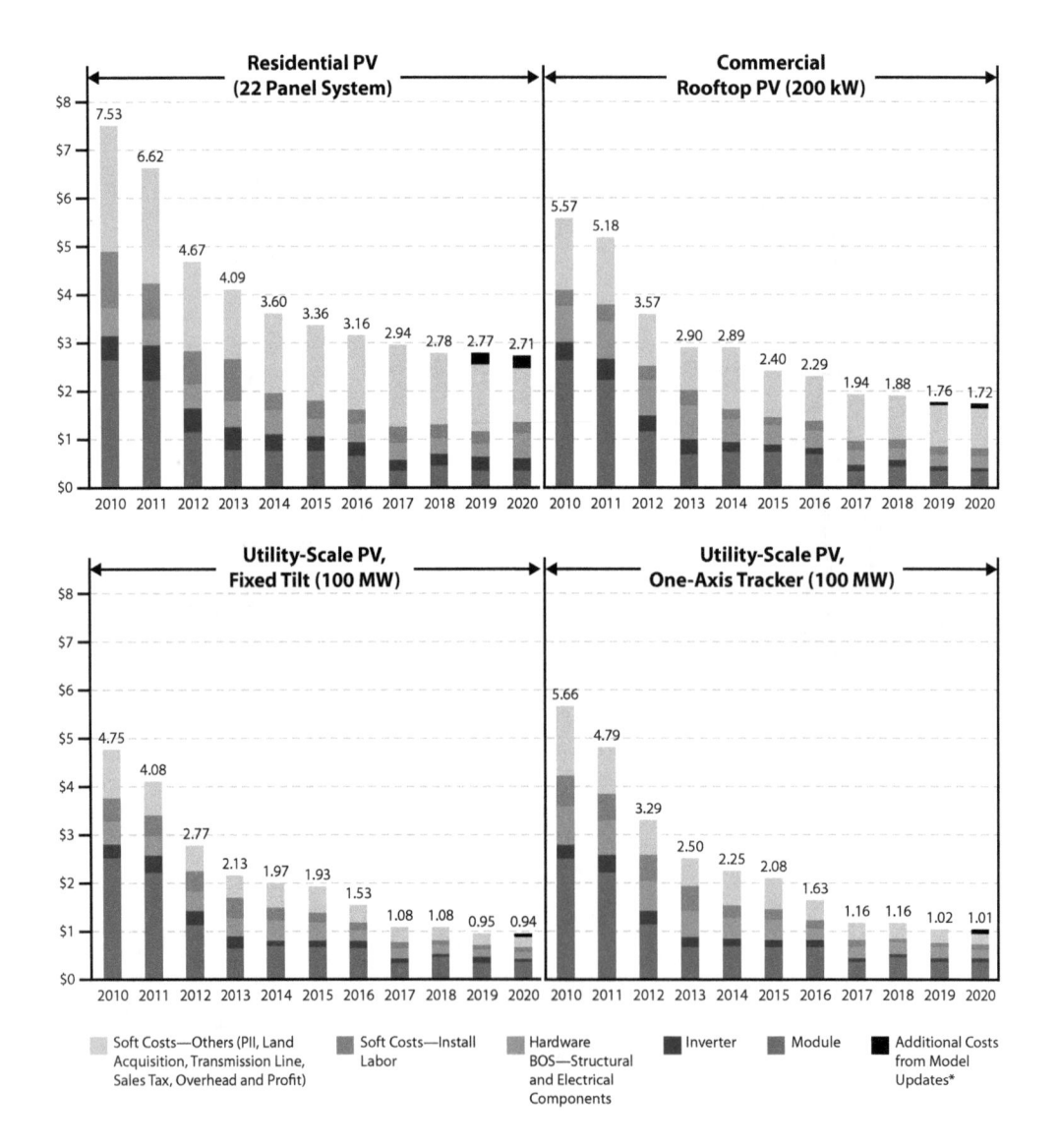

FIGURE 3.11 | Installed PV System Costs, 2010 to 2020.
Source: National Renewable Energy Laboratory

Newer Technologies Several emerging technologies promise to increase productivity, efficiency, and affordability.

Building Integrated Photovoltaics (BIPVs). While most buildings have surfaces that could easily contribute to solar energy production, they can also detract from the structure's aesthetic appeal. BIPVs integrate PVs into traditional exterior materials and features such as windows (PV glass) and cladding. The most versatile product is PV glass, which has transparent photovoltaic cells. The PV glass lets daylight enter a building while also producing energy. It can be installed in both new structures and in old buildings that are being renovated.

Thin-film solar cells are made from extremely thin and lightweight solar fabric compared to standard photovoltaic panels. This allows the film to be layered to harness up to 46 percent of the sun's energy, compared to 18 percent for conventional panels. Their flexibility also means that they can be used on curved surfaces. The lightness also makes it ideal for covering large expanses without the need for expensive structural reinforcement. They also are more effective in low light levels.

Solar-powered LED lighting systems are off-grid lighting systems that are transforming outdoor lighting like streets and pathways. The off-grid design results in significant savings since there is no need for expensive trench and cable installations. The systems are combined with PVs that produce energy during the day and stored in batteries. Controlling electronics greatly improves efficiency by customizing the light to the location or local weather patterns. These systems can also be installed in areas inaccessible to conventional lighting, improving public safety.

Concentrator photovoltaics (CPV) systems use lenses and curved mirrors to concentrate sunlight onto the photovoltaic surface, drastically increasing the electrical power production from each PV. These concentrators are often used with solar trackers to keep the focal point upon the cell as the sun moves across the sky.

Floatovoltaics are PV systems that float on or are affixed above the surface of water bodies, including irrigation canals, reservoirs, fishponds, quarried lakes, and tailing ponds. These systems save water for drinking and irrigation that would otherwise be lost through evaporation. They also tend to have higher efficiency, as the panels are kept at a cooler temperature. Floatovoltaic systems also reduce the need to use valuable land.

Solar updraft tower (SUT) systems generate electricity from low-temperature solar heat. Sunshine heats the air beneath an expansive greenhouse-like roofed collector structure surrounding the central base of a very tall chimney tower. The resulting convection causes a hot air updraft in the tower by the chimney effect. This airflow drives wind turbines placed in the chimney updraft or around the chimney base to produce electricity. Scaled-up versions of demonstration models are planned to generate significant power.

Perovskite solar cells (PSC) are a type of solar cell made from a perovskite-structured compound made from lead or tin halide-based material that acts as the light-harvesting active layer. Perovskite materials are cheap to produce and simple to manufacture.

Environmental Impacts of Solar Energy While electricity generated from solar energy does not directly emit greenhouse gases, there are indirect emissions from other stages of the solar life cycle, including manufacturing, materials transportation, installation, maintenance, and decommissioning. Most estimates of life-cycle emissions for PV systems are between 0.07 and 0.18 pounds of CO_2e per kilowatt-hour. CSP systems generate an estimated 0.04 to 0.9 kg of CO_2e per kilowatt-hour. In both cases, this is far less than the lifecycle emission rates for natural gas (0.3 kg of CO_2e/kWh) and coal (.6-1.6 kg of CO_2E/kWh).[15]

Other environmental impacts also need to be mitigated. These impacts vary depending on the type of technology. Utility-scale solar facilities may have land-use impacts, including land degradation and habitat loss. The land area requirements range from 3.5 to 10 acres per megawatt for PV facilities to 4 and 16.5 acres per megawatt for CSP facilities. Unlike wind facilities, solar projects have less opportunity to share the land with other uses, such as farming or ranching. These impacts can be mitigated by siting them on lower-quality locations such as brownfields, abandoned mine land, and transportation and transmission corridors. Smaller-scale solar PV arrays, built on homes or commercial buildings, also have minimal land use impact.

Water use can also be a concern. PV systems do not use water for power generation, but significant amounts of water are used in the manufacturing process. Like all thermal electric plants, CSP systems require water to produce steam to drive steam turbines connected to electrical power generators. Water is also used for cooling. Water use depends on the plant design, plant location, and the type of steam turbine and cooling system.

Lastly, solar power systems require components manufactured from hazardous chemicals and materials. In PV systems, most of these are used to clean and purify the semiconductor surface, similar to the general semiconductor industry. These chemicals include hydrochloric acid, sulfuric acid, nitric acid, hydrogen fluoride, 1,1,1-trichloroethane, and acetone. PV cells also contain several more toxic materials, including gallium arsenide, copper-indium-gallium-diselenide, and cadmium-telluride. Workers face risks associated with inhaling silicon dust containing these chemicals. If not handled and disposed of properly, these materials could pose serious environmental or public health threats. Care must ensure workers are not harmed by chemical exposure and that waste products are disposed of properly. Since these chemicals are rare and expensive, manufacturers and waste managers have a strong financial incentive to make sure they are recycled rather than thrown away.

Hydropower

Hydropower refers to the use of falling or fast-moving water to produce electricity or power machines. Hydropower systems convert the *potential* (gravitational) and *kinetic* (motion) energy of water to produce power. Hydropower is considered a form of sustainable energy because it is continually renewed by the Earth's water cycle. Hydropower is also an indirect form of solar energy because the water source is rainwater, which occurs due to the evaporation of water from bodies of water and the Earth's surface due to the heat of the Sun.

Hydropower is an attractive alternative to fossil fuels as it does not directly produce carbon dioxide or other atmospheric pollutants, does not require fuel purchase, and provides a relatively consistent source of power. International and national institutions often view hydropower as a low-carbon means for rural economic development. Nonetheless, hydropower has significant environmental and socio-economic impacts. It is also geographically constrained in terms of where it can be developed since it requires a sufficient source of elevated water.

Some evidence indicates that hydropower technology dates to ancient Greek civilization, while other sources suggest it first emerged in China around the same period.[16] The earliest applications were water wheels and watermills, where the weight of the water caused the wheel to turn. This mechanical energy was then used in processes like milling (grinding), rolling, hammering, and sawing.

At the beginning of the Industrial Revolution in Britain, hydropower was used in new manufacturing inventions such as Richard Arkwright's water frame—used to spin cotton—which was one of the world's first factory systems. As the Industrial Revolution grew, waterpower was displaced by steam power in larger mills and factories. However, it was still used during the eighteenth and nineteenth centuries for many smaller operations, such as gristmills and sawmills.

Hydropower became a source for generating electricity during the late nineteenth century. The first hydroelectric plant serving customers was opened in the state of Wisconsin. Within a decade, hundreds of hydropower plants were constructed in North America, where they were primarily used to power mills and light some local buildings. By the turn of the century, hydropower plants were spreading around the globe. Germany developed the first three-phase hydroelectric system in 1891, and Australia launched the first publicly owned plant in the Southern Hemisphere in 1895. In 1895, the world's largest hydroelectric development was created at Niagara Falls. In China, in 1905, a hydroelectric plant was built on Xindian creek near Taipei, with an installed capacity of 500 kW.

In the twentieth century, hydroelectric power developments became the focus of national and regional economic policy. The New Deal in the 1930s supported the construction of multipurpose hydro projects, such as the Hoover and Grand Coulee dams and a system of dams in the Tennessee River Watershed constructed by the Tennessee Valley Authority. By 1940, hydropower generated 40 percent of the electricity in the United States. From the 1940s to 1970s, spurred initially by World War II and strong post-war economic and population growth, state-owned utilities constructed massive hydropower developments throughout Western Europe and the Soviet Union, North America, and Japan. Low-cost hydropower was seen as one of the best ways to meet growing energy demand and was often tied to energy-intensive industries such as aluminum smelters and steelworks.

A case in point is the Bonneville Power Project on the Columbia River. The aluminum industry was the first major industrial customer of Columbia River power. The electrolysis technique used to produce aluminum from bauxite requires enormous amounts of electricity delivered steadily and inexpensively. With Bonneville Dam coming online in 1938, the region became attractive to the aluminum industry. Boeing became the primary customer for aluminum from Northwest smelters. It has been estimated that electricity from Grand Coulee Dam alone provided the power to make the aluminum in about one-third of the planes built during World War II.[17]

Over the last decades of the twentieth century, Brazil and China became world leaders in hydropower development. In Brazil and Paraguay, the Itaipu Dam became the world's largest dam when it opened in 1984. It has recently been eclipsed in size by the Three Gorges Dam in China. Hydropower developments have declined due to adverse environmental and socioeconomic impacts and financial challenges resulting from immense construction costs. Many prospective projects have been halted worldwide.[18] Lending and financial support from international institutions, most notably the World Bank, dried up in the late 1990s, particularly affecting hydropower construction in the developing world.

Advantages and Disadvantages of Hydropower Hydropower has historically been one of the most inexpensive ways to generate electricity. Once a dam is constructed and the equipment installed, the energy source derived from flowing water is free. It is renewable yearly by snow and rainfall. There are no GHG emissions, pollution, or waste released in the production of hydropower. Hydropower is flexible and reliable since the release of water can be controlled. Furthermore, since water is a naturally recurring resource, there are no concerns of price fluctuations, production strikes, issues of transportation, or other national security issues. In addition, hydropower dams are often justified as offering many co-benefits such as flood control, irrigation, rural economic development, and recreational opportunities.

Hydropower is highly controversial for numerous reasons. Containing rivers within dams disrupts wildlife and other natural resources. Dams present an obvious obstacle to migrating fish. Dams block the downstream movement of juvenile fish to the waters where they will spend their adult lives—the ocean for salmon and steelhead or a lake or river for resident fish like trout, bull trout, or sturgeon. Adult fish are also prevented from swimming upstream to spawn. Fish ladders and even water-filled fish elevators are often installed. However, there is often no fish passage for juvenile or adult fish for many dams worldwide.

Another issue that has plagued large hydro projects since the beginning is the forcible eviction of people from their land, as witnessed in the heyday of North American Dam construction from the 1930s to the 1970s and in China, Canada, and Chile. This becomes very controversial, particularly for indigenous communities that have maintained a particular way of life in the watershed for many generations.

Hydroelectric Power Capacity Trends Hydropower is the largest source of renewable electricity generation, producing an estimated 4,370 terawatt-hours (TWh) of the roughly 26,000 TWh of total global electricity in 2020 (17 percent).[19] This electricity is produced by about 60,000 large hydroelectric dams worldwide, with an additional 3,700 currently planned or under construction. However, capacity growth has decreased in recent years and is not on track to contribute significantly to a net-zero trajectory called for in the Paris Agreement. Reaching the 5,870 TWh of electricity generation the scenario envisions for 2030 requires a 3 percent (48 GW) average annual growth in generation capacity. Although several large projects are under construction in China, India, Ethiopia, and Southeast Asia, capacity growth is far below 3 percent.

Some additional generation capacity can be gained through modernization refurbishments. The hydroelectric infrastructure in many advanced economies dates to the 1940s through the 1980s, and almost 40 percent (476 GW) of the global capacity is over 40 years old (the average age is 32). With infrastructure this old, major equipment modernization is required to improve performance and increase flexibility. In countries like the United States with many aging plants, these investments are essential to maintain or increase output.

Increasing hydropower capacity is also being challenged by the increasingly common practice of dam removal, the process of demolishing dams to return natural water flow to rivers, restore fish passage, and conserve river and watershed systems. Currently, more dams are being removed than built in North America and Western Europe. Dam and hydropower policy has been consistently shifting towards restoring the state of rivers and water systems. A total of 1,449 dam removals occurred between 1953 and 2016. While most of these dams were old and small, recent removals have been larger. In 2021, 57 dams were removed in the United States, reconnecting more than 2,131 miles of rivers.

Conventional Hydropower Technologies   There are two main types of conventional hydroelectric facilities:

Run-of-the-river systems rely on the river's natural current to produce electricity. Run-of-the-river systems may have a limited amount of storage, in which case the storage reservoir is referred to as *pondage* (see Figure 3.12 below). A plant without pondage is subject to seasonal river flows and thus operates as an intermittent energy source. Both types may have a *weir* that diverts water flow to the hydro turbines.

Impoundment systems accumulate water in reservoirs created by dams on streams and rivers (see Figure 3.13 below). Water is released through hydro turbines as needed to generate electricity. Most large hydropower facilities are of this type. They comprise three parts: 1) a dam to control water flow, 2) an upstream reservoir where water is stored, and 3) an electric plant where the electricity is produced. The flow of water behind the dam powers the blades in a turbine that spins a generator to produce electricity. The electricity is then transported over long-distance electric lines to homes, factories, and businesses.

Pumped Storage Hydropower   One of the challenges utilities deal with is ramping up electricity at times of high demand. *Pumped-storage hydropower (PSH) facilities* can be used to store energy to use when demand is high. Water is pumped from a water source up to a storage basin or reservoir located at a higher elevation. When additional power is needed, water is released to power turbines located below. PSHs function like a giant battery, storing energy and releasing it when needed.

FIGURE 3.12 | Chief Joseph Dam Run-of-the River Hydropower Station.
Image Source: USACE Digital Visual Library

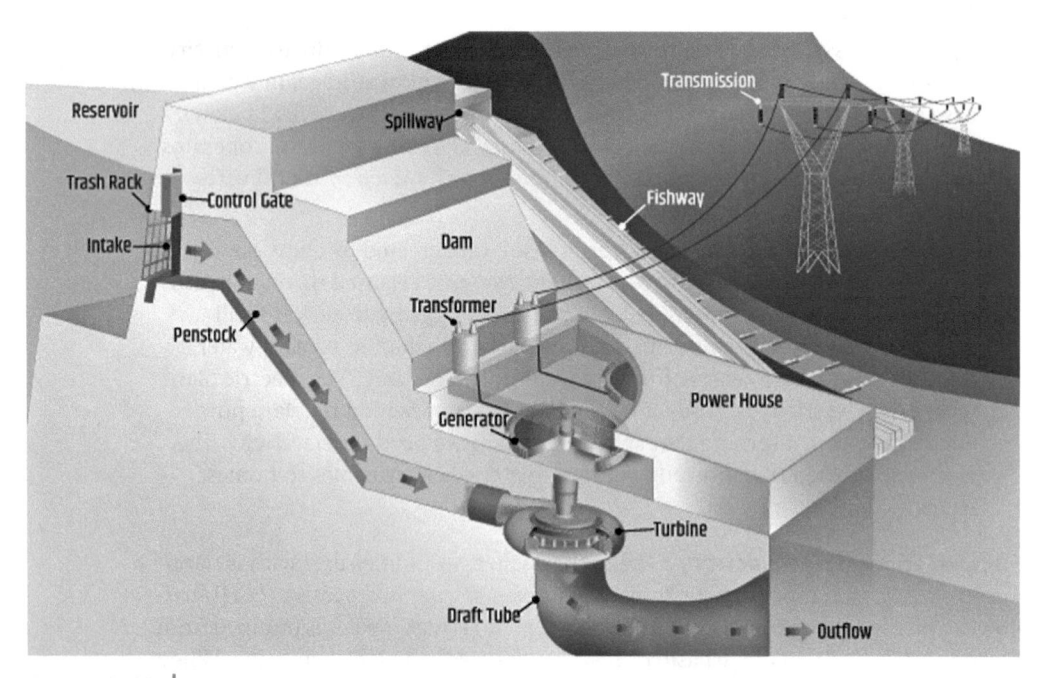

FIGURE 3.13 | Components of an Impoundment Hydroelectric Facility.
Source: https://www.energy.gov/eere/water/water-power-information-resources

The upper basin is usually filled when electricity demand and wholesale electricity prices are relatively low. It is then released during peak demand periods and when wholesale electricity prices are relatively high. PSH facilities can also effectively store energy from intermittent renewable energy sources, such as solar or wind. While pump storage facilities have a net negative electricity generation balance (they use more electricity than they produce), they allow more generation capacity during peak demand.

Oceanic Energy Another form of hydropower can be the energy from the ocean. About 70 percent of the Earth's surface comprises oceans that contain thermal energy and mechanical energy in the form of waves and tides. There are three main types of ocean energy.

Ocean thermal energy taps into the thermal energy from the sun. The heat energy stored in the ocean generates electricity using the *ocean thermal energy conversion* (OTEC) process. There is a temperature difference between the colder layers at the bottom and the warmer layers at the top, particularly in tropical regions. A temperature difference of at least 36°F (or 20°C) is required to form a thermodynamic cycle. The two challenges to this technology are cost and location. There is a substantial initial investment needed to make this technology a reality. There are only a few hundred land-based sites in the tropics where OTEC plants can be developed.[20]

Tidal power is the conversion of energy from tides into usable forms of power. Tides are created by the gravitational pull of the moon and sun along with the rotation of the Earth. Tidal power is the only technology that uses the orbital characteristics of the Earth-moon system and, to a lesser extent, the Earth-sun system. A tidal generator converts the energy of tidal flows into electricity. Greater tidal variation and higher tidal current velocities increase the potential of a site for tidal electricity generation. While tidal power is practically inexhaustible, it is not currently widely used due to relatively high cost and limited availability of sites with sufficiently high tidal ranges or flow velocities, limiting its total availability. As better technologies emerge and costs decrease, tidal energy has the potential for future renewable energy production.

Wave power is produced by waves formed by wind blowing over the surface of open water in oceans and lakes. Ocean waves contain tremendous energy. This wave power can be captured to generate electricity using various wave energy converters (WECs). A group of WECs deployed in the same location is called a *wave farm*. Compared to other established renewable energy sources, wave-power generation is not a widely employed commercial technology. However, there continues to be interest due to its high power density relative to other renewable energy sources. Many different approaches are being developed for converting wave energy to electricity, including placing devices on or just below the surface of the water and anchoring devices to the ocean floor.

Environmental Impacts of Hydropower Although hydropower facilities do not directly emit GHG emissions, many other negative environmental impacts exist. As was stated earlier, dams may obstruct fish migration. Turbines kill and injure fish that pass through the turbine. A dam and reservoir can also change river flow, water chemistry, and water temperatures, all of which can affect the river's ecology and physical characteristics. These changes may negatively affect the native habitat in and around the river. Reservoirs may inundate vast natural areas, agricultural land, human communities, and archeological sites. A reservoir and the operation of the dam may also result in the relocation of people.

Manufacturing the concrete and steel in hydropower dams requires material and equipment that produce GHG emissions. GHGs are also produced in reservoirs because of aerobic and anaerobic decomposition of the biomass in the water. The amount of GHGs emitted depends on many site-specific and regional factors. However, given the long operating lifetime of a hydropower plant (50 to 100 years), these emissions are offset by the emissions-free hydroelectricity. Overall, they emit significantly fewer GHGs than fossil fuel plants. The Three Gorges Dam on the Yangtze River in China caused the relocation of over 1 million residents.

Biomass Energy

Biomass is the organic material that comes from plants and animals. Biomass contains stored *chemical energy* from the sun. Plants produce biomass through photosynthesis. Animals build biomass by consuming plants or other animals. *Biomass energy*, or *bioenergy*, can be produced by burning biomass directly for heat or converting it to liquid and gaseous fuels through various conversion processes.

Biomass energy was the primary form of energy used worldwide until the industrial revolution and the emergence of fossil fuels. There is a resurgence of interest in biomass to produce *biofuels* for transportation or electricity generation.

Biofuel Production Trends   Biomass continues to be an essential fuel in developing countries. Currently, biomass contributes about 10 percent of the global energy supply. Two-thirds is used in developing countries for cooking and heating, and one-third is converted to biofuels for transportation and electricity generation. Currently, 3.7 percent of transport fuels come from renewable sources, of which biofuels constitute 93 percent.[21]

Biofuel output is expected to expand by 28 percent (1.1 EJ) by 2028. The United States leads in volume increases, but much of this growth is a rebound from the drop caused by the pandemic. Asia accounts for almost 30 percent of new biofuel production, overtaking European output by 2026. Recent ethanol-friendly policies in India and blending targets for biodiesel in Indonesia and Malaysia are responsible for most of the growth in Asia. India is projected to become the third-largest market for ethanol demand worldwide by 2026.

Bioenergy Technologies   Throughout human history, direct combustion (burning) was the most common method for converting biomass to usable energy, particularly for heating homes, water, and cooking food. Since the industrial revolution, biomass has also been used for industrial process heat, transportation (rail and ship steam engines), and generating electricity in steam turbines.

In recent decades, technologies have been developed that convert biomass into liquid and gaseous fuels through *biomass conversion (or bioconversion) pathways*. Bioconversion pathways include various combinations of three components: 1) feedstock, 2) conversion process, and 3) fuel type (see Figure 3.14 below).

The primary sources of biomass, called *feedstocks*, for bioconversion include:

- **Wood and wood wastes,** including residues from forestry and forest product industry processes.
- **Agricultural crops and waste materials,** including starches from grains, oils from oilseeds, and tallow from livestock.
- **Food waste,** including food scraps, animal fat, and residual cooking oils.
- **Municipal solid waste,** including paper, cotton, wool products, and food, yard, and wood waste.
- **Animal waste,** including both animal manure and human sewage.

Biomass is converted to usable energy through various conversion pathway processes, including:

- **Biological conversion.** Biological conversion includes *fermentation* to convert biomass into various alcohols and *anaerobic digestion* to produce natural gas. The most common alcohol produced is ethanol, used as a vehicle fuel. Renewable natural gas—also called *biogas* or *biomethane*—is

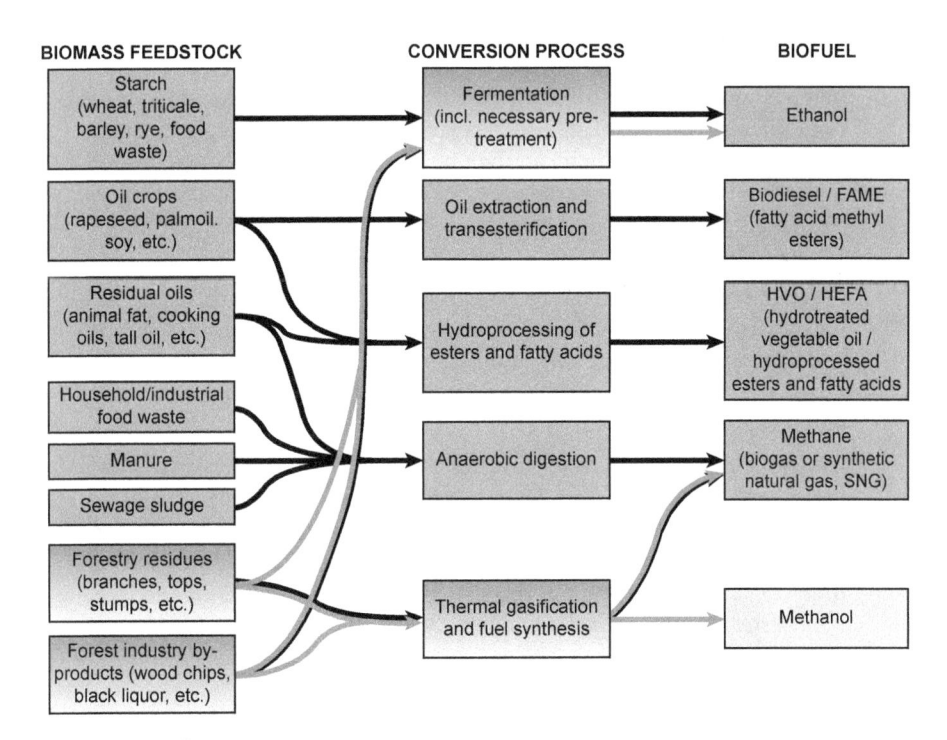

FIGURE 3.14 | Biomass to Sustainable Fuel Pathways.
Source: Michael Martin, Elisabeth Wetterlund, Roman Hackl, Kristina M. Holmgren, & Philip Peck (2017): Assessing the aggregated environmental benefits from by-product and utility synergies in the Swedish biofuel industry, Biofuels, DOI: 10.1080/17597269.2017.1387752

produced in anaerobic digesters at sewage treatment plants and dairy and livestock operations. It also forms in and can be captured from solid waste landfills. Properly treated renewable natural gas has the same uses as fossil fuel natural gas.

- **Chemical conversion.** A chemical conversion process known as *transesterification* is used for converting vegetable oils, animal fats, and greases into fatty acid methyl esters (FAME), which are used to produce biodiesel.
- **Thermochemical conversion.** Thermochemical conversion of biomass includes *pyrolysis* and *gasification*. Pyrolysis entails heating organic material in a low oxygen environment, producing fuels such as charcoal, bio-oil, renewable diesel, methane, and hydrogen. Gasification involves heating organic materials to extremely high temperatures to produce a gas called synthesis gas or *syngas*. Syngas can be used as a fuel for diesel engines, heating, and generating electricity in gas turbines. The syngas can be further processed to produce liquid fuels.

Finally, various types of liquid and gaseous fuels are the product of conversion:

- **Ethanol (CH_3CH_2OH)** is an alcohol produced by fermenting plant starches and sugars—mainly corn starch in the United States—but other technologies are emerging that convert the sugars from cellulose and hemicellulose, the nonedible fibrous material in plants. During fermentation, microorganisms (e.g., bacteria and yeast) metabolize plant sugars to produce ethanol, which can then be blended with gasoline to increase octane and cut down carbon monoxide and other emissions. Roughly 97 percent of gasoline in the United States contains some ethanol.
- **Biodiesel** is produced primarily by combining alcohol with new and used vegetable oils and animal fats, resulting in a low-carbon replacement for petroleum-based diesel fuel. Biodiesel is non-toxic, biodegradable, and can be blended with petroleum diesel, including B100 (pure biodiesel, the most common blend) and B20 (a blend containing 20 percent biodiesel and 80 percent petroleum diesel).
- **Biogas** is a mixture of gases, primarily methane, carbon dioxide, and hydrogen sulfide, produced from raw materials such as agricultural waste, manure, municipal waste, plant material, sewage, green waste, and food waste. It is a renewable energy source. Biogas is produced by anaerobic digestion with anaerobic microorganisms inside an *anaerobic digester*, *biodigester*, or a *bioreactor*.
- **Methanol (CH_3OH),** also called methyl alcohol, wood alcohol, or wood spirits, is the simplest alcohol. Historically, methanol was produced in the wood distillation process. While most methanol today is made from natural gas, biomass feedstocks are increasingly used as a climate-friendly replacement. Most methanol is used to make transportation fuels and as an industrial solvent to produce inks, resins, adhesives, dyes, and pharmaceutical ingredients.

Environmental Impacts of Bioenergy   Bioenergy is a unique type of renewable energy. Unlike solar, wind, and hydropower, which do not produce direct GHG emissions and other pollutants, biomass does emit GHG and other pollutants into the atmosphere. When we use biomass for heat, electricity, or fuel, it releases carbon dioxide into the atmosphere. However, the carbon in biomass is already part of the biogenic (short) carbon cycle. No additional carbon is added from biomass, whereas fossil energy pulls carbon out of the Earth's crust, where it is sequestered in the geologic (long) carbon cycle. Additionally, sources of biomass energy, such as trees and agricultural crops, also capture and sequester carbon during photosynthesis. If trees and other plants absorb as much carbon dioxide as they emitted during the biomass combustion process, the carbon cycle remains in balance.

Unfortunately, in real-life practice, it's not that simple. The carbon impact of bioenergy depends on many factors, including the feedstock sourcing, conversion technologies used, regrowing efforts, and the carbon impact of the fossil energy resource it's replacing. Assessment of total lifecycle (GHG) emissions is necessary to determine which fuel pathways can qualify.

For example, consider the production of ethanol from agricultural crops like corn. Converting corn to fuel and burning that fuel in combustion engines results in the emission of GHGs. Fossil fuels are also used in the production of corn, in the form of diesel fuel to drive farm vehicles and for fertilizer. On the other hand, these emissions are offset by the CO_2 captured when future crops used to make the ethanol are grown. As a result, vehicles running on high-level blends of ethanol produce less net CO_2 than conventional vehicles per mile traveled. A 2020 analysis by Argonne National Laboratory found that using corn-based ethanol in place of gasoline reduces GHG emissions by 40 percent. Using cellulosic ethanol provides an even greater benefit—with reductions from 88 percent to 108 percent—than fossil fuels, depending on biomass feedstocks used.[22]

Beyond the GHG emissions from bioenergy, there are other environmental consequences to consider:

Land-use: Land use change from biofuel production releases a significant amount of carbon from soil and plant biomass, creating a "carbon debt" that can take years to repay. Besides increasing GHG emissions, changes in land use can have other environmental consequences, such as soil erosion, nutrient depletion, water consumption, and loss of biodiversity.

Air quality: Production and use of biofuels can negatively impact air quality. Facilities producing ethanol from corn and cellulosic feedstocks tend to have greater air pollutant emissions relative to petroleum refineries on a per-BTU basis. Ethanol blends also tend to increase nitrous oxide emissions, even though the vehicles were equipped with modern emissions controls.[23]

Water quantity and quality: large amounts of water are used in every stage of growing biofuel crops, particularly for irrigation. Crops such as sugar cane, oil palm, and corn have relatively high water requirements. The amount of irrigation water needed in lower rainfall areas can be significant. Biofuel crop production can also affect water quality. For example, converting pastures, woodland, and wetlands into cornfields may increase soil erosion and excess nitrogen and phosphorous runoff into surface and groundwaters. Pesticides and other chemicals can also wash into water bodies. Of the principal feedstocks, corn requires the most fertilizer and pesticides per hectare.

Soil: Changes in land use and intensification of biofuel crop production can potentially harm soil conditions. These impacts can be mitigated using various strategies, including conservation tillage and crop rotations. Removing plant residues for biofuels can reduce soil quality and increase erosion. Perennial plants such as palm, sugar cane, or switchgrass can also improve soil quality by increasing soil cover and organic carbon levels compared with annual crops like oilseed, corn, and grains.

Biodiversity and habitat: Increased biofuel production has been associated with the loss of grasslands and wetlands in ecologically sensitive areas, particularly in the Midwest United States, Brazil, and Indonesia. The resulting loss of habitat and the "simplification" of landscapes negatively impact pollinators, birds, and soil-dwelling organisms and disrupt ecosystem services in terrestrial and aquatic habitats.

Not all biomass energy solutions are created equal. We must make careful choices about the type of biomass we harvest for fuel and how we harvest it. Advancements in research and technology and policy development can help ensure that future investments in bioenergy are more environmentally friendly.

Geothermal Power

Geothermal power comes from the heat contained inside the Earth. Most of the geothermal energy is trapped under the Earth's crust in the form of hot magma. In some areas, this geothermal energy is closer to the Earth's surface, where it heats rocks or groundwater. Most geothermal resources are found along major tectonic plate boundaries, such as the "Ring of Fire," which encircles the Pacific Ocean and Iceland.

When magma comes near the Earth's surface, it heats groundwater trapped in porous rock or water running along fractured rock surfaces and faults. Hydrothermal features have two common ingredients: water (hydro) and heat (thermal). Geothermal energy is a renewable energy source because heat is continuously produced inside the Earth. People use geothermal heat for bathing, heating buildings, and generating electricity.

Geothermal Energy Trends Geothermal electricity generation increased by 2 percent in 2020, falling below the growth rate of the previous five years, with a capacity increase of less than 200 MW annually. Geothermal energy development is not on track with the Paris net-zero emissions goals, which require 13 percent annual increases in generation from 2021 to 2030. Policies to help reduce costs and mitigate predevelopment risks are needed to increase geothermal-based power generation.

Geothermal Power Technologies Some geothermal energy technologies use the Earth's temperatures near the surface, while others require drilling miles into the Earth. These technologies can be divided into three basic types:

- Direct use and district heating systems
- Geothermal power plants
- Geothermal heat pumps

Direct use and district heating systems. Ancient Roman, Chinese, and Native American cultures used hot water from springs or reservoirs for bathing, cooking, and heating. Today, many hot springs are still used for bathing, and many people believe the hot, mineral-rich waters have health benefits. Geothermal energy is also used to heat individual buildings directly and to heat multiple buildings with *district heating systems.* Such as the buildings in Reykjavik, Iceland. Industrial applications of geothermal energy include food dehydration (drying), gold mining, and milk pasteurizing.

Geothermal electricity generation requires water or steam at high temperatures (300° to 700°F). Geothermal power plants are generally built where geothermal reservoirs are located within a mile or two of the Earth's surface. The United States is the leading producer of geothermal electricity generation, with about 16 billion kWh in 2021, or equal to about 0.4 percent of total utility-scale electricity generation in the United States. Beyond the United States, 26 countries generate about 72 billion kWh of electricity from geothermal energy. Indonesia was the second-largest geothermal electricity producer at nearly 14 billion kWh, equal to about 5 percent of Indonesia's total electricity generation. Kenya was the eighth-largest geothermal electricity producer at about 5 billion kWh, but it had the largest percentage share of its total annual electricity generation from geothermal energy at about 46 percent.

Geothermal heat pumps (GHPs) are heating/cooling systems for buildings that use a heat pump to transfer heat to or from the ground or water. Taking advantage of the relative constancy of temperatures of the Earth through the seasons, GHPs are among the most energy-efficient technologies for heating and cooling buildings and water heating. GHPs use far less energy than burning fossil fuels in a boiler or furnace or using electrical resistance heaters.

Geothermal Environmental Impacts Utility-scale geothermal plants produce an average of 45 kg of CO_2 equivalent emissions per megawatt-hour of generated electricity (kg CO_2eq/MWh), significantly lower than the 1,001 kg of CO_2 equivalent per megawatt-hour for coal-fired power plants. Plants that emit high levels of pollutants are usually equipped with emission-control systems that capture the emissions. The hot water from geothermal sources may contain toxic chemicals, such as mercury, arsenic, boron, antimony, and salt.

Geothermal developments have minimal land and freshwater requirements compared to either renewable or fossil fuel installations. They use much less freshwater. Geothermal power stations can disrupt the natural cycles of geysers and can cause small earthquakes.

Geothermal heat pumps use 25 to 50 percent less electricity than conventional heating and cooling systems. Even better, if a renewable energy source generates the electricity, there are zero greenhouse gas emissions from system operation. However, there are GHG emissions associated with manufacture, installment, decommission, etc.). Even when the source of electricity is not GHG-free, the emissions associated with heat pumps are still almost always less than conventional heating/cooling systems, including conventional air conditioners, natural gas, oil furnaces, and electrical resistance heaters.

Hydrogen and Hydrogen Fuel Cells

Hydrogen is the simplest element, with each atom having only one proton. Hydrogen is also the most abundant element in the universe. The sun and stars are essentially giant balls of hydrogen and helium gases. On Earth, hydrogen exists only in compound form with other elements in liquids, gases, or solids. Hydrogen combined with oxygen is water (H_2O). *Hydrocarbons* are hydrogen combined with carbon to form different compounds found in natural gas, coal, and petroleum.

Hydrogen is an *energy carrier*, defined as a substance that contains energy that can be transported from one place to another and then converted into other energy forms such as heat, mechanical work, or chemical processes. Hydrogen fuel is produced by separating it from water, fossil fuels, or biomass. Hydrogen is a clean fuel that, when consumed in a fuel cell, produces only water. Hydrogen has the highest energy content of any fuel by weight. Pure hydrogen is a highly flammable gas, and safety is a consideration during storage, transport, and use.

Hydrogen Fuel Production Trends In recent years, close to 70 MW of production capacity was installed annually. However, this progress falls well short of what is needed to meet net-zero goals. Moreover, low-carbon hydrogen fuel demand is almost exclusively limited to road transport. Therefore, more efforts are needed in demand creation and in reducing emissions associated with hydrogen production.

Hydrogen Fuel Technologies Hydrogen fuel can be produced through several technologies.

Thermal processes involve *steam reforming*, a high-temperature process in which steam reacts with a hydrocarbon fuel to produce hydrogen. Fossil fuels and biomass can be reformed to produce hydrogen fuel. Today, about 95 percent of all hydrogen fuel is produced from steam reforming of natural gas.

Electrolysis processes separate water into oxygen and hydrogen *electrolyzer*, which functions much like a fuel cell in reverse—instead of using the energy of a hydrogen molecule like a fuel cell does, an electrolyzer creates hydrogen from water molecules. If the electricity used in the process is from renewable power, such as solar or wind, the resulting pollutant-free hydrogen is called *green hydrogen*. The rapidly declining cost of renewable energy is one reason for the growing interest in green hydrogen. Some experts argue green hydrogen is essential because certain aspects of the economy are difficult to electrify and therefore will require fuels for the foreseeable future.

Solar-driven processes use light as the energy for hydrogen production. These solar-driven processes include photobiological, photoelectrochemical, and solar thermochemical conversion. Photobiological processes use photosynthesizing bacteria and green algae to produce hydrogen. Photoelectrochemical processes use semiconductors to separate water into hydrogen and oxygen. Solar thermochemical processes use concentrated solar power to drive water splitting reactions.

Biological processes use microbes such as bacteria and microalgae to produce hydrogen through biological reactions. In microbial biomass conversion, the microbes break down organic matter like biomass or wastewater to produce hydrogen, while in photobiological processes the microbes use sunlight as the energy source.

Hydrogen Fuel Cells *Fuel cells* are electrochemical energy devices that convert stored chemical energy into electricity. Hydrogen fuel cells combine hydrogen and oxygen into water, producing heat and electricity. Unlike fossil fuel, hydrogen fuel cells don't directly emit GHGs or other pollutants. Hydrogen itself is not toxic. Hydrogen fuel cells are also more efficient (35 percent conversion rate) compared to gasoline or diesel engines (20 percent conversion rate). In addition to electricity, fuel cells produce water and heat. The energy efficiency of a fuel cell is generally between 40 and 60 percent; however, if waste heat is captured in a cogeneration scheme, efficiencies of up to 85 percent can be obtained.[24]

Fuel cells are also highly scalable and have few moving parts to maintain or repair. Because they are quiet, clean, and reliable, they can be located anywhere and are especially suited for dense urban areas but also are good options for rural areas, vehicles and portable devices, and spaceflight.

Environmental Impacts of Hydrogen Fuel and Fuel Cells Hydrogen is the most abundant element in the universe. Hydrogen fuel cells provide an inherently clean source of energy, with no direct emissions or adverse environmental impact during operation as the byproducts are simply heat and water. Unlike biofuel or hydropower, hydrogen doesn't require large areas of land to produce. Hydrogen fuel technology provides a high-density source of energy with high energy efficiency. The charge time for hydrogen fuel cells is extremely rapid, on par with conventional internal combustion engines. Hydrogen fuel cells do not produce noise or visual pollution.

Conversely, there are still challenges to overcome to realize the full potential of hydrogen as a key enabler for a future decarbonized energy system. Despite being the most abundant element in the Universe, extracting hydrogen from water requires a significant amount of energy to achieve. This energy is greater than the hydrogen fuel created. If the energy for this conversion comes from fossil fuels, the GHG emission reductions may be minimal or nonexistent. Precious metals such as platinum and iridium are typically required as catalysts in fuel cells. The mining of these materials comes with environmental costs. Hydrogen is a highly flammable fuel source, which brings understandable safety concerns.

ENERGY STORAGE

Renewable energy has the potential to help us reach a 1.5°C climate future. And yet, the actual business of renewable energy continues to struggle against the petrochemical industry. The problem is rooted in cost parity, often referred to as the *levelized cost of energy* (LCOE). While cost parity has been achieved with renewable energy production technologies like onshore wind, there continues to be one area that continues to struggle: *energy storage*. Energy storage is defined as the capture of energy produced at one time for use later to reduce imbalances between energy demand and energy production.

Energy storage is not a problem with fossil fuels. The energy is stored in the fuel itself, which can be transported by pipeline, ship, rail, truck, and vehicle gas tanks to be used when and where it's needed. Such is not the case with some sources of renewable energy, which can be affected by environmental, seasonal, and daily cycles that limit their availability. As such, renewable energy cannot always consistently produce energy at all hours of the day—this is called *intermittency*.

The solution to intermittency is storage. The ability to store excess energy produced by renewable energy during peak cycles gives power grids the ability to tap into those reserves when the cycles dip, negating intermittency. Yet despite recent technological advances, storage continues to limit the growth of renewable energy. Recent studies have shown that the use of large-scale batteries in the United States could both help reduce renewable energy infrastructure costs and provide over 80 percent of the nation's power demands through sustainable energy.[25] Energy storage is sometimes referred to as the "holy grail" of renewable energy. Storage makes energy produced from solar and wind available whenever it is needed. Shifting energy from daytime to nighttime and from high wind to low wind periods is critical for solar energy to compete with fossil fuels. When the costs of shifting renewable energy reach parity with fossil fuels, it is likely that renewable sources will replace our current fossil fuel generators.

Up until now, lithium-ion has dominated energy storage, with upwards of a 60 percent market share. There are several reasons why alternative technologies have become a key topic in the storage industry. Yet there are huge problems with lithium-ion technology. Lithium-ion batteries are extremely expensive, and while costs continue to decline, it will take many years or decades to reach grid parity. Additionally, lithium-ion technologies use cobalt, considered by many experts to be a "conflict mineral" in that it is mined in areas of armed conflict and often traded illicitly to finance the fighting. This has led to a push for more alternatives that are ethically better for the environment and for national security reasons. Another key argument against lithium-ion is the inherent fire hazard the systems pose. Instances of fire over the past few years brought this topic of safety to the forefront. Lastly, lithium-ion batteries degrade, resulting in major impacts on the system as it progresses through its life.

More and more utilities are looking to alternative technology pilot projects. While there are countless experimental technologies, they tend to fall into the following categories.

Gravity Batteries

A *gravity battery* is a category of energy storage technology that stores gravitational energy by using excess energy from the grid to raise a mass to generate gravitational potential energy, which is then dropped to convert potential energy into electricity through an electric generator. There are several types of gravitational batteries.

Pumped-storage hydroelectricity (PSH), discussed earlier in this chapter, is the most common form of grid-energy storage. PSH uses water, which is pumped from a lower reservoir to a higher reservoir before being released through turbines to create energy.

Rail energy storage is where excess renewable energy is used to power heavy train cars uphill during times of low energy demand. The potential energy is released later by using regenerative braking. A utility-scale facility is being constructed in the Pahrump Valley, Nevada.

Lifted Weight Storage (LWS) technology uses excess renewable electricity to lift heavy weights vertically several hundred meters high and generate energy when the weights are lowered. Such systems could theoretically be installed almost anywhere, compared to the limited siting options for PSH and rail energy storage.

Buoyant gas container storage stores energy by using renewable energy to pull the containers down into water with a winch. The cycle is then reversed, and electricity is generated when the containers are released and rise. Relatively little infrastructure is required, and the batteries can be sited near major population centers.

FLOW BATTERIES

A *flow battery* is a cross between a conventional battery and a fuel cell. Liquid electrolyte of metallic salts is pumped through a core that consists of a positive and negative electrode, separated by a membrane. The ion exchange that occurs between the cathode and anode generates electricity. Flow batteries typically have a higher energy efficiency than fuel cells, but lower than that of lithium-ion batteries. High material costs and low energy density have limited their adoption.

COMPRESSED AIR ENERGY STORAGE

With *compressed air energy storage (CAES)*, air is pumped into tanks or underground during off-peak hours when electricity is cheaper. When energy is needed, the air is released to turn an electricity generator. A challenge of CAES systems is the management of energy produced by the compression of air, which not only reduces operational efficiency but can damage the system. CAES systems can store energy for longer periods of time and have less upkeep than traditional batteries.

THERMAL ENERGY STORAGE

Thermal energy storage facilities use temperature to store energy in rocks, salts, water, or other materials that are then kept in insulated environments. When energy is needed, the thermal energy is released by pumping cold water onto the material to produce steam, which spins turbines. Thermal efficiency can range from 50 to 90 percent depending on the type of thermal energy used.

SOLID-STATE BATTERIES

Solid-state batteries have multiple advantages over lithium-ion batteries in large-scale grid storage. Solid-state batteries have higher energy densities and are much less prone to fire than lithium-ion batteries. Their smaller volumes and higher safety make solid-state batteries well suited for large-scale grid applications. However, solid-state battery technology is considerably more expensive than lithium-ion batteries.

Hydrogen

As discussed earlier in the chapter, *hydrogen* and *hydrogen fuel cells* have a far greater energy storage density than lithium-ion batteries. The production of hydrogen requires significant amounts of energy, so the way it's produced is critical to GHG emission performance.

Flywheels

While not suitable for long-term storage, *flywheels* can be very effective for load-leveling and load-shifting applications. Flywheels have long life cycles, high energy density, low maintenance costs, and quick response speeds. Motors store energy in flywheels by accelerating their spins to very high speeds. The motor then uses that stored kinetic energy to generate electricity by going into reverse.

Implications for Businesses

Today, the business case for transitioning to renewable energy is no longer limited to corporate social responsibility. There are now compelling business reasons for making a strong push into renewable resources:

Cost Parity

Until recently, there was truth to the perception that renewable energy technologies were too expensive. But that is quickly changing. Renewables increasingly undercut the cost of fossil energy development and operations. And the cost of renewable technologies continues to fall. In 2020, the cost of concentrating solar power (CSP) fell by 16 percent, onshore wind by 13 percent, offshore wind by 9 percent, and solar PV by 7 percent. With costs at low levels, renewables give firms a strong business case to transition from fossil fuels to net zero operations.

Energy Price Fluctuations Exposure

We write these words as the war in Ukraine rages, which has led to skyrocketing fossil fuel costs. While energy prices are one of the most important business planning considerations, they are also among the most uncontrollable. Many firms are committing to 100 percent renewable energy by 2030 or earlier to increase energy price predictability and maintain tighter control over profit margins. With the rise of cheaper, more effective renewable energy solutions, making the transition to renewables increasingly makes business sense.

INCREASED DEMAND IN OTHER SECTORS

Even though renewables offer bottomless sources of energy, there is still a need to convert that energy into electricity, store it, and deliver it when and where it's needed. Emerging renewable energy technologies, including both production systems and storage, are proving to be a significant growth market. A good example is Tesla's multi-billion-dollar investment in gigafactories that manufacture EV vehicles, batteries, and solar power systems. With the increasing realization that they are in the energy business, not the fossil fuel business, big energy companies like BP, Shell, Chevron, and Exxon are increasingly investing in renewables.

INVESTMENT OPPORTUNITIES

There has never been a better time for firms and institutional and private investors to embrace renewable energy. As costs continue to fall and governments implement climate-friendly policies, these investment opportunities will expand dramatically. One recent report shows that the Paris Agreement policy provisions will open over $29 trillion in opportunities for climate-smart investment by 2030. As a result of massive cost reductions, solar photovoltaic (PV) and wind power are now mainstream. In 2020, global investment in renewables was nearly $350 billion—more than twice the amount invested in fossil fuel power generation. Other examples include the green buildings market, which has doubled every three years for the past decade.[26]

CONCLUSION

Many countries are looking to phase out coal by 2025 or 2030. If power-generating companies are to remain viable businesses, they will need to decarbonize their operations. Government subsidies to incentive the transition to renewables is likely to play a major role, as will cap-and-trade and taxes imposed on carbon-emitting industries. In the future, emissions will only head downwards, and so businesses and investors should invest accordingly. It is likely to prompt more and more businesses to look at how they themselves can aim for net-zero emissions, further driving the pace and scale of change. Delaying the transition could leave businesses exposed. The momentum is solidly behind the renewable energy transition. As the "virtuous cycle" of renewable energy gains momentum, the opportunities for businesses and for the world at large should be enormous.

Keywords

- » Acid mine drainage
- » Active solar energy
- » Aeolian processes
- » Anaerobic
- » Anthracite
- » Biodiesel
- » Bioenergy
- » Biofuels

- Biogas
- Biomass
- Biomass conversion (bioconversion) pathways
- Bituminous coal
- Bridge fuel
- Building Integrated Photovoltaics
- Chemical energy
- Clean coal technologies
- Coal
- Compressed air energy storage (CAES),
- Concentrated solar power
- Concentrating Linear Fresnel Reflectors
- Conservation of Energy
- Conventional hydroelectric facilities
- Crude Oil
- Dish Stirling
- District heating systems
- Electrical energy
- Electrical grid
- Energy
- Energy Efficiency
- Ethanol
- Floatovoltaics
- Flow battery
- Flywheel
- Fossil fuels
- Fuel rods
- Fugitive emissions
- Geothermal energy
- Geothermal heat pumps
- Gravitational energy
- Gravity battery
- Hydraulic fracturing
- Hydroelectric power
- Hydrogen fuel cells
- Hydropower
- Impoundment hydropower
- Intermittency
- Kinetic energy
- Levelized cost of energy (LCOE)
- Lignite
- Mechanical energy
- Methanol
- Motion energy
- Mountaintop removal
- Nacelle
- Natural Gas
- Non-renewable energy
- Nuclear energy
- Nuclear fission
- Ocean thermal energy
- Oil
- Parabolic troughs
- Passive solar energy
- Peat
- Perovskite solar cells
- Petroleum
- Photovoltaic cells
- Potential energy
- Pumped-storage hydropower
- Radiant Energy
- Radioactive Waste
- Renewable energy
- Run-of-the-river hydropower
- Shale gas
- Solar energy
- Solar panel
- Solar power
- Solar-powered LED lighting
- Solar power towers
- Solar updraft tower
- Sound energy
- Strip mining
- Subbituminous coal
- Thermal energy
- Thin-film solar cells
- Tide energy
- Underground mining
- Valley fill
- Wave energy
- Wind energy
- Wind farms
- Wind turbines
- Yellowcake

Discussion Questions

1. Describe the categories and forms of energy.
2. What are the primary challenges with the "business as usual" approach in using conventional forms of energy? Discuss in detail.
3. Of the sources of conventional, non-renewable energy, which have we been most successful at transitioning away from? Which will be the most difficult to transition away from?
4. What do you think of nuclear energy as a solution to climate change?
5. Why is there a need for clean, renewable energy? What are the challenges posed by the way we derive energy at present?
6. What are the issues related to incorporating renewable energy in the developed world? Developing nations?
7. Wind power is one of the fastest growing energy sources today; however, there are some drawbacks. Discuss the major issues concerning this renewable energy.
8. How do the advantages of solar energy compare to the disadvantages? Does one outweigh the other?
9. Can plant-based energy replace our current dependence on coal, oil, and natural gas?
10. Governments oftentimes create subsidies and other projects to help industries take off. What sort of role can the government have in encouraging the use and development of clean energy?
11. Which form of renewable energy do you think has the greatest potential to become adaptable in everyday use? Why?
12. Of the other renewable energy sources listed, such as geothermal, oceanic, tidal, and wave energy, which source holds the greatest potential in the United States? Use online sources to research this question.
13. What energy storage solutions hold the most promise for the transition to renewable energy?

Recommended Websites

- Center for Climate and Energy Solution – www.c2es.org/
- International Renewable Energy Agency – www.irena.org/
- National Renewable Energy Laboratory – www.nrel.gov/
- U.S. Department of Energy – www.energy.gov/
- The Intergovernmental Panel on Climate Change – www.ipcc.ch/

Endnotes

[1] BP Global. (n.d.). Statistical review of world energy: Energy Economics. *BP Global*. Retrieved September 10, 2022, from https://www.bp.com/en/global/corporate/energy-economics/statistical-review-of-world-energy.html.

[2] BP Global. (n.d.). Statistical review of world energy: Energy Economics. *BP Global*. Retrieved September 10, 2022, from https://www.bp.com/en/global/corporate/energy-economics/statistical-review-of-world-energy.html

[3] BP Global. (n.d.). Statistical review of world energy: Energy Economics. *BP Global*. Retrieved September 10, 2022, from https://www.bp.com/en/global/corporate/energy-economics/statistical-review-of-world-energy.html

[4] *Renewable energy*. (2021, November 10). Center for Climate and Energy Solutions. Retrieved September 10, 2022, from https://www.c2es.org.

[5] BP Global. (n.d.). Statistical review of world energy: Energy Economics. *BP Global*. Retrieved September 10, 2022, from https://www.bp.com/en/global/corporate/energy-economics/statistical-review-of-world-energy.html

[6] International Renewable Energy Agency. (n.d.). International Renewable Energy Agency. *IRENA*. Retrieved September 10, 2022, from https://www.irena.org/.

[7] Windustry. (n.d.). *How much do wind turbines cost?* Retrieved September 10, 2022, from https://www.windustry.org/how_much_do_wind_turbines_cost.

[8] *Renewable energy*. (2021, November 10). Center for Climate and Energy Solutions. Retrieved September 10, 2022, from https://www.c2es.org.

[9] Windustry. (n.d.). *How much do wind turbines cost?* Retrieved September 10, 2022, from https://www.windustry.org/how_much_do_wind_turbines_cost.

[10] NREL. (n.d.). Life cycle assessment harmonization. *NREL.gov*. Retrieved September 10, 2022, from https://www.nrel.gov/analysis/life-cycle-assessment.html.

[11] Masterson, V. (2021, July 5). Renewables were the world's cheapest source of energy in 2020, new report shows. *World Economic Forum*. Retrieved September 10, 2022, from https://www.weforum.org/agenda/2021/07/renewables-cheapest-energy-source/

[12] Singh, D. pal. (n.d.). *Levelized cost of energy, levelized cost of storage, and levelized cost of hydrogen*. Lazard.com. Retrieved September 10, 2022, from https://www.lazard.com/perspective/levelized-cost-of-energy-levelized-cost-of-storage-and-levelized-cost-of-hydrogen/.

[13] Bojek, P. (2021). Solar PV: analysis. *International Energy Agency*. Retrieved September 10, 2022, from https://www.iea.org/reports/solar-pv.

[14] National Renewable Energy Laboratory. (2021) U.S. solar photovoltaic system and energy storage cost benchmark: Q1 2021. Golden, CO: NREL.

[15] Intergovernmental Panel on Climate Change. (2011). IPCC special report on renewable energy sources and climate change mitigation. *IPCC*. Retrieved September 10, 2022, from https://www.ipcc-wg3.de/srren-report/.

[16] Munoz-Hernandez, G. A., Mansoor, S. P., & Jones, D. I. (2013). *Modelling and controlling hydropower plants*. London, UK: Springer-Verlag.

[17] Northwest Power and Conservation Council. (n.d.). Aluminum. Retrieved September 10, 2022, from https://www.nwcouncil.org/reports/columbia-river-history/aluminum/

[18] World Energy Council. (n.d.). Charting the upsurge in hydropower development 2015. *World Energy Council*. Retrieved September 10, 2022, from https://www.worldenergy.org/publications/entry/charting-the-upsurge-in-hydropower-development-2015

[19] *Renewable energy.* (2021, November 10). Center for Climate and Energy Solutions. Retrieved September 10, 2022, from https://www.c2es.org.

[20] U.S. Department of Energy. (2011e). Ocean thermal energy conversion. Retrieved from www.eere.energy.gov/basics/renewable_energy/ocean_thermal_ energy_conv.html

[21] U.S. Energy Information Administration. (2021). Renewables: Fuels & Technologies. IEA. Retrieved September 10, 2022, from https://www.iea.org/fuels-and-technologies/renewables

[22] Argonne National laboratory. (2002). *Ethanol blends: Providing a renewable fuel choice.* Retrieved September 11, 2022, from https://afdc.energy.gov/files/u/publication/ethanol_blends.pdf

[23] EPA Clean Air Task Force. (2018, July 9). EPA's report on the environmental impacts of biofuels. *Clean Air Task Force.* Retrieved September 10, 2022, from https://www.catf.us/2018/07/epa-report-environmental-impacts-biofuels/.

[24] Energy.gov. (n.d.). *Fuel cells fact sheet.* Retrieved September 10, 2022, from https://www.energy.gov/eere/fuelcells/articles/fuel-cells-fact-sheet

[25] Shaner, M., Davis, S., Lewis, N., & Caldeira, K. (2018). Geophysical constraints on the reliability of solar and wind power in the United States. *Energy & Environmental Science, 11,* 914–925.

[26] International Finance Corporation. (2018, November 29). IFC report identifies more than $29 trillion in climate investment opportunities in cities by 2030. Press release. *IFC.* Retrieved September 11, 2022, from https://pressroom.ifc.org/all/pages/PressDetail.aspx?ID=18420

CHAPTER 4

Ecosystem Services: Water, Forests, Wildlife, and Biodiversity

LEARNING OBJECTIVES

By the end of this chapter, you will be able to do the following:

- » Define Ecosystem services.
- » Discuss the relationship between various ecosystem services and climate.
- » Discuss the various methods of forest stewardship.
- » List the certification programs for sustainable forestry.
- » Understand the importance of urban forests.
- » Explain the importance of preserving wilderness.
- » Discuss the Endangered Species Act of 1973 (ESA).
- » Research the issues concerning economics and biodiversity.

Chapter Overview

Humanity has always depended on the services and benefits derived from the natural world. *Natural capital* is defined as the world's stocks of natural assets, including geology, soil, air, water, and all living things.[1] From this natural capital flow a wide range of values and benefits, collectively referred to as *ecosystem services*, that make human life possible. The water we drink, the air we breathe, the food we eat, the clothes we wear, and the buildings we live in are all derived from the natural world. Beyond these apparent benefits, less visible ecosystem services include climate regulation, flood control, and the pollination of crops. Even less visible are cultural ecosystem services such as the inspiration derived from wildlife and the natural world.

Today, over half of the global gross domestic product depends on nature.[2] Thirteen of the eighteen business sectors comprising the FTSE 100—representing $1.6 trillion in market capitalization—have production processes that fundamentally depend on material resources from nature.[3] This demand for natural systems is predicted to grow in the coming decades as the world population increases by 2 billion people and world economy doubles by 2050.[4]

At the same time, human actions are also diminishing the capability of ecosystems to meet our needs. For example, while the global demand for wood grows, we are also converting more and more of the Earth's forests to other uses such as agriculture and urban spaces. As demand for ocean fisheries increases, those fisheries are declining from habitat degradation and overfishing. As the demand for freshwater increases, we continue to modify river basins in ways that negatively impact flow regimens and water quality.

The United Nations Millennium Ecosystem Assessment[5] categorizes ecosystem services as:

- *Provisioning Services* or the provision of food, clean air and water, fuel, materials, and other goods;
- *Regulating Services* such as climate (carbon), water, disease regulation, and pollination;
- *Supporting Services* such as soil formation, biodiversity, and nutrient cycling; and
- *Cultural services* including education, aesthetics, recreation, tourism, and cultural heritage.

We covered air and water in the atmosphere and hydrosphere sections of Chapter 2. In this chapter, we will focus on three other types of natural capital from which ecosystem services are derived: forests, wildlife, and biodiversity.

Sustaining the capacity of ecosystem services into the future is both a supply-side and a demand-side challenge. On the supply-side, policy and management interventions can often help protect, conserve, and regulate the flow of ecosystem benefits over time. Such conservation interventions require a substantial understanding of the ecological and social systems involved. Every country has developed conservation systems, from the national to the local level, involving government regulatory and land management agencies and the private non-profit sector.

On the demand side, since the flow of these ecosystem services is limited, use and consumption rates must be kept within replenishment rates to sustain them long-term. For instance, only so much water may be available to withdraw from a river basin without endangering the fish and wildlife that depend on it. Only so many trees can be harvested today to ensure that trees are available to harvest tomorrow and not impair forest ecosystem functions like biodiversity and hydrologic regimes.

Types of Ecosystem Services

Ecosystem services can be categorized into five categories: biospheric, ecological, social, amenity, and resource. Using forests as an example, the figure below illustrates these general categories and corresponding benefits for forest ecosystems.

Biospheric Services

Natural ecosystems are a critically important source of both terrestrial and aquatic biodiversity. Forests, for instance, contain most of the Earth's terrestrial species, including 60,000 different tree species, 68 percent of mammal species, 75 percent of bird species, and 80 percent of amphibian species.[6]

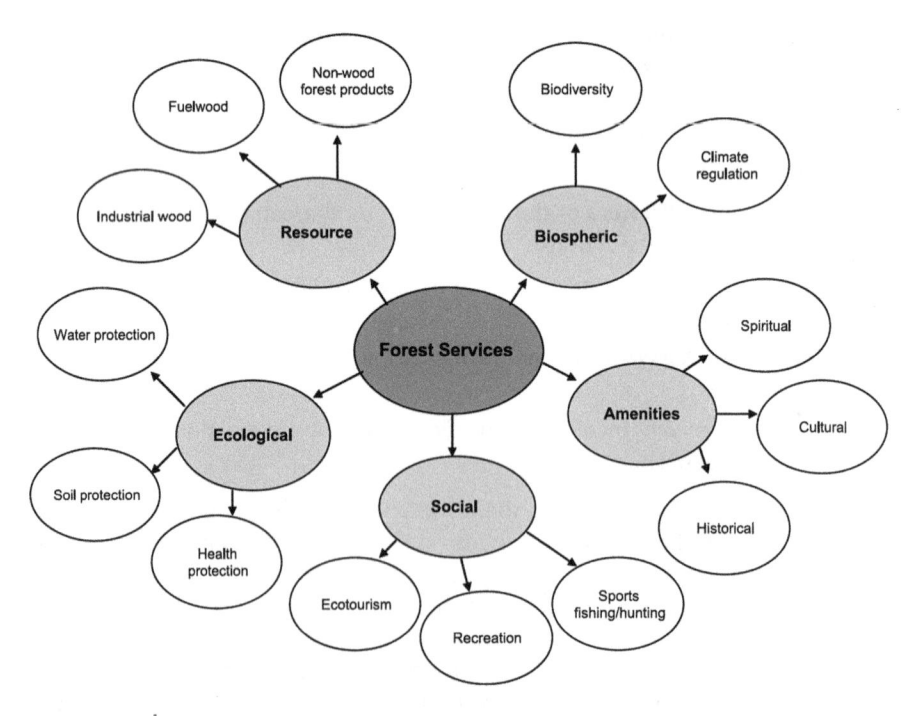

Figure 4.1 | Types of Forest Ecosystem Services.
Source: https://www.millenniumassessment.org/

Natural ecosystems also play an important role in global climate regulation and mitigation. They absorb greenhouse gases, regulate water flows, and protect coastal communities from extreme events and sea level rise. In addition, they provide plants and animals with routes to more resilient habitats.

Ecological Services

Virtually all the world's freshwater supply comes from natural ecosystems, with 75 percent of the total supply coming from forested watersheds. Nearly half of the world's largest cities draw their drinking water from forest watersheds. Natural ecosystems help control the water cycle by regulating precipitation, evaporation, and flows. Forests filter pollutants out of the water, prevent soil erosion, and absorb nutrients and sediment. Layers of the forest canopy, branches, and roots can store and release water vapor, which controls rainfall. They can also help reduce the impacts of floods from storms by blocking and slowing down the flow of runoff.

Trees and forests are among the most effective methods of maintaining healthy soil and preventing erosion. Trees have various properties that control soil erosion, including expansive root systems, large canopies, and their transpiration processes.

In terms of human health, natural ecosystems improve human health in multiple ways. Spending time in nature promotes physical and mental health by reducing stress. Natural ecosystems are natural pharmacies that contain many substances with medicinal or nutritional value. Wild foods are an essential part of the diet of vulnerable population groups worldwide. Research has shown that healthy natural ecosystems may help regulate infectious diseases.

Social Services

The world's natural ecosystems contain multiple social values. Nearly 200 million people worldwide rely on forests and other wildlands for subsistence, particularly in developing countries. Forests and rangelands also provide jobs for over 13 million people worldwide and another 41 million jobs in forest-related sectors. They offer outdoor recreational opportunities for hundreds of millions of people, along with millions of jobs in the nature-based tourism and hunting/fishing industries.

Amenity Services

Natural ecosystems provide non-market benefits of spiritual, cultural, and historical value. Forests and people have co-evolved over time, with people shaping the character of most forests and the forests, in turn, shaping human cultures and spiritual beliefs.[7] Forests are sacred places for many cultures, with the existence of "sacred groves" in many societies protected for hundreds and even thousands of years. Forests provide spiritual and recreational services to millions of people through forest-based tourism, which has become a central component of the world tourism economy.

Resource Services

Even in our modern, petroleum-driven, digital world, we are still highly dependent on the timber, fuel, and fiber goods derived from forests. The production of timber and non-timber forest products has increased significantly over the past decades. And like other economic sectors, the forest product industry has become increasingly globalized.

For the near future, global wood supplies are predicted to remain adequate for most market demands, if not in surplus. And this will likely be accomplished while we also end the age of deforestation. In some cases, sustainably harvested wood products will find market niches as environment and climate-friendly alternatives to products derived from fossil fuels. In other instances, forest products derived from unsustainable sources or harvesting practices may be replaced by other more sustainably derived wood products or non-wood products.

Ecosystem Management

Some ecosystem services, such as the biospheric and ecological, are compatible and complimentary. Others are conflicting and mutually exclusive, such as biospheric services and some forms of resource extraction. This requires tradeoffs to balance various service needs. Increasingly, natural resource managers employ an *ecosystem management* approach to balance the ecosystem service functions of natural environments. The primary goal of ecosystem management is to ensure the long-term sustainability of ecosystem functions while meeting socioeconomic, political, and cultural needs.[8]

Core principles[9] of ecosystem management include:

1. **Systems thinking:** Management has a holistic perspective instead of focusing on a particular level of biological hierarchy in an ecosystem (e.g., only conserving a specific species; only preserving ecosystem functioning).

2. **Ecological boundaries:** Ecological boundaries are clearly and formally defined. Management is place-based and may require working across political or administrative boundaries.

3. **Ecological integrity:** Management focuses on maintaining or reintroducing native biological diversity and preserving natural disturbance regimes and other key processes that sustain resilience.

4. **Data collection:** Broad ecological research and data collection is needed to inform effective management (e.g., species diversity, habitat types, disturbance regimes, etc.).

5. **Monitoring:** The impacts of management methods are tracked, allowing their outcomes to be evaluated and modified if needed.

6. **Adaptive management:** Management is an iterative process in which methods are continuously reevaluated as new scientific knowledge is gained.

7. **Interagency cooperation:** As ecological boundaries often cross administrative boundaries, management requires cooperation among various agencies and private stakeholders.
8. **Organizational change:** Successful management implementation requires shifts in the structure and operation of land management agencies.
9. **Humans and nature:** Nature and people are intrinsically linked, and humans shape and are shaped by ecological processes.
10. **Values:** Humans play a key role in guiding management goals, which reflect a stage in the continuing evolution of social values and priorities.

FOREST ECOSYSTEMS AND FOREST ECOSYSTEM MANAGEMENT

Forest ecosystems are critical refugia for the Earth's terrestrial biodiversity. They also play an essential role in the Earth's biogeochemical systems, like the carbon cycle discussed in Chapter 2. At the same time, the world's forests are also a source of essential ecosystem services for people. These services are incredibly diverse, including values such as climate change mitigation, conservation of biological diversity, freshwater supply, subsistence resources for rural and indigenous communities, employment generation, and recreational and tourism opportunities. Over 75 percent of the freshwater supply that humans depend on comes from natural forests, often located hundreds of miles away from population centers. Urban forests improve the quality of life for billions of people worldwide while also providing critical wildlife habitats.

However, the area and condition of the world's forests have declined since the Industrial Revolution. The amount of overall forest cover has decreased by

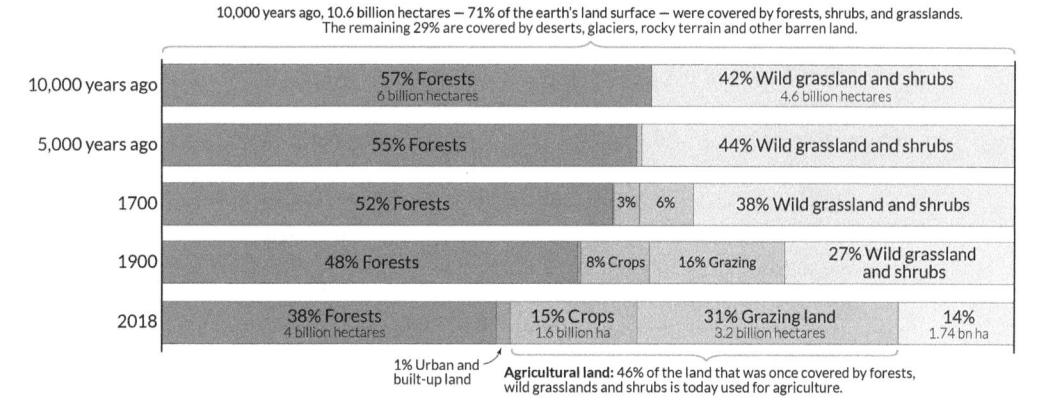

FIGURE 4.2 | World Forest Cover, 10,000 Years Ago to Present.
Source: Our World in Data – https://ourworldindata.org/world-lost-one-third-forests
https://ourworldindata.org/deforestation

approximately 40 percent, an area the size of the United States, with most of that loss happening in the past century. While urbanization accounts for about 1 percent of this loss, the most significant cause is what we eat, not where we live. Crops and grazing land now occur on 46 percent of the habitable land on the planet.

Twenty-nine countries have lost over 90 percent of their forest cover, and forests have disappeared entirely in 25 others. Across the rest of the world, fragmentation and other forms of degradation have impaired the ecological and human service functions of remaining forests.[10]

WHY ARE TEMPERATE FORESTS INCREASING WHILE TROPICAL FORESTS CONTINUE TO DECLINE?

Today, the Earth's *temperate forests*, including in Europe, North America, and Australia, are increasing. In Europe, for instance, forests have increased by 9 million hectares, an area the size of Portugal, between 1990 and 2015. In the United States, the total forest area increased by 7.3 million hectares between 1990 and 2020, an area larger than the state of West Virginia. At the same time, the world's *tropical forests* continue to decline by 10 million hectares per year,[11] an area larger than Greece. Most of this loss is in the Amazon and parts of Africa and Asia.

These contrasting examples represent opposite ends of the spectrum regarding the current fate of the world's forests. While the reasons for the disparity are complex, they are deeply rooted in economics and global geopolitics. The figure below shows that the world's temperate forests have been exploited by the industrial economy for much longer than tropical forests. Biomass from temperate forests fueled the early Industrial Revolution and the economic success of the developed world. While the steam engine was the technology that launched the industrial revolution; it was wood from the temperate forests that fueled it.

The temperate forests of Europe and North America were the first to be exploited at a massive scale. It was only when temperate forest feedstocks became scarce that coal began to replace wood in industrial processes and heating. As energy demand shifted to fossil fuels, the temperate forests of the developed world could be conceived of and exploited in more diverse ways, including conservation, biodiversity protection, landscape maintenance, and more sustainable forest product use. Consequently, much of the world's temperate forests are far from their original "old-growth" condition but are highly managed and regulated to conserve and protect these diverse values.

No longer needed for fuel, demand still increased for other temperate forest products such as building materials, pulp for paper, and other wood products. The relative scarcity of temperate forest biomass, combined with the increasing wealth in industrialized countries, allowed them to "offshore" their forest product needs to less developed temperate regions like Scandinavia and Canada, and eventually to the tropics. Thus, tropical forest exploitation became an integral part of colonialism, imperialism, and the expansion of capitalist economic systems, along with the oppression and subjugation of peoples in those tropical regions. It also led to the transferal of diseases, invasive plants and animals, land-use change, and administrative systems to all corners of the tropics.

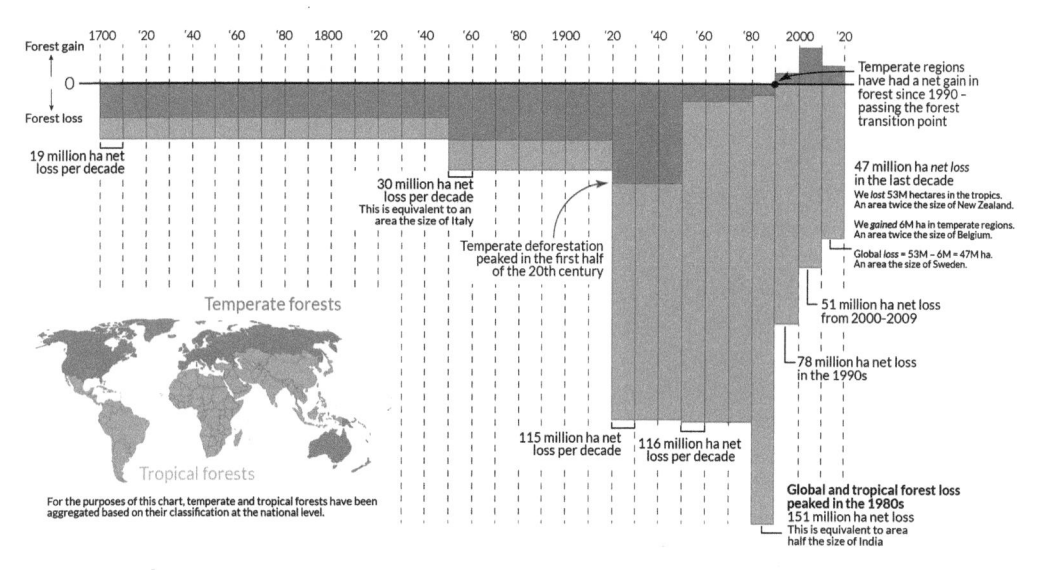

FIGURE 4.3 | Decadal Forest Cover Loss Over the Past 300 Years.
Source: Our World in Data – https://ourworldindata.org/deforestation

While preindustrial human societies utilized and modified tropical forests since the Pleistocene, economic exploitation by industrial capitalism occurred late relative to temperate forests and is still happening today. As people and politicians in temperate regions increasingly call for better protection of what they regard as a globally significant resource, people and politicians in those tropical countries sometimes take issue with what they see as an outdated colonialist outlook and imposition on their sovereignty. Countries in temperate regions are understandably accused of hypocrisy given their historical record of decimating their own forests.

BRINGING AN END TO OUR LONG HISTORY OF DEFORESTATION

While the future of the world's forests may appear gloomy, especially given the projected increases expected in the human population, there are reasons to believe that deforestation can be ended in the coming decades. Indeed, it's already happening. Deforestation rates have steadily declined from 78 million hectares per decade in the 1990s to 47 million in the last decade.[12]

Why is deforestation decreasing? As seen in the figure above, countries tend to follow a predictable forest cover pattern as their economies develop. Forests decrease as population and demand for agricultural land increase. Eventually, however, they reach the so-called *forest transition point* where they begin to regrow more forests than they lose. There are two main paths to reach the forest transition point. One emerges from scarcity where most or all forest cover is lost, and there is nowhere else to go but up. The other more preferred path is through various conservation and economic development policy interventions that shift pressure away from forest exploitation. Of these interventions, the most effective are likely those that accelerate the adoption of improved agricultural practices that reduce the demand to convert forests to agriculture. Better practices for crop yields decrease per capita demand for agricultural land, thus reducing the need to convert tropical forests to agricultural uses.

In temperate countries, the forest transition point was reached by the 1990s. Since then, temperate regions have added millions of hectares of forest cover. Many temperate region countries not only ended deforestation but increased their forest cover. In contrast, tropical forests passed peak deforestation in the 1980s but have not yet passed the transition to reforestation. While some tropical countries like Costa Rica have reached the forest transition point and are regrowing their lost forests, others like Brazil are still far behind. Accelerating when these countries reach the forest transition point will require concerted effort, likely involving financial incentives from wealthier temperate region nations.

The history of worldwide deforestation is a tragic story. But there is hope that forest transitions are happening and that we in this generation can bring an end to forest loss around the planet. By understanding where and why deforestation and forest transitions are happening and actions that can be taken to incentivize those transitions, we can accelerate the transition and minimize the amount of forest we lose along the way.

FOREST PRODUCT SUPPLY AND DEMAND TRENDS

Ending deforestation does not mean ending societal demand for the products and services we obtain from forests. Global timber harvest has increased by 60 percent since 1980, even as many countries passed the forest transition point and began expanding their forest cover. Demand for forest products is expected to continue to grow in the near future.[13]

Many factors affect the global demand for wood and wood products. These include the prices of wood and wood products, the price of substitute products, population and income levels, and trends in consumer preferences. Also, since most forest products are intermediate goods used in other economic sectors (e.g., building materials used in construction), technological innovations in those sectors have a significant impact on the demand for forest products, either through efficiencies or the use of alternative materials such as metals, plastics, cement, agricultural fiber, etc.

Technological innovation in materials is replacing the need for sawn timber in many products. For instance, engineered products made from low-value species, small-dimension logs, or wood waste is replacing sawn wood products in dimensional lumber and finish materials like flooring and siding. Similarly, digital information technologies are reducing the need for paper, with many industries completely removing paper from their business operations. A growing interest in environmentally friendly products means that consumers will increasingly evaluate the environmental acceptability of forest products compared to non-forest substitutes.

Forest Ownership and the Delivery of Ecosystem Services

Forest land ownership profoundly impacts how forests are managed and the benefits derived from them. Forest ownership systems vary considerably depending on country and context. The three broadest categories of forest ownership are public, private, and hybrid (see Table 4.1 below).

In a small number of countries, namely the Russian Federation, Georgia, Cyprus, Turkey, and some Central Asian nations, virtually all forests are owned by the nation-state. Conversely, in Portugal and Norway, almost all forests are privately owned by individuals, families, and corporations. In most countries, however, there is a mix of public, private, and hybrid ownership. In North America, the United States, Canada, and Mexico all have mixed ownership schemes. However, the proportions vary significantly, owing to each country's differing legal and socioeconomic systems, cultural traditions, and histories. In the United States, 37 percent of forests are public, with most of those owned at the federal level. Most of the balance (63 percent) is held privately, along with some tribal entities. In Canada, while the share of public forests is 91 percent, only 1.7 percent is owned at the national level, whereas provincial governments own the balance. Mexico has gone in a very different direction, with over 70 percent of the forests controlled by 35,000 indigenous and rural communities.

Generally, forest ownership determines the types of ecosystem service values provided (see Table 4.2 below). Private forests tend to be managed for extractive values (i.e., timber and non-timber forest products) while public forests tend to be managed for ecological, cultural/historic, and recreation values. Areas controlled by indigenous and local communities vary widely in their management focus depending on those communities' history, cultural traditions, and economic needs.

TABLE 4.1 | Types of Forest Ownership.

Public • State at national level • State at subnational government scale • Local government
Private • Individuals and families • Business entities • Non-governmental organizations (NGOs)
Hybrid • Tribal and indigenous communities • Other common ownership
Unknown • Ownership undefined due to vague or nonexistent property ownership laws

Source: Adapted from https://unece.org/forests/forest-ownership-unece-region
   https://www.millenniumassessment.org/

TABLE 4.2 | Types of Forest Services by Forest Ownership Type.

Types of Forest Services	Emphasis Level by Ownership Type		
	Public	Private	Hybrid (Indigenous and Local Communities)
Biospheric services: biodiversity, climate regulation	High	Low	High
Ecological services: soil and water protection, health protection	High	Low	High
Social services: recreation, tourism, sports, fishing/hunting	High	Low	High
Amenities: historical, cultural, spiritual	High	Low	High
Resource services: wood products, non-wood forest products, fuel wood	Low to medium	High	Low to high

SUSTAINABLE FORESTRY

Given the importance of the world's forests, we must ensure that human demands don't compromise their capacity to deliver the full range of ecological, social, and economic benefits they provide in the future. *Sustainable Forestry* and *Sustainable Forest Management* (SFM) is generally recognized as how this can be accomplished.

The United Nations Food and Agriculture Organization (FAO) defines SFM as:

> The stewardship and use of forests and forest lands in a way, and at a rate, that maintains their biodiversity, productivity, regeneration capacity, vitality, and their potential to fulfill, now and in the future, relevant ecological, economic and social functions, at local, national, and global levels, and that does not cause damage to other ecosystems.[14]

In this context, SFM is a holistic process of planning and implementing forest stewardship practices that deliver the full range of social, ecological, and economic benefits, balance competing needs, and maintain and enhance forest functions into the future. It deals with the overall administrative, legal, economic, social, scientific, and technological dimensions of forest stewardship. Depending on the social and ecological context, SFM can be applied at varying degrees of human intervention, ranging from complete forest protection to sustainable extraction of forest goods and services.

While outright deforestation is declining worldwide and may be eliminated in the coming decades, many of the world's forests, especially in tropical and subtropical regions, are still being lost. This is sometimes the result of inadequate forest policies, legislation, management frameworks, and incentives to promote sustainable forest management. It is also often the result of insufficient funding or management capacity. Where forest management plans exist, they often emphasize wood product extraction and ignore the many other intangible but nonetheless important products and services that forests offer.

The Montréal Process Working Group is arguably the leading intergovernmental organization promoting SFM. The group developed the following internationally recognized criteria and indicators for sustainable forest management, covering 90 percent of the temperate and boreal forests as well as many of the world's tropical and sub-tropical forests (see Figure 4.4 below).

Criterion 1: Conservation of Biological Diversity
- Biophysical Characteristics of Forests
- 9 Indicators
- Flora, Fauna, Conservation Efforts

Criterion 2: Maintenance of Productive Capacity
- Production and Capacity of Physical Outputs
- 5 Indicators
- Wood Products, Nonwood Forest Products

Criterion 3: Maintenance of Ecosystem Health and Vitality
- Forest Disturbances Processes
- 2 Indicators
- Biotic (Insects, Invasive Species), Abiotic (e.g., fire, weather)

Criterion 4: Conservation of Soil and Water Resources
- Characteristics and quality of forest soils and water
- 5 Indicators
- Soil and water condition, Conservation, Maintenance

Criterion 5: Maintenance of Forest Contribution to Global Carbon Cycles
- Sequestered carbon and flux in forests
- 3 Indicators
- Forests, Wood Products, Energy

Criterion 6: Socioeconomic Benefits
- Broad Array of socioeconomic conditions and output
- 20 Indicators
- Production and Consumption, Investment, Jobs, Recreation

Criterion 7: Legal, Institutional, and Economic Framework
- Capacity to support sustainable management
- 10 Indicators
- Laws and Regulations, Data and Information, Policies

FIGURE 4.4 | Montréal Process Criteria and Indicators.
Source: https://montreal-process.org/index.shtml

The Montréal Process has helped many member countries improve their sustainable forest management practices. For instance, New Zealand has seen a 50 percent increase in the forest area that is sustainably harvested, an increase in plantation forests (thus reducing extractive demand on natural forests), and an increased focus on the health and safety of forest industry workers.

SUSTAINABLE FOREST CERTIFICATION

For decades, forest protection strategy focused on getting the public, and through them politicians, to support policies to end deforestation, the clear-cutting of old-growth forests, and to protect biodiversity. Met with limited success, in the 1990s forest advocates began to turn their attention to consumers, forest product markets, and the forest industry. Out of this shift in strategy emerged the idea of *forest certification*. Today, forest certification has arguably become the most common mechanism worldwide for implementing and incentivizing SFM practices.

Forest certification is an extension of the concept of *product certification*, or *product qualification*, in which products must pass performance and quality assurance tests based on specific qualification criteria. Such certification schemes were first used to ensure product safety but are now used to protect and safeguard other social values, including environmental values like the Earth's forests.

The certification concept is compelling in that it caters to multiple forest interests. For forest owners and the forest industry, it is a mechanism for marketing and accessing consumer markets. For consumers and buyers, it provides information on the environmental impacts of products. For governments, it is a soft policy instrument for promoting SFM. For environmental groups, it is a means to protect non-market forest values like biodiversity.

Like other product certification schemes, the basic idea behind forest certification is to connect consumers with information about the origins of their products. If products are sustainably sourced, consumers will be more willing to purchase them, often at premium prices. Conversely, if products are derived from unsustainable sources, like timber from old-growth forests, consumers will find alternatives or only purchase them at discounted prices. This sourcing information is typically obtained by determining the *chain of custody*.

The impact of forest certification is mixed. About 1 billion acres, or about 25 percent of the world's forests, are certified.[15] In the United States, recent data shows that about 95.4 million acres, representing about 13 percent of total forests, have been certified with at least one certification system. Most of the world's certified forests are in temperate and boreal regions, particularly in Europe. The approach has been notably unsuccessful in tropical countries, where only about 10 percent of certified forests are located.

The forest certification process involves an independent third party (called a certifier or certification body) that assesses the quality of forest management as measured by SFM criteria or standards. The certifier provides written assurance that products or processes conform to the standards.

The Forest Stewardship Council (FSC) and the Sustainable Forestry Initiative (SFI) are two of the most well-known forest certification organizations. The FSC program was created and continues to be managed by environmental NGOs in response to the failure of politicians and international organizations to address forestry issues, particularly in tropical regions. SFI was established by the American Forest and Paper Association as an alternative to FSC.[16] While FSC and SFI are both accredited by the Programme for the Endorsement of Forest Certification (PEFC), FSC is generally considered more comprehensive and rigorous.

Does forest certification work? In some temperate and boreal forests, it does seem to have had a positive impact. Yet even in these forest systems, there is limited evidence that certification has improved market competitiveness, without which there is little incentive for forest enterprises to incur the higher costs associated with SFM or to submit themselves to stricter controls than those at present. The problem is particularly serious in the tropical forests of developing countries. Hopefully, this will improve with time as certification systems become more robust and markets respond accordingly. If not, forests will continue to be unsustainably exploited, or consumers will turn to substitutes that are not subject to sourcing requirements.

URBAN FORESTS

Urban forests play a critical role in providing ecosystem services to urban populations. They moderate the local climate, remove air pollution, slow wind and stormwater, and filter sunlight. They are critical in cooling the urban heat island effect and reducing the number of ozone days that plague major cities in peak summer months. Urban forests protect local biodiversity, providing habitats and networks for numerous species within fragmented urban landscapes. They add beauty and structure to urban landscapes, reduce noise, provide places to recreate, strengthen social cohesion, and increase property values.[17]

Urban forests comprise all trees in the urban area, including individual street trees, clusters of trees in parks and greenways, and forests in outer metropolitan areas. Urban forests take many forms, including city parks, city forests, pocket parks, public squares, public gardens, greenways, riparian corridors, rooftops, and nurseries.

Urban areas occupy 4 percent of the world's land area and currently contain over 10 billion trees representing over 100 species. But we could do even better. An estimated 110 billion trees could be supported in urban environments across the globe, thereby greatly increasing the benefits described above.[18]

The business community has become involved in tree planting to offset their carbon footprint and burnish their environmental records. While these investments have typically been in rural areas, businesses are increasingly looking at cities and urban areas as places to invest in forest projects. Amazon recently announced a $4.37 million commitment to tree planting initiatives in Berlin. Bank of America partners with American Forests on the Tree Equity initiative to support non-profits and local partners across the globe in implementing urban forest projects to bring both trees and jobs to low- and moderate-income areas. In communities where Microsoft is building data centers, it is also investing in urban forestry projects to bring environmental and health benefits to low-income neighborhoods.

Businesses also realize they can earn carbon credits for urban tree projects. For many years, carbon removal and storage were seen as the only benefit of trees. Urban tree projects were less attractive to businesses because the carbon dioxide removal impacts were limited. However, urban forest projects are increasingly attractive because the many ancillary benefits can multiply the carbon credits' value. Such bundled credits include carbon and the health benefits of urban trees, creating a credit scheme like carbon removal offsets.

BIODIVERSITY

As we discussed earlier in the chapter, natural ecosystems provide many functions that go far beyond what can be measured in economic terms. These include many different biospheric, ecological, amenity, and social benefits that, while difficult to quantify in economic terms, nonetheless provide immense value to both the health of the planet and human beings. Of these values, biodiversity is one of the most critical to planetary survival.

The United Nations *Convention on Biodiversity* (CBD) defines biodiversity as:

> . . . variability among living organisms from all sources including, inter alia, terrestrial, marine and other aquatic ecosystems and the ecological complexes of which they are part; this includes diversity within species, between species, and of ecosystems.[19]

The CBD definition covers biodiversity at all levels: genetic, species, and ecosystem diversity.

- *Genetic diversity* is all the different genes in all the living species, including individual plants, animals, fungi, and microorganisms.
- *Species diversity* is all the different species and the differences within and between species.
- *Ecosystem diversity* is all the different habitats, biological communities, ecological processes, and variations within individual ecosystems.

Biodiversity conservation is a common concern of humankind, including the business community. Biodiversity enriches our lives in many ways, some of which are difficult to quantify, including our emotional, psychological, spiritual, and economic well-being. Humans have always depended on the Earth's biodiversity for:

- *Food:* species that are hunted, fished, and gathered, as well as those cultivated for agriculture, forestry, and aquaculture.
- *Shelter and warmth:* timber and other forest products and fibers such as wool and cotton.
- *Medicines:* both traditional and modern medicines derived from biological resources and processes.[20]

Biodiversity also provides many indirect human services we take for granted. Insects, bats, birds, and other animals pollinate our crops. Recent declines in honeybee populations threaten the pollination services required for many crops. Parasites and predators can act as natural pest controls. Various "decomposer" organisms recycle organic materials and maintain the productivity of the soil.

Biodiversity also provides scientific insight into human health problems. For example, researchers are looking at how marine animals use oxygen during deep-water dives for clues to treat strokes, shock, and lung disease. Genetic diversity is also crucial in terms of evolution. The loss of individuals, populations, and species decreases the variety of genes—the material needed for species and populations to adapt to changing conditions or for new species to evolve.

Yet ever-expanding human civilization has a profound impact on the Earth's biodiversity. Species are becoming extinct at the fastest rate known in history. Most of these extinctions are tied to human activity. These activities include:

- *Habitat loss and destruction,* particularly the conversion of natural ecosystems for agriculture and other forms of development.
- *Alterations of ecosystem composition,* like removing a predator species, can profoundly affect other species and the ecosystem.
- *The introduction of exotic (non-native) species* can disrupt entire ecosystems and impact populations of native plants or animals.
- *The over-exploitation* (over-hunting, over-fishing, or over-collecting) of a species or population.
- *Pollution and contamination* can affect all levels of biodiversity.
- *Global climate change* can alter the conditions that species and populations need to survive.[21]

Many industrial materials derive directly from biological sources, including building materials, fibers, dyes, solvents, rubber, and oils. Loss of biodiversity is increasingly a risk factor that businesses must consider.[22] Recognizing the global scale of these threats, in 1992 the *Convention on Biological Diversity* (CBD), a multilateral treaty known informally as the *Biodiversity Convention*, was ratified. Now signed by 196 countries, the CBD compels every country to develop national-level strategies to meet the following strategic goals:[23]

- *Strategic Goal A:* Address the underlying causes of biodiversity loss by mainstreaming biodiversity across government and society
- *Strategic Goal B:* Reduce the direct pressures on biodiversity and promote sustainable use
- *Strategic Goal C:* To improve the status of biodiversity by safeguarding ecosystems, species, and genetic diversity
- *Strategic Goal D:* Enhance the benefits to all from biodiversity and ecosystem services
- *Strategic Goal E:* Enhance implementation through participatory planning, knowledge management, and capacity building

Unfortunately, most independent analyses conclude that we are not meeting these goals and that biodiversity will continue to decline until 2050 due to land development, overexploitation, climate change, pollution, and invasive species. While declining biodiversity will hurt people and businesses worldwide, it will be particularly hard on local communities, indigenous peoples, and the world's poor, given their reliance on biodiversity.

ENDANGERED AND THREATENED SPECIES

An endangered species is a species that is likely to become extinct in the near future, either worldwide or in a particular political jurisdiction.[24] Whether a species is endangered is decided by determining its *conservation status*, which indicates whether it still exists and how likely it is to become extinct in the near future.[25] Determining conservation status depends not only on the number of individuals remaining but also on population trends over time, breeding success, and known threats.

Various conservation status systems exist at the international, multi-country, national, and local levels as well as for consumer use.

International Union for Conservation of Nature Red List

Established in 1964, The *International Union for Conservation of Nature* (IUCN) *Red List of Threatened Species*[26] is the world's most comprehensive source on the conservation status of species. Including more than 116,000 species, the Red List assigns a species one of nine different categories.

Extinct (EX) A species is classified as extinct when there is not a reasonable doubt that the last of that species has died.

Extinct in the Wild (EW) The classification given to animals that are known only by living members kept in captivity or as a naturalized population outside its range due to massive habitat loss.

Critically Endangered (CR) A critically endangered species is considered to face an extremely high risk of extinction in the wild.

Endangered (EN) An endangered species faces a very high risk of extinction in the wild.

Vulnerable (VU) A vulnerable species is considered to face a high risk of extinction in the wild.

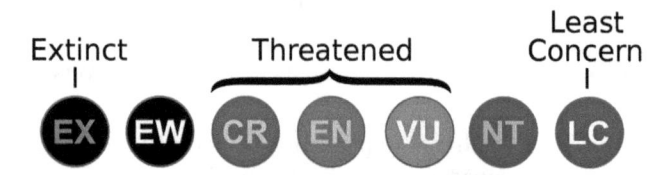

FIGURE 4.5 | IUCN Red List Conservation Status Spectrum.
Source: Peter Halasz/Creative Commons Attribution 2.5 Generic.

Near Threatened (NT) A near threatened species does not qualify for a threatened category (Vulnerable, Endangered, or Critically Endangered) but is close to or likely to qualify for one of these categories in the near future.

Least Concern (LC) A species receives this classification when it does not qualify as Near Threatened, Vulnerable, Endangered, or Critically Endangered.

Data Deficient (DD) A species is data deficient when there is insufficient data on the population or distribution of the species to determine its status.

Not Evaluated (NE) This classification is given to all species that the IUCN has not yet assessed.

Convention on International Trade in Endangered Species of Wild Fauna and Flora (CITES)

The *Convention on International Trade in Endangered Species of Wildlife Fauna and Flora* (CITES) is a multilateral treaty that lists species to ensure that international trade in wild animals and plants does not threaten their survival. When ratified in 1975, CITES initially focused on the demand for luxury goods such as furs in Western countries. However, it has expanded to look at worldwide demand for luxury goods such as elephant ivory or rhinoceros horn. CITES now lists thousands of species.

Multi-National Systems

There are several different multi-country systems around the world. In the European Union, the *Birds and Habitats Directives* evaluate and list the conservation status of bird species and habitats within the EU.[27] Similarly, NatureServe conservation status focuses on North America, Latin America, and the Caribbean.[28] The Red Data Book of the Russian Federation is used within the Russian Federation and accepted in parts of Africa.[29]

National Systems

Most countries have conservation status systems and lists. For instance, in the United States, the Endangered Species Act of 1973 requires the Endangered Species List. In Canada, the Committee on the Status of Endangered Wildlife in Canada (COSEWIC) assesses and designates which endangered wild species are to be included on their list. In Australia, the Environment Protection and Biodiversity Conservation Act 1999 (EPBC Act) requires a list of threatened species, ecological communities, and threatening processes. In Japan, the Ministry of Environment publishes a Threatened Wildlife of Japan Red Data Book.

BUSINESS IMPLICATIONS

It might be assumed that risks to natural capital and ecosystem services are confined to resource-intensive industries like mining, forestry, and agriculture. In these industries, business practices can have damaging effects that lead to supply-chain disruptions, fluctuating prices, smaller crop yields, and a loss of pollinators.

However, many less resource-intensive industries rely on natural capital and ecosystem services in subtle but important ways. Businesses can also be affected indirectly as more attention is placed on natural capital systems by the public and policymakers.

One example of potential business implications is access to capital. As demand for natural capital resources increases, policymakers and resource managers adopt conservation interventions to manage the demand, including regulatory limits on the commercial use of land and resources, subsidy reforms, taxes and fines, ecological recovery targets, and trade directives. As is already happening with fossil fuel markets, investors will likely be less likely to invest in enterprises at risk of "stranded assets" created by future conservation interventions.

Businesses also risk the continued degradation of natural capital assets, reducing their capacity to deliver ecosystem services that companies rely on. One in five firms worldwide could face significant operational risks from collapsing ecosystems.[30] This includes companies directly dependent on nature as a part of their business model (e.g., beverage industry dependence on freshwater, food industry dependence on pollinators, construction industry dependence on building materials). Disruption of natural capital feedstocks could drastically impact supply chains and financial performance. Impacts could also be indirect, as in the case of reputational damage to a company's brand. Consumers, investors, policymakers, employees, and communities increasingly expect businesses to minimize their environmental impact to preserve their social license to operate.

As the business world transitions to a low-carbon economy, companies will be increasingly expected to demonstrate not just their decarbonization strategies but also how they are reducing negative impacts on other natural capital resources. This will include adopting business practices consistent with the sustainable use and management of natural capital.

Conclusion

This chapter reviewed issues concerning natural capital assets and the ecosystem services that flow from them. Biodiversity loss can directly impact businesses by disrupting their supply chains, increasing regulatory compliance costs, and eroding social license. Investors are already considering how to direct capital toward companies that demonstrate climate-friendly practices. As the business world transitions to a low-carbon economy, companies will be increasingly expected to show not just their decarbonization strategies but also how they are reducing negative impacts on other natural capital resources. This will include adopting business practices consistent with the sustainable use and management of natural capital.

Keywords

- Biodiversity
- Chain of custody
- Conservation status
- Convention on Biodiversity
- Convention on International Trade in Endangered Species of Wild Fauna and Flora (CITES)
- Ecosystem diversity
- Ecosystem management
- Ecosystem services
- Endangered species
- Forest certification
- Forest management
- Forest Stewardship Council (FSC)
- Forest transition point
- Genetic diversity
- Indicator species
- International Union for Conservation of Nature (IUCN) Red List
- Montréal Process
- Natural capital
- Programme for the Endorsement of Forest Certification (PEFC)
- Species diversity
- Sustainable Forest Management
- Sustainable Forestry
- Sustainable Forestry Initiative (SFI)
- Temperate forests
- Tropical forests
- Urban forests

Discussion Questions

1. What are ecosystem services and natural capital, and what is their role in the world's economy?
2. Describe the ecosystem management approach to managing ecosystem services and natural capital.
3. Why are temperate forests increasing while tropical forests continue to decline?
4. What are types of forest ownership, and what types of ecosystem services do each best contribute to the economy?
5. How does sustainable forest certification work? Do you think it's an effective method for protecting forest resources globally?
6. How do the various forest certification programs differ?
7. Forest certification programs have been criticized for their relationship to business and environmental advocacy groups. Research the controversy over certification.
8. What role do urban forests play in our society?
9. Why do we enact laws to protect endangered species? Discuss the role biodiversity plays in nature.
10. Illegal trade in wild animals and plants is a global problem. Describe efforts to stop this type of international trade.

Recommended Websites

- Global Assessment Report on Biodiversity and Ecosystem Services – ipbes.net/global-assessment
- Natural Capital Finance Alliance – https://naturalcapital.finance/
- NatureServe – www.natureserve.org/
- Exploring Natural Capital Opportunities, Risks and Exposure – encore.naturalcapital.finance/en
- Programme for the Endorsement of Forest Certification (PEFC) – www.pefc.org/
- UN FAO State of the World's Forests 2022 – www.fao.org/publications/sofo/en/
- Convention on Biological Diversity – www.cbd.int/
- The IUCN Red List of Threatened Species – www.iucnredlist.org/
- Convention on International Trade in Endangered Species of Wild Fauna and Flora – cites.org/eng

Endnotes

[1] Natural capital. (2021). Convention on Biological Diversity. Retrieved September 11, 2022, from https://www.cbd.int/business/projects/natcap.shtml

[2] Russo, Amanda. (2020, January 19). Half of the world's GDP moderately or highly dependent on nature, says new report. *World Economic Forum*.

[3] International Finance Corporation. (2018, November 29). IFC report identifies more than $29 trillion in climate investment opportunities in cities by 2030. Press release. *IFC*. Retrieved September 11, 2022, from https://pressroom.ifc.org/all/pages/PressDetail.aspx?ID=18420

[4] United Nations Department of Economic and Social Affairs, Population Division (2022). World Population Prospects 2022: Summary of Results. UN DESA/POP/2022/TR/NO. 3.

[5] Millennium Ecosystem Assessment. (n.d.). The millennium ecosystem assessment. United Nations, https://www.millenniumassessment.org/en/index.html.

[6] FAO and UNEP. (2020). *The state of the world's forests 2020: Forests, biodiversity and people*. Rome: United Nations Food and Agriculture Organization. https://doi.org/10.4060/ca8642en.

[7] de Groot, R. S., Ramakrishnan, P. S., van de Berg, A., Kulenthran, T., Muller, S., Pitt, D., Wascher, D., & Wijesuriya, G. (2005). Cultural and amenity services. In R. Hassan, R. Schols, & N. Ash (Eds.), *Ecosystems and human well-being: Current state and trends*. Washington, DC: Island Press.

[8] Szaro, R. C., Sexton, W. T., & Malone, C. R. (1998). The emergence of ecosystem management as a tool for meeting people's needs and sustaining ecosystems. *Landscape and Urban Planning, 40*(1–3), 1–7. https://doi.org/10.1016/s0169-2046(97)00093-5.

[9] Grumbine, R. E. (1994). What is ecosystem management? *Conservation Biology, 8*(1), 27–38.

[10] FAO and UNEP. (2020). *The state of the world's forests 2020: Forests, biodiversity and people*. Rome: United Nations Food and Agriculture Organization. https://doi.org/10.4060/ca8642en.

[11] FAO and UNEP. (2020). *The state of the world's forests 2020: Forests, biodiversity and people*. Rome: United Nations Food and Agriculture Organization. https://doi.org/10.4060/ca8642en.

[12] United Nations Food and Agriculture Organization. (n.d.). Global forest ecosystem assessment. UN FAO. https://fra-data.fao.org/

[13] Independent Evaluation Group. (2014). Managing forest resources for sustainable development: An evaluation of the world bank group's experience. Washington, DC: World Bank Group. https://openknowledge.worldbank.org/handle/10986/35158.

[14] FAO and UNEP. (2011). *The state of the world's forests 2011: Forests, biodiversity and people*. Rome: United Nations Food and Agriculture Organization. https://www.fao.org/state-of-forests/en/.

[15] Programme for the Endorsement of Forest Certification. (n.d.) *PEFC*. https://pefc.org/.

[16] Gutierrez Garzon, A. R., Bettinger, P., Siry, J., Abrams, J., Cieszewski, C., Boston, K., Mei, B., Zengin, H., & Yesil, A. (2020). A comparative analysis of five forest certification programs. *Forests, 11*(8), 863. https://doi.org/10.3390/f11080863.

[17] FAO and UNEP. (2022). *The state of the world's forests 2022: Forests, biodiversity and people*. Rome: United Nations Food and Agriculture Organization. https://www.fao.org/state-of-forests/en/.

[18] Crowther, T. W., et al. (2015). Mapping tree density at a global scale. *Nature, 525*(7568), 201–205. https://doi.org/10.1038/nature14967.

[19] Natural capital. (2021). Convention on Biological Diversity. Retrieved September 11, 2022, from https://www.cbd.int/business/projects/natcap.shtml

[20] The Ecological Society of America. Biodiversity. https://www.esa.org/blog/tag/biodiversity/.

[21] The Royal Society. (n.d.) What is the human impact on biodiversity? *Royal Society*. https://royalsociety.org/topics-policy/projects/biodiversity/human-impact-on-biodiversity/.

[22] Hanson, C., Ranganathan, J., & Iceland, C. (2012, February 7). The Corporate Ecosystem Services Review. *World Resources Institute*. Retrieved from https://www.wri.org/research/corporate-ecosystem-services-review

[23] Strategic plan for biodiversity 2011–2020, including Aichi biodiversity targets. (2020, January 21). *Convention on Biological Diversity*. https://www.cbd.int/sp/.

[24] U.S. Department of the Interior. (n.d.). What are the differences between endangered, threatened, imperiled, and at-risk species? *U.S. Geological Survey*. https://www.usgs.gov/faqs/what-are-differences-between-endangered-threatened-imperiled-and-risk-species.

[25] *IUCN Red List of Threatened Species*. (2012). United Nations International Union for the Conservation of Nature. https://www.iucnredlist.org/.

[26] *IUCN Red List of Threatened Species*. (2012). United Nations International Union for the Conservation of Nature. https://www.iucnredlist.org/.

[27] Sundseth, K. (2014). *The EU birds and habitats directives*. Luxembourg: European Commission. https://ec.europa.eu/environment/nature/info/pubs/docs/brochures/nat2000/en.pdf

[28] InfoNatura. (n.d.). About the data: Conservation status. *NatureServe.org*. Retrieved on April 10, 2007 from https://web.archive.org/web/20130921055302/http://www.natureserve.org/infonatura/Lnsstatus.htm.

[29] Red Data Book of the Russian Federation. (n.d.). Red book of rare and endangered species. *Red Data Book of Russia*. https://redbookrf.ru/.

[30] Swiss Re Group. (2020, September 23). *A fifth of countries worldwide at risk from ecosystem collapse as biodiversity declines, reveals pioneering Swiss Re index*. Swiss Re Group. Retrieved April 6, 2022, from https://www.swissre.com/media/press-release/nr-20200923-biodiversity-and-ecosystems-services.html

CHAPTER 5

Sustainable Agriculture and Food

LEARNING OBJECTIVES

In this chapter, we will do the following:

» Describe the role of innovation in the development of our modern agriculture and food systems.
» Discuss sustainable agriculture.
» Discuss the foods we eat.
» Describe the difference between conventional and sustainable agriculture.
» Recognize the differences between natural and organic foods.
» Examine companies involved in the food industry.
» Discuss malnutrition.

CHAPTER OVERVIEW

The food industry is one of the largest industries in the world. In the United States alone in 2020, 19.7 million full- and part-time jobs—10.3 percent of total U.S. employment—were in the agricultural and food sectors, which include grocery stores, restaurants, food and beverage manufacturers, as well as agriculture.[1] Its importance to the global economy cannot be understated, as it accounts for 4 percent of global gross domestic product (GDP) and more than 25 percent of GDP in some of the least developed countries. Sustainability issues within this industry include producing safe and healthy food and nutrition.

When it comes right down to it, farmers are businesspeople. Like other businesses, farmers are constantly looking to maximize available labor and technology, reduce spending, and maximize revenue to be profitable. They are continually searching for ways to balance the need to maximize yields, address consumer demand for quality and safety, and price their products for sale in a hyper-competitive market. They do all this while working at the whims of Mother Nature. Storms, drought, pests, and diseases can all impact their bottom line.

In this environment, farmers are constantly making decisions about which crops to plant, which animals to raise, how much water to use, which and how much fertilizer, herbicides, and pesticides to apply, and which technology to acquire. Every decision impacts not only their profitability but also ecological systems, GHG emissions, supply chains, and the health of both agricultural workers and consumers.

This chapter begins with a brief history and current state of agriculture and food systems, focusing on comparing conventional versus sustainable agriculture systems. We review global food consumption patterns and the GHG emissions associated with that consumption. We discuss trends shaping the future of sustainable agriculture. We explore the continuing growth in the organic food industry and how producers and regulators have responded. After a discussion on what we eat, we review the plight of the malnourished. Then, we look at several corporate approaches to sustainability, including Monsanto, McDonald's, Cargill, Kraft Heinz, Walmart, and Danone.

A Brief History of Agriculture and Food Systems

Agriculture, or farming, is the practice of cultivating the soil, growing crops, or raising livestock for human use, including the production of food, feed, fiber, fuel, or other valuable products.[2] At its simplest, agriculture is the manipulation of ecosystems and natural processes for human benefit.

Homo sapiens arrived on the evolutionary scene about 196,000 years ago.[3] For most of that time, they did not practice agriculture: food and other material needs were acquired from the wild. Then about 12,000 years ago, humans discovered how to plant seeds. Within a few thousand years, they learned how to select for genes to produce desired characteristics in plant crops to increase yields. Domestication of animals began in about 8500 BCE with pigs in Western Asia, sheep and goats in the Fertile Crescent, and cattle in the areas of modern Turkey and Pakistan.[4] By 5000 BCE, agriculture was practiced in every continent except Australia.[5]

Each breakthrough in agriculture contributed to the gradual transition from a hunter-gatherer society toward agrarian cultures focused on cultivating crops and raising animals for food and material needs. As agrarian cultures developed, populations grew, and the permanence and size of development increased. With that permanence, farmers could no longer move to new areas when soils were exhausted of nutrients. This encouraged innovations, such as crop rotation, intercropping, and irrigation. These and other innovations have progressively increased the intensity and efficiency of agriculture and food production systems.

Intensive Agriculture and The Green Revolution

Beginning in developed countries during the 1950s and 1960s, agricultural production increased dramatically due to technology and practice initiatives known collectively as the *Green Revolution*. Eventually, such agricultural intensification practices spread to the developing world, enabling countries like India and China to become more self-sufficient and avoid mass famine and starvation. These initiatives included widespread adoption of scientific methods of farming, the latest technological advances, consolidation of land into larger, more economically efficient holdings, and mechanization in the form of petroleum-driven machinery. Together they comprised a sweeping "package of practices" that quickly overtook "traditional" farming methods.[6]

The key elements of the Green Revolution can be categorized into three sectors: irrigation, development of modern pesticides and fertilizers, and genetically developed crop varieties. Advances in these sectors are collectively credited with ending worldwide famine and saving millions, if not billions, of lives. Without the Green Revolution, countries worldwide may not have been able to escape massive food shortages.

Today, ever-increasing agricultural intensification has become the norm in most countries. The transition from traditional agriculture has been so widespread that what was once seen as revolutionary has become what is referred to as *conventional agriculture* or, more derogatorily, *industrial agriculture*. For the rest of this chapter, we will refer to modern intensive agriculture practices as conventional agriculture.

Socioeconomic Impacts of Conventional Agriculture

While the Green Revolution has allowed food production to keep pace with the world population, it also had far-reaching socioeconomic and environmental impacts. Researchers generally agree that the transition from traditional to conventional agriculture helped billions of people rise out of poverty and reduced food insecurity around the globe. The transition also required farmers to go into debt to finance the required technology and production levels. This locked farmers into increasing dependency on high-energy inputs, synthetic chemicals, expensive technologies, and genetically modified organisms. In many cases, especially for small farmers, this resulted in bankruptcy and loss of their farmland. Mechanization also eliminated sources of employment from rural economies around the world.

This led to increased rural-urban migration. On the other hand, increased food production led to cheaper food for urban dwellers, enabling them to spend on other goods and services to improve their well-being and quality of life. Overall, the Green Revolution increased income and GDP per capita, whereas if it had never happened, it could have reduced GDP per capita in the developing world by half.[7]

In terms of human health, it is widely agreed that the intensive agriculture practices of the Green Revolution substantially reduced infant mortality in the developing world, primarily because of crop varieties with higher yields, caloric content, and protein.[8] Conversely, intensive agriculture has also created negative health impacts. Exposure to agrochemical pesticides and fertilizer may have adverse health impacts, particularly pesticide poisoning and a higher risk of certain cancers. The World Health Organization and UN Environmental Program estimated approximately 1 million human pesticide poisonings annually, with some 20,000 ending in death.[9]

Environmental Impact of Conventional Agriculture

Agricultural intensification is hotly debated regarding its overall impact on the Earth's ecosystems. It is generally agreed that the expansion of conventional agriculture has profoundly impacted the environment. Over half of the Earth's habitable land has been converted from natural ecosystems to agriculture, resulting in the biodiversity crisis discussed in Chapter 4. Figure 5.1 below shows that

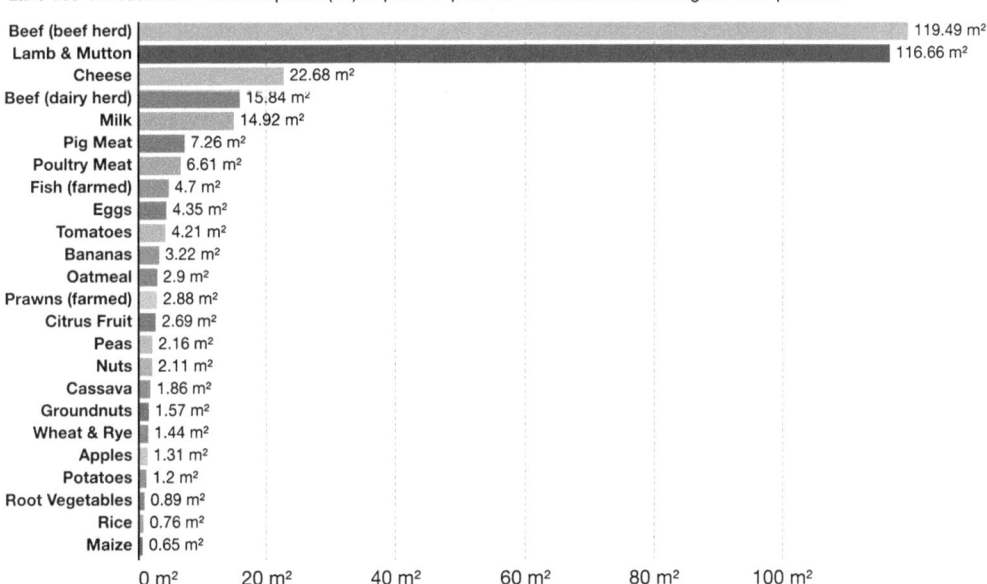

Land use is measured in meters squared (m²) required to produce 1000 kilocalories of a given food product.

Food	Land Use (m²)
Beef (beef herd)	119.49 m²
Lamb & Mutton	116.66 m²
Cheese	22.68 m²
Beef (dairy herd)	15.84 m²
Milk	14.92 m²
Pig Meat	7.26 m²
Poultry Meat	6.61 m²
Fish (farmed)	4.7 m²
Eggs	4.35 m²
Tomatoes	4.21 m²
Bananas	3.22 m²
Oatmeal	2.9 m²
Prawns (farmed)	2.88 m²
Citrus Fruit	2.69 m²
Peas	2.16 m²
Nuts	2.11 m²
Cassava	1.86 m²
Groundnuts	1.57 m²
Wheat & Rye	1.44 m²
Apples	1.31 m²
Potatoes	1.2 m²
Root Vegetables	0.89 m²
Rice	0.76 m²
Maize	0.65 m²

Figure 5.1 | Land Use of Foods per 1000 Kilocalories.
Source: Poore, J., & Nemecek, T. (2018). Additional calculations by Our World in Data. OurWorldInData.org/environmental-impacts-of-food • CC BY

animal agriculture comprises 77 percent of global agricultural land. While livestock takes up most of the world's agricultural land, it only produces 18 percent of the calories and 37 percent of the total protein consumed.

The conversion of natural ecosystems to conventional agriculture has profoundly impacted the Earth's wild biodiversity. Of the 28,000 species listed under threat of extinction on the IUCN Red List, agriculture conversion is the reason for 24,000 of them.[10] Of the total biomass of mammals (excluding humans), 94 percent is livestock, with livestock outweighing wild mammals by a factor of 15 to 1.4.

Conventional agriculture has also profoundly impacted agricultural biodiversity, or *agrodiversity*. Agrodiversity has declined significantly with the adoption of agriculturally intensive practices, leading to concerns about the vulnerability of the world food supply to pests and pathogens and the loss of valuable genetic traits bred into traditional varieties over thousands of years.[11]

The environmental impact of agriculture is not limited to biodiversity. Agriculture and food production also consumes nearly 75 percent of worldwide freshwater withdrawals.[12] Of the total ocean and freshwater eutrophication (nutrient pollutants) worldwide, 78 percent is caused by agriculture.[13]

And lastly, agriculture is the source of over a quarter (26 percent) of global greenhouse gas emissions.[14] Breaking down these emissions, the figure below shows that the largest share of emissions (53 percent) is from livestock and fish production, animal feed production, and land use for livestock (see Figure 5.2).

While these impacts, particularly from animal agriculture, are indeed profound, the question must be asked: What would the impacts be if the transition to conventional agriculture had never happened? One perspective is that agricultural intensification allowed more food to be grown on less land, reducing the need to convert natural systems to agriculture. Conventional agriculture is characterized in part by a low *fallow* ratio, meaning that land does not need to be set aside for a period to restore its nutrients and control pests. This is possible because of the higher use of petroleum-based fertilizers, herbicides, and pesticides. Similarly, petroleum-driven mechanization meant that vast amounts of land were no longer needed to produce feed for draft animals (1 acre for every 2–3 acres in production). Together, this allowed for greatly improved crop yields per unit of land area. Food production could increase without expanding into natural areas to feed a growing human population.[15]

The counter hypothesis is that conventional agriculture practices like irrigation, petrochemical fertilizers, and genetically developed crops allowed agriculture to expand into areas where traditional agriculture could not be practiced economically.

While this debate may never be resolved, we can agree that conventional agriculture must better address social and ecological concerns in the future. Agricultural scientist M. S. Swaminathan has called for an *Evergreen Revolution* that adds an ecological and social justice dimension to conventional agriculture.[16] Recognizing this imperative, ecologist E. O. Wilson wrote:[17]

> The problem before us is how to feed billions of new mouths over the next several decades and save the rest of life at the same time, without being trapped in a Faustian bargain that threatens freedom and security. No one

knows the exact solution to this dilemma. The benefit must come from an Evergreen Revolution. The aim of this new thrust is to lift food production well above the level obtained by the Green Revolution of the 1960s, using technology and regulatory policy more advanced and even safer than those now in existence.

What also seems clear is that the next phase of agriculture development will need to come to grips with the immense and disproportionate impact of animal agriculture. Reducing these impacts will be crucial to climate change mitigation, biodiversity conservation, water conservation, and nutrient management. Some impacts can be mitigated through even greater food production intensifi-

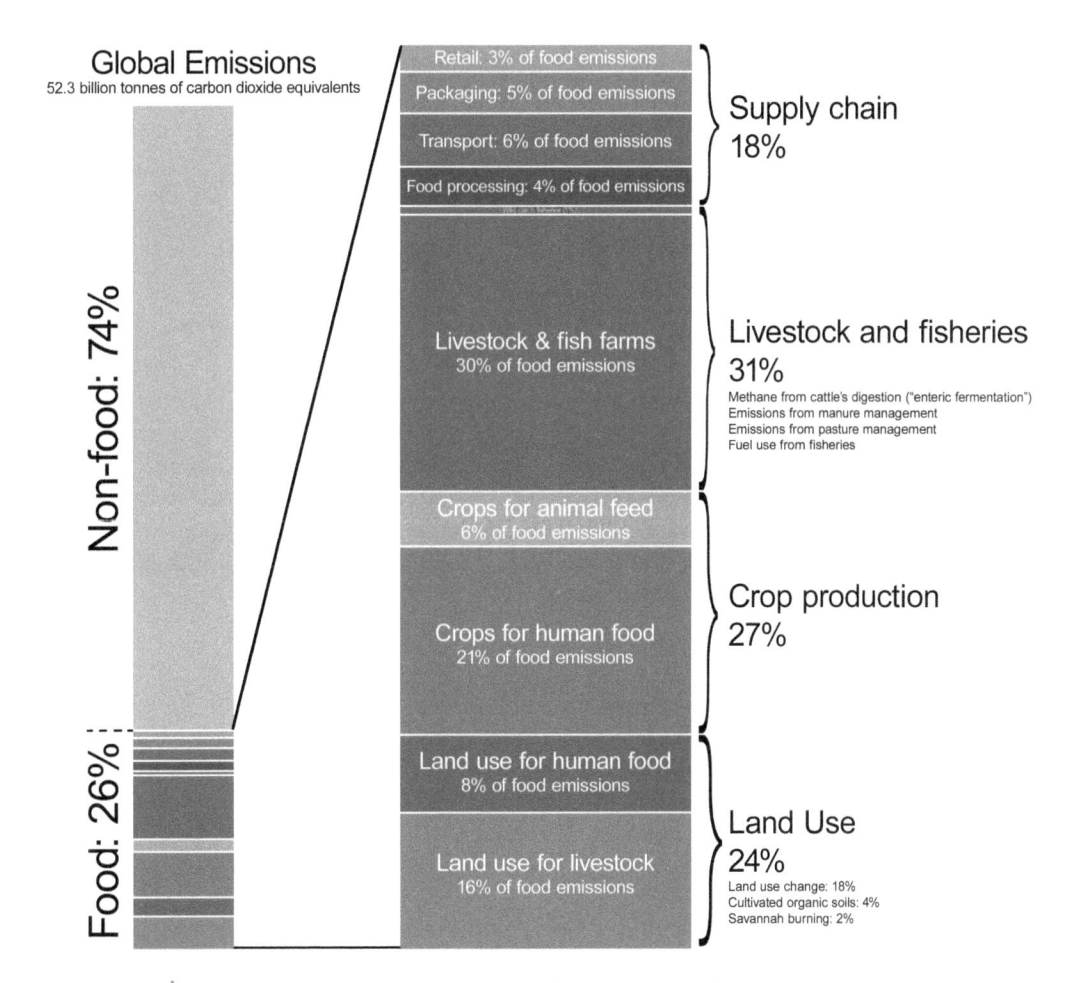

Global Emissions
52.3 billion tonnes of carbon dioxide equivalents

Non-food: 74%
Food: 26%

- Retail: 3% of food emissions
- Packaging: 5% of food emissions
- Transport: 6% of food emissions
- Food processing: 4% of food emissions

Supply chain 18%

- Livestock & fish farms: 30% of food emissions

Livestock and fisheries 31%
Methane from cattle's digestion ("enteric fermentation")
Emissions from manure management
Emissions from pasture management
Fuel use from fisheries

- Crops for animal feed: 6% of food emissions
- Crops for human food: 21% of food emissions

Crop production 27%

- Land use for human food: 8% of food emissions
- Land use for livestock: 16% of food emissions

Land Use 24%
Land use change: 18%
Cultivated organic soils: 4%
Savannah burning: 2%

FIGURE 5.2 | Global Greenhouse Gas Emissions from Food Production.
Source: Joseph Poore & Thomas Nemecek (2018). Reducing food's environmental impacts through producers and consumers. Published in *Science*. OurWorldinData.org – Research and data to make progress against the world's largest problems. Licensed under CC-BY by the author Hannah Ritchie.

cation through improved animal agriculture practices, including animal health and breeding practices, feed efficiency, composting, manure management, and anaerobic digesters.

But these gains are not likely to be sufficient. It will also likely require a societal shift toward a plant-based diet or at least less carbon-intensive forms of animal protein like farm-raised fish and poultry. Such a shift would allow lands currently used for animal production to be converted to human food production, greatly improving the per acre efficiency of calorie production for human consumption. Whether we like it or not, the tremendous environmental and health payoffs of a shift to a plant-based diet will likely be a big part of the next revolution in agriculture intensification.

However, a societal shift to a plant-based diet, which is generally less expensive than a meat-based diet, means that people will have more money to spend in other ways. The gains may be minimal if that added spending is on carbon-intensive products and services. Therefore, we need to decarbonize not only agriculture but also other sectors of the economy.

Trends Shaping the Future of Sustainable Agriculture

From the domestication of wheat in 8500 BCE in the Fertile Crescent to the moldboard iron plow in China in 500 BCE and the gasoline-powered tractor in 1892, technological innovation has always been a core dimension of agriculture. Today, farmers manage their operations with drones and satellites, monitor soil and micro-weather conditions with remote sensors, and utilize sophisticated software to decrease the need for fertilizers and pesticides, increasing efficiency and reducing fuel use. Emerging technologies expected to be an essential part of agriculture in the future include the following.

Biotechnology

Biotechnology is one of the oldest tools that farmers have for improving crops. Over eons, biotechnological innovations like crossbreeding have produced hardier plants and animals that increase yields. Today, modern scientific lab methods like *genetic engineering* enable scientists to directly modify the DNA of crops and animals to improve characteristics like resistance to disease, size, and nutritional content. *Genetically modified organisms* (GMO) are the result of this genetic engineering.

Although these methods are controversial—opponents fear that modified crops could introduce unforeseen and potentially devastating effects—proponents point to how crops can be made more productive and resistant to insects and disease and better able to respond to local conditions, such as more severe droughts or higher amounts of moisture. The new gene editing CRISPR technology can also be used to increase productivity and disease resistance by altering specific traits.

DRONES

Farmers continue to find more uses for drones to manage crops more efficiently. At first, drones were deployed to spray crops with chemicals. Other emerging uses include taking aerial photos to assess crops and capturing data from sensors that can be mined to determine the health of crops as well as weed populations. Drones can also drop tree seeds for reforestation projects.

BLOCKCHAIN TECHNOLOGY

Blockchain technology is commonly associated with buying and selling cryptocurrencies, but it also has applications in agriculture. Blockchain technology tracks transactions securely and accurately. Using blockchain in agriculture allows for tracking agricultural products from farm to consumer. Agricultural supply chains are already using it to determine where outbreaks of salmonella and other food poisoning causes originated.

ARTIFICIAL INTELLIGENCE

Artificial intelligence (AI) systems analyze data to help farmers determine when and where to plant crops and feed livestock or even when to sell to get the best prices. Data can help farmers apply fertilizers in a more timely and accurate manner. The more farmers know before they grow, the better they can allocate resources and, ultimately, use fewer chemicals and fuel.

WHAT THE WORLD EATS

According to the UN Food and Agriculture Organization (FAO), the average global food availability per person is projected to grow by 4 percent per year, reaching just over 3,025 kcal/day in 2030.[18] This global average, however, doesn't show a significant difference among regions (see Figure 5.3 below). While middle-income countries are projected to increase their per capita food intake most significantly, diets in low-income countries will remain unchanged.

The composition of diets also influences global health outcomes. At the worldwide level, fats and staples will account for about 60 percent of the additional calories over the next decade and provide 63 percent of the available calories by 2030. High-income countries will continue to have the highest proportion of calories coming from animal products, fats, and sweeteners. In high-income countries, per capita consumption of animal protein is expected to level off because of growing health and environmental concerns. These consumers are expected to increasingly replace red meat with poultry, dairy, and nut products.

Conversely, lower-middle-income and lower-income countries will continue to depend mainly on staples such as rice, wheat, maize (corn), millet, sorghum, and roots and tubers (potatoes, cassava, yams, and taro). Fruits and vegetable consumption in these countries is expected to continue to provide only 7 percent of the available calories, far short of the World Health Organization's (WHO)

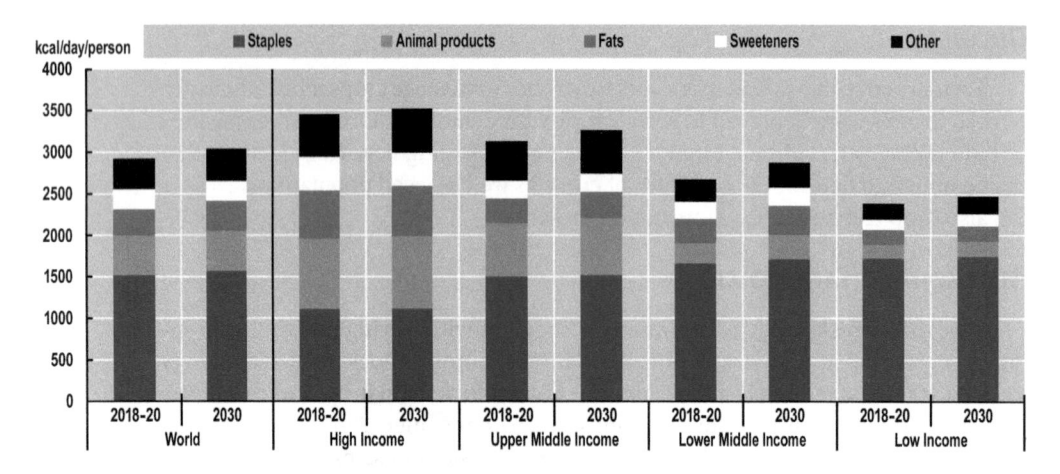

FIGURE 5.3 | Per Capita Availability of Main Food Groups, By Country Income Group.
Source: FAO (2021). FAOSTAT Food Balances Database, http://www.fao.org/faostat/en/#data/FBS; OECD/FAO (2021), "OECD-FAO Agricultural Outlook," OECD Agriculture statistics (database)

recommendations. In middle-income countries, consumption of animal products and fish is expected to increase by 11 percent, narrowing the consumption gap with high-income countries.

Like trends in crop production, a large share of the projected 14 percent production growth in livestock and fish will come from productivity improvements such as intensive feeding methods, improved genetics, and better herd management practices. Aquaculture production is expected to overtake wild-capture fisheries in 2027 and account for 52 percent of all fish production by 2030. This intensification is expected to reduce the demand to convert forests and natural ecosystems to agricultural uses, particularly in tropical regions.

MALNUTRITION

While citizens of the rich countries of the world struggle with issues of obesity and rush to one fad diet after another in search of a thin figure, close to 800 million global citizens are *undernourished*; in other words, they do not eat the minimum amount of food calories required for health. Of these, approximately 110 million are Chinese. More than half of Central Africa is undernourished. Other countries with severe hunger problems affecting over half the population include Somalia (75 percent), Burundi (66 percent), the Democratic Republic of the Congo (64 percent), Afghanistan (58 percent), Eritrea (57 percent), Haiti (56 percent), Mozambique (54 percent), and Angola (51 percent).

Malnutrition is a socioeconomic fact of life. As income levels decrease into poverty, the chance of malnutrition increases. Food prices are directly influenced by the price of fuel. Increases in oil prices lead to increases in the prices of fertilizers and agricultural chemicals, the cost of running farm equipment, and transportation costs. When food prices increase, and incomes either decline or stay static, food scarcity ensues, leading to undernourishment, malnourishment, and death.

According to the World Bank ("Population Growth Rate," 2001), the world population is currently growing at 1.2 percent per year (1 percent in the United States), with projections calling for a doubling of the world's population of 6.4 billion people by the year 2060. The food supply will be an issue. Corn and other cereal grains comprise 80 percent of the world's food supply, and the rate of growth in production is not projected to keep up.

Factors affecting food production include soil degradation and erosion, an inadequate water supply for irrigation, pollution, and fuel availability.

Malnutrition is the direct cause of 300,000 deaths per year; worldwide, 53 percent of the deaths of children under five years of age are due to malnutrition.

Approximately 852 million people were classified as undernourished in 2002. Malnutrition results from deficiencies in iron, iodine, vitamin A, and zinc. Poverty is the leading cause of malnutrition. People are too poor to purchase adequate food. This leads to chronic infections and early death.

Ready-to-use therapeutic foods (RUTF) have proven to help treat malnutrition. Malnourished patients in Maradi, Niger, received these foods and 6,200 were cured, while 1,000 died.

CONVENTIONAL VERSUS SUSTAINABLE AGRICULTURE

There are two broad categories of agriculture employed in the modern world: conventional and sustainable. Conventional agriculture, also referred to as *intensive agriculture*, is described in the sections above. Sustainable agriculture embraces the same principles as the triple bottom line (TBL)—to achieve environmental, economic, and social goals. Sustainable agriculture is sometimes framed as a response to the adverse outcomes associated with conventional agriculture.

Sustainable agriculture is generally defined as farming that meets society's present food and textile needs without compromising the ability of current or future generations to meet their needs. More specifically, sustainable agriculture is defined in U.S. federal law as an integrated system of plant and animal production practices having a site-specific application that will, over the long-term:[19]

- satisfy human food and fiber needs;
- enhance environmental quality and the natural resource base upon which the agricultural economy depends;
- make the most efficient use of nonrenewable resources and on-farm resources and integrate, where appropriate, natural biological cycles and controls;
- sustain the economic viability of farm operations;
- and enhance the quality of life for farmers and society.

Sustainable agriculture integrates the three main objectives of sustainability: environmental health, economic profitability, and social and economic equity. Environmental health includes:

- building healthy soil and preventing erosion,
- managing water wisely,
- minimizing air and water pollution,
- storing carbon on farms,
- increasing resilience to extreme weather,
- and promoting biodiversity.

Economic and social dimensions of sustainable agriculture include:

- profitable farms of all sizes,
- supporting the next generation of farmers,
- fair treatment of workers,
- racial equity and justice, including access to healthy food for all,
- and prioritization of people and communities over corporate interests.

Unlike organic and local food movements, which are positioned as alternatives to conventional agriculture, proponents of sustainable agriculture see it as a reform of conventional agriculture, integrated across the entire agriculture and food system supply chain, from growers, processors, and distributors, to retailers, consumers, and waste managers.[20] In particular, sustainable agriculture tends to be associated with the reform of the conventional production practices of growers, especially when used in combination, including the following.

Crop rotating and diversity – Planting a variety of crops can improve soil health and reduce pests. Such practices include intercropping (planting a mix of crops in the same area) and complex multiyear crop rotations.

Cover crops and perennials – Cover crops such as clover, rye, or hairy vetch can be planted during the off-season when soils might otherwise be left bare. Perennial crops keep soil covered and maintain living roots in the ground year-round. Together they can protect and build soil health, prevent erosion, control weeds, and reduce the need for fertilizers and pesticides.

Reducing or eliminating tillage – No-till or low-till methods involve planting seeds directly into undisturbed soil, thus reducing erosion and improving soil health.

Integrated pest management (IPM) – IPM includes a range of mechanical and biological controls that keep pest populations under control while minimizing the use of chemical pesticides.

Integrating livestock and crops – Conventional agriculture keeps plant and animal production separate, with animals living far from the areas where their feed is produced, and crops growing far away from abundant manure fertilizers. A growing body of evidence shows that a smart integration of crop and animal production can make farms more efficient and profitable by reducing nutrient management costs.

Agroforestry – Integrating trees or shrubs into farm operations can provide shade, shelter, and moisture that protect plants, animals, and water resources while offering additional income from fruit or nut crops.

Managing whole systems and landscapes – Examples of integrating uncultivated and less intensively cultivated areas into farm operations include natural vegetation buffers, particularly along streams, which can help control erosion, reduce nutrient runoff, support pollinators, and increase biodiversity.

The key concept underlying these practices is diversification. When it comes to effective, sustainable agriculture, the most effective systems are more diverse and complex—like nature itself.

ORGANIC FARMING AND FOOD

According to the UN Food and Agriculture Organization (FAO), organic agriculture is defined as the following:

> . . . a holistic production management system which promotes and enhances agro-ecosystem health, including biodiversity, biological cycles, and soil biological activity. It emphasizes the use of management practices in preference to the use of off-farm inputs, taking into account that regional conditions require locally adapted systems. This is accomplished by using, where possible, agronomic, biological, and mechanical methods, as opposed to using synthetic materials, to fulfill any specific function within the system.[21]

While both organic and sustainable agriculture are perceived as sustainable, they achieve it through different means. Organic farming focuses on the inputs used in production (e.g., no GMO seeds and animals, no synthetic fertilizer or pesticides, and no irradiation of products). In contrast, sustainable farming focuses on the physical treatment of the land (e.g., no-till, cover crops, buffer zones, etc.). Organic poultry and beef must also meet strict standards set by the USDA to attain that label. Their feed must be organic, they must not be injected with antibiotics or growth hormones, and they must not be confined all the time. Free range means the bird is not in a cage and is raised in an open environment.

Organic farming can be considered sustainable agriculture, but not all sustainable agriculture is organic. In addition to the environmental and socioeconomic benefits of sustainable agriculture described above, organic agriculture may have additional economic and health benefits. Research has shown that farmers who converted from traditional to organic methods had lower crop yields, but these losses were offset by reduced fuel costs.[22] Research has also shown that while there is no demonstrable difference between the nutritional value of organic versus conventionally grown food, organic foods are associated with reduced incidence of infertility, congenital disabilities, allergies, otitis media, pre-eclampsia, metabolic syndrome, high BMI, and non-Hodgkin's lymphoma.[23]

Given the potential health benefits of organic agriculture, it may be helpful to consider the level of pesticide residues in various types of produce. According to the Environmental Working Group Shoppers Guide to Pesticides in Produce,[24] the twelve fruits and vegetables contaminated with the most pesticide residue include:

1. strawberries
2. spinach
3. kale, collard, and mustard greens
4. nectarines
5. apples
6. grapes
7. bell and hot peppers
8. cherries
9. peaches
10. pears
11. celery
12. tomatoes

The EWG's "Clean 15" are fruits and vegetables with the lowest pesticide residues, including:

1. avocados
2. sweet corn
3. pineapple
4. onions
5. papaya
6. sweet peas (frozen)
7. asparagus
8. honeydew melon
9. kiwi
10. cabbage
11. mushrooms
12. cantaloupe
13. mangoes
14. watermelon
15. sweet potatoes

In the United States, the label *certified organic* means that produce has been grown according to the Organic Foods Production Act of 1990. A USDA inspection must qualify the designation, which can read, "100% Organic," "Organic," and "Made with organic ingredients." If the produce contains 73 percent or fewer organic ingredients, it can only list the ingredients on the information panel.[25]

Buy Local: The Local Food Movement

Another response to conventional agriculture is the local food, or locavore, movement. The term locavore literally means "local eater." The underlying idea is that our globalized food system is very fossil-fuel dependent, mainly because of the large distances food is transported.[26] While seductive, the idea of less *food miles* translating into more sustainable food systems has not been supported by the research. Numerous studies have demonstrated that locally and sustainably grown foods release more greenhouse gases than food made on factory farms. This is mainly because of the GHG emissions efficiencies obtained from agriculture intensification. Given their decreased production efficiency, more localized food systems may also increase global food insecurity.[27]

In response, the local food movement has broadened to other justifications, including healthier food, environmental benefits, and economic or community benefits. Local food systems, it is argued, can support communities by increasing community interaction and more sociable behavior, creating local jobs, and supporting local farm businesses unable to access global markets. Since local foods are transported while they are still fresh and are often sold directly from producer to consumer, they may not require as much processing or packaging as other foods transported over long distances. Thus, they often contain fewer added sugars or preservatives. The term "local" is sometimes synonymous with sustainable or organic practices, which can also arguably provide added health benefits described earlier in the chapter. Many local farmers also practice sustainable agriculture practices like crop rotation, no-till planting, integrated pest management, and agroforestry.

Today, the idea of food miles has mostly been overtaken by the need to look more comprehensively at the environmental, economic, and social impacts of food systems. For instance, many calculators now exist to help consumers determine their *foodprint* (see foodprint.org). Like other forms of life cycle analysis, a foodprint can include multiple parameters to quantify the overall impact of food. Some foodprint calculators also capture the social and ethical costs of food production, such as farm worker justice or share of revenues received by farmers.

How and What Should We Eat?

We're approaching two decades since the publication of journalist Michael Pollan's book, *The Omnivore's Dilemma*[28] and the film *Food, Inc.*,[29] which is based on a book of the same title. Together, they launched a genre of books and media that have impacted the way we think about the food we eat and the food systems that produce it.

Pollan posed this basic question: What should we eat as omnivores—that is, humans—since we can eat practically anything edible? He explores this by tracing the supply chain of four meals. The first represents the height of industrial agriculture, a meal from McDonald's eaten while in a moving car. The second represents what he calls "industrial organic." The third is from a small, diversified farm in Virginia. The fourth is a "perfect meal" in which he grew, gathered, or hunted (almost) everything that he ate.

Pollan pays particular attention to corn production as indicative of the industrial agriculture system. He traces corn from the farm to the market and points out that humans eat so much corn that we are almost made of corn from the corn syrup that goes into our soft drinks, the corn feed that the animals we eat consume, and all the various by-products of corn. In this film, the production of chicken, beef, and pork is shown and described as inhumane and unsustainable.

The dilemma is that we must make ethical and health choices. Do we eat organic? Do we eat only fair trade? Do we become vegans or vegetarians? Should we eat red meat? Should we eat carbohydrates? Should we eat more fat? Pollan noted that the French are healthier on average than Americans, despite consuming more chocolates, wines, and cheeses, and that is because of the amount of food Americans consume. He also investigated the plight of the small farmer. By focusing on a small farm in Iowa of 470 acres, he discussed the difficulty of competing with the large conglomerates that dominate agriculture. A 470-acre farm produces enough to feed 129 people yet still struggles to survive.

The takeaway message is that society has moved away from a system in which our local environment and culture dictated the food we ate. In our globalized economy, where those of us in high-income countries can eat any food from anywhere, we now make our food decisions based on government regulation, food science, and big-industry marketing and advertising. The problem is, given the epidemic of food-based health issues (obesity, diabetes, heart disease, hypertension, stroke, etc.), these forces make poor substitutes for healthy, wholesome food options. Pollan gives extensive coverage of Monsanto to illustrate the legal clout of the large food conglomerates.

Pollan concludes by advocating that we change our eating habits to be more old-fashioned and small-scale. This conclusion has been criticized as privileged, expensive, and impractical as a strategy for feeding a global population of 8 billion people. In defense of Pollan, he wrote *The Omnivore's Dilemma* before so much attention was paid to climate change and GHG emissions from food production. The diet he recommended in the book may have higher emissions than one from conventional agriculture.

In his most recent writing, particularly *Cooked: A Natural History of Transformation*,[30] Pollan has incorporated climate change impacts into his recommendations, many of which more closely resemble a move toward high-tech, intensive, sustainable agriculture rather than a return to pre-industrial, low-intensity systems.

SUSTAINABILITY AT FOOD COMPANIES

The criticism of "Big Ag" from writers like Pollan has not gone unanswered by the agriculture industry. Some companies have acknowledged, at least grudgingly, the urgent need to rethink our food systems in more climate-friendly ways and to distribute economic benefits more fairly, in ways that are socially just. Central to these discussions is engaging and incentivizing farmers to adopt climate-friendly practices, particularly using carbon markets and other mechanisms to pay farmers for ecosystem services. USDA Deputy Secretary Jewel Bronaugh emphasized the agency's support for scaling up ecosystem markets, voluntary conservation programs, and methane digesters, stating, "It's past time to take the challenges of climate change and turn them into opportunity."[31]

Others, primarily from the meat, dairy, and commodity crop industries, have been more defensive, focusing their message on the progress they claim they have already made within their supply chains. There is a defensiveness from farmers and agriculture businesses about the public's demands for more climate-friendly and sustainable food. They tend to see the public and advocacy groups as uninformed about the realities of agriculture while still demanding sweeping reforms in the industry.

Given this tension, it's worthwhile to look at what some of the most prominent corporate players are doing in response.

Monsanto and "Roundup Ready" Crops

In 2018, Bayer purchased Monsanto, the biggest player in the agriculture industry. Monsanto's first genetically engineered product was bovine growth hormone, released in 1994 to increase milk production. The issue became controversial when consumer and environmental groups protested. Monsanto is most recognized as the owner of Roundup, a systemic, broad-spectrum glyphosate-based herbicide, along with a line of "Roundup Ready" seeds. Roundup Ready seed lines are genetically modified to contain a gene encoded with a glyphosate-tolerant enzyme. The result is glyphosate-tolerant crops, enabling farmers to apply Roundup herbicide to control weeds without killing crops, thereby increasing yields. Monsanto also touted Roundup as environmentally friendly and non-toxic to humans and animals since it broke down so quickly after it was applied.

Monsanto's first Roundup-resistant seeds were soybeans, released in 1996. Sales took off, and by 2010 Roundup Ready crops accounted for about 90 percent of the soybeans and 70 percent of the corn and cotton grown in the United States. Globally, at their peak, Roundup herbicide and Roundup Ready seed lines represented about 50 percent of Monsanto's revenues.[32] The global glyphosate market is estimated at $7.6 billion USD in 2020 and is projected to reach $8.9 billion USD by 2026, with nearly 70 percent of that occurring outside of the United States.[33]

There have been concerns and critiques regarding Roundup since Monsanto first released it in the 1970s. Many of these concerns regard the health risks associated with glyphosate-based herbicides. Mounting research evidence confirmed these concerns, and in 2015 the World Health Organization's International Agency for Research on Cancer (IARC) classified glyphosate as "probably carcinogenic," meaning it likely causes cancer. This became even more alarming when in 2022, the Centers for Disease Control (CDC) announced the results of a study finding measurable levels of glyphosate in 80 percent of urine samples tested in the United States.

By the time Bayer bought Monsanto in 2018, thousands of lawsuits linking Roundup to a form of cancer known as non-Hodgkin's lymphoma had been filed in courts nationwide. The first case to make it to trial in 2018 resulted in a $289 million judgment against Bayer/Monsanto. This was followed by two guilty verdicts in 2019, totaling over $2 billion in compensatory and punitive damages. These findings motivated Bayer/Monsanto to seek settlements with the plaintiffs. As of May 2022, Monsanto has reached settlement agreements in nearly 80 percent (about 100,000) Roundup lawsuits totaling over $11 billion. There are still between 26,000 and 30,000 active Roundup lawsuits. Bayer has set aside almost $15 billion to settle future cases.

The other primary concern with Roundup and other glyphosate-based herbicides is "superweeds." Farmers sprayed so much Roundup that weeds quickly evolved to survive it. Today, Roundup-resistant horseweed, pigweed, and giant ragweed are forcing farmers to return to more expensive, petroleum-intensive techniques and more toxic herbicides that they had abandoned long ago.

As a result of this negative backlash, in 2021, Bayer announced that it would remove Roundup from the consumer market in 2023.

With the new name of Bayer Crop Science, the rebranded mission of the company is to "transform agriculture and drive a more sustainable food system." In the short term, this means continuing with its focus on "seed trait improvement" (a euphemism for GMOs) and crop protection (a euphemism for chemical herbicides). Long-term, Bayer claims several ambitious sustainability goals, including reducing the environmental impact of its herbicidal products, decreasing GHG emissions, and improving the livelihoods of smallholder farmers.[34]

Time will tell if these become real changes or simply a rebranding of past practice.

McDonald's and the Climate Impacts of Beef

The 2004 documentary *Super Size Me* depicted a man who ate at McDonald's every day for a month and gained 28 pounds. The lesson McDonald's learned was to no longer encourage customers to increase the order size, which was their usual practice. Supersizing the french fries increases the calories and the price. McDonald's took a public relations hit because of the film. Companies like McDonald's, Walmart, and Coca-Cola must often deal with public backlash when their business practices are called into question.

McDonald's accounts for more beef consumption (nearly 2 percent of the world's total beef consumption) than any other company, sold through its 39,000 restaurants in 119 countries.[35] GHG emissions linked to this meat production come from deforestation and land conversion, feed production, and methane emitted by the cows themselves. Combined with its other emissions, McDonald's accounts for about 53 million metric tons of carbon dioxide per year, more than the country of Norway.[36] With that number rising yearly, climate advocates have called on the company to reduce its emissions.

For over a decade, McDonald's has pledged to reduce GHG emissions from its animal product operations. In 2011 it launched the Global Roundtable for Sustainable Beef, an industry-sponsored group focused on more sustainable cattle production systems. In 2018 the company promised to purchase some of its beef from sustainable sources and trim the climate intensity of its food and packaging by 31 percent by 2030. It went a step further in 2021, vowing to zero out its entire climate footprint by 2050.

A recent in-depth examination by Bloomberg, however, calls into question the sincerity of these efforts. The analysis concludes that the company has failed to reduce the climate impact of its beef, casting doubt on its overall climate commitment. For instance, while the company says it has reduced the emissions intensity of its food and packaging by 6 percent since 2015, overall emissions have gone up by 7 percent.[37]

The challenge McDonald's faces is convincing its growers and suppliers to adopt greener practices. The company's hamburgers account for only a fraction of the meat products that come from a cow. The higher-end cuts go to other distributors and consumers, limiting the ability of McDonald's to influence its supply chain effectively. Farmers and ranchers are skeptical about changing their practices for

McDonald's when they aren't getting that pressure from other buyers. Producers also question who will pay for changes in production practices and infrastructure.

Despite this lack of progress, McDonald's deserves credit for initiating these efforts with its suppliers. Time will tell if they can use their purchasing power to drive meaningful change in the beef supply chain.

CARGILL AND DEFORESTATION

Cargill is the largest privately held company in the United States, with annual earnings of $116 billion. Its primary business areas are agriculture, livestock nutrition and protein, food processing, and trade-related financial services. Cargill has a noble mission: to help meet the growing food needs of the global population. Some of its companies are Cargill Ocean Transport, Cargill Cocoa & Chocolate, Diamond Crystal Salt, and Truvia.

Cargill has the ambitious mission of having the world's most sustainable food supply chains. The company has three interrelated sustainability goals:

1. *Climate:* Reduce GHG emissions in operations by 10 percent by 2025 and in supply chains by 30 percent by 2030.

2. *Land and Water:* Transform agricultural supply chains to be deforestation-free by 2030 and achieve sustainable water management in operations.

3. *People:* Promote and respect human rights as outlined by the UN Universal Declaration of Human Rights. Improve the livelihoods of 10 million farmers by 2030.

Cargill has also committed to greater transparency as a means of being accountable to these goals. They do this via their ESG Scorecard and a reporting hub that provides information on progress towards the company's sustainability commitments. On its Scorecard, the company claims a 4 percent reduction in GHG emissions from operations and 52 percent implementation of sustainable water management at their facilities. Less significant gains are reported in other areas. In 2022 Cargill launched a program to pay farmers for production practices that lower emissions by capturing carbon in soils. In recent years, some environmental advocacy groups have praised the company for its promises to do better.

Despite its claims, Cargill has a long record of controversies involving food contamination, workplace injuries, anti-competitive practices, fraught labor relations, child labor, and environmental violations such as deforestation.[38] Environmental groups have repeatedly highlighted how Cargill is lagging on its 2020 commitments.[39] The most recent controversy regards the company's commitment to ending deforestation in Brazil, where it buys large quantities of soy from local farmers. Much of this soy is grown on land converted from natural forests.

Given its immense size and global reach, Cargill does have the power to clean up agriculture supply chains, improve the livelihood of small farmers and agriculture workers, and improve food safety. So far, the company's record is mixed. The public, policymakers, and investors will continue to pressure agricultural companies like Cargill to limit their environmental impacts and increase transparency.

Kraft Heinz and Shareholder Pressure

With over $26 billion in annual sales as of 2020, Kraft Heinz is North America's third-largest food and beverage company and the fifth largest in the world.[40] In addition to the Kraft and Heinz brands, they include over 20 other brands among which are Kool-Aid, Jell-O, Gevalia, Grey Poupon, Oscar Mayer, and Philadelphia Cream Cheese. Since Kraft is a major buyer of agricultural products across the world, it has a strong interest in sustainable agriculture and the purchasing power to influence its supply chains.

Beginning in 2017, shareholder investment groups began to submit shareholder resolutions related to GHG emissions, supply chain sustainability, and human rights issues. These investment groups included Domini Impact Investments, Calvert Investment Management, and Catholic Responsible Investments.

Shareholder democracy through proxy voting is a relatively new strategy for compelling companies to improve their commitment to environmental and social issues. Proxy voting is the primary means for shareholders to communicate their views about a company's management. While non-binding, proxy vote proposals enable investors to drive attention to social issues. The proxy vote process has resulted in more shareholders and company management engagement.

One of the most common areas of shareholder proxy votes is around companies' environmental and sustainability performance, along with transparency around that performance. The number of ESG-related proxy proposals has increased significantly over the last decade. Most proxy proposals are withdrawn before a vote because of negotiation with management to implement changes. For proxy resolutions that do come to a vote, the percentage of shareholders voting in support has increased steadily in recent years. Investors are also increasingly supportive of dissident board nominees who support greater commitment to climate and sustainability.[41]

This appears to be what has happened at Kraft Heinz in recent years. Some ESG resolutions were withdrawn after negotiated agreements with management to reform ESG efforts. Others that came to a vote did not pass but garnered significant minority support from shareholders. This pressure motivated Kraft Heinz to improve its environmental and human rights efforts.

One of the most significant of these efforts is that the company pledged to achieve net zero GHG emissions across its global operations and supply chains by 2050. Short-term, it has promised to reduce these emissions by 50 percent by 2030. To accomplish this, the company has committed to:

- promoting regenerative and sustainable practices across the company's agricultural supply chain
- transitioning to circular and recyclable consumer packaging
- procuring most of the company's electricity from renewable sources by 2025
- transitioning on-site manufacturing facilities to renewable energy sources.[42]

One example of how the company is transitioning into green packaging is the development of a paper-based, renewable, and recyclable bottle made from 100 percent sustainably sourced wood pulp. Heinz is the first sauce brand to test its condiment products' potential paper bottle packaging.

Kraft Heinz's environmental record is relatively positive, even though they were relatively latecomers to sustainability and ESG reporting. It will be interesting to see if this shareholder strategy of proxy voting on ESG issues is effective at creating enduring change at the company and if it will become more widely practiced by shareholders at other companies.

WALMART, SCOPE 3 EMISSIONS, AND TRANSPORT

Walmart is the world's largest retail chain, with over 10,500 stores in 24 countries. According to Fortune Global 500, Walmart is the world's largest country by revenue, with $570 billion USD in annual revenues. With over 2.2 million employees, it is also the world's largest private employer.[43] Walmart was one of the earliest companies to adopt a sustainability program and tout its leadership in corporate environmental responsibility. Some of its earliest sustainability efforts focused on shipping efficiency, recycling, and energy efficiency.

In recent years, Walmart's sustainability efforts have focused on climate change and reducing GHG emissions. Like other companies, Walmart's emissions come from three types of emissions. Scope 1 and 2 emissions come from the company's direct operations and the energy it purchases, respectively. Walmart has pledged to reduce Scope 1 and 2 emissions by 35 percent by 2025 and 65 percent by 2040 and to accomplish this without relying on purchasing offsets. It plans to do this by adopting new energy efficiency measures, using lower carbon energy sources, and powering 50 percent of its global operations with renewable energy sources by 2025 and 100 percent by 2035.

The third source of Walmart's emissions are Scope 3 emissions. Scope 3 emissions are from assets not directly owned or controlled by the company but from the suppliers in its supply chain and the distribution of those products.[44] While the Scope 1 and 2 emissions from Walmart's huge retail store footprint are massive, far and away its largest sources of emissions are the Scope 3 emissions from its supply chain. This is because most of the products Walmart carries come from third-party suppliers.

To reduce Scope 3 emissions, in 2017 the company launched Project Gigaton, with the goal of diverting one billion metric tons, or one gigaton, of CO_2 emissions from global supply chains by 2030. A gigaton of avoided GHG emissions is the equivalent of taking more than 211 million passenger vehicles off U.S. roads for an entire year. Project Gigaton focuses on Scope 3 emissions by engaging all the company's suppliers and motivating them to decarbonize their products.

There are two complex challenges for Walmart in reducing these Scope 3 emissions. The first is compelling its growers, processors, and manufacturers to decarbonize their production processes. As discussed in the examples above, this is a huge task. But given Walmart's immense purchasing power, and other buyers like Target and Amazon pushing for similar emission reductions, they may be able to drive meaningful reductions.

Probably the more difficult challenge is shipping. Most of Walmart's products are transported by maritime shipping, which has a massive carbon footprint. Between 2018 and 2020, goods imported by Walmart, Target, Amazon, and IKEA using maritime transport accounted for 20 million metric tons of GHG emissions. Nearly 90 percent of global trade is transported by container ships.[45]

This is particularly challenging for Walmart, given its reliance on the ocean carrier CMA CGM. CMA CGM is the biggest polluter amongst ocean carriers, accounting for 68 percent of Walmart's ocean shipping emissions in 2020. CMA CGM is one of the world's biggest buyers of fossil gas vessels, which emit 70–82 percent more lifecycle greenhouse gas emissions than those fueled with petroleum distillate marine gas oil.[46]

Unlike other consumer products like clothing and electronics, most of Walmart's food products are produced domestically and therefore do not require ocean shipping. However, these food products are transported large distances around North America by rail and truck. Rainier cherries from Washington State go to Walmart stores in Florida. Ocean Spray juices from Massachusetts are shipped to California. Yet a great deal also comes from Central and South America and is shipped by ocean freight or air, depending on the product type.

If Walmart and other large retailers can pressure their transport partners toward zero-emissions solutions, they could propel the decarbonization of retail product distribution. For instance, Walmart is already working with CMA CGM on warehousing and last-mile transport solutions, which could be seen as an opportunity to build zero-emission shipping into their growth model. CMA CGM is already taking the first steps toward low-carbon shipping using biomethane rather than traditional marine fuels.[47]

DANONE AND ESG DISCLOSURE

One strategy for getting large companies to be more sustainable is to require transparency about what companies are doing to manage environmental, social, and governance risks. As a result, government regulatory bodies, stock exchanges, and the public are increasingly mandated ESG reporting. ESG reporting is the disclosure of environmental, social, and corporate governance data. Variously referred to as environmental reporting, environmental disclosure, and ESG disclosure, the goal is to make ESG reporting a business norm that incentivizes real action towards a sustainable economy. It also enables companies to demonstrate that their ESG goals are genuine, not just greenwashing and empty promises.

One of the tenets of ESG reporting is the third-party review of the disclosed data. One of the biggest and most well-respected of these organizations is CDP (formerly the Carbon Disclosure Project), an independent international nonprofit organization. Firms use the CDP platform to disclose their ESG impact and progress. In 2021, over 14,000 organizations disclosed their environmental information through CDP.[48]

As we discussed earlier, food processing and packaging companies face enormous ESG challenges because of the far-reaching nature of their supply chains. As a result, few of these companies achieve high ratings from CDP. One example is Danone, the multinational food products company based in Paris. Danone was ranked as one of the most valuable food brands worldwide in 2021, with net sales of about €24.28 billion, ranking it third globally in terms of brand worth behind Nestlé and Unilever.[49] In 2021, CDP gave Danone an A rating for its three main ESG reporting metrics—climate change, forests, and water security—making it one of only 14 companies worldwide to accomplish this out of the over 14,000 firms that reported their ESG data.

Danone's journey toward sustainability began in 2015 with the pledge to achieve carbon neutrality throughout its entire value chain by 2050 (Scopes 1, 2, and 3). Any GHG emissions they were not able to eliminate would be offset. To accomplish this, Danone became a member of the *Science-Based Targets initiative* (SBTi) working group to define 1.5°C pathways for the Agriculture, Forest, and Land sectors.

To reach its Net Zero goal, Danone adopted a multi-pronged strategy:

- reduce its emissions intensity by 50 percent on its full scope of responsibility (Scopes 1, 2, and 3) between 2015 and 2030 and reduce its absolute emissions by 30 percent on Scopes 1 and 2 between 2015 and 2030
- transforming agricultural practices of its supply chain; keeping more carbon in the ground
- eliminating deforestation from its supply chain
- Danone's main actions to accomplish these goals are:
- reduction of greenhouse gas emissions from milk and dairy ingredients supplies by changing farming practices and improving the efficiency of processing techniques
- transformation of packaging design (target of 100 percent recyclable, reusable, or compostable packaging by 2025) and materials (target of 50 percent use of recycled polyethylene terephthalate, also called PET, to halve its use of virgin PET from fossil fuels), as well as the acceleration of reuse models
- reduction of energy consumption from operations (based on energy efficiency improvement) and the use of renewable energies
- development of new plant-based alternatives with a lower carbon footprint than dairy products.

What stands out in Danone's strategy is the company's willingness to publicly state its intention to move away from animal-based products and replace them with plant-based products with a lower ESG footprint. This is a high-profile demonstration of the product substitution approach discussed earlier in the chapter.

It hasn't been all smooth sailing for Danone. Its ESG numbers improved significantly from 2015 to 2019. Yet progress in recent years has flattened. While this may be partly because of more stringent reporting requirements by CDP, it may also be because Danone has implemented the more straightforward projects and is now wrestling with the more intractable Scope 3 emissions embodied in its supply chain. Danone has also been accused of outsourcing its ESG impacts in ways that don't show up in its Scope 3 emissions data.[50] It's likely that CDP's disclosure requirements will be more rigorous about such outsourced emissions in the future.

Conclusion

The agriculture industry is, of course, responsible for the food that goes into our bodies. Ultimately, the whole concept of sustainability revolves around human health and well-being. The diets of developed and emerging countries are quite different from developing countries. In the developed world, we take for granted that the food we consume is safe and rely upon the government to fix standards that will protect us, while in the developing world, there is still huge concern over malnutrition and hunger. Fixing these systemic inequities will be essential to future efforts to make our agriculture and food systems more sustainable.

This chapter covered the critical aspects of sustainable agriculture. We reviewed the principles that go into organic food and studied some of the practices that put meat on the table. The intelligent consumer should know how their food arrives at the table. Knowledge of this process may alter one's dietary practices and drive the industry toward more sustainable products and practices.

Keywords

- Agriculture
- Agriculture intensification
- Agrodiversity
- Agroforestry
- Agronomic practices
- Artificial Intelligence (AI)
- Biotechnology
- Blockchain technology
- Breeding
- Certified organic
- Contamination
- Conventional agriculture
- Crop ration
- ESC disclosure
- ESG reporting
- Evergreen revolution
- Fallow
- Food miles
- Free range
- Genetically modified organisms (GMOs)
- Genetic engineering
- Glyphosate
- Green Revolution
- Grower houses Irradiation
- Integrated pest management (IPM)
- Intensive Agriculture
- Local Food Movement
- Locavore
- Malnutrition
- Natural
- No-till
- Organic farming
- Product substitution
- Roundup Ready crops
- Salinization
- Sustainable agriculture
- Sustainable seafood

Discussion Questions

1. Visit your supermarket and find foods that are labeled natural. Determine how they qualify for that designation.
2. Is there evidence of sustainable seafood at your local fish counter?
3. How did the Green Revolution change agriculture and food systems?
4. Has agricultural intensification increased or decreased the conversion of natural ecosystems to agriculture?
5. What are the main crops in your state or region? What evidence of sustainability practices can you find in local growers?
6. What are some examples of innovative technologies you can see in your region that are changing the way agriculture and food systems work?
7. How can a small farm succeed in today's market?
8. Why do you believe there has been a drop in the consumption of red meat in the United States?
9. Some countries have seen meat consumption decline; others have seen it increase. What are the driving forces in meat consumption?
10. A national politician recently criticized the U.S. government's program to combat obesity. Why would a government pursue a program like this?
11. What could be done to reduce cases of malnutrition across the world?

Recommended Websites

- The United Nations Food and Agriculture Organization (FAO) – www.fao.org/home/en
- U.S. Department of Agriculture – www.usda.gov/
- Alternative Farming Systems Information Center – www.nal.usda.gov/programs/afsic
- Appropriate Technology Transfer for Rural Areas (ATTRA) – attra.ncat.org/
- National Organic Program – www.ams.usda.gov/about-ams/programs-offices/national-organic-program
- SARE and Sustainable Agriculture Network – www.sare.org/
- American Farmland Trust – farmland.org/
- Center for Agriculture in the Environment – https://farmland.org/about/how-we-work/research/NationalSustainableAgricultureCoalition-sustainableagriculture.net/
- Organic Consumers Association – www.organicconsumers.org/
- Organic Trade Association – www.organicitsworthit.org/
- The Women's Agricultural Network – www.uvm.edu/extension/agriculture/womens-agricultural-network

Endnotes

[1] U.S. Department of Agriculture. (2021, September 23). Agriculture and food sectors and the economy. *USDA Economic Research Service.* https://www.ers.usda.gov/data-products/ag-and-food-statistics-charting-the-essentials/ag-and-food-sectors-and-the-economy/

[2] Agriculture. (n.d.). Oxford Reference. Retrieved from https://www.oxfordreference.com/view/10.1093/oi/authority.20110803095356555

[3] Trinkaus, E. (2005). Early modern humans. *Annual Review of Anthropoly, 34*(1), 207–230.

[4] Clutton-Brock, J. (1999). *A natural history of domesticated mammals.* Cambridge, UK: Cambridge University Press.

[5] Trinkaus, E. (2005). Early modern humans. *Annual Review of Anthropoly, 34*(1), 207–230.

[6] Farmer, B. H. (1986). Perspectives on the 'Green Revolution' in South Asia. *Modern Asian Studies, 20*(1), 175–99.

[7] Gollin, D., Hansen, C. W., & Wingender, A. M. (2021). Two blades of grass: The impact of the green revolution. *Journal of Political Economy, 129*(8), 2344–2384. https://doi.org/10.1086/714444.

[8] von Der Goltz, J., Dar, A., Fishman, R., Mueller, N. D., Barnwal, P., McCord, G. C. (2020). Health impacts of the Green Revolution: Evidence from 600,000 births across the developing world. *Journal of Health Economics, 74,* 2020, 102373.

[9] Pimentel, D. (1996). Green revolution agriculture and chemical hazards. *The Science of the Total Environment, 188,* S86–S98.

[10] IUCN Red List of Threatened Species. (2012). United Nations International Union for the Conservation of Nature. https://www.iucnredlist.org/

[11] Pilipinas, K. M. (2007). Historical and political perspectives on IRRI, and its impact on Asian rice agriculture. In V. M. Lopez, P. A. Z. dela Cruz, J. L. Benosa, & F. P. Concepcion (Eds.), *The Great Rice Robbery: A Handbook on the Impact of IRRI in Asia.* Penang, Malaysia: Pesticide Action Network Asia and the Pacific.

[12] FAO. (2011). Food and Agriculture Organization of the United Nations. London: Rome and Earthscan.

[13] Poore, J., & Nemecek, T. (2018). Reducing food's environmental impacts through producers and consumers. *Science, 360*(6392), 987–992.

[14] Poore, J., & Nemecek, T. (2018). Reducing food's environmental impacts through producers and consumers. *Science, 360*(6392), 987–992.

[15] Davies, P. (2003). An historical perspective from the green revolution to the gene revolution. *Nutrition Reviews, 61*(6), S124–34.

[16] Swaminathan, M. S. (2006). An evergreen revolution. *Crop Science, 46*(5), 2293–2303.

[17] Swaminathan, M. S. (2006). An evergreen revolution. *Crop Science, 46*(5), 2293–2303.

[18] Food and Agriculture Organization of the United Nations. (n.d.). OECD/FAO, FAOSTAT Food Balances Database. *Faostat.* Retrieved from https://www.fao.org/faostat/en/#home.

[19] USDA National Institute of Food and Agriculture. (n.d.). Sustainable agriculture programs. *USDA.gov.* https://www.nifa.usda.gov/grants/programs/sustainable-agriculture-programs

[20] CCAFRICA24 / Standards Can Improve Food Safety and Competitiveness across Africa. *CODEXALIMENTARIUS FAO-WHO.* https://www.fao.org/fao-who-codexalimentarius/news-and-events/news-details/en/c/1603899/

21. CCAFRICA24 / Standards Can Improve Food Safety and Competitiveness across Africa. *CODEXALIMENTARIUS FAO-WHO.* https://www.fao.org/fao-who-codexalimentarius/news-and-events/news-details/en/c/1603899/
22. Langemeier, M., & O'Donnell, M. (2020, September 8). Conventional vs. organic grains: 5-year comparison of returns. *AgFax.* https://agfax.com/2020/09/08/conventional-vs-organic-grains-5-year-comparison-of-returns/
23. Vigar, Vanessa, et al. (2019, December 18). A systematic review of organic versus conventional food consumption: Is there a measurable benefit on human health?" *Nutrients,* MDPI. https://www.ncbi.nlm.nih.gov/pmc/articles/PMC7019963/.
24. Environmental Working Group. EWG's 2022 shopper's guide to pesticides in produce. EWG's Summary. https://www.ewg.org/foodnews/summary.php.
25. U.S. Department of Agriculture. (n.d.). Labeling organic products. *USDA Agricultural Marketing Service.* https://www.ams.usda.gov/rules-regulations/organic/labeling.
26. Dunne, J. B., Chambers, K. J., Giombolini, K. J., & Schlegel, S. A. (2010). What does 'local' mean in the grocery store?: Multiplicity in food retailers' perspectives on sourcing and marketing local foods. *Renewable Agriculture and Food Systems, 26,* 46–59.
27. Shaw, J. S. (2012). Book review: The locavore's dilemma: In praise of the 10,000-mile diet, by P. Desrochers & H. Shimizu. *The Independent Review, A Journal of Political Economy, 17*(4). https://www.independent.org/publications/tir/article.asp?id=934.
28. Pollan, M. (2006). *The omnivore's dilemma: A natural history of four meals.* New York: Penguin.
29. Kenner, R. (2010). *Food, Inc.* [Motion picture]. Los Angeles: Magnolia Pictures.
30. Pollan, M. (2013). *Cooked: A natural history of transformation.* New York: Penguin Press.
31. Held, L. (2021, December 9). At an annual sustainability gathering, big AG describes its efforts to control the narrative. *Civil Eats.* https://civileats.com/2021/12/09/at-an-annual-sustainability-gathering-big-ag-describes-its-efforts-to-control-the-narrative/.
32. Kamin, D. (2019, May 14). *It's in the weeds: Herbicide linked to human liver disease* [press release]. San Diego, CA: UC Health, UC San Diego. https://health.ucsd.edu/news/releases/pages/2019-05-14-herbicide-linked-to-human-liver-disease.aspx.
33. Globe Newswire. (2022, May 3). Global glyphosate market to reach $8.9 billion by 2026. News Room, Globe Newswire. https://www.globenewswire.com/news-release/2022/05/03/2434796/0/en/Global-Glyphosate-Market-to-Reach-8-9-Billion-by-2026.html.
34. Bayer. (n.d.). The strategy of Bayer. *Bayer Global.* https://www.bayer.com/en/strategy/strategy.
35. Elgin, B. (2021, December 1). Emissions of methane from cows: McDonald's carbon footprint remains high. *Bloomberg.* https://www.bloomberg.com/news/articles/2021-12-01/the-carbon-footprint-of-mcdonald-s-menu-very-big.
36. Elgin, B. (2021, December 1). Emissions of methane from cows: McDonald's carbon footprint remains high. *Bloomberg.* https://www.bloomberg.com/news/articles/2021-12-01/the-carbon-footprint-of-mcdonald-s-menu-very-big.
37. Elgin, B. (2021, December 1). Emissions of methane from cows: McDonald's carbon footprint remains high. *Bloomberg.* https://www.bloomberg.com/news/articles/2021-12-01/the-carbon-footprint-of-mcdonald-s-menu-very-big.
38. Mattera, P. (2021, June 29.) Cargill: Corporate rap sheet. *Good Jobs First.* https://www.corp-research.org/cargill
39. Tabuchi, H., Rigny, C., & White, J. (2017, February 24). Amazon deforestation, once tamed, comes roaring back. *The New York Times.*

40. Kraft Heinz Company. (2021, November 19). Form 8-K. *U.S. Securities and Exchange Commission*. Retrieved February 11, 2021 from https://ir.kraftheinzcompany.com/sec-filings
41. Lasdon, E. (2022, April 26). The ABCs of proxy voting and its role in ESG. ClimeCo. Retrieved 23 Aug. 2022, from https://climeco.com/the-abcs-of-proxy-voting-and-its-role-in-esg/
42. Environmental Social Governance. (n.d.). The Kraft Heinz Company. Retrieved from https://www.kraftheinzcompany.com/esg/
43. Fortune Magazine. (2022, August 1). Walmart: 2022 Fortune 500. *Fortune*. https://fortune.com/company/walmart/fortune500/.
44. U.S. Environmental Protection Agency. (n.d.). Scope 3 inventory guidance. *Environmental Protection Agency*. https://www.epa.gov/climateleadership/scope-3-inventory-guidance
45. *The Economist* staff. (2017, March 11). Green finance for dirty ships. *The Economist*. www.economist.com/finance-and-economics/2017/03/11/green-finance-for-dirty-ships.
46. Pavlenko, N., Comer, B., Zhou, Y., Clark, N., & Rutherford, D. (2020). The climate implications of using LNG as a marine fuel. The International Council on Clean Transportation. www.stand.earth/publication/climate-implications-using-lng-marine-fuel
47. Zuber, D. (2022). *Walmart's dirty shipping problem*. Pacific Environment. Retrieved from https://www.pacificenvironment.org/walmart-dirty-shipping/
48. CDP. (2021, October 14). CDP reports record number of disclosures and unveils new strategy to help further tackle climate and ecological emergency. *Carbon Disclosure Project*. https://www.cdp.net/en/articles/media/cdp-reports-record-number-of-disclosures-and-unveils-new-strategy-to-help-further-tackle-climate-and-ecological-emergency.
49. Shahbandeh, M. (2022, November 11). Topic: Danone. *Statista*. https://www.statista.com/topics/2428/danone/#dossierKeyfigures.
50. Naik, G. (2020, February 4). Cost of environmental damage linked to Nestlé, Danone and Mondelez rises sharply. *S&P Global*.

Part III

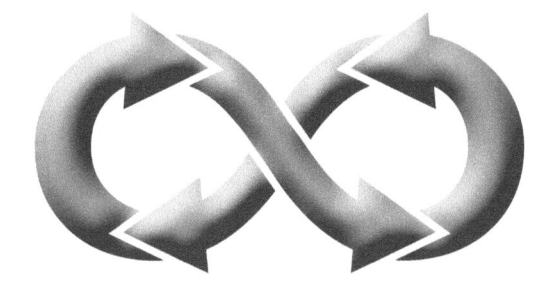

Stakeholder Interest and Choices

CHAPTER 6

Sustainable Strategies and Frameworks

LEARNING OBJECTIVES

By the end of this chapter, you should be able to do the following:

- » Explain the concept of sustainable value creation.
- » Understand the precepts of natural capitalism.
- » Examine activities via the natural step.
- » Discover examples of industrial ecology and biomimicry.
- » Compare and contrast the principles of the cradle-to-cradle (C2C) approach with biomimicry.
- » Explain the environmental management system (EMS) and environmental stewardship.
- » Compare and contrast various tools and processes used for sustainable strategies.

CHAPTER OVERVIEW

This chapter will discuss the overall strategies and frameworks employed by organizations focused on sustainability. The chapter will start with why organizations desire to pursue sustainability, followed by the concept of sustainable value creation, followed by a discussion of natural capitalism. Next, the chapter will move into a section on the various frameworks available such as the natural step, industrial ecology, C2C, biomimicry, and so on. This chapter will also present some other tools organizations use to develop strategies focused on sustainability.

The topics covered will include natural capitalism, life cycle assessment (LCA), natural step, industrial ecology, C2C, biomimicry, environmental stewardship, EMS, sustainable operating systems (SOS), sustainable value stream mapping, and the Sustainability Balanced Scorecard (SBSC).

Why Sustainable Strategy?

Given that our world is facing dual pressures of increased demand from an expanding population and declining natural resources of basic ecological stores, it is but a natural response that sustainable strategy is the paradigm for consumption and production. Due to the strategic importance of this area, we have devoted this chapter to reviewing the various frameworks that attempt to define, classify, and embed sustainability.

Sustainable Value Creation

A model of shareholder value was developed by Stuart Hart and Mark Milstein (2003). As shown in Figure 6.1, the vertical axis of this model represents time, and this axis reflects the organization's management of the current business while simultaneously creating future technology and markets. The horizontal axis represents space, and this axis reflects the organization's need for growth and to protect the internal organization's capabilities while simultaneously incorporating new

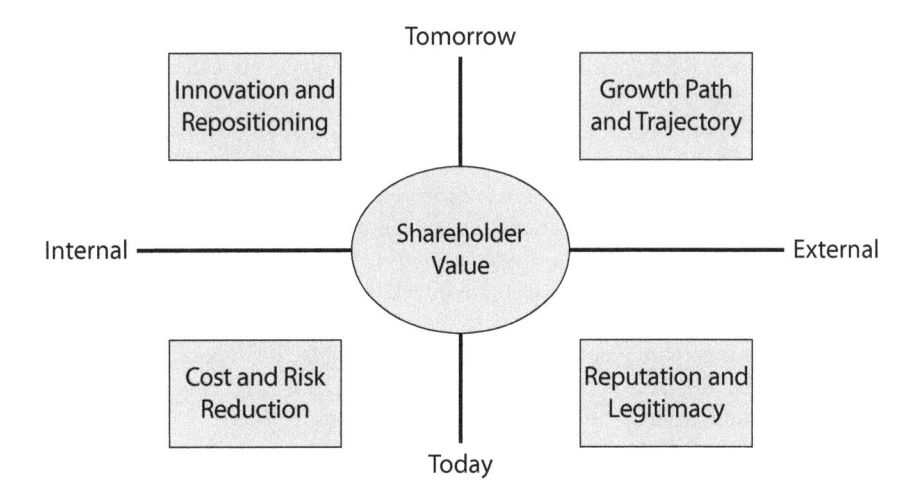

Figure 6.1 | Shareholder Value.
Source: Hart & Milstein (2003).

perspectives and knowledge from outside. The concept is to balance the need to focus on core capabilities while being aware of fresh, external perspectives. Putting both the time and space dimensions in the model yields a matrix of four distinct areas—(1) risk reduction, (2) reputation, (3) innovation, and (4) growth—wherein each is critical to the goal of generating shareholder value. Sustainable value creation is built around the same two dimensions—(1) time and (2) space—as shareholder value creation. In addition, as shown in Figure 6.2, this framework also includes social and environmental challenges.

Global Drivers of Sustainability

There are four sets of drivers that need to be addressed for global sustainability. The first set of drivers relates to the negative impact of industrialization—namely, pollution, waste, and material consumption. The second set relates to groups like nongovernmental organizations (NGOs) and their growing impact on society. The third set of drivers includes the emerging disruptive technologies, such as genomics, nanotechnology, biomimicry, renewable energy, and so on, that have the potential to make the energy and material-intensive industries obsolete. The fourth set of drivers relates to global concerns about an increase in population, poverty, and inequity arising from globalization.

According to the sustainable value framework, each driver and its strategies and business practices correspond to a dimension of shareholder value. For the lower left quadrant of Figure 6.2, organizations can create value by following a pollution prevention strategy by minimizing emissions and waste. The immediate payoff is one of cost and risk reduction. Indeed, empirical evidence shows that profits increase for companies pursuing pollution prevention and waste reduction (Christmann, 1998; Sharma & Vredenburg, 1998). Some industry examples are Dow Chemical's Waste Reduction Always Pays (WRAP), Chevron's Save Money and Reduce Toxins (SMART), 3M's Pollution Prevention Pays (3P), and so on (Hart & Milstein, 2003).

For the lower right quadrant of Figure 6.2, organizations can increase confidence by engaging stakeholders. The ideal strategy for a company would be to integrate stakeholder views into business processes to gain a payoff of reputation and legitimacy. Some actions are cause-related marketing, life cycle management, industrial ecology, and so on. As an example of the latter, organizations can convert wastes into inputs. In 1997, Collins and Aikman Floorcoverings, now called Tandus Flooring, Inc., converted the old carpet into the new carpet backing. This product, ER3 (environmentally redesigned, restructured, and reused), has helped increase market share for the company (Buffington, Hart, & Milstein, 2002). Another example is from Nike, which faced a growing backlash regarding its labor and environmental practices and made a turnaround by engaging stakeholders to address social and environmental issues (Hart & Milstein, 2003).

For the upper left quadrant of Figure 6.2, organizations would develop the sustainable competencies of the future for a resultant payoff of innovation and repositioning. Companies that can engage disruptive technologies that address the needs of society will drive economic growth. Firms that fail to lead in such

Sustainable Value Model

Tomorrow

- **Drivers**
  - Disruption
  - Clean Tech
  - Footprint

  Strategy: Clean Technology
  Develop the sustainable competencies of the future
  Corporate Payoff: Innovation and Repositioning

- **Strategy: Sustainability Vision**
  Create a shared roadmap for meeting unmet needs
  Corporate Payoff: Growth Trajectory

  Drivers
  - Population
  - Poverty
  - Inequity

Internal ———— **Sustainable Value** ———— **External**

- **Drivers**
  - Pollution
  - Material Consumption
  - Waste

  Strategy: Pollution Prevention
  Minimize waste and emissions from operations
  Corporate Payoff: Cost and Risk Reduction

- **Strategy: Product Stewardship**
  Integrate stakeholder views into business process
  Corporate Payoff: Reputation and Legitimacy

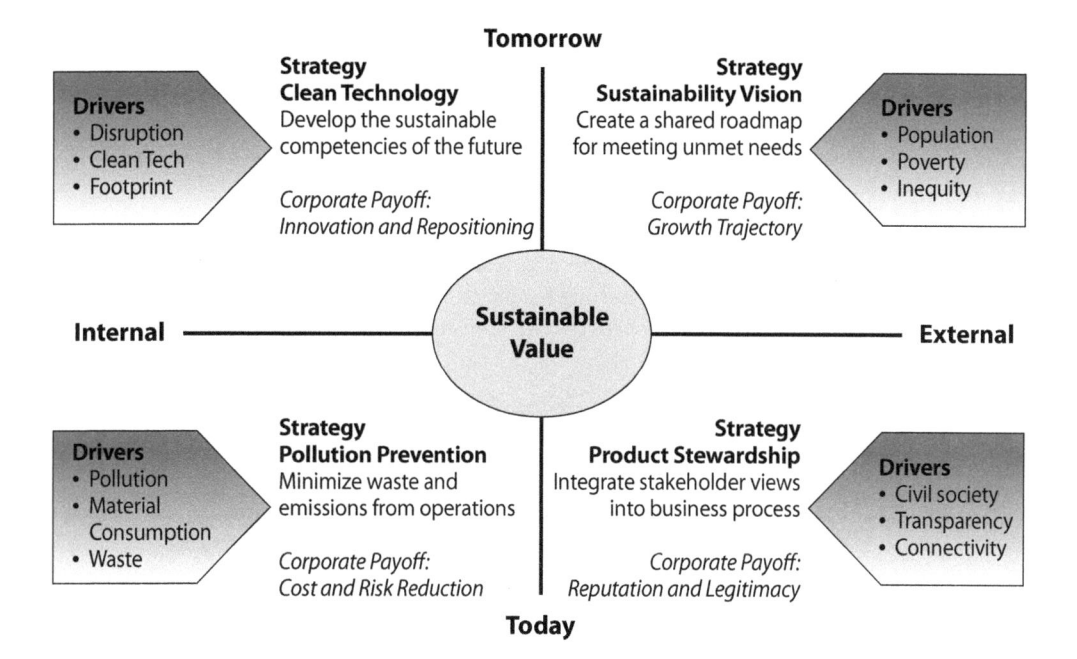

  Drivers
  - Civil society
  - Transparency
  - Connectivity

Today

FIGURE 6.2 | Sustainable Value Model.
Source: Hart & Milstein (2003).

technologies are not likely to be future market players (Hamel, 2000). For example, British Petroleum (BP) and Shell invested in renewable technologies; Toyota and Honda incorporated hybrid power systems into their cars; General Electric (GE), Honeywell, and United Technologies are investing in small-scale energy systems; and Cargill and Dow are developing biologically based polymers that will enable renewable feedstocks. Another commendable example is DuPont, which transformed itself from a gunpowder and explosives manufacturer into a chemical company in the late 1800s and then transformed into a renewable resource company focused on sustainable growth in the 1990s (Holliday, 2001). Firms that invest in clean solutions create organizational structures that support the innovative process (Hart & Milstein, 2003).

For the upper right quadrant of Figure 6.2, organizations ought to create a shared road map for meeting unmet needs for a resultant payoff of a sustainable growth trajectory. In other words, firms that make a compelling sustainability vision have the potential to unlock future markets. For example, Grameen Bank opened a new pathway for business growth (Counts, 1996). Another example of a multinational corporation is Hindustan Unilever Limited (HLL), which developed products specifically aimed at the rural poor in India and provided affordable soaps and shampoos to this market (Balu, 2002). In another example, Hewlett-Packard (HP) created a research and development lab in India to understand this burgeoning market. Other companies like Johnson & Johnson, Dow,

DuPont, Coca-Cola, and Procter & Gamble are attempting to leverage their skills to meet the basic needs of the world's poor (Hart & Milstein, 2003).

In conclusion, the opportunity to create sustainable value is huge but unexploited. Organizations can choose the best strategy on the sustainable value framework and work toward the achievement of sustainable goals.

Ladder of Sustainability

Sustainability can be designed into any area of an organization. The ladder of sustainability contains numerous rungs, each representing an area of the organization. The idea is to take progressive steps toward attaining TBL (Holmes, n.d.). The rungs are listed as follows:

1. *Products or services:* This is the first area that should be considered. Are the products made using toxic materials? Are renewable materials used in the products?
2. *Processes:* Are the processes efficient in that they use minimal resources? Is the process geared toward the entire life cycle (C2C versus cradle to grave)?
3. *Business model:* A model of leasing might be more sustainable than selling. In the case of Interface, the reuse of carpet was not aligned with profit when it was used to sell the carpet. Once the model was changed to leasing carpets, there was an incentive to collect old carpets and reuse the material.
4. *Company focus:* All company employees need to be on board to focus on the innovation required for sustainability to become a reality.
5. *The brand identity of the company:* Sustainability can be a great branding tool and can be used to create a market niche. Companies like The Body Shop and Ben & Jerry's were highly successful in this area.
6. *Supplier web and value chain:* The commitment to sustainability can extend to all its partners, suppliers, and other value chain members. In the case of Walmart, the entire value chain needs to align with the new sustainability goals.
7. *Industry leadership and advocacy role:* Once a company has succeeded in the first six areas, it can become an advocate for the movement (Holmes, n.d.).

Players Within the Organization

For the internal success of any initiative, all the employees must be involved. The TBL goals call for teams of people who can deliver results. The three groups of people are the (1) leaders, (2) stakeholders, and (3) the change support group.

Leaders: A company needs at least one executive-level sponsor to execute a TBL strategy. The role of the executive-level sponsor is to give or get authorization, support, and resources for necessary activities.

Stakeholders: This group is responsible for implementing a TBL plan. Education and training are required to attain buy-in at this level and build group capacity.

Change support: Since the change can be large and complex, a change support team is required to enable a broad-scale migration. This team acts as a facilitator, gathering resources and spotting and solving problems (Holmes, n.d.).

Some sustainability gurus like McDonough, Braungart, and Lovins call for the next Industrial Revolution to be sustainable in business. The goal of the Industrial Revolution was to create financial value; the challenge in this next era is to create financial, social, and ecological value simultaneously.

Natural Capitalism

Our global economy is dependent on natural resources and ecosystem services. The Industrial Revolution, which began in the mid-18th century, gave rise to modern industrial capitalism and opened up immense possibilities for material development. However, the gains of the Industrial Revolution came at a great cost to nature with resultant loss of topsoil, fall of water tables, and a loss of species and biodiversity.

The three authors Amory Lovins, Hunter Lovins, and Paul Hawken, state that we need a new approach: natural capitalism. Amory and Hunter Lovins cofounded the Rocky Mountain Institute, a nonprofit think tank that analyzes the efficient and restorative use of resources. Amory Lovins is considered to be an authority on energy policy and was named one of the world's 100 most influential people in 2009 by *Time Magazine*. Paul Hawken is an environmentalist, entrepreneur, and author who has written about the impact of commerce on living systems and has served as a consultant on industrial ecology and environmental policy.

By definition, natural capital is the store of commodities produced by nature in its 3.8 billion-year development process. These everyday commodities range from water and minerals to soil and air. In addition, it includes all living systems, from grasslands to rainforests and oceans to coral reefs. These living systems supply the nonrenewable resources and, in addition, also replenish the basic services in nature, such as regeneration of the atmosphere, flood management, water storage and purification, soil fertilization, waste processing, and buffering against the extremes of weather (Marx, 2001).

The present rates of use and degradation are unsustainable in that there will be little left by the end of the next century. This is of great concern since the decline of this stock of natural capital will also impact vital life-giving services. Natural capitalism addresses the "critical interdependency between the production and use of human-made capital and the maintenance and supply of natural capital." A particular economy needs four types of capital to function properly:

1. Human capital, in the form of labor and intelligence, culture, and organization
2. Financial capital consisting of cash, investments, and monetary instruments
3. Manufactured capital, including infrastructure, machines, tools, and factories
4. Natural capital made up of resources, living systems, and ecosystem services (Lovins, Lovins, & Hawken, 2000).

Our economy is based upon using the first three forms of capital—(1) human, (2) financial, and (3) manufactured—to convert natural capital into items needed for basic living: food, shelter, transportation, and so on. This industrial system does not assign any value to natural resources and the social and cultural systems that are the basis of human capital. Hence, natural capitalism calls for an expanded set of values that would include accounting for natural and human capital. It proposes four central strategies or shifts in business practices so that the ecosystem services are truly valued (Lovins, et al., 2000).

Shift #1: Radical resource productivity: Using resources more effectively means getting more product from each ton of natural material extracted. This step can slow resource depletion, lower pollution, and provide employment.

Shift #2: Biomimicry: Industrial systems can be redesigned using principles from nature. This idea focuses on eliminating waste and toxicity in the system. Production models ought to emulate nature, wherein waste from any system is food for another system.

Shift #3: Service and flow economy: In traditional goods-based business models, consumers acquire goods, consume them, and discard them. In a solutions-based business model, the producer owns the goods and encourages "take back" when the productive life is over, resulting in incentives for remanufacturing and recycling. A shift to leasing models can lead to a decline in material flow and waste.

Shift #4: Investment in natural capital: Businesses need to take leadership to restore, sustain, and expand the planet's ecosystems for future provision of products and services. Without this investment, natural capital stocks will decline, and ecological problems will increase, leading to societal pressures through costly and inefficient governmental actions (Senge, 2000).

Natural capitalism has been utilized in certain industries. Some of these applications can be found in the sustainable tourism industry (Kuo & Hsiao, 2008), transportation agencies (Ramani, 2011), and the concrete industry (Mehta, 2001). Though the ideology of natural capitalism is sustainably sound, it has yet to be fully embraced by industries.

Natural Step

The Natural Step was developed by Swedish oncologist Dr. Karl Henrik-Robert in 1989 and is a systems-thinking-based framework that combines environmental problems with ecological principles. The framework consists of three parts:

1. the four system conditions
2. the funnel
3. strategies for action

Dr. Henrik-Robert worked with children battling leukemia and began to suspect environmental causes as sources of cancer. He worked with other scientists to find a set of irrefutable scientific principles on which to base his work. This work led Dr. Henrik-Robert to develop the four system conditions for sustainability.

Four System Conditions for Sustainability

In a sustainable society, nature is not subject to systematically increasing:

1. *concentrations of substances extracted from the Earth's crust*

   The first system condition states that to convert to a sustainable society, there must be no more extraction of metals, minerals, fossil fuels, etc. from the Earth's crust. The buildup of these extractive materials invariably leads to other environmental problems.

2. *concentrations of substances produced by society*

   The second system condition calls for eliminating synthetic chemicals and compounds, especially those that do not break down easily. Chemicals such as DDT are very hard to get rid of, especially once these leach into the food chains and water tables.

3. *degradation by physical means*

   The third system condition calls for an end to the degradation and destruction of natural environments. Examples would be the overfishing of the oceans, the overharvesting of forests, and the decline of biodiversity.

4. *and people are not subject to conditions that undermine their ability to meet their needs.*

   The fourth system condition calls for meeting the needs of all people and species fairly. For example, paying farmers low wages to grow cash crops such as cocoa would violate this condition ("The Four System Conditions," n.d.).

In short, The Natural Step addresses what we take from nature, what we make that impacts nature, what we maintain in nature, and what and how we share with others. In The Natural Step framework, the four system conditions act as a compass that can guide companies or organizations toward sustainability practices.

The Funnel

As a metaphor, The Natural Step uses a "funnel" to describe the current situation and the goal of sustainability. Please refer to Figure 6.3a for a description of the funnel.

The funnel needs to be visualized from the left-hand side. The upper wall of the funnel represents the availability of natural resources and the ability of the ecosystem to provide these resources. The lower wall of the funnel represents the increasing demand for these natural resources to provide our basic needs, such as food, shelter, clothing, transportation, and so on. Looking into the mouth of the funnel leads to a visualization that, given the increase in population and consumption levels, the demand for ecosystem resources is growing while nature's ability to regenerate ecosystems is declining.

The two walls of the funnel indicate that human demand is outstripping the supply of natural resources. To be sustainable, the shape of this funnel must be opened up by a decrease in our impacts and a restoration of the life support systems. The walls of the funnel can only be opened up with innovative and creative solutions to achieving sustainability ("The Funnel," n.d.).

STRATEGIES FOR ACTION

The Natural Step's strategies for action include four elements referred to as ABCD. Please refer to Figure 6.3b.

1. *Awareness and visioning:* Articulating a common understanding of sustainability within an organization and envisioning what the organization would look like in a sustainable future
2. *Baseline mapping:* Conducting a sustainability "gap analysis" to see which of the organization's activities are counter to principles of sustainability. Mapping current operations allow an organization to identify critical sustainability issues and the business implications of these.
3. *Creative solutions:* People are asked to brainstorm potential solutions to the issues identified in the previous step. In a technique termed backcasting, people begin with the end in mind and move toward a shared vision of sustainability, with each action moving toward further improvement.

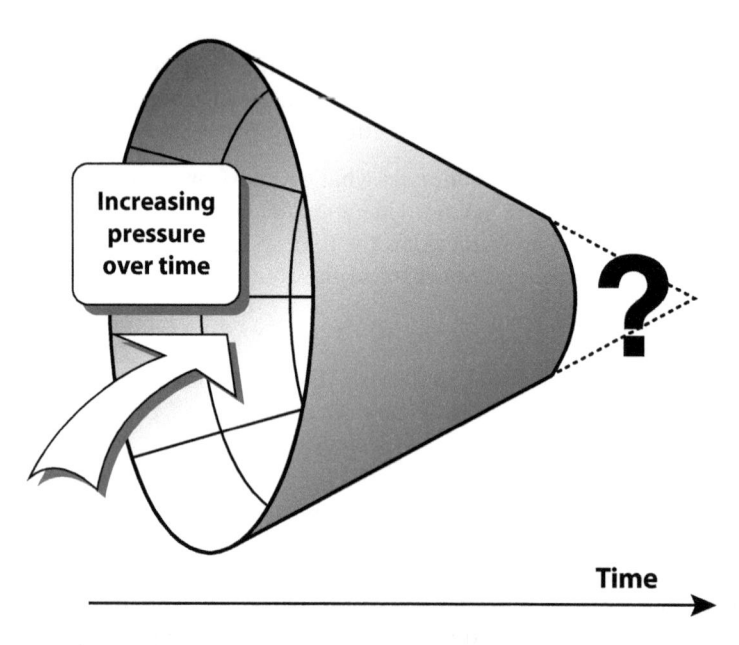

FIGURE 6.3a | TNS Resource Funnel.
Source: The funnel (n.d.).

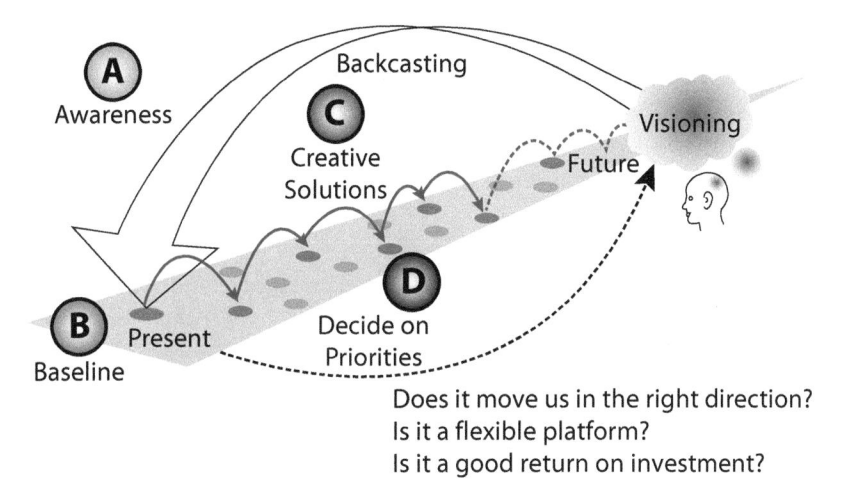

FIGURE 6.3b | Applying the ABCD Method.
Source: Applying the ABCD Method (n.d.).

4. *Decide on priorities:* Prioritizing measures to move the organization toward sustainability. Backcasting determines whether decisions and actions are moving the organization toward the desired steps outlined in Step A (Applying the ABCD Method, n.d.).

Some companies that have employed The Natural Step (TNS) include McDonald's Sweden, Nike, and IKEA. More details on the functioning of this organization can be found on The Natural Step's website: www. naturalstep.org.

There have been quite a few applications of TNS with most of the applications being concentrated in the architecture/construction/engineering sectors. The U.S. Green Building Council's Leadership in Energy and Environmental Design (LEED) incorporated the principles of The Natural Step (Zimmerman & Kilbert, 2007) and Sweden's Natural Step chapter has partnered with major businesses to promote organizational transformation towards sustainable development (Bradbury & Clair, 1998). The principles of TNS have also been used by numerous companies, ranging from Electrolux and Mitsubishi to McDonald's and Interface Carpets to Nike and Walmart, as they seek to enhance their environmental management systems (Burns, 1999; Asmus, 1998; Martin & Schouten, 2014).

A word of caution: One critique of TNS is that it is primarily designed as a persuasive argument and is not wholly based on sound science (Upham, 2008).

INDUSTRIAL ECOLOGY

Industrial ecology is a Ss" (Industrial Ecology, 2009). It is sometimes also referred to as "the Science of Sustainability" in that it promotes a broad scientific solution to sustainability problems. One of the basic tenets of industrial ecology is "the shifting of industrial process from linear or open-loop systems, in which resource and capital investments move through the system to become waste, to a closed-loop system where wastes become inputs for new processes" (Garner & Keoleian, 1995).

Industrial ecology utilizes systems analysis to frame the interaction between industrial systems and natural systems. The key concepts of industrial ecology are as follows:

Systems Analysis

The systems view, or approach, is integral to understanding the relationship between human activities and environmental problems since this viewpoint recognizes the interrelationships between industrial and natural systems. As an example, a manufacturer of a certain product would look at product life cycle stages and analyze the impact of the product on the consumer and the ecosystem. With this viewpoint, the manufacturer can design the product while keeping both its consumption and disposal constraints.

Material and Energy Flows and Transformations

An environmental impact analysis entails "material and energy flows and their transformation into products, byproducts, and wastes throughout the industrial system" (Garner & Keoleian, 1995). For example, a material flow diagram of a battery might illustrate how much of the product becomes scrap. Further efforts can be made to use this waste as an input for some other processes within the industrial system. This process would result in reducing the negative environmental impact and in improving the efficiency of the system. The ultimate goal is to reduce the overall environmental burden of an industrial system (Garner & Keoleian, 1995).

Multidisciplinary Approach

Since environmental problems are complex by nature, a variety of fields—economics, public policy, law, ecology, business, and engineering—can be utilized to solve these problems. In addition, in the case where current technologies are upgraded, these need to be matched by changes in consumer behavior and changes in public policy and legal standards.

Analogies to Natural Systems

Over millions of years of evolution, the natural system has evolved from a "linear (open) system to cyclical (closed) system in which there is a dynamic equilibrium between the various biological, physical, and chemical processes in nature" (Garner & Keoleian, 1995). The system is cyclical since all the organisms feed and pass on wastes that, in turn, are consumed by other organisms. There exists a high degree of integration and interconnectedness within the natural system along with a complex system of feedback mechanisms that trigger reactions in case certain limits are reached (Garner & Keoleian, 1995).

LINEAR (OPEN) VERSUS CYCLICAL (CLOSED) LOOP SYSTEMS

In a linear system, resources are consumed, and wastes are disposed into the environment. By contrast, in a cyclical system, resources and wastes are constantly recycled and reused within the system. A central concept in industrial ecology is the evolution of the industrial system from a linear system to a cyclical system.

The Type I system portrays a linear process whereby materials and energy enter the system and are transformed into products and wastes before they exit the system. Refer to Figure 6.4 for an illustration of the Type I system. This system needs a large and constant supply of raw materials since there is no recycling or reuse taking place. This system is unsustainable since it needs an infinite supply of raw materials and energy and has limited space to accommodate the wastes.

The *Type II* system portrays the industrial system at present wherein some wastes are recycled or reused whereas a majority of the wastes still leave the system. Refer to Figure 6.5 for an illustration of the Type II system.

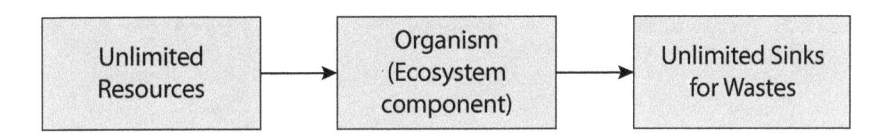

FIGURE 6.4 | Type I System.
Source: Allenby (1992).

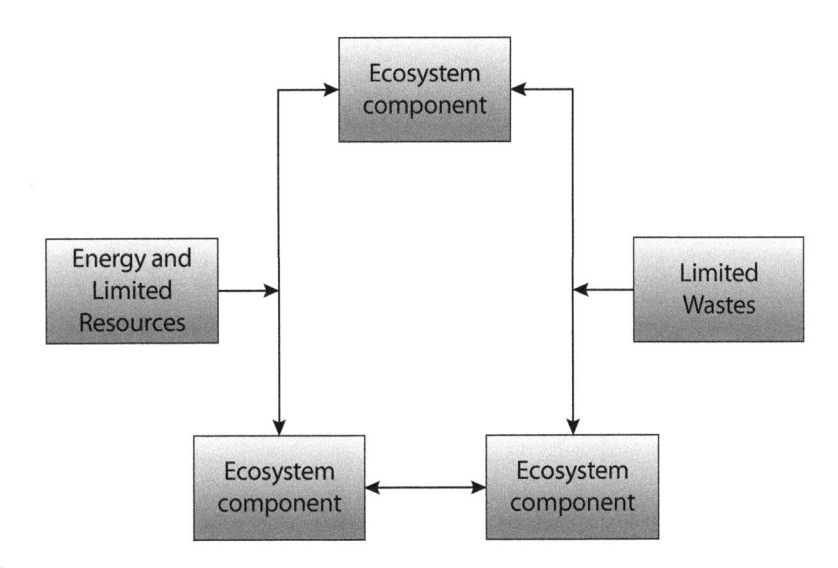

FIGURE 6.5 | Type II System.
Source: Allenby (1992).

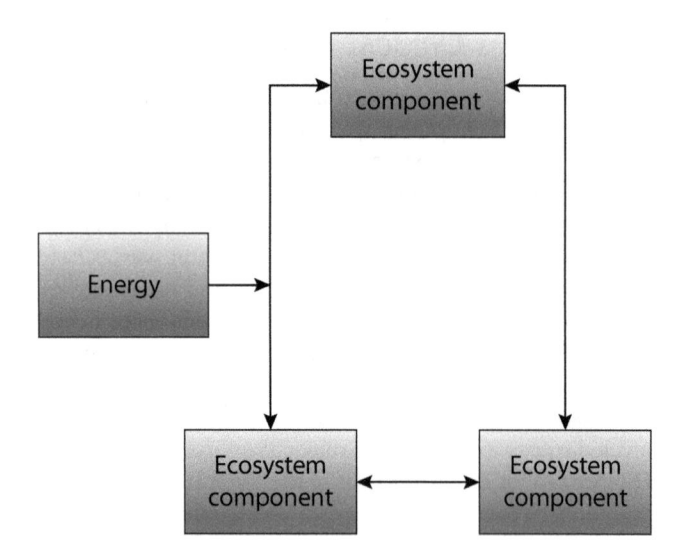

FIGURE 6.6 | Type III System.
Source: Allenby (1992).

The *Type III* system portrays the ideal dynamic equilibrium state of ecological systems, wherein energy and wastes are recycled and reused by other organisms and processes within the system. Refer to Figure 6.6 for an illustration of the Type III system. A perfect closed industrial system would only require solar energy, and all the by-products would be reused. This Type III system represents a sustainable state, and it epitomizes the ideal goal of industrial ecology.

In terms of geography, the entire Earth can be viewed as a natural/physical environmental system within which humans are mere players who have had and continue to have an impact. An essay from Brown (n.d.) includes information about the Earth as a natural system, energy in the system (open system), matter in the system (closed system), and the evolution of the environment (Brown, n.d.).

EXAMPLES OF INDUSTRIAL ECOLOGY

Barceloneta, Puerto Rico

In Barceloneta, Puerto Rico, a symbiotic relationship exists mainly among pharmaceutical companies, a waste management firm, and a water treatment plant (see Figure 6.7). The relationship began in the 1970s, as Puerto Rico's lower taxes attracted several pharmaceutical firms to the island. Around that time, the U.S. Environmental Protection Agency (EPA) also mandated that firms have a water treatment plant to manage the wastewater coming from the various production plants (Ashton, 2008). In response to this need, the firms pooled their funds together to share the operating costs of the treatment plant. This also allowed them to recover solvents from their processes. Furthermore, an exchange of solvents developed from this process, as firms realized that they may benefit

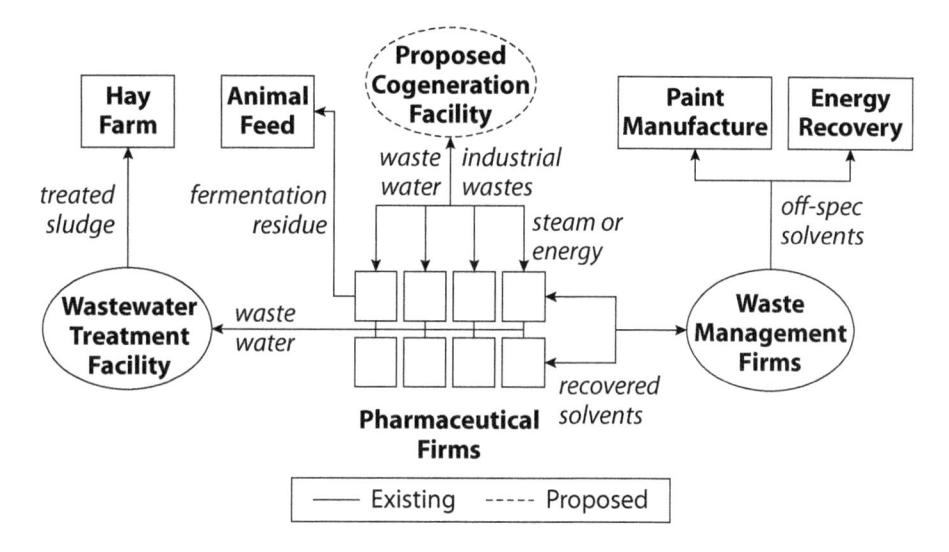

FIGURE 6.7 | Barceloneta, Puerto Rico.
Source: Ashton (2008).

from one firm's "wasted" solvent that can be recovered (Ashton, 2008). The ecosystem grew richer with the entrance of a waste management firm in the 1970s as well. This firm was able to make use of many of the solvents that were of no use to the pharmaceutical companies. This company would sell the recovered resources to other companies on the island—companies that were not directly linked to the pharmaceutical plants' water treatment symbiosis (Ashton, 2008). Furthermore, fermentation residue from the pharmaceutical plants benefited farmers' development of animal feed. Also, the treated sludge from the water treatment plant would be used by hay farmers to grow hay (Ashton, 2008).

Kouvola, Finland

Another strong example of an industrial ecosystem exists in Kouvola, Finland (see Figure 6.8). Kouvola's main industry is the UPM-Kymmene Corporation's (Kymi) paper and pulp mill (Sokka, 2010). The Kymi mill was established in 1874 and over time has grown to be the center of the region's industrial ecosystem. The mill interacts with a power plant, three chemical plants, a water treatment plant, and a sewage plant. The power plant utilizes wood and residual waste from the mill to provide the mill with electrical power. Moreover; the output from the power plant also provides the entire town of Kouvola with its electricity and heat (Sokka, 2010). The three chemical plants providing resources to Kymi are powered by Kymi. The Kymi mill also provides the chemical plants with purified water and other resources for their processes. Specifically, the calcium carbonate plant takes in the carbon dioxide given off by Kymi for its chemical processes (Sokka, 2010). In another process within the ecosystem, a sewage plant provides sludge to a water treatment plant, which receives wastewater from Kymi. The sludge acts as

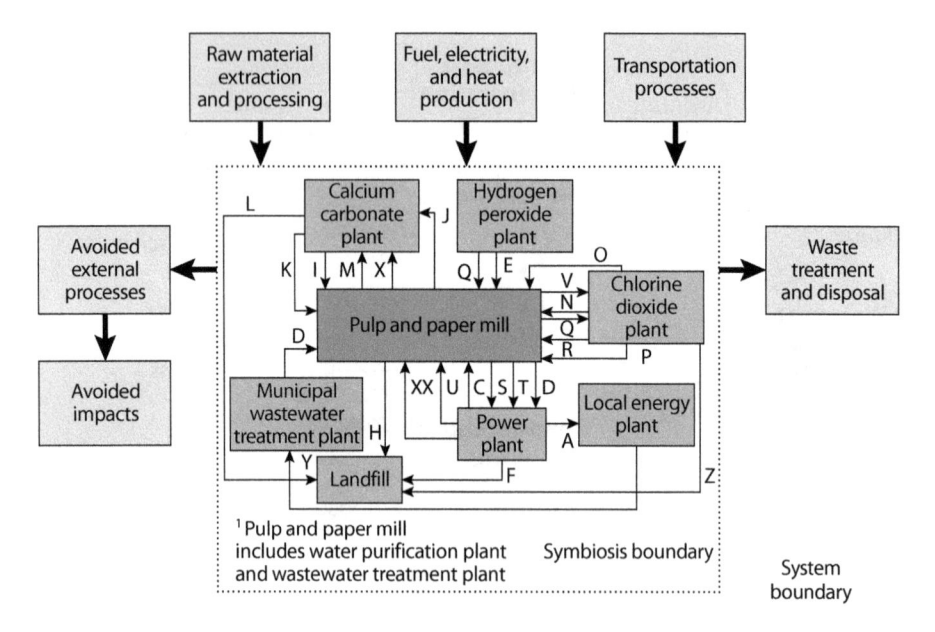

FIGURE 6.8 | Kouvola, Finland.
Source: Sokka (2010).

an expedient for purifying the wastewater (Sokka, 2010). This ecosystem not only benefits the participating firms but also the local municipality's residents, as they receive electricity and heat due to the efficient operation of the industrial ecosystem.

Cape Charles, Virginia

Within the United States, an attempt to build the first eco-industrial park occurred at Cape Charles, Virginia (see Figure 6.9). An eco-industrial park is like an industrial ecosystem, in the sense that the participating firms are acting toward reducing waste and conserving resources as responsible global citizens. However, unlike an industrial ecosystem, it does not appear that the participants need to work together as they would in a "food web"—as an ecosystem. The Cape Charles Sustainable Technology Park project began around 1996. The park serves the local community as a preserved wetland, where industries and residential homes can coexist with the natural ecosystem. The pavement of the park is porous, reducing water runoff during storms.

The park utilizes the natural wetland environment as a water retention system (Duran, n.d.). Furthermore, one of the companies in the park—a water purification company—has designed its building with ecofriendly features. The building consists of several solar panels for assisting with providing electricity to the building. Also, it has additional insulation for heat and cooling energy savings (Duran, n.d.). A German wind power company is planning on installing large windmills in the park to power not only the firms within the park but also the 3,000 nearby homes. The park not only has benefited the environment but has also brought

FIGURE 6.9 | Cape Charles, Virginia.
Source: Duran (n.d.).

more employment to the town (Duran, n.d.). As an incentive to maintain and increase ecological responsibility in the park, lease rates decrease as a company reduces its carbon footprint. The park manages an environmental responsibility scorecard for each company participating. The scores are not only based on eco-friendly measures but also local employment, thus enhancing the local economy and environment (Duran, n.d.).

The local and regional industrial system approach is found in two examples from Finland where the local forest industry system is based on renewable resources, waste materials, and energy utilization all arising from forestry companies: a sawmill, a paper mill, a pulp mill, and a forest industry power plant. The waste energy that is generated as a by-product of the energy production is, in turn, utilized for the production of heat and to process steam. Furthermore, regional city energy supply systems in Finland are arranged around power plants that can utilize waste energy (Korhonen, 2001). Another example of industry ecology is in food production aimed at minimizing nutrient pollution. The industrial ecology principles can be used to analyze nutrient cycling in complex systems (Fernandez-Mena, et al., 2016).

LIFE CYCLE ASSESSMENT

One of the tools used to support industrial ecology is the Life Cycle Assessment framework (LCA), which provides a methodology for analyzing the environmental consequences of products or processes from *cradle to grave*. In other words, an LCA is used to determine the total environmental impact of a product. This impact involves accounting for all the inputs and outputs from the birth to the death of the product including stages of design, raw material extraction, material production, assembly, usage, and final disposal.

The LCA framework comprises four stages: (1) goal definition and scoping, (2) inventory analysis, (3) impact assessment, and (4) interpretation. Refer to Figure 6.10 for an illustration. In the goal definition and scoping stage, the product or process is defined along with the boundaries of assessment. In the second stage—inventory analysis—all the inputs and outputs in the product's life cycle are examined including the usage of energy and materials. The next stage is impact analysis in which the environmental impacts of the first stage are evaluated. Next comes the interpretation stage in which the results of the previous two stages are evaluated ("Life Cycle Assessment: Principles and Practice," 2006).

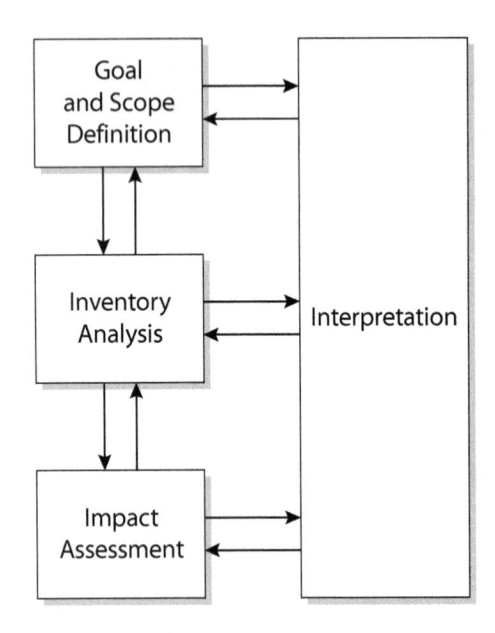

FIGURE 6.10 | Life Cycle Assessment Framework.
Source: Graedel & Allenby (2009).

The life cycle approach has also been used a lot in international discussions and negotiations around sustainable development. Indeed, the plan for implementation that came out of the World Summit on Sustainable Development (WSSD) calls for scientific approaches, like the LCA, to develop production and consumption policies while mitigating the environmental and health impacts ("Life Cycle Initiative Publications," n.d.).

There has been a plethora of life cycle approach applications. In food production and agriculture, LCA has been used in milk production (Eidi, 2002), tomato ketchup (Andersson, et al., 1998), and food products in general (Roy, et al., 2009). In the energy sector, LCA has been used to assess renewable energy technologies (Pehnt, 2006), and to assess electricity generation derived from coal, natural gas, oil, nuclear, biomass, solar, and wind (Turconi, et al. 2013). LCA has also been used in the building and construction sector (Cabeza, et al., 2014), process systems engineering (Pontalier & Sablayrolles, 2012), and to assess waste management strategies (Cherubini, 2009). Eco-industrial parks also offer possibilities to implement sustainable development policies using LCA principles (Gibbs & Deutz, 2007).

CRADLE-TO-CRADLE AND BIOMIMICRY

Two other concepts can also provide a new way of thinking about sustainability. The first concept is C2C, taken from design stating that products ought to be designed so that there is no waste or that the wastes produced can be used by another production process. The second, biomimicry, is taken from biology and states that nature is the best teacher for sustainability.

CRADLE-TO-CRADLE

This concept is derived from the book titled *Cradle-to-Cradle*, written by William McDonough and Michael Braungart in 2002. The C2C framework (McDonough & Braungart, 2002) calls for a new way of designing human systems to solve the conflicts between economic growth and environmental health. The framework identifies three key design principles in the intelligence of natural systems, which can inform human design:

1. *Waste equals food:* In nature, waste does not exist because the processes of each organism contribute to the health of the whole ecosystem. One organism's waste is food for another, and nutrients flow indefinitely in C2C cycles of birth, decay, and rebirth. In other words, waste equals food. Engineers and designers can use this principle to select safe materials and optimize products and services, creating closed-loop material flows that are safe and sustaining (McDonough & Braungart, 2002).

2. *Use current solar income:* Living things thrive on the energy of the sun, and trees and plants manufacture food from sunlight. C2C systems, ranging from buildings to manufacturing, can use solar energy, a renewable resource (McDonough & Braungart, 2002).

3. *Celebrate diversity:* Natural systems also thrive on diversity. Healthy ecosystems are made up of complex communities of living things, where each organism fits within a system. The engineers can use this principle by considering this C2C maxim: "All sustainability is local." The principle is that optimal sustainable design solutions need to get information locally, must draw on local energy and material flows, and ultimately, must "fit" within local natural systems (McDonough & Braungart, 2002).

Cradle-to-cradle has been used in pharmaceuticals and personal care products (PPCPs). These PPCPs are considered trace environmental pollutants and have been identified in surface and ground waters and sediments and sewage sludges. These pollutants primarily originate from consumer use and though these do degrade over time, their continued usage and disposal in wastewaters cause them to be persistent in the environment. Very little is known about the environmental or human health hazards that might be caused by the chronic levels of these substances. Cradle-to-cradle stewardship is used to capture the options available to minimize the release of PPCPs into the environment (Daughton, 2003).

BIOMIMICRY

Biomimicry is the "conscious emulation of life's genius to solve human problems" in design, industry, and elsewhere, according to Janine Benyus (1997), who wrote a book on the topic. The basic assumption is that over 4 billion years, natural selection and evolution have given us sustainable, diverse, complex, and efficient solutions to energy use and population growth. At present, humankind has the technology to understand how these solutions in nature work, and these can be applied to current problems. Examples range from mimicking spider silk and applying ideas from prairies and forests to agriculture. Rather than simply exploit nature's design, biomimicry advocates learning from nature. The three precepts are as follows:

1. Nature is a model for sustainable designs and processes.
2. Nature is the measure for successful solutions.
3. Nature is our mentor.

In short, living things have done everything we want to do, without guzzling fossil fuel, polluting the planet, or mortgaging their future. What better models could there be? Benyus writes,

> This time, we come not to learn about nature so that we might circumvent or control her, but to learn from nature, so that we might fit in, at last, and for good, on the Earth from which we sprang . . . [That ingenuity displays recurrent] laws, strategies, and principles. Nature runs on sunlight. Nature uses only the energy it needs. Nature fits form to function. Nature recycles everything. Nature rewards cooperation. Nature banks on diversity. Nature demands local expertise. Nature curbs excesses from within. Nature taps the power of limits (Benyus, 1997).

Benyus combined biomimicry with industrial ecology to come up with ten principles of an economy that would mimic nature:

1. *Use waste as a resource:* All waste is food. All living things use energy from sunlight and give up by-products of energy in the form of heat.
2. *Diversify and cooperate to fully use the habitat:* Symbiosis and specialization can help businesses collaborate on energy efficiency, remanufacturing, etc.
3. *Gather and use energy efficiently:* Use fossil fuels more efficiently while shifting to solar and renewables in the long run.
4. *Optimize rather than maximize:* Focus on quality over quantity.
5. *Use materials sparingly:* Reduce packaging and switch to businesses providing services rather than selling products.
6. *Don't foul the nests:* Reduce toxins and decentralize production.
7. *Don't draw down the resources:* Invest in ecological capital and reduce the use of renewable feedstocks to permit regeneration.
8. *Remain in balance with the biosphere:* Limit greenhouse gas (GHG) emissions and other pollutant emissions that disrupt climate cycles.
9. *Run-on information:* Create feedback loops and reward good environmental behavior.
10. *Shop locally:* Use local resources and reduce unnecessary transportation (Benyus, 1997).

There are numerous industrial applications of biomimicry wherein companies are researching to apply nature's principles to the design of products. The Mercedes-Benz Bionic was modeled after a tropical coral reef-dwelling fish called the boxfish. The design of the boxfish is extremely aerodynamic, and the Bionic has a low vehicle drag coefficient of 0.19 that, in turn, helps the Bionic travel approximately 70 miles per U.S. gallon. In addition, akin to its marine-dwelling prototype, the Bionic employs the use of hexagonal structures in its shell that have proven to be extremely durable and space-efficient when employed in architecture ("Design of New Mercedes-Benz Bionic Car," 2005).

Another company, Sto Corp., has developed Lotusan paint, an exterior paint that employs the self-cleaning, hydrophobic properties of the lotus plant wherein the water molecules touch a surface, immediately bead together, and roll off due to repulsion between water and the nonpolar substance. In addition, the structure of the plant enables dirt particles to adhere to the water droplet so they can be removed from the plant, thus enabling the self-cleaning properties of the paint. The Lotusan paint claims to be able to extend the surface life of exterior surfaces while simultaneously decreasing cleaning costs for building owners and has proven to be highly resistant to water damage, dirt, mold, and even UV rays (Sto Corp. Lotusan Videos, n.d.). This same technology is also being examined by GE to further understand its potential applications on metal surfaces. Ideally, if able to synthesize into a spray coating, the lotus effect could be useful as a quick fix for deicing aircraft.

Some of the other examples of biomimicry are as follows:

- The company Whalepower implemented tubercles in the wind turbines to reduce drag.
- The front end of the Shinkansen bullet train is modeled after the kingfisher beak to reduce noise and increase speed and efficiency.
- Sick chimpanzees go to trees from the Vernonia genus, and researchers are looking to test the chemical compounds on these trees for treating parasites in humans.
- EvoLogics developed a high-performance underwater modem that emulates dolphins' unique frequency modulating acoustics to send early warnings for tsunamis ("What Could Nature Teach Us?" n.d.).
- Numerous other examples of biomimicry applications can be found in architecture (Rao, 2014); textiles and textile technology (Eadie & Ghosh, 2011; Das, 2017); urban infrastructure design (Kenny, et al. 2012); sustainable engineering (Reap, et al. 2005); skin design (Radwan & Nouran, 2016); product and technology innovation (Lurie-Luke, 2012); urban planning (Taylor, 2017); and 3D concrete printing (du Plessis, 2021) among others.

ENVIRONMENTAL STEWARDSHIP AND SUSTAINABILITY

Stewardship means taking care of something. Sustainability is about using resources responsibly so that there is enough left for future generations. What do these terms mean together? How can an individual, an organization, or a community be stewards of the environment so that sustainability is attainable? What actions can you, as an individual, take to make it so?

An organization aims to balance making money with sustainability within its operations. Through this balance, this organization may take into account the needs of future generations. In practice, numerous opportunities consider environmental sustainability. The following is a list of such environmentally sustainable practices:

- *Manufacturing:* Use recycled and toxin-free materials, reuse and recycle transport packaging, incorporate pollution prevention programs, and set energy and water efficiency goals.
- *Suppliers:* Reduce packaging of raw materials and provide greener and less toxic supplies.
- *Product impact:* Reduce overall environmental impact and increase end-of-life recycling.
- *Office operations:* Recycle paper and reduce paper usage, purchase recycled office supplies, and use email.
- *Purchasing:* Set up environmentally preferable purchasing, purchase non-toxic and recycled supplies, request bulk supplies, and screen purchases.
- *Transportation:* Encourage teleconferencing, the usage of mass transit, and alternative fuel vehicles for carpooling and minimize trip miles through efficient routing of product and raw material supply.
- *Food service:* Provide reusable dinnerware, implement recycling programs, donate excess food, establish composting programs, and encourage energy and water efficiency.
- *Facility management and housekeeping:* Maximize energy efficiency in lighting, heating, and cooling; install water-saving devices such as low-flow toilets and showerheads; use the least toxic cleaning materials and employ green building techniques in maintenance.
- *Landscaping:* Evaluate fertilizers, pesticides, and herbicides; landscape to conserve water; monitor watering systems to use only when needed and establish composting programs.
- *Interactions with the public:* Inform the public and customers about sustainability efforts ("Stewardship Initiative Sustainability Definition," 2002).

This list can be a starting point for any organization to start implementing environmental sustainability within their day-to-day operations. While this list is by no means exhaustive, it can serve as a baseline, and once organizations start realizing cost benefits, further opportunities for savings can be realized.

The Environmental Protection Agency's Approach to Environmental Stewardship

Stewardship has had a long history across many cultures. In the United States, communities of Native Americans are considered to be the first practitioners of environmental stewardship. In the past decades, the consequences of poor environmental stewardship were often not as dire since the economy and the population was smaller and the technologies were much simpler than they are today. Despite this fact, there have been documented cases of serious human-caused environmental problems (Diamond, 2005). At present, both individuals and organizations are starting to realize that ecologically sustainable choices are economically sustainable and in their best interest.

Consider the following statement:

> Over the next 50 years, while the world's population is forecast to increase by 50 percent, global economic activity is expected to increase roughly fivefold. Conventional demand studies suggest that global energy consumption is likely to rise nearly threefold and manufacturing activity at least threefold, driven largely by industrialization and infrastructure growth in developing regions. Global throughput of material is also likely to triple, according to conventional projections (Matthews, et al., 2000).

Most people want a cleaner environment, a robust resource base, and a stronger economy that supports all individuals. However, the economy, the resource base, and environmental quality are all influenced by the day-to-day choices made by individuals, companies, communities, and government organizations. These choices range from product design to housing and transportation, from city planning to government procurement and operations, and so on.

Many of these choices are and ought to lie beyond the direct control of the government. However, the government can help by creating opportunities that enable and encourage environmental stewardship. The EPA and its state partners (at government levels) have launched a series of programs aimed to encourage environmental stewardship.

According to the EPA, its mission "is to protect human health and the natural environment." For a long time, the EPA approached its mission through regulations at the point of discharge. In the 1990s, pollution prevention was added to the earlier approach.

As illustrated in Figure 6.11, this environmental responsibility has evolved from simple compliance to continuous improvement that employs metrics to report on environmental performance. Furthermore, with the use of metrics and targets aimed at reducing the environmental footprint, there has been a further

Compliance Acceptance of meeting standards and requirements → **Continuous Improvement** Use of measurement and reporting to improve environmental performance → **Goals and Targets** Use of targets, measure, and reports to reduce environmental footprint → **Sustainability-based Strategies** Focus on long-lasting solutions to promote sustained env. quality

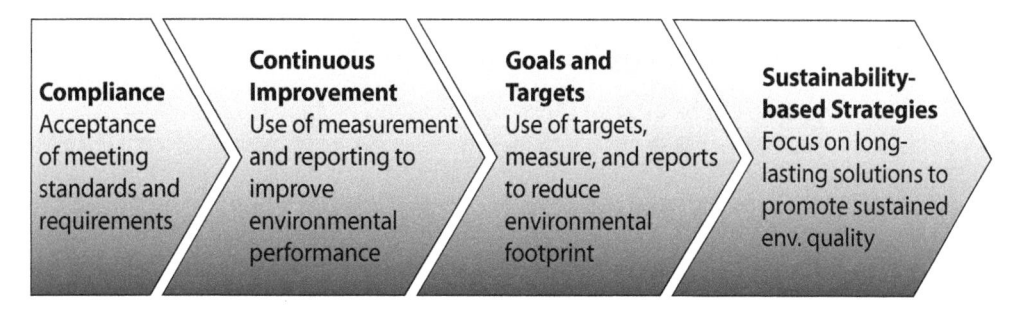

FIGURE 6.11 | Evolution of Environmental Stewardship.
Source: U.S. Environmental Protection Agency Environmental Stewardship Staff Committee (2005).

evolution to a "focus on long-standing solutions to promote sustained environmental quality. Environmental stewardship is also attractive since it allows private entities to participate in achieving sustainable environmental results" (U.S. EPA Environmental Stewardship Staff Committee, 2005).

Tools for Sustainability

There are numerous options available for organizations that wish to incorporate principles of sustainability within their operations or strategy. These options range from tools such as EMS and total quality environmental management (TQEM) to process evaluators such as sustainable value stream mapping. A brief discussion of these tools and processes follows next. Depending upon the type of organization, these tools and processes can be employed at various stages of the path toward sustainability.

Environmental Management System

EMS is a tool used to manage an organization's environmental programs in a planned, systematic, and documented way. It is a "continual cycle of planning, implementing, reviewing and improving the processes and actions taken by an organization to meet its business and environmental goals" (EMS, n.d.).

How to Develop an EMS

An EMS is usually built on the plan-do-check-act cycle (PDCA cycle). The diagram in Figure 6.12 illustrates this process. The first step is to develop an environmental policy. The next step in the process is planning the EMS and then implementing the EMS. The last step in the process concerns checking the EMS using system checks and controls. The EMS is a process of continual improvement whereby an organization is constantly reviewing and revising the system.

- *Plan:* Planning, including identifying environmental aspects and establishing goals
- *Do:* Implementing, including training and operational controls
- *Check:* Checking, including monitoring and corrective action
- *Act:* Reviewing, including progress reviews and acting to make needed changes to the EMS (EMS, n.d.).

The EMS can be used for most organizations, ranging from traditional manufacturing to services to governmental agencies. Some of the key elements of EMS are as follows:

- A policy statement that defines the organization's commitment to the environment
- Identification of significant environmental impacts of the products and services
- Development of objectives and targets for setting the environmental goals

- Implementation of plans to meet objectives and targets
- Training to get employees on board
- Management review

The EMS can result in numerous benefits in both business and environmental areas. It can do the following:

> improve environmental performance, enhance compliance, prevent pollution and conserve resources, reduce/mitigate risks, attract new customers and markets, increase efficiency, reduce costs, enhance employee morale, enhance the image with the public, regulators, lenders, and investors, and achieve/improve employee awareness of environmental issues and responsibilities. (EMS, n.d.)

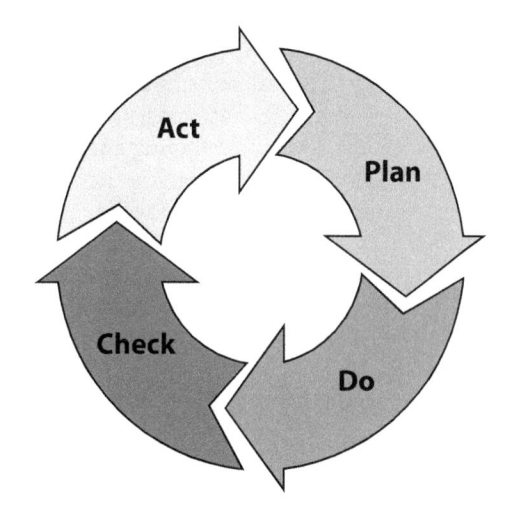

FIGURE 6.12 | Plan-Do-Check-Act Cycle. *Source:* http://en.wikipedia.org/wiki/File:PDCA_Cycle.svg

However, any such system has its set of associated costs, which include costs of internal resources, costs for training of personnel, costs for technical resources, and so on.

TOTAL QUALITY ENVIRONMENTAL MANAGEMENT

There have been other systems that deserve mention. One, in particular, is the TQEM, a process for applying total quality management approaches to corporate environmental strategies. The TQEM was created by the Global Environmental Management Initiative (GEMI), a coalition of 26 companies, including IBM, AT&T, and Kodak. There are four basic elements of TQEM:

1. *Customer identification:* Customer preferences determine environmental quality. The internal customers comprise the company's employees, and the external customers comprise buyers, environmental groups, and the general public.
2. *Continuous improvement:* Both the management and the employees of a company should work toward the improvement of environmental performance.
3. *Doing the job right the first time:* To eliminate environmental risks, the employees should isolate and get rid of potential environmental problems.
4. *A systems approach:* All components of the TQEM system need to be designed to work together to achieve desired goals ("TQEM," n.d.).

In its TQEM primer, GEMI stated that to analyze and condense information, the TQEM tools—such as the cause and effect diagram, the Pareto chart, the control charts, flowcharts, and histograms—can be used ("TQEM: The Primer," 1993).

Sustainable Value Stream Mapping

Several metrics are used to measure environmental performance, such as energy use, water use, and air emissions, that are not optimized in a lean process. Value stream mapping analyzes the proportion of process time that added value. However, this tool does not address resources and waste. To fill this gap, Simons and Mason (2002) developed sustainable value stream mapping by adding a metric (supply chain carbon dioxide divided by the market weight of the product) to the mapping process. For example, Simons and Mason (2002) applied this process tool to food supply chains and recommended producing food closer to the point of consumption (Venkat & Wakeland, 2006).

Sustainable Operating System

The SOS is a process that organizations can use to prioritize their goals to achieve sustainability. In this manner, SOS is akin to a process that lets organizations examine the business case for sustainability on a topic-by-topic basis (Blackburn, 2007). There are four elements to an SOS: (1) the drivers, (2) the efficient enablers, (3) the pathway elements, and (4) the evaluators.

The drivers make sure that the organization is motivated toward sustainability continuously. The main driver is the champion or the leader who puts sustainability on the business agenda and gets the dialogue started. Another important driver is to sell sustainability to the management. Since sustainability is a vague term with numerous connotations, this term must be defined clearly and could be translated into a sustainability policy. The last drivers are the reward and accountability mechanisms meant to keep the focus and the motivation on achieving sustainability objectives (Blackburn, 2007).

The efficient enablers allow the organization to assume its sustainability efforts efficiently. The core team and a deployment team are essential to the organizational structure needed in this process. In addition, deployment and integration are the other efficient enablers needed to spread sustainability throughout the organization (Blackburn, 2007).

For the pathway elements, each organization needs to develop its SOS standards. These could range from previously set standards like OSHAS (Occupational Health and Safety Assessment Series), ISO 9001 or 14001, The Natural Step, and so on. A set of priorities is also needed to sift through the numerous possible actions toward sustainability (Blackburn, 2007).

Three elements of the evaluators assist an organization in keeping track of its progress. These are as follows: creating goals and metrics, measuring and reporting progress, and engaging stakeholders and attaining feedback (Blackburn, 2007).

An organization ought to notice a substantial effect once the four elements of the SOS are documented, and the process is operating within a continuous PDCA cycle (Blackburn, 2007).

SUSTAINABILITY BALANCED SCORECARD

The SBSC is based on the balanced scorecard (BSC), a management tool proposed by Kaplan and Norton (1996). The BSC is a tool for organizations that seek to manage the demands of various stakeholders and translate strategies into action. The BSC contains four perspectives:

1. *The financial perspective:* Measures the financial gains provided to its shareholders
2. *The customer perspective:* Focuses on customer needs and satisfaction
3. *The internal perspective:* Focuses on the performance of the key internal processes
4. *The organization learning:* Focuses on the organization's people and infrastructure (Kaplan & Norton, 1996).

The SBSC provides a broader scope by integrating all three dimensions of sustainability. In addition to the four perspectives of the BSC, a fifth perspective can be included to address stakeholder issues. Since the BSC contains both financial and non-financial aspects, it also has the potential to address sustainability management. However, the BSC is only a tool, and it is still imperative to define a sustainability policy and strategy.

Hence, the SBSC offers corporations an opportunity to translate sustainability vision and strategies into action. In addition, the SBSC provides the integration of environmental and social aspects and objectives into the core management of companies (Bieker, 2003).

CIRCULAR ECONOMY

Our current economy is linear: materials are extracted from Earth, used to make products, and the waste is then thrown back into the environment. The basic concept of a circular economy is simple: stop waste from being produced in the first place.

There are three basic design principles in a circular economy:

- *Eliminate waste and pollution:* Waste and pollution should be viewed as design flaws rather than inevitable by-products of manufactured products. A change in this mindset, accompanied by new materials and technology, can ensure that waste and pollution are not created in the first instance.
- *Circulate products and materials:* Design products to be reused, repaired, and remanufactured. Keep food and packaging in circulation so that these do not end up in landfills.
- *Regenerate nature:* There is no concept of waste in nature. Everything is food for something else—a fallen leaf feeds the forest. Natural resources can be enhanced by returning nutrients to the soil and other systems.

A basic premise of a circular economy is the transition to renewable energy and materials. The circular economy decouples economic activity away from the consumption of finite resources. The current, linear system is essentially a "take-make-waste" system: how we manage resources, make and use products, and what is done with the materials after manufacture and consumption. It is also similar to a systems approach, like the earlier approaches, that tackles global challenges of climate change, pollution, and biodiversity. The circular economy provides a way to transform the current throwaway economy into one in which waste would be eliminated, resources would be circulated, and nature would be regenerated.

EXAMPLE: RENAULT, EUROPE'S FIRST CIRCULAR ECONOMY FACTORY FOR VEHICLES

Renault is a pioneer of the circular economy in the automotive industry. They aim to extend the life of vehicles and components and keep materials in use, reducing the use of virgin materials. Renault has achieved this aim in different parts of the manufacturing process by:

- remanufacturing vehicle components such as gearboxes and turbo compressors
- increasing recycled plastic content
- creating a second life for electric batteries

In late 2020, Groupe Renault established their Refactory, Europe's first dedicated circular economy factory for vehicles and mobility. This Refactory is located in Flins, about 40 km west of Paris, and will serve as the new hub for Groupe Renault's circular economy activities. The 237-hectare factory complex will be developed between 2021 and 2024 and will support circular economy innovation across the entire life cycle of vehicles. The top-line ambition for the Refactory is to create mobility solutions with a negative CO_2 balance by 2030 while at the same time generating employment for 3,000 people.

Circular economy at Refactory

The complex will comprise an ecosystem of four interconnected and complementary areas as listed below:

1. *Extend the life of vehicles—"Retrofit":* The goal is to recondition vehicles, thereby converting them to less carbon-intense versions. One option being considered is to include a specialist 3D printing service for manufacturing rare parts.
2. *Solutions for the production, storage, and management of green energies— "Re-energy":* Here, the goal is to optimize the first life of batteries, give used batteries a second life, manage end-of-life batteries, and explore new energy sources such as hydrogen.
3. *Optimize the management of resources to support the ecosystem—"Re-cycle":* The goal is to incorporate the dismantling of end-of-life vehicles, remanufacturing parts, and reusing and recycling materials.
4. *Promote innovation and knowledge sharing—"Re-start":* The goal here is to accelerate research and disseminate knowledge about the circular economy (The Circular Economy, 2020).

Conclusion

Numerous strategies and frameworks are available to organizations committed to pursuing sustainability. From thinking perspectives of natural capitalism to The Natural Step, from design parameters of industrial ecology to C2C and biomimicry, from tools such as EMS to SOS and processes such as sustainable value stream mapping to SBSC, there exist a comprehensive set of strategies available to examine the impact of activities on the environment, the economy, and the community.

Keywords

- Cradle-to-Cradle (C2C)
- Environmental management system (EMS)
- Four system conditions Industrial ecology
- Ladder of sustainability Life cycle assessment (LCA)
- Plan-do-check-act cycle (PDCA cycle)
- Shareholder value
- Sustainability Balanced Scorecard (SBSC)
- Sustainable operating system (SOS)
- Sustainable value creation
- Sustainable value stream mapping
- Total quality environmental management (TQEM)

Discussion Questions

1. What are the four drivers and the four quadrants of the sustainable value framework? Can you think of examples of companies in each of the four quadrants?
2. List the seven rungs of sustainability. Discuss which rungs might be the easiest and the hardest to attain.
3. In terms of natural capitalism, how can we redesign systems and incentives so that more value is placed on natural resources rather than industrial products?
4. Can you think of an application of industrial ecology within your community? Within your college or university?
5. Brainstorm to conduct a preliminary LCA of bottled water (plastic).
6. How can a computer manufacturer use the C2C principles to design a laptop?
7. Of the ten biomimicry principles listed, which ones can you apply to your daily life? Can you research any other company that has incorporated biomimicry principles into the design of their products?
8. There are three types of systems listed under systems thinking. Can you think of any organization moving from Type II to Type III?
9. Research your local or city government to determine if they use a form of EMS in their daily operations.

10. Of all the tools and processes mentioned in the last section of this chapter, which one might have the greatest applicability at your workplace? Discuss.
11. Use the four system conditions of The Natural Step to examine some everyday actions. For example:
    - Buying a latte in a cup from the corner cafe
    - Buying a pair of sneakers
    - Purchasing a new laptop
    - Getting a new car

Recommended Websites

- Biomimicry 3.8 – biomimicry.net/
- United States Environmental Protection Agency – www.epa.gov
- Natural Capitalism – www.natcap.org

CHAPTER 7

Role of the Consumer

LEARNING OBJECTIVES

By the end of this chapter, you should be able to do the following:

- » Discuss consumption and its link to ecosystem services.
- » Evaluate the link between consumption and the environment.
- » Detail sustainable food, drink, housing, clothing, and transportation choices.
- » Explain the role of consumers.
- » Discuss the ecological footprint and compute the carbon footprint.
- » Examine the future of consumption.

CHAPTER OVERVIEW

This chapter explores the role of consumers. As the global drivers of population and affluence increase consumption, there is more and more stress on the limited natural resources. What is the role of individuals, as consumers, in making sustainable choices in the categories that have the greatest ecological impact: food, drink, housing, and transportation? How does one go from reckless consumption toward a more sustainable consumption? Our choices as consumers are some of the most powerful ways we have of communicating to companies what we buy and what we condone. Furthermore, how can businesses assist in promoting sustainable consumption?

LIMITS TO CONSUMPTION

The average U.S. citizen consumes 18 tons of natural resources per person annually and generates an even higher volume of waste. One of the first economists to analyze consumption was John Kenneth Galbraith (1958), whose article "How Much Should a Country Consume?" called for analysis into problems that might be caused by consumption. Herman Daly (1999) stated that since energy resources are limited, there ought to be limits on consumption. Daly's (1999) work was important since it linked economic growth to a decline in well-being that came from social and environmental sacrifices made in the pursuit of growth. The theoretical work suggests that consumption must be viewed in its social and ecological context.

GLOBAL DRIVERS

Consumption around the world is driven by population growth and economic development and will rise as consumers in emerging economies demand goods and services. The world population hit the 7 billion mark in November 2011, and it is anticipated to reach 9.5 billion by 2050 (World Population Clock). Around 60 percent of gross domestic product (GDP) is from consumer spending on goods and services. The projected rise in the GDP of emerging countries like China, India, and Brazil is expected to increase the number of middle-class consumers. According to figures by Goldman Sachs, about 70 million people each year enter into an income equivalent to between $6,000 and $30,000 in purchasing power. If this trend continues, the middle class will comprise almost 80 percent of the world's population (O'Neill, 2008). There is now an emergence of the *global middle class*. The combination of two forces—(1) globalization and (2) economic integration—gives consumers increased access to products and services.

However, there is an inherent inequality. The market pressure created by affluent spending and consumption comes at a price wherein many are excluded. Currently, 4 billion people earn less than $3,000 USD per year. Expenditure on food tends to dominate the budgets of these low-income consumers. With a rise in the income levels, the amount spent on food often declines, the amount spent on transportation and telecommunication rises, and the amount spent on housing remains relatively constant. For example, low-income consumers comprise 95 percent of the population in Africa, which incur 71 percent of expenditure (Hammond, Kramer, Katz, & Walker, 2007). According to estimates by the World Wildlife Fund (WWF), three planets would be required were everyone to consume like the average citizen from the United Kingdom, and five planets to live like the average North American (WWF, 2006).

However, this consumerism does not necessarily translate to happiness. The New Economics Foundation's (WBCSD, 2008) *Happy Planet Index* discovered that people can live happy lives without using more than their "fair share" of the Earth's resources. No country combines high GDP with low life satisfaction. However, many less affluent countries achieve high life satisfaction (WBCSD, 2008). This contradicts the popular notion that money (and consumption) can buy happiness.

LINK TO EARTH'S ECOSYSTEMS

Global consumption has a direct linkage to the Earth's ecosystems, two-thirds of which are in decline. According to the Millennium Ecosystem Assessment (MA), 60 percent of nature's essential resources are degraded (WBCSD, 2008). In addition, almost 30 percent of the Earth's terrestrial area has been turned into urban areas or farms (WBCSD/Earthwatch Institute/World Resources Institute/International Union for the Conservation of Nature, 2006). Almost one-third of the Earth's plants and animals have been extinct since 1970 (WWF, 2006). Approximately 10 percent to 30 percent of mammal, bird, and amphibian species are threatened with extinction (IUCN, 2007). Studies indicate that current extinction rates could increase by a factor of 10 (WBCSD, 2008).

Biodiversity loss and changes to ecosystem services come from a set of direct drivers: habitat change, climate change, invasive alien species, and pollution (WBCSD, 2008). The sobering fact is that despite all the technological advances, scientists have not been able to create soil or seeds or life. For this reason alone, consumption needs to be curtailed and contained.

ECOLOGICAL IMPACT

According to the One Planet Business report, the highest levels of ecological impact are on food and drink, followed by household equipment and housing. Food, transportation, and housing have the most significant impacts (WWF UK, 2006). Housing uses the most materials and energy (WWF UK, 2006). For this reason, food, transportation, and housing will be discussed in greater detail in the next section.

Patterns of consumption levels vary considerably by geography, income, and demographics. Sustainability challenges also vary markedly per type of economy (see Figure 7.1). Though poorer countries emit the least amount of greenhouse gases (GHGs), they are most vulnerable to the loss of biodiversity and ecosystems. They are also vulnerable to flooding, reduced access to clean, fresh water, and health and social problems (Sustainable Consumption Research Exchanges, 2008). Affluent consumers in wealthy nations need to be aware of their impacts, especially on the disadvantaged populations across the globe.

Type of Economy	Example Countries	Main Sustainability Challenge
Consumer	United States, Japan, Western Europe	Dramatically lowering resource use while maintaining economic output (Factor 10)
Emerging	China, Southeast Asia	Leapfrogging to sustainable structures of consumption and production without copying Western examples
Developing	African countries, some in South America	Developing dedicated solutions for the "low income segment of the population," providing a basis for sustainable growth

FIGURE 7.1 | Sustainable Consumption Challenges.
Source: SCORE! (2008)

Consumption Choices

According to Figure 7.2, the highest impact is in the categories of food, drink, and housing. Other categories of significant impact include clothing, recreation, hotels/restaurants, and transportation (WBCSD, 2008).

Given that most of the expenditures are on food, drink, housing, clothing, and transportation, it is worthwhile to explore these choices in more detail. How can consumers make more informed and sustainable choices in these primary areas of impact?

Food and Drink

There is a synergy that exists in the sense that what is good for an individual is ultimately good for society and good for the world. Food is fuel for the body. How humans feel is directly related to what they eat. In a society, there needs to be demand for organically grown fruits and vegetables. At the same time, farmers who are practicing sustainable ways of farming by conserving water and reducing the use of pesticides and synthetic fertilizers need to be supported. While it is tempting to grab convenient, packaged foods, eating fresh, healthy, and organic food is healthier and more sustainable.

Produce

Human bodies require five to nine servings of fruits and vegetables per day, but often that produce is exposed to chemicals in the form of pesticides and fertilizers. The best choice is to eat organic produce since it is grown without synthetic pesticides, fertilizers, antibiotics, or added hormones. As a result, it contains one-third of the pesticides found in conventional produce. The chapter on food (Chapter 3) listed the fruits and vegetables that are most exposed to pesticides, and the "Clean 15" list contained the fruits and vegetables that were exposed to an average of two pesticides. Another trend is to buy locally from farmers' markets or local produce stands. Food that needs to be transported long distances is usually treated with fungicides and shipped before it is fully ripened. *Food miles* refers to how long the food has traveled before it is consumed. There are benefits to buying local food, and a good option is to join a community-supported agriculture (CSA) group in the local area. These CSA farms charge members a fee to purchase shares of each season's harvest. The website www.localharvest.org can be used to find a local CSA group.

Meat and Poultry

Beef, chicken, pork, and lamb compose the main portion of most meals. There has been a call for eating lower on the food chain, and there are good reasons for this argument. The commercialization and mass production of meat has lowered the price of meat. Still, the risks of foodborne illnesses such as E. coli, Salmonella, Campylobacter, and Listeria monocytogenes have gone up. Ground meat is especially vulnerable since it is derived from more than one animal. In addition, hormones and antibiotics are routinely given to animals to promote growth, and these residues stay in the meat after processing. Animals suffer severe

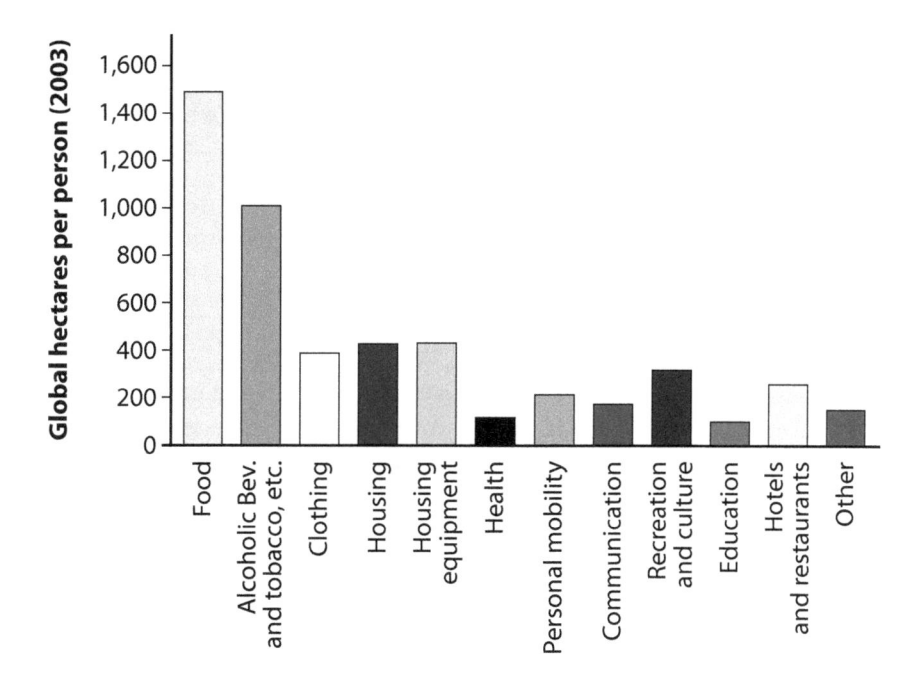

FIGURE 7.2 | Ecological Footprint Per US $1 Million.
Source: WBCSD (2008)

stress when raised in industrial settings. Oftentimes, the animals in feedlots are cramped, surrounded by waste, and fed an unnatural diet. Choose free-range meat since it comes from animals raised in pastures without hormones and antibiotics. Meats labeled as grass-fed are a good choice since the animals are raised on pasturelands and stored grasses. For poultry and eggs, some labels state *freefarmed*, cage-free, or free-range, implying that the bird was given some outdoor access. In the absence of other labels, look for meat labeled certified organic.

Seafood

Fish is considered a good source of protein and omega-3 fatty acids, but heavy metal contamination is a concern when eating seafood. In addition, since the advent of commercial fishing, the oceans are being fished out at an alarming and unsustainable rate. Wild fish caught at sea contain mercury and polychlorinated biphenyls (PCBs). Mercury builds up in the fish muscle, so it cannot be removed. Since mercury can harm brain development, pregnant women are advised not to eat fish. Commercial fishing has plundered the oceans, and an estimated 75 percent of the world's fish species are close to collapse. The worldwide populations of tuna, swordfish, cod, and halibut have been reduced by 90 percent. Look for seafood certified by the Marine Stewardship Council (MSC) (Garlough, Gordon, & Bauer, 2008). About half of the world's supply of fish now comes from fish farms. Though farming is a feasible solution to the falling wild fish populations, there are certain challenges present. Some cages or net pens are overcrowded, and antibiotics or anti-parasite pesticides can spill over into the waterways. Farmed fish can escape from farms and spread disease to the wild fish and interbreed, causing a dilution of the gene pool (Garlough, et al., 2008).

Dairy

Milk, cheese, and yogurt are enjoyed in numerous diets. However, using hormones and chemicals in cows' milk is a concern. Recombinant bovine growth hormone (rBGH) is a genetically engineered hormone injected into cows to increase milk production. This hormone is of concern since it never went through long-term safety testing by the U.S. Food and Drug Administration (FDA). A study in Canada found that rats absorbed this hormone; hence, rBGH was not approved in Canada. rBGH also stimulates the production of IGF-1, an insulin growth factor, which can cause cell division and tumor growth. The United States is one of the few countries where dairy farmers can use rBGH. Certified organic milk is usually free of rBGH (Garlough, et al., 2008).

Water

Water is a basic and essential need for all living beings, and it is the most plentiful substance in our bodies and on the planet. Indeed, the longest a human can survive without water is only three days. There has been much discussion of the environmental damage from bottled water. First, the water inside bottles is not regulated as much as tap water, and there is no saying where the water comes from. In many cases, this bottled water is more contaminated than tap water. In addition, bottled water contains a host of issues. The flexible plastic water bottles leach phthalates, chemicals that mimic the female hormone estrogen. Estrogenic endocrine disrupters are linked to health problems for both men (low sperm counts, lower energy, and decreased sex drive) and women (early puberty and increased rates of breast and ovarian cancers). In terms of environmental costs, bottled water costs more to transport as 1.5 billion gallons of fuel are needed per year, whereas tap water is delivered through an energy-efficient infrastructure. The most damaging environmental concern comes from the manufacture of 1.5 million plastic bottles (from petrochemicals) every year, and most of these bottles end up in landfills (Horn, 2006). A sustainable solution is filtered water, whereby a water filter is attached to the faucet to eliminate impurities. There are numerous water filters in the market, ranging from simple carbon filters and faucet-mounted filters to expensive systems like reverse osmosis systems and ultraviolet light filters.

Coffee and Tea

The coffee plant is a rainforest shrub with red berries that mainly grows in Africa and Latin America. Traditionally, coffee plants were grown in shade, under the rainforest canopy, which served as a habitat for migratory birds. Most of these plantations are being moved to full sun farms as the production increases fivefold. Coffee plantations are also referred to as farming sweatshops since the workers and farmers are paid very little for the harvest. In the early 1990s, coffee producers received 30 percent of the total coffee income, but this has dropped to 8 percent or less. As a consumer, look for the certified organic label to ensure that the beans were not treated with synthetic pesticides. Fairtrade-certified coffee is purchased directly from producers or cooperatives, and this practice states that the growers get a higher percentage of their share. Lastly, it is better for the environment to purchase coffee that is *shade grown*, and the two certifications are Rainforest Alliance and Bird Friendly (Garlough, et al., 2008). Tea production is also subject to similar problems of pesticide usage and low wages for pickers. Though a handful of brands own 90 percent of the market, organic and fair-trade certified teas are increasingly appearing in health food stores and specialty stores.

Beer and Wine

Beer is made from barley, hops, some yeast, and perhaps wheat. The commercial production of these grains involves using herbicides, insecticides, fungicides (hops are susceptible to fungus), and fertilizers. Certified organic beer is made with 95 percent organic ingredients, and the beer must be processed in breweries that do not use harsh acids or chemicals for cleaning. Organic beer sales increased by 40 percent in 2005 to $19 billion. Purchasing local beer is also a sustainable choice, and microbreweries are gaining popularity.

Conventionally grown wine grapes are also subject to fumigants, insecticides, fungicides, and herbicides. The pesticide methyl bromide has been used to kill insects, weeds, and nematodes before the planting of vines. Organic wine is made with 95 percent organic ingredients and does not contain added sulfites. Some wines are also organically processed without synthetic chemical agents. Depending on the location, locally grown wines might also be available (Garlough, et al., 2008).

HOUSING

A home is a big investment in financial terms, and the housing sector uses the most materials and energy. Home represents a space where leisure time is spent with families and friends. However, it also represents the space where sustainability ideals can be put into practice. Small changes such as filtering the water, recycling, composting, using natural products in lawncare and cleaning, and using energy-efficient appliances can all save money and make homes more sustainable.

Better Housekeeping

When homes are cleaned, the idea is to eliminate dirt, grime, and other germs. What is surprising is the number of chemicals and toxins hidden within the very cleaners that are used. The most hazardous are drain cleaners, oven cleaners, toilet bowl cleaners, and other products that contain chlorine or ammonia. In addition, fumes created by chemicals in cleaning products contribute to indoor air pollution.

One of the most common ways to incorporate sustainability at home is to increase the home's efficiency. Some of the simple steps to accomplish this goal include sealing the cracks around doors and windows with sealant to prevent heat loss, turning down the thermostat since a 2-degree change can result in 8 percent savings in heating or cooling bills, replacing lightbulbs with compact fluorescent lightbulbs since these are much more efficient than the traditional incandescent bulbs, turning off the lights and appliances when not in use, conserving water by taking quick showers instead of long baths, purchasing recycled paper and being prudent about buying disposable products, and looking for the Energy Star label when purchasing appliances (Horn, 2006).

For cleaning homes, chemically laden cleaners can be skipped, and almost all cleaning can be accomplished by using baking soda, white vinegar, lemon juice, borax, liquid soap, and so on. As an alternative, nontoxic cleaners such as Method and Seventh Generation can be purchased. Most suburban homes have a yard that, in the United States, consumes more than one-third of all the pesticides in the world. A sustainable option is to convert the yard into an organic garden. Use natural fertilizers and pull out weeds by hand (Horn, 2006).

A home can also be redesigned to be more sustainable. Nowadays, most retailers carry products that are green by design. An increasing number of design professionals, from interior designers to architects, understand this concept and are willing to employ the principles in home design. At first thought, it might seem that green home goods will be expensive. However, many green options are designed to save money in the long run. Some of the simple tips in designing or redesigning a home to make it more sustainable or green include purchasing Forest Stewardship Council (FSC) certified wood furniture, choosing natural fibers for upholstery and carpets, purchasing window shades made from bamboo or wood, using organic mattresses and comforters, and so on (Garlough, et al., 2008).

Modern appliances are designed to make life easier—from dishwashers to air conditioners and refrigerators—and it is hard to imagine a house without these appliances. However, these appliances also burden the planet in terms of their electricity consumption. At present, the current U.S. household dedicates 20 percent of its energy bill to the powering of appliances and electronics. In addition, the current U.S. household emits 9,900 pounds of carbon dioxide annually. Some tips for appliances and electronics include choosing Energy Star products and appliances, installing a fan to cool the house, defrosting the refrigerator regularly, checking that the air purifier does not emit ozone, washing clothes in cold water cycles, drying clothes on a clothesline or drying rack, using rechargeable batteries and recycling old batteries, turning off the computer when done with work, using power strips in rooms with many appliances and switching off the power strip when appliances are not in use, disposing of e-waste responsibly, reusing or recycling, donating old computers to nonprofit organizations, and using LED or solar powered flashlights (Garlough, et al., 2008).

Sustainable Building and Retrofitting

Many architects and contractors are turning to green construction to satisfy the demand for green homes. Indeed, a new home can be designed in such a way as to be green, incorporating issues like size, building materials, ventilation, insulation, and energy efficiency. However, many of these elements can be incorporated into the remodeling of a home. From a sustainability point of view, it is better to remodel an existing home than to build a brand new one.

The first basic step is to insulate for efficiency. Installing a programmable thermostat can minimize energy usage by shutting off when the house is unoccupied and setting the home into varying temperature zones. Smart landscaping can help with energy savings. In a colder climate, planting a row of trees can block cold winds, and in the summer, a tree can be positioned to block the summer sun. Shades can be used to cool the house in summer and opened to warm the house with natural sunlight in winter. Another idea to cool the house is to open the windows on the northern side of the house. To warm the house in winter, close off unused rooms. Covered porches or awnings can reduce cooling bills along with the installation of fans. The installation of storm windows can help with insulation in cooler climates (Horn, 2006).

The second step is to use sustainable building materials: Ceramic tiles or natural stone flooring are more sustainable options than carpets or vinyl. Solid wood cabinetry is a better choice for kitchen cabinets since particleboard is treated with formaldehyde. Some alternative building materials have come on the market in the past few years, such as concrete, modular construction, mortarless blocks, straw bale with cement stucco skin, and used and recycled materials from other construction projects (Horn, 2006).

The third step is to look at power sources and determine whether the house can be retrofitted with renewable power sources such as solar, wind, and geothermal. In the case of solar power, a home can meet its hot water needs with a solar panel on the roof. A more extensive solar array can meet all the power needs of a home. Residential wind turbines are rather expensive, ranging from $3,000 to $5,000. But these costs can be offset if they are used for powering entire communities. In the case of geothermal, heat pumps can be installed that cool the house in summer and heat it in the winter.

CLOTHING

The process of clothing manufacturing has many environmental implications. Polyester is made from petroleum, and the required crude oil to make it increases the demand and, with it, additional emissions. Cotton has a significant environmental impact, as it has been subject to pesticides and insecticides. Much of the cotton is exported to China and other countries where it is woven and assembled. Each year, Americans purchase more than 1 billion garments made in China: an average of four pieces of clothing for every U.S. citizen (Claudio, 2007).

Americans throw away 68 pounds of clothing per year. Much clothing is donated to charities, but only one-fifth is ever used again (Claudio, 2007). Instead, the charities sell clothing to textile recyclers at 5 to 7 cents per pound. One company, Trans-Americas Trading Company, recycles used clothing into fiber used to stuff upholstery.

Some companies have sought a niche in *eco-fashion*. The International Organization for Standardization (ISO) defines eco-fashion as "identifying the general environmental performance of a product within a product group based on its whole life-cycle to contribute to improvements in key environmental measures and to support sustainable consumption patterns" (Claudio, 2007). Patagonia makes fleece clothing from plastic soda bottles, estimating that they have saved more than 86 million bottles from landfills.

TRANSPORTATION

It is said that a car is the second most expensive item for a household after the purchase of a home. The transportation choices have a direct linkage to the carbon footprint. One of the most impactful decisions is to live near work. Commuting to and from work is expensive in terms of time, energy, and the environment. A job closer to home can lead to a better quality of life. Some companies offer alternatives to commuting such as working from home, teleconferencing, etc. If a commute to work is unavoidable, consider taking public transportation since it is much more fuel efficient than driving alone. Some communities or organizations also offer carpooling as an alternative (Horn, 2006).

There are some ways to keep cars running more efficiently. Some ways to boost gas mileage are to check that the tires are properly inflated, get a tune-up, replace air filters, and take off the roof rack when not in use (Horn, 2006). When in the market for a new car, consider the electric or hybrid versions, the alternative fuel option, and the flexible fuel option.

- *Electric cars:* Electric cars have experienced a surge in demand, partly due to federal regulations and partly due to increased production by car manufacturers. The United States is the latest country to pass the tipping point, with 5 percent of new car sales powered by electricity, a threshold signaling the start of mass EV adoption. Companies ranging from BMW to Ford to Volkswagen are each targeting 50 percent or more of their global sales to be fully electric by the end of the decade. The challenges to electric cars are universal: lack of public charging stations, the limited supply and the high price tag of the vehicles, and the lack of public knowledge. However, with mass adoption, these challenges might be addressed sooner rather than later (Randall, 2022).
- *Hybrids:* Some countries, especially in Europe, were quicker to adopt plug-in hybrids that have smaller batteries backed by a gasoline-powered engine. Virtually all automobile manufacturers are now offering EV, PHEV, and hybrid models. EV and hybrid versions generally cost more, upwards of $3,500 to $6,000 more, than a conventional version. There are tax credits and carpool lanes offered to incentivize the sale of hybrids, but the demand for these vehicles will depend on the consumer demand and the price of gasoline.
- *Flexible fuel tanks:* Most General Motors (GM), Ford, and Chrysler cars and trucks can run on a mix of 85 percent ethanol and 15 percent gasoline (E85), gasoline only, or a mixture of the two. Though about 2.3 million of these cars are on the road, only a few use this option due to the difficulty of finding fuel. There are only about 609 ethanol stations, and most of these are located in the Corn Belt region, with most being located in Minnesota.
- *Biodiesel:* This fuel is renewable and domestically produced. It can be manufactured from animal or vegetable fats, and it is safe and biodegradable. A blend of 20 percent biodiesel with 80 percent petroleum diesel can be used in conventional diesel engines. However, the engines require some modification if biodiesel were to be used in its pure form (Horn, 2006).

Role of Consumers

Given all this information on food, drink, housing, clothing, and transportation, it is still important to understand more about consumer attitudes and behaviors. There are many factors: availability, affordability, convenience, and force of habit (WBCSD, 2008).

There is rising awareness of environmental and social issues. About 96 percent of Europeans surveyed agreed that protecting the environment is important (Directorate of the Environment, 2008). Almost one in four U.S. adults agree with a set of values that includes "environmentalism, feminism, global issues and spiritual searching" (WBCSD, 2008). The people in this group are well educated, relatively affluent, and are the consumers likely to purchase hybrid cars (WBCSD, 2008).

Globally, a survey of consumer choice and environment in 14 countries found that consumers "feel empowered when it comes to the environment and are taking some action in their daily lives to reduce consumption and waste" (WBCSD, 2008). Another global survey also found that consumers are willing to act on environmental concerns. The largest rise in awareness came from U.S. consumers (WBCSD, 2008).

Furthermore, consumers in both rapidly developing and developed markets report that they would prefer to buy from companies with high reputations in environmental and social responsibility (Directorate of the Environment, 2008).

However, people do not always act on environmental and social concerns. A McKinsey survey globally found that 53 percent of consumers were concerned about environmental and social issues, and 13 percent were willing to pay more but currently did not do so (*The McKinsey Quarterly* from WBCSD, 2008).

Barriers to Change

What is the reason for the difference between what people say they are willing to do and their actual consumer behavior? The four most significant factors were as follows: (1) lack of understanding, (2) comfortable lifestyle/greed, (3) associated higher costs and taxes, and (4) the "tragedy of the commons." The last factor reflects an "I will if you will" mentality (WBCSD, 2008).

Some consumers are prone to the *rebound effect*—a tendency to use products *more* in response to efficiency improvements, reducing the expected benefits (Sussex Energy Group/UK Energy Research Centre, 2007). For example, consumers in the United States reportedly increase their use of air-conditioning by up to 50 percent when they switch to a green energy supply. Rebound effects have also been observed in home heating and personal transportation (WBCSD, 2008).

In addition, there also exists confusion around numerous labels and environmental claims. Some products are certified by a local or national authority that is internationally recognized and respected. Some of the examples of third-party labels include *organic* (e.g., U.S. Department of Agriculture [USDA], Rainforest Alliance, Soil Association), *healthy* (e.g., National Heart Foundation Approved, low glycemic index/gluten-free), *sourced from sustainable sources* (e.g., FSC, Sustainable Forestry Initiative [SFI], MSC), *dolphin friendly* (e.g., Greenseas), *ethically sourced* (e.g., Fairtrade), and *eco-friendly* (e.g., EU Flower) (WBCSD, 2008).

Still, labels help foster sustainable consumption. Many products designed to be environmentally responsible did not meet the basic expectations of the consumer (such as electric cars and recycled paper).

Consumers trust each other more than labels or any other source of information (WBCSD, 2008). While consumers do not trust brands, they believe in their purchasing power (WBCSD, 2008). Consumers are also turning to peer-published blogs on the Internet for information. It seems that companies need to be savvy to address the barriers to behavior change to effectively communicate the message of their products to the consumers.

Ecological Footprint and Carbon Footprint

By its very nature, human activity has an impact on the planet. However, the idea of sustainable consumption is that if we are mindful of our activities on the planet, we can make decisions to reduce our impact. The two tools most commonly used are the ecological footprint and the carbon footprint.

The ecological footprint, developed by Mathis Wackernagel and William Rees, examines the ecological capacity required to support the consumption of products ("Ecological Footprint," n.d.). In addition, it also measures the waste generated by this consumption. The ecological footprint of the commute from home to work can be calculated. In the same manner, it can be computed for an entire community or an organization.

The ecological footprint varies by development and consumption level. The largest ecological footprint belongs to the U.S. consumer, who uses about 24 acres to support their lifestyle. As a comparison, Germans have an ecological footprint of 13 acres compared to Indians, who have an ecological footprint of 2 ("Ecological Footprint," n.d.). Among the wealthier nations, the Europeans and the Japanese can serve as models because they have a high quality of life and footprints that are half the size of North Americans. Some of this is related to more efficient use of resources in Europe and Japan. This serves as a reminder that quality of life does not depend on large resource use ("Ecological Footprint," n.d.). For all global citizens to live an American or Canadian lifestyle, it would take "two more earths to satisfy everyone, three more still if population should double, and twelve earths altogether if worldwide standards of living should double over the next forty years" (Lovins, Lovins, & Hawken, 2000).

Humanity's combined footprint is more than the Earth's capacity. The challenge of sustainability is to find ways to create fulfilling lives while reducing our impact on the planet. The ecological footprint shows us how much we use so that we can make more sustainable choices.

A carbon footprint measures the impact of activities on the environment. The primary footprint measures the direct carbon dioxide emissions from travel choices and energy consumption. The consumer has direct control over these emissions. The secondary footprint is more complex since it measures indirect carbon dioxide emissions from the life cycle of the products used ("Carbon Footprint," n.d.). More consumption translates to a greater footprint. There are online calculators that let individuals and corporations estimate their footprint (see the appendix). Some of these calculators compute travel emissions by car or air; the other calculators can compute home emissions. Most carbon footprint calculator sites also provide simple tips to reduce the footprint from a consumer or business perspective. Please refer to the mini case at the end of this chapter to calculate a carbon footprint.

PROJECT DRAWDOWN

Project Drawdown is an organization devoted to finding solutions to help the world reach "drawdown"—the point in the future when levels of greenhouse gases in the atmosphere stop climbing and start to steadily decline, thereby stopping catastrophic climate change—as quickly, safely, and equitably as possible (drawdown.org). Project Drawdown published a book on climate solutions, edited by Paul Hawken, in 2017, promoting it as the most comprehensive set of climate solutions. The solutions, one hundred in number, offer substantive ways to reverse global warming. Most of these solutions can be found in energy, agriculture, forests, industries, buildings, transportation, and so on.

The publication lists different scenarios for CO_2 reductions. Drawdown Scenario 1 is roughly in line with a 2°C temperature rise by 2100, while Drawdown Scenario 2 is roughly in line with a 1.5°C temperature rise at the century's end.

The top ten solutions from Project Drawdown with the biggest potential impact as of 2022 are as follows in Figure 7.3:

Thorough descriptions of these and other areas are described on the site. For the individual consumer, what they eat, how they prepare and discard food, and family planning are areas one must consider. Increasing the availability of plant-based meat substitutes is one step in that direction. Burger King's "Impossible Whopper" is perhaps the most publicized foray into this area (Project Drawdown).

SOLUTION	SCENARIO 1 *	SCENARIO 2 *
Reduced food waste	88.50	102.20
Plant-rich diets	78.33	103.11
Family planning and education	68.90	68.90
Refrigerant management	57.15	57.15
Tropical forest restoration	54.45	85.14
Onshore wind turbines	46.95	143.56
Alternative refrigerants	42.73	48.75
Utility-scale solar photovoltaics	40.83	111.59
Clean cooking	31.38	76.34
Distributed solar photovoltaics	26.65	64.86

FIGURE 7.3 | Project Drawdown Top Ten Solutions.

FUTURE OF CONSUMPTION

Sustainable consumption is a systemic challenge in which all the players, from businesses to governments and consumers to civil society, have the power to effect change. Consumers need the support of businesses, governments, and NGOs to lead sustainable lifestyles. Businesses have a role to play since they can help define sustainable products and assist in mainstreaming sustainable consumption (WBCSD, 2006). Individuals can make a number of incremental improvements in the way they live. Although these differences may seem to make the smallest impact on the environment, the more people who practice living in an eco-friendly manner, the better.

The automobile and mode of transportation are a good place to start. The simple action of consolidating errands can reduce fuel. How often is it necessary to rush out to the grocery store for one item? A reduction in driving saves on fuel. What many consider a primitive mode of transport—the bicycle—for many in the world is the only way they can get around. Not only does it save on fuel, but it improves one's cardiovascular health. One can place a basket on the bike, lock it, and go anywhere without having to pay for parking.

The switch to alternative fuel vehicles is also a wise choice. Commuters want to go as far as possible on as little fuel as possible. Hybrid or electric vehicles have increased in popularity not only for their fuel efficiency but also for the reduction in emissions. Do the math: If gasoline goes for $4.00 per gallon and the vehicle is driven for 10,000 miles per year, a 20 mpg auto requires 500 gallons of fuel, while a 30 mpg auto requires 333 gallons. The difference of 167 gallons saves $668 per year. If the vehicle is driven for 15,000 miles, the savings would be over $1,000. The problem, at present, is that the increased cost of an EV or hybrid makes it difficult to justify the cost.

Public transportation obviously offers tremendous cost advantages where it is available. Public transit can save one individual an average of $9,700 annually based on July 2012 gasoline rates (American Public Transportation Association, 2012). As gasoline prices trend upward, these savings become larger in magnitude. The challenge is to find an efficient public transportation option that is both convenient and reliable.

An energy audit of a house is sometimes available from the local energy company. Heat and cooling may escape through poor windows and leaks in the walls and doors. Old furnaces are also less efficient, and a replacement can pay for itself in savings in only a few years. Half of the home energy expenses come from the heating and cooling, and a homeowner should make sure they have as tight a home as possible.

Home conversion to solar heating usually requires a costly retrofit; therefore, one would assume they would live in the home long enough to realize payback on the investment. However, in times of an energy crunch, the home may actually increase in value due to the savings in energy.

Conclusion

As individuals and consumers, we have a big role in sustainable consumption. Despite the popular myth of retail therapy, well-being is not necessarily correlated with high consumption. As discussed in this chapter, consumers in both developing and affluent nations have a responsibility to address consumption since we are losing Earth's basic ecosystem services at an unsustainable rate. Consumer choices have a significant impact based on the choices made in the consumption of food, drink, housing, clothing, and transportation. Though these are primary areas, sustainable choices can be extended to other areas such as recreation, health, communication, and education, among others. As shown by the *Happy Planet Index* (WBCSD, 2008), a high consumption level does not guarantee happiness. It might be time to fill life with value instead of stuff.

Keywords

- Biodiesel
- Carbon footprint
- Certified organic
- Consumption
- Drawdown Project
- Ecological footprint
- Ecological impact
- Ecosystems
- Electric cars
- Energy Star
- Fairtrade certified
- Flexible fuel
- Food miles
- Rainforest Alliance

Discussion Questions

1. What are the global drivers of consumption? What steps can be taken by affluent and emerging economies to curb consumption?
2. Of all the stresses on the earth's ecosystem, which one seems most pertinent? Discuss.
3. What sustainable choices can a consumer make in food and drink purchases? Which ones make the most sense to you?
4. Go to www.localharvest.org and find the CSA group closest to you.
5. Why is the common usage of antibacterials detrimental to the environment?
6. Refer to the information on household cleaners. Which product would you stop using, given the chemicals it contains?
7. What are some steps to increase the efficiency of a home?
8. What are some simple tips for appliances and electronics? Does your home contain any of these energy-saving appliances or electronics?
9. Use Google to find a carbon calculator to compute your carbon footprint (see also Chapter 11.) Compare your footprint to that of others in the class.

10. There are numerous electric cars and hybrids slated to enter the automotive market. Research some of these cars on the web and discuss which of these cars you would consider.
11. What role can businesses play in sustainable consumption? Can you think of a company that promotes such practices?
12. What do you think are the biggest hurdles for consumers when it comes to switching to more sustainable consumer habits?

Mini Case: Carbon Footprint

Three friends—Alyssa, James, and Xavier—were sitting in a café discussing their commuting choices and whether these choices were sustainable. Their discussion follows:

Alyssa: Okay, guys, I live with my parents, and I take the train to school. So in a sense, my footprint should be lowest, right?

James: But your parents have a massive house. It's almost 6,000 square feet! Can you imagine the energy that goes into heating the house in Chicago winters?

Alyssa: Well, you drive your car from the suburbs to the city for school every day! I cannot imagine that being good for the Earth.

Xavier: Guys, I have the best deal. I live in an apartment in the city and walk to school. Now that is a perfect solution.

James: Wait a minute, Xavier. You are an international student. Don't you, like, fly to Spain every month or so?

Xavier: I guess so. But I bet it's better than driving around everywhere.

Alyssa: Well, I hardly fly, and I don't even own a car, so I bet my lifestyle is the best.

Xavier: I would not be so sure. We see cars and airplanes emitting carbon dioxide, but a great deal of energy goes into homes.

Mini Case Questions

1. Alyssa lives in a 6,000-square-foot home with her parents and two siblings in a Chicago suburb. Calculate her home's carbon footprint.
2. James drives a 2010 Jeep Cherokee, and the annual mileage is about 12,000 miles. Calculate his vehicle's carbon footprint.
3. Xavier flies home to Madrid and back to Chicago for school four times a year. Calculate his airline carbon footprint.
4. Discuss the results with your classmates. Whose footprint is the largest? The smallest? Are the results surprising to you?

5. Please go to one of the following websites for the carbon footprint computations:

> *Cool Climate Network:* https://coolclimate.berkeley.edu/
> *The Nature Conservancy:* https://www.nature.org/en-us/
> *Terrapass:* www.terrapass.com/carbon-footprint-calculator/
> *Carbon Footprint:* www.carbonfootprint.com/calculator.aspx

Recommended Websites

- e-Stewards Recycler Finder – e-stewards.org/find-a-recycler/
- AutoGuide – www.hybridcars.com/index.php
- Local Harvest – www.localharvest.org/
- Organic.org – www.organic.org/
- World Business Council for Sustainable Development – www.wbcsd.org

APPENDIX

Top Ten Sustainable Steps

Greg Horn, in his book Living Green: A Practical Guide to Simple Sustainability, offers ten simple steps to becoming sustainable:

1. *Organic eating:* Organic food tastes better and is much healthier than regular, conventional food. In the United States, for each 1 percent increase in organic food consumption, pesticide and herbicide use are reduced by over 10 million pounds.
2. *Carbon neutral:* For a small sum of money, the carbon footprint can be offset. There are numerous carbon calculators, some of which will be discussed in Chapter 11.
3. *Recycling:* This step can cut the waste stream by up to 75 percent. An average U.S. consumer produces 1,609 pounds of waste per year. If all the glass, paper, and metal were recycled, it would save 162 million tons of materials going into landfills per year.
4. *Disposables:* Switching to a glass from a water bottle and a coffee mug from a Styrofoam cup would save $244 billion bottles and cups made of petrochemical-based plastics from ending up in landfills each year.
5. *Natural personal care:* Keep toxic chemicals off human bodies and out of the environment. A simple check: if something is not edible, it should not be applied to the body.

6. *Natural lawn care:* A suburban lawn uses six times the hazardous chemicals per acre than conventional farming. A switch to natural lawn care would save billions of pounds of synthetic fertilizers, pesticides, and herbicides from entering the environment.
7. *Green cleaners:* Each day, about 32 million pounds of chemicals are dumped down the drain from household cleaning chemicals. A switch to green alternatives keeps these chemicals out of the water supply.
8. *Filtered tap water:* The filtering process removes chlorine and fluoride and comes at a fraction of the cost of bottled water.
9. *Increased energy efficiency:* Insulation of homes and driving fuel-efficient cars, such as EVs and hybrids, can dramatically reduce the use of fossil fuels.
10. *Information:* A subscription to green news sources including blogs and podcasts helps in communication on sustainability resources, tips, and tools (Horn, 2006).

Household Cleaners

The following is a list of common household cleaners, the lurking chemicals, and the alternatives available.

All-Purpose cleaners: Some of these cleaners contain DEA and TEA, and others contain butyl cellosolve that is easily absorbed through the skin and can cause damage to kidneys, liver, and reproductive systems. Any product containing ammonia can cause respiratory irritation. As an alternative, buy natural all-purpose cleaners in a health store or make your own all-purpose cleaner by dissolving four tablespoons of baking soda in one quart of warm water.

Disinfectants: Most disinfectants contain pesticides to kill bacteria, and their effectiveness is questionable since these products cannot kill germs in the air. Most disinfectants contain APES that are hormone disruptors and Triclosan. A better option is to wash foods thoroughly before cooking and thaw meat in the refrigerator rather than on the countertop. Soapy water or white vinegar can be used to clean surfaces. Another alternative is to mix half a cup of borax with a gallon of hot water to disinfect.

Glass cleaners: The common window cleaners contain butyl cellosolve, a neurotoxin that can damage the liver, kidneys, and red blood cells. In addition, these cleaners may also contain ammonia that can irritate airways. As an alternative, glass cleaner can be made with a cup of water mixed with a quarter cup of white vinegar or a tablespoon of lemon juice.

Furniture polish: Many brands contain formaldehyde, a carcinogen, or petroleum distillates that can damage nerves. For dusting and polishing, combine one-half cup of white vinegar and a few drops of olive oil. Silver can be scrubbed with toothpaste to remove tarnish. Copper can be cleaned with a paste of salt and white vinegar, and brass can be cleaned with a paste made of one cup of flour, one cup of white vinegar, and one teaspoon of salt. Less toxic brands of furniture cleaners can also be purchased.

Toilet cleaners: Most cleaners contain corrosive agents that are irritating to the eyes, sinuses, and airways. Some cleaners also contain sodium bisulfate, which can trigger asthma attacks. For homemade cleaner, mix one cup of borax with one-quarter cup of white vinegar and let it sit for a few hours. Almost 99 percent of bacteria can be killed by ordinary vinegar.

Drain cleaners: The chemicals in these products are the most corrosive, containing sodium hydroxide and sodium hypochlorite, which can damage eyes and skin permanently and are lethal if ingested. Instead, keep drains clear by putting in metal or plastic screens available at hardware stores. In case of a clog, use a snake plumbing tool to remove the blockage. To disinfect drains, pour a cup of straight vinegar down twice a week.

Scrubs and cream cleansers: The abrasive agents in scrubs contain silica, which is harmful when inhaled, or chlorine bleach, which irritates airways. A paste of baking soda and water cleans stains on most countertops, showers, tubs, and toilets.

Soaps and detergents: For dishwashing liquids, choose clear gels since the dyes can be contaminated with lead or arsenic. For laundry detergents, choose fragrance-free and vegetable-based products. Stay clear of antibacterial detergents and products with bleach and harsh fragrances.

Cloth cleaners: Half of the trees cut in North America are used to make paper products. Wood pulp is also being sourced from South America and China. For home cleaning, use a cloth cleaner made from cotton since these can be used, washed, and reused. If paper products cannot be avoided, try to purchase recycled products (Garlough et al., 2008).

PERSONAL CARE

The following is a list of common personal hygiene products, the lurking chemicals, and available alternatives (Horn, 2006).

1. *Choose natural, organic fiber clothes:* Find clothes made from 100 percent natural fibers like cotton, silk, linen, hemp, or Tencel. Some examples of brands are Patagonia and Prana.

2. *Purchase chemical-free kids' clothing:* Avoid fire-retardant clothing that contains polybrominated Biphenyl ether (PDBE), which has been linked to development problems for the brain and thyroid. Buy bedding, diapers, and clothing made from organically grown fibers. For diapers, choose reusable brands like gDiapers that come with a flushable inner lining.

3. *Find a green dry cleaner:* Green dry cleaners are beginning to use nontoxic chemicals and other technologies to replace harmful chemicals such as PERC and hexane.

4. *Buy safe personal care products:* Though the adage, "Don't put it on your skin if you would not eat it" sounds shocking, it simply means that personal care items should be made from natural oils, herbs, vitamins, and minerals. The Food and Drug Administration (FDA) does not regulate cosmetics and

only gets involved if a product is proven to be hazardous. Some of the worst products in terms of chemical additives are as follows:

- Antiperspirants
- Sunscreens and sunblocks
- Soaps and shampoos
- Hair dyes and hair spray
- Toothpaste and mouthwash
- Lipstick
- Mascara
- Eye shadow, blush, and face powder
- Perfumes and aftershaves

5. *Filter shower and bath water:* Two-thirds of the daily chlorine exposure comes from showering. An inexpensive carbon filter attached to a showerhead can cut this exposure.

6. *Natural feminine hygiene products:* Tampons are made from rayon, a petrochemical-based fiber, or from cotton containing pesticide residues. Sanitary napkins also contain fibers bleached with dioxin. Choose reusable products like the silicone DivaCup or washable cloth sanitary napkins instead.

CHAPTER 8

Role of the Corporation

LEARNING OBJECTIVES

By the end of this chapter, you should be able to:

» Present the chrysalis economy.
» Discuss why sustainability is more than green.
» Define corporate social responsibility (CSR) and link it to sustainability.
» Understand the phases of CSR and how to make a case for CSR.
» Discuss the benefits and challenges of CSR.
» Explain green supply chains and sustainable value chains.
» Examine the role of logistics, transportation, and green procurement.
» Map out a business case for sustainability.

CHAPTER OVERVIEW

This chapter discusses the role of the corporation. Is the sole responsibility of a corporation to generate profits for its shareholders, or does a business need to do more? What is the impact of a corporation on the community? What are the methodologies available to corporations that would like to be more socially responsible? This chapter focuses on the topics of CSR, green supply chains, and the business case for sustainability.

The Chrysalis Economy

The preceding chapters of the book presented renewable resources such as air, water, food, forests, and clean energy. We discussed sustainable strategies and the role of consumers in sustainable consumption. Next, we turn our attention to the global economy and corporations. What might a sustainable global economy look like?

A sustainable global economy will arise in an era of severe technological, economic, social, and political metamorphosis. The present pattern of wealth creation and distribution is simply unsustainable. The present economy is highly destructive of natural and social capital, and the divide between the rich and the poor is ever widening. Since these patterns of wealth creation will lead to worsening environmental and social problems, there will be increasing pressure to transition to sustainable development (Elkington, 2004).

Figure 8.1 illustrates four main types of companies, or *value webs*, in this path toward a chrysalis economy—(1) corporate locusts, (2) corporate caterpillars, (3) corporate butterflies, and (4) corporate honeybees.

Corporate Locusts

These companies operate with an unsustainable business model in that they operate in a manner that overwhelms the carrying capacity of social systems. These companies are termed *destructive locusts* since they destroy social and environmental value, and most of these are found rampant in parts of Africa, Asia, Latin America, and Russia. The key characteristics of corporate locusts are as follows:

- Destruction of natural, human, social, and economic capital
- An unsustainable burn rate
- A business model that is unsustainable in the long run
- Tendency to swarm, overwhelming the carrying capacity of ecosystems
- Incapacity to foresee negative system effects
- An unwillingness to learn from mistakes (Elkington, 2004)

When companies act like corporate locusts, governments have had to take charge in controlling the worst offenders. In a global economy, environmental protection regulation needs to be extended beyond formal jurisdictions.

	Low Impact	High Impact
Regenerative (increasing returns)	Butterflies	Honeybees
Degenerative (decreasing returns)	Caterpillars	Locusts

Figure 8.1 | Corporate Characteristics.
Source: Elkington (2004)

Corporate Caterpillars

The impacts of these companies are more local, and as a result, harder to isolate. These caterpillars have the following characteristics:

- Depend on *high burn rate* in the form of renewable capital
- Operate on an unsustainable business model
- Operate in sectors where other companies are moving toward sustainable growth
- Have the potential to transform toward more sustainable growth

In this case, governments need to provide conditions for businesses to evolve while employing regulatory incentives to ensure that the development keeps in pace with environmental and sustainable objectives (Elkington, 2004).

Corporate Butterflies

These are small companies that are easy to spot. These companies are covered in the media and are highly conspicuous. Examples include Patagonia, The Body Shop, Ben & Jerry's, and others. These butterflies have the following characteristics:

- A sustainable business model
- Strong commitment to CSR
- Wide network
- Involvement in symbiotic networks
- High visibility and powerful representation for small companies

Corporate butterflies tend to occur in *pulses*. One pulse occurred in the 1960s with the boom in whole food and renewable energy. Another wave came in the 1990s with organic food, ecotourism, and social investments. Governments can help corporate butterflies by encouraging change that would move companies from the caterpillar to the butterfly stage (Elkington, 2004).

Corporate Honeybees

This is the area that companies, innovators, entrepreneurs, and government agencies and investors will seek out in the coming years. Ideally, in a sustainable global economy, there would be a steady hum of corporate honeybees and economic versions of beehives. The impact would be sustainable and strongly regenerative. The honeybees would have the following characteristics:

- A sustainable business model based on innovation
- A set of clear ethics-based business principles
- Strategic sustainable management of natural resources
- Evolution of powerful symbiotic relationships
- Sustainable production of natural, human, social, institutional, and cultural capital

- Capacity to moderate the impacts of corporate caterpillars in its supply chain (Elkington, 2004)

The attention around sustainability will lead to patterns of change in corporate behavior. Some companies might choose to remain degenerative yet try to improve their image by mimicking butterfly and honeybee traits. But no corporation can remain in the locust stage forever. Given the right set of drivers in the form of leadership or stakeholder demand, any corporation can start its transformative journey (Elkington, 2004).

Sustainability Is More Than Green

Of the world's 100 largest economic entities, most are corporations, not countries. This immense power calls for greater responsibility as society wants to hold global businesses accountable to meet the challenges facing our planet. What we are seeing are increasing limits on growth in the world and less credit. For this reason, companies need to develop and execute a strategy for sustainability. This is much more than a green strategy. The reason being that sustainability is much bigger than simply being green. Sustainability takes into account every dimension of the business environment: social, economic, and cultural, as well as natural (Werbach, 2009).

In a large picture, a sustainable business means a business that can thrive in the long term. Sustainability is much more than a public relations push. Sustainability is bigger than an occasional agreement to ongoing efforts to save the planet. If sustainability is to be realized fully and implemented well, it can drive a bottom-line strategy to save costs; a top-line strategy to reach a new consumer base; and a talent strategy to get, keep, and develop creative employees. This kind of true sustainability has four equal components:

1. Social, to address conditions that affect us all, including poverty, violence, injustice, education, public health, and labor and human rights.
2. Economic, to help people and businesses meet their economic needs. For people, that means securing food, water, shelter, and creature comforts; for businesses: turning a profit.
3. Environmental, to protect and restore the Earth—for example, by controlling climate change, preserving natural resources, and preventing waste.
4. Cultural, to protect and value the diversity through which communities manifest their identity and cultivate traditions across generations (Werbach, 2009).

Corporate Social Responsibility

What is the role of a corporation or a company? The actual word *company* comes from Latin—cum and panis, which mean "breaking bread together" (Arndt, 2003). Given that this terminology suggests some synergistic role, what are some of the views on the role of a company in the present age?

Let us consider two opposing views. Milton Friedman, a Nobel laureate, argued against CSR since it distracted business leaders from making money. Indeed, in an article titled "The Social Responsibility of Business Is to Increase Its Profits," he emphatically stated, "There is one and only one social responsibility of business—to use its resources and engage in activities designed to increase its profits" (Friedman, 1970).

Furthermore, he stated, "Few trends could so undermine the very foundations of our free society as the acceptance by corporate officials of a social responsibility other than to make as much money for their stockholders as possible" (Friedman, 1962).

David Packard of Hewlett-Packard (Carmichael, n.d.), said the following:

> Why are we here? Many people assume, wrongly, that a company exists solely to make money. People get together and exist as a company so that they are able to accomplish something collectively that they could not accomplish separately—they make a contribution to society.

Hence, whereas Milton Friedman stated that the main responsibility for a company was to make money and increase profits, David Packard was of the view that a company needs to do more than just make money: The company needs to contribute to society. It is the latter viewpoint that is becoming more prevalent in that companies need to provide a value to society, one that goes beyond the company's bottom line.

CSR stands for the social role or responsibility that a corporation has toward the society that it operates within. CSR is also known by some other terms, some of which are *corporate or business* responsibility, *business or corporate* citizenship, community relations, corporate stewardship, social responsibility, or strategic philosophy (Werther & Chandler, 2011).

Definition

Sustainable business and CSR are part of a cluster of terms that include sustainable development, socially responsible business, green management, corporate citizenship, and ethical business.

CSR has been defined in terms of sustainability, and sustainability has been defined in terms of CSR. CSR is commonly promoted as a means to achieve sustainability. This view is held both by researchers (Young, 2004) and practitioners (Frame, 2005). Some researchers see CSR and sustainable business as being synonymous (LaMe, 2005), while others have stated that sustainability can be viewed as a broader concept compared to CSR and that sustainability "embraces a wider, time-dependent definition of a benefit to society and focuses on results rather than standards of behavior" (Foot & Ross, 2004). At the simplest level, it calls for corporations to behave responsibly and pursue sustainable development goals.

History of Corporate Social Responsibility

According to Wilson (2003), the earliest CSR efforts can be traced back to the early Greek society, though Seeger and Hipfel (2007) noted that CSR has been around since the 1930s. The first formal definition of social responsibility was given by Howard R. Bowen (1953) in 1953 and it stated, "It refers to the obligations of businessmen to pursue those policies, to make those decisions, or to follow those lines of action which are desirable in terms of the objectives and values of our society" (Carroll, 1999).

Milton Friedman (1970) is the most cited critic, noting that businesses best serve societies by operating efficiently, hiring workers, paying taxes, and increasing shareholder value. Despite Friedman's criticism, businesses have adopted CSR. Allen (2004) described the uneven evolution of CSR from the 1950s to the present day. Business for Social Responsibility (BSR) was formed in 1992 and CSR Europe in 1996.

The past 25 years have witnessed the emergence and rapid growth of sustainability initiatives. Sustainable development entered the discourse in 1972 at the UN Conference on the Human Environment at Stockholm. The business community embraced the sustainability concept in 1991 with the formation of the Business Council for Sustainable Development. Since then, sustainability has gained wider acceptance, and the original organization has grown into the World Business Council for Sustainable Development (WBCSD) with 175 international member companies (Drexhage & Murphy, 2010).

The Paris Agreement of 2015 established global objectives in carbon reduction, with the United States one of only a few countries failing to sign the agreement until President Biden assumed the presidency in 2021. The United Nations Climate Change Conference held in Glasgow in 2021 further established global commitments to reduce carbon emissions.

CSR is about how companies manage the business processes to produce an overall positive impact on society.

> Corporate Social Responsibility is the continuing commitment by business to behave ethically and contribute to economic development while improving the quality of life of the workforce and their families as well as of the local community and society at large. (Holme & Watts, 2000)

In the United States, early CSR reports focused on philanthropy. The companies made profits, paid taxes, and then donated a certain share of the profits to charitable causes. As CSR developed, this notion progressed to include protection and improvement of the lives of workers. The current CSR reports cover issues that impact almost every area of operations from hiring and training workers to ethics and governance to responsible purchasing, environmental impact, and supply chain policies (CSR, n.d.). In contrast, the European model looks at operating the core business in a socially responsible way, complemented by investment in communities for solid business case reasons. The application of CSR would vary from culture to culture since there will be a difference in values or priorities across cultures (Baker, 2004).

Phases of Corporate Social Responsibility

CSR's role changes as society's demands and expectations change. The CSR movement had four main phases. It started with a reactive phase, wherein CSR was viewed as a public relations function intended for damage control when companies made mistakes with the community and the environment. In the second phase, some of these companies started to incorporate process efficiencies in manufacturing and services and started to establish relationships with stakeholders including nongovernmental organizations (NGOs). In the third phase of integration, companies created key performance indicators that were then used to publicly report on various functional business units. The knowledge garnered from this stage fed into the fourth stage of value creation, where brand enhancement, product development, and R&D looked for solutions to social issues that impacted the bottom line (Smalheiser, 2006).

The main advantage of a well-executed CSR is that it builds business value in many ways: by enhancing brand image, establishing a cooperative relationship with government, and attracting investors. In addition, a company can attract and retain motivated employees, enter new markets, position the company to partner for governments and NGOs, and improve risk avoidance (Smalheiser, 2006). The following examples illustrate how companies are building business value and gaining strategic advantage.

Examples

Business strategy: How does a company serve global markets in various stages of development in order to secure goodwill and support that would protect its investments and secure a broad credibility? The Marathon Oil Corporation started a malaria eradication and treatment program in Equatorial Guinea in conjunction with the local government and NGOs that led to a massive drop in new incidents of malaria. In addition, the company installed a workforce program that will enable local people to acquire skills necessary to earn employment at the company.

Overcoming obstacles: Becton, Dickinson and Company (BD), a New Jersey-based technology company making medical devices, also focuses on global health issues. The company has the social networks, expertise, and resources to work closely with local organizations to help treatment of diseases. BD also manufactures single use syringes that minimize the rate of infections caused by reusing these syringes.

Fertile ground: In areas of environmental innovation, General Electric's (GE) *ecomagination* works in areas of product and packaging design, water stewardship, and greenhouse gas mitigation. Canada's Domtar Corporation had a history of obtaining timber rights from public lands. As a company committed to sustainable forestry, its operations are based on sustainable forestry standards.

Brand building: As consumers become sensitive to environmental issues, companies attempt to develop new products. Waste Management, the largest trash-removal company in the United States, is also the largest recycler. The company is a leading convertor of waste to energy and operates 17 plants that process 24,000 tons of solid waste per day. It has more than 100 landfill projects that convert methane into clean energy. The company converts its landfill areas to wildlife habitats, thus providing more than 17,000 acres of land devoted to wetlands and wildlife (Smalheiser, 2006).

Making the Case for Corporate Social Responsibility

In general terms, the case for CSR can be made on moral grounds. The point to be made is that since the corporation exists within society, it needs the infrastructure, the employees, and the consumer base from this very society. However, not everyone can be convinced on the moral argument alone. How can the upper management of companies, the C-suite, be convinced that adoption of CSR would be good for their company? Porter and Kramer (2006) made four arguments to support their case: "moral obligation, sustainability, license to operate, and reputation" (p. 81).

The first argument, one of moral obligation, states that companies ought to "do the right thing." Specifically, the message is that businesses "achieve commercial success in ways that honor ethical values and respect people, communities, and the natural environment" (Porter & Kramer, 2006). In areas of financial reporting, moral obligations are easy to understand and apply. However, most corporate social choices involve balancing competing values, interests, and costs. For example, Google's entry into China has resulted in a conflict over censorship and Chinese government mandates. A pharmaceutical company has no direct way of knowing how to allocate its revenues between subsidizing care, developing cures for the future, or providing investor dividends (Porter & Kramer, 2006).

The second argument is derived from sustainability, and it places importance on environmental and community stewardship. Going back to the Brundtland Commission's definition of sustainability, "meeting the needs of the present without compromising the ability of future generations to meet their own needs" usually invokes the triple bottom line approach of economic, social, and environmental performance. In this approach, companies ought to operate in ways that improve their long-term performance while avoiding short-term pitfalls arising from environmental or societal concerns. For example, DuPont saved over $2 billion from energy use reductions since 1990, and McDonald's reduced its solid waste by 30 percent from changes to materials used to wrap its food. However, in some other areas, sustainability is used in vague terms—transparency is more *sustainable* than corruption or philanthropy, leading to *sustainability* of a society (Porter & Kramer, 2006).

The third argument comes into play when companies identify a set of social issues pertinent to the stakeholders, engage in a dialogue with the community, and make decisions. This thinking is prevalent in companies that depend on government approval, such as mining or other extractive industries, and in companies whose operations, by nature, are hazardous, such as chemical manufacturing. The inherent challenge is that companies that seek to placate stakeholders run the risk of ceding the control of their CSR agendas to external parties (Porter & Kramer, 2006).

The fourth argument concerns the reputation of the company and seeks to appease external stakeholders. In industries like chemical manufacturing and energy, this strategy is pursued like an insurance policy in case of a crisis. Companies like Ben & Jerry's, Patagonia, and The Body Shop stand out due to their long-term commitment to social issues. However, the social impact is tough to determine, and there is no way to quantify the benefits of social investment (Porter & Kramer, 2006).

The important point to note is that there needs to be integration between business and society. A healthy society needs successful companies since these companies create jobs, wealth, and innovation that lead to an increase in the standard of living. In turn, a successful company needs a healthy society since education and health care are essential to having a productive workforce. In coming up with their corporate social agenda, a company needs to be responsive to its stakeholders and, furthermore, look for ways to achieve social and economic benefits in a strategic manner (Porter & Kramer, 2006).

Porter and Kramer (2006) also classified CSR in two main categories: responsive and strategic. Responsive corporate social responsibility (CSR) companies act as good citizens and mitigate harmful value chain impacts. An example of the former role is GE's program to adopt underperforming high schools. GE helps with donations, and the GE managers mentor students. An example of the latter role is B&Q, a chain of home supply centers based in England that has begun to analyze its entire product line against a list of social issues in order to determine which products might pose a social responsibility risk (Porter & Kramer, 2006).

Strategic corporate social responsibility aims to identify initiatives whose social and business benefits stand out in scope. It also taps shared value by investments in aspects that strengthen the competitive advantage for the company. For example, Toyota's Prius is a car model that has produced competitive advantages and environmental benefits. Nestlé works directly with small farmers in developing countries in order to source basic commodities such as milk, coffee, and cocoa. Another good example is Whole Foods Market, which emphasizes purchasing from local farmers; screening out foods that contain any of 100 common ingredients considered to be environmentally damaging; constructing stores using a minimum amount of virgin raw materials; purchasing wind credits; and offsetting all its electricity consumption. Examples also include initiatives from large companies. Sysco aims to preserve small family farms and offer local produce to customers; GE aims to focus on developing water purification technology; and Unilever aims to meet the needs of the poorest populations worldwide (Porter & Kramer, 2006).

RELEVANCE OF CORPORATE SOCIAL RESPONSIBILITY

There are four main environmental forces causing CSR to gain relevance: (1) increasing affluence, (2) globalization, (3) ecological sustainability, and (4) brands.

Increasing Affluence

CSR tends to be more prevalent in affluent nations where consumers can afford to be picky in the products they purchase. However, the relevance of CSR is just as important in developing nations as multinational corporations are increasingly being held responsible for their overseas actions. One example is the infamous case of Nike and its subcontractors in which CEO Phil Knight was reluctant to accept responsibility for the company's overseas labor practices (Werther & Chandler, 2011).

Globalization

The media are quick to report any *corporate mistakes* to the consumers. In addition, the Internet facilitates instant communication among consumer groups located worldwide, enabling them to coordinate action such as product boycotts. Consumers are better informed and are more diligent when it comes to their choices. For the companies, the market is also being shaped by grassroots campaigns. Hence, it is in the best interest of a corporation to listen to bottom-up concerns and respond in a proactive manner (Werther & Chandler, 2011).

Ecological Sustainability

From growing affluence and change in society's expectations comes an increased concern for the environment. Firms perceived to be indifferent to their environmental responsibilities are likely to be criticized and penalized. Some firms have recognized this shift and responded by taking positive steps. For example, Walmart has started integrating some aspects of sustainability into their operations (Werther & Chandler, 2011).

Brands

Great strides have been made toward the integration of CSR into the core culture of companies. For example, companies such as Chevron, GE, Microsoft, and HP have made public commitments to CSR and have reported on their CSR performance. Companies also want to be included on *Fortune's* annual list of the best companies to work for. In Europe, companies are required to report on their social and environmental performance (CSR, n.d.). Brands are highly crucial since a popular brand increases leverage, which in turn impacts sales and revenues. A strong corporate brand is of immeasurable value to the company, and CSR can assist in the branding of a corporate image.

Positive Brand Building

British Petroleum (BP) spent $200 million to reposition itself as an environmentally sound and socially responsible company. This is in stark contrast to ExxonMobil, which has to constantly battle NGO attacks and consumer boycotts. In response to the 2010 Gulf of Mexico oil spill, BP agreed to pay an estimated $7.8 billion in settlement charges (Fisk, 2012). The Body Shop takes an aggressive stand on fair trade and other social issues and attracts consumers via this fair trade stance. The clothing company Benetton also advertises on social issues that it deems are important to consumers (Werther & Chandler, 2011).

Brand Insurance

Nike faced consumer boycotts and NGO attacks in the mid-1990s. However, Nike has turned itself around and is now known as a committed corporate citizen. It publishes an annual CSR report and has appointed a VP for corporate responsibility. Merck & Co. took a socially responsible stance when it announced that "medicine is for the patients, not for the profits." The most cited example is Merck donating the medicine Mectizan to combat river blindness, an infectious disease in Africa and Latin America (Werther & Chandler, 2011).

Key Corporate Social Responsibility Areas

What are the main areas that companies tend to report in CSR? The four main areas that emerged from the "Winning with Integrity" framework by Business in the Community in 2000 ("Key CSR Issue Areas," n.d.) are as follows:

Marketplace: What is the value created by the goods and services produced by the company? In turn, what cost does the business impose on the community it operates within and the society at large?

Environment: Can companies begin to tackle their environmental footprint? Can companies control their GHG emissions via efficiency measures? Can companies satisfy customer needs with minimal environmental impact?

Workplace: How does a company attract, recruit, and retain skilled people? There is evidence that people want to work for companies that stand out in corporate reputation, including social responsibility.

Community: Is the company viewed as a good influence on the community? At what level are the employees of the company involved within the community? ("Key CSR Issue Areas," n.d.).

These four key areas of CSR reporting are the ones that emerged as more important. Next, as we analyze some of the common CSR policies, note that most of these policies impact these four areas.

Corporate Social Responsibility Policies

In general terms, CSR refers to running a business while keeping an account of the social and environmental impact of the business. In practical terms, CSR calls for developing policies that incorporate responsible practices within daily business operations and for the reporting on progress actually made toward these practices.

Some of the common CSR policies include the following:

- adoption of internal controls reform in the wake of accounting scandals;
- commitment to diversity in hiring employees and barring discrimination;
- management teams that view employees as assets;
- workplaces that integrate the views of line employees into decision-making processes;
- adoption of operating policies that exceed compliance with social and environmental laws;
- advanced resource productivity, focused on the use of natural resources in a more productive, efficient, and profitable fashion; and
- taking responsibility for conditions under which goods are produced directly or by contract employees (CSR, n.d.).

CSR is only one part of the overall corporate strategy. How can companies achieve progress toward a more competitive environmental approach? Porter and van der Linde (1995) suggested the following four options:

1. Measure direct and indirect environmental impacts
2. Recognize the opportunity cost of underutilized resources
3. Create a bias in favor of innovation-based, productivity-enhancing solutions
4. Become more proactive in defining relationships with regulators and environmentalists

BENEFITS OF CORPORATE SOCIAL RESPONSIBILITY

There are numerous businesses that recognize the benefits of CSR. However, those that are investing in CSR face a new set of challenges. CSR can be viewed as a public relations ploy, and there are numerous companies that do the minimum, for example, by funding a development project or two in an area in which they operate. In order to move ahead, companies need to consider the social and environmental impact of their policies alongside profit when making investment strategy decisions and incorporating management practices. Surveys state that business leaders are called upon to play an increasingly larger role in solving social issues, from education to environment (Bielak, Bobini, & Oppenheim, 2007). The biggest argument against CSR is familiar: there is a lack of tangible economic benefit since both opinion and research on this relationship has been divided.

Businesses have shown that *strategic* CSR supports business objectives along with accruing certain intangible benefits such as increasing brand awareness, attracting a talented workforce, and improving relations with regulators. A survey of MBA candidates stated that they look at reputation when considering where to work after graduating. Social responsibility is one of the factors that drive reputation (Butcher, 2009), and 77 percent of consumers will not buy from companies they distrust (Butcher, 2009). As a result, companies must respond to the demand for more ethical business processes and actions.

An International Business Report by Grant Thornton on CSR states the following:

> Four of the top five [corporate social responsibility] initiatives were directly associated with people and their workplace—active promotion of workforce health and well-being (71 percent of respondents); provision of apprenticeships and work experience (67 percent); promotion of diversity/equality in the workplace (64 percent) and allowing flexible working (62 percent). In many countries [. . .] a large proportion of respondents say they have taken action on waste management and have also acted to improve energy efficiency. (MacBeath, 2008)

Some of the other areas that companies are focusing on are product life cycle management, strategic sourcing and procurement, logistics, and continuous process improvement.

Business leaders are committed to incorporating CSR into their strategies (Riddleberger & Hittner, 2009). As a policy, program, or process, CSR is strategic when it results in supporting the core business activities (Burke & Logsdon, 1996).

The way to support the purpose of CSR within firms is by the concept of value creation. In specific terms, "under what conditions does a firm jointly serve its own strategic business interests and the societal interests of its stakeholders?" (Burke & Logsdon, 1996, p. 495). In the study by Burke and Logsdon (1996), value creation is most effective when the following factors are considered:

- centrality—closeness of fit to the firm's mission and objectives;
- specificity—ability to capture private benefits by firm;
- proactivity—degree to which the program is planned in anticipation of emerging social trends and in the absence of crises;
- voluntarism—the scope for discretionary decision-making and the lack of externally imposed compliance requirements;
- visibility—observable, recognizable credit by internal and/or external stakeholders for the firm; and
- value creation—identifiable, measurable economic benefits that the firm expects to receive (Cavett-Goodwin, 2007).

For the most positive impact, businesses need to focus on efficient operations balanced with diverse social and environmental ecosystems. CSR is a necessity rather than a choice given the increasing scrutiny from stakeholders (Butcher, 2009).

Most of the current CSR theories are focused on four main aspects: (1) meeting objectives that yield long-term profits, (2) employing business power responsibly, (3) combining social demands and (4) being ethical. The CSR theories can be classified into four groups: (1) instrumental, (2) political, (3) integrative, and (4) value theories (Garriga & Mele, 2004). The instrumental theories are the ones in which the corporation's social activities serve as a means to achieve economic results. The political theories focus on the power of corporations in society and how this power can be employed responsibly. The integrative theories state that the corporation can focus on the satisfaction of social demands. Lastly, the value theories are based on the responsibilities of corporations to society (Garriga & Mele, 2004).

CHALLENGES OF CORPORATE SOCIAL RESPONSIBILITY

One weakness of CSR is the lack of measures of performance, something that can lead to unsubstantiated claims. Even the examples provided in the preceding discussion on companies like BP, Marathon Oil Corporation, Nike, and so on are open to debate. However, there is one process that aims to set forth a common set of guidelines, the Global Reporting Initiative (GRI; www.gri.org). This process incorporates the active participation of various global stakeholders ranging from businesses to environmental and labor organizations. More details on GRI will be discussed in Chapter 10 of this book.

CSR has also been undermined as an initiative. There are three main failings that have attributed to this failure. These points are as follows:

1. CSR has been restricted to the largest companies and to a specific PR department within these companies.
2. CSR has adopted a model akin to the quality management model that results in incremental improvements.

3. CSR does not always make economic sense and, in the short term, companies that push their costs to society are rewarded (Visser, 2001).

Visser proposed a radical, or holistic, CSR dubbed CSR 2.0. The four DNA codes for this CSR 2.0 are (1) value creation, (2) good governance, (3) societal contribution, and (4) environmental integrity. The strategic goals for each of these are, respectively: economic development, institutional effectiveness, stakeholder orientation, and sustainable ecosystems (Visser, 2001).

THE WORLD'S MOST SUSTAINABLE COMPANIES

The World Economic Forum has unveiled a ranking of sustainable companies, from a review by Corporate Knights of over 8,000 companies. It becomes clear by a visit to each of these firm's websites how strongly the quest for sustainability means to these companies (Tatler, https://www.tatlerasia.com/power-purpose/business/most-sustainable-companies-2021).

1. Schneider Electric SE, France
2. Orsted A/S, Denmark
3. Banco do Brasil SA, Brazil
4. Neste Oyj, Finland
5. Stantec, Inc., Canada
6. McCormick & Company, Inc., United States
7. Kering SA, France
8. Metso Outotec, Finland
9. American Water Works Company, Inc., United States
10. Canadian National Railway Co., Canada
11. Rexel SA, France
12. Atlantica Sustainable Infrastructure PLC, United Kingdom
13. Cisco Systems, Inc., United States
14. Storebrand ASA, Norway
15. Owens Corning, United States
16. Eisai Co., Ltd, Japan
17. Cascades, Inc., Canada
18. Brambles, Ltd., Australia
19. Iberdrola SA, Spain
20. Taiwan Semiconductor Manufacturing Co., Ltd., Taiwan

The full list of all 100 top-ranking most sustainable corporations of 2021 can be found at Corporate Knights.

Green, Sustainable Supply Chains

A supply chain is the planning and management of all activities involved in manufacture of a product or provision of a service. A green, sustainable supply chain can be defined as follows:

> The process of using environmentally friendly inputs and transforming these inputs through change agents—whose byproducts can improve or be recycled within the existing environment. This process develops outputs that can be reclaimed and re-used at the end of their life-cycle thus, creating a sustainable supply chain. (Penfield, 2007)

The point of a green, sustainable supply chain is to reduce costs while helping the environment. Though the trend of developing a green supply chain is getting popular, most companies are not sure where to start. Indeed, most large corporations have no green supply chain policy in place. A survey conducted by management consultant group BearingPoint found that 35 percent of companies have already established a green supply chain. The interest in green supply chains is linked to size: "54 percent of companies with turnover in excess of $700 million claim to have established a Green Supply Chain" (Green Supply Chain Management, n.d.). In the past few years, companies have been attempting to minimize cost, increase efficiency, and improve supply chain visibility. The focus on green supply chains does not have to undermine these prior goals. Some best practices have emerged from the companies that are greening their supply chains.

Align the Green Supply Chain with Business Goals

A company should identify how a transition to a green supply chain can help achieve business goals. For example, if a company wants to reduce its energy costs, it should explore more energy efficient equipment. If the overall goal is one of cost reduction, then the move to a green supply chain should align with the business goal (Murray, 2010).

Use the Green Supply Chain to Improve Processes

Companies that green their supply chains should review all their business processes to determine areas where a greener approach can improve their business. This might identify the inefficiencies along the supply chain, such as wastage of raw materials, underutilized raw materials, and inefficient equipment (Murray, 2010).

Green Suppliers and Material Refurbishment

Companies should aim to find suppliers who have not sacrificed the quality of their product in an attempt to minimize their environmental impact. In this manner, companies can begin to green their supply chains before any material reaches their site. In addition, companies should pay close attention to their return process since a refurbishment program can offer more purchasing options to the customers and widen the customer base while improving the environmental impact of the products (Murray, 2010).

It is important to have strong leadership in place before a transition to a green supply chain can be made. A simple plan to implement a green supply chain will not be realized without the necessary resources, both financial and personnel.

TEN STEPS TO CREATING A SUSTAINABLE SUPPLY CHAIN

The supply chain of any product comprises various steps that include resource extraction, transportation, production, packaging, distribution, sales, consumer use, and disposal. Each stage in the supply chain has repercussions on the environment, and a sustainable-minded company would need to account for all these steps along the way. The following steps have been taken by some business leaders—Starbucks, Walmart, Disney, Gap, Timberland, and HP—in an attempt to green their supply chains (Kaestner, 2007):

1. *Start with the top:* Top-level management support is critical. With sustainable supply chains, the chief executive, the finance director, and the board all need to support the initiative (Baker, 2011). Any large-scale initiative that impacts the whole corporation needs top-level approval.
2. *Make the business case:* The benefits of a sustainable supply chain must be outlined internally to employees and managers and externally for risk reduction and development of a positive brand. The business case is also essential in order to get top-level support (Baker, 2011). More details on articulating a business case are provided later in the chapter.
3. *Develop a code of conduct:* Various certification schemes need to be assessed to develop a code of conduct. In those instances where the certification schemes do not suffice, internal standards can be developed. As an example, Starbucks developed its own Corporate Average Fuel Economy (CAFE) standards (Kaestner, 2007). Companies can apply these standards internally and also communicate these efforts externally. A two-way process—listening and broadcasting—is crucial (Baker, 2011).
4. *Collaborate with critics:* For companies that have been criticized by media, this step is perceived as being sincere. For example, Home Depot worked with the Rainforest Action Network, Starbucks allied with the Rainforest Alliance, and Walmart asked the Environmental Defense Fund (EDF) to open an office in Arkansas (Kaestner, 2007).
5. *Use scorecards to rate suppliers:* Every supplier has its own set of standards and taken collectively, these standards can lead to confusion. A better alternative is to develop scorecards to rate suppliers in order to improve performance and to document efforts for auditors.
6. *Verify through third-party certification:* Companies need to get third-party verification via an external audit. When companies develop their own standards and audit themselves, the external stakeholders are skeptical of the results.
7. *Team up with competitors:* There is a need for similar supply chain standards within an industry, a goal that competitors could team up to accomplish. Too many standards with different reporting structures lead to unnecessary confusion.

8. *Take corrective action:* Certain companies do not engage their suppliers due to the possibility of failing a compliance audit. Valid certification schemes need to be used to identify and dismiss failing suppliers.

9. *Empower suppliers to build capacity:* Companies ought to engage their suppliers to get them to improve their performance before dismissing them. For example, Starbucks advises farmers to use fewer chemicals to maintain soil health (Kaestner, 2007).

10. *Encourage transparency:* Internal standards and codes of conduct are necessary, but companies need to communicate their efforts publicly to promote awareness. Companies also need to be clear about their own standards, both in the application of standards and in the communication of these standards (Kaestner, 2007).

To develop a sustainable supply chain strategy, it is of utmost importance to get management approval, to develop credible standards by collaborating with nonprofits, to assist suppliers to attain best practices, and to keep customers informed about company efforts. More details on how many companies actually follow these 10 steps are provided in the Green Procurement section. Though these steps might seem overwhelming at first, the benefits of a sustainable supply chain lead to reducing costs while minimizing the impact on the environment.

In an effort to save money and the environment, companies can take a closer look at operation in three areas: (1) facility design, equipment, and systems; (2) logistics and transportation; and (3) green procurement. A win-win approach whereby a green retrofit can lead to cost savings can be embraced by even the most critical opponents within a corporation.

FACILITY DESIGN, EQUIPMENT, AND SYSTEMS

Facility Design

Traditional lightbulbs can be converted to fluorescents for energy savings. Skylights and photo sensors can be used to adjust lighting. Solar panels can be used for heating water and generating power. Geothermal heat pumps (GHPs, discussed in Chapter 5) can be used for further cost savings. The installation of the right dock seals can also save money by preventing energy loss. An energy provider can identify cost savings for a specific facility (Hill, 2010).

Equipment

Fuel cells, more efficient than internal combustion engines, can reduce carbon dioxide emissions by up to 45 percent. Conveyer systems can be designed to be energy efficient. Turn off conveyers when not in use and employ motors and sensors to shut down and power the conveyer systems back up. Automated systems for storage, retrieval, and transportation might cost less given the trade-off in energy costs. Maintenance needs to be kept on track since delays lead to cost inefficiencies (Hill, 2010).

Systems

Various systems can offer further cost reductions. An important strategic consideration is in locating warehouses and inventories to satisfy customer demands at the lowest transportation and related energy costs. For inventory, picking routines can improve output while reducing energy costs. Warehouse management systems (WMS) can be used to select the right personnel and equipment to reduce travel distances and related energy costs. Also, companies are shifting to reusable packaging, containers, and pallets (Hill, 2010).

In terms of facility and warehouse design, the potential of cost savings from environmental initiatives is immense. The cost savings from reduction of energy wastages is an essential step to start tackling the *low-hanging fruit* for environmental savings. This reduction in energy costs frees up resources for other corporate initiatives.

Logistics and Transportation

Strategic choices in logistics and transportation allow for a greener supply chain without sacrificing the bottom line (Chan & Joy, 2008).

Strategic Consolidation Programs

Logistics companies can ship full truckloads by combining purchase orders. The suppliers and retailers can work to attain further cost efficiencies.

Warehouse Planning

Warehouses can be built in centralized locations to service retailers. An efficient provider operates in an area to provide maximum shipping potential.

Establishing a Strategic Route

Truck routing software is used to maintain efficiency. Also, software packages can integrate a biodiesel mapping system to locate fueling stations that provide alternative fuel.

Alternative Fuel

Biodiesel does not require any engine modifications since a truck can easily switch off between biodiesel and diesel. Numerous logistics providers have switched to biodiesel. As an example, States Logistics Services, Inc., has converted its transportation fleet to run on B99 (a blend of 1 percent petroleum diesel and 99 percent biodiesel) biodiesel fuel (Doherty, 2011).

Certification Programs

The U.S. Environmental Protection Agency (EPA) sponsors a program to reduce emissions. The SmartWay Transport Program holds carriers responsible for reducing emissions, but third-party logistics providers (3PLs) must also reduce their emissions by selecting greener carriers (Chan & Joy, 2008).

Logistics and transportation play an essential role in the carbon footprint of a corporation. Producing a green product is not enough: The storage and the subsequent transportation of this product must be designed with the environment implications in mind. Logistics companies investing in alternative fuels reduce operational costs. For example, UPS has 1,914 alternative fuel vehicles in its fleet and has one of the most technologically diverse alternative fuel fleets in the industry (Berman, 2011).

GREEN PROCUREMENT

Business Buying Power created a list of ways sustainable procurement can be environmentally positive (Svenson, Joanne, Business Buying Power, New Zealand, 17 May 2020).

- Reducing greenhouse gas emissions
- Improving energy efficiency and resource usage, in particular water, minerals, and land
- Minimizing air, water, and soil pollution
- Removing toxic substances from the manufacturing process
- Reducing waste and effluent, including eliminating unnecessary processes or packaging, and/or setting requirements for reuse and recycling
- Supporting sustainable agriculture
- Banning the use of materials produced because of deforestation of natural habitats and ecological conservation areas, such as palm oil
- Banning the exploitation of rare or endangered species
- Committing to ethical labor and employment practices, as well as fair trade
- Worker health and safety
- Promoting animal husbandry and care
- Supporting suppliers who have attained environmental and ethical certification.

8 benefits of sustainable procurement:

1. Care for our environment as well as animal, bird, and plant life
2. Care for our fellow human beings
3. Improved health outcomes
4. Economic benefits of having socially engaged enterprises sharing employment, resources, and financial benefits throughout the community
5. Commitment to controlling climate change
6. Supporting the well-being of the Earth for future generations
7. Feel-good factor for current and future employees
8. A bit of positive PR to show your customers that your company truly cares

9 ways to help your workplace become more sustainable:

1. Conserving paper and reusing it wherever possible
2. Participating in recycling programs

3. Using environmentally friendly hygiene and cleaning products
4. Using eco-friendly and efficient lighting and air conditioning
5. Implementing energy-efficient policies
6. Encouraging alternative transport options
7. Using certified environmentally sustainable and ethically sourced products such as tea and coffee
8. Minimizing or eliminating single-use plastics
9. Getting your local barista to make your favorite cup of coffee in your own cup, which will help reduce disposable cups and lids going to landfills

Office Supplies, Cleaning Products, and Computers

Information technology was identified as an industry leader. What products are being purchased based upon green criteria? The top three industries were cleaning products (78 percent), office supplies (57 percent), and computers and IT hardware (55 percent). Certification is important since there are many ratings for these product categories, such as the Forest Stewardship Council's (FSC) certification for paper and wood products, *Green Seal* for cleaning products, and the Electronic Product Environmental Assessment Tool (EPEAT) standard for computers (Davies, 2009).

Measuring Green Purchasing

Within purchasing, almost 73 percent of companies state that green criteria are important. Overall, 59 percent of companies stated that they have a green procurement policy and that green criteria are included in requests for proposal (RFPs). As recommended in the 10 steps that were given earlier, companies communicate green criteria to their suppliers and evaluate results. About one third of the companies surveyed publish a code of conduct for their suppliers. In addition, companies are also measuring performance using supplier scorecards. In terms of supplier evaluation, larger companies with revenues over $1 billion used ISO 14001 as a leading factor in their evaluations, whereas smaller companies relied on published CSR or sustainability reports (Davies, 2009).

Selling Green

About 84 percent of companies stated that there is a need for third-party standards or certifications for green products. More companies (50 percent) identified positive environmental performance as a reason to award or renew a contract versus companies (35 percent) that canceled a supplier's contract due to poor environmental performance. Though many buyers (61 percent) prefer independent certifications, about 45 percent use self-declaration and 33 percent use references to evaluate their suppliers (Davies, 2009).

In the previously given 10 steps, some advice was offered by leading companies. This section on green purchasing reports the results from a survey that attest to the importance of certifications, standards, codes of conduct, scorecards, and so on. The main point is that companies need to work with suppliers to convert their supply chains to green, sustainable supply chains.

Carbon Disclosure Project's Supply Chain Project

Another good source for finding sustainable and green supply chains is the Carbon Disclosure Project's (CDP) Supply Chain Program. This project aims to drive action on climate change by getting companies and their suppliers involved. CDP facilitates the computation of a corporation's carbon footprint by measuring direct GHG emissions and including the climate change risks and opportunities along the supply chain. For the purposes of disclosure, CDP provides a global process, and the information garnered can be used by senior management in large corporations. For corporations, one of the main reasons to sign as a member is to understand how suppliers are reducing their GHG emissions (CDP, n.d.). More information on CDP is provided in Chapter 10. In the survey on green purchasing, only 13 percent of companies surveyed ask their suppliers for GHG emissions data (Davies, 2009).

A BUSINESS CASE FOR SUSTAINABILITY

At times, sustainability officers at corporations struggle to articulate the business case, and they attempt to come up with the commercial benefits of social and environmental initiatives. So why is this business case so hard to find? David Bent (2009) provided six pointers on mapping a business case for sustainability:

1. *There is no "one size fits all" business case.* The business case needs to be specific to the company since every company has different issues of sustainability and drivers of shareholder value. **"Lesson: Focus on finding the business justification"** (Bent, 2009).

2. *The "societal case" doesn't make a business case.* Companies are making profits from resources that are *unsustainable*, such as bottled water. Though there might be greater overlap between the societal case and the business case in the future, for now, companies need to focus on their own business case. **"Lesson: Don't expect a justification for all the things the company needs to do"** (Bent, 2009).

3. *Opportunity trumps responsibility.* It is easy to get trapped into a checklist-compliance mode that looks at costs alone. However, corporate sustainability is about finding the route to be successful in the future. **"Lesson: Present sustainability as a way of unlocking opportunity for the company now and into the long term"** (Bent, 2009).

4. *The more you look, the more you find.* The process becomes self-fulfilling, and once companies start searching, they find more opportunities (Bent, 2009). Companies usually start by tackling the low hanging fruit of energy savings and find themselves moving on to bigger avenues. **"Lesson: Explore how to make sustainability commercial and improve the company's business case"** (Bent, 2009).

5. *Sustainability professionals and finance professionals speak different languages.* The former discusses benefits to society and the company,

and the latter is more focused on the financial benefits to the company. Sustainability change agents must learn to speak to the financial audience as well. **"Lesson: Frame the case for sustainability in terms that the finance director will understand"** (Bent, 2009).

6. *The "no business case, no permission" vicious cycle.* Permissions are needed to get funding from finance to prepare a business case, but the permission is not given without a business case, leading to a vicious cycle. **"Lesson: Plan small steps to create a virtuous circle of permission and results"** (Bent, 2009).

The present media and government initiatives are packed with initiatives for green businesses, green jobs, and emerging green economies, and these will be a central part of the new world now being created.

For any company that aims to achieve greater sustainability, it must articulate a strategic direction—an overarching goal that is consistent with the company strengths, is connected to its core business, is able to inspire personal contributions from its members, and is attainable within five to fifteen years.

Patagonia

An organization's commitment to sustainable practices should be reflected on its website. One firm that is serious about that commitment is the clothing retailer Patagonia. They boldly state, "The climate crisis is our business!" They then state:

> The climate crisis is an existential threat, and every part of Patagonia's business is implicated. We must radically reduce carbon emissions by transforming how we make our products. We must also double down on our work to help communities get off fossil fuels and protect nature, the original climate solution. And we must demand nothing short of systemic change from government and industry. The fight is on every front . . . . Purchasing offsets to get to carbon neutral doesn't erase the footprint we create and won't save us in the long run. If our goal were to cut emissions from our owned and operated stores, offices and distribution centers, we'd be good. But the bulk of our emissions—95 percent—comes from our supply chain and materials manufacturing. We take responsibility for all of it. (Patagonia, n.d.)

Conclusion

This chapter presented the role of businesses and corporations. It started with the large picture concept of a chrysalis economy that provides the grounding and argument as to why corporate sustainability is essential. The next section discussed why the concept of being sustainable means much more than simply being green. Next, we presented a detailed discussion on CSR—its phases, its benefits, and challenges. Then we presented a discussion on green supply chains to illustrate how corporations are attempting to make the supply chains more sustainable. The chapter ended with a discussion of how to make a business case for sustainability.

Keywords

- Business case for sustainability
- Chrysalis economy
- Corporate butterflies
- Corporate caterpillars
- Corporate honeybees
- Corporate locusts
- Corporate social responsibility (CSR)
- Green procurement
- Green supply chains
- Logistics and transportation
- Responsive corporate social responsibility (CSR)
- Strategic CSR
- Value creation

Discussion Questions

1. What is the role of a corporation? Does it exist simply to make money, or should businesses serve the needs of the society as well? Can you provide examples of companies in both cases?
2. Are sustainability and CSR linked together? Explain.
3. What are the four phases of CSR? Use the Internet and search the CSR reports of any particular company to find what phase it is operating within.
4. What are the four arguments given to make a case for CSR? Which of these would you feel most comfortable in promoting (for example, to a potential recruiter or at your company)?
5. Should CSR be responsive or strategic? Discuss with an example.
6. What are the six environmental forces causing CSR to be relevant? Which of these forces do you deem to be most relevant?
7. What are the benefits of CSR? Which one of these would be the most attractive to you? Would you prefer working at a company that commits to CSR?
8. What are the 10 steps to creating a sustainable supply chain? Which of these might be applicable at the company you work for?
9. How can companies encourage their suppliers to go green?
10. What is the role of transportation and logistics in a green supply chain? How about the role of green procurement? Are any of these initiatives being undertaken at your company? Your university?
11. Why is it important to make a business case for sustainability? Think of your role as an advocate of sustainability attempting to explain the business case to your peers.
12. What are corporate locusts and corporate caterpillars? Can you think of a corporate locust that is unwilling to change?
13. What are corporate butterflies and corporate honeybees? Can you think of examples where a particular company has gone from being a butterfly to a honeybee?

14. Research the CSR reports of some of the local companies in your area. Evaluate the report critically, given the knowledge gained from this chapter. For example, is the report an exercise in public relations (greenwashing), or did the company commit to some goals and make headway in the pursuit of these goals?

Recommended Case Studies

1. *Burt's Bees: Balancing Growth and Sustainability*, Product Number 410704-MMC-ENG, Harvard Business School Publishing.

    Learning objective: To understand the leadership challenges of implementing sustainable business practices and how to balance sustainability with growth. Case examines Burt's Bees' sustainability journey and in particular the important element of CSR as essentially a nonmarket strategy; committed companies can set industry standards to corporate acquisitions and how Burt's Bees can continue to pursue its social and environmental endeavors while growing as its own unit and within the larger parent company, Clorox.

2. *McDonald's Corporation: Managing a Sustainable Supply Chain*, Product Number 907414-PDF-ENG, Harvard Business School Publishing.

    Learning objective: To investigate how a major food service company takes a proactive role in sustainability of the food supply chain. McDonald's seeks to learn from a successful response to Greenpeace's Amazon deforestation campaign in order to make its supply chain more socially and environmentally responsible.

3. *Sustainability at Millipore*, Product Number 610012-PDF-ENG. Harvard Business School Publishing.

    Learning objective: To expose students to the challenges of conceptualizing *environmental sustainability* at an organization level and differentiating sustainability management from traditional environmental, health, and safety management. The case provides a background of the sustainability movement and reviews major sustainability frameworks (including The Natural Step, Carbon Footprints, and the Sustainability Hierarchy) and prevailing sustainability performance metrics.

Recommended Websites

- GreenBiz – www.greenbiz.com
- World Business Council for Sustainable Development – www.wbcsd.org

CHAPTER 9

Role of Governments and Nongovernmental Organizations

LEARNING OBJECTIVES

By the end of this chapter, you should be able to do the following:

» Understand the role of governments in promoting sustainability.
» Present the role of the U.S. Environmental Protection Agency (EPA).
» Explain Agenda 21 and the role of local governments.
» Discuss the history, growth, and funding of nongovernmental organizations (NGOs).
» Expand on the role of NGOs in social development, community development, and sustainable development.
» Explore NGOs and business partnerships.
» Discuss the role of NGOs and sustainable consumption.
» Present the five types of environmental NGOs.

Chapter Overview

This chapter presents the role of governments and NGOs in promoting sustainability. We start with the role of governments in advancing sustainability and provide some examples of legislation along with the role of the EPA. Next, we segue into the history and the growth of NGOs and the role of NGO funding as it relates to power. We discuss the role of NGOs in social development, community development, and sustainable development and present cases of partnerships between NGOs and businesses. We conclude with a detailed discussion on a specific category of NGOs: the environmental nongovernmental organizations (ENGOs).

Role of Governments

What role, if any, should governments play in promoting sustainability? Governments worldwide are beginning to recognize the challenge of sustainability, and this term is being addressed in public policy discussions. Any one government cannot work in this area alone; it is imperative to work with other governments in order to address the issue in a global context. According to a GlobeScan poll of experts, the leading role in achieving sustainability will be played by businesses (35 percent), followed by NGOs (30 percent), and governments (24 percent; Bell, 2002). Chapter 8 discussed the role of business in advancing sustainability, and this chapter will discuss the role of governments and NGOs in advancing sustainability.

Governments need to be able to anticipate the rising demand for sustainable products and services. Governments can play a key role in aiding the transition toward more efficient, less damaging economies. Those governments that can lead in this role would be able to set the agenda for their economies, industries, and citizens (Peck & Gibson, 2002).

In most developed countries, like the United States and Canada, the government is the largest employer, the largest landowner, and the largest fleet owner. The government is also the largest consumer of energy and has the largest impact on the environment. It stands to reason that governments should incorporate sustainability principles in their internal operations (Bell, 2002).

In developing countries, the role of the government assumes even greater significance. Within the realm of sustainability, governments ought to encourage companies to address the needs of the world's entire population (Prahalad & Hart, 2002).

According to a KPMG report, the government has four distinct roles in addressing sustainability concerns. These roles are as follows:

1. Policy development
2. Regulation
3. Facilitation
4. Internal sustainability management

CHAPTER 9 ∞ ROLE OF GOVERNMENTS AND NONGOVERNMENTAL ORGANIZATIONS | 253

GOVERNMENT ROLES IN SUSTAINABILITY

POLICY DEVELOPMENT
Development of new policies to steer and enable sustainability innovation

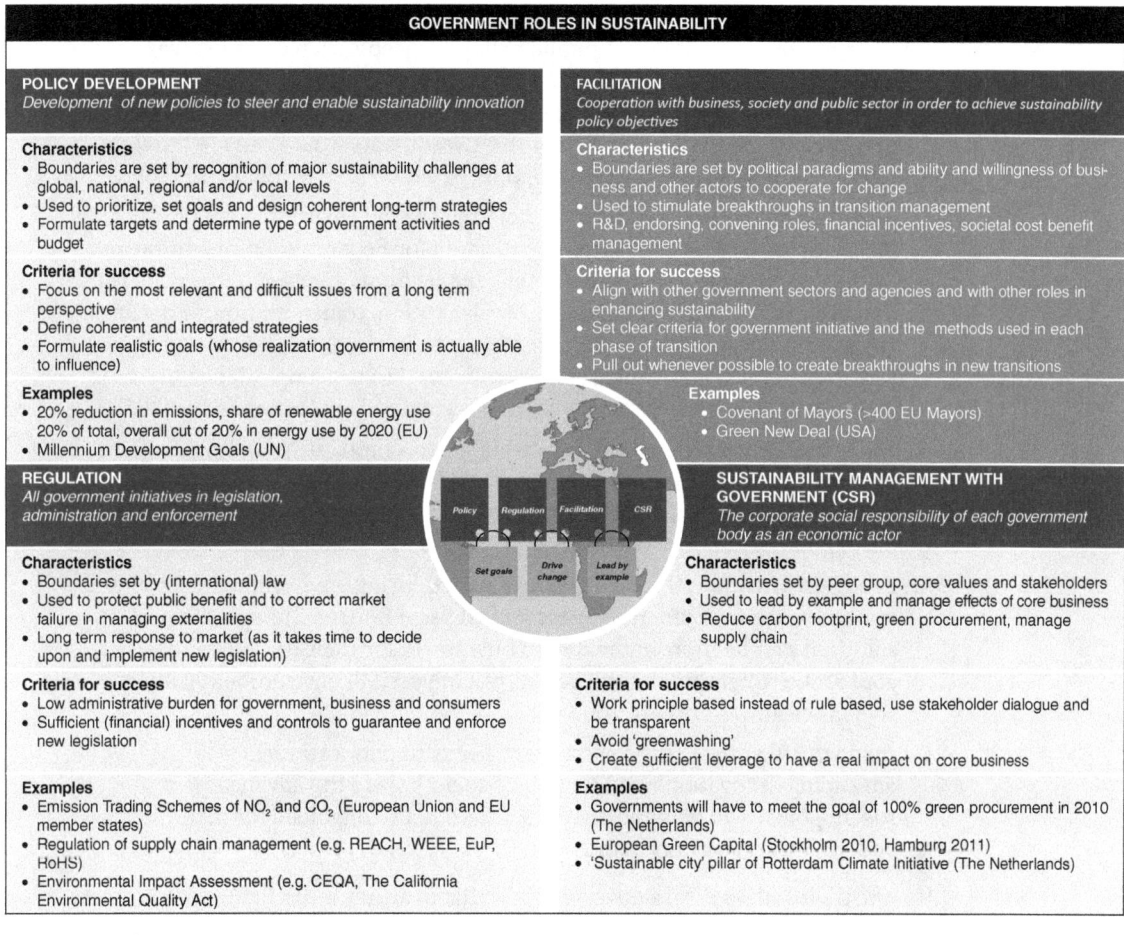

Characteristics
- Boundaries are set by recognition of major sustainability challenges at global, national, regional and/or local levels
- Used to prioritize, set goals and design coherent long-term strategies
- Formulate targets and determine type of government activities and budget

Criteria for success
- Focus on the most relevant and difficult issues from a long term perspective
- Define coherent and integrated strategies
- Formulate realistic goals (whose realization government is actually able to influence)

Examples
- 20% reduction in emissions, share of renewable energy use 20% of total, overall cut of 20% in energy use by 2020 (EU)
- Millennium Development Goals (UN)

FACILITATION
Cooperation with business, society and public sector in order to achieve sustainability policy objectives

Characteristics
- Boundaries are set by political paradigms and ability and willingness of business and other actors to cooperate for change
- Used to stimulate breakthroughs in transition management
- R&D, endorsing, convening roles, financial incentives, societal cost benefit management

Criteria for success
- Align with other government sectors and agencies and with other roles in enhancing sustainability
- Set clear criteria for government initiative and the methods used in each phase of transition
- Pull out whenever possible to create breakthroughs in new transitions

Examples
- Covenant of Mayors (>400 EU Mayors)
- Green New Deal (USA)

REGULATION
All government initiatives in legislation, administration and enforcement

Characteristics
- Boundaries set by (international) law
- Used to protect public benefit and to correct market failure in managing externalities
- Long term response to market (as it takes time to decide upon and implement new legislation)

Criteria for success
- Low administrative burden for government, business and consumers
- Sufficient (financial) incentives and controls to guarantee and enforce new legislation

Examples
- Emission Trading Schemes of NO_2 and CO_2 (European Union and EU member states)
- Regulation of supply chain management (e.g. REACH, WEEE, EuP, HoHS)
- Environmental Impact Assessment (e.g. CEQA, The California Environmental Quality Act)

SUSTAINABILITY MANAGEMENT WITH GOVERNMENT (CSR)
The corporate social responsibility of each government body as an economic actor

Characteristics
- Boundaries set by peer group, core values and stakeholders
- Used to lead by example and manage effects of core business
- Reduce carbon footprint, green procurement, manage supply chain

Criteria for success
- Work principle based instead of rule based, use stakeholder dialogue and be transparent
- Avoid 'greenwashing'
- Create sufficient leverage to have a real impact on core business

Examples
- Governments will have to meet the goal of 100% green procurement in 2010 (The Netherlands)
- European Green Capital (Stockholm 2010, Hamburg 2011)
- 'Sustainable city' pillar of Rotterdam Climate Initiative (The Netherlands)

FIGURE 9.1 | Four Government Roles to Spur Sustainability.
Source: Sustainable Insight (2009).

As shown in Figure 9.1, each of the policy-making, regulating, facilitating, and internal sustainability managing roles of government has its own characteristics and success factors. Combined, these roles have the potential to effectively support sustainability management through setting goals, driving change, and leading by example ("Sustainable Insight," 2009).

CHANGING ROLE OF GOVERNMENTS

Increasingly, governments are called to form partnerships ranging from the ones with other levels of government to ones with civil society organizations (CSOs) and the private sector. In terms of advancing sustainability, the government can also play a significant role. The five roles are discussed as follows:

1. *Visionary/Goal setter:* Governments need to provide vision and strategy to incorporate sustainability in public policy. Concepts such as natural capitalism (discussed in Chapter 6), eco-economy (Brown, 2009), and green economy (Milani, 2000) call for grand-scale transformations in systems dealing with energy, waste, water, and governance. Governments would need to develop strategies for a transition to an economy based on sustainability principles.

2. *Leader by example:* Governments can improve the environmental performance of public procurement (Organisation for Economic Co-operation and Development [OECD], 2002), whereby public funds are used in the construction of highways and buildings, power generation, transportation, and water and sanitation services. Green procurement can also provide impetus to innovative and environmentally friendly products. As an example, Japan used the procurement of low-emission automobiles to drive innovation (Bell, 2002).

3. *Facilitator:* Governments need to create "open, competitive, and rightly framed markets" that would include pricing of goods and services, dismantling subsidies, taxing waste and pollution, and so on. However, as Lester Brown (2002, p. 26) pointed out, "not one country has a strategy to build an eco-economy."

4. *Green fiscal authority:* Governments are exploring environmental taxes and market-based instruments for ecological fiscal reform. Though the market solutions can be more amenable to businesses for their flexibility, these approaches might not be the best at pricing certain environmental assets such as clean water (Bell, 2002).

5. *Innovator/Catalyst:* The government needs to play a strategic role in advancing innovation in all sectors of society since the advancement of sustainability will demand changes. There is a strong need for technological and policy innovation (Bell, 2002).

The traditional role of a government is that of an authority figure that protects public interests and regulates industries. This role is changing as governments are working collaboratively with other stakeholders from companies to CSOs. As the roles of governments change, so do their responsibilities. Indeed, the whole future of a sustainable world can be shaped by the policy decisions taken by governments, individually or in collective forums.

Policy Instruments

There are two basic policy instruments that can be employed by governments: (1) direct regulation and (2) market instruments and economic/fiscal measures.

Direct Regulation

The first form of public policy on the environment was direct regulation. These approaches are also termed *command and control* approaches since the taxes are set by the regulatory agency or the government, and the companies need to comply and pay these taxes. Though taxes are controversial and governments have faced pushback on the idea of carbon taxes, regulation is still an effective mechanism to ensure minimum performance from those players that are reluctant to comply.

Market Instruments and Economic/Fiscal Measures

This category includes any set of instruments that reward innovation in sustainability from the private sector. These instruments can include subsidies, taxes, ecolabeling schemes, and public procurement policies. The idea is that if the private sector is given enough motivation, the sector itself would come up with the best way to solve a problem. One such example was the cap and trade system, wherein the cap on emissions would be set by the regulatory agency, and companies would have an incentive to lower emissions and trade the extra permits. Research does indicate that market mechanisms are efficient, flexible, and more palatable to industry (Dhanda, 1999).

In addition, governments can also employ new policy instruments that expand the range of alternatives to regulation and legislation. The task of choosing the best "mix" from this wider array of possible options is not straightforward (Howlett & Ramesh, 1995), and research is ongoing to assess these various alternatives. For example, Italy is experimenting with a scheme that provides the consumer with a modest (1 percent) sales tax reduction on the price of green products. France, on the other hand, has introduced mandatory corporate sustainability reporting (Bell, 2002).

ROLE OF THE ENVIRONMENTAL PROTECTION AGENCY

In the United States, the largest regulatory organization is the EPA, which from the time of its inception acted as a watchdog for the environment, implementing pollution control regulations and ensuring that businesses met the legal requirements. As time progressed, the EPA's role changed from pollution control to pollution prevention.

The EPA Strategic Plan lays out the goals for the EPA for the next four years. As per this plan, the EPA is committed to protecting human health and the environment for all people, with an emphasis on communities it deems "overburdened and underserved." This plan renews commitment to the three basic principles at the EPA: "follow the science, follow the law, and be transparent." In addition, it adds a new fourth principle: advance justice and equity. This new principle aims to advance environmental justice and civil rights (EPA Strategic Plan, 2022).

LIST OF ENVIRONMENTAL PROTECTION AGENCY PROGRAMS FOR SUSTAINABILITY

There are numerous EPA policies and programs that have helped to shape policy. This is an archived list of programs managed by the EPA:

- Agriculture
- Air Quality
- Energy Efficiency and Global Climate Change
- Pollution Prevention
- Product Labeling

- Technology
- Transportation Programs
- Waste Management
- Water
- The EPA's Regional partnership programs

Local Governments for Sustainability

Much of the work on sustainability has been accomplished at the local level. One of the most comprehensive programs is Agenda 21, which calls for involvement at the local, national, and global levels. Agenda 21 articulates a series of environmental strategies for the management of natural resources and the monitoring and reduction of chemical and radioactive waste. It also contains socioeconomic plans to improve health care, develop sustainable farming development and fair trade policies, and reduce poverty (Agenda 21, n.d.-b). Furthermore, Agenda 21 requires local governments to develop their own "Local Agenda 21" for sustainable development. Agenda 21 is a large document with 40 chapters. The appendix to this chapter contains Chapter 27 of Agenda 21, one that discusses the role of NGOs.

Another local association is the International Council for Local Environmental Initiatives (ICLEI)—Local Governments for Sustainability, composed of over 2,500 local and regional government members. The members of ICLEI, representing more than 125 countries, influence sustainability policy and aim to drive local action for "low emission, nature-based, equitable, resilient and circular development." The main goal of ICLEI is to bring sustainability to the urban world, one that is rapidly developing (About us, 2022).

Nongovernmental Organizations

Definition

What is an NGO? The term NGO stands for nongovernmental organization. They are nonprofit entities centered around specific purposes or issues with local or international reach that operate independently from governments. The term NGO describes a range of groups and organizations from watchdog activist groups and aid agencies to development and policy organizations. Usually, NGOs are defined as organizations that pursue a public interest agenda, rather than commercial interests (Hall-Jones, 2006).

It is believed that the first international NGO was probably the Anti-Slavery Society, formed in 1839. However, the term *NGO* originated at the end of World War II when the United Nations sought to distinguish between private organizations and intergovernmental specialized agencies (Hall-Jones, 2006). NGOs are a complex mixture comprised of alliances and rivalries; businesses and charities; conservatives and radicals. The funding comes from various sources, and though NGOs are usually nonprofit organizations, there are some that operate for profit (Hall-Jones, 2006).

NGOs originate from all over the world and have access to different levels of resources. Some NGOs work on environmental preservation while others aim to advance human rights.

History of the Nongovernmental Organizations Movement

The first NGO was the Anti-Slavery Society, followed by the Red Cross and Caritas, a movement that arose at the end of the 19th century. Most of the other NGO movements were founded after the two world wars and, hence, were primarily humanitarian in nature. For example, Save the Children was formed after World War I, and CARE was formed after World War II (Hall-Jones, 2006). The decolonization of Africa in the 1960s led to a new way of thinking—one that focused on the causes of poverty rather than its consequences. The armed conflicts of the 1970s and 1980s (Vietnam, Angola, Palestine) led the European NGOs to take on the task of mediators for informal diplomacy. Their support for locals had an impact on the demise of the apartheid regime in South Africa and the dictatorships of Ferdinand Marcos in the Philippines and Augusto Pinochet in Chile. In addition, in the mid-1980s, the World Bank realized that NGOs were more effective and less corrupt than the typical government channels. The food crisis in Ethiopia in 1984 spurred a new market for "humanitarian aid" (Berthoud, 2001).

In the history of the NGO movement's growth, there have been several milestones. One of the first milestones was the role of the solidarity movement in the political transformation in Poland in the 1980s. The next was the impact of environmental activists on the 1992 Earth Summit in Rio de Janeiro. Another milestone was the Fifty Years Is Enough campaign in 1994. This was organized by the South Council and was aimed at the World Bank and International Monetary Fund (IMF) on the belief that these two institutions had been promoting and financing unsustainable development overseas that created poverty and destroyed the environment. The most recent milestone was the organization of the labor, anti-globalization, and environmental groups that protested and disturbed the Seattle World Trade Organization (WTO) meeting in 1999 (McGann & Johnstone, 2006).

Top 10 Most Influential NGOs in the World

The NGO ADVISOR, a Geneva-based independent media organization, compiles yearly rankings that feature the most impactful NGOs. These are the top 10 nonprofit organizations highlighted in the 2021 ranking:

1. BRAC International, established in 1972 and headquartered in Dhaka, is the largest nongovernmental development organization in the world. This NGO offers a wide range of services that create opportunities for social empowerment, education, health, livelihood, environmentalism, and disaster preparedness. It employs the largest workforce of any NGO—107,000 people—and its annual income was around $1.08 billion USD.

2. Médecins Sans Frontières (MSF) or Doctors without Borders, founded in 1972 and headquartered in Switzerland, is an international non-profit medical humanitarian organization that offers emergency medical assistance and guidance to people affected by armed conflicts, violence, epidemics, or natural disasters. It employs over 45,000 people and has reported an annual income of almost €2 billion.
3. Open Society Foundations, founded in 1993 in the United States, is a network of international and national nonprofit organizations working for justice, democratic governance, and human rights. It employs between 1,001 and 5,000 people and reported an income over $500 million USD.
4. The Danish Refugee Council, founded in 1956 in Denmark, is one of the leading international nonprofits that offer humanitarian support to refugees and internally displaced persons affected by violence, war, political crises, and natural disasters. It operates in 40 countries, employs 9,000 people, and has an operating income of about €430 million.
5. Ashoka, founded in 1980 in the United States, is an international nonprofit entity that focuses on empowering social leadership, entrepreneurship, and innovation. Ashoka is currently running projects in more than 90 countries, employs a little over 500 people, and had an operating income in 2019 of close to $65 million USD.
6. Mercy Corps, established in 1979 in the United States, is an international humanitarian nonprofit working in more than 40 countries around the world with a mission to alleviate suffering and poverty and assist those in need to build secure, productive, and just communities. The organization currently employs over 5,300 team members and lists a yearly operating income of $500 million USD.
7. JA Worldwide, established in 1919, is one of the world's largest youth-centered NGOs. The organization works in over 100 countries by assisting young people to gain the professional and entrepreneurial skillsets necessary to succeed. JA Worldwide employs about 4,000 people and has an annual operating income of about $370 million USD.
8. Acumen, founded in 2001, is an international NGO that aims to drive impact across the globe by investing in businesses that tackle poverty. It currently employs about 300 people and its last known operational income was a little over $33 million USD.
9. Cure Violence Global, established in 1995 in the United States, aims to reduce violence globally using disease control and behavior change methods. The organization currently employs about 700 people, has programs running in more than 50 cities worldwide, and has a yearly income of about $55 million USD.
10. Landesa, established in 1981 in the United States, forms partnerships with governments and other stakeholders to create opportunities for the world's poorest to lift themselves out of poverty. Landesa currently employs about 120 people and showed a yearly operating income of a little over $13 million USD (Ilasco, 2021).

GROWTH IN POWER

The real story is how these organizations have networked and impacted world politics.

Global politics have gone through a drastic shift resulting from the growth of nongovernmental agencies. NGOs or CSOs have moved from being in the background to having a presence in the midst of world politics and, as a result, are exerting their influence and power in policy-making on a global scale. Some organizations such as Amnesty International and Greenpeace have effectively become NGO brands and have helped make NGO a household word. At the 1992 Earth Summit in Rio, there was a large NGO presence. While 1,400 NGO members were involved in the official proceedings, another 17,000 NGO members staged an alternative forum to the meeting. Encouraged by their success, a larger group gathered in Beijing for the Fourth World Conference on Women (McGann & Johnstone, 2006).

How have NGOs gained this global attention? There are various strategies that have been employed. For example, some NGOs organize large-scale protests, capture international headlines, and gain notoriety. The two NGOs that were successful in organizing large-scale action around specific themes were Amnesty International, which focuses on human rights issues, and Greenpeace, which focuses on ecological issues (Berthoud, 2001). There are other NGOs that have organized meetings to challenge the legitimacy of the WTO, the G8, the World Bank, and the IMF. The effectiveness of these NGOs' efforts took governments and other global multilateral institutions by surprise. In response, these efforts forced the governments to figure out ways to involve NGOs in their decision-making. Now that their place in world politics is firmly established, most NGOs have moved from street protests to a policy-making role in the boardrooms of the United Nations, WTO, World Bank, and the IMF (McGann & Johnstone, 2006).

What are the factors that have led to the unprecedented growth of NGOs? Research by McGann and Johnstone (2006) has isolated six interrelated forces as follows:

1. *Democratization and the civil society ideal:* The emergence of civil society and the addition of more open societies have both led to an environment that was favorable to the proliferation of NGOs.

2. *Democratization and the civil society ideal:* The general public is bombarded with unsystematic and unreliable information. NGOs can collect data to make decisions, a role that is invaluable in developing countries where such information might not readily exist.

3. *Growth of state, nonstate, and interstate actors:* After World War II, there was a global trend toward increased democratization and decentralization that led to an increase in the number of nations or states after World War II. In addition, numerous intergovernmental organizations (United Nations, WTO, World Bank) were created and granted certain powers and functions. This led to unprecedented growth in the number of governmental organizations, NGOs, and nation-states.

4. *Improved communications technologies:* The growth of the Internet has led to an inexpensive, instant, and largely unregulated flow of information. In addition, the nature of the information age makes it very difficult to restrict the inflow of information from the perspective of authoritarian governments.

5. *Globalization of NGO funding:* The issue of funding is important since many organizations work with small budgets and staff. In many nations such as those in Africa, Asia, and Latin America, there are no tax incentives to fund NGOs. Hence, most of the funding flows from developed countries to developing or transitional countries. However, foreign funding raises questions about the credibility of an organization. Furthermore, the issues of funding, transparency, and accountability become more complicated when NGOs cross national borders.

6. *Paralysis and poor performance of the public sector:* There has been an erosion of confidence in government leaders and institutions. The never-ending scandals involving public officials combined with the poor performance of policymakers have led citizens to question the legitimacy of governments. When the institutions are considered ineffective and the nation-state is distrusted, the NGOs operating on a local, grassroots level have emerged so that these deficiencies can be addressed.

Role of Nongovernmental Organizations

Given this unprecedented growth in the numbers and financial power of NGOs, how has the role changed or matured? What we see is that NGOs can have a huge impact. These NGOs are unfettered, not answerable to specific agendas, and, in many instances, can act independently.

Even though NGOs are highly diverse organizations, the one common goal is that they are not focused on short-term targets, and thus, they devote themselves to long-term issues like climate change, malaria prevention, or human rights. In addition, public surveys state that NGOs often have public trust, which makes them a useful proxy for societal concerns (Hall-Jones, 2006).

Next, we will discuss four important roles of NGOs. These roles are (1) social development, (2) sustainable community development, (3) sustainable development, and (4) sustainable consumption.

Social Development

NGOs play an important role in global social development—work that has helped facilitate achievements in human development as measured by the UN Human Development Index (HDI).

One of the major strengths of NGOs is their ability to maintain institutional independence and political neutrality. Even though NGOs need to collaborate with governments in numerous instances, failure to maintain neutrality and autonomy may severely compromise the NGOs' legitimacy. Unfortunately, if a government insists upon political allegiance, NGOs encounter the dilemma of either violating the neutrality position or failing to provide needed services to the population. Indeed, some NGOs have been asked to leave troubled countries due to political reasons (Asamoah, 2003).

The major advantages that NGOs bring to this role include "flexibility, ability to innovate, grass-roots orientation, humanitarian versus commercial goal orientation, non-profit status, dedication and commitment, and recruitment philosophy" (Asamoah, 2003). The drawbacks of working with NGOs are similar to the advantages that were previously listed. In addition, some other disadvantages include "over-zealousness, restricted local participation, inadequate feasibility studies, conflicts or misunderstandings with host partner, inflexibility in recruitment and procedures, turf wars, inadequately trained personnel, lack of funding to complete projects, lack of transparency, inability to replicate results, and cultural insensitivity" (Asamoah, 2003).

SUSTAINABLE COMMUNITY DEVELOPMENT

NGOs have shown leadership in promoting sustainable community development. Due to their particular ideology and nature, NGOs are good at reaching out to the poor and remote communities and mobilizing these populations. They can also empower these populations to regain control of their lives and can work with and strengthen local organizations. In addition, such NGOs can carry out projects more efficiently and at lower costs than government agencies and, most importantly, promote sustainable development (Nikkhah & Redzuan, 2010).

The five dimensions of sustainable community development are as follows:

1. Increasing local economic diversity
2. Self-reliance: development of local markets, local production, local processing, greater cooperation among local economic entities
3. Reduction in the use of energy combined with recycling and management of waste products
4. Protection and enhancement of biological diversity and stewardship of natural resources
5. The commitment of sustainable communities to social justice (Bridger & Luloff, 1999).

Since NGOs are professionally staffed organizations aimed at the reduction of human suffering and the development of poor countries (Streeten, 1997), they have a significant role to play in supporting women, men, and households. The roles of such NGOs include "counseling and support service, awareness-raising and advocacy, legal aid and microfinance" (Desai, 2005). The long-term aim of these NGOs is to assist in sustainable community development through activities such as capacity building and self-reliance (Langran, 2002). This can be done by funding projects, contributing to awareness, and promoting the self-organization of various groups (Baccaro, 2001).

A case study in Vietnam illustrates that NGOs play an important role in promoting sustainable community development (Hibbard & Tang, 2004). Usually, this is accomplished by providing three basic functions: (1) service delivery (e.g., relief, welfare), (2) education, and (3) public policy advocacy (Stromquist, 2002). The idea is that NGOs can promote sustainable community development via three functions: (1) microfinance, (2) capacity building, and (3) self-reliance. NGOs ought to develop local products and local markets; develop social, capital, and human resources; encourage and motivate people to participate in activities; and act as network liaisons between communities and systems. In this manner, the long-term goal of sustainable community development would be achieved (Nikkhah & Redzuan, 2010).

Sustainable Development

NGOs have played a significant role in promoting sustainable development at the international level. NGOs are going beyond their primary focus on governments and starting to address large corporations. In this vein, NGOs have focused attention on the social and environmental impacts of business activity, helped in part by advances in information and communications technology. The brands of multinational corporations have also been vulnerable to pressure from activists and from NGOs on the corporation's labor, environmental, or human rights record. As the downstream customers are targeted, even the supply chain partners and suppliers are feeling the pressure (Hall-Jones, 2006).

In response to such concerns, many corporations are embracing a stakeholder approach that looks at the impact of business activity on customers, employees, communities, and other interested groups. There are numerous visible manifestations of this shift. The primary one has been an increased attention to social and environmental affairs. Many corporations are taking responsibility for their actions and are starting to report on the impact of their activities. A secondary shift is more heartening: Many companies have designed management structures that integrate sustainable development concerns (Hall-Jones, 2006).

NGOs can take most of the credit for creating these trends. The question remains as to how the business world should react to NGOs in the future. Should companies gear themselves in preparation of attacks from hostile critics? Should companies engage NGOs to become helpful partners? Depending upon their philosophy, not all NGOs are willing to collaborate with the private sector. Some NGOs observe at a distance and monitor, publicize, and criticize cases where companies fail to consider their impacts upon the community. However, other NGOs are willing to allocate some of their resources to working along with businesses to further corporate social responsibility (CSR; Hall-Jones, 2006).

Agenda 21 of the United Nations has a chapter dedicated to the role of NGOs in partnering for sustainable development. Please refer to the appendix for the full text of this chapter.

Sustainable Consumption

NGOs can also play an important role as partners to business/industry in promoting sustainable consumption. Some of the instances when this partnership has been successful is in categories such as product development, sustainable housing, labeling, the World Wildlife Fund (WWF), green purchasing, marine stewardship, and so on. The basic premise is: can NGOs influence behavioral change? Specifically, there are two questions that need to be asked: (1) How are

NGOs educating households to change their consumption behavior, and (2) how can NGOs be potential partners to businesses in promoting sustainable consumption (Kong, Saltzmann, Steger, & Ionescu-Somers, 2002)?

A range of projects shows that NGOs are engaging businesses to promote sustainable consumption. Some of the interesting approaches are as follows:

Using Strategic Means to Point Out Problems

NGOs are encouraging households to exercise their power as shareholders. If shareholder power is substantial, this can raise public awareness and change business policies. For example, Friends of the Earth's (FoE) Green Paycheck Campaign tells individuals how to use their shareholder power and screen their investments so that "money becomes a tool for change" (Kong, et al., 2002).

Assessing Environmental Impacts of Products

NGOs rank products and services based on their environmental performance and impacts. The idea is that consumers can then pick and choose what products or brands they would purchase. For example, many consumer organizations have adopted a commitment to sustainability in their mission statements, such as in Austria, Germany, Sweden, Norway, and the Netherlands, and their assessment of products reaches consumers via magazines, websites, and other publications (Kong, et al., 2002).

Greening the Supply of Products and Services

NGOs are developing or designing products that will minimize the environmental impacts of consumption. The consumer is simply offered an alternative of more sustainable consumption, and this choice is deemed empowering. For example, the WWF is engaging the retail sector to offer more sustainable food products. It also cooperates with the catering sector to design WWF Weeks for the menu and one permanent WWF dish. This campaign has been successful in increasing demand for organic products in Switzerland (Kong, et al., 2002).

Focusing on Market Forces

Creating a green demand that will drive changes in supply, NGOs are providing information through labels that would empower consumers to make informed choices. For example, WWF has worked with the industry to design labeling schemes to help in the launch of independent certification bodies. The Forest Stewardship Council (FSC) was created in 1993 to protect the world's forest by a coalition of NGOs, businesses, and government entities. Unilever and WWF started the Marine Stewardship Council (MSC) to establish a certification scheme for sustainable fishing (Kong, et al., 2002).

Forming Extensive Networks of Different Stakeholders

NGOs enter into collaborations with other NGOs and businesses to highlight issues and jointly look for solutions. For example, the Green Purchasing Network (GPN) promotes green purchasing among consumers, businesses, and other governmental organizations in Japan. It consists of 2,150 members including Sony, Fuji, Toyota, Honda, Canon, and Mitsubishi among others (Kong, et al., 2002).

Business Partnerships

Corporations have partnered with NGOs when looking to tackle social and environmental issues that matter to the company. Some leading examples include GSK's partnership with Save the Children to help reduce child mortality, the Aviva-British Red Cross collaboration to help communities with disaster preparedness and response, Lifebuoy's partnership with NGOs to promote hand hygiene, and Danone's partnership with the Ramsar Convention on Wetlands and the International Union for Conservation of Nature to restore natural ecosystems that support disadvantaged rural communities (Mizar, 2019).

In the past, corporate philanthropy was the main driver for business-NGO collaboration. The new wave of collaboration is different. The present trend is toward strategic partnerships aimed at addressing internal operational issues and the external impacts of corporate activity. Within the partnerships, NGOs and trade unions are involved in decisions that impact core business practices. As a result, CSR has evolved from what companies do with their profits to looking at how companies make those profits (Bendell, 2010).

One notable trend has been that of development NGOs promoting sustainable development among other companies. As an example, the British NGO called the Fairtrade Foundation initiated a pilot project to assist companies in developing codes of practice to guide relationships with their suppliers. Another initiative, launched in 1998, contained a broader mandate and came with UK government backing. The Ethical Trading Initiative (ETI) is a network of companies, NGOs, and trade union organizations working together to identify and promote good labor practices, including monitoring and independent verification. Some of the members include supermarket chains J. Sainsbury and Tesco, garment industry players Levi Strauss and the Pentland Group, and NGOs Oxfam and Save the Children (Bendell, 2010).

NGOs are helping in the establishment of certification systems that would help companies to monitor, measure, and communicate their social and environmental best practices. As an example, the WWF, an environmental NGO, has helped in the FSC accreditation, certification, and labeling scheme that endorses products from properly managed forests. Rather than waiting for time-consuming regulatory agreements, the NGO spearheaded the creation of a new organization for moving the industry toward sustainability (Bendell, 2010).

Corporate and not-for-profit partnerships are on the rise. The 2018 Corporate-NGO Partnerships Barometer from C&E Advisory, a UK-based consultancy, has found that 86 percent of corporate respondents and 88 percent of NGO respondents see the role of corporate-NGO partnerships growing in importance over the next few years (Mizar, 2019).

Other Examples

Corporate partnerships are a challenge for any non-profit organization, but these partnerships can be especially tough for smaller organizations. There are a few examples where cooperation between a business and an NGO resulted in a synergistic relationship.

FORON & Greenpeace

Greenpeace, known for its extreme activist stunts, has worked with industry to promote solutions for a better environment. In 1992, Greenpeace partnered with German company FORON to develop the first ten "Greenfreeze" technology refrigerators, appliances that were completely free of chlorofluorocarbons (CFCs), hydrochlorofluorocarbons (HCFCs), and hydrofluorocarbons (HFCs). Greenpeace Germany and FORON quickly moved to market and within three weeks of the development of the new product, the launch had secured 70,000 orders from German households.

LEGO & WWF

WWF has worked with a range of local and international partners to pursue key environmental priorities from deforestation to overfishing to sustainable palm oil. With LEGO, the partnership aimed to work with the LEGO Group's global suppliers in order to reduce total greenhouse gas emissions by 10,000 tons. Through its partnership with WWF, LEGO has committed to cutting the energy it uses to create each LEGO® element by 10 percent and become carbon positive by the end of 2016 (Greentumble, 2022).

One of the major risks for small NGOs working to build a corporate program is the "transactional partnership" trap, which leads to a mere contractual relationship, rather than something more transformational and two-way. A meaningful partnership is one in which shared goals are at the core of the strategy and impact is achieved for both partners.

These five examples show how genuine impact can be achieved by small organizations through proactive and purposeful collaboration with businesses.

The Sweet Partnership

The Entrepreneurial Refugee Network (TERN) is a pioneering social enterprise that teamed up with Ben & Jerry's in 2017 to reach a shared goal: empowering refugee entrepreneurs in the UK. This partnership set up the Ice Academy, an innovative incubator program for refugees to receive training and mentoring. The Ice Academy provides part-time employment as well as invaluable access to finances, resources, networks, and opportunities (Awad, 2019).

The Purposeful Partnership

On Purpose is a community that helps young professionals achieve a meaningful career change to put purpose before profit. Their one-year Fellowship Programme lets interns spend time in different organizations. One corporate partner is Lightful, a social impact company developing technology for social good. The paid interns learn new skills, repurpose their existing ones, and gain exposure to a huge network of companies and professionals, making it easier for them to find job opportunities once the fellowship ends. At the same time, they are adding value to Lightful and its team (Awad, 2019).

The Shared Goal Partnership

Women Win leverages the power of sports and play to empower women through building leadership skills and supporting them to exercise their rights. In 2006 Standard Chartered Bank launched its Goal Programme with Women Win as one of the primary partners. Goal is a curriculum for girls aged 12–18 using sports to build their social capital and develop their economic and social skills. With a target of reaching 500,000 girls by 2018, Standard Chartered and Women Win scaled the initiative by licensing the Goal curriculum to other local partners across Asia and Africa (Awad, 2019).

The Mapped Partnership

Mapping areas before a crisis is an efficient way to support humanitarian work, as it enables emergency responders to reach those in need faster and more efficiently. The Humanitarian OpenStreetMap Team (HOT) revolutionizes disaster management in remote areas through map data, in collaboration with local communities and corporate partners. As part of their 2016 Missing Maps Project, they trained Accenture employees to chart vulnerable "unmapped" areas in a global digital volunteering "mapathon." Employees mapped at their desks (or in groups) for as little as one hour at a time. This helped Accenture create a sense of community within and across their global offices, while actively making a difference in supporting humanitarian work and disaster response in remote areas (Awad, 2019).

The Learning Partnership

In 2017, international law firm DLA Piper launched "Know Your Rights," a pro bono program that delivers training and advice to empower refugees and increase their legal knowledge and integration. After a successful launch in Belgium, the firm went on to establish partnerships in several European countries, including with the French NGO Terre d'Asile. DLA Piper delivers the program by leveraging their own corporate relationships with clients such as Nike, Amazon, and BNP Paribas, who teach additional classes alongside their local NGO partners (Awad, 2019).

When common goals are shared, the gains can be far greater than a simple marketing exercise. Services, resources, and expertise can be leveraged to transform both businesses and social good causes.

Caveats

Not all NGO-business collaborations are always fruitful. As an example, challenges arose in the creation of a certification scheme for banana plantations. In the case of Chiquita's partnership with the Rainforest Alliance, the scheme started with the NGO certifying bananas, but over time, this certification grew to coffee and other fruits. The critics argued that this was a case of greenwashing since the partnership did not tackle the most important issues in banana production (Bendell, 2007).

Why do partnerships fail?

A high percentage—around 80 percent—of cross-sector partnerships, fail. According to a consultancy report, there are four leading causes of partnership development failure.

1. *Choosing the Wrong Partner*

   It is important that partners understand their counterparts' motivations, goals, incentives, and constraints before committing to a partnership. While it is rare for partners to have complete alignment across the board, partners need to do sufficient due diligence to identify potential sources of significant disagreement or conflict.

   Case in point: an argument between two partners—one a representative of a major bilateral government donor agency, the other an executive at a well-known agricultural development NGO. The donor and the NGO were two of the lead partners in a cross-sector partnership, along with several leading multinational agribusinesses. The multimillion-dollar partnership was meant to strengthen the seed industry in West Africa—critical to enhancing food security in the region. On the surface, the partners were all highly interested in agriculture in West Africa, and they all believed that the seed industry was a critical component of food security in the region. Yet some of the partners felt strongly that genetically modified organisms (GMOs) were critical to increasing yields and should play a central role in any solution and other partners were passionately opposed to GMOs for a variety of environmental and ideological reasons. This fundamental divide on whether or not to support GMOs made it almost impossible for partnership development. Had these partners invested the time to understand the perspectives, priorities, and approaches of the other partners, they would have quickly realized that despite having a shared goal, they diverged significantly on the means to achieve it.

2. *Choosing the Wrong Solution*

   At times, the problem is not the actual partners, but the solution the partners are developing or propagating. As an example, Playpumps International was a high-profile partnership that collapsed after it was discovered that the solution—a merry-go-round water pump powered by children playing—had numerous conceptual and design flaws. The merry-go-round would have to spin 24 hours a day to supply enough water for a typical village. Many of these wells were located in areas where children simply did not play. Lastly, the partners failed to appreciate how important and expensive maintenance would be. After spending millions of dollars and installing more than a thousand pumps, Playpumps was shut down following exposés in the news media.

   A partnership needs to be grounded in smart solution design. This means reaching out to local stakeholders to understand the context, making sure the right problem is being solved, and leaning in and testing solutions in ways that include rigorous monitoring, evaluation, and learning. This is important to help partners adapt and pivot away from poor solutions before investing many millions of dollars.

3. *Falling Short on Governance*

   There are times that partnerships fail because of poor or weak governance and decision-making among the partners. In the case of the West Africa agribusiness partnership, the partners had established an elaborate governance structure that made it difficult to make decisions quickly. In addition, the governance structure lacked transparency—several partners and key stakeholders were totally in the dark as to how decisions within the partnership were being made. This made a difficult situation even worse.

   Partnership governance structures can take many forms: from informal working groups to elaborate tiered governance boards. Regardless of the structure chosen, successful partnership development seeks to balance three governance elements: equity, transparency, and decision-making.

4. *Failing to Secure Internal Buy-in*

   The next major partnership development pitfall takes place behind the scenes, within the individual partner organizations. Many cross-sector partnerships fail due to a lack of internal buy-in and support. In other words, the partners are ready to go, but the internal team isn't truly on board. For this reason, an essential part of the partnership development process is to sell the collaboration concept internally and to keep communication open — celebrating successes and building momentum.

   Each partner also needs to be realistic about the internal costs and requirements of the partnership and should be ready to make a clear and persuasive case for how the partnership helps their own team meet their goals (despite the costs). If you can't make that case and gain the enthusiastic support of your leadership and team, you need to stop and reassess (Schmida, 2021).

Environmental Nongovernmental Organizations

ENGOs are the NGOs that work directly for the preservation of the environment. There is a linkage between environmental protection and democracy in that democracy enhances the protection of the environment (Holden, 2002). Indeed, Principle 10 of the Rio Declaration states, "Environmental issues are best handled with the participation of all concerned citizens, at the relevant level" (United Nations Conference on Environment and Development [UNCED], 1992). This viewpoint is further reiterated by the Johannesburg Declaration which also restates the need for "broad-based participation in policy formulation, decision-making and implementation at all levels" as well as the "need [for] more effective, democratic and accountable international and multilateral institutions" (United Nations, 2002, Principles 26, 31).

Role of Environmental Nongovernmental Organizations

The ENGOs provide for "popular participation and influence" in environmental politics (Holden, 2002, p. 139). This influence can be noted by the following two examples. First, Greenpeace has 3.25 million supporters worldwide (Greenpeace, 2022). Second, FoE has an estimated 1 million supporters and 75 member groups worldwide with 5,000 local activist groups (FoE International, 2002, p. 3).

According to the World Commission on Environment and Development (WCED), ENGOs play "an indispensable role . . . in identifying risks, in assessing environmental impacts and designing and implementing measures to deal with them, and in maintaining the high degree of public and political interest required as a basis for action" (WCED, 1987, p. 326).

ENGOs have become key players in environmental politics at all levels from local to global. As an example, FoE can play an important role in matters from local planning disputes to global environmental conferences (Pricen & Finger, 1994, pp. 4–6). Hence, ENGOs are vital democratic entities for the promotion of environmental sustainability.

However, ENGOs have also been questioned or criticized on two fronts. The first criticism is on grounds of efficacy; that is to say, ENGOs have insufficient influence to promote environmental sustainability. The second criticism contends that ENGOs are not always democratic institutions. For example, Greenpeace is a protest organization that aims to shape the views of its own members rather than represent these views (Bell, 2003).

THE SPLIT: FROM TWO GROUPS TO FIVE

The environmental movement seems to have split into two groups—one that partners with businesses and the other that does not. Christine McDonald, former media manager of Conservation International (CI), discussed the practice of ENGOs that accept corporate industrial donations without holding them accountable. She further stated that this relationship between ENGOs and corporations has led to the system of co-optation, whereby the result is greenwashing (McDonald, 2008).

There is an ideological distinction between the two camps of environmentalists: the dark greens and the bright greens. NGOs such as Greenpeace and FoE are dark greens in that they call for radical social change and confront corporations. The bright greens, on the other hand, such as CI and the Environmental Defense Fund (EDF) work within the system, with the partnership of corporations, to solve these environmental problems (Hoffman, 2009).

Research suggests that this gap between purity and pragmatism is getting wider. However, both the camps need to work together since the ability of moderate ENGOs is enhanced by the presence of the radical ENGOs (Conner & Epstein, 2007).

Andrew Hoffman used social networking tools and came up with five different types of ENGOs: (1) isolates, (2) mediators, (3) bridges, (4) independents, and (5) captives. Refer to Hoffman (2009) for a complete listing of the five categories of ENGOs.

Isolates

The ENGOs in this group refuse to partner with corporations. They form an ideological core that does not concern itself with the corporate sector's issues. Examples are Greenpeace, The Wildlife Society, FoE, and others (Hoffman, 2009).

Mediators

The ENGOs in this group are central to the corporate network and maintain sectoral links. These ENGOs are pragmatic and able to influence change due to their corporate ties. For example, the only five ENGOs that are part of the U.S. Climate Action partnership are in this group. These are (1) EDF, (2) The Nature Conservancy, (3) Natural Resources Defense Council (NRDC), (4) World Resources Institute, and (5) WWF (Hoffman, 2009).

Bridges

The first of the hybrid groups among the previous two extremes maintains a narrow spectrum of sectoral links. These ENGOs channel between a specific set of corporate sector issues and the rest of the group. For example, the Center for Clean Air Policy is a bridge focused on solving climate, air quality, and energy problems, yet it maintains ties with the oil and gas sectors (Hoffman, 2009).

Independents

The second hybrid group is located on the periphery of the corporate network but maintains a wide variety of links, which gives them more autonomy than others. These ENGOs are good at generating innovative solutions that involve collaboration among various sectors. An example is the River Network, which helps freshwater protection organizations (Hoffman, 2009).

Captives

The last of the hybrid group is also on the periphery of the corporate network, and their sectoral links are very limited, mostly tied to marine, firearms, and beer and alcohol. These ENGOs have greater credibility with the sectors they engage with, but this role makes them vulnerable to a small subset of biased influence from one set of corporate interests (Hoffman, 2009).

BLESSED UNREST

Paul Hawken (2007) described blessed unrest as a movement that is made of citizens and organizations that are united by their shared beliefs. This movement includes NGOs, nonprofit organizations, people who call themselves environmental activists, and others who protest labor injustices or support local farming. Hawken (2007) said, "Life is the most fundamental human right, and all of the movements within the movement are dedicated to creating the conditions for life, conditions that include livelihood, food, security, peace, a stable environment, and freedom from external tyranny" (pp. 67–68).

The book *Blessed Unrest: How the Largest Social Movement in History Is Restoring Grace, Justice, and Beauty to the World* by Paul Hawken contains an appendix that lists concerns from climate change to child labor and green banking to global governance. In Hawken's estimates, this movement is composed of 2 million organizations. More importantly, *Blessed Unrest* makes a link between the environment and issues of social justice and culture. Hawken (2007) said, "Sustainability, ensuring the future of life on earth, is an infinite game, the endless expression of generosity on behalf of all" (p. 187).

Conclusion

There are countless NGOs worldwide and these organizations have played a significant role in social development, sustainable community development, and promoting sustainable consumption. Businesses that wish to reach out to all their stakeholders can benefit from a productive relationship with NGOs. In addition, there is a category of NGOs called ENGOs that focus on environmental concerns. There are a large number of ENGOs ranging from the Audubon Society to WWF.

Lastly, two of the principles of Agenda 21 are relevant to sustainability. These principles are as follows:

1. The right to development must be fulfilled so as to equitably meet the developmental and environmental needs of the present and future generations.

2. In order to achieve sustainable development, environmental protection shall constitute an integral part of the development process and cannot be considered in isolation from it (Agenda 21, n.d.-a).

Keywords

- Agenda 21
- Blessed unrest
- Environmental nongovernmental organizations (ENGOs)
- Global social development
- International Council for Local Environmental Initiatives (ICLEI)— Local Governments for Sustainability
- International nongovernmental organizations (INGOs)
- Nongovernmental organizations (NGOs)
- Sustainable community development
- Sustainable consumption
- Sustainable development

Discussion Questions

1. What is the role of government in advancing sustainability? Do you think that governments can serve as leaders in this role?

2. As a web exercise, explore your frequently visited websites to find information that can be used for sustainability within business and personal use. Is there any information related to sustainability initiatives?

3. When were NGOs created? What were some of the historical reasons that led to this creation?

4. How do NGOs attain their funding? Do some of these sources of funding pose a conflict of interest?

5. Which NGO is the richest in the world? Has this ranking changed in recent years? What are the eight biggest NGOs discussed in the chapter?

6. What are the six factors that contributed to the growth of NGOs?
7. How can NGOs promote the following three areas: (1) social development, (2) community development, and (3) sustainable consumption? Discuss these roles in detail.
8. Should businesses or corporations partner with NGOs? What are the advantages or disadvantages of this relationship?
9. What is an ENGO? What are the five types of ENGOs? Discuss the differences between these ENGOs.
10. Research any three NGOs mentioned in the chapter. Go to the official website of these NGOs and discuss the role of each NGO in detail.
11. Can you think of any NGO and business partnership that has been particularly beneficial or disturbing?
12. What is the role of Agenda 21? Can you find a local chapter of Agenda 21 in your community?

Recommended Websites

- Audubon Society – www.audubon.org/
- Business for Social Responsibility – www.bsr.org/
- CARE – www.care.org/
- Conservation International – www.conservation.org/
- Catholic Relief Services – crs.org/
- CSR Wire – www.csrwire.com/
- Doctors Without Borders – www.doctorswithoutborders.org/
- United States Environmental Protection Agency – www.epa.gov
- Friends of the Earth – www.foe.org/
- Future 500 – www.future500.org/
- Greenpeace – www.greenpeace.org/
- InterAction – www.interaction.org/
- Kiva – www.kiva.org/
- Mercy Corps – www.mercycorps.org/
- Marine Stewardship Council – www.msc.org/
- Oxfam International – www.oxfam.org/
- Save the Children – www.savethechildren.org/
- International Rescue Committee – www.theirc.org/
- Division for Sustainable Development – www.un.org/esa/dsd/agenda21/res_agenda21_00.shtml
- United Nations Environment Programme – www.unep.org
- World Vision – www.worldvision.org/
- World Wildlife Fund – www.wwf.org

Appendix

TABLE 9.1 | Sustainable Development Programs.

Country	Sample of Sustainable Development Research Programs
Austria (individual programs)	Austrian Landscape Research; Austrian Program on Technology for Sustainable Development; PFEIL 05 Program for Research and Development in Agriculture, Forestry, Environment and Water Management.
Belgium (umbrella program and sub-programs)	Scientific Support Plan for a Sustainable Development Policy 1 (Sustainable management of the North Sea, global change and sustainable development, Antarctica 4, sustainable mobility, norms for food products, Telsat 4, levers for a sustainable development policy and supporting actions); Scientific Support Plan for a Sustainable Development Policy 2 (Sustainable modes of production and consumption, global change, eco-systems and biodiversity, supporting actions and mixed actions); Scientific Support to an Integration of Notions of Quality and Security of the Production Environments, Processes and Goods in a Context of Sustainable Development.
Germany (umbrella program and sub-programs)	Research on the Environment (Research on sustainable economic management, regional sustainability, research on global change, socioecological research)
The Netherlands (umbrella program with structured and coordinated individual programs)	Economy, Ecology and Technology (EET); Dutch Initiative for Sustainable Development (NIDO); Sustainable Technology Development Project[2] HABIFORM (Expertise network – multiple use of space)
Sweden (individual programs)	Urban and Regional Planning Infrasystems for Sustainable Cities; The Sustainable City; Economics for Sustainable Development; Sustainable Forestry in Southern Sweden; Sustainable Food Production; Sustainable Coastal Zone; Sustainable Management of the Mountain Region; Paths to Sustainable Development – Behavior, Organizations, Structures (Ways Ahead) Innovation Systems Supporting a Sustainable Growth
UK (individual programs)	Environmental Strategy Research Program; Towards a Sustainable Urban Environment; EPSRC Infrastructure and Environment Program; Environment Agency Sustainable Development R&D Program; Sustainable Development Commission; Sustainable Technologies Initiative – LINK Program

Source: Hargroves & Smith (2005).

Note: The table shows the three main program types for organizing research for sustainable development: (1) umbrella programs, (2) subprograms, and (3) individual programs.

TABLE 9.2 | List of Environmental NGOs

List of Mediator Nongovernmental Organizations (NGOs) CERES Conservation International (CI) Environmental Defense Fund (EDF) National Audubon Society Natural Resources Defense Council (NRDC) The Nature Conservancy Wildlife Conservation Society Wildlife Habitat Council World Resources Institute World Wildlife Fund (WWF) **List of Bridge NGOs** Center for Clean Air Policy Rainforest Alliance Scenic Hudson Student Conservation Association **List of Independent NGOs** American Forests American Rivers Pheasants Forever Rainforest Action Network River Network Soil and Water Conservation Society	Whitetails Unlimited Wildlife Forever **List of Captive NGOs** African Wildlife Foundation Bat Conservation International Defenders of Wildlife Delta Waterfowl Foundation Dian Fossey Gorilla Fund Ducks Unlimited Environmental and Energy Study Institute Fauna & Flora International Fish America Foundation International Wildlife Coalition—USA Izaak Walton League of America Jane Goodall Institute Land Trust Alliance National Council for Air and Stream Improvement National Wildlife Federation Quail Unlimited RARE Sierra Club The Wilderness Society Trout Unlimited Wildlife Trust Worldwatch Institute

Source: Data from Hoffman (2009).

Appendix A: Agenda 21 Chapter 27

Strengthening the Role of Non-governmental Organizations: Partners for Sustainable Development

PROGRAMME AREA

Basis for action

1. Nongovernmental organizations play a vital role in the shaping and implementation of participatory democracy. Their credibility lies in the responsible and constructive role they play in society. Formal and informal organizations, as well as grass-roots movements, should be recognized as partners in the implementation of Agenda 21. The nature of the independent role played by non-governmental organizations within a society calls

for real participation; therefore, independence is a major attribute of non-governmental organizations and is the precondition of real participation.

2. One of the major challenges facing the world community as it seeks to replace unsustainable development patterns with environmentally sound and sustainable development is the need to activate a sense of common purpose on behalf of all sectors of society. The chances of forging such a sense of purpose will depend on the willingness of all sectors to participate in genuine social partnership and dialogue, while recognizing the independent roles, responsibilities and special capacities of each.

3. Non-governmental organizations, including those non-profit organizations representing groups addressed in the present section of Agenda 21, possess well-established and diverse experience, expertise and capacity in fields which will be of particular importance to the implementation and review of environmentally sound and socially responsible sustainable development, as envisaged throughout Agenda 21. The community of non-governmental organizations, therefore, offers a global network that should be tapped, enabled and strengthened in support of efforts to achieve these common goals.

4. To ensure that the full potential contribution of non-governmental organizations is realized, the fullest possible communication and cooperation between international organizations, national and local governments and non-governmental organizations should be promoted in institutions mandated, and programmes designed to carry out Agenda 21. Non-governmental organizations will also need to foster cooperation and communication among themselves to reinforce their effectiveness as actors in the implementation of sustainable development.

Objectives

5. Society, Governments and international bodies should develop mechanisms to allow non-governmental organizations to play their partnership role responsibly and effectively in the process of environmentally sound and sustainable development.

6. With a view to strengthening the role of non-governmental organizations as social partners, the United Nations system and Governments should initiate a process, in consultation with non-governmental organizations, to review formal procedures and mechanisms for the involvement of these organizations at all levels from policy-making and decision-making to implementation.

7. By 1995, a mutually productive dialogue should be established at the national level between all Governments and non-governmental organizations and their self-organized networks to recognize and strengthen their respective roles in implementing environmentally sound and sustainable development.

8. Governments and international bodies should promote and allow the participation of non-governmental organizations in the conception, establishment and evaluation of official mechanisms and formal procedures designed to review the implementation of Agenda 21 at all levels.

Activities

9. The United Nations system, including international finance and development agencies, and all intergovernmental organizations and forums should, in consultation with non-governmental organizations, take measures to:

   a. Review and report on ways of enhancing existing procedures and mechanisms by which non-governmental organizations contribute to policy design, decision-making, implementation and evaluation at the individual agency level, in interagency discussions and in United Nations conferences;

   b. On the basis of subparagraph (a) above, enhance existing or, where they do not exist, establish, mechanisms and procedures within each agency to draw on the expertise and views of non-governmental organizations in policy and programme design, implementation and evaluation;

   c. Review levels of financial and administrative support for non-governmental organizations and the extent and effectiveness of their involvement in project and programme implementation, with a view to augmenting their role as social partners;

   d. Design open and effective means of achieving the participation of non-governmental organizations in the processes established to review and evaluate the implementation of Agenda 21 at all levels;

   e. Promote and allow non-governmental organizations and their self-organized networks to contribute to the review and evaluation of policies and programmes designed to implement Agenda 21, including support for developing country non-governmental organizations and their self-organized networks;

   f. Take into account the findings of non-governmental review systems and evaluation processes in relevant reports of the Secretary-General to the General Assembly, and of all pertinent United Nations organizations and other intergovernmental organizations and forums concerning implementation of Agenda 21, in accordance with the review process for Agenda 21;

   g. Provide access for non-governmental organizations to accurate and timely data and information to promote the effectiveness of their programmes and activities and their roles in support of sustainable development.

10. Governments should take measures to:

    a. Establish or enhance an existing dialogue with no-governmental organizations and their self-organized networks representing various sectors, which could serve to: (i) consider the rights and responsibilities of these organizations; (ii) efficiently channel integrated non-governmental inputs to the governmental policy development process; and (iii) facilitate non-governmental coordination in implementing national policies at the programme level;

    b. Encourage and enable partnership and dialogue between local non-governmental organizations and local authorities in activities aimed at sustainable development;

c. Involve non-governmental organizations in national mechanisms or procedures established to carry out Agenda 21, making the best use of their particular capacities, especially in the fields of education, poverty alleviation and environmental protection and rehabilitation;

d. Take into account the findings of non-governmental monitoring and review mechanisms in the design and evaluation of policies concerning the implementation of Agenda 21 at all levels;

e. Review government education systems to identify ways to include and expand the involvement of non-governmental organizations in the field of formal and informal education and of public awareness;

f. Make available and accessible to non-governmental organizations the data and information necessary for their effective contribution to research and to the design, implementation and evaluation of programmes.

Means of implementation

(a) *Financing and cost evaluation*

11. Depending on the outcome of review processes and the evolution of views as to how best to build partnership and dialogue between official organizations and groups of non-governmental organizations, relatively limited but unpredictable, costs will be involved at the international and national levels in enhancing consultative procedures and mechanisms. Non-governmental organizations will also require additional funding in support of their establishment of, improvement of or contributions to Agenda 21 monitoring systems. These costs will be significant but cannot be reliably estimated on the basis of existing information.

(b) *Capacity-building*

12. The organizations of the United Nations system and other intergovernmental organizations and forums, bilateral programmes and the private sector, as appropriate, will need to provide increased financial and administrative support for nongovernmental organizations and their self-organized networks, in particular those based in developing countries, that contribute to the monitoring and evaluation of Agenda 21 programmes, and provide training for non-governmental organizations (and assist them to develop their own training programmes) at the international and regional levels to enhance their partnership role in programme design and implementation.

13. Governments will need to promulgate or strengthen, subject to country-specific conditions, any legislative measures necessary to enable the establishment by nongovernmental organizations of consultative groups, and to ensure the right of non-governmental organizations to protect the public interest through legal action.

Source: www.un.org/esn/dsd/agenda21/res_agenda21_27.shtml

Part IV

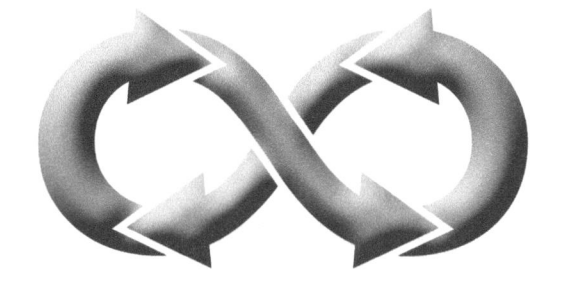

Strategies for a Sustainable Future

CHAPTER 10

Transparent Reporting, Measurement, and Standards

LEARNING OBJECTIVES

By the end of this chapter, you should be able to do the following:

» Understand the need for reporting and transparency.
» Present voluntary reporting on sustainability.
» Discuss frameworks such as GRI, CDP, and UN Global Compact.
» Compare and contrast various standards such as ISO 14001 and AA1000.
» Present other ratings and indices such as DJSI, FTSE.

CHAPTER OVERVIEW

This chapter discusses the role of reporting and transparency and the importance of these roles for companies. We explain the importance of voluntary reporting on sustainability and the GRI, and we will outline the ISO standards. Furthermore, we include a discussion of the UN Global Compact along with the 10 principles underlying the compact. We will end with a discussion on other standards that exist in the marketplace. The appendix to the chapter contains the speech of former UN secretary-general Mr. Kofi Annan calling for the UN Global Compact.

Reporting

Why does a company want to report? What are the incentives for companies to share information on their performance? What kinds of reports exist in the marketplace?

Reporting on performance can help a company drive internal change in numerous ways. First, it forces the company to acknowledge sustainability issues and assess if any gaps exist. If these gaps are communicated internally, the company leaders can show managers and employees what needs to be done and rally support for a cause or an action. In this manner, the sustainability report can serve as a part of the check-in standard plan-do-check-act cycle (PDCA cycle). Furthermore, this change can also come about via a benchmarking study whereby data are collected and compared to a best-in-class company. Lastly, the sustainability reports that spur change also invite comments and scrutiny from external stakeholders (Blackburn, 2007).

Reporting on sustainability performance is one of the primary ways for a company to manage its impact on sustainable development. It is now widely accepted that a company has a responsibility to the local community, environment, and social conditions (refer to the *Global Compact Speech* by Kofi Annan in the appendix). Reporting is valuable since it allows companies to measure, track, and improve their performance on various issues such as energy consumption, water usage, and so on. As any manager knows, if a company can measure an issue, it can be managed more effectively. In addition, sustainability reporting also promoted accountability and transparency. When the company reports information across a public domain, its stakeholders can track the company's performance on themes around the environment, community relations, and so on. A particular company's performance can be compared to other competitors. For example, how does Starbucks compare with Dunkin Donuts? Starbucks has made a commitment to purchase fair trade coffee. Has Dunkin Donuts made a similar commitment?

Why is transparency important? Trust is an important, yet elusive, goal for a company. It would be terribly unwise for a company to report only its achievements or good stories. It is only a matter of time before some stakeholder or media finds the full details. A company would be prudent not to invite suspicions of cover-ups. Hence, the best approach for a company is to report significant achievements and acknowledge weaknesses along with the steps that need to be taken to address these weaknesses (an action plan). By openly sharing information, a company can convey good-faith estimates regarding sustainability. As an example, the 2003 reports of ABN AMRO Bank, a Netherlands company, shared information in sidebars labeled as dilemmas. These sidebars contained discussions on animal rights, environmental degradation in a developing country, military defense contracts, and other topics (Blackburn, 2007). There are numerous other companies—for example, Shell and Nike—that keep reporting even in the presence of public criticisms.

What are the reasons that companies give for reporting? Since most of the reporting is voluntary, it is worthwhile to explore the reasons for reporting. A survey conducted in 2002 of 200 business leaders in 50 countries stated the reasons that companies reported on their sustainability performance.

Why Companies Report on Sustainability Performance

1. Drives constructive change in the management of sustainability issues
2. Educates employees on the issues
3. Aligns the organization to areas of needed improvement
4. Hastens the resolution of problems before they magnify
5. Builds stakeholder trust
6. Enhances company reputation for honesty
7. Strengthens relationships with stakeholders

Benefits of Sustainability Reporting

What are the benefits of sustainability reporting to corporate responsibility? A company needs to publish a public sustainability report for the sake of its stakeholders' information needs. In addition, companies need to be focused on issues outside of the company (Brownlie, n.d.).

A survey of business leaders cited the top benefits of sustainability reporting as improving stakeholder relations and management of sustainable development issues. The survey respondents stated that the benefits of social and environmental performance reporting outweigh the costs. A survey by KPMG (Brownlie, n.d.) indicated that businesses adopt sustainability reporting to do the following:

- Reduce operating costs and improve efficiencies
- Develop innovative products and services for access to new markets
- Improve reputation and brand value
- Recruit and retain excellent people
- Gain better access to investor capital
- Enhance the public value of the company
- Reduce liabilities through integrated risk management (Brownlie, n.d.)

Indeed, if reporting is so beneficial, why are more companies not doing so? This is because the list of reasons for not reporting is much longer (Blackburn, 2007, p. 314).

Why Companies Do Not Report on Issues

1. Embarrassed about performance
2. Key competitors aren't reporting on the issue; no competitive advantage
3. Afraid of releasing proprietary information that could hurt business

4. Concerned about reporting information that could create a security risk
5. Concerned about possible litigation on the issue
6. Afraid it will stir up certain stakeholders and create public relations problems
7. Afraid the media will criticize the company for its failings
8. Don't fully understand the issue
9. Not aware of the issue
10. Believe that their trade association is adequately addressing the issue
11. Believe the issue isn't significant/material enough to be a priority
12. Not concerned about improving performance on the issue
13. Believe the cost and effort of reporting would be excessive (Blackburn, 2007, p. 315)

Reporting can be mandatory or voluntary in nature. Some companies report voluntarily since these companies find the reasons to do so to be compelling. However, most companies report since they are required to do so by law. The mandatory reports can come from a variety of legal requirements. The most common requirement comes about as pollutant-disclosure laws. Herein, companies are required to report on the emissions of toxic pollutants. In the United States, the Emergency Planning and Community Right-to-Know Act (EPCRA) was passed in 1986. The EPCRA requires reporting of toxic emissions under Toxics Release Inventory (TRI), and this law led to the passage of other versions of similar legislation. Other countries that have similar registries of emissions include Canada, the Czech Republic, Hungary, Norway, Poland, and Yugoslavia. On a global scale, the Organisation for Economic Co-operation and Development (OECD) has been asked to develop registries similar to TRI in member states. Another requirement of mandatory reporting is in cases when social and environmental information is included in financial reports. For example, in the case of contaminated disposal sites, the Securities and Exchange Commission (SEC) rules require that companies declare fines in excess of $100,000.

There are numerous tools in the area of Sustainability Reporting. The rest of the chapter will be divided into three areas to cover the spectrum of tools: Frameworks; Standards; and Ratings and Indices. Frameworks refer to principles, initiatives, or guidelines that can be used by organizations to assist them in their disclosure efforts. Standards are similar to frameworks but usually contain more formal documentation that can highlight the requirements and specifications that can be used to ensure that sustainability efforts are achieved. Lastly, ratings or indices are similar to third-party evaluations for an organization's sustainability efforts.

Frameworks

Global Reporting Initiative (GRI)

There are numerous frameworks for voluntary reporting on sustainability. At present, the GRI standard has become the *de facto* international reporting standard.

GRI was established in 1997 by the partnership of Ceres and the United Nations Environment Programme (UNEP). The broad mission was to develop "globally applicable guidelines for reporting on the economic, environmental, and social performance of corporations, governments, and nongovernmental organizations (NGOs)" (Stappen, 2009). GRI works as a collaborative effort in that it incorporates the active participation of multiple stakeholders from corporations to nongovernmental organizations worldwide. This multi-stakeholder aspect leads to GRI's broad applicability, and it has become the de facto international standard in sustainability reporting ("What Is GRI," n.d.).

The GRI reporting framework lays out the principles and the indicators that can be employed by organizations wanting to measure and report their economic, social, and environmental performance ("What Is GRI?" n.d.). The sustainability-reporting framework provides guidance for organizations to disclose their sustainability reporting. This framework is relevant to organizations of all shapes and sizes worldwide and is developed through individuals from over 60 countries that represent many institutions. There are guidelines that should be used as the basis for all reporting. The guidelines consist of principles, guidelines, and standard disclosures. The core guidelines are the G3 guidelines ("RG: Sustainability Reporting Guidelines," n.d.).

The first draft of the guidelines was released in 1999, and the framework encompassed the triple bottom line of economic, environmental, and social issues. These guidelines then evolved into the G2 in 2002. In 2006, the third generation of these guidelines, the G3, was released. Since the founding of GRI, three subsequent versions of the third-generation guidelines have been issued, namely G2, G3, and G3.1. A multi-stakeholder approach was used to create the G3.1 standards. In addition, sector supplements that serve as guidelines for different industry sectors are provided. In addition, the fourth generation of standards, G4, is currently being developed.

GRI Standards

The sustainability reporting standards are grouped into three categories, the most recent version being the 2023 standards. The three categories are:

- **Universal:** These standards apply to all reporting companies. These include general disclosures on organizational details, the entities included in reporting, the reporting period, frequency and contact point, and external assurances. The universal standards also include material disclosures about the reporting business's operation. These are often sector-specific, which leads to the next category of standards.

- **Sector-Specific:** There are four sectors for which GRI has developed standards to support material disclosures. These include basic materials and needs; industrial; transportation, infrastructure, and tourism; and other services and light standards.
- **Topic-Specific:** The topic-specific standards dive deeper into economic, environmental and social impacts. Reporting companies will make disclosures on anti-corruption and marketing presence; materials and energy; and human rights and diversity, among others. The level of detail reported for each topic will depend on the company's operations (GRI Framework, 2021).

WHO REPORTS AND WHY?

Of the more than 50,000 multinational corporations, fewer than 1 percent use the GRI framework in some capacity (Elkington & Lee, 2006). In addition, most of these are composed of large companies that presumably have higher expectations from the public. Of the largest group, all the companies in the chemicals, forestry, and pharmaceuticals sectors report on their corporate social responsibility (CSR).

A growing number of companies do understand the primary importance of corporate reporting, which is one of the competitive advantages. Other benefits include better management of environmental, social, and governance impacts and overall risk; enhancement of company brands and reputation; and greater ability to attract and retain customers and talent. There are other companies that adopt a reactive stance and might initiate reporting in order to comply with a checklist or as a public relations strategy. However, these approaches are shortsighted. When a reactive or defensive approach is not linked to the overall strategy, it often is delegated to corporate communications or public relations. Without an overarching direction from the top management, the managers of departments that are responsible for reporting might fail to grasp strategic issues or they might be unwilling or unable to engage in meaningful debates on impacts or challenges (Elkington & Lee, 2006).

Given all this information, is the GRI really helpful as a tool for reporting on the sustainability performance of a company? A report lists the potential benefits and drawbacks of the GRI.

BENEFITS OF THE GLOBAL REPORTING INITIATIVE

- It provides a holistic framework that follows the TBL: social, environmental, and economic aspects.
- The reporting information is consistent across different organizations.
- It is widely accepted across the globe.
- Organizations across the globe can be compared to one another.
- It can be used to measure and benchmark performance.
- Being flexible, it can be implemented incrementally and used across sectors and geographical contexts.

- Support and integration of other tools and standards, such as the AA1000 Series, a principle-based set of standards, is included (GRI, n.d.; GRI Guidelines, n.d.).

Limitations of the Global Reporting Initiative

- Labor-intensive, especially for smaller companies
- Does not measure pollution prevention
- No guidance provided on data collection or preparation of reports
- Limited usage in social enterprise sector
- No accreditation or external evaluation provided
- Reports impacts, not positive outcomes (GRI, n.d.; "GRI Guidelines," n.d.).

To summarize, the GRI is an excellent tool for companies that want to report on their sustainability performance. As many as 73 percent of the world's 250 largest companies complete their annual sustainability reports in accordance with the GRI (GRI Framework, 2021).

UN Global Compact

The United Nations UN Global Compact is an initiative to encourage businesses all over the world to adopt sustainable policies and to report on the implementation of these policies. The Secretary General of the UN Kofi Annan, in his address to the World Economic Forum on January 31, 1999, announced the Global Compact. Please refer to the appendix for the text of this statement.

The uniqueness of the Global Compact is that it is both global and local, private and public, and voluntary yet accountable ("Overview of the UN Global Compact," 2010). The Global Compact promotes ten principles across diverse areas such as human rights, labor, environment, and anticorruption. At present, the Global Compact is one of the largest voluntary corporate voluntary initiatives in the world with over 16,169 corporate participants and stakeholders from more than 161 countries (Overview, 2022).

These principles are as follows.

Human Rights

- Principle 1: Businesses should support and respect the protection of internationally proclaimed human rights; and
- Principle 2: make sure that they are not complicit in human rights abuses ("The Ten Principles," 2022).

Labor

- Principle 3: Businesses should uphold the freedom of association and the effective recognition of the right to collective bargaining;
- Principle 4: the elimination of all forms of forced and compulsory labor;

- Principle 5: the effective abolition of child labor; and
- Principle 6: elimination of discrimination in respect to employment and occupation ("The Ten Principles," 2022).

Environment
- Principle 7: Businesses should support a precautionary approach to environmental challenges;
- Principle 8: undertake initiatives to promote greater environmental responsibility; and
- Principle 9: encourage the development and diffusion of environmentally friendly technologies ("The Ten Principles," 2022).

Anti-Corruption
- Principle 10: Businesses should work against corruption in all its forms, including extortion and bribery ("The Ten Principles," 2022).

CARBON DISCLOSURE PROJECT

The Carbon Disclosure Project (CDP) is a UK-based not-for-profit organization that facilitates environmental disclosures of firms with institutional investors. Every year, CDP sends out a questionnaire and collects data from large firms across the globe and across different industrial sectors (CDP, 2022). Thousands of organizations from across the world measure and disclose their greenhouse gas emissions, water usage, and climate change strategies through the CDP.

The Investor CDP encourages companies to be transparent with their emissions and to improve their understanding of the strategic risks and opportunities of climate change. Hence, the Investor CDP focuses on three key areas of climate change strategy: management; risks and opportunities; and emissions.

CDP also gathers data on public disclosure, supply chain, and water disclosure projects. The CDP Water Disclosure provides water-related data from a subset of the world's largest 500 companies listed in the FTSE Global Equity Index Series, that are focused on sectors that are water-intensive or exposed to water-related risks. In 2010, the CDP Cities project was launched and this project gathers data from a group of the largest cities in the world (Hanks, 2022).

The CDP is considered to be the most comprehensive collection of self-reported environmental data and it has the largest database of corporate climate change information. In 2019, over 8,400 companies with over 50 percent of global market capitalization disclosed environmental data through CDP. This data, in addition to the over 920 cities, states, and regions that disclosed data, makes CDP's platform one of the richest sources of information globally on how companies and governments are driving environmental change (CDP, Green Finance).

World Business Council for Sustainable Development

The World Business Council for Sustainable Development (WBCSD) global organization is led by the CEOs of about 200 companies. The council provides a forum for its 200 member companies—who represent most business sectors, all continents, and combined revenue of over $8.5 trillion USD—to share best practices on sustainable development issues and to develop innovative tools that change the status quo. The members of this council represent 35 countries and 20 industrial sectors and have a global network of 70 national and regional partners.

WBCSD has outlined three imperatives: Climate Action, Equity Action, and Nature Action. Furthermore, the WBCSD has highlighted six pathways to work on these imperatives. The pathways are:

- Built Environment
- Energy
- Food and Agriculture
- Health and Well-being
- Products and Materials
- Transport and Mobility

The projects that have been undertaken by the WBCSD range from Built Environment to Global Agribusiness to Sustainable Plastics (About Us, 2022).

GHG Protocol

The Greenhouse Gas Protocol is a joint initiative between the World Resources Institute and WBCSD. It was created to serve as an international standard for corporate accounting and reporting emissions. Over time, it became a widely accepted tool, especially for accounting tools to track GHG emissions.

The GHGP provides accounting and reporting standards, sector guidance, calculators, and training for organizations and governments. It has also created a comprehensive, global, standardized framework for measuring and managing emissions from both public and private sectors and across supply chains to reduce greenhouse gas emissions. As per reports, nine out of ten Fortune 500 companies that report to CDP use this framework (Greenhouse Gas Protocol, 2022).

Standards

International Organization for Standardization Standards

The issue of environmental impact is becoming an increasingly important topic globally. The pressure to comply is coming from numerous sources: governments, regulation and trade agencies, customers, employees, and shareholders. In addition, social pressures are also building up from numerous interested parties, such as consumers and environmental nongovernmental organizations (ENGOs). Hence, other standards besides the GRI need to be explored to meet this need for compliance.

ISO 14001

The ISO was started in 1996 and is located in Geneva. The purpose of the ISO standards is to facilitate and support international trade by developing standards that would be accepted and recognized worldwide. The standard is designed to maintain the balance between profitability and reducing environmental impact. These standards are developed by technical committees and tend to have worldwide support since the members of the technical committees represent various national organizations. The purpose of these standards is to put forth a process that can evaluate the lifetime impact of the product on the environment ("ISO Standards for Life Cycle Assessment [LCA]," 2006).

ISO 14001 states how any organization can implement an effective environmental management system (EMS). The ISO 14001 is comprised of the following five steps:

1. [Following] general requirements
2. [Adhering to] environmental policy
3. Planning implementation and operation
4. Checking and corrective action
5. [Undergoing] management review ("ISO 14001 Environment," n.d.).

These steps lead an organization to identify aspects of the business that have an impact on the environment in order to understand the applicable environmental laws. The next stage is to come up with a management process for continual improvement. The system can be periodically assessed, and if compliant, the organization can be registered to ISO 14001 ("ISO 14001 Environment," n.d.).

According to ISO 14001, a particular company ought to start with an environmental review if it does not have an EMS in place. The four steps involved in setting an environmental review are as follows:

1. Identify the environmental aspects of the organization.
2. Clarify the legal requirements that apply to these environmental aspects.
3. Examine the current environmental management policies, procedures, and practices.
4. Refine the scope of the EMS ("ISO 14001 2004 Introduction," n.d.).

However, if a company does have an EMS in place, then a gap analysis is needed to update to the new standards ("ISO 14001 2004 Introduction," n.d.). One of the broad appeals of the ISO 14001 is in regards to its relevance. The standards can be applied to almost every organization, including the following:

- Single site to large multinational companies
- High-risk companies to low-risk service organizations

- Manufacturing, process, and service industries, including local governments
- All industry sectors including public and private sectors
- Original equipment manufacturers and their suppliers ("ISO 14001 Environment," n.d.)

Besides the 14000 series, there are numerous other standards in the series that serve as guidelines. Some of these guidelines are given as follows.

- ISO 14004: provides guidance on the development and implementation of environmental management systems
- ISO 14010: provides general principles of environmental auditing (now superseded by ISO 19011)
- ISO 14011: provides specific guidance on auditing an environmental management system (now superseded by ISO 19011)
- ISO 14012: provides guidance on qualification criteria for environmental auditors and lead auditors (now superseded by ISO 19011)
- ISO 14013/5: provides audit program review and assessment material.
- ISO 14020+: provides guidance on labeling issues
- ISO 14030+: provides guidance on performance targets and monitoring within an Environmental Management System
- ISO 14040+: covers life cycle issues ("Other 14000 Series Standards," 2002).

ISO 26000: SOCIAL RESPONSIBILITY

The ISO 26000 is an international standard that provides an organization with guidance on how to be more socially responsible. This set of standards can be used as a tool to transition from good intentions to good actions. As well as being the "right thing" to do, the application of ISO 26000 is increasingly viewed as a way of assessing an organization's commitment to sustainability and its overall performance. However, this set of standards contains voluntary guidance, not requirements; hence, it cannot be used as a certification standard like ISO 9001:2008 and ISO 14001:2004.

Importance of ISO 26000

Sustainability encompasses the three aspects of a business: (1) to provide goods and services profitably, (2) to preserve the environment, and (3) to operate in a socially responsible manner. As pointed out in the TBL approach, an organization needs to respect the 3 Ps: (1) people, (2) planet, and (3) profit.

Despite all the high-level declarations of principles related to social responsibility and individual social responsibility programs, the challenge is how to put the principles into practice. Furthermore, the term *social responsibility* has numerous connotations, and it can be challenging to put the principles into practice. Moreover, the previous initiatives have tended to focus on CSR while ISO 26000 provides guidance not only for companies but also for public sector organizations of all types (Frost, 2011). The expertise of these standards is also in articulating international agreements based on two levels of consensus: (1) among the principal categories of stakeholders and (2) among countries (Frost, 2011).

Benefits of ISO 26000

ISO 26000 provides guidance on numerous issues such as the trends, core issues, principles, and practices of SR. They also provide guidance on promoting, integrating, and implementing SR within an organization; engaging with stakeholders; and, finally, communicating information about SR (Frost, 2011).

The intent of ISO 26000 is to assist organizations in contributing to sustainable development and to go beyond legal compliance. Furthermore, ISO 26000 promotes a common understanding of social responsibility. While applying the ISO 26000, an organization needs to take into consideration diversity in terms of cultural, economic, environmental, legal, political, and societal factors while staying consistent with international norms of behavior (Frost, 2011).

What Benefits Can Be Achieved by Implementing ISO 26000?

The performance on SR can have immense influence on the reputation and competitive advantage for the organization. In addition, the organization can also attract and retain workers, customers, and clients. Social responsibility can influence the morale, commitment, and productivity of employees as well as impact the perceptions of investors and donors. Last but not least, social responsibility has the potential to influence the relationship with stakeholders ranging from companies and suppliers to governments and from customers to the community within which the organization operates (Frost, 2011).

Challenges

The application of social responsibility can be challenging. The presence of cultural differences, competing priorities, and other unique variables can lead to confusion regarding the *right* action. There are certain areas that are accepted in certain cultures and banned in other cultures. The standards state "a situation's complexity should not be used as an excuse for inaction" ("ISO 26000 and the Definition of Social Responsibility," 2011). The seven principles of socially responsible behavior as outlined in the standard are "accountability, transparency, ethical behavior, respect for stakeholder interests, respect for the rule of law, respect for international norms of behavior, and respect for human rights" ("ISO 26000 and the Definition of Social Responsibility," 2011).

AA1000

In addition to the GRI and ISO 26000, the AA100 standards can also be used to meet stakeholder engagement. The AA1000 Stakeholder Engagement Standard (SES) is a global standard that aims to set the benchmark for good-quality engagement. It is a generally applicable framework that organizations can use to assess, design, implement and communicate quality stakeholder engagement. This standard:

- Provides a simple, relevant, and practical framework for implementing high-quality stakeholder engagement.

- Outlines how to rethink an organization's approach to engagement by empowering stakeholders as active contributors in the creation of value for the organization.
- Describes how to integrate stakeholder engagement within an organization's governance, strategy, and operations (Thiry, 2020).

As per the AA1000 standard, stakeholder engagement must be embedded in the organization's culture and core functions. It should promote:

1. **Inclusivity:** Organizations should actively engage with stakeholders to understand their expectations about the organization's governance, policies, strategies, practices, and performance.
2. **Materiality:** Organizations should be transparent in how they report their performance on issues that are material to stakeholders.
3. **Responsiveness:** Organizations should develop innovative and sustainable responses to issues that matter to their stakeholders—both for the present and the future.

Ratings and Indices

Dow Jones Sustainability World Index (DJSI World)

The DJSI is the first index that tracks the financial performance of sustainability-driven companies worldwide. The index consists of the top 10 percent of the largest 2,500 stocks in the S&P Global Broad Market Index based on their sustainability and environmental practices. Due to numerous investors searching for socially conscious investments, the DJSI World is a popular benchmark for private wealth managers.

As of May 31, 2022, some of the index's top 10 include Microsoft Corp., Alphabet Inc., UnitedHealth Group Inc., Taiwan Semiconductor Manufacturing Co. Ltd., and AbbVie Inc. The companies view membership in the index as an opportunity to enhance shareholder awareness of environmental efforts and they often issue press releases announcing their index membership (Chen, 2022).

The companies listed in the DJSI World are reevaluated each year and those companies that fail to show consistent progress may be removed from the index. A company may be excluded from the index if it is not behaving in accordance with sustainability guidelines and on a variety of ethical exclusions, including its exposure to alcohol, gambling, tobacco, armaments, firearms, nuclear power, nuclear weapons, and adult entertainment (Chen, 2022).

FTSE4Good Index Series

The FTSE4Good Index Series is a list of environmental, social, and governance (ESG) stock indexes that include companies with positive reputations for corporate responsibility. It contains several individual stock indexes, each tailored to a particular geographic region. For example, the series includes specific indexes for companies in the United States, Australia, Japan, and Latin America, among others.

Investors can use the indexes either for individual stock selection or as the basis for investment products such as mutual funds and exchange-traded funds (ETFs). Investors can thus use the index as a reference point for individual stock selection, such as by selecting investments from the index's top holdings. For example, the top holdings of the index based in the United States at the end of 2019 included several well-known technology companies such as Apple, Microsoft, Alphabet, and Meta (formerly Facebook).

The companies must score highly in measures of environmental, social, and corporate governance (ESG) practices in order to be included in the FTSE4Good Index Series. This ensures that the companies also have strong policies in areas such as environmental sustainability of supply chains; respect for human rights, labor relations and workplace safety; and lack of real or perceived corruption (Fernando, 2022).

MSCI KLD Database (Formerly KLD)

The MSCI KLD 400 Social Index is an index focusing on companies that maintain high environmental, social, and corporate governance (ESG) standards. It was previously known as the Domini 400 Social Index and was named after Amy Domini, one of the founders of KLD Research & Analytics.

The MSCI KLD 400 Social Index represents 400 publicly traded companies that maintain high ESG ratings. As such, the index forms part of a broader universe of tools and investment products designed for investors concerned about the social and environmental impact of the assets they hold.

The potential candidates for the MSCI KLD 400 Social Index have an excellent record on issues such as the treatment of employees, the safety of their products, the environmental sustainability of their supply chains, and their corporate practices. Examples of businesses excluded from consideration include companies dealing in alcohol, tobacco, gambling, and weapons technology.

The index is deliberately focused on large-cap stocks, requiring candidates to be based in the United States and listed on either the New York Stock Exchange (NYSE) or the Nasdaq exchange. Companies that fail to maintain the requisite ESG ratings will be replaced by other companies that score more favorably, based on an ongoing review that takes place in April of each year (Fernando, 2022b).

Other Registries

In recent years, external stakeholders such as NGOs and financial institutions have started asking companies for information on their environmental performance. For example, over 80 percent of global Fortune 500 companies publish reports that disclose their sustainability performance. Some of the examples of key reporting formats and sustainability indexes are presented in Table 10.1 and are discussed as follows:

CERES

This organization is a group of investors, environmental organizations, and other organizations working with companies and investors to address sustainability challenges. The primary mission of the organization is "integrating sustainability into capital markets for the health of the planet and its people." In addition, it has laid out a Ceres 20-20 Vision whereby it aims to achieve a sustainable global economy by the year 2020. The plan has four pillars, each with specific ambitious goals:

1. We need honest accounting that abolishes the folly of free pollution.
2. We need higher standards of business leadership.

TABLE 10.1 | Examples of Key Reporting Formats and Sustainability Indices.

Organization	Description
Reporting Formats	
GRI (Global Reporting Initiative)—G3 reports	Based on triple bottom line; international standard used by more than 1200 companies for corporate reporting on environmental, social and economic performance www.globalreporting.org
Ceres & Tellus Institute Facility Reporting Project	Consistent and comparable economic, environmental, and social reporting guidance for US facilities www.ceres.org
World Business Council for Sustainable Development	Global association of companies dealing only with business and sustainable development www.wbcsd.org
Reporting Repositories	
Corporate Register	Free directory of CSR, sustainability, and environmental reports issued by the companies worldwide www.corporateregister.com
Carbon Disclosure Project	Voluntary, annual reporting of GHG emissions worldwide www.cdproject.net
SD Indexes	
Dow Jones Sustainability Index (DJSI)	First global index tracking financial performance of leading sustainability-driven companies worldwide www.sustainability-index.com
Corporate Knights Global 100	100 Most Sustainable Companies across the globe as defined by a Canadian media company www.corporateknights.ca

Source: Phyper & MacLean (2009).

3. We need bold solutions that accelerate green innovation.
4. We need smart new policies that reward sustainability performance ("Our Vision for a Sustainable Global Economy," n.d.).

Corporate Register

Corporate Register is based in the United Kingdom and it aims to provide "the global, central reference point for all CSR-related information" ("About Corporate Register," n.d.). While a majority of the content is available free to the stakeholders, a fee is charged for advanced users who need more detailed content. Some of the reports that have been provided include the following:

- An online directory of CSR/Sustainability reports
- CSR/Sustainability reporting directories for the three most significant reporting guidelines currently available: The Global Reporting Initiative, AccountAbility AA1000AS, and the Global Compact
- Free directory of service providers in the CSR reporting field
- Announcement service for new CSR reports and CSR events
- Global and independent awards for CSR reporting ("About Corporate Register," n.d.).

The two audiences for this site are the stakeholders who need to track and access CSR-related information, and companies who need to share their CSR reports and news with the global audience ("About Corporate Register," n.d.).

Corporate Knights Global 100

Corporate Knights is a Canadian media company that publishes an annual ranking of the world's most sustainable companies called the Global 100. The 2012 list is topped by pharmaceutical maker Novo Nordisk, Brazil's Natura & Co., Norwegian energy company Statoil, the Danish biotech firm Novozymes, and ASML Holding, a Dutch manufacturer of photolithography machines used in the semiconductor industry.

Here are the criteria used to determine the Global 100—a *sustainability* ranking—for 2012:

1. Energy productivity
2. Greenhouse gas (GHG) productivity
3. Water productivity
4. Waste productivity
5. Innovation capacity
6. Percentage of taxes paid
7. CEO to average employee pay
8. Safety productivity

9. Employee turnover
10. Leadership diversity
11. Clean capitalism paylink (MacDonald, 2012)

The concern is that more than half of these criteria—numbers 5 through 10—"have nothing to do with sustainability" (MacDonald, 2012). It seems that "sustainability doesn't mean 'sustainability' anymore—it just means all the good stuff that business does" (MacDonald, 2012). A ranking on sustainability that considers environmental performance in only half the criteria is misleading at the least.

Caveats of Reporting

What are the potential downsides of voluntary and mandatory reporting? In terms of reporting on nonfinancial performance, too many surveys and metrics can lead to low response rates that can invalidate the accuracy of the results. In addition, poor performers can design their own metrics with attractive titles, give themselves good scores, and deceive stakeholders. Another concern is that increased measurement can decrease social performance. In the case of child labor restrictions, it is assumed that children not working in factories will attend school. However, the alternative can be that the child is employed in a more dangerous industry, such as prostitution. Hence, the unintended consequences of metrics can actually *decrease* overall welfare. This drawback is an issue for many nonfinancial performances (Levine & Chatterji, 2006).

In the case of ISO 14000 standards, can weak monitoring and sanctioning systems minimize shirking behavior and improve environmental performance? Research has shown that the ISO certified facilities do manage to reduce their pollution emissions more than noncertified facilities (Potoski Prakash, 2005). Other studies have illustrated that global diffusion of ISO 14001 standards could be due to the companies' desires to appear legitimate in the eyes of external stakeholders (Darnall, 2006). External stakeholders also play an important role in assisting firms to gain competitive advantages. Since the ISO 14001 standards focus on processes instead of outcomes, the involvement of stakeholders facilitates the communication of credible information on the standard. In this manner, by involving external stakeholders, a company can transform certification into an organizational capability (Delmas, 2001).

Conclusion

Reporting, once considered voluntary, is now becoming a de facto requirement for most companies that are concerned about their public image. Fortunately, there are numerous standards that exist for companies to choose from—ranging from international standards such as GRI and ISO 14001 to smaller, local standards such as Ceres and DJSI World. To illustrate gains in environmental performance, a company needs to be able to report and verify its accomplishments. In this age of media scrutiny and consumer backlash, to not do so would invite criticisms of greenwashing that in turn would undermine any efforts made by the organization.

Keywords

- AA1000
- Carbon Disclosure Project (CDP)
- Ceres
- Corporate Knights
- Corporate Register
- Dow Jones Sustainability World Index (DJSI)
- Environmental, social, and governance (ESG) disclosures
- FTSE4Good
- GHG (Greenhouse Gas) Protocol
- Global Reporting Initiative (GRI)
- ISO 14001
- ISO 26000
- ISO standards
- MSCI KLD
- Sustainability reporting
- UN Global Compact
- United Nations Environment Programme (UNEP)
- World Business Council for Sustainable Development (WBCSD)

Discussion Questions

1. What is the purpose of reporting? Why should organizations report on their performance?
2. Should reporting on sustainability be voluntary or required by law? What might be a better approach to getting companies to report on sustainability?
3. Discuss the GRI standards. Browse through the list of companies that have published reports with the GRI. Do you think this list is a representative sample of companies?
4. Find a local company that follows the ISO 14000 standards. Discuss how this company implements the ISO 14001 standards.
5. What is the advantage of ISO 26000 standards for companies looking to implement social responsibility issues into their operations?
6. Go to the WBCSD website. Click on the case studies and select any one case study to discuss.
7. Research the official website of GRI. What local area companies can you find that have published GRI reports?
8. Research a medium to large local company. Does it publish a report on sustainability—for example, a GRI report, CSR report, or something similar?
9. Browse through the DJSI. What is the purpose of publishing such indices? What value is provided by this service?
10. What are the top 10 companies in the Global 100 list published by Corporate Knights. Go to the website (www.global100.org) to determine what companies are on the list. Were you surprised by the results?
11. Which of the 10 principles of the UN Global Compact do you think would be hardest to comply with at the company you work for? Why is this the case?

Recommended Websites

- Ceres – www.ceres.org
- Corporate Knights – www.corporateknights.ca
- Corporate Register – www.corporateregister.org
- Global 100 Resources – www.global100.org
- Global Reporting Initiative – www.globalreporting.org
- ISO – www.iso.org
- United Nations Global Compact – www.unglobalcompact.org/

APPENDIX

GLOBAL COMPACT SPEECH, KOFI ANNAN, SECRETARY GENERAL, UN, JANUARY 31, 1999

Secretary-General Proposes Global Compact on Human Rights, Labour, Environment, in Address to World Economic Forum in Davos

Following is the address of Secretary-General Kofi Annan to the World Economic Forum in Davos, Switzerland, on 31 January:

I am delighted to join you again at the World Economic Forum. This is my third visit in just over two years as Secretary-General of the United Nations.

On my previous visits, I told you of my hopes for a creative partnership between the United Nations and the private sector. I made the point that the everyday work of the United Nations—whether in peacekeeping, setting technical standards, protecting intellectual property or providing much-needed assistance to developing countries—helps to expand opportunities for business around the world. And I stated quite frankly that, without your know-how and your resources, many of the objectives of the United Nations would remain elusive.

Today, I am pleased to acknowledge that, in the past two years, our relationship has taken great strides. We have shown through cooperative ventures—both at the policy level and on the ground—that the goals of the United Nations and those of business can, indeed, be mutually supportive.

This year, I want to challenge you to join me in taking our relationship to a still higher level. I propose that you, the business leaders gathered in Davos, and we, the United Nations, initiate a global compact of shared values and principles, which will give a human face to the global market.

Globalization is a fact of life. But I believe we have underestimated its fragility. The problem is this. The spread of markets outpaces the ability of societies and their political systems to adjust to them, let alone to guide the course they take. History teaches us that such an imbalance between the economic, social and political realms can never be sustained for very long.

The industrialized countries learned that lesson in their bitter and costly encounter with the Great Depression. In order to restore social harmony and political stability, they adopted social safety nets and other measures, designed to limit economic volatility and compensate the victims of market failures. That consensus made possible successive moves towards liberalization, which brought about the long post-war period of expansion.

Our challenge today is to devise a similar compact on the global scale, to underpin the new global economy. If we succeed in that, we would lay the foundation for an age of global prosperity, comparable to that enjoyed by the industrialized countries in the decades after the Second World War. Specifically, I call on you—individually through your firms, and collectively through your business associations—to embrace, support and enact a set of core values in the areas of human rights, labour standards, and environmental practices.

Why those three? In the first place, because they are all areas where you, as businessmen and women, can make a real difference. Secondly, they are areas in which universal values have already been defined by international agreements, including the Universal Declaration, the International Labour Organization's Declaration on fundamental principles and rights at work, and the Rio Declaration of the United Nations Conference on Environment and Development in 1992. Finally, I choose these three areas because they are ones where I fear that, if we do not act, there may be a threat to the open global market, and especially to the multilateral trade regime.

There is enormous pressure from various interest groups to load the trade regime and investment agreements with restrictions aimed at preserving standards in the three areas I have just mentioned. These are legitimate concerns. But restrictions on trade and investment are not the right means to use when tackling them. Instead, we should find a way to achieve our proclaimed standards by other means. And that is precisely what the compact I am proposing to you is meant to do.

Essentially there are two ways we can do it. One is through the international policy arena. You can encourage States to give us, the multilateral institutions of which they are all members, the resources and the authority we need to do our job.

The United Nations as a whole promotes peace and development, which are prerequisites for successfully meeting social and environmental goals alike. And the International Labour Organization, the United Nations High Commissioner for Human Rights and the United Nations Environmental Programme strive to improve labour conditions, human rights and environmental quality. We hope, in the future, to count you as our allies in these endeavours.

The second way you can promote these values is by taking them directly, by taking action in your own corporate sphere. Many of you are big investors, employers and producers in dozens of different countries across the world. That power brings with it great opportunities—and great responsibilities.

You can uphold human rights and decent labour and environmental standards directly, by your own conduct of your own business.

Indeed, you can use these universal values as the cement binding together your global corporations, since they are values people all over the world will recognize as their own. You can make sure that in your own corporate practices you uphold and respect human rights; and that you are not yourselves complicit in human rights abuses.

Don't wait for every country to introduce laws protecting freedom of association and the right to collective bargaining. You can at least make sure your own employees, and those of your subcontractors, enjoy those rights. You can at least make sure that you yourselves are not employing under-age children or forced labour, either directly or indirectly. And you can make sure that, in your own hiring and firing policies, you do not discriminate on grounds of race, creed, gender or ethnic origin.

You can also support a precautionary approach to environmental challenges. You can undertake initiatives to promote greater environmental responsibility. And you can encourage the development and diffusion of environmentally friendly technologies.

That, ladies and gentlemen, is what I am asking of you. But what, you may be asking yourselves, am I offering in exchange? Indeed, I believe the United Nations system does have something to offer.

The United Nations agencies—the United Nations High Commissioner for Human Rights, the International Labour Organization (ILO), the United Nations Environment Programme (UNEP)—all stand ready to assist you, if you need help, in incorporating these agreed values and principles into your mission statements and corporate practices. And we are ready to facilitate a dialogue between you and other social groups, to help find viable solutions to the genuine concerns that they have raised. You may find it useful to interact with us through our newly created website, www.un.org/partners, which offers a "one-stop shop" for corporations interested in the United Nations. More important, perhaps, is what we can do in the political arena, to help make the case for and maintain an environment which favours trade and open markets.

I believe what I am proposing to you is a genuine compact, because neither side of it can succeed without the other. Without your active commitment and support, there is a danger that universal values will remain little more than fine words—documents whose anniversaries we can celebrate and make speeches about, but with limited impact on the lives of ordinary people. And unless those values are really seen to be taking hold, I fear we may find it increasingly difficult to make a persuasive case for the open global market.

National markets are held together by shared values. In the face of economic transition and insecurity, people know that if the worst comes to the worst, they can rely on the expectation that certain minimum standards will prevail. But in the global market, people do not yet have that confidence. Until they do have it, the global economy will be fragile and vulnerable—vulnerable to backlash from all the "isms" of our post-cold-war world: protectionism; populism; nationalism; ethnic chauvinism; fanaticism; and terrorism.

What all those "isms" have in common is that they exploit the insecurity and misery of people who feel threatened or victimized by the global market. The more wretched and insecure people there are, the more those "isms" will continue to gain ground. What we have to do is find a way of embedding the global market in a network of shared values. I hope I have suggested some practical ways for us to set about doing just that.

Let us remember that the global markets and multilateral trading system we have today did not come about by accident. They are the result of enlightened policy choices made by governments since 1945. If we want to maintain them in the new century, all of us—governments, corporations, non-governmental organizations, international organizations—have to make the right choices now.

We have to choose between a global market driven only by calculations of short-term profit, and one which has a human face. Between a world which condemns a quarter of the human race to starvation and squalor, and one which offers everyone at least a chance of prosperity, in a healthy environment. Between a selfish free-for-all in which we ignore the fate of the losers, and a future in which the strong and successful accept their responsibilities, showing global vision and leadership.

I am sure you will make the right choice.

CHAPTER 11

Carbon Markets
Offsets and Standards

LEARNING OBJECTIVES

By the end of this chapter, you should be able to do the following:

» Present the concept of carbon neutrality.
» Explain the Kyoto Protocol.
» Discuss the details of carbon markets.
» Compare and contrast the various types of offsets.
» Present the market standards.
» Discuss proceedings of the Conference of the Parties (COP17) Durban.

CHAPTER OVERVIEW

This chapter discusses the concept of carbon neutrality and then presents the state of the carbon markets, including the mandate from the Kyoto Protocol. We examine the concept of carbon offsets and provide examples of the market. The purpose of the chapter is to present the logic of carbon markets and how they work—especially in the space of market instruments aimed at lowering carbon emissions. How did this market develop and where is it headed? Why does this market spark such heated debates? Does it encourage people to change consumption habits or merely provide a quick fix? We then discuss carbon offsets in detail and extend the discussion to carbon standards.

INTERNATIONAL CLIMATE AGREEMENTS

To understand carbon markets and offsets, it is important to understand the various international climate agreements that have been implemented over the past three decades. These agreements were the impetus behind carbon markets and offsets, particularly those that are compulsory in nature and still play an important role in those markets to this day.

The aim of the *United Nations Framework Convention on Climate Change* (UNFCCC) is to prevent dangerous human-caused changes to the Earth's climate. It was signed by 154 states at the *United Nations Conference on Environment and Development* (UNCED), informally known as the Earth Summit, held in Rio de Janeiro 1992.

The *Kyoto Protocol*, which was signed in 1997 and ran from 2005 to 2020, was the first implementation of measures under the UNFCCC. Essentially, the Kyoto Protocol is a legally binding agreement that states that industrialized countries will reduce their collective emissions of greenhouse gases (GHGs), carbon dioxide, methane, nitrous oxide, sulfur hexafluoride, hydrofluorocarbons (HFCs), and perfluorocarbons (PFCs) by 5.2 percent compared to the year 1990. The basic tenet of the Kyoto Protocol is that industrialized nations needed to reduce their emissions first. The developed, industrialized countries promised to reduce their emissions by an average of 5.2 percent by 2012, representing about 29 percent of the world's total greenhouse gas emissions.[1] The United States' position on the Kyoto Protocol was originally a subject of controversy and frustration amongst the international community. The United States is a member of the UNFCCC and it signed the Kyoto Protocol in 1998 during the Clinton administration. However, the United States dropped out of the protocol in 2001 at the beginning of the George W. Bush administration. The Bush administration's position was that the agreement was unfair since it only called for industrialized nations to limit emissions reductions and that doing so would hurt the U.S. economy.[2]

During the Obama Administration, two additional agreements were forged. The *Doha Amendment* (2012) and the *Paris Climate Agreement* (2015) both extend the Kyoto Protocol to further curb GHG emissions. Furthermore, the Paris Agreement replaces the Kyoto Protocol and includes commitments from most major GHG emitting countries to reduce their emissions. President Trump pulled the United States from the Paris Agreement. On his first day in office, January 20, 2021, President Biden began the process of rejoining the Paris Climate Agreement, which took effect on February 19, 2021.[3] Collectively, these international climate agreements offer three different mechanisms that enable countries to meet their emission targets. These three mechanisms are:

- The *International Emissions Trading Mechanism:* the countries that have excess emission credits can engage in carbon trading and sell these excess credits to other countries that need to meet targets.
- The *Clean Development Mechanism:* countries with limiting commitments may implement emission-reducing projects in developing countries to earn certified emission reduction credits.
- The *Joint Implementation Mechanism:* countries with limiting commitments may also earn emission reduction credits from a project in another country.[4]

Net Zero versus Carbon Neutrality

At the core of all the carbon market dimensions of the international climate agreements is the concept of *net zero*. Net zero refers to the global state of equilibrium in which *all* greenhouse gases going into the atmosphere are balanced by removal out of the atmosphere. It's the point at which human-caused global warming stops. The Paris Agreement underlines the need for net zero, requiring nations to "achieve a balance between anthropogenic emissions by sources and removals by sinks of greenhouse gases in the second half of this century."[5] The "net" in net zero is important because it will be virtually impossible to reduce global emissions to zero on the timescale needed. In addition to making deep cuts in emissions, we also need to scale up removals. For these additional removals to be effective, they must be long-lasting and not leak back into the atmosphere over time.

In contrast, *carbon neutrality* refers specifically to carbon emissions and not other GHGs. At its most basic, carbon neutrality is the state of balance between the amount of carbon that is emitted and the amount that is absorbed.[6] Also, the concept of carbon neutrality is often applied at different scales, from individual consumers and firms to nations and the entire planet. In essence, while both terms refer to the balance between GHG emissions and removals, carbon neutrality is narrower than net zero but can be applied at many different scales. For instance, businesses often set carbon neutrality goals, meaning after decarbonizing their operations where possible, they invest in "carbon sinks"—projects to offset their remaining emissions.

The concept of carbon neutrality offers the participants an opportunity to take personal responsibility for the global warming implications of their lifestyles. Rather than merely discussing climate change scenarios, it offers an opportunity to be part of a solution. In this context, environmental commodity markets and retail markets for voluntary carbon neutrality provide many solutions for participants. Both markets are still seeking broader public interest. Standards of what qualifies as a valid offset are still evolving. As an intangible commodity, it is difficult for an environmentally conscious consumer to make a distinction between a high and low-quality offset.

There are five basic steps to achieving carbon neutrality. The first step is to assess a carbon footprint. Numerous web-based calculators let individuals and corporations estimate their footprints (see the appendix). The second step is to implement emissions reduction measures such as energy efficiency, conservation, technology, re-engineering, and greener buildings. Steps three through five happen when further reductions can no longer take place due to technology or monetary constraints. The third step involves computing the remaining carbon emissions. In the fourth step, offsets are purchased for the remaining amount in the previous step. Finally, the fifth step is to communicate carbon neutrality to the market. This step mostly applies to public companies or corporations.[7]

CARBON MARKETS

The UNFCCC defines a *carbon market* as "a trading system through which countries may buy or sell units of greenhouse-gas emissions in an effort to meet their national limits on emissions, either under the Kyoto Protocol or under other agreements, such as that among member states of the European Union." The term comes from the fact that carbon dioxide is the predominant greenhouse gas, and other gases are measured in units called CO_2e, or "carbon-dioxide equivalents."[8]

Carbon markets falls into two categories: (1) *cap-and-trade*, and (2) *carbon offset markets*.

Cap-and-Trade

Cap-and-trade refers to government regulatory programs designed to limit, or cap, GHG emissions, particularly carbon dioxide, from industrial activity. The cap is in the form of permits issued to GHG-emitting companies by regulatory bodies. Firms that exceed the cap must purchase additional credits, while companies that cut their emissions may sell or trade unused credits. The cap on pollution credits ratchets down over time, giving corporations an incentive to find cheaper alternatives. Cap-and-trade proponents claim that it is a politically palatable alternative to a carbon tax. Critics say the cap is often set too high, giving companies an excuse to avoid investing in cleaner alternatives.

Carbon Offset Markets

Carbon offsets refer to GHG emission reductions—or an increase in carbon removals and storage—used to compensate for emissions occurring elsewhere. A carbon offset credit represents one metric ton of CO_2, or an equivalent amount of other GHGs certified by governments or independent certification bodies. Carbon offset credits are transferrable instruments that a buyer can "retire" to claim the underlying reduction in their own GHG emission goals. Proponents argue that carbon offsets make it easier and more cost-effective for organizations to meet their climate goals. Critics question the effectiveness of offsets projects to really produce the level of emission reductions or sequestration that they claim.

Carbon offset programs can be voluntary or mandatory in nature. Historically, mandatory programs were operated by governmental bodies that certified offset credits for regulatory purposes (compliance programs), while nongovernmental organizations served voluntary buyers (voluntary programs). In recent years, both types of programs began serving both types of markets. Each carbon offset program issues its own labeled "brand" of credit.

Mandatory offset programs generally include offset credit units recognized by the Kyoto Protocol. For instance, the UN Clean Development Mechanism covering developing nations issues offset credits called *Certified Emissions Reductions*, or *CERs*. Voluntary carbon markets enable businesses to offset their emissions outside of regulatory regimes. Firms can purchase offsets either through the voluntary or compliance markets. Trading and demand in the voluntary market are created only by voluntary buyers, whereas in a compliance market, demand is created by a regulatory mandate.

A list of major mandatory and voluntary carbon offset programs is presented in the tables below.

TABLE 11.1 | Major Mandatory Carbon Offset Programs.

Programs	Geographic Coverage	Label Used for Offset Credits
UN Clean Development Mechanism (CDM)	Developing Nations	Certified Emission Reduction (CER)
California Compliance Offset Program	United States	Air Resources Board Offset Credit (ARBOC)
Joint Implementation (JI)	Developing Nations	Emission Reduction Unit (ERU)
Regional Greenhouse Gas Initiative (RGGI)	Northeast U.S.	RGGI CO_2 Offset Allowance (ROA)
Alberta Emission Offset Program (AEOP)	Alberta, Canada	Alberta Emissions Offset Credit (AEOC)
Washington State Climate Commitment Act (CCA)	Washington State	Offset Credit

Source: Adapted from: https://www.offsetguide.org/understanding-carbon-offsets/carbon-offset-programs/

TABLE 11.2 | Major Voluntary Carbon Offset Programs.

Program	Geographic Coverage	Label Used for Offset Credits
American Carbon Registry	U.S., some international	Emission Reduction Ton (ERT)
Climate Action Reserve (CAR)	U.S., Mexico	Climate Reserve Ton (CRT)
The Gold Standard	International	Verified Emission Reduction (VER)
Plan Vivo	International	Plan Vivo Certificate (PVC)
The Verified Carbon Standard	International	Verified Carbon Unit (VCU)

Source: Adapted from: https://www.offsetguide.org/understanding-carbon-offsets/carbon-offset-programs/

Carbon offset programs are often criticized for the quality of the credits and social justice concerns. A number of independent studies have identified serious problems with some carbon offset credits. For example, recent studies of the world's largest offset programs—the Clean Development Mechanism (CDM) and Joint Implementation (JI)—found that 60–70 percent of offset credits may not represent valid GHG reductions.[9] This relates to the concept of *additionality*. GHG reductions are considered additional only if they occurred as a result of the market for offset credits. If the reductions would have happened without selling carbon offset credits, then they are not additional. Additionality is essential for the quality of carbon offset credits—if their associated GHG reductions are not additional, then purchasing offset credits in lieu of reducing your own emissions will make climate change worse.

Other critics have highlighted instances of carbon offset projects that harm local communities or result in broader environmental damage.[10] Offsets, it is argued, allow polluters to continue operations that negatively impact poor and marginalized communities.

Overall, the pros and cons of carbon markets and carbon offsets can be summarized as follows.

Pros:

- Makes economic sense
- Easy to adopt
- Social/individual involvement
- Voluntary market
- Improves corporate image
- Builds awareness

Cons on Moral Grounds:

- Easy on sacrifice and big on consumerism
- Minimizes need to change business operations or lifestyle
- Purchase forgiveness with money
- Allow wealthy individuals or organizations to buy themselves out of responsibility to reduce emissions
- Transfers climate impacts to poor and marginalized communities

Cons on Policy Side:

- Market in climate neutrality can blunt public support for binding limits on emissions or a tax on GHG fuels
- Development of greener and cleaner technologies might be hindered
- Flawed principle: gives the impression that the people in rich countries need not change their lifestyle to reduce global warming

To address the above concerns, several online tools exist for evaluating the quality and social justice impacts of carbon offset programs. One resource is the Carbon

Offset Guide (www.offsetguide.org) developed by the Carbon Offset Research and Education (CORE) initiative of the Stockholm Environment Institute (SEI) and Greenhouse Gas Management Institute (GHGMI) to promote offset programs and policies that maximize benefits while minimizing negative impacts. Companies and consumers are pursuing carbon neutral status increasingly and at a surprisingly fast rate. Some of the world's largest companies purchase carbon offsets, including Alphabet, Cemex, Disney, General Motors, Microsoft, PG&E, Salesforce, Shell, and Unilever. In fact, at least 36 percent of S&P 500 companies now buy carbon offsets.[11] The total value of the voluntary carbon market alone exceeded more than $1 billion USD in November 2021, up from $305.8 million USD in 2021.[12]

While concerns about carbon market programs remain, companies and organizations will increasingly look to use every tool at their disposal to achieve emission reduction goals. If used responsibly, carbon markets and offset program can help accelerate action to reach net zero and carbon neutrality. Due diligence is recommended to help businesses in the assessment and identification of "good quality" offsets to ensure offsetting provides the desired additional environmental benefits, and to avoid reputational risk associated with poor quality offsets.

Carbon Offset Programs

There are a wide variety of carbon offsetting projects. Some are in agriculture and forestry, while others are in waste management and carbon sequestration. Programs can vary considerably with regard to the actual validity of GHG reductions that result. Some examples of carbon offsetting projects are as follows:

- Forestry: tree planting projects have the potential to restore deforested areas. Since trees absorb and store carbon, tree planting projects are often the easiest for consumers to understand
- Agriculture: certain techniques and technologies can be provided to farmers that maximize resources and reduce waste in crop-growing cycles
- Aviation: flight paths can be optimized using artificial intelligence algorithms to minimize emissions and the creation of contrail clouds
- Renewable energy: these projects replace fossil fuel use with clean, renewable energy, such as that generated by a solar farm or wind turbine
- Water management: projects that aim to get clean water to areas where water is polluted or chemically contaminated
- Waste management: projects that capture methane generated in waste disposal landfills
- Carbon sequestration: certain projects use carbon capture and storage technologies that put carbon in areas where it is unlikely to be released into the atmosphere, such as deep undergrown in geologic formations
- Energy efficiency: projects that aim to improve the existing infrastructure efficiency, for example, home insulation systems[13]

The five basic steps to achieving carbon neutrality are described earlier in this chapter. The first step is to assess the organization's carbon footprint. Numerous web-based calculators let individuals and corporations estimate their footprints (see the appendix). Many organizations and companies are willing to help individuals and companies calculate carbon footprints and sell offsets.[14] One such organization is the CoolClimate Network, a consortium of universities, businesses, governments, and nonprofit organizations dedicated to the broad dissemination of climate solutions (coolclimate.org). They have developed a site with a range of GHG calculator tools for both individuals/households and businesses. For this example, let's use the individual household calculator. This calculator is comprehensive in that it allows one to compute one's footprint in each of the following areas: home, travel, food, goods, and services.

For example, if you own a car, you can enter the miles driven per year and the average miles per gallon. As an example, let's say you have one gasoline vehicle that gets 40 miles per gallon and you drive 20,000 miles per year. Upon entering the data, the calculator yields a total car footprint of 5.62 metric tons of CO_2e per year. One can also use this calculator to find the carbon footprint of an upcoming flight. As an example, one extended (>3,000 miles) round-trip flight from Chicago to London results in 1.38 tons of CO_2e emissions per leg for a total of 2.67 tons. Once all the data is inputted, the calculator gives you an overall carbon footprint. This website then allows you to "take action" by providing suggestions for decarbonizing each activity. The CoolClimate Network's business calculator works in a similar way. Emissions can be calculated for all aspects of a firm's operations. While comprehensive, the online tool is a broad-brush estimate. For a more detailed analysis, much more sophisticated tools can be employed. Such analyses can be conducted internally, or by external consulting firms specializing in Life-Cycle-Analysis (LCA) and carbon emission calculation.

Conclusion

This chapter offers a basic understanding of carbon neutrality, the carbon market, carbon offsets, and the standards surrounding the offset market. Given the large and rising number of offset providers in the highly unregulated and often misunderstood carbon offset industry, this chapter highlights areas of concern for consumers and other stakeholders. The chapter offers insight into the standards environment for offset providers since the numerous standards themselves need to be standardized.

Given that so much attention is paid to environmental sustainability, the public needs to be educated about the various policy prescriptions. As long as the purchaser of carbon credits remains naïve about the process, uninformed about standards, confused by conflicting claims, and overwhelmed by choice, neither the fundamental values of a right to health and a sustaining physical environment nor the benefits of a balanced, equitable and fair global carbon emission standard can truly be realized.

Keywords

- Additionality
- Cap-and-trade
- Carbon footprint
- Carbon market
- Carbon neutrality
- Carbon offset markets
- Certified Emissions Reductions (CERs)
- Clean Development Mechanism
- Doha Amendment
- Gold Standard
- International Emissions Trading Mechanism
- Joint Implementation Mechanism
- Kyoto Protocol
- Net zero
- Paris Climate Agreement
- United Nations Conference on Environment and Development (UNCED)
- United Nations Framework Convention on Climate Change (UNFCCC)
- Voluntary Carbon Standard (VCS)
- Voluntary Offset Standard (VOS)

Discussion Questions

1. What is the logic behind the cap-and-trade system? Do you think this mechanism can help reduce air pollution in the United States?
2. Why do organizations want to go carbon-neutral? What are the reasons behind this goal?
3. What is the present stance of the United States on the Kyoto Protocol?
4. The market solutions are more popular in the United States, and the command-and-control strategies are more popular in Europe. Why is this so?
5. How do carbon offsets work? Would you consider purchasing offsets the next time you travel?
6. Go to the top five carbon offset providers mentioned in Table 11.3 and determine the price of offsetting your next air travel trip. How do the costs compare? What reasons contribute to the difference?
7. Why do we need certification and standardization in the carbon offset markets?
8. Go to the top five carbon offset providers mentioned in Table 11.3. Which of these standards—Gold Standard, the VCS 2007, the VOS, Plan Vivo—are used by these providers?
9. Go to the appendix and calculate the carbon footprint of your car and your house. What steps can you take to reduce your footprint?
10. In conclusion, do you think carbon offsets are good or bad? Justify your position using factual data.
11. Research the Kyoto Protocol online and the followup conferences in Cancún, Copenhagen, Durban, and Qatar. Do you think that all nations should agree to binding targets or not? Discuss your reasoning.

Recommended Website

- United Nations Climate Change: Kyoto Protocol – unfccc.int/kyoto_protocol/items/2830.php

Endnotes

[1] Tardi, C. (2022, August 12). What is the Kyoto Protocol? Definition, history, timeline, status. *Investopedia*. Accessed August 2022 at https://www.investopedia.com/terms/k/kyoto.asp

[2] Tardi, 2022

[3] Tardi, 2022

[4] Tardi, 2022

[5] United Nations. (2016). Paris Agreement. United Nations Treaty Collection. https://treaties.un.org/pages/ViewDetails.aspx?src=TREATY&mtdsg_no=XXVII-7-d&chapter=27&clang=_en

[6] European Parliament. (2019) What is carbon neutrality and how can it be achieved by 2050? *European Parliament president's website*. https://www.europarl.europa.eu/news/en/headlines/society/20190926STO62270/

[7] Trexler Climate + Energy Services, Inc., 2006

[8] United Nations Climate Change. (n.d.) Glossary of climate change acronyms and terms. https://unfccc.int/fr/processus-et-reunions/la-convention/lexique-des-changements-climatiques-acronymes-et-termes#c

[9] Cames, M., Harthan, R. O., Füssler, J., Lazarus, M., Lee, C. M., Erickson, P., & Spalding-Fecher, R. (2016). *How additional is the clean development mechanism?* Berlin, Germany: Öko-Institut.

[10] Lo, A. Y., Cong, R. (2022). Emission reduction targets and outcomes of the Clean Development Mechanism (2005–2020). *PLOS Climate*, 1(8), e0000046. https://doi.org/10.1371/journal.pclm.0000046

[11] Ecosystem Marketplace Insights Team. (2022, August 3). VCM reaches towards $2 billion in 2021: New market analysis published from Ecosystem Marketplace. *Ecosystem Marketplace*. https://www.ecosystemmarketplace.com/articles/the-art-of-integrity-state-of-the-voluntary-carbon-markets-q3-2022/

[12] Globe Newswire, (2022, February 3). Voluntary carbon offsets market size [2022–2027] is projected to reach USD 700.5 Million, with 11.7% CAGR. *Market Reports World*. Retrieved from https://www.globenewswire.com/news-release/2022/02/03/2378160/0/en/Voluntary-Carbon-Offsets-Market-Size-2022-2027-is-Projected-to-Reach-USD-700-5-Million-with-11-7-CAGR-Growth-Rate-Share-Emerging-Technologies-Key-Players-Regional-and-Global-Indust.html

[13] Lutkevich, B. (2020) Definition: Carbon offset. TechTarget. Retrieved from https://www.techtarget.com/whatis/definition/carbon-offset

[14] Trexler Climate + Energy Services, Inc., 2006

Appendix

Carbon Calculators

Note: These calculators are only rough estimators. Hence, the same trip can yield different results. Depending upon the trip, these calculators can provide a starting point.

Table 11.3 | Carbon Footprint Calculators.

Companies	Websites	Types
Airplane Travel Emissions		
Atmosfair	www.atmosfair.de/index.php?id=5&L=3	Location to location detail, with layovers.
Climate Care	www.climatecare.org/living/calculator_info/index.cfm	Location to location, as well as house and car emissions.
Offsetters	www.offsetters.ca/calculators_flights.htm	Location to location detail.
Business Emissions Calculators		
Climate Friendly	www.climatefriendly.com/business.php	One of very few business calculators. Includes factory and office electricity, fleet fuel, and corporate air travel.
Car Travel Emissions		
Certified Clean Car	www.certifiedcleancar.com/menu/cleannow/foryou/index.htm	Input exact car make and model.
Target Neutral	www.targetneutral.com/TONIC/carbon.do?method=init	Calculate up to 4 cars at once.
TerraPass	www.terrapass.com/road/carboncalc.php	Input exact car make and model.
Clean Air Pass	www.cleanairpass.com/treecanada	Input exact car make and model.
Other Notable Calculators		
Carbon Counter	www.carboncounter.org/test.php?testPath=estimate&nextStep=1	Calculate "estimated" or "exact" emissions.
Sustainable Travel International	www.sustainabletravelinternational.org/offset/index.php?p=hotel	Include hotel emissions.
World Land Trust	www.carbonbalanced.org/personal/calculator/calctravel.asp	Includes hotel, boat, flight emissions.
Atmos Clear	www.atmosclear.org/calculator_tran.php	Includes household and recreational equipment, from leaf blowers to jet skis.

Source: Clean Air-Cool Planet (2006).

CHAPTER 12

Designing Sustainable Cities and Communities

LEARNING OBJECTIVES

By the end of this chapter, you will be able to do the following:

» Discuss the sustainability plan highlights of major cities across the world.
» Understand the components of a sustainable city plan.
» Discuss the city's contribution to corporate sustainability.

CHAPTER OVERVIEW

This chapter reviews the sustainability plans of some of the major cities of the United States, Europe, South America, and Africa. Since businesses must operate within the context of the local community, a community plan is important in aiding the efforts of businesses. Conversely, cities must expect the employers of its citizens to make an effort to follow the plan.

Business must rely on local city services, including water supply and sewage, fire and police protection, trash pickup, educational systems for children, public transportation, and road repair. Most of these services are taken for granted until something goes amiss. Taxpayers complain about increasing property taxes and at the same time complain about decreases in services.

Many aspects of a facility location decision are tied to the effectiveness of local cities and communities in providing services, tax incentives, and amenities. This chapter will look at some major cities across the world and their sustainability programs. These programs impact the local businesses in many ways.

- By reducing energy consumption, they can save money for other needed services.
- By improving green space, they improve the quality of life of their local citizens.
- By reducing air pollution, they improve the health of their citizens.
- By improving mass transit, they not only reduce air pollution, but also save money for their citizens.

Cities studied in this chapter include the following:

United States:
- Los Angeles
- Salt Lake City
- Seattle
- Phoenix
- Chicago
- Boston
- New York City
- Atlanta
- New Orleans

International Cities:
- London
- Paris
- Hong Kong
- Montreal
- Vancouver
- Mexico City
- Mumbai
- Curitiba
- Melbourne

A City Sustainability Portfolio

Edward Glaeser (2011), in his book *Triumph of the City*, wrote the following:

> If the future is going to be greener, then it must be more urban. Dense cities offer a means of living that involves less driving and smaller homes to heat and cool. Maybe someday we'll be able to drive and cool our homes with almost no carbon emissions, but until then, there is nothing greener than blacktop.

Glaeser (2011) offered an interesting, counterintuitive argument in defense of city living. He argued convincingly that city living makes ecological sense: "Cities are much better for the environment than leafy living. Residing in a forest might seem to be a good way of showing one's love of nature, but living in a concrete jungle is actually far more ecologically friendly."

Glaeser's statement makes sense due to the aggregation of population and the infrastructure that enables a more efficient use of resources. Any city should have a complete sustainability program, and this should be highlighted on the city website. A comprehensive portfolio would include the following:

- A comprehensive water agenda, detailing policies on water conservation and water quality
- Efforts to utilize alternative energy
- A public transportation agenda to increase its support and use of alternative fuel vehicles in the system
- A policy on urban forestry to promote the city's tree coverage
- A health and safety network for its citizens
- Efforts to improve air quality in the city
- A complete recycling program
- The promotion of open spaces, parks, and trails
- Markets for locally and organically produced food

Los Angeles

Los Angeles, the United States' second-most populated city, suffers from several handicaps: geography, pollution, and an underutilized mass transit system. The beautiful weather attracts some 11 million residents, but the layout of the city forces many to drive. The geography of the Los Angeles Basin is such that the polluted air often sits without moving—a problem also experienced in Denver and Salt Lake City. Despite these handicaps, Mayor Villaraigosa set a goal to transform Los Angeles into one of the greenest cities.

Only 6 percent of Los Angeles's energy comes from wind power, with the majority of energy coming from coal plants in Arizona and Utah. A major thrust of Southern California Edison is to expand its solar power. All new public buildings must meet Leadership in Energy and Environmental Design (LEED) standards.

Water has always been a valuable commodity in this arid basin. Water conservation is almost routinely practiced in Los Angeles, and low-flow toilets and showerheads are required at all residences. L.A.'s ambitious "Green New Deal" was introduced in 2019 by Mayor Eric Garcetti (plan.lamayor.org). It set goals in thirteen areas:

- Environmental justice
- Renewable energy
- Local water use

- Clean and healthy buildings
- Housing and development
- Mobility and public transportation
- Zero emission vehicles
- Industrial emissions and air quality monitoring
- Waste and resource recovery
- Food systems
- Urban ecosystems and resilience
- Prosperity and green jobs

L.A. hopes to achieve these major goals of this program in the following years:

- 2021: Plant 90,000 trees
- 2030: 100 percent electric vehicle fleet
- 2035: Recycle 100 percent of wastewater
- 2035: Source 70 percent of water locally
- 2045: 100 percent renewable energy
- 2050: Divert 100,000 tons of waste from landfills
- 2050: 100 percent net zero

Salt Lake City

Situated in a beautiful setting at the base of the Wasatch Range, Salt Lake City has a strong interest in keeping its natural beauty. Several times each year, Salt Lake City experiences the malady of the inversion, in which a hazy smog settles on the city and stays for several days, causing poor air quality.

Salt Lake City's sustainability program is titled "SLCgreen." It contains goals in four areas:

- Waste and recycling
- Local food
- Sustainable business resources
- Climate and air quality plan

Among its goals are to reduce greenhouse gas emissions by 80 percent between 2009 and 2040 and to achieve 100 percent renewable energy by 2030.

Salt Lake City built one of the United States' first LEED certified buildings in preparation for the 2002 Olympic Games—the Olympic Oval in Kearns.

A list of the city's accomplishments include the following:

- Passed an ordinance requiring all county buildings to meet LEED standards
- Obtained LEED certification for the Intermodal Hub and Unity Center
- Purchased acres of open space

- Performed technical audits of city buildings, implementing energy saving measures
- Has a climate action plan
- Updated zoning ordinances in accordance with sustainable practices
- Prohibited bottled water in municipal buildings

The comprehensive sustainability policy can be found at codelibrary.amlegal.com

SEATTLE

Seattle has been recognized as a forward-thinking city in its sustainability efforts for some time (Seattle Office of Sustainability and the Environment). As 80 percent of Americans live in cities, it recognized the importance of striving to meet sustainability goals. In 2000, it was the first city to adopt green building goals and in 2005, Seattle City Light was the first large utility to become carbon neutral.

The Climate Action Plan was first adopted in 2006 and revised in 2013 and 2018. Among its targets are a 64 percent reduction of passenger vehicle and building emissions from a 2008 base to 2030. It intends to achieve 91 percent by 2050.

Like many Western cities with mild climates, Seattle suffers from a homelessness problem that detracts from its sustainability efforts. This is also true of Portland, San Francisco, and L.A., among others. Extreme poverty and mental illness are prominent within this population, to the point that the treatment of the problem was an issue in the 2021 mayoral election. Private donors pledged to radically reduce this problem in downtown Seattle, reducing the numbers.

PHOENIX

The biggest environmental issue for Phoenix is water availability. Phoenix is located in the Arizona desert with the least rainfall of any of the major cities in the United States, and water is a prized commodity. The temperature often rises above 110 degrees Fahrenheit in the summer, and watering a green lawn is very expensive. Most yards are covered with rocks, not grass, a design technique called xeriscaping. Because water is such a valuable commodity, the average Phoenician uses 120 gallons of water per day, compared to an average of 160 in other southwestern cities.

On the website Grist.org, Lisa Selin Davis (2010) wrote the following:

> Phoenix is a less-natural shade of brown; a ring of smoggy pollution known locally as the Brown Cloud shadows the city. And that's not the only affront to the environs here. Anyone flying in can see the patches of fierce green lawns that paint the landscape, along with the swimming pools; the man-made lake in the suburb of Tempe; evaporating 452 million gallons of water each year; the sear of single family homes spilling across the desert; the traffic clogging the ribbons of highways; and the heat snakes squiggling from all that boiling bitumen. The 517-square-mile city—the fifth largest and fourth fastest growing in America—just survived its second-driest winter on record and is deep in drought. So how is it that this poster child for sprawl and environmental ills is being hailed—albeit by its own government—as an exemplar of sustainability?

Phoenix set a climate action plan in 2009. The city chose 10 measures to reduce emissions, including renewable energy, energy efficiency, alternative fuels, and landfill methane collection efficiency.

The impetus for this plan was Arizona's risk from global warming. If warming continues at the present rate of 1.4 degrees every 50 years, it will result in a 15 percent annual reduction in runoff from the Colorado River, a 40 percent decrease in water basin storage, and a 45 to 56 percent decline in hydroelectric power. Arizona's forests would be depleted by 15 to 30 percent, and incidents of skin cancer would increase.

Examples of Phoenix's sustainability programs include the following:

- Adoption of energy conservation standards in building codes
- Residential recycling program
- Pedestrian-friendly zoning code standards
- Light rail service increased by 37 miles
- A heat-island task force to study ways to reduce urban temperatures
- Water conservation, wetlands habitat restoration, and aquifer recharge projects
- Urban forestry program to increase trees
- Recycled asphalt overlay program for noise reduction and street maintenance
- District cooling projects that chill water at night for daytime cooling ("Phoenix: Living Like It Matters," 2008)

One of the novel approaches Phoenix has taken to reduce greenhouse gas emissions is to install energy efficient traffic signals. The conversion to light emitting diode (LED) technology reduces electricity use by 54 percent. All 500 city buses use clean-burning fuel or alternative fuels.

A federal grant created a partnership with Arizona State University and Arizona Public Service to create Energize Phoenix, a program designed to save energy and create jobs. The first major project was the Green Rail Corridor. Goals of the program include reducing home energy consumption by 30 percent, commercial energy use by 18 percent, and carbon emissions by 50,000 metric tons per year while also promoting energy efficiency. The Global Institute of Sustainability at Arizona State University is the research center for this project ("City of Phoenix Receives $25 Million Grant," 2010).

In 2020, Phoenix set new goals for 2050. Among the goals were zero waste participation accomplished by education and training; building of a new compost facility; further extending the light rail to 60 miles, and adding 150 added miles of paths, greenways, and bikeways.

Urban sprawl has been a byproduct of Phoenix's growth in population and has added another level of difficulty in sustainability efforts (City of Phoenix Environmental Sustainability Goals).

CHICAGO

Chicago's Green Action Plan is due for a revision in 2022. Chicago, situated on the banks of Lake Michigan, plans to develop the Chicago River banks into a "second shoreline," with riverwalks and urban redesign. Green design is an import aspect of the Action Plan, including plans for rain gardens, green roofs, drainage swales, and permeable paving.

Permeable alleys are aspects of the green design, utilizing open spaces to hold water. Chicago has issues with basement flooding and efforts are made to rechannel water.

Other features within the Action Plan are the Nature and Wildlife Plan, establishing 4,800 acres at 98 sites to protect and expand ecosystems for the benefit of both people and wildlife, and a Solar Express plan making solar energy in homes more affordable. 117 miles of on-street bike lanes help reduce traffic in the city and CTA has a program titled Going Green to reduce emissions. The Green Taxi Program promotes the use of alternative energy fuels in taxis.

In 2021, Chicago initiated a Waste Strategy for individuals and organizations, including 63 recommendations for waste reduction.[1]

BOSTON

Boston amended its zoning codes to require all new construction projects exceeding 50,000 square feet to earn LEED new construction points. Mayor Menino signed an order in 2007 establishing the goal of an 80 percent reduction in emissions by 2050.

Boston embarked on a social marketing campaign to increase recycling. The Public Works Department campaign was called "Recycle more, trash less." They tested the feasibility of collecting residential recyclables (plastic, metal, and glass) in one container, known as single stream collection. The pilot for this approach realized a 52 percent increase in recycled trash.

The city of Boston received over $300 million in a stimulus package from the American Recovery and Reinvestment Act (ARRA) in 2009. The city employed a novel approach to the analysis of the success of this stimulus—the sustainable return on investment (SROI).

> The sustainability analysis recognizes the increasing importance of environmental, energy and social factors when evaluating the use of public funding. In fact, ARRA funding requires consideration of: rapid implementation, green industry creation, energy efficiency and security, greenhouse gas reduction, job creation, and return on investment. The competitive funding programs for ARRA funds, whereby Boston competes for funding opportunities with communities across the country, are increasingly requiring a public benefit-cost analysis and estimation of environmental and energy benefits such as reduced greenhouse gas emissions and reduced dependency on oil and gas consumption. Consequently, this study has developed an innovative approach to measuring sustainability benefits and return on investment based on HDR's sustainable return on investment (SROI) approach. Sustainability

benefits are measured over time in terms of energy cost savings, emissions reductions, water preservation, travel time savings, safety, and accelerated development value for a subset of Boston's ARRA investments. (Boston Redevelopment Authority, 2010)

Their analysis projected 2,861 new jobs in Massachusetts with an increase of personal income of $245 million and $410 million in added tax revenue. The sustainability benefits included the following:

- 34.4 million fewer kWh of electricity consumed
- 277,000 therm reduction of gas used
- 23,750 hundreds of cubic feet of water preserved
- 25,150 fewer tons of greenhouse gas emissions
- $5.7 million per year savings in direct energy bills
- $2.4 million savings per year in reduced water and sewer costs
- $0.9 million per year in reduced greenhouse gas emissions (Boston Redevelopment Authority, 2010)

By 2022, Boston focused upon six initiatives:

1. Community Choice Electricity: Citizens can calculate their electricity costs and compare different providers to choose between them.
2. Building Emissions Reduction and Disclosure Ordinance: Boston has a goal of net zero emissions by 2050. Buildings are required to report energy and water use to the city annually.
3. Climate ready: To deal with climate change, Boston has programs to study heat resilience and protect the city from rising sea levels and flooding.
4. Renew Boston Trust: Using electricity cost savings, buildings can finance additional methods of energy efficiency.
5. Zero Waste: The campaign to reduce, repair, and reuse includes a number of toolkits, guides, and lists for consumers.
6. Archaeology: Boston employs an archeology team to protect sites and landmarks.[2]

NEW YORK CITY

On Earth Day 2007, the mayor of New York City, Michael Bloomberg, announced an environmental sustainability plan for New York City: PlaNYC 2030. The plan includes 100 strategies on the environment, economics, and quality of life. Three key areas are (1) air quality, (2) climate change, and (3) transportation.

Strategies to improve air quality include the following:

- Require filters to reduce pollution inside school buses
- Convert taxis to clean and efficient hybrid models
- Enforce anti-idling laws along heavy truck routes

- Require cleaner fuels for the Staten Island Ferry and other private ferries
- Install new boilers in several dozen schools

Strategies geared toward climate change issues include the following:

- Make government buildings more energy-efficient
- Launched energy planning board to coordinate planning on energy supply and demand
- Had volunteers coat rooftops with reflective coating to reduce cooling costs
- Invested $25 million in energy efficiency improvements in the Castle Hill Houses in the Bronx
- Tested high-efficiency LED lights in parks and roadways

Strategies toward improving transportation include the following:

- Implemented bus corridors on existing roads.
- More than 200 miles of bike lanes were installed in the five boroughs.
- Created pedestrian plazas in Herald Square and Times Square (Kassel, 2009).

The updated NYC approach revealed eight programs and initiatives:

1. One NYC 2050: This program introduced nine volumes designed to improve the quality of life for NYC citizens. The term "Green New Deal," adopted by several politicians, may have originated here.
2. NYC Accelerator: This is a 2012 program that offers free guidance on cost saving and energy efficient building upgrades, designed to help reach the goal of 80 percent reduction in greenhouse gas emissions by 2050.
3. Environmental justice: Communities with low income and high percentages of people of color are disproportionally affected by poor environmental outcomes. Local laws 60 and 64 are designed to address environmental justice.
4. Divest/invest: This program encourages the divestiture of investments from fossil fuels and encourages investments in climate solutions like wind and solar.
5. GHG Inventories: This site provides data on where NYC emissions come from.
6. Energy and water performance map: Data is provided on these key areas on this site.
7. NYC Carbon Challenge: This program is a voluntary initiative in which companies take a pledge to reduce carbon emissions by 30 percent or more.
8. GreeNYC: this is a how-to site for citizens who can find ways to reduce waste and energy at home, at the workplace, and on the go.[3]

Atlanta

The economic and transportation hub of the South, Atlanta sits at 1,000 feet of elevation, the highest elevation of any major city in the South and East. For many years, Atlanta has experienced traffic congestion on its major arteries: I-20,

I-75, I-85, and I-285. Georgia 400 was constructed as an alternative route to help ease traffic. Basically, Atlanta is a suburban community with few residents living in the city center. The Sustainable Atlanta Initiative in 2007 set goals for a higher quality of life in the city. The core for the quality of life was as follows:

- Clean air
- Zero waste
- Water efficient
- Efficient buildings
- Abundant green space
- Green jobs
- Clean energy
- Social and economic equity
- More accessible transit options
- Walkability (Mahoney, 2008)

The first year of the Sustainability Initiative, the carbon footprint was reduced by 5.6 percent, measured in metric tons of carbon dioxide. The city seeks grants to fund projects totaling $105 million. The stimulus funds are aimed at replacing inefficient lighting; installing automatic building controls and reflective roofing; upgrading water conservation; and increasing solar thermal and photovoltaic energy.

Atlanta initiated an incentive recycling system in which residents could receive rewards, gift cards, and products in exchange for the use of recycling carts. Other initiatives included the following:

- *Buildings:* An ordinance was passed requiring all new city construction projects to be LEED certified.
- *Planning and land use:* The BeltLine Project converts 22 miles of abandoned railroad corridors and 2,900 acres of land into a system of transit and greenways.
- *Green space:* A city ordinance maintains the maximum amount of tree cover within the city.
- *Local food:* The city will promote more healthy food and economically viable local farms.
- *Watershed protection:* This plan is to improve water quality through watersheds. The plan is in three phases: (1) water quality monitoring, (2) watershed assessment, and (3) watershed protection plan.
- *Clean air:* Atlanta was one of the cities that endorsed the Kyoto Protocol, which was never passed by the U.S. Congress. The city outlawed truck or bus idling for more than 15 minutes.

At the Hartsfield–Jackson Airport, the following took place:

- Encouraged airlines to use single engine taxiing when possible
- Encouraged the use of alternative fuel vehicles

- Partnered with Delta Air Lines and the Metropolitan Atlanta Rapid Transit Authority (MARTA) in a remote baggage check-in at the MARTA airport station
- Constructed an end-around taxiway to reduce the arrival times to reach the gates
- Constructed a rental car facility served by an automated people mover

The 4th- and 5th-grade curricula added a series of lessons and activities to educate students on the environment (Mahoney, 2008).

Atlanta relies on a network of innovators to accomplish sustainability goals. Rubicon spearheads the efforts to accomplish zero waste. Georgia Power and the Pulte Group developed a model for "smart neighborhoods" in association with Alarm.com, Green Marbles, Hannah Solar, Mercedes Benz Energy, and Sunverge Energy.

The state set a standard for smaller cities to accomplish the designation of "smart community," with a challenge to reduce greenhouse gas emissions.[4]

WASHINGTON, D.C.

The nation's capital calls its program the Green DC Agenda. Washington, D.C., follows a five-step methodology proposed by the International Council for Local Environmental Initiatives (ICLEI)—Local Governments for Sustainability. The five milestones to follow are as follows:

1. Inventory greenhouse gas emissions
2. Set an emissions reductions target
3. Develop a plan
4. Implement the plan
5. Monitor implementation progress (Green DC Agenda, 2010)

The first milestone was reached in 2006. Washington, D.C., discovered that 61 percent of emissions came from its 500 city facilities, 21 percent came from the electricity used to pump and treat wastewater, 7 percent from streetlights and traffic signals, and 7 percent from the vehicle fleet. The unaccounted 4 percent apparently comes from politicians.

City operations have reported a number of successes: Government electric customers buy electricity at a reduced rate and purchase 10 percent renewable energy. D.C. promotes alternative work schedules and flexible commuting options for employees. Approximately 360 vehicles were removed from the fleet to be replaced by alternative fuel vehicles. Geographic information system (GIS) technology was used to plan more efficient trash, recycling, and waste collections.

Ten SmartBike stations with 100 shared bicycles were installed. Forty miles of bike paths and 1,000 bicycle racks were installed. About 69,000 LED streetlights were installed.

Sports fields have been lit with computer-controlled high-efficiency lighting. Parklands have managed pollution with rain gardens, bioswales, and other stormwater techniques (Green DC Agenda, 2010).

The plan was updated as Sustainable DC 2.0 by Mayor Bowser. The overarching plan included Clean Energy DC, Climate Ready DC, Zero Waste DC, and Carbon Neutral DC.

An annual progress report revealed that DC reduced emissions by 31 percent from 2006 to 2021. 52 percent of commuter trips were done either by bike, walking, or public transportation, with a goal of 75 percent. The goal of 50 percent of building use of renewable energy was far off target, however, with a present state of 7 percent.[5]

SAN FRANCISCO

Out west, one of the United States' most beautiful cities is situated on an earthquake fault that has several times caused major catastrophes. San Francisco grades its progress in sustainability according to achievements in 14 areas:

- Air quality
- Biodiversity
- Economy and economic development
- Environmental justice
- Food and agriculture
- Hazardous materials
- Human health
- Municipal expenditures
- Parks, open space, and streetscapes
- Public information and education
- Solid waste
- Transportation
- Water and wastewater (SFEnvironment, 2010)

An aspect of the economic plan is to recruit emerging environmental industries. A sustainable tourism industry has been established that includes education, green spaces, and habitat restoration.

San Francisco has financial incentives available for businesses that perform ISO 14000 audits, rewarding those that make corrections. The city has perhaps the most expensive housing in the United States and suggests that businesses assist employees in down payments for mortgages.

In the area of community, San Francisco lists these accomplishments:

- Mixed use affordable housing has been increased.
- Open and green spaces have been increased.
- Neighborhood boards have been established.
- Percentage of local contractors and minority and woman-owned businesses has increased.
- Tax incentives for owners of lots suitable for garden projects have been targeted.

- Recycling and composting centers have been established in multiple locations.
- Neighborhood sustainability resource centers have been set up.
- Household retrofits to reduce energy and water use have increased.
- Purchase of green products and services has increased.

Few cities have an active food policy within their sustainability program. The goals of the San Francisco program are as follows:

- To increase individual, public, and private-sector participation in a sustainable food system.
- To establish and coordinate a community-based policy and educational program to achieve a sustainable food system.
- To ensure access by all people at all times to enough nutritious, affordable, safe, and culturally diverse food for an active, healthy life.
- To create, support, and promote regional sustainable agriculture.
- To maximize food and agricultural production within the city itself.
- To recycle all organic residuals, eliminate chemical use in agriculture and landscaping, and use sustainable practices that enhance natural biological systems throughout the city (SFEnvironment, 2010).

SF Environment offers a complete plan covering why San Francisco is frequently cited as one of the greenest cities in the United States.[6]

PORTLAND

Located in the Pacific Northwest, Portland, Oregon, was rated by SustainLane.com as the top sustainability city in the United States. Portland benefits from a mild, albeit wet, climate and has an environmentally conscious population.

Portland's 2009 plan has six major goals:

- *Goal One:* Establish a citywide sustainability team to manage strategic goal implementation.
  » The existing team was voluntary and the movement was to staff with city employees.
- *Goal Two:* Enhance and implement the city's green building policy, sustainability initiatives, and practices.
  » This goal entailed certifying completion of green building projects.
- *Goal Three:* Grow sustainability expertise among community firms.
  » Here, the intention is to reach minority and women contractors.
- *Goal Four:* Expand sustainable economic development.
  » Portland intends to offer trade shows, recruit new sustainable businesses, and introduce a sustainability institute.

- *Goal Five:* Reduce energy use as well as climate and environmental impacts.
  - » The goal is to purchase 100 percent renewable energy and find new ways to reduce the carbon footprint.
- *Goal Six:* Enhance sustainability culture through education and training (City of Portland and Multnomah County, 2009).

Portland's Climate Action Plan includes a 40 percent reduction in emissions by 2030. Portland had an ambitious goal of enabling 90 percent of residents to either walk or bicycle to meet basic daily, nonwork needs. By 2030, Portland hopes for a 30 percent reduction in daily vehicle miles traveled.

From 1990 to 2008, the population had increased more than 20 percent. At the same time, carbon emissions showed a total net loss as the per person emissions dropped from 14.7 to 11.9 metric tons per year. Meanwhile, passenger miles per day per person increased from 17.4 to 18.5 (City of Portland and Multnomah County, 2009).

New Orleans

Hurricane Katrina crippled New Orleans in 2006. After suffering tremendous casualties and property losses, approximately one third of the population relocated out of the city. Forced to rebuild, the city of New Orleans used the opportunity to write a sustainability plan to aid their efforts.

The plan was coauthored by Earthea Nance, the city of New Orleans director of infrastructure and environmental planning; Wynecta Fisher, the city of New Orleans director of environmental affairs; Jeffrey Schwartz, a professor at the Department of Urban Studies and Planning at MIT; and David Quinn, a professor in the Department of Architecture at MIT. They created a road map around six areas:

1. Green Buildings and energy efficiency
2. Alternative energy
3. Waste reduction, reuse, and recycling
4. Transportation and clean fuels
5. Environmental outreach and justice
6. Flood risk reduction ("GreeNOLA: A Strategy for a Sustainable New Orleans," 2012)

An important aspect of the plan was to reorganize city government to add an Energy Office and a Disaster Mitigation Office. One certainty for New Orleans is that due to its geography, it certainly will be hit by devastating hurricanes in the future. What is possible is to find ways to mitigate the damage.

New Orleans is pursuing housing certification standards with incentive packages. Louisiana Senate Bill 90 gives tax credits for up to $25,000 for solar energy and thermal systems. New Orleans models the new plan after the best practices in these cities:

- Portland—The low-income weatherization program, with sliding scale fees and rebates
- Houston—Weatherization of inner-city homes by a utility, CenterPoint Energy
- Seattle—BuiltGreen certification
- Chicago—The Chicago construction standard and the Green Permit Program
- Austin—All new homes zero net energy by 2015
- Atlanta—EarthCraft House Program offered

The commercial building program is modeled after Portland and Chicago. Portland's G/Rated program and Chicago's Green Permit program accelerate the permit process for green buildings.

New Orleans cites the best practices of these cities in establishing its alternative energy program:

- Seattle—Seattle City Light achieved zero net emissions through the purchase of renewable energy credits.
- Salt Lake City—Residents can purchase wind power for a flat rate.
- Portland—Oregon Energy Trust uses a surcharge to finance energy incentives.
- Boston—8.6 percent of the total energy use is through renewable sources.
- Austin—A goal of 30 percent renewable energy by 2015 has been set.

The state of Louisiana established a Coastal Restoration and Hurricane Protection Authority that focused around four objectives: (1) reduce economic losses of a storm, (2) promote a sustainable coastal ecosystem, (3) provide habitats to support commercial and recreational activities, and (4) sustain the unique heritage of coastal Louisiana by protecting historic properties and traditional living cultures. The U.S. Army Corps of Engineers is at work to protect the levee that gave way after Katrina. Small secondary levees are being built around critical public or commercial facilities for protection.

Hurricane Katrina gave New Orleans a hard-learned lesson. As one of the United States' most beloved cities, its sustainability plan probably has more cogent meaning, for its very survival is at stake.

Resilience is a pervading theme for the city as it plans for sea levels to rise by 1 to 6 feet by 2100, and an increase in the number of hot days per year. The goal is a 50 percent reduction in greenhouse gas emissions by 2030.

A 2014 comparison of major cities showed that New Orleans was doing a good job in limiting pollution on a per capita basis.[7]

Pollution per capita (metric tons)

Houston	15.22	New Orleans	9.34
Portland	12.47	Los Angeles	8.31
Chicago	12.34	San Francisco	5.37
Seattle	9.38		

Top Sustainable Cities

There are several ways to rank the most sustainable cities in the United States and the world. Here is one approach to ranking the top cities in the United States and the world:

United States
1. Portland
2. Seattle
3. St. Paul, Minnesota
4. San Diego
5. Washington, D.C.
6. San Francisco
7. Boston
8. Denver
9. Sacramento
10. Los Angeles
11. Silver Springs, Maryland
12. New York City
13. San Bernardino, California
14. Honolulu
15. Phoenix[8]

World
1. Copenhagen, Denmark
2. Zürich, Switzerland
3. Bristol, UK
4. London, UK
5. San Francisco
6. New York City
7. Paris
8. Tokyo
9. Reykjavík, Iceland
10. Berlin
11. Stockholm, Sweden
12. Singapore
13. Ljubljana, Slovenia
14. Montevideo, Uruguay
15. Vancouver, Canada[9]

London

In the United Kingdom, London fog is a combination of pollution and climate, and one study estimated the poor air quality results in over 4,000 deaths per year. The air quality is the biggest challenge for London. Proposals from the mayor of London include the following:

1. All buses must meet European emissions standards.
2. Taxis older than 10 years must be removed and replaced with alternative fuel vehicles.
3. Larger vans and minibuses must meet the Euro 3 standards.
4. Work is to be done with boroughs on traffic management to smooth driving.
5. New developments must be air quality neutral or better.
6. Dust emissions must be reduced from construction sites.
7. Homes and public buildings should be retrofitted to improve energy efficiency.
8. Public awareness will be raised to encourage all Londoners to reduce their emissions from travel choices to energy efficiency (Johnson, 2009).

London was especially aware of the need to preserve their green space and make a good presentation at the 2012 Olympic Games. In the mayor's position on green space, he wrote the following:

> With the increasing impact of climate change, open space and water are more important than ever. London will make more of its green infrastructure to provide eco system services (the processes operating in the natural environment on which we depend and can often benefit from): to help manage surface water and regulate temperatures, to facilitate walking and cycling, and as a network, for recreation, to support healthier lifestyles, and for peace and reflection. Defra's "Making Space for Water" (March 2005) emphasizes the importance of green space and of restoring rivers to manage the risk of flooding. Reinstating flood plains provides a natural increase in the flood storage capacity of the whole river, which contributes to flood protection downstream. It also creates important new habitats where wildlife can flourish. (Johnson, 2009)

London shared the 2008 Sustainable Transport Award with Paris, based primarily on its 2003 congestion pricing program, which increased motor vehicle fees and taxed fuel-burning vehicles.

The London Sustainability Plan was updated in May 2018 and integrated air quality, green infrastructure, climate change mitigation, waste, ambient noise, and a strategy for the low carbon circular economy. The goal was to achieve net zero carbon by 2030.[10]

Paris

Paris, the beloved city in France—a city with only one skyscraper—has always been concerned with its appearance. Paris presented its sustainable development, environment, and climate plan at the C40 Tokyo Conference in 2008. One goal was to cut traffic in the city by 25 percent by increasing public transportation by 12 percent. The Paris Metro and RER systems make it one of the world's easiest cities to commute in, unless you are stuck in the roundabout circling the Arc de Triomphe.

Walking and cycling are emphasized, and there are 215,000 subscribers to the Velib bicycle share system, which has 15,000 available bikes. Paris saw good results from 2002 to 2007, with an 11 percent reduction in car traffic resulting in a 9 percent drop in carbon dioxide emissions and a 32 percent drop in nitrogen oxide emissions. Cycling has increased by 48 percent since 2002.

Washington Post reporter Alexandra Topping (2007) described their Velib system:

> The system is designed to encourage short journeys. After paying your subscription fee and picking up a bike, the first half-hour is free.
>
> The second half-hour costs one euro, the third costs two euros and a fourth would cost an added four euros, to encourage people to stick to the half-hour system.
>
> But you can take a bike out, as many times as you like in a day—and each time it's free for the first 30 minutes. "This is utilitarian way of getting around," explained Velib project manager Celine Lepault. "The Velibs are for everyone, but tourists should realize they are simply a way of getting from A to B. If they want to take a bike for the day, they should hire one from a rental shop."
>
> There are now 14,197 sleek gray bikes around town. They are elegant, sturdy machines made more for cruising than for speed, with three gears, large padded seats and good hand brakes on the "sit-up" handle bars. By the end of the year, there are to be 20,600 bikes at 1,450 stations—or about one station every 900 feet.
>
> The Velib system is complicated and possibly nerve-racking. So why bother? Quite simply, the Velib does exactly as its name promises. It gives you the liberty to discover Paris at your own pace, under your own steam. Most journeys take less than 30 minutes (it takes about 15 minutes to cycle from the Musee d'orsay to the Eiffel Tower, for example), and instead of popping up at the sights like a touristy mole, you discover all the hidden attractions in between. (Topping, 2007)

The highways in France have extremely high tolls that limit traffic. This puts more commuters on trains. Similar to London, congestion pricing has been introduced to the city to curb traffic.

In 2019, the Paris Climate Action Plan adopted the UN Sustainable Development goals, with an ambition for carbon neutral achieved by 2050.[11]

HONG KONG

One of Asia's most beautiful coastal cities, Hong Kong has serious problems with air quality. In 2008, Hong Kong's Council for Sustainable Development reported on approaches to improve the air. Hong Kong packs 7 million people into 1,100 square kilometers, making it four times the population density of Los Angeles.

Total emissions of respirable particulates have been reduced by 60 percent since May 2003. Hong Kong has been a leader in performing environmental assessments since the early 1990s. The environmental audit prior to the building of the new airport resulted in minimizing environmental damage. Another example was the scrapping of an excavation project from Mirs Bay.

The recommendations of the council included the following:

- High air pollution days will be denoted with a color-coded system that designates the worst days as "red," limiting use of private vehicles, nonessential electrical, and diesel equipment. Schools should postpone outdoor activities on such days.
- Congestion road pricing, similar to London and Paris, will be introduced with penalties for vehicles with high pollution outputs.
- Cleaner fuel options should be pursued for public vehicles.
- Increased pedestrian areas will be available.
- Strict building codes to reduce energy consumption will be enforced.
- Mandates for ecolabels for electrical equipment and appliances will be given.
- The government should educate the public in ways to reduce energy consumption.
- A dialogue with Guangdong, China, to tackle cross-boundary emissions should be pursued (Council for Sustainable Development, 2008).

Several companies such as IKEA, 7-Eleven, Wellcome, and Mannings formed the Dairy Farm International Group and embarked on a campaign to educate pre-kindergarten children on environmental issues. They called these children "little green ambassadors." The four retailers claimed that this program resulted in the reduction of plastic bag consumption by 30 million per year. Every Tuesday at these companies is designated "No plastic bag day."

The long-term decarbonization strategy was established in 2019.

https://www.enb.gov.hk/sites/default/files/susdev/html/en/council/lds_ped_e.pdf

MONTREAL

Montreal, the cosmopolitan French-Canadian city, has monitored its air quality since the 1960s. One of the issues has been the popularity of burning wood as a heat source in winter. In the winter of 2007, the number of poor air quality days in the Rivière-des-Prairies district was five times greater than in the downtown area and was even higher than in the refinery section of the city. In the summer, the numbers were reversed. The Rivière-des-Prairies area is a suburban area. Despite public awareness campaigns, the public has been reluctant to give up its wood-burning fires. However, there has been overall improvement. Montreal had 44 poor air quality days in 2007, a 40 percent decrease from 2003.

Montreal has a self-service bike rental network, established in 2009. The bike stations are located in every Metro station and can be returned at any other station. Almost half—46 percent—of Montreal commuters took public transportation, bicycled, or walked to work in 2006. The cycling network contained 502 kilometers of bike paths (about 310 miles).

The Coolest Cities technical report on Canada's six major cities' sustainability performance made the following recommendations for Montreal:

1. Develop systems for consistent, frequent estimates of GHG emissions from urban personal transportation and ensure results are readily available to city departments and to the public.
2. Provide estimates of future GHG emissions for any significant infrastructure or policy development.
3. Ensure land use and transportation plans are implemented, and develop additional initiatives to meet GHG reduction targets.
4. Increase participation of multiple departments and across municipalities in planning and information sharing.
5. Track progress toward meeting GHG reduction targets and estimate the impact of infrastructure (City of Montreal, 2007).

Montreal introduced electric trolley buses linked to overhead wires in 2011, and beginning in 2012, all new buses were hybrids (Bailie & Beckstead, 2010).

Montreal's third sustainable action plan was issued in 2016, and a fourth set is scheduled for 2022.

https://montreal.ca/en/articles/sustainable-montreal-2016-2020-8944

Vancouver

Canada's site of the 2010 Winter Olympic Games, Vancouver set up a sustainability framework in 2002. They established this framework with a noble vision:

> Metro Vancouver seeks to achieve what humanity aspires to on a global basis—the highest quality of life embracing cultural vitality, economic prosperity, social justice and compassion, all nurtured in and by a beautiful and healthy natural environment. We will achieve this vision by embracing and applying the principles of sustainability, not least of which is an unshakeable commitment to the well being of current and future generations and the health of our planet, in everything we do. As we share our efforts in achieving this vision, we are confident that the inspiration and mutual learning we gain will become vital ingredients in our hopes for a sustainable common future. (Metro Vancouver, 2010)

Notable achievements Vancouver listed since that time include the following:

- Vancouver's Board of Directors made sustainability the region's primary philosophy
- Received the International Gas Union Grand Prix for its 100-year plan
- Participated in the Johannesburg UN World Summit on Sustainable Development (WSSD)
- Won the Canadian Municipalities Sustainable Community Award for energy co-generation at the Annacis Waste Water Treatment Plant
- Installed a turbo-generator as a source of sustainable energy recovery at the Burnaby Waste-to-Energy Facility

- The first waste transfer station built to LEED standards was commissioned
- Launched the Sustainability Community Breakfast series
- Acquired Burns Blog, an ecological area
- Launched a television series, the *Sustainable Region*
- Cohosted the World Urban Forum III
- Announced the Affordable Housing Strategy
- Adopted sustainable purchasing policy
- Adopted a corporate policy for the design and construction of green buildings
- Held the first Sustainability Summit, a regional initiative to set a common vision for the future
- Established a regional facility for organic food waste composting
- First filtered water has been delivered to areas of Metro Vancouver (Metro Vancouver, 2010)

Vancouver has a goal of carbon neutral new construction by 2030.

MEXICO CITY

One of the world's most populous cities, Mexico City also fights a battle with its air quality. Eighty-eight percent of its GHG emissions come from energy consumption. Mexico City set a Green Plan into motion in 2007. The city government does not doubt the evidence of climate change, as it can point to a change in the intensity and seasonality of rains, increased annual temperatures, and increased incidences of severe weather.

The main components of the Green Plan are related to energy, water consumption, transportation, soil conservation, economic development, waste generation, and environmental education. The Mexico City government set four objectives:

1. To influence the behavioral patterns, habits, and attitudes of Mexico City's population so that it will contribute to the mitigation of climate change and enact adaptation measures.

2. To attract investment and financing for greenhouse gas emission mitigation projects aimed at overcoming obstacles to the implementation of adopted measures.

3. To position Mexico City and its government as leaders in national and international efforts to mitigate greenhouse gas emissions in the context of the commitments assumed by Mexico in the United Nations Framework Convention on Climate Change (UNFCCC).

4. To set out guidelines for public policies in the mitigation of and adaptation to climate change in Mexico and to generate a multiplier effect in the country and the world.

The Mexico City Climate Action Program has two global aims, the first being the mitigation of GHG emissions and the second, adaptation to climate change:

> Aim 1: To reduce carbon dioxide equivalent emissions by 7 million tons during the 2008 to 2012 period.
>
> Aim 2: To initiate an integrated program for adaptation to climate in Mexico City and have it fully functional by 2012 (Secretaría del Medio Ambiente Gobierno del Distrito Federal, 2008).

The plan to reduce GHG emissions consisted of 26 actionable items:

1. Sustainable housing: Installing solar heating and energy and water saving systems
2. Sustainable buildings: Establishing environmental certification
3. Renewable energy programs: Promoting solar water heating and solar energy
4. Energy efficiency in government: Efficient lighting in buildings; efficient street lighting; efficiency in the electrical transportation system
5. Efficient home lighting program: Distribution of 10 million compact fluorescent lamps
6. Improvement of water pump control systems: Reduction of energy consumption
7. Reduction of emissions from septic systems
8. Energy improvement of water pump equipment
9. Expansion of hydroelectric plants
10. Infrastructure improvement through leak suppression and pipe rehab
11. Home water savings: Promoting low-flow toilets and water saving accessories
12. Reduction of mud emissions from biological treatment plants
13. Construction of 300 km of bike paths
14. Implementation of streetcar corridor from historic city center to Buenavista
15. Alternative energy for public transportation
16. Replacement of obsolete vehicles with energy efficient units
17. Establish vehicle inspection program for freight trucks
18. Replace medium-capacity vehicles with high-capacity city vehicles
19. Implement nine transportation corridors with 200 km of restricted lanes
20. Replace taxis with new vehicles
21. Construct Subway Line 12
22. Increase bus transportation for students
23. Construct compost production plant
24. Exploit biogas from landfill
25. Construct integrated recycling center
26. Modernize and automate separation plants, compost plants, and transfer centers (Secretaría del Medio Ambiente Gobierno del Distrito Federal, 2008)

Mexico City has shown improvement. In 1990, there were 333 days in which the ozone level was above the national standard of 0.11 parts per million. The minister of the environment was quoted as saying, "We couldn't even see our astonishing volcanoes the Popocatépetl and the Iztaccihuatl because of the polluted air" ("Mexico City Presents," 2011). By 2009, the number of days had been reduced to 180 and the number of hours per day that the standard was exceeded had dropped to 1.5 hours from 4.9.

Mexico City was the second major city to outlaw plastic bags in stores, with San Francisco being the first. Mumbai, India, soon followed suit.

Mexico City's Climate Action Plan covered 2014–2020 and has not been updated due to the COVID-19 pandemic. The Plan had five strategic priorities:

- Urban and rural energy transition
- Containment of urban sprawl
- Environmental improvement
- Sustainable improvement of natural resources and biodiversity preservation
- Building resilience

Mumbai

Mumbai is the largest city in India and the financial capital of the country. It has a population of 13 million and a population density of 27,209 per square kilometer. In the "Mumbai Sustainability and Corporate Citizenship Protocol," released by Shri Jayant Patil, the Honorable Minister for Finance and Planning, they make this insightful comment:

> With its ever increasing population, deteriorating environmental conditions, income disparities, scarcity of land resources, Sustainability of City becomes a major agenda for Mumbai.
>
> This is not possible without striking a balance between Corporate Governance and Public Governance, because these are two faces of the same coin and it is not possible to improve one, without the other. Talking of this balance is easier said than done. This requires a constant dialogue between Corporate Boards, Government, NGOs and Citizens making concerted efforts for creating a buy-in by all the stakeholders. The code of conduct for Ministries, Government officials and regulators is as important as they are for Corporate Boards, Communities, Customers, and Citizens at large.
>
> We believe Sustainable community development is the ability to make development choices, which respects the relationship between the three "E's"—Economy, Ecology, and Equity. (Patil, 2010. Mumbai Sustainability and Corporate Citizenship Protocol, prepared by Asian Center for Corporate Governance & Sustainability.)

In this passage, Mumbai's government is the first to acknowledge a partnership with corporations and businesses and to admit that they cannot accomplish sustainability without support.

Mumbai sets out 12 principles:

1. Water conservation to help meet future needs
2. Air pollution control for better quality of life
3. Effective land utilization
4. Waste management and restoration
5. Increased distribution of wealth throughout the social strata. In this principle Mumbai states the following:

    "Ensure that economic activities and institutions at all levels promote human development in an equitable manner. Guarantee people the right of potable water, clean air, food security, uncontaminated soil, shelter and safe sanitation. Recognize the ignored, protect the vulnerable, serve those who suffer and enable them to develop and enhance their capabilities, in order to earn their livelihood in a sustainable manner."

6. Ensure gender equality and equity. Mumbai makes several notable comments here:
    » "Eliminate discrimination in all forms as that based on color, race, sex, sexual orientation, religion, language, ethnicity, and social origin."
    » Secure the human rights for women and girls and end all violence against them.
    » "Promote the active participation of women in all aspects of economic, political, civil, social, cultural life as full and equal partners, decision makers, leaders, and beneficiaries."
    » Affirm the right of indigenous peoples to their spirituality, knowledge, lands and resources and to their related practice of sustainable livelihoods.
    » Uphold the right of all, without discrimination, to a natural and social environment supportive of human dignity, bodily health and spiritual well being with special attention to right of indigenous people and minorities.

7. Empowerment through education.
8. A culture of tolerance, nonviolence, and peace
9. Uphold the conditions of human settlement as a prime necessity of life
10. Transparency and accountability in governance.
11. Right to information
12. Effective implementation of right to information. (Patil, 2010)

However, Mumbai was rated as one of the least sustainable cities in the world in 2015 (Sustainable Cities Index, Aracddis.com).

Curitiba

A city widely known as one of the first to advertise itself as *green*, Curitiba's reputation led to rapid growth and with that, increasing problems of urbanization.

In the 1960s, then with a population of 430,000, Mayor Ivo Arzua Pereira assembled a team of architects and urban planners to help minimize urban sprawl. The Curitiba Master Plan was adopted in 1968 and featured a central two-lane street restricted to buses and local traffic between one-way streets. The center of the commercial district, the Rua Quinze de Novembro, was converted to pedestrian-only use, and an industrial zone was moved to the outskirts of the city. At the time of the original plan, there was only 5 square feet of open space per resident. By adding parks and preserving green space, today's figure is 559 square feet per resident. Approximately 1.3 million trees were planted, 16 parks were created, and 1,000 plazas were established (Gnatek, 2003).

The population climbed to 900,000 in the 1980s, so the city expanded the transportation system, protected a number of green areas from development, and established a recycling program.

The city's population continued to climb, reaching 1.4 million by 1992, and the city had attracted Renault, Chrysler, and Audi plants to its industrial portfolio. Buses carrying 270 passengers were added to the transit system. Curitiba hosted the World Cities Forum that year, increasing its reputation as a world leader in sustainable urban planning.

Today, the city has grown to 2 million people. The city is very aggressive in helping its residents find employment and offers training centers for $1 in courses such as auto mechanics, hairdressing, typing, and electrical work so that the unemployed can gain skills. Recycling was introduced in Curitiba's schools, and the schoolchildren encouraged their parents to recycle at home. Today, two thirds of the garbage is recycled (Sustainable Communities Network, 2010). Recycling is enhanced through an exchange for bus tokens.

MELBOURNE

The Australian Climate Change Bill proposes legislation to reduce GHG emissions by at least 20 percent by 2020. This aggressive target is accompanied by a number of strategies aimed at accomplishing that goal:

- Reduce emissions from coal-fired generators.
- Provide more support for solar power.
- Establish grants for research in energy.
- Introduce a retrofit for households.
- Offer rebates for solar hot water installations.
- Set up a carbon exchange program for offsets.
- Support the electric vehicles market.
- Install cogeneration plants in hospitals.
- Introduce climate change into the public school curriculum ("Summary of Key Actions," 2010).

Melbourne subscribes to the multi-city Climate Change Mitigation Strategy for 2050 and the Paris Climate Agreement.[12]

BEST CITIES TO SURVIVE THE ZOMBIE APOCALYPSE

There are rankings for cities in almost every category one might come up with, so LawnLove, a lawn care company, ranked according to emergency preparedness using 23 metrics. In many ways, the planning behind emergency preparedness is similar to a sustainability plan—if planners want the city to be sustainable, one must survive unplanned events.

So, if one is concerned about the eventuality of zombies taking over the city, here are the top ten cities for zombie survival, scored according to overall preparedness, public health, vulnerability, infrastructure, supplies, protection, and mobility. We are uncertain how these ranks were determined.

TABLE 12.1 | 2021's Best Cities for Surviving a Zombie Apocalypse.

Overall Rank (1 = Best)	City	Overall Score	Public Health Rank	Vulnerability Rank	Infrastructure Rank	Supplies Rank	Protection Rank	Mobility Rank
1	Huntington Beach, CA	52.15	19	182	147	47	4	20
2	Bellevue, WA	50.61	2	48	22	15	39	71
3	Alexandria, VA	49.85	8	107	44	35	48	10
4	Minneapolis, MN	48.92	21	55	10	105	146	9
5	Vancouver, WA	48.75	57	32	47	30	56	12
6	Seattle, WA	48.61	3	56	32	176	122	7
7	St. Paul, MN	47.51	55	31	5	123	138	13
8	Fort Collins, CO	47.13	7	125	20	81	34	61
9	Fort Lauderdale, FL	46.99	68	166	90	2	6	129
10	Hollywood, FL	46.97	103	165	95	10	3	105

Source: https://lawnlove.com/blog/best-cities-zombie-preparedness/

BUSINESS IMPLICATIONS

Businesses make location decisions—where do they establish a plant or a corporate or regional headquarters—and these decisions are made with a number of factors. The city infrastructure and financial incentives are key factors, as are transportation and labor costs, the economic climate, and quality of life. Companies may elect to move from one city to another due to poor support or a deficiency in any of the important factors. A sustainability portfolio that is actively implemented is a barometer of the city's capabilities and priorities and is an important consideration in any location decision.

Quality of life is impacted by a city's approach to sustainability. Parks and recreation in beautifully designed spaces beautify a city and make for an attractive place to live, but that must be supported by an infrastructure that maintains the face of the city.

It goes both ways—cities help business, but business must also help the city. Once a business establishes itself in a community, it must participate in the efforts to make the city sustainable. The city plays a part in job satisfaction.

LEED Certification

The U.S. Green Building Council (USGBC) has established the LEED certification for green buildings. The certification, as is evident from the many cities that are requiring all government buildings to become certified, has become a standard for U.S. cities.

The basic categories for new construction are as follows:

Sustainable sites	26 points
Water efficiency	10
Energy and atmosphere	35
Materials and resources	14
Indoor environmental quality	15
Innovation and design	6
Regional priority	4
Total	110 points

Certification	40 to 49 points	Gold	60 to 79 points
Silver	50 to 59 points	Platinum	80 points

Conclusion

The majority of major cities across the world have mapped a comprehensive sustainability plan that sets an agenda for the next 10 to 20 years. However, these documents are written by politicians who will undoubtedly be out of office when the final report card is given two or three decades in the future.

The movement in Melbourne to actually legislate emissions reductions will not be effective unless they have a mechanism of enforcement, and that may come in the form of luxury taxes on SUVs, taxes on air passengers, and so on.

What is illustrated in this chapter is that these cities have a sustainability plan, and that is an important first step. The second step is to have ways to meet the goals set forth in the plan.

Keywords

- American Recovery and Reinvestment Act (ARRA)
- Australian Climate Change Bill
- International Council for Local Environmental Initiatives (ICLEI)— Local Governments for Sustainability
- LEED certification
- Mexico City Climate Action Program
- Mumbai Sustainability and Corporate Citizenship Protocol
- Single stream collection
- Sustainable Atlanta Initiative
- Sustainable Building Initiative
- Sustainable return on investment (SROI)
- Volatile organic compounds (VOCs)

Discussion Questions

1. Does your city have a sustainability plan? If so, how does it compare to some of the cities reviewed in this chapter?
2. What are the major components of a city sustainability plan?
3. What considerations should smaller cities, with populations ranging from 50,000 to 500,000, make in writing a sustainability plan?
4. Is it necessary for a smaller town to consider a sustainability plan?
5. Compare other airports—for example, Chicago's O'Hare and Atlanta's Hartsfield–Jackson—with the plan at LAX.
6. Why do cities pursue LEED certification for their buildings?
7. Could the shared bike systems of Portland and Paris work in congested cities like New York City and San Francisco? What about spacious cities like Salt Lake City, Denver, and Jacksonville?
8. How does public transportation figure into a city's sustainability plan?
9. How do cities in desert communities—for example, Phoenix, Las Vegas, and Tucson—differ in their water policies from water-rich cities—for example, Portland, Seattle, and Chicago?
10. Compare the proportions of green space in major cities. How does the protection of parks and recreational locations influence sustainability plans?
11. What are the arguments for and against city living as a way to be more ecologically sound?

Recommended Websites

- Global Institute of Sustainability and Innovation – www.sustainability.asu.edu
- United States Green Building Council – www.usgbc.org

Endnotes

[1] City of Chicago. (n.d.). 2021 Waste Strategy. Retrieved from https://www.chicago.gov/city/en/progs/env/2021-waste-strategy.html.

[2] City of Boston. (n.d.). Environment. Retrieved from https://www.boston.gov/departments/environment.

[3] NYC Mayor's Office of Climate and Environmental Justice. (n.d.). Adapt NYC. Retrieved from https://www1.nyc.gov/site/sustainability/index.page.

[4] Central Atlanta Progress. (n.d.). The Sustainable Atlanta Initiative in 2007. Retrieved from https://www.atlantadowntown.com/cap/areas-of-focus/sustainability.

[5] District of Columbia. (n.d.) Sustainable DC. Retrieved from https://sustainable.dc.gov/.

[6] San Francisco Planning. (n.d.). Sustainable City. Retrieved from https://sfplanning.org/project/sustainable-city.

[7] City of New Orleans. (n.d.). Resilience and Sustainability. Retrieved from https://nola.gov/resilience-sustainability/

[8] Nowacki, L. (2022, October 17). The 15 most sustainable cities in the U.S. in 2022. *RocketHomes*. Retrieved from https://www.rockethomes.com/blog/housing-market/most-sustainable-cities-in-the-us

[9] Owens, Eric. (2021, September 23). 17 most sustainable cities in the world (2022). *The Sustainable Living Guide*. Retrieved from https://thesustainablelivingguide.com/most-sustainable-cities/.

[10] Greater London Authority. (n.d.). London Environment Strategy. Retrieved from https://www.london.gov.uk/what-we-do/environment/london-environment-strategy

[11] City of Paris. (n.d.). Paris Climate Action Plan. Retrieved from https://cdn.paris.fr/paris/2019/07/24/1a706797eac9982aec6b767c56449240.pdf

[12] City of Melbourne. (n.d.) Sustainability for Melbourne. Retrieved from https://www.melbourne.vic.gov.au/about-melbourne/sustainability/Pages/sustainability-for-melbourne.aspx.

CHAPTER 13

Green Marketing

LEARNING OBJECTIVES

By the end of this chapter, you will be able to do the following:

» Know the basic rules of green marketing.
» Understand greenwashing: trying to pass a company off as green when it is questionable.
» Explain the five green *P*s.
» Discuss the consumer groups that marketers target.

CHAPTER OVERVIEW

Companies must use all of their marketing tools to sell products. Through effective promotion, sales, and distribution, a company will attempt to get their goods into the hands of waiting customers. The basic principles of marketing still apply when it comes to "green" marketing, a term that has come to encompass environmental and socially conscious goods.

This chapter will review the basic principles of green marketing and study the best and worst approaches to promoting these products. We will review the five green *P*s and discuss the demographic factors of green consumers.

GREEN MARKETING

Companies that seek to leverage their eco-friendly products employ marketing techniques that have several labels. It has been called green marketing (Ottman, 1998), environmental marketing (Coddington, 1993), ecological marketing (Henlon, 1976), eco-marketing (Fuller & Butler, 1998), and finally, sustainable marketing (Fuller, 1999).

Fuller (1999) defined sustainable marketing as meeting customer needs with an ecologically compatible process of development and distribution.

For our purposes, we will use the term *green marketing*, because it appears to have attained the most use in practice.

All organizations seek to establish a sustainability presence for a number of reasons. It may be because they truly believe in it. It may be because their competitors are involved and they need to keep up, or it might be that their buyers may want to know their stance. Marketing this presence is becoming more and more critical.

For a company to actually market their products as green, there must be a number of considerations, including authenticity, commitment, and a programmatic approach.

1. Authenticity—The company should have a genuine claim to the environmentally or ecologically beneficial. Grant (2007) gave a number of marketing claims producers made in the United Kingdom:

   - Organic
   - Carbon neutral
   - Recycled
   - Free of genetic modification
   - Dolphin-friendly
   - Biodegradable
   - Energy efficient
   - Additive-free
   - Not tested on animals
   - Fair-trade
   - Free range
   - Sweatshop-free clothing
   - Vegan
   - Forest Stewardship Council (FSC)-certified (forestry)
   - European eco label
   - UK fuel economy label
   - Energy Star
   - Confidence in textiles
   - Marine Stewardship Council (MSC)

Claims of this type in the United States must pass the muster of the Federal Trade Commission (FTC), which monitors false advertising. The point is that the claim should be genuine, for if it were later found to be false, the resultant public relations would be a nightmare.

2. *Commitment*—The company itself should actively pursue the quest for sustainability. It should be a universal commitment from the president of the organization down through the ranks.
3. *A programmatic approach*—Sustainability is much more than recycling aluminum and paper and only watering the lawn on odd-numbered days. A complete program aimed at addressing a complete, holistic approach should be established prior to embarking on green marketing. Failures in one aspect of the triple bottom line can make all other good efforts go to waste—for example, selling fair trade coffee while employing underage workers.

This chapter reviews the principles of green marketing and gives examples of companies that have succeeded or failed in this endeavor. We will review the problems associated with greenwashing, a practice in which firms attempt to make false claims or to distract from other environmental problems. Finally, we will review a number of companies that have successfully employed green marketing.

Marketing has always relied upon a number of factors to help place a product in a customer's hands. It starts with marketing research to discover the attributes a customer wants in a product. Product development then embarks with a design strategy intended to approach that ideal mix of customer attributes. The sales team is charged with targeting the relevant buying groups and securing purchases. Advertising is charged with finding the media outlets that may increase customer demand through effective commercials or ads. The supply chain is responsible for the timely delivery of the product so that the customer is satisfied with the purchase. Customer relationship management (CRM) tracks customers' buying habits to maximize the marketing research aspects.

The classic 5 *P*s of marketing are product, price, place, promotion, and people. Each of these must be carefully considered if a company is going to use being green as their marketing strategy.

1. *Product:* Is the product completely vetted? Are all claims legitimate, proven, and certified? Is the product packaging recyclable?
2. *Price:* If the product costs more to deliver, are customers willing to pay extra for the product, given its environmental superiority over competing products? Marketing research and focus groups will help answer this question.
3. *Place:* What stores would be the most appropriate to capture the demographic that would buy this product? In what area of the country would sales be optimal?
4. *Promotion:* To what media outlets would the potential customers be most likely to pay attention? What nongovernmental organizations might be willing to partner with this particular product?
5. *People:* Do we have the support people who identify with the values presented by this product?

Conventional marketing is out. Green marketing is in. Effectively addressing the needs of consumers with a raised environmental consciousness cannot be achieved with the same assumptions and formulas that guided consumer marketing in the high-production-high-consumption postwar era. New strategies and innovative product and service offerings are required (Ottman, 1998, p. 45).

PATHS TO DEVELOPING SUSTAINABLE PRODUCTS

Unruh and Ettenson (2011) stressed a three-pronged approach to green product development. Path #1 was to accentuate, emphasizing the existing green attributes the company already possesses. They provide the example of the Brita water filter, which took advantage of the move away from plastic water bottles by pointing out the environmental advantages of their filter. However, companies risk public backlash if they have other products in their portfolio that do not pass muster. Unruh and Ettenson gave the example of British Petroleum's (BP) "Beyond Petroleum" campaign, which sought to emphasize other product areas. *Fortune* magazine's reaction was "Here's a novel advertising strategy—pitch your least important product and ignore your most important one" (Murphy, 2002). In light of the BP oil spill in the Gulf of Mexico, it is doubtful BP will push a "Beyond Petroleum" campaign in the immediate future. The only ads BP sponsored in 2010 were apologetic commitments to cleaning up the spill.

Path #2 is to acquire—buy firms that improve the green portfolio. Small firms that have sound ecological practices—for example, Ben and Jerry's and Stonyfield Farm—were both purchased by larger firms.

Path #3 is to architect. Build your own products. The Toyota Prius hybrid car is an example. Whichever path a company takes, Unruh and Ettenson (2011) pointed out that it must be cognizant of any environmental "skeletons" in the portfolio that may exist and to ascertain whether new green claims are credible and not candidates for cries of greenwashing—a practice of making hollow environmental claims that do not have merit.

THE RULES OF GREEN MARKETING

Consultant Jacquelyn Ottman (2010) illustrated five simple rules of green marketing:

1. *Know your customer:* Ottman's example was Whirlpool's introduction of a chlorofluorocarbon (CFC)-free refrigerator. Whirlpool had to increase the price of their refrigerator to a level that customers were not willing to pay.
2. *Empower consumers:* Give them the feeling that the purchase of the product actually makes a difference.
3. *Be transparent:* Skepticism abounds about environmental claims, so the product should have legitimate claims.
4. *Reassure the buyer:* The product should perform the task it is designed to do and not forsake functionality for environmental claims.
5. *Consider your pricing:* Make sure customers feel the extra cost is warranted.

Ottman's (2010) tips on implementing these rules include the following:

1. Think and act holistically. Green "thinking" should be part of every product and service decision the company makes.
2. Engage consumers on an emotional level in order to build brand equity. Try to make customers feel good and responsible about their purchase.
3. Communication is critical to success and will help avoid accusations of greenwashing. As stated earlier in this chapter, authenticity is paramount.
4. Eco-innovation can be used to grow top-line sales. With mature product lines, this may be a creative way to prolong the product life cycle by improving the environmental aspects of the product.
5. Aim for an ideal goal of zero environmental impact. Company-wide programs seeking real gains beyond recycling should be considered as a place to start.

A study by Fraj-Andrés, Martinez-Salinas, and Matute-Vallejo in 2009 supported the hypothesis that "environmental marketing positively influenced the firm's operational and commercial performance."

GREENWASHING

Greenwashing is defined by the firm TerraChoice as "the act of misleading consumers regarding the environmental practices of a company or the environmental benefits of a product or service." In Australia, concerns about false green claims led to the Green Marketing and the Trade Practices Act that states, "Firms which make environmental or green claims should ensure that their claims are scientifically sound and appropriately substantiated." France's consumer protection agency rules that cars should only be depicted in advertisements placing them in traffic scenes, rather than immersed in nature. The U.S. FTC established rules for environmental claims and can fine companies that mislead consumers.

THE SEVEN SINS OF GREENWASHING

1. *Sin of the hidden trade-off:* Suggesting a product is green, but not considering the trade-offs involved. Paper, for example, may be listed as environmentally preferable; however, that disregards the other aspects of the timber industry.
2. *Sin of no proof:* A claim that cannot be substantiated.
3. *Sin of vagueness:* A poorly defined claim. "All natural" can mean just about anything. What does "non-toxic" actually mean?
4. *Sin of irrelevance:* A claim that is unimportant. CFC-free is a frequent claim, but since CFCs are banned anyway, the claim is irrelevant.
5. *Sin of the lesser of two evils:* A claim that may be true, but is intended to distract the consumer from other issues. An example is the fuel-efficient SUV, which might get the best mileage in its class, but nowhere close to the fuel efficiency of a smaller sedan.
6. *Sin of fibbing:* Making a completely false claim. This can lead to fines from the FTC.

7. *Sin of worshipping false labels:* Making false endorsement claims. In Canada, one manufacturer of paper towels used a certification-like emblem on its product and claimed, "This product fights global warming" (TerraChoice, 2012).

The site Earth.org called out greenwashers (Robinson, 2021). The publicity garnered from sites like this is damaging, so it is wise not to alter reality.

Some of the companies named as greenwashers, to be certain, are making attempts to change their image through positive actions. Others, however, try to change the public perception simply by advertising.

GREEN MARKETING SEGMENTS

Ottman (1998) classified consumers as *dark green*—consumers who will pay added costs to buy green products; *light green*—consumers who lean green but are not willing to pay extra costs; and *basic brown*—those who just don't care.

Ottman (1998) further classified the dark green consumers into four groups:

1. *Resource conservers:* These consumers wear classic clothing, are prone to carrying cloth shopping bags to the grocery store, and would never be found with bottled water. All their appliances are Energy Star, and their lightbulbs are compact fluorescent bulbs. They are conscious of energy consumption and try to minimize. To appeal to these consumers, marketers need to emphasize the longevity and reusability of the products.
2. *Health fanatics:* They eat organic foods, use sunscreen, and buy nontoxic products. Green marketers should hone in on health benefits. Finding shelf space at a natural foods store—for example, Whole Foods—would be a good start.
3. *Animal lovers:* Individuals who may be vegetarian or vegan or may be members of PETA (People for the Ethical Treatment of Animals) would never buy leather or fur. They often contribute to groups that protect animals. To appeal to these individuals, advertising should be sought in specialty magazines like *PAWS* or *Animal Fair*, or partner with organizations like the ASPCA (American Society for the Prevention of Cruelty to Animals).
4. *Outdoor enthusiasts:* Campers and hikers whose idea of a good time is a day at REI. They seek products that reduce their impact on the environment—clothing made from recycled products, for example. To appeal to this group, they should advertise in the *Sierra Club* magazine or *Backpacker* magazine and look for opportunities to partner with national parks.

The Boston consulting firm Cone LLC and Boston College Center for Corporate Citizenship surveyed 1,080 consumers and developed five guidelines for green marketing based upon the responses.

1. Be precise. Claims should be specific and quantify the environmental impact.
2. Be relevant. Show the connection between the product and the environment.
3. Be a resource. Provide appropriate consumer information.
4. Be consistent. Avoid contradictory signals, i.e., the gas-guzzling SUV in nature.
5. Be realistic. Nothing is perfectly green (Cone LLC, 2008).

The Ogilvy Earth Handbook

Ogilvy Earth, the sustainability arm of the firm Ogilvy & Mather, provides the handbook *From Greenwash to Great* (Ogilvy Earth, 2010). They divide the marketing campaign into three distinct phases: (1) planning your approach, (2) developing communications, and (3) launching and beyond.

Planning Your Approach

- *Focus on fundamentals:* Form a team to plan through the supply chain and map a plan. Hellmann's Mayonnaise switched to using free-range eggs, for example.
- *Get out ahead:* Ogilvy mentioned GE (also listed in the greenwashing villains) and its CEO, who instructed his firm to be aggressive in its sustainability efforts.
- *Partner for content and credibility:* Look for a third party with which to join forces. Clorox, for example, partnered with the Sierra Club.

Developing Communications

- *Make honesty a priority:* Tell the truth. Period. Patagonia offers a nice touch by illustrating the path an article of clothing takes to get on your body.
- *Find strength in humility:* "Frame your brand's achievements in a way that acknowledges your limitations and includes a commitment to try harder" (Ogilvy Earth, 2010).
- *Embrace the detail:* Provide all the details, and be truthful about their implications. One example is Coca-Cola's claim of "30% plant-based 100% recyclable bottles."
- *Show, don't tell:* Demonstrate your products so customers can witness their performance.

Launching and Beyond

- *Become a first responder:* Be proactive in responding to criticisms. Greenpeace accused Timberland of "slaughtering the Amazon" for its leather procurement practices. Timberland's response was to partner with Greenpeace for help finding different suppliers.
- *Commit for the long term:* This is not a short-term solution (Ogilvy Earth, 2010).

Corporate Examples

Any corporation that desires to market its products with sustainability as a compelling feature must establish proof that it merits that designation. Allbirds, a casual shoe company (Allbirds.com), publishes a statement of verification of the products' carbon footprints. This is an example of a real attempt to practice what they preach.

Some major companies make climate pledges. For example, Microsoft pledges carbon neutrality by 2030, and Amazon by 2040. Scorecards are a necessary statement of resources that organizations trying to claim sustainability for marketing purposes should include on their websites.

Amazon's Climate Pledge Arena is the first carbon neutral arena, a marvelous structure that houses the Seattle Storm, the Seattle Kraken hockey team, and concerts.

Fifty Years of Green Marketing

Fast Company's (2012) website (www.fastcompany.com/pics/50-year-historygreen-marketing) chronicled the 50-year history of green marketing. Important dates in corporate green marketing include the following:

- 1969—Santa Barbara oil spill concerns are raised.
- 1970—First Earth Day.
- 1977—GE ceases dumping PCBs into Hudson River. The Occidental Chemical Love Canal disaster.
- 1980—Superfund created to clean up hazardous waste sites.
- 1980s—Volkswagen begins testing solar-powered cars.
- 1980—ARCO Solar produces more than 1 megawatt of photovoltaic modules.
- 1984—Union Carbide's fertilizer plant leaks methyl isocyanide in Bhopal, India.
- Mid-1980s—DuPont sells substitutes for CFC refrigerants.
- 1989—Exxon Valdez spills 11 million gallons of crude oil into Prince William Sound.
- 1990—76 percent of Americans call themselves "environmentalists."
- 1990—Apple introduces first environmental policy.
- 1993—Clorox makes *Fortune's* list of top companies in environmental management.
- 1993—Nike launches Reuse-a-Shoe program.
- 1999—Honda Insight and Toyota Prius are introduced.
- 2002—Jury rules that Monsanto Chemical is responsible for polluting Anniston, Alabama, with toxic PCBs.

2002—U.S. Department of Agriculture (USDA)-certified organic labeling is introduced.

2007—Home Depot Eco-Options program is introduced.

2009—Wal-Mart institutes sustainability labeling system ("A 50 Year History of Green Marketing," 2012).

ECOTOURISM

Many tourists have taken advantage of "ecotourism"—travel that is specifically designed to reduce the impact on the environment. The International Ecotourism Society (TIES) defines ecotourism as "responsible travel to natural areas that conserves the environment and improves the well-being of local people."

The ecotourism principles espoused by TIES (n.d.) are as follows:

- Minimize impact.
- Build environmental and cultural awareness and respect.
- Provide positive experiences for both visitors and hosts.
- Provide direct financial benefits for conservation.
- Provide financial benefits and empowerment for local people.
- Raise sensitivity to host countries' political, environmental, and social climates.

One of the best websites for ecotourism is the New York Times travel guide (www.travelnytimes.com/travel/guides/eco-tourism/overview.html). A recent selection of tours included Québec, Galapagos, Guyana, Belize, and Costa Rica.

Several travel guides are available for those interested in ecotourism and its benefits. *The Lonely Planet Code Green* (Lorimer, 2006) is but one example of books directed at those who intend to travel but are cognizant of treading lightly and leaving a minimal footprint.

THE FEDERAL TRADE COMMISSION ENVIRONMENTAL STANDARDS

The U.S. FTC has established standards regarding environmental marketing claims. Violation of these standards can result in a fine.

THE GENERAL PRINCIPLES

In general, the FTC states that the marketing disclosure must be clear and understandable. It must establish whether the claim relates to the product itself, or the packaging. For example, a box of aluminum foil may be labeled *recyclable*, but it is unclear whether the claim relates to the product or the box. If any part of the product is not recyclable, the advertising is considered deceptive.

Overstatements of fact can get a company into trouble. The claim "50 percent more recycled content" may be true if the product has gone from 2 percent to 3 percent, but it is still trivial. Comparative claims also must be valid, when it relates to a competitive product. "The most recycled content of all brands" must be supported.

The claim of *degradable* must have scientific backing to establish a claim. Similarly, claims of *compostable* must be supported with scientific proof. Also, *recyclable* must have evidence. An aluminum can that states, "Please recycle" carries a message that it is recyclable, and this is, in fact, warranted by evidence. However, any product with the same message that cannot be recycled is using deception.

The phrases *ozone safe* and *ozone friendly* can be misrepresented. If a product does no damage to the ozone but still contributes to smog, the claim is deceptive.

The FTC provides numerous examples on its website. Here are several found in the *Guides for the Use of Environmental Marketing Claims* (FTC, 2007):

> A product is advertised as environmentally preferable. This claim is likely to convey to consumers that this product is environmentally superior to other products. If the manufacturer cannot substantiate this broad claim, the claim would be deceptive. The claim would not be deceptive if it were accompanied by clear and prominent qualifying language limiting the environmental superiority representation to the particular product attribute or attributes for which it could be substantiated, provided that no other deceptive implications were created by the context.
>
> A trash bag is marketed as "degradable," with no qualification or other disclosure. The marketer relies on soil burial tests to show that the product will decompose in the presence of water and oxygen. The trash bags are customarily disposed of in incineration facilities or sanitary landfills that are managed in a way that inhibits degradation by minimizing moisture and oxygen. Degradation will be irrelevant for those trash bags that are incinerated and, for those disposed of in landfills, the marketer does not possess adequate substantiation that the bags will degrade in a reasonably short period of time in a landfill. The claim is therefore deceptive.
>
> A nationally marketed lawn and leaf bag is labeled compostable. Also printed on the bag is a disclosure that the bag is not designed for use in home compost piles. The bags are in fact composted in yard trimmings composting programs in many communities around the country, but such programs are not available to a substantial majority of consumers or communities where the bag is sold. The claim is deceptive because reasonable consumers living in areas not served by yard trimmings programs may understand the reference to mean that composting facilities accepting the bags are available in their areas. To avoid deception, the claim should be qualified to indicate the limited availability of such programs, for example, by stating, "Appropriate facilities may not exist in your area." Other examples of adequate qualification of the claim include providing the approximate percentage of communities or the population for which such programs are available.

A packaged product is labeled with an unqualified claim "recyclable." It is unclear from the type of product and other context whether the claim refers to the product or its package. The unqualified claim is likely to convey to reasonable consumers that both the entire product and its packaging that remain after normal use of the product, except for minor, incidental components, can be recycled. Unless each such message can be substantiated, the claim should be qualified to indicate what portions are recyclable.

A product in a multi-component package, such as a paperboard box in a shrink-wrapped plastic cover, indicates that it has recycled packaging. The paperboard box is made entirely of recycled material, but the plastic cover is not. The claim is deceptive since, without qualification, it suggests that both components are recycled. A claim limited to the paperboard box would not be deceptive.

An advertiser notes that disposal of its product generates "10% less waste." The claim is ambiguous. Depending on contextual factors, it could be a comparison either to the immediately preceding product or to a competitor's product. The 10% less waste reference is deceptive unless the seller clarifies which comparison is intended and substantiates that comparison, or substantiates both possible interpretations of the claim.

The seller of an aerosol product makes an unqualified claim that its product "Contains no CFCs." Although the product does not contain CFCs, it does contain HCFC-22, another ozone depleting ingredient. Because the claim "contains no CFCs" may imply to reasonable consumers that the product does not harm the ozone layer, the claim is deceptive" (FTC, 2007).

The FTC's document contains many similar examples of deceptive and fair claims that companies have made of their products.

Business Implications

Green marketing is something that businesses must be very careful about. Claims have to be justifiable and authentic or a campaign can cause irreparable damage. One might even question whether a company conducts a green campaign because they truly believe in the spirit of the campaign or because they simply are after another customer demographic.

There are consumers out there who will pay more to be ethically, socially, and environmentally proactive. The decision to campaign about a company's activities in this domain should be backed with proof, or else the greenwashing sites will embarrass the company publicly.

Conclusion

Companies may find it advantageous to advertise the environmental advantages of their products because many of today's consumers will pay attention to their claims. As a result, care and diligence must go into the making of these claims to assure that they are legitimate.

This chapter listed the sins of greenwashing and portions of the general principles of the FTC. Bad publicity is the result of an unwarranted claim, and that can cause loss of goodwill with customers. Therefore, all effort should be made to provide scientific proof to substantiate a claim. Once a company enters the marketplace with an advertisement, it is too late to discover that the product has not been properly vetted and there are holes in the argument of its environmental superiority.

The most important aspect of green marketing is authenticity—to have a valid claim that the company can promote. A company that cannot back up its claims risks being tagged with the label of a *greenwasher*.

Keywords

- Accentuate
- Acquire
- Architect
- Authenticity
- Customer relationship management (CRM)
- Five green *P*s
- Green marketing
- Greenwashing
- Responsible Appliance Disposal (RAD) Program
- Sustainable marketing

Discussion Questions

1. Define sustainable marketing.
2. What are the basic requirements for successful green marketing?
3. What are the five green *P*s?
4. Describe Ottman's rules of green marketing.
5. What are the seven sins of greenwashing?
6. Select several periodicals and scan the advertisements for examples of green marketing. Is there any level of greenwashing involved?
7. Examine the comparative advertisements in one industry—i.e., automobiles or computers. What degree of green marketing do you find among the competitors?
8. Describe green marketing attempts from companies considered to be in "dirty" industries: steel, chemical, energy, and so on.
9. Discuss the public relations efforts of companies that have experienced significant environmental catastrophes: ExxonMobil, BP, and others.
10. Ecotourism is aimed at environmentally conscious consumers. Locate some advertisements for tours and note their ecological features.

Recommended Websites

- 24/7 Wall St. – www.247wallst.com
- Amtrak – www.amtrak.com
- The International Ecotourism Society – www.ecotourism.org
- Earth.org – www.earth.org
- Fast Company – www.fastcompany.com
- GreenBiz – www.greenbiz.com
- Green Marketing – www.greenmarketing.com
- Greenwashing – www.greenwashing.com
- The New York Times, Travel – www.travel.nytimes.com/travel/guides/eco-tourism

References

1992 Conference on Sustainability in Rio de Janeiro. Division for Sustainable Development. (1992). Rio Declaration on Environment and Development. www.un.org/esa/dsd/agenda21/

2009/10 blueprint for sustainability: The future at work. (2010). Ford Motor Company. Retrieved from http://corporate.ford.com/dodsr09-blueprint-summary.pdf

2011 North American environmental report highlights. (2012). Honda. Retrieved from http://corporate.honda.com/environment/2011-report/statement.aspx

60% upsurge in GRI reports in 2010. (2010, November 3). Retrieved from www.globalreporting.org/information/news-and-press-center/Pages/60-percent-upsurge-in-GRI-reports-in-2010-.aspx

A more eco friendly existence. (2018, October 27). *Green Living Tips*. Retrieved September 10, 2022, from https://www.greenlivingtips.com/

A more sustainable supply chain. (2020, November 16). *Harvard Business Review*. Retrieved September 10, 2022, from https://hbr.org/2020/03/a-more-sustainable-supply-chain

A survey of organizations, providers and research involved in the effort to understand and deal with climate change. (n.d.). Retrieved from www.kyotoprotocol.com

About Corporate Register. (n.d.). CorporateRegister.com. Retrieved 2009 from www.corporateregister.com/about.html

About ICLEI. (n.d.). ICLEI—Local governments for sustainability. Retrieved March 2011 from www.iclei.org/index.php?id=about

About us. (n.d.). WBCSD: World Business Council for Sustainable Development. https://www.wbcsd.org/Overview/About-us

Advantages of solar energy. (n.d.). Retrieved from www.millionsolarroofs.com/advantagesofsolarenergy.html

Affordable-Alternative-Energy.com. (n.d.). *Nanotechnology and solar energy*. Retrieved from www.affordable-alternative-energy.com/nanotechnology-and-solar-energy.html

Agenda 21 of the United Nations, Section 9.11. (1992). Retrieved from www.un.org/esa/dsd/agenda21/

Agenda 21. (n.d.-a). *Answers*. Retrieved March 2012 from www.answers.com/topic!agenda-21#ixzz1pIXqZtjU

Agenda 21. (n.d.-b). *Chapter 27: Strengthening the role of non-governmental organizations: Partnering for sustainable development*. Retrieved from http://habitat.igc.org/agenda21/a21-27.htm

References

Agriculture. (n.d.). Oxford Reference. Retrieved from https://www.oxfordreference.com/view/10.1093/oi/authority.20110803095356555

Aguilar, S., Appleton, A., Dafoe, J., Doran, P., Kosolapova, E., McColl, V., Mead, L., & Recio, E. (2011). *Summary of the Durban Climate Change Conference.* Retrieved March 2012 from www.iisd.ca/vol12533e.html

Agyeman, J., Bullard, R. D., & Evans, B. (Eds.). (2003). *Just sustainabilities: Development in an unequal world.* Cambridge, MA: MIT Press.

AirNow. (n.d.). Retrieved from www.airnow.gov/index.cfm?action=airnow.main

Allen, C. (2004). *A rose by any other name? A discursive typology of the terms business social responsibility and sustainability in New Zealand.* Paper presented at the First International Critical Discourse Analysis Conference, Valencia, Spain.

Allenby, B. R. (1992). Industrial ecology: The materials scientist in an environmentally constrained world. *MRS Bulletin, 17*(3), 46–51.

Alter, L. (2007). *Forest Ethics' naughty and nice list of treekillers.* Treehugger.com. Retrieved from www.treehugger.com/corporate-responsibility/forest-ethics-naughty-and-nice-list-of-treekillers.html

American Public Transportation Association. (2012). *July transit savings report.* Retrieved August 2012 from www.apta.com/mediacenter/pressreleases/2012/Pages/120726TransitSavings.aspx

Anastasiadis, P., & Metaxas, G. (2010). *Sustainable city and risk management.* Paper presented at the first WIETE Annual Conference on Engineering and Technology Education, Pattaya, Thailand. Retrieved from www.wiete.com.au/conferencesnst_wiete/11-07-Metaxas.pdf

Anderson, S., & Cavanagh, J. (2000, December 4). *Top 200: The rise of corporate global power.* Institute for Policy Studies. Retrieved from http://www.corpwatch.org/article.php?id=377

Andersson, K., Ohlsson, T., & Olsson, P. (1998). Screening life cycle assessment (LCA) of tomato ketchup: A case study. *Journal of Cleaner Production, 6*(3–4), 277–288. https://doi.org/10.1016/S0959-6526(98)00027-4.

Andrews, R. N. L. (2006). *Managing the environment, managing ourselves: A history of American environmental policy.* New Haven, CT: Yale University Press.

Annan, K. (1999). Global Compact speech, press release SG/SM/6881. Retrieved from www.un.org/News/Press/docs/1999/19990201.sgsm6881.html

Applying the ABCD Method. (n.d.). *The Natural Step.* Retrieved May 29, 2012, from www.naturalstep.org/en/abcd-process

Archer, C., & Jacobson, M. (2003, May 13). Evaluation of global wind power. *Journal of Geophysical Research, 108.*

Argonne National laboratory. (2002). *Ethanol blends: Providing a renewable fuel choice.* Retrieved September 11, 2022, from https://afdc.energy.gov/files/u/publication/ethanol_blends.pdf

Arvizu, S. (2008, February 14). *Green marketing done right: Burt's Bees new campaign.* TriplePundit. Retrieved from www.triplepundit.com

As You Sow. (2022, February 16). *Clean200 continues to outperform MSCI ACWI Global Index, leaves index of dirty energy companies in the dust.* https://www.asyousow.org/press-releases/2022/2/15/clean200-outperform-msci-acwi-global-index

Asamoah, Y. (2003). NGOs, social development and sustainability. *Foreign Aid Rating.* Retrieved September 12, 2010, from www.foreignaid.com/thinktank/articles/NGOsAndSocialDevelopment.html

Ashton, W. S. (2008). Understanding the organization of industrial ecosystems: A social network approach. *Journal of Industrial Ecology, 12*(1), 34–51.

Asmus, P. (1998). A template for transition: How Mitsubishi and the rainforest action network found the natural step. *Corporate Environmental Strategy, 5*(4), 50–59.

Association of American Railroads. (2007). *Overview of American rail-roads*. Washington, DC: Author.

Awad, J. (2019). 5 successful corporate partnerships with small NGOs. Bond. Retrieved from https://www.bond.org.uk/news/2019/04/5-successful-corporate-partnerships-with-small-ngos

Baccaro, L. (2001). Civil society, NGOs, and decent work policies: Sorting out the issues. *IILS Discussion Paper, 127*.

Baker, M. (2004, June 4). *Corporate Social Responsibility—What does it mean?* Retrieved from www.mallenbaker.net/csr/definition.php

Baker, M. (2011, November 10). *Supply chains: Forging stronger links*. Strategy Management, UK: Ethical Corporation. Retrieved from www.ethicalcorp.com/ supply-chains/supply-chains-forging-stronger-links

Balu, R. (2002). Strategic innovation: Hindustan lever. *Fast Company, 47*, 120–125.

Barnhill, D. (2006, October). *Deep ecology*. Retrieved from www.eoearth.org/article/Deep_Ecology

Bar-On, Y. M., Phillips, R., & Milo, R. (2018). The biomass distribution on Earth. *Proceedings of the National Academy of Sciences of the United States of America, 115*(25), 6506–6511. ISSN 0027-8424. PMCID PMC6016768.

Bayer. (n.d.). The strategy of Bayer. *Bayer Global*. https://www.bayer.com/en/strategy/strategy.

Bell, D. (2003, April 16). *Sustainability through democratisation? Assessing the role of environmental NGOs in a liberal democracy. NGOs, sustainability and democracy*. Paper presented at the Political Studies Association Annual Conference, Leicester.

Bell, D. V. J. (2002). *The role of government in advancing corporate sustainability*. Background paper, York University, Toronto, Canada. Retrieved April 2012 from www.g8.utoronto.ca/scholar/2002/bell111062002.pdf

Bendell, J. (2007). Chiquita. *International Institute for Sustainable Development*. Retrieved from www.bsdglobal.com/viewcasestudy.aspx?id=109

Bendell, J. (2010). Opposites attract. *International Institute for Sustainable Development*. Retrieved from www.bsdglobal.com/ngo/opposites.aspx

Bent, D. (2009). Six key lessons on mapping out a business case for sustainability initiatives. GreenBiz.com. Retrieved May 2010 from www.greenbiz.com/ blog/2009/10/20/six-key-lessons-mapping-out-business-case-sustainability-initiatives#ixzzOmzXDsW3u

Benyus, J. M. (1997). *Biomimicry: Innovation inspired by nature*. New York: William Morrow and Company.

Berinstein, P. (2001). *Alternative energy: Facts, statistics, and issues*. Westport, CT: Oryx Press.

Bernard, S. M., Samet, J. M., Grambsch, A., Ebi, K. L., & Romieu, I. (2001). The potential impacts of climate variability and change on air pollution: Related health effects in the United States. *Environmental Health Perspectives, 109*(2), 199–209.

Berthoud, O. (2001, August). NGOs: Somewhere between compassion, profitability and solidarity. *Envio Digital*, Number 21. Retrieved from www.envio.org.ni/ articulo/1526

Bieker, T. (2003). Sustainability management with the balanced scorecard. In S. Karner, I. Oehme, & U. Seebacher (Eds.), *Corporate sustainability*. Conference proceedings at the 5th International Summer Academy on Technology Studies, Deutschlandsberg, Austria.

Biello, D. (2008, April 25). Solar power lightens up with thin-film technology. *Scientific American*. Retrieved from www.scientificamerican.com/article. cfm?id=solar-power-lightens-up-with-thin-film-cells

Blackburn, W. (2007). *The sustainability handbook: The complete management guide to achieving social, economic and environmental responsibility*. Washington, DC: Environmental Law Institute.

Bloch, M. (2010). Green business—The triple bottom line. *Green Living Tips*. Retrieved January 26, 2010, from www.greenlivingtips.com/articles/264/1/Triple-bottom-line.html

Bojek, P. (2021). Solar PV: analysis. *International Energy Agency*. Retrieved September 10, 2022, from https://www.iea.org/reports/solar-pv.

Boston Redevelopment Authority. (2010). Economic and sustainability benefits of Boston's ARRA investments. Retrieved from www.cityofboston.govl . . . I SROI%20Analysis%20 Report_tcm3-18467.pdf

Bourne, J. K., Jr. (2010). The deep dilemma. *National Geographic, 218*(4), 40–61.

Bowen, M. (1953). *Social responsibilities of the businessman*. New York: Harper.

BP Global. (n.d.). Statistical review of world energy: Energy Economics. *BP Global*. Retrieved September 10, 2022, from https://www.bp.com/en/global/corporate/energy-economics/statistical-review-of-world-energy.html

Bradbury, H., & Clair, J. A. (1999). Promoting sustainable organizations with Sweden's Natural Step. *AMP, 13*, 63–74. https://doi.org/10.5465/ame.1999.2570555

Braden, P. (2006, September 16). Paying the freight for polluting the air: Europe takes the lead. *The New York Times*, p. 8.

Bridger, J. C., & Luloff, A. E. (1999). Toward an interactional approach to sustainable community development. *Journal of Rural Studies, 15*(4), 377–387.

Broekhoff, D. (2007, July 18). Testimony before the House Select Committee on Energy Independence and Global Warming. *Voluntary carbon offsets: Getting what you pay for*. U.S. House of Representatives. Retrieved from http://pdf.wri.org/20070718_broekhoff_testimony.pdf

Bromley, D. W. (2008). Sustainability. In S. N. Durlauf & L. E. Blume (Eds.), *The new Palgrave dictionary of economics* (2nd ed.). New York: Palgrave Macmillan.

Brown, B. (n.d.). Essay: Earth as a natural/physical environmental system. *National Geographic*. Retrieved from www.nationalgeographic.com/xpeditions/guides/ geogsummary.pdf

Brown, F. (2009, August 24). Percentage of global population living in cities, by continent. *Guardian*.

Brown, F. (2009, September 2). Meat consumption per capita. *Guardian*. Retrieved from www.guardian.co.uk/environment/datablog/2009/sep/02/meat-consumption-per-capita-climate-change

Brown, L. (2002, March/April). The eco-economic revolution: Getting the market in sync with nature. *The Futurist*, p. 26.

Brown, L. (2009). *Plan B 4.0: Mobilizing to save civilization*. Earth Policy Institute. New York: Norton.

Brown, L. R. (1981). *Building a sustainable society*. New York: Norton.

Browne, Lord J. (2000). *Conservation awards dinner*. Speech presented at the conservation awards dinner, London. Retrieved from www.bp.com/genericarticle.do?categoryId=98&contentId=2000484

Brownlie, M. (n.d.). Bringing concrete expression to corporate responsibility: The fundamental role of sustainability reporting. *Corporate Responsibility*. Retrieved 2009 from www.responsiblepractice.corrilenglish/standards/gri/

Buffington, J., Hart, S., & Milstein, M. (2002). *Tandus 2010: Race to sustainability*. Chapel Hill, NC: Center for Sustainable Enterprises, University of North Carolina.

Burke, L., & Logsdon, J. M. (1996). How corporate social responsibility pays off. *Long Range Planning, 29*(4).

Burns, S. (1999). The natural step: A compass for environmental management systems. *Corporate Environmental Strategy, 6*(4), 329–342. https://doi.org/10.1016/S1066-7938(00)80049-4

Business for Social Responsibility. (2006, December). Offsetting emissions: A business brief on the voluntary carbon market. *The Ecosystem Marketplace*.

BusinessGreen blog. (2007). Latest offset standard draws criticism. Retrieved from https://www.businessgreen.com/blog-post/1810666/latest-offset-standard-draws-criticism

Butcher, D. (2009). Promoting corporate social responsibility. Retrieved November 8, 2009, from http://news.thomasnet.com/IMT/archives/2009/08/promoting-corpo rate-social-responsibility-global-view-of-sustainability.html

Cabeza, L. F., Rincón, L., Vilariño, V., Pérez, G., & Castell, A. (2014). Life cycle assessment (LCA) and life cycle energy analysis (LCEA) of buildings and the building sector: A review. *Renewable and Sustainable Energy Reviews, 29*, 394–416. ISSN 1364-0321, https://doi.org/10.1016/j.rser.2013.08.037.

Callicott, J. B., & Mumford, K. (1997). Ecological sustainability as a conservation concept. *Conservation Biology, 11*(1), 32–40. https://doi.org/10.1046/j.1523-1739.1997.95468.x.

Cames, M., Harthan, R. O., Füssler, J., Lazarus, M., Lee, C. M., Erickson, P., & Spalding-Fecher, R. (2016). *How additional is the clean development mechanism?* Berlin, Germany: Öko-Institut.

Carbon Concierge. (2008). *Carbon offset providers evaluation matrix*. Retrieved from www.climatetrust.org/pdfs/COPEM.pdf

Carbon Disclosure Project. (n.d.). Retrieved from www.cdproject.net/en-US/Pages/HomePage.aspx

Carbon footprint. (n.d.). Green Student U. Retrieved August 2012 from www.greenstudentu.com/encyclopedia/carbon_footprint

Carmichael, E. (n.d.). *Lesson #2: Always leave the doors to innovation open*. Retrieved January 2012 from www.evancarmichael.com/Famous-Entrepreneurs/ 1947/Lesson-2-Always-Leave-the-Doors-to-Innovation-Open.html

Carroll, A. (1999). Corporate social responsibility. *Business and Society, 38*, 3.

Carson, R. (1962). *Silent spring*. New York: Houghton Mifflin.

Cash, S. B., Goddard, E. W., & Lerohl, M. (2006). Canadian health and food: The links between policy, consumers, and industry. *Canadian Journal of Agricultural Economics, 54*, 605–629.

Cavett-Goodwin, D. (2007). Making the case for corporate social responsibility. *Culturalshifts.com*. Retrieved from http://culturalshifts.com/archives/181

CCAFRICA24 / Standards Can Improve Food Safety and Competitiveness across Africa. *CODEXALIMENTARIUS FAO-WHO*. https://www.fao.org/fao-who-codexalimentarius/news-and-events/news-details/en/c/1603899/

CDP. (2021, October 14). CDP reports record number of disclosures and unveils new strategy to help further tackle climate and ecological emergency. *Carbon Disclosure Project*. https://www.cdp.net/en/articles/media/cdp-reports-record-number-of-disclosures-and-unveils-new-strategy-to-help-further-tackle-climate-and-ecological-emergency.

Central Atlanta Progress. (n.d.). The Sustainable Atlanta Initiative in 2007. Retrieved from https://www.atlantadowntown.com/cap/areas-of-focus/sustainability.

Chandler, A. D. (1980). Industrial revolutions and institutional arrangements. *Bulletin of the American Academy of Arts and Sciences, 33*(8), 33. https://doi.org/10.2307/3823248.

Changing the Face of Medicine. (2015, 3 June). Alice Hamilton. *U.S. National Library of Medicine, National Institutes of Health*. https://cfmedicine.nlm.nih.gov/physicians/biography_137.html

Chen, D. (2022, July 6). Dow Jones Sustainability World Index. *Investopedia*. Retrieved from https://www.investopedia.com/terms/d/djones-sustainability-world.asp

Cherubini, F., Bargigli, S., & Ulgiati, S. (2009). Life cycle assessment (LCA) of waste management strategies: Landfilling, sorting plant and incineration. *Energy, Elsevier, 34*(12), 2116–2123. doi: 10.1016/j.energy.2008.08.023

Chicken industry report. (1997, May 26). *Feedstuffs*.

Chiras, D. D. (2010). *Environmental science* (8th ed.). Sudbury, MA: Jones and Bartlett.

Chiras, D. D., Reginald, J. P., & Owen, O. S. (2002). Natural resource conservation (8th ed.). Upper Saddle River, NJ: Prentice Hall.

Christmann, P. (1998). Effects of best practices of environmental management on cost advantage: The role of complementary assets. *Academy of Management Journal, 43*(4), 660–680.

City of Boston. (n.d.). Environment. Retrieved from https://www.boston.gov/departments/environment.

City of Chicago. (n.d.). 2021 Waste Strategy. Retrieved from https://www.chicago.gov/city/en/progs/env/2021-waste-strategy.html.

City of Melbourne. (n.d.) Sustainability for Melbourne. Retrieved from https://www.melbourne.vic.gov.au/about-melbourne/sustainability/Pages/sustainability-for-melbourne.aspx.

City of Montreal. (2007). *Environmental assessment report*. Retrieved from www.rsqa.qc.ca.

City of New Orleans. (n.d.). Resilience and Sustainability. Retrieved from https://nola.gov/resilience-sustainability/

City of Paris. (n.d.). Paris Climate Action Plan. Retrieved from https://cdn.paris.fr/paris/2019/07/24/1a706797eac9982aec6b767c56449240.pdf

Clarke, T. (2008). In T. Lohan (Ed.), *Water consciousness* (194–195). San Francisco: AlterNet Books.

Claudio, L. (2007). Waste couture: Environmental impact of the clothing industry. *Environmental Health Perspectives, 115*(10), 449–454.

Clean Air-Cool Planet. (2006). *A Consumers' Guide to Retail Carbon Offset Providers*. Retrieved from www.cleanair-coolplanet.org.

Cleveland, C. (2010, June 9). Exxon Valdez oil spill. *The Encyclopedia of Earth*. Retrieved from www.eoearth.org/article/Exxon_Valdez_oil_spill

Climate and energy. (n.d.). Wal-Mart.com. Retrieved from www.walmartstores/sustainability

Clutton-Brock, J. (1999). *A natural history of domesticated mammals*. Cambridge, UK: Cambridge University Press.

Coal energy. (n.d.). Retrieved from www.odec.ca/projects/2006/wong6j2/coal.html

Compassion Over Killing. (n.d.). *A COK report: Animal suffering in the broiler industry*. Retrieved from www.chickenindustry.com/ch/broilerindustryreport

Conlin, J. (2007, February 25). Going green, one spring break at a time. *The New York Times*.

Connelly, J., & Smith, G. (2003). *Politics and the environment: From theory to practice*. London, UK: Routledge.

Conner, A., & Epstein, K. (2007). Harnessing purity and pragmatism. *Stanford Social Innovation Review, 5*(4), 61–66.

Consumer trends. (2012). Greenbiz. Retrieved September 10, 2022, from https://www.greenbiz.com/topics/consumer-trends?page=22

Convention on Biological Diversity. United Nations Environment Programme. https://www.cbd.int/.

Corporate Social Responsibility. (n.d.). *CA: As you sow*. Retrieved from www.asyousow.org/csr/

Costanza, R., Mitsch, W. J., & Daly, J. W, Jr. (2006). A new vision for New Orleans and the Mississippi Delta, applying ecological economics and ecological engineering. *Frontiers in Ecological Environment, 4*(9), 465–472.

Country comparison: Infant mortality rate. (2012). CIA: The World Factbook. Retrieved from www.cia.gov/library/publications/the-world-factbooldrankorder/2091rank.html

Counts, A. (1996). *Give us credit.* New York: Times Books.

Craven, G. (2009). *What's the worst that could happen?* New York: Perigee.

Crowe, C. (2022). What you need to know about the AA1000 stakeholder engagement standard. *Borealis.* Retrieved from https://www.boreal-is.com/blog/aa1000-stakeholder-engagement-standard

Crowther, T. W., et al. (2015). Mapping tree density at a global scale. *Nature, 525*(7568), 201–205. https://doi.org/10.1038/nature14967.

Cruise ship pollution: Overview. (n.d.). Oceana.org. Retrieved from www.ocean.org/en/our-work/stop-ocean-pollution/cruise-ship-pollution/overview

Crutzen, P. J., & Stoermer, E. F. (2000). The Anthropocene. *Global Change Newsletter, 41*, 17–18.

Daly, H. (1999). *The first annual Feasta lecture.* Dublin, Ireland: Trinity College.

Darnall, N. (2006). Why firms mandate ISO 14001 certification. *Business and Society, 45*(3), 354–381.

Das, S., Shanmugam, N., Kumar, Ajay, & Jose, S. (2017). Potential of biomimicry in the field of textile technology. *Bioinspired, Biomimetic and Nanobiomaterials, 6*(4), 224–235.

Daughton, C. G. (2003). Cradle-to-cradle stewardship of drugs for minimizing their environmental disposition while promoting human health. I. Rationale for and avenues toward a green pharmacy. *Environmental Health Perspectives 111*(5). doi.org/10.1289/ehp.5947

David Suzuki Archives. David Suzuki Foundation. https://davidsuzuki.org/expert/david-suzuki/.

Davies, J. (2009). What does it mean when procurement goes green? *GreenBiz.com.* Retrieved May 2010 from www.greenbiz.com/blog/2009/11/19/what-does-it-mean-when-procurement-goes-green ?page=full#ixzzUmzXs6kxH

Davies, P. (2003). An historical perspective from the green revolution to the gene revolution. *Nutrition Reviews, 61*(6), S124–34.

Davis, L. S. (2010, June 7). What Phoenix, the poster child for environmental ills, is doing right. Retrieved from www.grist.org/article/Phoenixl/PALL

de Groot, R. S., Ramakrishnan, P. S., van de Berg, A., Kulenthran, T., Muller, S., Pitt, D., Wascher, D., & Wijesuriya, G. (2005). Cultural and amenity services. In R. Hassan, R. Schols, & N. Ash (Eds.), *Ecosystems and human well-being: Current state and trends.* Washington, DC: Island Press.

de La Hamaide, S. (2007, April 26). Bangladesh seeks World Bank loan for solar power. *Reuters.*

de Villiers, M. (2001). *Water: The fate of our most precious resource.* Boston: First Mariner Books.

Dean, C. (2007, May 22). Executives on a mission: Saving the planet. *The New York Times.*

Decision summary—Durban Climate Negotiations (COP17). (2011, December 12). *Climate Connect Limited.* Retrieved March 2012 from www.climate-connect.co.uk/ . . . /Durban%2000P%2017T020Summary

Delmas, M. (2001). Stakeholders and competitive advantage: The case of ISO14001. *Production Operation Management, 10*(3), 343–358.

DePalma, A. (2006, April 22). Gas guzzlers find price of forgiveness. *The New York Times.*

Desai, V. (2005). NGOs, gender mainstreaming, and urban poor communities in Mumbai. *Gender & Development [Special issue: Mainstreaming: A Critical Review], 13*(2), 90–98.

Design of new Mercedes-Benz Bionic car inspired by fish body shape. (2005). DaimlerChrysler Release. Retrieved December 2011 from http://news.mongabay.com/2005/0710-DaimlerChrysler.html

Dhanda, K. (1999). A market-based solution to acid rain: The case of sulfur dioxide (SO_2) trading program. *Journal of Public Policy & Marketing, 18*(2), 1–15.

Diamond, J. (2005). *Collapse: How societies choose to fail or succeed.* New York: Viking.

Directorate of the Environment. (2008, March). European Commission/Eurobarometer 295, Attitudes of European Citizens towards the Environment.

District of Columbia. (n.d.) Sustainable DC. Retrieved from https://sustainable.dc.gov/.

Doherty, K. (2011). Top 20 green supply chain partners. *Food Logistics.* Retrieved August 2012 from www.foodlogistics.com/article/10281442/top-20-green-supply-chain-partners?page=6

Dr. Robert Bullard. (n.d.). Dr. Robert Bullard: Father of Environmental Justice. *DrRobertBullard.com.* https://drrobertbullard.com/.

Dreo, J. (2006, March 9). Sustainable development. Retrieved from http://en.wikipedia.org/wiki/File:Sustainable_development.svg

Drexhage, J., & Murphy, D. (2010). *International Institute for Sustainable Development, sustainable development: From Brundtland to Rio 2012.* New York: United Nations Headquarters.

du Plessis, A., Babafemi, A. J., Paul, S. C., Panda, B., Tran, J. P., & Broeckhoven, C. (2021). Biomimicry for 3D concrete printing: A review and perspective. *Additive Manufacturing, 38,* 101823.

Duncan, A. (2001). *The definition of sustainability depends on who is speaking.* Oregon State University Extension Service. Retrieved from http://oregonfuture.oregonstate.edu/part1/pf1_02.html

Dunne, J. B., Chambers, K. J., Giombolini, K. J., & Schlegel, S. A. (2010). What does 'local' mean in the grocery store?: Multiplicity in food retailers' perspectives on sourcing and marketing local foods. *Renewable Agriculture and Food Systems, 26,* 46–59.

Duran, R. (n.d.). Eco-industrial parks: Just common sense. *Business Xpansion Journal.*

Eadie, L., & Ghosh, T. K. (2011). Biomimicry in textiles: Past, present and potential. An overview. *Journal of the Royal Society, Interface, 8*(59), 761–775. http://doi.org/10.1098/rsif.2010.0487

Earthwatch Institute. (n.d.). Company biodiversity action plan.

Ebert, R. (2009, June 17). Food, Inc: First we make them miserable, and only then kill and eat them. *RogerEbert.com.* Retrieved from https://www.rogerebert.com/reviews/food-inc-2009

Ecological footprint. (n.d.). Retrieved October 2009 from www.sustainablesonoma.org/keyconcepts/footprint.html

Econation. (2021, November 28). Sustainable economy: What is a sustainable economy. *Econation.* https://econation.one/sustainable-economy/

Ecosystem Marketplace Insights Team. (2022, August 3). VCM reaches towards $2 billion in 2021: New market analysis published from Ecosystem Marketplace. *Ecosystem Marketplace.* https://www.ecosystemmarketplace.com/articles/the-art-of-integrity-state-of-the-voluntary-carbon-markets-q3-2022/

Ehrenfeld, J. (2008). *Sustainability by design: A subversive strategy for transforming our consumer culture.* New Haven, CT: Yale University Press.

Eide, M. H. (2002). Life cycle assessment (LCA) of industrial milk production. *The International Journal of Life Cycle Assessment, 7*, 115–126. https://doi.org/10.1007/BF02978855

Elgin, B. (2021, December 1). Emissions of methane from cows: McDonald's carbon footprint remains high. *Bloomberg.* https://www.bloomberg.com/news/articles/2021-12-01/the-carbon-footprint-of-mcdonald-s-menu-very-big.

Elkington, J. (2004). Enter the triple bottom line. Retrieved from www.johnelkington.com/TBL-elkington-chapter.pdf

Ellen MacArthur Foundation. (2020). The Circular Economy. Retrieved from https://ellenmacarthurfoundation.org/topics/circular-economy-introduction/overview

Emerson, R. W. (1983). *Essays & lectures.* New York: The Library of America.

Energy Information Administration. (2012). *International energy statistics.* London: Author.

Energy.gov. (n.d.). *Fuel cells fact sheet.* Retrieved September 10, 2022, from https://www.energy.gov/eere/fuelcells/articles/fuel-cells-fact-sheet

Environmental Management System. (n.d.). Retrieved from www.epa.gov/EMS/info/index.htm

Environmental responsibility: Doing more with less. (n.d.). McDonalds.com. Retrieved from www.aboutmcdonalds.com/mcd/sustainability/our_focus_areas/ environmental_responsibility.html

Environmental Social Governance. (n.d.). The Kraft Heinz Company. Retrieved from https://www.kraftheinzcompany.com/esg/

Environmental stewardship. (n.d.). Starbucks.com. Retrieved from www.starbucks. corn/responsibility/environment/

Environmental sustainability: Helping customers and partners shrink their footprints. (n.d.). Cargill.com. Retrieved from www.cargill.com/corporate-responsibi lity/environmental-sustainability/others-footprints/index.jsp

Environmental Working Group. EWG's 2022 shopper's guide to pesticides in produce. EWG's Summary. https://www.ewg.org/foodnews/summary.php.

EPA. (2022, April 14). Inventory of U.S. greenhouse gas emissions and sinks: 1990–2019. *United States Environmental Protection Agency.* https://www.epa.gov/ghgemissions/inventory-us-greenhouse-gas-emissions-and-sinks

EPA Clean Air Task Force. (2018, July 9). EPA's report on the environmental impacts of biofuels. *Clean Air Task Force.* Retrieved September 10, 2022, from https://www.catf.us/2018/07/epa-report-environmental-impacts-biofuels/.

EPA Strategic Plan. U. S. Environmental Protection Agency. Retrieved from https://www.epa.gov/planandbudget/strategicplan

Epicurious Staff. (2006, November 6). *How to eat fewer pesticides.* Environmental Working Group. Retrieved from www.ewg.org/news/how-eat-fewer-pesti cides-0

European Parliament. (2019) What is carbon neutrality and how can it be achieved by 2050? *European Parliament president's website.* https://www.europarl.europa.eu/news/en/headlines/society/20190926STO62270/

European Photovoltaic Industry Association. (2009, April). *Global market outlook for photovoltaics until 2013* (pp. 3–4). Brussels, Belgium: Author.

European Wind Energy Association. (2009, February). *Wind now leads EU power sector* [Press release]. Brussels, Belgium: Author.

Evelyn, J. (1670). Sylva, or A discourse of forest-trees, and the propagation of timber in His Majesties dominions: As it was deliver'd in the Royal Society the XVth of October, [MD]CLXII, upon occasion of certain quæries propounded to that illustrious assembly, by the honourable the principal officers, and Commissioners of the Navy. Published by expresse order of the Royal Society. London: Printed for Jo. Martyn and Ja. Allestry. http://name.umdl.umich.edu/A38811.0001.001

FAO. (2011). Food and Agriculture Organization of the United Nations. London: Rome and Earthscan.

FAO and UNEP. (2011). *The state of the world's forests 2011: Forests, biodiversity and people*. Rome: United Nations Food and Agriculture Organization. https://www.fao.org/state-of-forests/en/.

FAO and UNEP. (2020). *The state of the world's forests 2020: Forests, biodiversity and people*. Rome: United Nations Food and Agriculture Organization. https://doi.org/10.4060/ca8642en.

FAO and UNEP. (2022). *The state of the world's forests 2022: Forests, biodiversity and people*. Rome: United Nations Food and Agriculture Organization. https://www.fao.org/state-of-forests/en/.

Fargione, J., Hill, J., Tilman, D., Polasky, S., & Hawthorne, P. (2008). Land clearing and the biofuel carbon debt. *Science, 319*(5867), 1235–1238.

Farmer, B. H. (1986). Perspectives on the 'Green Revolution' in South Asia. *Modern Asian Studies, 20*(1), 175–99.

Fast Company Staff. (2012). A 50 year history of green marketing. Retrieved from www.fastcompany.com/pics/50-year-history-green-marketing#1

Federal Trade Commission. (2007). *Guides for the use of environmental marketing claims* (Part 260). Washington DC: Author.

Feenstra, T. L., van Genugten, M. L., Hoogenveen, R. T., Wouters, E. F., Rutten-van Molken, M. P. (2001). The impact of aging and smoking on the future burden of chronic obstructive pulmonary disease: A model analysis in the Netherlands. *American Journal of Respiratory and Critical Care Medicine, 164*(4), 590–596.

Fernandez-Mena, H., Nesme, T., & Pellerin, S. (2016). Towards an agro-industrial ecology: A review of nutrient flow modelling and assessment tools in agro-food systems at the local scale. *Science of The Total Environment, 543*(A), 467–479.

Fernando, J. (2022a). FTSE4Good Index. *Investopedia*. Retrieved from https://www.investopedia.com/terms/f/ftse4good-index.asp

Fernando, J. (2022b). MSCI KLD 400 Social Index. *Investopedia*. Retrieved from https://www.investopedia.com/terms/d/domini_400.asp

Fettig, T. (2007). Harvesting the wind [Episode 6]. In M. Willoughby (Producer), e2: Energy [DVD]. Arlington, VA: PBS Home Video.

FigBytes. (n.d.). GRI framework: What is it and why is it important? *FigBytes*. https://figbytes.com/blog/gri-framework-what-is-it-why-is-it-important/

Fisk, M. (2012, May 3). BP oil spill judge tentatively approves $7.8 billion pact. *Bloomberg Businessweek*.

Food and Agricultural Organization of the United Nations. (2007). Retrieved from http://faostat.fao.org/ site/340/default.aspx

Food and Agriculture Organization of the United Nations. (n.d.). OECD/FAO, FAOSTAT Food Balances Database. *Faostat*. Retrieved from https://www.fao.org/faostat/en/#home.

Forest Stewardship Council. (n.d.). The 10 principles: Ten rules for responsible forest management. Retrieved from www.fsc.org/the-ten-principles.103.htm

Foroudastan, S., & Dees, O. (2006). Solar power and sustainability in developing countries. *International Conference on Renewable Energy for Developing Countries*. Retrieved from www.mtsu.edu/.../Solar%20Power%20and%20

Fortune Magazine. (2022, August 1). Walmart: 2022 Fortune 500. *Fortune*. https://fortune.com/company/walmart/fortune500/.

Fossil Fuel. (n.d.). The advantages of coal. Retrieved from http://fossil-fuel.co.uld coal/advantages-of-coal

Fraj-Andrés, E., Martinez-Salinas, E., & Matute-Vallejo, J. (2009). A multidimensional approach to the influence of environmental marketing and orientation on the firm's organisational performance. *Journal of Business Ethics, 88,* 263–286.

Friedman, M. (1962). Capitalism and freedom. Chicago, IL: University of Chicago Press.

Friedman, M. (1970). The social responsibility of business is to increase its profits. *New York Times Magazine,* 32–33, 122–126.

Friedman, T. L. (2007, July 8). Live bad, go green. *The New York Times.*

Friends of the Earth International. (2002). *Annual report 2001: Friends of the Earth International.* Amsterdam, Netherlands: Author.

Frost, R. (2011). The essentials. *ISO Focus+, The Magazine of the International Organization for Standardization, 2*(3). Retrieved from www.iso.org/iso/iso_focusplus_march_2011_social-responsibility.pdf

Fuller, D. (1999). Sustainable marketing. Thousand Oaks, CA: Sage.

Galbraith, J. K. (1958). How much should a country consume? In H. Jarrett (Ed.), *Perspectives on conservation: Essays on America's natural resources* (89–99). Baltimore, MD: Johns Hopkins University Press.

Gardner, T. (2010, May 26). *Global CO_2 emissions to rise 43 percent by 2035: EIA.* Planet Ark. Retrieved August 12, 2010, from http://planetark.org/enviro-news/ item/58178

Garlough, D., Gordon, W., & Bauer, S. (2008). *Green guide: The complete reference for consuming wisely.* Washington, DC: National Geographic Society.

Garner, A., & Keoleian, G. (1995). *Industrial ecology: An introduction, pollution prevention and industrial ecology.* Retrieved from www.umich.edu/—nppcpub/resources/compendia/INDEpdfs/INDEintro.pdf

Garriga, E., & Mele, D. (2004). Corporate social responsibility theories: Mapping the territory. *Journal of Business Ethics, 53,* 51–71.

General Motors sustainability report. (n.d.). Retrieved from www.gmsustainability.com

Genetically engineered foods. (n.d.). WholeFoodsMarket.com. Retrieved from http://wholefoodsmarket.com/values/genetically-engineered.php. Courtesy of Whole Foods Market. Whole Foods Market is a registered trademark of Whole Foods Market IP, L. P.

Geothermal Heat Pumps. (2011). Energy efficiency and renewable energy. Retrieved from www.energysavers.gov/your_home/space_heating_cooling/index.cfm/mytopic=12640

Getting to know us. (n.d.). McDonalds.com. Retrieved from www.aboutmcdonalds.com/mcd/our_company.html

Gibbs, D., & Deutz, P. (2007). Reflections on implementing industrial ecology through eco-industrial park development. *Journal of Cleaner Production, 15*(17), 1683–1695. https://doi.org/10.1016/j.jclepro.2007.02.003.

Gilman, R., & Gilman, D. (1991). *Ecovillages and sustainable communities: A report for Gaia Trust.* Gaia Trust.

Gipe, P. (2004). *Wind power for home, farm, and business: Renewable energy for the new millennium.* White River Junction, VT: Chelsea Green Publishing Company.

Glaeser, E. (2011). *Triumph of the city.* New York: Penguin Press.

Glanz, J. (2009, December 11). Geothermal power. *The New York Times.* Retrieved from http://topics.nytimes.com/top/news/business/energy-environment/geothermal-power/index.html

Gleick, P. H., & Cohen, M. J. (2008). The world's water 2008–2009. In *The biennial report on freshwater resources.* Washington, DC: Island Press.

Glickman, D. (1996, September 13). *Secretary's memorandum, 9500-6, sustainable development.* Baltimore, MD: U.S. Department of Agriculture, Office of the Secretary.

Global Reporting Initiative. (n.d.-a). Pollution prevention P2, EPA. Retrieved from www.epa.gov/p2/pubs/resources/p2measgri.htm

Global Reporting Initiative. (n.d.-b) GRI Framework. Retrieved from https://www.globalreporting.org/standards/

Global responsibility report. (2012). Walmart.com. Retrieved from www.walmartstores.com/sustainability/7951.aspx

Global strategy on diet, physical activity, and health. (n.d.). World Health Organization. Retrieved from www.whoint/dietphysicalactivity/dieden/index.html

Global Wind Energy Council. (2009). *Global wind 2008 report, renewable energy house*. Brussels, Belgium: Author. Retrieved from www.gwec.net/index.php?id=153

Globe Newswire. (2022, February 3). Voluntary carbon offsets market size [2022–2027] is projected to reach USD 700.5 Million, with 11.7% CAGR. *Market Reports World*. Retrieved from https://www.globenewswire.com/news-release/2022/02/03/2378160/0/en/Voluntary-Carbon-Offsets-Market-Size-2022-2027-is-Projected-to-Reach-USD-700-5-Million-with-11-7-CAGR-Growth-Rate-Share-Emerging-Technologies-Key-Players-Regional-and-Global-Indust.html

Globe Newswire. (2022, May 3). Global glyphosate market to reach $8.9 billion by 2026. News Room, Globe Newswire. https://www.globenewswire.com/news-release/2022/05/03/2434796/0/en/Global-Glyphosate-Market-to-Reach-8-9-Billion-by-2026.html

Gnatek, T. (2003). *Curitiba's urban experiment.* Retrieved from www.pbs.org/frontlineworldfiellows/brazi11203

Gold, M. V. (1999). *Sustainable agriculture: Definition and terms*. Baltimore, MD: U.S. Department of Agriculture.

Gollin, D., Hansen, C. W., & Wingender, A. M. (2021). Two blades of grass: The impact of the green revolution. *Journal of Political Economy, 129*(8), 2344–2384. https://doi.org/10.1086/714444.

Gore, A. (2007, July 7). So, Al Gore, what's the one thing we can all do to tackle climate change? *The Independent*. Retrieved from www.independent.co.uk/environment/climate-change/so-al-gore-whats-the-one-thing-we-can-all-do-to-tackle-climate-change-456269.html

Graedel, T. E., & Allenby, B. R. (2009). Industrial ecology and sustainable engineering. Englewood Cliffs, NJ: Prentice Hall.

Grant, J. (2007). The green marketing manifesto. West Sussex, England: Wiley.

Greater London Authority. (n.d.). London Environment Strategy. Retrieved from https://www.london.gov.uk/what-we-do/environment/london-environment-strategy

Green Finance Platform. (n.d.). Carbon disclosure project. Retrieved from https://www.greenfinanceplatform.org/organization/carbon-disclosure-project.

Green Supply Chain Management. (n.d.). *Bearing point management and technology consultants*. Retrieved from https://www.bearingpoint.com/en/insights-events/insights/green-supply-chain-management/

GreenBiz Staff. (2007a). Case studies in sustainable grocery supply chains. *Greenbiz.com*. Retrieved July 19, 2007, from www.greenbiz.com/toolbox/printer.cfm?LinkAdvID=83325

GreenBiz Staff. (2007b). $100K award for sustainability opens for nominations. *Greenbiz.com*. Retrieved from www.greenbiz.com/news/news_third .cfm?NewsID=35812

GreenBiz Staff. (2007c). Businesses embracing green procurement, survey finds. *Greenbiz.com*. Retrieved from www.climatebiz.com/sections/news_detail .cfm?NewsID=35700

GreenBiz Staff. (2007d). Sonoco helps manufacturers cut landfill waste. *Greenbiz.com*. Retrieved from www.greenbiz.com/news!printer.cfm?NewsID36l 32

GreenBiz Staff. (2008). BT- and Cisco-sponsored paper says sustainability breeds innovation and profitability. *Greenbiz.com*. Retrieved April 2012 from www.greenbiz.com/print/1601

Green-e. (2007). The Green-e climate standard. Center for Resource Solutions. https://www.green-e.org/docs/climate/Green-eClimateStandard_V2.1.pdf

Greenpeace. (2003). *Greenpeace: About us*. Retrieved July 4, 2003, from www.greenpeace.org/aboutus/

Greentumble. (2017, March 14). Working together for the environment: Great examples of industry partnerships with NGOs. *Greentumble*. Retrieved from https://greentumble.com/working-together-for-the-environment-great-examples-of-industry-partnerships-with-ngos/

Grumbine, R. E. (1994). What is ecosystem management? *Conservation Biology, 8*(1), 27–38.

Guerin, B. (2007, July 2). European blowback for Asian biofuels. Asia Times.

Gutierrez Garzon, A. R., Bettinger, P., Siry, J., Abrams, J., Cieszewski, C., Boston, K., Mei, B., Zengin, H., & Yesil, A. (2020). A comparative analysis of five forest certification programs. *Forests, 11*(8), 863. https://doi.org/10.3390/f11080863.

Hall-Jones, P. (2006). The rise and rise of NGOs. *Public Service International*. Retrieved from https://archive.globalpolicy.org/component/content/article/176-general/31937.html

Hamel, G. (2000). Leading the revolution. Boston: Harvard Business School Press.

Hamilton, K., Bayon, R., Turner, G., & Higgins, D. (2007). *State of the voluntary carbon markets 2007: Picking up steam*. San Francisco: Ecosystem Marketplace & New Carbon Finance. Retrieved from http://ecosystemmarketplace.com/documents/acrobat/StateoftheVoluntaryCarbonMarket18July_Final.pdf

Hamilton, K., Sjardin, M., Marcello, T., & Xu, G. (2008). *Forging a frontier: State of the voluntary carbon markets*. San Francisco: Ecosystem Marketplace & New Carbon Finance. Retrieved from http://ecosystemmarketplace.com/documents/cms_documents/2008_StateofVoluntaryCarbonMarket.4.pdf

Hammond, A., Kramer, W., Katz, R., & Walker, C. (2007). *The next 4 billion: Market size and business strategy at the base of the pyramid*. Washington, DC: World Resources Institute and International Finance Corporation/World Bank Group.

Hanks, J. (n.d.). Carbon Disclosure Project. Retrieved from http://www.enviropaedia.com/topic/default.php?topic_id=305

Hanson, C., Ranganathan, J., & Iceland, C. (2012, February 7). The Corporate Ecosystem Services Review. *World Resources Institute*. Retrieved from https://www.wri.org/research/corporate-ecosystem-services-review

Harack, B., & Laskowski, K. (2010, November 29). 31 ways to reduce paper usage. *Vision of Earth*. Retrieved from www.visionofearth.org/live-green/31-ways-to-reduce-paper-usage/

Hargroves, K., & Smith, M. (2005). The natural advantage of nations: Business opportunities, innovation, and governance in the 21st century. London: The Natural Edge Project, Earthscan.

Hart, S., & Milstein, M. (2003). Creating sustainable value. *Academy of Management Executive, 17*, 2.

Harwood, R. R. (1990). A history of sustainable agriculture. In C. A. Edwards, R. Lal, J. P. Madden, R. H. Miller, & G. House (Eds.), Sustainable agricultural systems (pp. 3–19). Ankeny, IA: Soil and Water Conservation Society.

Hauserman, J. (2007). *Florida's coastal and ocean future, a blueprint for economic and environmental leadership*. New York: National Resources Defense Council. Reprinted with permission from the National Resources Defense Council.

Hawken, P. (1994). *The ecology of commerce: How business can save the planet*. London, UK: Weidenfeld & Nicolson.

Hawken, P. (2007). *Blessed unrest: How the largest social movement in history is restoring grace, justice and beauty to the world*. London: Penguin Books.

Hawken, P. (Ed.). (2017). *Drawdown: The most comprehensive plan ever proposed to reverse global warming*. Penguin Books: New York City.

Held, L. (2021, December 9). At an annual sustainability gathering, big AG describes its efforts to control the narrative. *Civil Eats*. https://civileats.com/2021/12/09/at-an-annual-sustainability-gathering-big-ag-describes-its-efforts-to-control-the-narrative/

Henlon, K. E. (1976). Ecological marketing. Columbus, OH: Grid.

Hibbard, M., & Tang, C. C. (2004). Sustainable community development: A social approach from Vietnam. *Community Development Society, 35*(2), 87–105.

Higgins, M. (2006). How to keep flying and staying green. *The New York Times*, p. 6.

Hill, J., Nelson, E., Tilman, D., Polasky, S., & Tiffany, D. (2006). Environmental, economic, and energetic costs and benefits of biodiesel and ethanol biofuels. *Proceedings of the National Academy of Sciences of the United States of America, 103*(30), 11206–11210.

Hill, J. M. (2010). Getting started with greening your supply chain. *GreenBiz.com*. Retrieved May 2010 from www.greenbiz.com/blog/2010/04/12/getting-started-greening-your-supply-chain?page=full#ixzzOmzWjYprU

History.com Editors. (2009, Oct. 27). George Washington Carver. History.com, A&E Television Networks. Retrieved from https://www.history.com/topics/black-history/george-washington-carver.

Hoffman, A. J. (2009). Shades of green. *Stanford Social Innovation Review*, 40–49.

Holden, B. (2002). Democracy and global warming. London: Continuum.

Holliday, C. (2001). Sustainable growth, the DuPont way. *Harvard Business Review, 79*(8), 129–132.

Holmes, J. (n.d.). *Sustainability and the triple bottom line*. Retrieved from http://enterprisedevelop.com/resources/pdf/EDG%20Sustainable%20Enterprise%20.pdf

Horn, G. (2006). Living green: A practical guide to simple sustainability. Topanga, CA: Freedom Press.

House-Energy. (n.d.). *Solar energy costs payback*. Retrieved from www.houseenergy.com/

Howlett, M., & Ramesh, M. (1995). Studying public policy: Policy cycles and policy subsystems. Toronto: Oxford University Press.

Huff, E. (2011). Solar cell breakthrough achieves 90% efficiency at fraction of costs. *NaturalNews.com*. Retrieved March 2012 from www.naturalnews.com/028691_ solar_cells_efficiency.html#ixzz1 Oegw80Eo

Human Development Index. (n.d.). Human development reports, United National Development Programme. Retrieved August 2012 from http://hdr.undp.org/en/statistics/hdi/

Hunter, M. L. (Ed.). (1999). *Maintaining biodiversity in forest ecosystems*. Cambridge, UK: Cambridge University Press.

Hydropower development: The economic impact of hydropower. (2010). Economy Watch.

Hydropower: Going with the flow. (2012). National Geographic Society. Retrieved from http://environment.nationalgeographic.com/environment/global-warming/hydropower-profile/

Ilasco, I. (2021, December 23). Top 10 largest NGOs in the world. *Development Aid*. Retrieved from https://www.developmentaid.org/news-stream/post/124777/top-10-largest-ngos-in-the-world

Independent Evaluation Group. (2014). Managing forest resources for sustainable development: An evaluation of the world bank group's experience. Washington, DC: World Bank Group. https://openknowledge.worldbank.org/handle/10986/35158

InfoNatura. (n.d.). About the data: Conservation status. *NatureServe.org*. Retrieved on April 10, 2007 from https://web.archive.org/web/20130921055302/http:/www.natureserve.org/infonatura/Lnsstatus.htm.

Intergovernmental Panel on Climate Change. (n.d.). *IPCC*. https://www.ipcc.ch/.

Intergovernmental Panel on Climate Change. (2011). IPCC special report on renewable energy sources and climate change mitigation. *IPCC*. Retrieved September 10, 2022, from https://www.ipcc-wg3.de/srren-report/.

Intergovernmental Panel on Climate Change. (2018). Special report: Global warming of 1.5°C. *IPCC*. https://www.ipcc.ch/sr15/.

International Finance Corporation. (2018, November 29). IFC report identifies more than $29 trillion in climate investment opportunities in cities by 2030. Press release. *IFC*. Retrieved September 11, 2022, from https://pressroom.ifc.org/all/pages/PressDetail.aspx?ID=18420

International Renewable Energy Agency. (n.d.). International Renewable Energy Agency. *IRENA*. Retrieved September 10, 2022, from https://www.irena.org/.

International Union for the Conservation of Nature. (2007). Red list 1996–2007. Retrieved from www.iucnredlist.org/info/2007RL_Stats_Table/0201.pdf

ISO 14001 2004 introduction. (n.d.) Praxiom Research Group Limited. Retrieved 2009 from www.praxiom.com/iso-14001-intro.htm

ISO 14001 environment. (n.d.). British Standards Institute. Retrieved 2009 from www.bsigroup.com/en/Assessment-and-certification-services/management-systems/Standards-and-Schemes/ISO-14001/

ISO 26000 and the definition of social responsibility. (2011). Retrieved March 2012 from www.triplepundit.com/2011/03/iso-26000-definition-social-responsibility

International Organization for Standardization. (2006, March 3). New ISO 14064 standards provide tools for assessing and supporting greenhouse gas reduction and emissions trading. *ISO.org*. Retrieved from http://www.iso.org/iso/home/news_index/news_archive/news.htm?refid=Ref994

IUCN Red List of Threatened Species. (2012). United Nations International Union for the Conservation of Nature. https://www.iucnredlist.org/

Johnson, P. M., & Mayrand, K. (Eds.). (2006). *Governing global desertification: Linking environmental degradation, poverty, and participation*. Oxfordshire, UK: Routledge.

Jonnes, J. (2011). What is a tree worth? *The Wilson Quarterly*. Retrieved from www.wilsonquarterly.com

Kaestner, N. (2007). Ten steps to create a sustainable supply chain. *GreenBiz.com*. Retrieved May 2010 from www.greenbiz.com/blog/2007/05/23/ten-steps-create-sustainable-supply-chain#ixzzOmVBGfTlh

Kamin, D. (2019, May 14). *It's in the weeds: Herbicide linked to human liver disease* [press release]. San Diego, CA: UC Health, UC San Diego. https://health.ucsd.edu/news/releases/pages/2019-05-14-herbicide-linked-to-human-liver-disease.aspx

Kaplan, R., & Norton, D. (1996). *The balanced scorecard: Translating strategies into action*. Boston: Harvard Business School Press.

Karl-Henrik, R. (2022). *The Natural Step story: Seeding a quiet revolution*. Gabriola Island, BC: New Society Publishers.

Kassel, R. (2009, October 29). Moving the city along the road to sustainability. *GothamGazette.com*. Retrieved from http://old.gothamgazette.com/article/20091029/7/3077/

Kenner, R. (2010). *Food, Inc.* [Motion picture]. Los Angeles: Magnolia Pictures.

Key corporate social responsibility issue areas. (n. d.). *Business Respect*. Retrieved May 2010 from www.businessrespect.net/issues.php

Kenny, J., Desha, C., Kumar, A., & Hargroves, C. (2012). Using biomimicry to inform urban infrastructure design that addresses 21st century needs. In A. Allen. (Ed.), *1st International Conference on Urban Sustainability and Resilience: Conference Proceedings* (pp. 1–13). London, UK: University College London.

Kirschner, A. (2010). Understanding poverty and unemployment on the Olympic peninsula after the spotted owl. *The Social Science Journal, 47*(2), 344–358. doi: 10.1016/ j.socij. 2009.11.002

Klappenbach, L. (2021). The Biomes of the World. *ThoughtCo.* thoughtco.com/the-biomes-of-the-world-130173.

Kollmuss, A., & Bowell, B. (2006, December). Voluntary offsets for air-travel carbon emissions. *Tufts Climate Initiative*. Retrieved from http://sustainability.tufts.edu/pdf/TCI_Carbon_Offsets_Paper_April-207.pdf

Kollmuss, A., Zink, H., & Polycarp, C. (2008). Making sense of the voluntary carbon market: A comparison of carbon offset standards. Germany: World Wildlife Fund.

Kong, N., Saltzmann, O., Steger, U., & Ionescu-Somers, A. (2002). Moving business/industry towards sustainable consumption: The role of NGOs. *European Management Journal, 20*(2), 109–127.

Korhonen, J. (2001). Regional industrial ecology: Examples from regional economic systems of forest industry and energy supply in Finland. *Journal of Environmental Management, 63*(4), 367–375. ISSN 0301-4797, https://doi.org/10.1006/jema.2001.0477.

Kraft Foods sustainability goals and agriculture fact sheet (2011). Kraft Foods. Retrieved from www.kraftfoodscompany.com/SiteCollectionImages/ImageRepository/news/mmr05112011/2011.05%20FACT%20Goals°/0204°/020Sustainability%20Release%20 FINAL.pdf

Kraft Heinz Company. (2021, November 19). Form 8-K. *U.S. Securities and Exchange Commission*. Retrieved February 11, 2021 from https://ir.kraftheinzcompany.com/sec-filings

Krimmel, M. (2007, February 12). Transforming Los Angeles into a sustainable city. *World Changing*.

Kuo, N.-W., & Hsiao, T.-Y. (2008). An exploratory research of the application of natural capitalism to sustainable tourism management in Taiwan. *Journal of Cleaner Production, 16*(1), 116–124.

Laine, M. (2005). Meanings of the term sustainable development in Finnish corporate disclosures. *Accounting Forum, 29,* 395–413.

Lambert, E. (2021, February 23). *When green investments pay off*. Chicago Booth Review. Retrieved from https://www.chicagobooth.edu/review/when-green-investments-pay?sc_lang=en

Land Rover. (n.d.). Retrieved from www.landrover.com/gb/en/lr/aboutland-rover/sustainability/

Langemeier, M., & O'Donnell, M. (2020, September 8). Conventional vs. organic grains: 5-year comparison of returns. *AgFax*. https://agfax.com/2020/09/08/conventional-vs-organic-grains-5-year-comparison-of-returns/

Langran, L. V. (2002). *Empowerment and the limits of change: NGOs and health decentralization in the Philippines*. Unpublished doctoral dissertation, University of Toronto.

Lasdon, E. (2022, April 26). The ABCs of proxy voting and its role in ESG. ClimeCo. Retrieved 23 Aug. 2022, from https://climeco.com/the-abcs-of-proxy-voting-and-its-role-in-esg/

Lasley, E. A., Jones, H. B., Jr., Easterling, E. H., & Christensen, L. A. (1988). The U.S. broiler industry. Commodity Economics Division, Economic Research Service, U.S. Department of Agriculture. Agricultural Economic Report. No. 591.

Lemelson. (n.d.). A national leader in advancing invention education. *Lemelson-MIT*. Retrieved September 10, 2022, from https://lemelson.mit.edu/

Lemonick, M. D. (2009). Top 10 myths about sustainability. *Scientific American, 19*(1), 40–45. https://doi.org/10.1038/scientificamericanearth0309-40.

Leopold, A. S. (1949). The land ethic. In *A Sand County Almanac and Sketches Here and There*. New York: Oxford University Press.

Levasseur, É. (1889). *La population française: Histoire de la population avant 1789 et démographie de la France comparée à celle des autres nations au XIX siècle, précédée d'une introduction sur la statistique.* Vol. 1. Paris, France: Arthur Rousseau.

Levine, D. I., & Chatterji, A. K. (2006). Breaking down the wall of codes: Evaluating non-financial performance measurement. *California Management Review, 48*(2), 29–51.

Licht, F. O. (2009). World fuel ethanol production. *World Ethanol and Biofuels Report, 7*(18).

Life cycle assessment: Principles and practice. (2006). Retrieved June 2012 from www.epa.gov/nrmrl/std/lca/lca.html

Life cycle initiative publications. (n.d.). Retrieved October 2009 from http://jp1.estis.net/sites/lcinit/default.asp?site=lcinit&page_id=138F5949-6997-4BE6-A553-585E92C22EE4#1cirap

Lo, A. Y., Cong, R. (2022). Emission reduction targets and outcomes of the Clean Development Mechanism (2005–2020). *PLOS Climate, 1*(8), e0000046. https://doi.org/10.1371/journal.pclm.0000046

Logistics. (n.d.). Wal-Mart.com. Retrieved from www.walmartstores/sustainability

Lohan, T. (2008). Water consciousness. San Francisco: AlterNet Books.

Lomborg, B. (2001). *The skeptical environmentalist.* Cambridge, UK: Cambridge University Press.

Lorimer, K. (2006). *Lonely planet green guide.* Victoria, Australia: Lonely Planet.

Louaillier, K. (2008). 5 myths about bottled water. In T. Lohan (Ed.), *Water consciousness* (pp. 58–71). San Francisco: AlterNet Books.

Love, G. J., Lan, S.-P., & Shy, C. M. (1982). A study of acute respiratory disease in families exposed to different levels of air pollution in the Great Salt Lake Basin, Utah, 1971–1972 and 1972–1973. *Environmental Health Perspectives, 44*, 169–174.

Lovins, A., Lovins, H., & Hawken, P. (2000). Natural capitalism: The next Industrial Revolution. New York: Little, Brown.

Lowe's (n.d.). *Lowe's policy on sustainability*. Retrieved from www.lowes.com/kd_Lowes+Policy+on+Sustainability_12863 85507_

Luck, T. (2008, February 26). The world's dirtiest cities. *Forbes*.

Lurie-Luke, E. (2014). Product and technology innovation: What can biomimicry inspire? *Biotechnology Advances, 32*(8), 1494–1505.

Lutkevich, B. (2020) Definition: Carbon offset. TechTarget. Retrieved from https://www.techtarget.com/whatis/definition/carbon-offset

Lyon, Thomas P., Delmas, M. A., Maxwell, J. W., Bansal, P., Chiroleu-Assouline, M., Crifo, P., Durand, R., Gond, J.-P., King, A., Lenox, M., Toffel, M. W., Vogel, D., & Wijen, F. (2018). CSR needs CPR: Corporate sustainability and politics. *California Management Review, 60*(4), 5–24.

MacDonald, C. (2012, January 30). Global 100 flawed on corporate sustainability. *Business Ethics, Canadian Business*. Retrieved from https://archive.canadianbusiness.com/blogs-and-comment/global-100-flawed-on-corporate-sustainability/

Macmillan, T. (2007). *Meat consumption: Trends and environmental implications.* Brighton, United Kingdom: Food Ethics Council.

Mahara, D., & Mukwita, A. (2002, August 28). Zambia rejects gene-altered U.S. corn. *Los Angeles Times.*

Mahoney, M. (2008). *City of Atlanta energy and climate initiatives.* City of Atlanta. Retrieved from www.environmentaltrademission.orgl . . . IETM%20-%20 Presentation%)

Main, E. (2007). Shifting into neutral. *The Green Guide.* Retrieved from www.thegreenguide.com/doc/119/neutral

Marino, V. (2007, April 29). A starring role for "green" construction. *The New York Times.* Retrieved September 10, 2022, from https://www.nytimes.com/2007/04/29/realestate/commercial/29sqft.html

Marsh, G. P. (1864). *Man and nature: Or, physical geography as modified by human action.* New York: Scribner.

Martin, D. M., Schouten, J. W. (2014). Sustainable Marketing through the Natural Step. In R. Varey & M. Pirson (Eds.), *Humanistic marketing.* Humanism in Business Series. Palgrave Macmillan, London. https://doi.org/10.1057/9781137353290_18

Masterson, V. (2021, July 5). Renewables were the world's cheapest source of energy in 2020, new report shows. *World Economic Forum.* Retrieved September 10, 2022, from https://www.weforum.org/agenda/2021/07/renewables-cheapest-energy-source/

Mathews, M. S. (2000). The Kyoto Protocol to the United Nations Framework Convention on climate change: Survey of its deficiencies and why the United States should not ratify this treaty. *Dickinson Journal of Environmental Law and Policy, 9*(1), 193–226.

Mattera, P. (2021, June 29.) Cargill: Corporate rap sheet. *Good Jobs First.* https://www.corp-research.org/cargill

Matthews, E., Amann, C., Bringezu, S., Fischer-Kowalski, M., Hüttler, W., Kleijn, R., Moriguchi, Y., Ottke, C., Rodenburg, E., Rogich, D., Schandl, H., Schütz, H., Van Der Voet, E., & Weisz, H. (2000). *The weight of nations: Material outflows from industrial economies* (p. V). Washington, DC: World Resources Institute.

Mayo Clinic Staff. (2011, October 12). Water: How much should you drink every day? Mayo Clinic. Retrieved from www.mayoclinic.com/health/water/NU00283

McComb, B. C. (2008). Wildlife habitat management. Boca Raton, FL: CRC Press.

McDonald, C. (2008). *Green Inc.: An environmental insider reveals how a good cause has gone bad.* Guilford, CT: Globe Pequot.

McDonough, W., & Braungart, M. (2002). Cradle to cradle: Remaking the way we make things. New York: North Point Press.

McGann, J., & Johnstone, M. (2006). The power shift and the NGO credibility crisis. *The International Journal of Not-for-Profit Law, 8*(2).

McNeill, J. R., & Engelke, P. (2014). *The great acceleration: An environmental history of the anthropocene since 1945.* Cambridge, MA: The Belknap Press of Harvard University Press.

McPherson, E. G., Nowak, D. J., & Rowntree, R. A. (Eds.). (1994). *Chicago's urban ecosystem: Results of the Chicago Urban Forest Climate Project.* Radnor, PA: U.S. Department of Agriculture, Forest Service.

MeetGreen. (n.d.). Retrieved from www.meetgreen.com/

MeetGreen. (2021). Glossary. *MeetGreen.com.* https://meetgreen.com/event-resources/glossary/

Mehta, K. P. (2001). Reducing the environmental impact of concrete. *Concrete international 23*(10), 61–66.

Metro Vancouver. (2010). *Metro Vancouver sustainability framework.*

Milani, B. (2000). *Designing the green economy.* Lanham, MD: Rowman & Littlefield.

Millennium Ecosystem Assessment. (n.d.). The millennium ecosystem assessment. United Nations, https://www.millenniumassessment.org/en/index.html.

Mitchell, J. (1970). Big yellow taxi. On *Ladies of the canyon* [Record]. New York: Warner Brothers and Siquomb Publishing Co.

Mizar, S. P. (2019, March 31). Successful corporate-NGO partnerships: Key qualities define fruitful collaborations between businesses and charities. *Financial Management*. https://www.fm-magazine.com/issues/2019/apr/successful-corporate-ngo-partnerships.html

Monsanto. (n.d.). *Biotechnology*. Retrieved from www.monsanto.com/products/pages/biotechnology.aspx

Montreal Process Working Group. (1999). The Montreal Process: Forests for the future. Retrieved from www.rinya.maff.go.jp/mpci/rep-pub/1999/ broch_e.html#5

Morelli, J. (2011). Environmental sustainability: A definition for environmental professionals. *Journal of Environmental Sustainability, 1*(1), 1–10. https://doi.org/10.14448/jes.01.0002.

Morikawa, M., Morrison, J., & Gleick, P. (2007). Corporate Reporting on Water, 2007. Retrieved from www.pacinst.org/reports/water_reportinglcorporate_reporting_on_water.pdf

Morton, O. (2006). Solar energy: A new day dawning?: Silicon Valley sunrise. *Nature, 443*, 19–22.

Mountain Association for Community Economic Development. (n.d.). Retrieved from https://mtassociation.org/

Muir, J. (1916). *A thousand-mile walk to the Gulf*. Boston and New York: Houghton Mifflin Company.

Munoz-Hernandez, G. A., Mansoor, S. P., & Jones, D. I. (2013). *Modelling and controlling hydropower plants*. London, UK: Springer-Verlag.

Murphy, C. (2002, September 30). Is BP beyond petroleum? Hardly. *Fortune*.

Murray, J. (2007, October 21). Study finds greener companies outperform rivals. *Business Green*. Retrieved from www.greenbiz.com/news/2007/10/21/study-finds-greener-companies-outperform-rivals

Murray, L. (2010). Consider the turkey. *Encyclopaedia Brittanica Advocacy for Animals*. Retrieved from http://advocacy.britannica.com/blog/advocacy/2010/11/consider-the-turkey-3/

Murray, M. (2010). Green supply chain best practices. *About.com: Logistics/supply chain*. Retrieved May 2010 from http://logistics.about.com/od/greensupply chain/a/GSC_Best_Prac.htm

Naess, A. (1989). *Ecology, community and lifestyle: Outline of an ecosophy* (D. Rothenberg, Trans. Ed.). Cambridge: Cambridge University Press.

Naik, G. (2020, February 4). Cost of environmental damage linked to Nestlé, Danone and Mondelez rises sharply. *S&P Global*.

NASA. (n.d.). Global warming versus climate change. *NASA*. https://climate.nasa.gov/resources/global-warming-vs-climate-change/

National Audubon Society. (n.d.). John James Audubon: A complicated history. National Audubon Society. Retrieved 29 Apr. 2021, from https://www.audubon.org/content/john-james-audubon

National Renewable Energy Laboratory, U.S. Department of Energy. (2008, October 20). Photovoltaic solar resource of the United States. Retrieved from http://www.nrel.gov/gis/images/map_pv_national_lo-res.jpg

National Renewable Energy Laboratory. (2021) U.S. solar photovoltaic system and energy storage cost benchmark: Q1 2021. Golden, CO: NREL.

Natural capital. (2021). *Convention on Biological Diversity*. Retrieved September 11, 2022, from https://www.cbd.int/business/projects/natcap.shtml

Nelson, G. (1970). *America's last chance* (p. 8). Waukesha, WI: Country Beautiful.
Nelson, L. (2007). Solar-water heating resurgence ahead? *Solar Today, 2*(3), 28.
Nestle, M. (2006). *What to eat*. New York: North Point Press.
Nikkhah, H. A., & Redzuan, M. B. (2010). Role of NGOs in promoting empowerment for sustainable community development. *Journal of Human Ecology, 30*(2), 85–92.
NOAA Global Monitoring Laboratory. (n.d.). The NOAA annual greenhouse gas index (AGGI): An introduction. *NOAA Global Monitoring Laboratory/Earth System Research Laboratories*. Retrieved 30 October 2020 from https://gml.noaa.gov/aggi/.
Northwest Power and Conservation Council. (n.d.). Aluminum. Retrieved September 10, 2022, from https://www.nwcouncil.org/reports/columbia-river-history/aluminum/
Nowacki, L. (2022, October 17). The 15 most sustainable cities in the U.S. in 2022. *RocketHomes*. Retrieved from https://www.rockethomes.com/blog/housing-market/most-sustainable-cities-in-the-us
NREL. (n.d.). Life cycle assessment harmonization. *NREL.gov*. Retrieved September 10, 2022, from https://www.nrel.gov/analysis/life-cycle-assessment.html
NYC Mayor's Office of Climate and Environmental Justice. (n.d.). Adapt NYC. Retrieved from https://www1.nyc.gov/site/sustainability/index.page
Office Depot. (n.d.). Environmental stewardship. Retrieved from www.community.officedepot.com/paperproc.asp
Ogilvy Earth. (2010). *From greenwash to great: A practical guide to green marketing*. New York: Ogilvy Mather.
O'Neill, J. (2008, July 15). Boom time for the global bourgeoisie. *Financial Times*.
Oregon Environmental Council. (2010). *A sustainable economy*. Retrieved from www.oeconline.org/our-worldeconomy
Organisation for Economic Co-operation and Development. (2002). *OECD governments agree to take the lead on buying "green"* [press release]. Retrieved from www.oecd.org
Orr, D. W. (1992). Ecological literacy: Education and the transition to a postmodern world. SUNY series in constructive postmodern thought. Albany, NY: State University of New York Press.
Other 14000 Series standards. (2002). Retrieved March 2011 from www.iso14000-iso14001-environmental-management.com/iso14000.htm.
Ottman, J. (1998). *Green marketing*. New York: BookSurge.
Ottman, J. (2010, February 6). A smart new way to segment green consumers. *Greenmarketing.com*.
Our vision for a sustainable global economy. (n.d.). *Ceres*. Retrieved August 2012 from www.ceres.org/about-us/what-we-do/our-vision/our-vision
Overend, R. P., & Milbrandt, A. (2007). Potential carbon emissions reductions from energy efficiency and renewable energy by 2030. In C. F Kutscher (Ed.), *Tackling climate change in the U.S*. Boulder, CO: American Solar Energy Society.
Owens, Eric. (2021, September 23). 17 most sustainable cities in the world (2022). *The Sustainable Living Guide*. Retrieved from https://thesustainablelivingguide.com/most-sustainable-cities/.
Pachauri, R. K., & Reisinger, A. (Eds.). (2007). *IPCC fourth assessment report: Climate change 2007*. Geneva, Switzerland: IPCC.
Palmer, J. (2008). Renewable energy: The tide is turning. *New Scientist*.
Patel, R. (2007). *Stuffed and starved*. Brooklyn, NY: Melville House Publishing.
Pavlenko, N., Comer, B., Zhou, Y., Clark, N., & Rutherford, D. (2020). The climate implications of using LNG as a marine fuel. The International Council on Clean Transportation. www.stand.earth/publication/climate-implications-using-lng-marine-fuel

PBS. (n.d.). *Silence of the bees*. Retrieved from www.pbs.org/wnet/nature/episodes/ silence-of-the-bees/introduction/3 8/

Peck, S., & Gibson, R. (2002). Pushing the revolution. *Alternatives Journal, 26*(1).

PEFC. (n.d.). *Forest certification*. Retrieved from https://pefc.org/discover-pefc/what-is-pefc.

Pehnt, M. (2006). Dynamic life cycle assessment (LCA) of renewable energy technologies. *Renewable Energy, 31*(1), 55–71.

Perlack, R. D., Wright, L. L., Turhollow, A. F., Graham, R. L., Stokes, B. J., & Erbach, D. C. (2005). *Biomass as feedstock for a bioenergy and bioproducts industry: The technical feasibility of a billion-ton annual supply*. Oak Ridge, TN: Oak Ridge National Laboratory.

Phyper, J. D., & MacLean, P. (2009). *Good to green*. New York: Wiley.

Pilipinas, K. M. (2007). Historical and political perspectives on IRRI, and its impact on Asian rice agriculture. In V. M. Lopez, P. A. Z. dela Cruz, J. L. Benosa, & F. P. Concepcion (Eds.), *The Great Rice Robbery: A Handbook on the Impact of IRRI in Asia*. Penang, Malaysia: Pesticide Action Network Asia and the Pacific.

Pimentel, D. (1996). Green revolution agriculture and chemical hazards. *The Science of the Total Environment, 188*, S86–S98.

Pollan, M. (2006). *The omnivore's dilemma: A natural history of four meals*. New York: Penguin.

Pollan, M. (2013). *Cooked: A natural history of transformation*. New York: Penguin Press.

Poore, J., & Nemecek, T. (2018). Reducing food's environmental impacts through producers and consumers. *Science, 360*(6392), 987–992.

Pope, C. A. (1989). Respiratory disease associated with community air pollution and a steel mill, Utah Valley. *American Journal of Public Health, 79*(5), 623–628.

Population growth rate. (2001). World Bank. Retrieved from www.worldbank.org/depweb/english/modules/social/pgr/index.html

Porter, M. E., & Kramer, M. R. (2006). Strategy and society: The link between competitive advantage and corporate social responsibility. *Harvard Business Review*, 78–92.

Porter, M. E., & van der Linde, C. (1995). Green and competitive. *Harvard Business Review*, 120–134.

Portney, P. R., & Mullahy, J. (1990). Urban air quality and chronic respiratory disease. *Regional Science and Urban Economics, 20*(3), 407–418.

Potoski, M., & Prakash, A. (2005). Covenants with weak swords: ISO 14001 and facilities' environmental performance. *Journal of Policy Analysis and Management, 24*(4), 745–769.

Poultry marketplace. (n.d.). Agriculture and Agri-Food Canada. Retrieved February 28, 2012, from www.agr.gc.ca/poultry/consm_eng.htm

Power, M. E., Tilman, D., Estes, J. A., Menge, B. A., Bond, W. J., Mills, L. S., Daily, G., Castilla, J. C. Lubchenco, J., & Paine, R. T. (1996). Challenges in the quest for keystones. *BioScience, 46*, 609–620.

Prahalad, C. K., & Hart, S. L. (2002). The fortune at the bottom of the pyramid. *strategy+business, 26*, 1–14.

Presidio Buzz. (2009). Nuclear energy: Pros and cons. Retrieved from www.triplepundit.com/2009/02/nuclear-energy-pros-and-cons/

Pricen, T., & Finger, M. (1994). Introduction. In T. Pricen & M. Finger (Eds.), *Environmental NGOs in world politics*. London, UK: Routledge.

Product Certification Program Standard. Retrieved from http://resource-solu

Profiling food consumption in America. (2009). In Factbook (Chp. 2). Retrieved from www.usda.gov

Programme for the Endorsement of Forest Certification. (n.d.) *PEFC*. https://pefc.org/.

Public sector sustainability under the spotlight. (1999, April). *Government sustainability*. Retrieved from www.governmentsustainability.co.uk/

PV costs down significantly from 1998–2007. (2009). *Renewable Energy World*.

PV costs set to plunge for 2009/10. (2008). *Renewable Energy World*.

Radwan, G. A. N., & Osama, N. (2016). Biomimicry, an approach, for energy efficient building skin design. *Procedia Environmental Sciences, 34*, 178–189.

Ramalho, Tania. (2013). Chico Mendes: Brazilian labour leader and conservationist. *Encyclopædia Britannica*. Chicago, IL: Encyclopædia Britannica, Inc. Retrieved from https://www.britannica.com/biography/Chico-Mendes.

Ramani, T. L., Zietsman, J., Gudmundsson, H., Hall, R. P., & Marsden, G. (2011). Framework for sustainability assessment by transportation agencies. *Transportation Research Record, 2242*(1), 9–18. doi:10.3141/2242-02.

Randall, T. (2022, July 13). U.S. crosses the electric car tipping point for mass adoption. Retrieved from https://driving.ca/auto-news/industry/u-s-crosses-the-electric-car-tipping-point-for-mass-adoption

Rauh, V. A., Whytt, R. M., Garfinkel, R., Andrews, H., Hoepner, L., Reyes, A., Diaz, D., Camann, D., & Perera, F. P. (2004). Development effects of exposure to environmental tobacco smoke and material hardship among inner-city children. *Neurotoxicology and Teratology, 26*(3), 373–385.

Reap, J., Baumeister, D., & Bras, B. (2005). Holism, biomimicry and sustainable engineering. *ASME International Mechanical Engineering Congress and Exposition*, 423–431.

Red Data Book of the Russian Federation. (n.d.). Red book of rare and endangered species. *Red Data Book of Russia*. https://redbookrf.ru/.

Renewable energy. (2021, November 10). Center for Climate and Energy Solutions. Retrieved September 10, 2022, from https://www.c2es.org.

Retiere, C. (2007, May 7). Rural Areas Get Increased Hydro Power Capacity. *Xinhua*.

Revkin, A. (2007, April 29). Carbon-neutral is hip, but is it green? *The New York Times*.

RG: Sustainability Reporting Guidelines. (n.d.). Version 3.1, The Netherlands: Global Reporting Initiative. Retrieved from www.globalreporting.org

Richardson, A. (2006). Carbon credits—Paying to pollute? *3rd Degree*. Retrieved from http://3degree.cci.ecu.edu.au/articles/view/781

Robért, K. H. (2010). *The Natural Step*. Retrieved from www.naturalstep.org/

Rogers, P. P., Jalal, K. E., Lohani, B. N., Owens, G. M., Yu, C. C., Dufornaund, C. M., & Bi, J. (1997). *Measuring environmental quality in Asia*. Manila, Philippines: Asian Development Bank.

Roy, P., Nei, D., Orikasa, T., Xu, Q., Okadome, H., Nakamura, N., & Shiina, T. (2009). A review of life cycle assessment (LCA) on some food products. *Journal of Food Engineering, 90*(1), 1–10.

Royte, E. (2008). Disney (waste) land. Retrieved from www.onearth.org/article/disney-wasteland

Russell, J. (2007). Are emissions offsets a carbon con? *Ethical Corporation*. Retrieved from www.greenbiz.com/news/reviews_third.cfm?NewsID=34804

Russo, Amanda. (2020, January 19). Half of the world's GDP moderately or highly dependent on nature, says new report. *World Economic Forum*. https://www.weforum.org/press/2020/01/half-of-world-s-gdp-moderately-or-highly-dependent-on-nature-says-new-report

Rydaker, A. (2007, April 16). Biomass for electricity & heat production. Paper presented at Bioenergy North America, Chicago, IL.

San Francisco Planning. (n.d.). Sustainable City. Retrieved from https://sfplanning.org/project/sustainable-city.

Schlosser, E. (2005). *Fast food nation: The dark side of the all-American meal*. New York: Harper.

Schmer, M. R., Vogel, K. P., Mitchell, R. B., & Perrin, R. K. (2008). Net energy of cellulosic ethanol from switchgrass. *Proceedings of the National Academy of Sciences of the United States of America, 105*(2), 464–469.

Schmida, S. (2021, December 16). 4 main causes of development failure. *Resonance Global*. Retrieved from https://www.resonanceglobal.com/blog/main-causes-of-partnership-development-failure

Seafood sustainability. (n.d.). WholeFoodsMarket.com. Retrieved from http://wholefoodsmarket.com/values/seafood.php

Searchinger, T., Heimlich, R., Houghton, R. A., Dong, F., Elobeid, A., Fabiosa, J., Tokgoz, S., Hayes, D., & Yu, T. H. (2008). Use of U.S. croplands for biofuels increases greenhouse gases through emissions from land-use change. *Science, 319*(5867), 1238–1240.

Seeger, M., & Hipfel, S. (2007). Legal versus ethical arguments: Contexts for corporate social responsibility. In G. Cheney, J. Roper, & S. May (Eds.), *The debate over corporate social responsibility*. New York: Oxford University Press.

Senge, P. M., Smith, B., Kruschwitz, N., Laur, J., & Schley, S. (2008). *The necessary revolution: How individuals and organizations are working together to create a sustainable world*. New York: Penguin Random House.

Sessions, G. (Ed.). (1995). *Deep ecology for the 21st century*. Boston: Shambala.

Seuss, Dr. (1971). *The lorax*. New York: Random House.

Shahbandeh, M. (2022, November 11). Topic: Danone. *Statista*. https://www.statista.com/topics/2428/danone/#dossierKeyfigures.

Shaner, M., Davis, S., Lewis, N., & Caldeira, K. (2018). Geophysical constraints on the reliability of solar and wind power in the United States. *Energy & Environmental Science, 11*, 914–925.

Sharma, S., & Vredenburg, H. (1998). Proactive corporate environmental strategy and the development of competitively valuable organizational capabilities. *Strategic Management Journal, 19*(8), 729–753.

Shaw, J. S. (2012). Book review: The locavore's dilemma: In praise of the 10,000-mile diet, by P. Desrochers & H. Shimizu. *The Independent Review, A Journal of Political Economy, 17*(4). https://www.independent.org/publications/tir/article.asp?id=934.

Shuster, E. (2009). *Tracking new coal-fired power plants*. Pittsburgh, PA: Department of Energy, National Energy Technology Laboratory.

Simons, D., & Mason, R. (2002). *Environmental and transport supply chain evaluation with sustainable value stream mapping*. Proceedings of the 7th Logistics Research Network Conference, Birmingham, AL.

Singh, D. pal. (n.d.). *Levelized cost of energy, levelized cost of storage, and levelized cost of hydrogen*. Lazard.com. Retrieved September 10, 2022, from https://www.lazard.com/perspective/levelized-cost-of-energy-levelized-cost-of-storage-and-levelized-cost-of-hydrogen/

Smalheiser, K. (2006, November 13). Value driven leadership: Responsible companies committed to tackling global societal woes have discovered they gain strategic advantage [Special advertising feature]. *Fortune*. Retrieved from www.timeincnewsgroupcustompub.com/sections/061113_CSRv2.pdf

Smith, A. (2002). *The wealth of nations*. Oxford, England: Bibliomania.com Ltd.

Sokka, L. (2010). Analyzing the environmental benefits of industrial symbiosis. Journal of Industrial Ecology, 15(1), 137–155.

Sonoco. (n.d.). *Zero waste consulting*. Retrieved September 10, 2022, from https://www.sonoco.com/capabilities/recycling/zero-waste-consulting

Sow housing. (2012). McDonalds.com. Retrieved from www.aboutmcdonalds.com/mcd/sustainability/library/policies_programs/sustainable_supply_chain/animal_welfare/sow_housing.html

Specter, M. (2014, August 18). Seeds of doubt. *The New Yorker.*

Stappen, R. K. (2009). Global Reporting Initiative, Forum: Science and Innovation for Sustainable Development, Advancing Science, Serving Society (ASSS). Retrieved August 2012 from http://sustsci.aaas.org/content.html?contentid=693

State of the Air. (2012a). Cleanest cities. *American Lung Association.* Retrieved from www.stateoftheair.org/2012/city-rankings/cleanest-cities.html

State of the Air. (2012b). Most polluted cities. *American Lung Association.* Retrieved from www.stateoftheair.org/2012/city-rankings/most-polluted-cities.html

Steelworks. (2007, April 24). Steel industry exploring new CO_2-reducing steel making processes. *United States Steel.* Retrieved from www.uss.com/corp/environment/documents/Steel%20Industry%20Exploring%20New%20CO2-Reducing%20Steel%20Making%20Processes.pdf

Stewardship at REI. (n.d.). REI. Retrieved from www.rei.com/stewardship.html

Stewardship initiative sustainability definition. (2002). Retrieved from www.p2pays.org/ref/38/37967.pdf. With permission from NC DENR's Division of Environmental Assistance and Outreach.

Sto Corp. (n.d.). Lotusan Videos. Retrieved December 2011 from www.stocorp.com.

Strandberg, C. (2013, October 23). 10 steps to developing an industry sustainability program. *Greenbiz.* Retrieved from https://www.greenbiz.com/article/10-steps-developing-industry-sustainability-program

Strategic plan for biodiversity 2011–2020, including Aichi biodiversity targets. (2020, January 21). *Convention on Biological Diversity.* https://www.cbd.int/sp/

Streeten, P. (1997). Non-governmental organizations and development. *Annals of the American Academy of Political and Social Science, 554,* 193–210.

Stromquist, N. P. (2002). NGOs in a new paradigm of civil society. *Current Issues in Comparative Education, 1*(1), 62–67.

Sturgis, S., (2009). Growth in renewable energy outpaces nuclear, fossil fuels. *Grist Magazine.*

Summary and analysis of COP17: The UN Climate Change Conference at Durban, Sustainable Solutions for the Environment. (2011). Retrieved from www.emergent-ventures.com/Summary-and-Analysis-of-COP17.pdf

Sundseth, K. (2014). *The EU birds and habitats directives.* Luxembourg: European Commission. https://ec.europa.eu/environment/nature/info/pubs/docs/brochures/nat2000/en.pdf

Sussex Energy Group/UK Energy Research Centre. (2007). *The rebound effect: An assessment of the evidence for economy-wide energy savings from improved energy efficiency.*

Sustainability moves centre-stage as international pressure grows. (2007). *Bioenergy Business, 1*(4).

Sustainable agriculture. (2009). Subchapter 1: Findings, Purposes, and Definitions, U.S. Code, Title 7, Chapter 64. Agricultural Research, Extension and Teaching. Sustainable City Code Revision Project. (n.d.). Retrieved from www.mayorsinnovation.org/pdf/5SaltLakeCity.pdf

Sustainable Communities Network. (2010). Brazil. Retrieved from www.sustainable.org/casestudies/INTL_af_curitiba.html.

Sustainable Consumption Research Exchanges. (2008). *System innovation for sustainability 1: Perspectives on radical changes to sustainable consumption and production.*

Sustainable insight. (2009). KPMG Global Sustainability Services. Retrieved February 20, 2010, from www.kpmg.com/GRJengssuesAndInsights/ArticlesPublications/Sustainability/Pages/Sustainable-Insight-April-2009.aspx

Sustainable Measures. (2010). Definitions of sustainability. Retrieved from www.sustainablemeasures.com/node/35

Swaminathan, M. S. (2006). An evergreen revolution. *Crop Science, 46*(5), 2293–2303.

Swart, R., Amman, M., Raes, E., & Tuinstra, W. (2004). A good climate for clean air: Linkages between climate change and air pollution. An editorial essay. *Climate Change, 66*(3), 263–269.

Swedish Energy Agency. (2008). *Energy in Sweden 2008* (pp. 96, 111). Sweden: Eskilstuna.

Sweet, W. V., Kopp, R. E., Weaver, C. P., Obeysekera, J., Horton, R. M., Thieler, E. R., & Zervas, C. (2017). *Global and regional sea level rise scenarios for the United States: NOAA Technical Report NOS CO-OPS 083*. NOAA/NOS Center for Operational Oceanographic Products and Services.

Swiss Re Group. (2020, September 23). *A fifth of countries worldwide at risk from ecosystem collapse as biodiversity declines, reveals pioneering Swiss Re index*. Swiss Re Group. Retrieved April 6, 2022, from https://www.swissre.com/media/press-release/nr-20200923-biodiversity-and-ecosystems-services.html

Szaro, R. C., Sexton, W. T., & Malone, C. R. (1998). The emergence of ecosystem management as a tool for meeting people's needs and sustaining ecosystems. *Landscape and Urban Planning, 40*(1–3), 1–7. https://doi.org/10.1016/s0169-2046(97)00093-5.

Tabuchi, H., Rigny, C., & White, J. (2017, February 24). Amazon deforestation, once tamed, comes roaring back. *The New York Times*.

Tardi, C. (2022, August 12). What is the Kyoto Protocol? Definition, history, timeline, status. *Investopedia*. Accessed Aug 2022 at https://www.investopedia.com/terms/k/kyoto.asp

Tavanti, M. (2010, September 30). Defining sustainability. *Sustainable DePaul, DePaul University*. https://sustainabledepaul.blogspot.com/p/defining-sustainability.html

Taylor Buck, N. (2017). The art of imitating life: The potential contribution of biomimicry in shaping the future of our cities. *Environment and Planning B: Urban Analytics and City Science, 44*(1), 120–140.

TerraChoice. (2012). *The sins of greenwashing*. Retrieved from http://sinsofgreen washing.org/

The 2008 US city rankings. (2012). Retrieved from www.sustainlane.com/us-cityrankings/

The Chicago Water Agenda. (2003). City of Chicago. Retrieved from www.cityofchicago.org/city/en/depts/water.html

The Context Group. (2006). Carbon offsets in context: Providers + advisors. Retrieved from www.econtext.co.uk/downloads/carbon_offset.pdf.

The Daily Green. (2010). The BP Gulf of Mexico oil spill update. TheDailyGreen.com. Retrieved from www.thedailygreen.com/environmental-news/latest/gulf-of-mexico-oil-spill

The Ecological Society of America. Biodiversity. https://www.esa.org/blog/tag/biodiversity/

The Economist staff. (2006a, August 3). Sins of emission. *The Economist*. https://www.economist.com/leaders/2006/08/03/sins-of-emission

The Economist staff. (2006b). Upset about offsets. *The Economist*. https://www.economist.com/business/2006/08/03/upset-about-offsets

The Economist staff. (2017, March 11). Green finance for dirty ships. *The Economist*. www.economist.com/finance-and-economics/2017/03/11/green-finance-for-dirty-ships.

The four system conditions (n.d). The Natural Step. Retrieved May 29, 2012, from www.naturalstep.org/en/the-system-conditions

The funnel. (n.d.). The Natural Step. Retrieved May 29, 2012, from www.natural step.org/the-funnel

The Global Warming Statistics. (n.d.). Global warming statistics. Retrieved from www.theglobalwarmingstatistics.org/the-global-warming-statistics.

The Green Belt Movement. (n.d.). Wangari Maathai: Biography. *The Green Belt Movement.* https://www.greenbeltmovement.org/wangari-maathai/biography.

The International Ecotourism Society. (n.d.). What is ecotourism? *Ecotourism.org.*

The Kyoto Protocol. (n.d.). Retrieved March 2012 from www.kyotoprotocol.com/

The Kyoto Protocol summary. (n.d.). Earth's Friends. Retrieved March 2012 from www.earthsfriends.com/kyoto-protocol-summary

The Royal Society. (n.d.) What is the human impact on biodiversity? *Royal Society.* https://royalsociety.org/topics-policy/projects/biodiversity/human-impact-on-biodiversity/.

The Wilderness Society. (n.d.). Our campaigns. Retrieved from http://wilderness.org/campaigns

Thiry, J.-C. (2020). What do you need to know about AA Stakeholder Engagement Standard, 2020.

Thompson, I., & Angelstam, P. (1999). Special species. In M. L. Hunter (Ed.), *Maintaining biodiversity in forest ecosystems.* Cambridge: Cambridge University Press.

Thoreau, H. D. (1854). *Walden; Or, life in the woods.* Boston, MA: Ticknor and Fields.

Tikkanen, Amy. (2020). Greta Thunberg: Swedith activist. *Encyclopædia Britannica.* Chicago, IL: Encyclopædia Britannica, Inc. Retrieved from https://www.britannica.com/biography/Greta-Thunberg.

Time for Change. (n.d.). *Pros and cons of nuclear power.* Retrieved October 2011 from http://timeforchange.org/pros-and-cons-of-nuclear-power-and-sustainability

Topping, A. (2007, September 21). Free wheeling. *The Washington Post.*

Total quality environmental management: The primer. (1993). Global Environmental Management Institute. Retrieved from http://gemi.org/resources/TQE_101.pdf

Total quality environmental management. (n.d.). BSD Global. Retrieved December 2011 from www.iisd.org/business/tools/systems_TQEM.asp

Toyota 2010 North America environmental report. (2010). Toyota.com. Retrieved from www.toyota.com/aboutienvironmentreport2010/

Trexler Climate + Energy Services, Inc., 2006

Trinkaus, E. (2005). Early modern humans. *Annual Review of Anthropoly, 34*(1), 207–230.

Tubiello, F. N., Salvatore, M., Cóndor Golec, R. D., Ferrara, A., Rossi, S., Biancalani, R., Federici, S., Jacobs, H., & Flammini, A., (2014). Agriculture, forestry and other land use by sources and removals by sinks. *United Nations Food and Agricultural Organization.* Retrieved from https://www.fao.org/3/i3671e/i3671e.pdf

Turconi, R., Boldrin, A., & Astrup, T. (2013). Life cycle assessment (LCA) of electricity generation technologies: Overview, comparability and limitations. *Renewable and Sustainable Energy Reviews, 28,* 555–565. ISSN 1364-0321, https://doi.org/10.1016/j.rser.2013.08.013.

Turk, J. (1989). *Introduction to environmental studies* (3rd ed.). Philadelphia: Saunders College Publishing.

Tyrvainen, L., Silvennoinen, H., & Kole, O. (2003). Ecological and aesthetic values in urban forests. *Urban Forestry & Urban Greening, 1*(3), 135–149.

Understanding the AQI. (n.d.). *AirNow.* Retrieved from www.airnow.gov/index.cfm?action=aqibasics.aqi

UNESCO. (2002). Education for sustainable development. https://www.unesco.org/en/education/sustainable-development

Union of Concerned Scientists. (2003). *Farming the wind: Wind power and agriculture fact sheet*. Cambridge, MA: Author.

United Nations. (2002). *Report of the World Summit on Sustainable Development*. New York: Author.

United Nations. (2016). Paris Agreement. United Nations Treaty Collection. https://treaties.un.org/pages/ViewDetails.aspx?src=TREATY&mtdsg_no=XXVII-7-d&chapter=27&clang=_en

United Nations Climate Change. (n.d.) Glossary of climate change acronyms and terms. https://unfccc.int/fr/processus-et-reunions/la-convention/lexique-des-changements-climatiques-acronymes-et-termes#c

United Nations Conference on Environment and Development. (1992). *Earth Summit 1992*. London: Regency.

United Nations Department of Economic and Social Affairs. (n.d.). The 17 Goals: Sustainable Development. *United Nations*. https://sdgs.un.org/goals.

United Nations Department of Economic and Social Affairs. (1992). Agenda 21. UNCED. Retrieved June 2012 from https://sdgs.un.org/publications/agenda21

United Nations Department of Economic and Social Affairs, Population Division. (2022). World population prospects 2022: Summary of results. UN DESA/POP/2022/TR/NO. 3.

United Nations Educational, Scientific, and Cultural Organization. (2002). *Education for sustainability*. Paris: Author.

United Nations Environment Programme. (2017). Indigenous people and nature: A tradition of conservation. *United Nations Environment Programme*. Retrieved from https://www.unep.org/news-and-stories/story/indigenous-people-and-nature-tradition-conservation

United Nations Food and Agriculture Organization. (n.d.). Global forest ecosystem assessment. UN FAO. https://fra-data.fao.org/

United Nations Framework Convention on Climate Change. (n.d.). Mechanisms under the Kyoto Protocol: Emissions trading, the clean development mechanism, and joint implementation. United Nations Climate Change. Retrieved March 2010 from http://unfccc.int/kyoto_protocol/mechanisms/items/1673.php

United Nations Global Compact. (2022). The Ten Principles. *United Nations Global Compact*. Retrieved from https://www.unglobalcompact.org/what-is-gc/mission/principles.

Unruh, G., & Ettenson, R. (2011). Growing green: Three smart paths to developing sustainable products. In G. Unruh & R. Ettenson (Eds.), *Greening your business profitably*. Boston: Harvard Business Review Press.

Upham, P. (2000). An assessment of The Natural Step theory of sustainability. *Journal of Cleaner Production, 8*(6), 445–454.

U.S. Census Bureau. (2012). Table 373: Selected national air pollutant emissions: 1970 to 2008. *2012 statistical abstract, geography and environment: Air quality*. Washington, DC: Author.

U.S. Department of Agriculture Forest Service. (n.d.). *Urban and community forestry*. Retrieved from www.fs.fed.us/ucf/program.html

U.S. Department of Agriculture. (n.d.). Retrieved from www.usda.gov/wps/portal/usda/usdahome?navid=ORGANICCERTIFICATION

U.S. Department of Agriculture. (n.d.). Labeling organic products. *USDA Agricultural Marketing Service*. https://www.ams.usda.gov/rules-regulations/organic/labeling.

U.S. Department of Agriculture. (2021, September 23). Agriculture and food sectors and the economy. *USDA Economic Research Service*. https://www.ers.usda.gov/data-products/ag-and-food-statistics-charting-the-essentials/ag-and-food-sectors-and-the-economy/

References

USDA National Institute of Food and Agriculture. (n.d.). Sustainable agriculture programs. *USDA.gov.* https://www.nifa.usda.gov/grants/programs/sustainable-agriculture-programs

U.S. Department of Energy Hydrogen Program. (n.d.). Hydrogen & our energy future. Retrieved from www1.eere.energy.gov/hydrogenandfuelcells/pdfs/hydro genenergyfuture_web.pdf

U.S. Department of Energy. (2010a). Fuel cell technologies program: Production. Retrieved from www1.eere.energy.gov/hydrogenandfuelcells/pdfs/doe_h2_production.pdf

U.S. Department of Energy. (2010b). Hydrogen and fuel cells technology program. Retrieved from www1.eere.energy.gov/hydrogenandfuelcells/pdfs/doe_h2_fuelcell_factsheet.pdf

U.S. Department of Energy. (2011a). Hydrogen and fuel cell technologies program: Storage. Retrieved from www1.eere.energy.gov/hydrogenandfuelcells/pdfs/doe_h2_storage.pdf

U.S. Department of Energy. (2011b). Safety, codes, and standards. Retrieved from www1.eere.energy.gov/hydrogenandfuelcells/pdfs/doe_h2_safety.pdf

U.S. Department of Energy. (2011c). Biodiesel. Retrieved from www.eere.energy.gov/basics/renewable_energy/biodiesel.html

U.S. Department of Energy. (2011d). Ethanol. Retrieved from www.eere.energy.gov/basicskenewable_energy/ethanol.html

U.S. Department of Energy. (2011e). Ocean thermal energy conversion. Retrieved from www.eere.energy.gov/basics/renewable_energy/ocean_thermal_ energy_conv.html

U.S. Department of Energy. (2011f). Renewable energy technologies. Retrieved from www.eere.energy.gov/basics/renewable_energy/

U.S. Department of Energy. (2011g). Tidal energy. Retrieved from www.eere.energy.gov/basics/renewable_energy/tidal_energy.html

U.S. Department of Energy. (2011h). Wave energy. Retrieved from www.eere.energy.gov/basics/renewable_energy/wave_energy.html

U.S. Department of Energy. (2012a). Advancing distributed energy storage. https://solarhighpen.energy.gov/article/advancing_distributed_energy_storage

U.S. Department of Energy. (2012b). Ethanol feedstocks. Retrieved from https://afdc.energy.gov/fuels/ethanol_feedstocks.html

U. S. Department of Energy and Environment. (2010). Green DC Agenda. Retrieved from www.green.dc.gov.

U.S. Department of the Interior. (n.d.). What are the differences between endangered, threatened, imperiled, and at-risk species? *U.S. Geological Survey.* https://www.usgs.gov/faqs/what-are-differences-between-endangered-threatened-imperiled-and-risk-species.

U.S. Energy Information Administration. (n.d.). Independent statistics and analysis. Ocean thermal energy conversion. *U.S. EIA.* Retrieved September 10, 2022, from https://www.eia.gov/energyexplained/hydropower/ocean-thermal-energy-conversion.php.

U.S. Energy Information Administration. (2010). Electric power monthly. EIA. Retrieved from www.eia.doe.gov/cneaf/electricity/epm/table1_1.html

U.S. Energy Information Administration. (2021). Renewables: Fuels & Technologies. IEA. Retrieved September 10, 2022, from https://www.iea.org/fuels-and-technologies/renewables

U.S. Environmental Protection Agency. (n.d.-a). List of programs. Environmental Protection Agency. https://archive.epa.gov/partners/web/html/index-5.html

U.S. Environmental Protection Agency. (n.d.-b). Scope 3 inventory guidance. *Environmental Protection Agency.* https://www.epa.gov/climateleadership/scope-3-inventory-guidance

U.S. Environmental Protection Agency. (2003). Municipal solid waste in the United States: 2001 facts and figures. EPA. Retrieved from www.epa.gov/osw/nonhaz/municipal/pubs/rnsw2001.pdf

U.S. Environmental Protection Agency. (2012). Basic information about estuaries: Why are estuaries important? EPA. Retrieved from http://water.epa.gov/type/oceb/nep/about.cfm#protect

U.S. Environmental Protection Agency Environmental Stewardship Staff Committee. (2005). Technical report prepared by EPA Environmental Stewardship Staff Committee for the EPA Innovation Action Council. Retrieved from www.epa .gov/innovation/pdf/techrpt.pdf

Velazquez, L., et al. (2006). Sustainable university: What can be the matter? *Journal of Cleaner Production, 14*(9–11), 810–819.

Vigar, Vanessa, et al. (2019, December 18). A systematic review of organic versus conventional food consumption: Is there a measurable benefit on human health?" *Nutrients*, MDPI. https://www.ncbi.nlm.nih.gov/pmc/articles/PMC7019963/.

Von Carlowitz, H. C. (1713). *Sylvicultura Oeconomica, Oder Haußwirthliche Nachricht Und Naturmäßige Anweisung Zur Wilden Baum Zucht*. Leipzig: J. Fr. Braun.

von Der Goltz, J., Dar, A., Fishman, R., Mueller, N. D., Barnwal, P., McCord, G. C. (2020). Health impacts of the Green Revolution: Evidence from 600,000 births across the developing world. *Journal of Health Economics, 74*, 2020, 102373.

Whole Foods. (n.d.). Sustainability and our future. *WholeMarketFoods.com*. Retrieved from www.wholefoodsmarket.com/values/sustainability.php

Why buy local? (2009, January 9). Sustainable Table. Retrieved from www.sustainabletable.org/issues/whybuylocal/#fn9

Wilderness Connect. (n.d.). History. Wilderness.net. Retrieved from https://wilderness.net/learn-about-wilderness/history/default.php

Wilderness History. (n.d.). History. Wilderness.net. Retrieved from https://wilderness.net/learn-about-wilderness/history/default.php

Wilderness Society. (2012). *Gaylord Nelson*. Retrieved from http://wilderness.org/ content/gaylord-nelson

Wilson, E. O. (2002). *The future of life*. New York: Random House.

Wind power. (2012). *The New York Times*. Retrieved from http://topics.nytimes.com/top/news/business/energy-environment/wind-power/index.html

Windustry. (n.d.). *How much do wind turbines cost?* Retrieved September 10, 2022, from https://www.windustry.org/how_much_do_wind_turbines_cost

World Alliance for Decentralized Energy. (2004). Bagasse cogeneration: Global review and potential (p. 32). Washington, DC: Author.

World Business Council for Sustainable Development. (2006a). *Business and ecosystems*. Switzerland: Author.

World Business Council for Sustainable Development. (2006b). *From challenge to opportunity: The role of business in tomorrow's society*. Switzerland: Author.

World Business Council for Sustainable Development. (2007). *Survey of sustainability experts*. GlobeScan.

World Business Council for Sustainable Development. (2008). *Sustainable consumption facts and trends: From a business perspective*. Switzerland: Author.

World Business Council for Sustainable Development. (2009). *What a way to run the world: WBCSD annual review 2008*. Retrieved from http://www.wbesd.ch/DocRoot/gUpF06N8whsB1rEquh4k/rapport_annuel_08.pdf.

World Business Council for Sustainable Development. (2021). Vision 2050: Time to transform. Retrieved from https://www.wbcsd.org/Overview/About-us/Vision-2050-Time-to-Transform.

World Commission on Environment and Development. (1987). *Our common future: Report of the World Commission on Environment and Development*. Oxford, UK: Oxford University Press.

World Energy Council. (n.d.). Charting the upsurge in hydropower development 2015. *World Energy Council*. Retrieved September 10, 2022, from https://www.worldenergy.org/publications/entry/charting-the-upsurge-in-hydropower-development-2015

World Population Clock. (n.d.). Worldometers. Retrieved from https://www.worldometers.info/world-population/#table-forecast.

World Resources Institute. (n.d.). Greenhouse gas protocol. WRI. https://www.wri.org/initiatives/greenhouse-gas-protocol

World Resources Institute. (2003). *World Resources Institute* (pp. 3–4). Washington, DC: Author.

World Wildlife Fund. (2006). *Living planet report*.

World Wildlife Fund UK. (2006). *One planet business*.

World Wind Energy Association. (2009). *World wind energy report*. Bonn, Germany: Author. Retrieved from www.wwindea.org/home/

Worldwatch Institute. (n.d.). Window to prevent catastrophic climate change closing; EU should press for immediate U.S. action. Retrieved January 6, 2012, from www.worldwatch.org/node/5340

Zeller Jr., T. (2009, February 27). Wave power for San Francisco? *The New York Times*. Retrieved from http://green.blogs.nytimes.com/2009/02/27/wave-power-for-san-francisco/

Zero waste. (n.d.). Wal-Mart.com. Retrieved from www.walmartstores/sustainability

Zimmerman, A., & Kibert, C. J. (2007). Informing LEED's next generation with The Natural Step. *Building Research & Information, 35*(6), 681–689. doi:10.1080/09613210701342367

Zuber, D. (2022). *Walmart's dirty shipping problem*. Pacific Environment. Retrieved from https://www.pacificenvironment.org/walmart-dirty-shipping/

Zumbo, J. (n.d.). *Wolves*. YellowstoneNationalPark.com. Retrieved from www.yellowstonenationalpark.com/wolves.htm

Index

ABN AMRO, 281
Accentuate approach, 345
Acid rain, 38, 85
Acquirement approach, 345
Additionality, carbon offsets, 307
Afghanistan, malnutrition in, 158
Africa, 134, 145, 158, 208, 212, 228, 257, 266, 313. *See also specific country*
African Wildlife Foundation, 274
Agenda 21 (United Nations):
   local governments, 256
   nongovernmental organizations (NGOs), 262, 274, 275
   principles, 271
Agriculture. *See* Sustainable agriculture
Agronomic practices, 161
Airlines, 322, 323
Air pollution:
   acid rain, 38, 85, 88
   air quality index, 330
   carbon dioxide emissions, 38
   carbon monoxide, 38, 88
   global warming, 17
   heat island effect, 141
   nitrogen dioxide, 88
   nitrogen oxide, 85
   ozone, 141
   particulate matter, 85
   sulfur dioxide, 38, 85, 88
   sustainable agriculture, 159
   troposphere, 38
Airports, 322, 323, 331

Alaska, Exxon Valdez oil spill, 8, 123, 236, 349
Alcoa, 21
Alcott, Bronson, 10
Aluminum, 107–108, 344, 351
American Forests, 141, 274*t*
American Recovery and Reinvestment Act (ARRA), 319
American Rivers, 274*t*
American Society for the Prevention of Cruelty to Animals (ASPCA), 347
Amnesty International, 259
Amtrak, 354
Anderson, Ray, 19, 21
Angola, 158, 257
Animal Fair, 347
Annan, Kofi, 281, 286, 298
Anti-Slavery Society, 256, 257
Appalachian Trail, 11
Appliances, 57, 62, 64*t*, 68*t*, 91, 213, 214, 265, 331, 347
Architectural approach, 345
Arizona, 315, 317, 318
Arkansas, 242
Arzua, Ivo, 336
ASML Holding, 295
Atlanta, Georgia:
   air quality, 321–323
   energy resources, 322
   Hartsfield-Jackson Airport, 322
   Leadership in Energy and Environmental Design (LEED), 322
   sustainability plan, 322–323

   Sustainable Atlanta Initiative (2007), 322
   water resources, 322
Atmos Clear, 312*t*
Atmosfair, 312*t*
AT&T, 201
Audi, 337
Audubon, John James, 11
Austin, Texas, 327
Australia:
   energy resources, 111
   greenwashing, 346
   Melbourne, 337
Australian Climate Change Bill, 337
Austria, sustainable development programs, 273
Authenticity, green marketing, 343–344
Automobile industry:
   biodiesel, 114, 216, 244
   boxfish design, 196
   carbon calculators, 312
   carbon dioxide emissions, 218
   consumer transportations, 180, 216, 220
   electric vehicles, 89, 219
   ethanol fuel, 114, 216
   flexible fuel vehicles, 216
   fuel efficiency, 67*t*, 216, 220, 346
   hybrid vehicles, 67*t*, 137, 216, 220
   zero-emission vehicle, 316
   See also specific company

Backpacker, 347
Balanced scorecard (BSC) approach, 203
Basic brown consumers, 347
Bat Conservation International, 274*t*
Beavers, 44
Becton, Dickinson and Company (BD), 233
Beef, consumption of, 166–167
Beer, 213
Bees, 229–230
Belgium, 273*t*
Benetton, 236
Ben & Jerry's, 182, 229, 234, 265, 345
Benzene, 89
Bicycling, 220, 323, 326, 330, 331
Biodiesel, 122, 114, 216, 244
Biofuel carbon debt, 115
Biomass resources, 44, 112–115
Biotechnology, 156
Bird Friendly, 213
Birds of America (Audubon), 11
Black liquor, 113
Blessed Unrest (Hawken), 270
Bloomberg, Michael, 320
Body Shop, The, 21, 182, 229, 234, 236
Boston, Massachusetts:
  energy resources, 319–320
  Leadership in Energy and Environmental Design (LEED), 319
  single stream collection, 319
  sustainability plan, 319–320
  sustainable return on investment (SROI), 319
  water resources, 320
Bottled water:
  consumerism, 212
  green marketing, 347
  health problems from, 212
Bovine growth hormone, 165, 212
Boxfish design, 196
B & Q, 235
Brands:
  brand building, 233, 236
  brand insurance, 236
  corporate social responsibility (CSR), 236
Braungart, M., 183, 195
Brazil:
  consumerism, 208
  Curitiba, 336–337

energy resources, 108
sustainability reporting, 284
tropical rainforest, 136
Brazzaville, Republic of the Congo, 158
Breeding, 144, 156
Bridge organizations, 270
Brita, 345
British Petroleum (BP):
  "Beyond Petroleum" campaign, 345
  corporate social responsibility (CSR), 236
  oil spill (Gulf of Mexico), 236, 345
  sustainability strategies, 181
Brundtland Report, 3, 234
Burt's Bees, 250
Burundi, 158
Bush, George W., 303
Business case for sustainability, 247–248
Business for Social Responsibility (BSR), 232

California, 11, 170, 328
  Los Angeles, 315–316
  San Francisco, 317
Campylobacter, 210
Canada:
  energy resources, 108
  greenwashing, 347
  Montreal, 331–332
  recombinant bovine growth hormone (rBGH), 212
  sustainability reporting, 284
  Vancouver, 328, 332–333
Canadian Boreal Forest, 40, 41, 139, 140, 141
Canadian Municipalities Sustainable Community Award, 332
Canon, 263
Cap and trade system, 74, 123, 255, 305
Captive organizations, 270
Carbon calculators, 223, 312
Carbon capture and storage, 73, 308
Carbon capture technology, 86
Carbon Counter, 312
Carbon dioxide emissions:
  carbon calculators, 218
  greenhouse gas (GHG), 55
Carbon dioxide offsets, 308

Carbon Disclosure Project (CDP), 170–172, 247, 287
Carbon footprint:
  calculator, 312
  carbon neutral, 171, 223, 304, 309
  consumerism, 222
  defined, 218
Carbon markets:
  cap and trade system, 305
  carbon capture and storage, 308
  carbon footprint, 304
  carbon neutral, 304–305
  carbon offsets, 305–309
  discussion questions, 310
  Internet resources, 311
  keywords, 310
  Kyoto Protocol, 303
  learning objectives, 302
  research overview, 302
  study guide, 309
  See also Carbon offsets
Carbon monoxide, 38, 88, 90, 114
Carbon neutral, 171, 223, 304, 309
Carbon offsets,
  additionality, 307
  advantages of, 307
  cap and trade system, 305
  carbon calculators, 312
  carbon dioxide offsets, 306
  certification, 305
  compulsory offsets, 303
  consumer reports, 309
  defined, 305
  disadvantages of, 307
  emission trading schemes, 304
  examples of, 304–308
  Gold Standard, 306
  market performance criteria, 308–309
  offset carbon market, 305–308
  Plan Vivo, 306
  renewable energy credits (RECs), 327
  Voluntary Carbon Standard (VCS), 310
  voluntary offsets, 304
  Voluntary Offset Standard (VOS), 310
Cargill, 167, 181

Index

Caribou, 41
Caritas, 257
Carson, Rachel, 12
Catholic Relief Services, 272
Center for Clean Air Policy, 270, 274
Centers for Disease Control and Prevention (CDC), 165
Central Africa, 158
Ceres, 274, 284, 294, 298
Certification:
  carbon offsets, 305
  forests, 140–141
  green supply chains, 245
  nongovernmental organizations (NGOs), 266
  See also Leadership in Energy and Environmental Design (LEED); Standardization
Certified Clean Car, 312*t*
Certified Emission Reductions (CERs), 304, 306
Chain of custody certification, 140
Chevron, 123, 180, 236
Chicago, Illinois, 319, 327
Chile, 108, 257
China:
  carbon dioxide emissions, 90
  consumerism, 208
  energy resources, 97, 107
  garment industry, 215
  greenhouse gas (GHG) emissions, 74
  Hong Kong, 331
  malnutrition, 158
Chiquita, 266
Chlorofluorocarbons (CFCs), 59, 60, 265, 345
Chrysalis economy, 228–230:
Chrysler Corporation, 216, 337
City sustainability plans:
  Atlanta, Georgia, 321–323
  Boston, Massachusetts, 319–320
  business implications, 338–339
  city rankings, 328
  Curitiba, Brazil, 336–337
  discussion questions, 340
  Hong Kong, 330–331
  international cities, 329–337
  Internet resources, 340
  key words, 340

Leadership in Energy and Environmental Design (LEED), 315, 316, 319, 322
learning objectives, 313
light-emitting diodes (LED), 318, 321
London, England, 329
Los Angeles, California, 315–316
Melbourne, Australia, 337
Mexico City, Mexico, 333–335
Montreal, Canada, 331–332
Mumbai, India, 335–336
New Orleans, Louisiana, 326–327
New York City, New York, 320–321
Paris, France, 329–330
Phoenix, Arizona, 317–318
Portland, Oregon, 325–326
research overview, 313
Seattle, Washington, 317
Salt Lake City, Utah, 316–317
San Francisco, California, 324–325
study guide, 339
sustainability portfolio, 314–315
U.S. cities, 315–328
Vancouver, Canada, 332–333
Washington, D.C., 323–324
Civil society organizations (CSOs), 253, 259
Clean Air Act, United States (1963), 8
Clean Air Pass, 312*t*
Clean Development Mechanism (CDM), 306, 307
Clean energy economy, 81
Cleaning products, 213, 246
Clear-cutting, 140
Climate, global warming, 52–53
  See also Air pollution
Climate Care, 312
Climate Friendly, 312
Clorox, 250, 348, 349
Clothing, 215
Coal, clean technologies, 124
Coca-Cola, 166, 182, 348
Coffee, 212–213
Collins and Aikman Floorcoverings, 180
Command and control approach, 254

Comprehensive Environmental Response, Compensation, and Liability Act (1980), 9
Conference of the Parties (COP 17), Durban, South Africa, 28, 74
Conservation International (CI), 269, 272, 274
Construction industry:
  green construction, 17, 214
  green jobs, 322
Contamination, 91, 143, 167, 211
Corporate butterflies, 229
Corporate caterpillars, 229
Corporate honeybees, 229
Corporate Knights Global 100, 240, 294, 295–296
Corporate locusts, 228
Corporate Register, 295
Corporate social responsibility (CSR):
  benefits, 238–239
  brands, 236
  challenges of, 239–240
  community level, 237
  CSR 2.0, 240
  defined, 231
  ecological sustainability, 236
  environmental level, 237
  European model, 232
  globalization impact, 236
  historical development, 231–232
  influence of, 235
  key areas, 237
  market level, 236
  moral grounds for, 234–235
  movement phases, 232–233
  policy components, 237–238
  profits, 231
  relevance of, 235–236
  responsive corporate social responsibility, 235
  strategic corporate social responsibility, 235
  strategy, 237
  sustainability reporting, 290
  sustainable value creation, 232–233
  theoretical approach, 239
  triple bottom line (TBL), 234
  U.S. model, 232
  workplace level, 238

Corporations:
  business case for sustainability, 247–248
  carbon calculators, 312
  case studies, 250
  chrysalis economy, 228–229
  competitive advantage, 17
  consumer loyalty, 17
  corporate social responsibility (CSR), 230–239
  discussion questions, 249
  environmental nongovernmental organization collaboration, 269
  global warming concerns, 17
  green supply chains, 241
  greenwashing, 18
  international pressures, 17–18
  Internet resources, 250
  key words, 249
  learning objectives, 227
  nongovernmental organization collaboration, 266–268
  public exposure, 18
  research overview, 227
  study guide, 248
  sustainability components, 230
  sustainability guidelines, 15–17
  sustainability motivation, 17–18
  sustainability stages, 21
  sustainable consumption, 217–219
  triple bottom line (TBL), 21–23
  waste reduction, 18
  See also Green marketing; Sustainability reporting
Cotton, 12, 107, 113, 142, 165, 215, 225, 226
CO₂ balance, 204
Cradle-to-cradle (C2C) approach, 22–23, 26, 194–195
Cradle to Cradle (McDonough and Braungart), 195
Cradle-to-grave approach, 22, 193
Curitiba, Brazil, 336–337
Customer relationship management (CRM), 334
Czech Republic, 283

DaimlerChrysler, 23
Dairy, 212
Dairy Farm International Group, 331
Dark green consumers, 347
DDT, 12, 185
Defenders of Wildlife, 7, 274*t*
Defra's Guidelines, 329
Degradable label, 351
Delta Air Lines, 323
Delta Waterfowl Foundation, 274
Deming, W. Edwards, 14
Democratic Republic of the Congo, 158
Denmark, 23, 258
Denver, Colorado, 315, 328
Dhaka, Bangladesh, 257
Dian Fossey Gorilla Fund, 274
Diet and nutrition:
  childhood obesity, 158
  global hunger rates, 158
  malnutrition, 158
Discharge water treatment, 89
Doctors Without Borders, 258
Domtar Corporation, 233
Dow Chemical, 180
Dow Jones Sustainability Index (DJSI), 292, 294
Drinking water, 9, 89, 91, 131
  bottled water, 212, 224, 247, 317, 347
Drivers of sustainability:
  model illustration, 181*t*
  sustainability strategies, 180–182
Ducks Unlimited, 7, 274
DuPont:
  corporate social responsibility (CSR), 234
  sustainability stage, 21
  sustainability strategies, 181–182

E. coli, 210
Earth Day, 8, 12, 320, 349
Earth Summit, Rio de Janeiro, Brazil (1992), 257, 259, 303
Earthwatch Institute, 209
Ecological footprint, 23, 27, 211*t*, 218
Ecological impact, 209
Eco Options program, 350
Ecotourism, 350

Electronic Product Environmental Assessment Tool (EPEAT), 246
Elkington, John, 21
Emergency Planning and Community Right-to-Know Act (1968), 9, 283
Emerson, Ralph Waldo, 10
Emission trading schemes, 253
Employment: *See* Green jobs
Endangered species, 144, 245
Endangered Species Act (1973), 25, 145
Energize Phoenix, 318
Energy efficiency:
  Energy Star, 17, 64*t*, 66*t*, 68*t*, 214, 347
  flexible fuel vehicles, 216
  hybrid vehicles, 67*t*, 216, 220
  light-emitting diodes (LED), 318
Energy resources:
  biodiesel, 114, 216, 244
  biomass, 44, 112
  black liquor, 113*t*
  carbon capture technology, 86
  clean energy economy, 92
  consumerism, 216
  discussion questions, 125
  ethanol fuel, 114, 216
  fossil fuels, 92, 96, 112, 119
  geothermal energy, 116–117
  geothermal heat pump (GHP), 117, 243
  green jobs, 248, 316, 322
  hydroelectric power, 107, 108–109, 318
  hydrogen, 118–119, 122
  hydrogen fuel cells, 118–119
  Internet resources, 125
  key words, 123–125
  learning objectives, 81
  natural gas, 83, 89–91, 113, 114
  nuclear energy, 82*t*, 83, 86, 91–92, 94
  oceanic energy, 111
  ocean thermal energy, 111
  oil, 86
  renewable energy, 94–97
  research overview, 81
  solar energy, 100–101
  study guide, 123
  tide energy, 111

wave energy, 111
wind energy, 97–100
Energy Star, 17, 64*t*, 66*t*, 68*t*, 214, 347
England, 51, 235
Environmental, social, and governance (ESG) disclosures, 170–172
Environmental and Energy Study Institute, 274*t*
Environmental Defense Fund (EDF), 242, 269, 274*t*
Environmental Management System (EMS), 200–201
Environmental nongovernmental organizations (ENGOs):
 corporate collaboration, 268
 group divisions, 269–270
 list of, 269–270
 role of, 268–269
Environmental stewardship:
 evolution of, 199*f*
 industry practices, 197–198
 sustainability strategies, 197–200
Environmental sustainability, 4
Environmental Working Group, 162
Equatorial Guinea, 233
Equity, 4
Eritrea, 158
Estrogen, 212
Ethanol fuel, 114
Ethical Trading Initiative (ETI), 264
Ethiopia, 109, 257
European Union (EU):
 biofuel, 17
 ecological footprint, 218
 genetically modified food, 166
 greenhouse gas (GHG) emissions, 303
 nongovernmental organizations (NGOs), 257
 Programme for the Endorsement of Forest Certification (PEFC), 141
 See also specific city or country
EvoLogics, 197
ExxonMobil, 236
Exxon Valdez oil spill (Alaska), 8, 349

Fairtrade, 217
Fair trade certified, 213
Fairtrade Foundation, 264
Fast Company, 349
Fauna & Flora International, 139, 145, 148, 274*t*
Fifty Years Is Enough (1994), 257
Financial capital, 183, 335
Finland:
 industrial ecology, 191–192
 urban forests, 141
Fish America Foundation, 274*t*
Fisher, Wynecta, 326
Fishing industry:
 consumerism, 211
 fish farms, 211
 Marine Stewardship Council (MSC), 211
 overfishing, 129, 185, 265
 See also Seafood
Five green *P*'s strategy, 344
Flexible fuel vehicles, 216
Food. *See* Sustainable agriculture; Sustainable food
Food, Inc. (2010), 163
Food miles, 162, 210
Food web, 44
Ford Motor Company, 216, 217
Forest management certification, 140
Forests:
 biodiversity management, 133–142
 business implications, 145–146
 chain of custody certification, 140
 forest management certification, 140
 greenwashing, 346
 Internet resources, 148
 key words, 147
 learning objectives, 128
 management of, 133–142
 Montreal Process, 139–140
 old-growth forest, 134
 Programme for the Endorsement of Forest Certification (PEFC), 141
 research overview, 129–130
 sustainability certification, 140–141
 sustainable forestry criteria, 139

Sustainable Forestry Initiative (SFI), 140
 tropical rainforest, 134–135
 urban forest, 141–142
Forest Stewardship Council (FSC), 140–141, 214, 246, 263, 343
Fortune, 236, 345, 349
Fossil fuels, 38, 54, 56, 62, 66, 73, 83, 92, 93, 97, 107, 115, 118, 120, 224
Fourth World Conference on Women (Beijing), 259
France:
 government role, 255
 greenwashing policy, 346
Free-range poultry, 161, 211, 348
Friedman, Milton, 231, 232
Friends of the Earth (FoE), 263, 272
Fruitland, 10
Fuji, 263
Fuller, Margaret, 10, 343

Garment industry, 215
G8, 259
General Electric (GE):
 corporate social responsibility (CSR), 233
 Ecomagination, 233
 greenwashing, 236
 sustainability stage, 21
 sustainability strategies, 181
General Motors (GM), 23, 216, 308
Genetically modified food, 152, 154, 156
Georgia, 137, 322
Geothermal energy, 82*t*, 116–117
Geothermal heat pump (GHP), 117
Germany:
 ecological footprint, 218–219
 sustainable development programs, 273*t*
Glaeser, E., 314, 315
Glasgow, Scotland, 8, 86, 232
Global Compact (United Nations):
 anti-corruption, 287
 environmental rights, 287
 human rights, 286
 labor rights, 286–287

principles, 286–287
sustainability reporting, 288
World Economic Forum (Switzerland, 1999), 298–301
Global Environmental Management Initiative (GEMI), 201
Global middle class, 208
Global Reporting Initiative (GRI), 239, 284, 285–286
 establishment of, 284
 policy benefits, 285–286
 policy limitations, 286
 reporting benefits, 285–286
 reporting corporations, 285–286
 triple bottom line (TBL), 284
Global social development, 260
Global warming, 17, 40, 52–53, 60–61, 69–70, 76, 91, 95, 219, 304, 318
GlobeScan, 252
Goldman Sachs, 208
Gold Standard, 306
Google, 234
Government role:
 agency example, 255–256
 command and control approach, 254
 developed countries, 252
 developing countries, 252
 discussion questions, 271–272
 ecological fiscal reform, 254–255
 facilitation, 253t, 254
 green marketing, 350–351
 innovation, 254
 internal sustainability management, 252
 Internet resources, 272
 key words, 271
 leadership, 253–254
 learning objectives, 252
 local governments, 256
 market mechanisms, 255
 organizational collaboration, 253–254
 policy development, 253t
 regulation, 253t
 research overview, 252
 strategic visionary goals, 254
 sustainable development programs, 273t–274t

 See also Legislation; Nongovernmental organizations (NGOs); *specific agency*
Grameen Bank, 181
Grand Coulee Dam (Washington), 107, 108
Great Britain:
 energy resources, 107
 environmental nongovernmental organizations (ENGOs), 268
 sustainable development programs, 273t
Greece, 134
Green construction, 17, 214
Greenhouse gas (GHG) emissions:
 carbon dioxide, 55–56, 61t, 90, 303, 305
 global comparisons, 74, 303
 global warming, 60, 61t
 hydrofluorocarbons (HFCs), 60, 265, 303
 methane, 37, 55, 57–58
 nitrous oxide, 58, 303
 perfluorocarbons (PFCs), 55, 303
 sulfur hexafluoride, 55, 303
Green jobs, 248, 316, 322
Green marketing, 343–353
Green Marketing and the Trade Practices Act (Australia), 346
Green Marketing Without the Greenwash (Ogilvy Earth), 348
Green Paycheck Campaign, 263
Greenpeace, 250, 259, 265, 268, 269, 348
Green Purchasing Network (GPN), 263
Green Rail Corridor (Phoenix), 318
Green Seal, 246
Greenseas, 217
Green Suppliers network, 241–242
Green supply chains:
 business goal alignment, 241
 business process improvement, 241
 certification programs, 244–245
 cleaning products, 246
 computers, 246

 corporations, 241–247
 defined, 241
 developmental guidelines, 242–243
 facility design, 243
 facility equipment, 243
 facility systems, 244
 green procurement, 245–247
 logistics and transportation, 244–245
 material refurbishment programs, 241–242
 office supplies, 246
 requests for proposals (RFPs), 246
 Supply Chain Program, 247
 warehouse management systems (WMS), 244
Greenwashing:
 defined, 18, 346
 green marketing, 346–347
 industry examples, 347
 legislation, 346
 nongovernmental organizations (NGOs), 266
 seven sins of, 346–347
Gross domestic product (GDP), 121, 151, 208
Guides for the Use of Environmental Marketing Claims (FTC), 351
Gulf of Mexico,

Haiti, 158
Happy Planet Index (2008), 208, 221
Hawken, 183, 219, 270
Heat island effect, 141, 318
Hellmann's Mayonnaise, 348
Hewlett-Packard (HP), 181, 231
Hindustan Unilever Limited (HLL), 181
Home Depot, 242, 350
Honda, 181, 263, 349
Honeywell, 181
Hong Kong, 330–331
Honolulu, Hawaii, 328
Horn, G., 223
Housing:
 appliances, 213, 214
 consumerism, 213, 217
 energy efficiency, 209
 green homes, 213–215
 home design, 213
 household cleaners, 213–214

INDEX | 391

Human capital, 22, 26, 183, 184
Humanitarian aid, 257
Hungary, 283
Hunting, 6, 131, 138*t*
Hurricane Katrina (2006), 326, 327
Hybrid vehicles, 67*t*, 181, 216, 217, 220, 270
Hydroelectric power, 106–112, 121
Hydrofluorocarbons (HFCs), 55, 59, 60, 265, 303
Hydrogen fuel cells, 118–119
Hydrological cycle, 35, 37*f*

IBM, 23, 201
Iceland, 116, 117
Ikea, 170, 187, 331
India, 8, 74, 109, 112, 152, 181, 208, 335
Indiana, 11
Indonesia, 112, 116, 117
Industrial ecology, 187–194
  defined, 187–188
  environmental impact analysis, 188
  global examples, 190–193
  life cycle assessment (LCA), 193–194
  linear-to-cyclical systems, 189–190
  model illustrations, 191*f*, 192*f*
  multidisciplinary approach, 188
  natural systems, 188
  system illustrations, 189*f*, 190*f*
  systems analysis, 188
  Type I system, 189*f*
  Type II system, 189*f*
  Type III system, 190*f*
Industrial Revolution, 40, 46, 47, 51, 55, 107, 133, 134, 183
Infant mortality rate, 153
InterAction, 272
Interface, 21, 182, 187
Intergovernmental Panel on Climate Change, 53
International Business Report, 238
International Council for Local Environmental Initiatives (ICLEI)-Local Governments for Sustainability, 256, 323

International Ecotourism Society, the (TIES), 350
International Gas Union Grand Prix, 332
International Monetary Fund (IMF), 257
International nongovernmental organizations (INGOs), 256–257
International Organization for Standardization (ISO), 215, 288–289
  ISO 14001, 289–290
  ISO 26000, 290–291
International Rescue Committee, 272
International Union for the Conservation of Nature (IUCN), 144, 209, 264
International Wildlife Coalition-USA, 274
International resources:
  Agenda 21, 256
  bottled water, 212
  carbon calculators, 312
  Carbon Footprint calculator, 219
  carbon markets, 218
  Cargill, 167
  city sustainability plans, 315
  consumerism, 223–224
  corporations, 239, 250
  Global Reporting Initiative (GRI),
  government role, 239
  green marketing, 346
  Natural Step framework, 185
  nongovernmental organizations (NGOs), 268
  sustainability, 29
  sustainability reporting, 294
  sustainability strategies, 188
  sustainable food, 167
  United States Department of Agriculture (USDA), 161
  U.S. Environmental Protection Agency (EPA), 17
  World Wildlife Fund (WWF), 263
Iowa, 163
Italy, 51, 255
Izaak Walton League of America, 7, 274*t*

Jane Goodall Institute, 274*t*

Japan:
  ecological footprint, 218
  green construction, 17
  nongovernmental organizations (NGOs), 263
Johannesburg, South Africa, 268, 332
Johnson & Johnson, 181
J. Sainsbury, 264
Justice, 332

Kenya, 117
Keystone species, 44–45
Knight, Phil, 235
Kodak, 201
Kouvola, Finland, 191–192
KPMG, 252, 282
Kraft Foods, 168–169
Kyoto Protocol (Japan, 1997), 74, 303–304

Labor force, *See also* Green jobs
Ladder of sustainability, 182
Lake Michigan, 319
Land Trust Alliance, 274*t*
Leadership in Energy and Environmental Design (LEED), 17, 187, 316, 319, 322, 339
Legislation, 21, 74, 137, 138, 164, 188, 255, 266, 283, 291, 303. *See also specific legislation*
Lemelson-MIT Award for Sustainability, 18
Lemelson-MIT Prize, 18
Leopold, Aldo, 11
Levi Strauss, 264
Life cycle assessment (LCA):
  cradle-to-grave approach, 193–194
  model illustration, 194*f*
Light-emitting diodes (LED), 318
Light green consumers, 347
Listeria, 210
Living Green (Horn), 223
Locomotive engines, 38, 41, 51
Logistics and transportation, 244–245
London, England, 329
Lonely Planet Code Green, The, 350
Los Angeles, California, 315–316, 328, 330

Lotusan paint, 197
Louisiana, 327
Love Canal (New York), 8, 349
Lung disease, 85, 143

MacKay, Benton, 11
Malaysia, 112
Malnutrition, 158–159
Mannings, 331
Manufactured capital, 183
Marathon Oil Corporation, 233, 239
Marcos, Ferdinand, 257
Marine ecology. *See* Fishing industry; Oceans; Seafood
Marine Stewardship Council (MSC), 211, 263, 272, 343
Marshall, Robert, 11
Massachusetts, 170, 320
Massachusetts Institute of Technology (MIT), 18
McDonald's, 166–167, 187, 234, 269
McDonough, W., 183, 195
Meat consumption, 163
Mediator organizations, 257, 269–270
Melbourne, Australia, 337
Mercedes-Benz, 196, 323
Merck & Company, 236
Mercury, 41, 85, 90, 117, 211
Mercy Corps, 258, 272
Methane, 37, 53, 55, 57–58, 61*t*, 64, 65*t*, 68*t*, 76, 88, 89, 90, 91, 113*f*, 114, 164, 166, 233, 303, 308, 318
Methyl bromide, 213
Mexico City, Mexico, 333–335
Mexico City Climate Action Program, 334
Microsoft, 141, 236, 292, 293, 308, 349
Milk production, 165, 194, 212, 235
Millennium Ecosystem Assessment, 129, 209
Minneapolis, Minnesota, 338*t*
Minnesota, 216
Mitsubishi, 187, 263
Monsanto, 151, 164, 165, 349
Montreal, Canada, 331–332
Montreal Process (1993), 139–140
Mozambique, 158

Muir, John, 7, 11
Mumbai, India, 335–336
Mumbai Sustainability and Corporate Citizenship Protocol, 335

Nance, Earthea, 326
National Audubon Society, 7, 11, 274*t*
National Forest Management Act, 7
National Heart Foundation Approved, 217
National Park Service, 11
National Renewable Energy Laboratory, 103*f*, 104*f*, 125
National Wildlife Federation, 7, 274*t*
Natural capital:
 defined, 129
 sustainability strategies, 183–184
 triple bottom line (TBL), 22
Natural gas, 83
Naturalists, 11, 12
Natural Resources Defense Council (NRDC), 270, 274*t*
Natural Step framework, 184–187
Nature Conservancy, The, 7, 223, 270, 274*t*
Necessary Revolution, The (Senge), 19
Nelson, Gaylord, 12
Nestle, 171, 235
Netherlands, 253*f*, 263, 273*t*, 281
New Economics Foundation, 208
New Orleans, Louisiana, 326–327
New York, Love Canal, 8, 349
New York City, New York, 320–321
New York Times, 350
New Zealand, 140, 245
Niger, 159
Nike, 180, 187, 235, 236, 239, 266, 281
Nitrogen dioxide, 38
Nitrogen oxide, 38, 85, 90, 330
Nitrous oxide, 55, 58–59, 61*t*, 65*t*, 88, 115, 303

Nongovernmental organizations (NGOs):
 Agenda 21 (United Nations), 256
 blessed unrest movement, 270
 bridge organizations, 270
 captive organizations, 270
 corporate collaboration, 263–268
 defined, 256–257
 discussion questions, 271–272
 environmental nongovernmental organizations (ENGOs), 268–270
 financial resources, 258
 global power, 259–260
 global social development, 260–261
 historical development, 257
 independent organizations, 270
 international nongovernmental organizations (INGOs), 257–258
 Internet resources, 272
 isolate organizations, 269
 key words, 271
 learning objectives, 251
 mediator organizations, 269–270
 organizational expansion, 257
 poverty impact, 256
 research overview, 252
 sustainable community development, 261–262
 sustainable consumption, 262–263
 sustainable development, 262
 See also Government role; *specific organization*
Norton, J. J., 203
Norway, 137, 166, 263, 283
Novo Nordisk, 295
Novozymes, 295
Nuclear accidents:
 Fukushima Daiichi, 92, 94
 Three Mile Island Pennsylvania, 8, 92
 Ukraine, 122
Nuclear energy, 91–94

Obesity, 158, 164
Occupational Health and Safety Assessment Series, 202
Ocean acidification, 71
Ocean thermal energy, 111
Offsetters, 312*t*
Ogilvy & Mather, 348
Oil, energy resources, 83, 86
Oil spills:
  British Petroleum (Gulf of Mexico), 236, 345
  Exxon Valdez (Alaska), 8, 123
Old-growth forest, 140
Omnivore's Dilemma, The (Pollan), 163, 164
One Planet Business, 209
Oregon, 325, 327
Organic farming:
  certified organic, 162
  meat production, 166
  sustainable agriculture, 159–160
Organic Foods Production Act (1990), 162
Organisation for Economic Co-operation and Development (OECD), 254, 283
Overfishing, 129, 185, 265
Oxfam, 264, 272
Ozone, 8, 16, 38, 39, 59, 60, 335, 351, 352

Packard, David, 231
Pakistan, 23, 151
Palm oil, 18, 245, 265
Paper products, 41, 225
Paris, France, 69, 116, 171, 204, 329–330
Particulate matter, 38, 85, 90
Patagonia, 21, 215, 225, 229, 234, 248, 348
Patil, Shri Jayant, 335
PAWS, 347
Pennsylvania, 8
Pentland Group, 264
People for the Ethical Treatment of Animals (PETA), 347
Perfluorocarbons (PFCs), 55, 59, 303
Pheasants Forever, 274*t*
Philadelphia, Pennsylvania, 168
Philanthropy, 232, 234, 264
Philippines, 257
Phoenix, Arizona, 317–318

Photovoltaics, 101–103, 105, 123, 219*f*, 322, 349
Phthalates, 212
Pinochet, Augusto, 257
Plan-do-check-act cycle (PDCA), 200, 202, 281
Plant-based energy, 25, 79
Plan Vivo, 306
Plastic bags, 331, 335
Plastic water bottles. *See* Bottled water
Poland, 23, 257, 283
Pollan, M., 163, 164
Pollutant-disclosure laws, 283
Pollution Prevention Pays (3P), 180
Polychlorinated biphenyls (PCBs), 211
Polyester, 215
Pork, 163, 210
Portfolio Manager, 17
Portland, Oregon, 317, 325–327
Portugal, 134, 137
Poultry, 44, 156, 157, 161, 210–211
Poverty impact, 13, 14, 152, 158, 159, 180, 230, 257, 258, 277, 317
Procter & Gamble, 182
Programme for the Endorsement of Forest Certification (PEFC), 141
Prologis, 17
Public transportation, 67*t*, 216, 220, 313, 315, 324, 330, 331
Puerto Rico, 190–191
Purified water, 191

Quail Unlimited RARE Sierra Club, 274*t*
Quinn, David, 326

Railroads, 322
Rainfall, 8, 108, 115, 131, 317
Rainforest Action Network, 242, 274*t*
Rainforest Alliance, 213, 217, 242, 266, 274*t*
Rainforests, 183
Ready-to-use therapeutic food (RUTF), 159
Recombinant bovine growth hormone (rBGH), 212
Recycling, consumerism, 213–214

Red Cross, 257, 264
Rees, William, 218
REI, 347
Renault, 204
Renewable energy, 94–119
Renewable energy credits (RECs), 327
Reporting. *See* Sustainability reporting
Responsive corporate social responsibility, 235
Reverse osmosis systems, 212
Rhinoceros, 145
River Network, 270, 274*t*
Robert, K. H., 184, 185
Rocky Mountain Institute, 183
Roundup, 165
Roundup-ready seeds, 165
Royal Dutch/Shell, 23
Russia, 137, 145, 228

7-Eleven, 331
Safe Drinking Water Act (1974), 9
Salmonella, 157, 210
Salt Lake City, Utah, 316–317, 327
San Francisco, California, 324–325, 335
Save Money and Reduce Toxins (SMART), 180
Save the Children, 257, 264
Scenic Hudson, 274*t*
Schwartz, Jeffrey, 326
Science of Sustainability, 187
Scotland, 8
Seafood, 211–212
Seattle, Washington, 317, 327, 349
Securities and Exchange Commission (SEC), 283
Senge, Peter, 19, 20, 21
Seventh, Generation, 21, 214
Sewage, 7, 38, 68, 113, 114, 191, 195
Shade grown coffee, 213
Shareholder value:
  model illustration, 179*f*
  sustainability strategies, 179–180, 232
Shell, 23, 123, 181, 281, 308
Sierra Club, 7, 11, 348
Sierra Club, 347
Silent Spring (Carson), 12
Simon, 17, 202
Single stream collection, 319

Skin cancer, 318
Smart electrical grids, 101
SmartWay Transport Program, 244
Soil and Water Conservation Society, 139f, 274t
Soil Association, 217
Soil erosion, 44, 115, 131
Soil management, 58
Solar power, 100–112
  advantages of, 108
  capacity trends, 101, 108–109
  conventional technologies, 109
  disadvantages of, 108
  environmental impacts, 106, 111–112
  hydropower, 106–108
  mainstream technologies, 101–104
  new technologies, 105–106
  oceanic, 111
  storage, 109–111
Somalia, 158
Sonoco Sustainability Solutions, 18
Sony, 23, 263
South Africa, 257
South Council, 257
Southern California Edison, 315
St. Paul, Minnesota, 338t
Starbucks, 242, 243, 281
Sto Corp, 197
Stonyfield Farms, 345
Strategic corporate social responsibility, 235
Student Conservation Association, 274t
Sulfur dioxide, 38, 85, 88
Sulfur hexafluoride, 55, 59, 303
Super Size Me, 166
Supply Chain Program, 247
Supply chains. *See* Green supply chains
Sustainability:
  areas of, 3–5
  defined, 2–5
  discussion questions, 29
  Internet resources, 29
  key words, 28
  myths, 13–15
  organizational benefits, 20
  organizational guidelines, 16–17
  organizational motivation, 17–18
  organizational priority, 19–20
  pollution historically, 7–8
  research overview, 23–28
  stages of, 21
  study guide, 28
  sustainable development defined, 3
  triple bottom line (TBL), 21–23
Sustainability Balanced Scorecard (SBSC), 179, 203, 205
Sustainability ethics, 5
Sustainability reporting:
  benefits of, 282
  Carbon Disclosure Project (CDP), 287
  Ceres, 294–295
  Corporate Knights Global, 295–296
  Corporate Register, 295
  corporate social responsibility (CSR), 290
  disadvantages of, 285
  discussion questions, 297
  Dow Jones Sustainability Index (DJSI), 292
  Global Compact (United Nations), 286–288
  Global Reporting Initiative (GRI), 285–286
  International Organization for Standardization (ISO), 288–292
  Internet resources, 298
  key words, 297
  learning objectives, 280
  legislation, 282
  life cycle assessment (LCA), 289
  limitations of, 286
  motivating factors, 282
  plan-do-check-act cycle (PDCA), 281
  pollutant-disclosure laws, 283
  reporting formats, 281–282
  transparency, 281
  World Business Council for Sustainable Development (WBCSD), 288
Sustainability software, 17
Sustainability strategies:
  biomimicry, 195–197
  case studies,
  cradle-to-cradle (C2C) approach, 194–195
  discussion questions, 205–206
  environmental stewardship, 197–200
  global sustainability drivers, 180–182
  industrial ecology, 187–194
  Internet resources, 206
  key words, 205
  ladder of sustainability, 182
  learning objectives, 178
  life cycle assessment (LCA), 193–194
  natural capital, 183–184
  Natural Step framework, 184–185
  organizational team members, 182–183
  research overview, 178–179
  shareholder value, 179
  sustainable value creation, 179–180
  triple bottom line (TBL), 182
  value of, 179–180
Sustainability tools:
  Environmental Management System (EMS), 200–201
  Sustainability Balanced Scorecard (SBSC), 203
  Sustainable Operating System (SOS), 202
  Total Quality Environmental Management (TQEM), 201
  value stream mapping, 202
Sustainable agriculture:
  agriculture industry, 165
  agronomic practices, 165
  biotechnology, 156
  breeding, 165
  contamination, 167
  crop diversity, 160
  defined, 4, 156
  discussion questions, 173
  genetically modified food, 165
  green jobs, 152
  high-pesticide fruits/vegetables, 162
  Internet resources, 173

irradiation, 161
key words, 172
learning objectives, 150
legislation, 157
low-pesticide fruits/vegetables, 162
media coverage, 163
omnivore's dilemma, 163
organic farming, 161–162
renewable energy, 151
research overview, 150–151
See also Sustainable food
Sustainable Atlanta Initiative (2007), 322
Sustainable city, 4. *See also* City sustainability plans
Sustainable community development, 4, 261–262
Sustainable consumption, 262–263
Sustainable economy, 4–5
Sustainable education, 5
Sustainable food:
 certified organic, 162
 consumerism, 208, 210–213
 defined, 5
 diet and nutrition, 158, 162
 discussion questions, 173
 egg production, 211
 food miles, 162
 global hunger rates, 158
 Internet resources, 173
 key words, 172
 labor force, 151
 learning objectives, 150
 legislation, 162
 local markets, 162–163
 malnutrition, 158–159
 milk production, 165, 212
 ready-to-use therapeutic food (RUTF), 159
 research overview, 150
 seafood consumption, 211–212
 social goals, 150–151
 See also Meat consumption; Meat production; Sustainable agriculture
Sustainable food companies:
 Cargill, 167
 Kraft Foods, 168–169
 McDonald's, 166–167
 Starbucks, 242, 281
 Wal-Mart, 169–170
 Whole Foods Market, 235

Sustainable Forestry Initiative (SFI), 140, 217
Sustainable marketing, 343
Sustainable Measures, 29
Sustainable Operating System (SOS), 179, 202
Sustainable processes, 5
Sustainable return on investment (SROI), 319
Sustainable society, 5, 185
Sustainable Transport Award (2008), 329
Sustainable Travel International, 312t
Sustainable university, 5
Sustainable value, 5
Sustainable value creation:
 corporate social responsibility (CSR), 232–233
 model illustration, 181t
 sustainability strategies, 179–180
SustainLane.com, 325
Sweden, 187, 263
 sustainable development programs, 273t
Sysco, 235

Tandus Flooring, Inc., 180
Target Neutral, 312t
Tea, 212–213
TerraChoice, 346
TerraPass, 223, 312t
Tesco, 264
Texas, 12
Textile industry, 85, 159, 197, 215
Thoreau, Henry David, 6, 10, 11
Thornton, Grant, 238
3M, 180
Three Mile Island Pennsylvania, 8, 92
Timberland, 242, 348
Time Magazine, 183
Total Quality Environmental Management (TQEM), 201
Toxics Release Inventory (TRI), 283
Toyota, 181, 235, 263, 345, 349
Trans-Americas Trading Company, 215
Transparency, 27, 167, 168, 170, 234, 243, 260, 261, 268, 280, 281, 291

Transportation:
 airlines, 322
 bicycling, 323, 326
 carbon calculators, 312t
 consumerism, 216–217
 corporation logistics, 244–245
 public transportation, 220
 railroads, 322
 See also Automobile industry
Triple bottom line (TBL):
 corporate social responsibility (CSR), 232
 cradle-to-cradle (C2C) approach, 232
 cradle-to-grave approach, 22–23
 economic measures, 21
 environmental measures, 21
 Global Reporting Initiative (GRI), 284
 importance of, 23
 model illustration, 22f
 people, 22
 planet, 22
 profit, 23
 social measures, 21
 sustainability strategies, 182
Triumph of the City (Glaeser), 314
Tropical rainforest, 134–135
Troposphere, 38
Trout Unlimited, 274t

Ukraine, 122
Ultraviolet light filters, 213
Unilever-Greenpeace Sustainable Palm Oil Coalition, 171, 235, 264, 308
Union Carbide (India), 8, 349
United Nations:
 Agenda 21, 27, 256, 271, 274–277
 Conference of the Parties (COP 17), 74
 Conference on Environment and Development (Rio de Janeiro, 1992), 268, 299, 303
 Conference on the Human Environment (Stockholm, 1972), 232
 Division for Sustainable Development, 272

Global Compact, 286–288
Human Development Index (HDI), 260
Kyoto Protocol (Japan, 1997), 303
World Economic Forum (Switzerland, 1999), 286
United Nations Environment Programme (UNEP), 284
United Nations Food and Agriculture Organization, 138
United Nations Framework Convention on Climate Change (UNFCCC), 303
United States:
  bee population, 143
  ecological footprint, 218–219
  energy resources, 83, 100, 107
  greenwashing, 346
  See also specific city or state
United States Army Corps of Engineers, 7, 327
United States Climate Action, 270
United States Department of Agriculture (USDA), 12, 161, 162, 164, 217, 350
United States Department of Energy, 125
United States Environmental Protection Agency (EPA):
  agency programs, 225–226
  environmental stewardship, 197–200
  Executive Orders, 225–226
  industrial ecology, 190–191
  polychlorinated biphenyls (PCBs), 211
  SmartWay Transport Program, 244
United States Federal Trade Commission (FTC), 344, 346, 350, 351, 352, 353
United States Food and Drug Administration (FDA), 212, 225
United States Forest Service, 11
United States Green Building Council (USGBC), 339

United Technologies, 181
University of Wisconsin, 11
Uranium, 83, 92, 93
Urban forest, 141–142
Urbanization, 35, 134, 336
Utah, 315

Value creation. *See* Sustainable value creation
Value stream mapping, 202
Vancouver, Canada, 332–333
Verified Carbon Standard, 306*t*
Vietnam, 257, 261
Virginia, 163, 192–193
Volatile organic compounds (VOCs), 39, 90
Voluntary Carbon Standard (VCS), 306, 308

Wackernagel, Mathis, 218
Walden (Thoreau), 10
Wal-Mart, 169–170, 182, 187, 236, 242
Warehouse management system (WMS), 244
Washington, 170, 306*t*
Washington, D.C., 323
Washington Post, 330
Waste Management, 68*t*, 190, 191, 194, 233, 256
Waste Reduction Always Pays (WRAP), 180
Water:
  bottled water, 212, 247, 347
  drinking water, 89, 91, 131
  hydrological cycle, 35
  purified water, 191
  sustainable agriculture, 115
  water cycle, 70, 107, 131, 214
Water cycle, 70, 107, 131, 214
Water filters, 212, 345
Water pollution, 37, 81, 160
Wave energy, 111
Wellcome, 331
Wetlands, 16, 35, 37, 40, 42, 58, 73, 115, 116, 192
Whalepower, 197
Whales, 44
Whirlpool, 345
Whitetails Unlimited, 274*t*
Whole Foods Market, 235, 347
Wilderness, 11–12

Wilderness Act (1964), 11
Wilderness Society, The, 7, 11–12
Wildlife Conservation Society, 274*t*
Wildlife Forever, 274*t*
Wildlife Habitat Council, 274*t*
Wildlife Society, 269
Wildlife Trust, 274*t*
Wilson, E. O., 154, 231
Wind energy, 97–100
Wine, 213
Wolves, 41, 44
Wood products, 132, 134, 136, 138, 139*f*, 246
World Bank, 108, 159, 257, 259
World Business Council for Sustainable Development (WBCSD), 16, 232, 288
World Commission on Environment and Development (WCED):
  Brundtland Report, 3
  environmental nongovernmental organizations (ENGOs), 269
World Economic Forum (Switzerland, 1999), 240, 286, 298
World Health Organization (WHO), 153, 157, 165
World Land Trust, 312*t*
World Resources Institute, 209, 270, 274*t*, 288
World Summit on Sustainable Development (WSSD), 194, 332
World Trade Organization (WTO), 257
World Vision, 272
Worldwatch Institute, 274*t*
World Wildlife Fund (WWF), 208, 262, 274*t*

Yangtze River Dam (China), 112
Yard, Robert Sterling, 11
Yellowstone National Park, 44
Yosemite National Park, 11
Yugoslavia, 283